EDITION

9th

THE IRONY OF DEMOCRACY
An Uncommon Introduction to American Politics

EDITION

9th

THE IRONY OF DEMOCRACY
An Uncommon Introduction to American Politics

 Thomas R. Dye
McKenzie Professor of Government and Public Policy
Florida State University

 Harmon Zeigler

Wadsworth Publishing Company
Belmont, California
A Division of Wadsworth, Inc.

Political Science Editor: *Peggy Adams*
Editorial Assistant: *Cathleen S. Collins*
Production Editor: *Ellen Brownstein*
Manuscript Editor: *Catherine Cambron*
Permissions Editor: *Karen Wootten*
Interior and Cover Design: *Sharon L. Kinghan*
Cover Photo: *Patrick Tregenza*
Art Coordinator: *Lisa Torri*
Interior Illustration: *L. M. Graphics*
Cartoon Researcher: *Sue C. Howard*
Typesetting: *Weimer Incorporated*
Printing and Binding: *Malloy Lithographing*

Printed in the United States of America

1 2 3 4 5 6 7 8 9 10—97 96 95 94 93

Library of Congress Cataloging-in-Publication Data

Dye, Thomas R.
  The irony of democracy: an uncommon introduction to American politics/Thomas R. Dye, Harmon Zeigler.—9th ed.
      p.   cm.
  Includes bibliographical references and index.
  ISBN 0-534-19848-1
  1. United States—Politics and government.   2. Elite (Social sciences)—United States.   3. Pluralism (Social sciences)—United States.   I. Zeigler, L. Harmon (Luther Harmon). [date].
II. Title.
JK271.D92   1993   92-34011
306.2'0973—dc20   CIP

To the Student

In asking you to read this book, your instructor wants to do more than teach about "the nuts and bolts" of American government, for this book has a theme; that is, only a tiny handful of people make decisions that shape the lives of all of us and, despite the elaborate rituals of parties, elections, and interest group activity, we have little direct influence over these decisions. This theme is widely known as *elitism*. Your instructor may not believe completely in this theory but may instead believe that many groups of people share power in the United States, that competition is widespread, that we have checks against the abuse of power, and that the individual citizen can personally affect the course of national events by voting, supporting political parties, and joining interest groups. This theory, widely known as *pluralism*, characterizes virtually every American government textbook now in print—except this one. Your instructor, whether personally agreeing with the elitist or with the pluralist perspective, is challenging you to confront our arguments and to deal directly with some troubling questions about democracy in the United States.

It is far easier to teach "the nuts and bolts" of American government—the constitutional powers of the president, Congress, and courts; the function of parties and interest groups; the key cases decided by the Supreme Court; and so on—than to tackle the question, "How democratic is American society?" It is easier to teach the "facts" of American government than to search for their explanations. Although this book does not ignore such facts, its primary purpose is to interpret them—to help you understand *why* our government works as it does.

The Irony of Democracy is not necessarily "antiestablishment." This book challenges the prevailing pluralistic view of democracy in the United States, but it neither condemns nor endorses American political life. Governance of the United States by a small, homogeneous elite is subject to favorable or unfavorable interpretation, according to one's personal values. Each reader is free to decide whether we as a society should preserve, reform, or restructure the political system described in these pages.

The Irony of Democracy is neither a conservative nor a liberal text-book. It does not apologize for elite rule or seek to defend American insti-tutions or leaders. On the contrary, we are very critical of politicians, bureaucrats, corporate chieftains, media moguls, lawyers, lobbyists, and special interests. But we do not advocate fruitless liberal nostrums prom-ising to bring "power to the people," or "citizen movements" that are them-selves led by elites with their own self-interest.

The Irony of Democracy is indeed an endorsement of democratic val-ues—individual dignity, limited government, freedom of expression and dissent, equality of opportunity, private property, and due process of law. Our elitist theory of democracy is not an attack on democratic govern-ment, but rather an effort to understand the realities of politics in a democracy.

To the Instructor

The Ninth Edition of *The Irony of Democracy* continues its classic theme—elitism in a democratic society. Despite the near-universal acceptance of pluralist ideology in American political science and American government textbooks, we remain unrepentant. *The Irony of Democracy* remains an *elitist* introduction to American government.

This is a textbook that will challenge your students to rethink everything they have been taught about American democracy—it is a book of ideas, not just facts.

Elite theory is contrasted to democratic theory and to modern pluralist political theory throughout the book, in examining the U.S. Constitution, American political history, power structures, public opinion, mass media, elections, parties, interest groups, the presidency, Congress, the bureaucracy, the courts, federalism, and protest movements.

Elite theory is employed as an analytic model for understanding and explaining American politics; it is *not* presented as a recommendation or prescription for America.

The Ninth Edition is a major revision, both theoretically and substantively, of this now classic text. We are tempted to label this our elite-bashing edition because it reflects our increasing disenchantment with narrow, self-serving elite behavior and the threats such behavior poses to mass confidence in democratic government. Our elitist theory of democracy has always recognized the potential for danger in mass movements led by extremist and intolerant demagogues, and we have always condemned elite resorts to repression. But we have become convinced that the principal threat to democracy in the United States today arises from irresponsible elites seeking relative advantage at the expense of shared societal values. We have always been critical of governmental, corporate, media, and interest group elites; but we believe that narrow, shortsighted, and self-serving elite behavior has now become so endemic that it threatens the fabric of the American economy and polity. Thus, throughout the book we have described this current elite distemper, sometimes in general discussions and occasionally in new special sections, such as "Greed in the Boardroom," "Bashing America for Fun and Profit," "Follow the Money: Interest Groups and the Budget," "George Bush: Managing Presidential Popularity," "Mortgaging the Future: Elite Fiscal Irresponsibility," "The Lush Life on Capitol Hill," and "Congressional Self-Recruitment." To be fair, we do give George Bush high marks in the Gulf War and compare his performance in that endeavor with the behavior of the nation's elite in the Vietnam era.

Our theoretical introduction to elitism, pluralism, and democracy in Chapter 1 has been recast to focus on the paradox of elitism in a democracy. We provide clear and concise definitions of elitism, pluralism, and democracy, and directly address the question of elitism versus pluralism. We have reshaped our essay "Elite and Mass Threats to Democracy" to reflect our concern with the current elite distemper. A summary section, "An Elitist Theory of Democracy," identifies the key questions posed by elite theory.

Acknowledgments

We offer our thanks to the people who reviewed the book in preparation of the Ninth Edition: Richard Bush, Southern Illinois University—Edwardsville; Randall Clemons, Mercyhurst College; Herbert J. Doherty, University of Florida—Gainesville; James L. Gibson, University of Houston—University Park; John Klemanski, Oakland University; Joseph F. Schuster, Eastern Washington University; A. B. Villanueva, Western Illinois University; Mitchell Weiss, Charles S. Mott Community College; and Mamoon A. Zaki, LeMoyne-Owen College.

We also thank the members of the team at Brooks/Cole who, as always, brought us smoothly through the production of the Ninth Edition: Craig Barth, Ellen Brownstein, Sharon Kinghan, and Lisa Torri. We are very grateful.

Thomas R. Dye

Harmon Zeigler

Contents

1

The Irony of Democracy

★ *Government is always government by the few, whether in the name of the few, the one, or the many.*

Harold Lasswell, The Comparative Study of Elites, *1952*

Elites—not masses—govern the United States. In an industrial, scientific, and nuclear age, life in a democracy, just as in a totalitarian society, is shaped by a handful of people. Despite differences in their approach to the study of power in the United States, political scientists and sociologists agree that "the key political, economic, and social decisions are made by 'tiny minorities.' "[1]

Elites are the few who have power; the *masses* are the many who do not. Power is deciding who gets what, when, and how; it is participation in the decisions that shape our lives; the masses are the many whose lives are shaped by institutions, events, and leaders over which they have little direct control. Harold Lasswell writes, "The division of society into elite and mass is universal," and even in a democracy "a few exercise a relatively great weight of power, and the many exercise comparatively little."[2]

Democracy is government "by the people," but the survival of democracy rests on the shoulders of elites. This is the irony of democracy: Elites must govern wisely if government "by the people" is to survive. The masses do not lead; they follow. They respond to the attitudes, proposals, and behavior of elites.

This book, *The Irony of Democracy*, explains American political life using elite theory. It presents the evidence of U.S. political history and contemporary political science to describe and explain how elites function in a modern democratic society. But before we examine American politics we must understand more about *elitism*, *democracy*, and *pluralism*.

THE MEANING OF ELITISM

The central proposition of elitism is that all societies are divided into two classes: the few who govern and the many who are governed. The Italian political scientist Gaetano Mosca expressed this basic concept as follows:

> In all societies—from societies that are very underdeveloped and have largely attained the dawnings of civilization, down to the most advanced and powerful societies—two classes of people appear—a class that rules and a class that is ruled. The first class, always the less numerous, performs all of the political functions, monopolizes power, and enjoys the advantages that power brings, whereas the second, the more numerous class, is directed and controlled by the first, in a manner that is now more or less legal, now more or less arbitrary and violent.[3]

Elites, not masses, govern *all* societies. Elites are not a product of capitalism or socialism or industrialization or technological development. All societies—socialist and capitalist, agricultural and industrial, traditional and advanced—are governed by elites. All societies require leaders, and leaders acquire a stake in preserving the organization and their position in it. This motive gives leaders a perspective different from that of the organization's members. An elite, then, is inevitable in any social organization. As the French political scientist Roberto Michels put it, "He who says organization, says oligarchy."[4] The same is true for societies as a whole. According to political scientist Harold Lasswell, "The discovery that in all large-scale societies the decisions at any given time are typically in the hands of a small number of people" confirms a basic fact: "Government is always government by the few, whether in the name of the few, the one, or the many."[5]

Elitism also asserts that the few who govern are not typical of the masses who are governed. Elites control resources: power, wealth, education, prestige, status, skills of leadership, information, knowledge of political processes, ability to communicate, and organization. Elites in the United States are drawn disproportionately from wealthy, educated, prestigiously employed, socially prominent, white, Anglo-Saxon, and Protestant groups in society. They come from society's upper classes, those who own or control a disproportionate share of the societal institutions: industry, commerce, finance, education, the military, communications, civic organizations, and law.

Elitism, however, does not necessarily bar individuals of the lower classes from rising to the top; elite theory admits of some social mobility that enables nonelites to become elites. In fact, a certain amount of "circulation of elites" (upward mobility) is essential for the stability of the elite system. Openness in the system siphons off potentially revolutionary leadership from the lower classes; moreover, an elite system is strengthened when talented and ambitious individuals from the masses enter governing circles. However, social stability requires that movement from nonelite to elite positions be a slow, continuous assimilation rather than a rapid or revolutionary change. Only those nonelites who have demonstrated their commitment to the elite system itself and to the system's political and economic values can be admitted to the ruling class.

Elites share a general consensus about the fundamental norms of the social system. They agree on the basic rules of the game, as well as on the importance of preserving the social system. The stability of the system, and even its survival, depends on this consensus. According to David Truman, "Being more influential, they [the elites] are privileged; and being privileged, they have, with very few exceptions, a special stake in the continuation of the system in which their privileges rest."[6] Elite consensus does not prevent elite members from disagreeing or competing with each other for preeminence. But competition takes place within a very narrow range of issues, and elites agree on more matters than they disagree on. Disagreement usually occurs over *means* rather than *ends.*

In the United States, the bases of elite consensus are the sanctity of private property, limited government, and individual liberty. Richard Hofstadter writes about American elite struggles:

The fierceness of political struggles has often been misleading; for the range of vision embodied by the primary contestants in the major parties has always been bounded by the horizons of property and enterprise. However much at odds on specific issues, the major political traditions have shared a belief in the rights of property, the philosophy of economic individualism, the value of competition; they have accepted the economic virtues of capitalist culture as necessary qualities of man.[7]

Elitism implies that public policy does not reflect demands of "the people" so much as it reflects the interests and values of elites. Changes and innovations in public policy come about when elites redefine their own values. However, the general conservatism of elites—that is, their interest in preserving the system—means that changes in public policy will be incremental rather than revolutionary. Public policies are often modified but seldom replaced.

Elites may act out of narrow self-serving interests or enlightened, "public-regarding" motives. Occasionally elites abuse their powers and position and undermine mass confidence in their leadership. At other times, elites initiate reforms designed to preserve the system and restore mass support. Elitism does not necessarily mean that the masses are exploited or repressed, although these abuses are not uncommon. Elitism means only that the responsibility for mass welfare rests with elites, not with masses.

Finally, elitism assumes that the masses are largely passive, apathetic, and ill informed. Mass sentiments are manipulated by elites more often than elite values are influenced by the sentiments of the masses. Most communication between elites and masses flows downward. Masses seldom make decisions about governmental policies through elections or through evaluation of political parties' policy alternatives. For the most part, these "democratic" institutions—elections and parties—have only symbolic value: they help tie the masses to the political system by giving them a role to play on election day. Elitism contends that the masses have at best only an indirect influence over the decision-making behavior of elites.

Americans frequently misunderstand elitism because the prevailing myths and symbols are drawn from democratic theory rather than elite theory. Therefore it is important to emphasize what elitism is *not* as well as what it is.

Elitism does not mean that those in power continually battle against the masses or that elites always achieve their goals at the expense of the public interest. Elitism is not a conspiracy to oppress the masses. It does not imply that power is held by a single, impenetrable, monolithic body or that those in power always agree on public issues. It does not prevent power from shifting over time or prohibit the emergence of new elites. Elites may be more or less selfish and self-interested, or more or less enlightened and public-regarding. They may be more or less monolithic and cohesive, or more or less pluralistic and competitive. Power need not rest exclusively on the control of economic resources; it may rest instead on other leadership resources—organization, communication, or information. Elitism does not deny the influence of the masses on elite behavior; it holds only that elites influence masses more than masses influence elites.

In brief, elite theory may be summarized as follows:

1. Society is divided into the few who have power and the many who do not. Only a small number of people allocate values for society; the masses do not decide public policy.
2. The few who govern are not typical of the masses who are governed. Elites are drawn disproportionately from the upper socioeconomic strata of society.
3. The movement of nonelites to elite positions must be slow and continuous to maintain stability and avoid revolution. Only nonelites who have accepted the basic elite consensus enter governing circles.
4. Elites share a consensus on the basic values of the social system and the preservation of the system. They disagree only on a narrow range of issues.
5. Public policy does not reflect the demands of masses but the prevailing values of the elite. Changes in public policy will be incremental rather than revolutionary.
6. Elites may act out of narrow self-serving motives and risk undermining mass support, or they may initiate reforms, curb abuse, and undertake public-regarding programs to preserve the system and their place in it.
7. Active elites are subject to relatively little direct influence from the apathetic masses. Elites influence masses more than masses influence elites.

THE MEANING OF DEMOCRACY

Ideally, *democracy* means individual participation in the decisions that affect one's life. Traditional democratic theory has valued popular participation as an opportunity for individual self-development: Responsibility for governing one's own conduct develops one's character, self-reliance, intelligence, and moral judgment—in short, one's dignity. The classic democrat would reject even a benevolent despot who could govern in the interest of the masses. As the English political philosopher J. S. Mill asked, "What development can either their thinking or active faculties attain under it?" Thus the argument for citizen participation in public affairs depends not on its policy outcomes but on the belief that such involvement is essential to the full development of human capacities. Mill argued that people can know truth only by discovering it for themselves.[8]

Procedurally, in the democratic model, a society achieves popular participation through majority rule and respect for the rights of minorities. Self-development presumes self-government, and self-government comes about only by encouraging each individual to contribute to the development of public policy and by resolving conflicts over public policy through majority rule. Minorities who have had the opportunity to influence policy but whose views have not won majority support accept the decisions of majorities. In return, majorities permit minorities to attempt openly to win majority support for their views. Freedom of speech and press, freedom to dissent, and freedom to form opposition parties and organizations are essential to ensure meaningful individual participation. This freedom of expression is also critical in ascertaining the majority's real views.

The underlying value of democracy is individual dignity. Human beings, by virtue of their existence, are entitled to life, liberty, and property. A "natural law," or moral tenet, guarantees every person liberty and the right to property, and this natural law is morally superior to human law. John Locke, the English political philosopher whose writings most influenced America's founding elites, argued that even in a "state of nature"—that is, a world of no governments—an individual possesses inalienable rights to life, liberty, and property. Locke meant that these rights are independent of government; governments do not give them to individuals, and no government may legitimately take them away.[9]

Locke believed that a government's purpose is to protect individual liberty. People form a "social contract" with one another in establishing a government to help protect their rights; they tacitly agree to accept government activity to protect life, liberty, and property. Implicit in the social contract and the democratic notion of freedom is the belief that governmental activity and social control over the individual must be minimal. This belief calls for removing as many external restrictions, controls, and regulations on the individual as possible without violating the freedom of other citizens.

Another vital aspect of classical democracy is a belief in the equality of all people. The Declaration of Independence states that "all men are created equal." Even the Founding Fathers believed in equality for all persons *before the law,* regardless of their personal circumstances. A democratic society cannot judge a person by social position, economic class, creed, or race. Many early democrats also believed in *political equality:* equal opportunity of individuals to influence public policy. Political equality is expressed in the concept of "one man, one vote."

Over time, the notion of equality has also come to include *equality of opportunity* in all aspects of American life: social, educational, and economic, as well as political. Political scientist Roland Pennock writes:

> The objective of equality is not merely the recognition of a certain dignity of the human being as such, but it is also to provide him with the opportunity—

equal to that guaranteed to others—for protecting and advancing his interests and developing his powers and personality.[10]

Thus the notion of equal opportunity has spread beyond political life to include education, employment, housing, recreation, and public accommodations. Each person has an equal opportunity to develop his or her capacities to their natural limits.

Remember, however, that the traditional democratic creed has always stressed *equality of opportunity* for acquiring education, wealth, and status, and not *absolute equality*. Thomas Jefferson recognized a "natural aristocracy" of talent, ambition, and industry, and liberal democrats since Jefferson have always accepted inequalities that arise from individual merit and hard work. Absolute equality, or "leveling," is not part of liberal democratic theory.

In summary, democratic thinking reflects the following ideas:

1. Popular participation in the decisions that shape the lives of individuals in a society.
2. Government by majority rule, with recognition of the rights of minorities to try to become majorities. These rights include the freedom of speech, press, assembly, and petition and the freedom to dissent, to form opposition parties, and to run for public office.
3. A commitment to individual dignity and the preservation of the liberal values of life, liberty, and property.
4. A commitment to equal opportunity for all individuals to develop their capacities.

ELITISM IN A DEMOCRACY

Democracy requires popular participation in government. (The Greek root of the word *democracy* means "rule by the many.") But popular participation in government can have different meanings. To our nation's Founders, who were quite ambivalent about the wisdom of democracy, it meant that the people would be given representation in government. The Founding Fathers believed that government rests ultimately on the consent of the governed. But their notion of republicanism envisioned decision making by *representatives* of the people, rather than direct decision making by the people themselves. The Founding Fathers were profoundly skeptical of direct democracy, in which the people initiate and decide policy questions by popular vote (thus, the U.S. Constitution has no provision for national referenda.) The Founding Fathers had read about direct democracy in the ancient Greek city-state of Athens, and they were fearful of the "follies" of direct democracy. James Madison wrote,

> Such democracies have ever been spectacles of turbulence and contention; have ever been found incompatible with personal security of the rights of

property and have in general been as short in their lives as they have been violent in their deaths.[11]

The Founding Fathers were most fearful that unrestrained *majorities* would threaten liberty and property and abuse minorities and individuals, "the weaker party and the obnoxious individual." They recognized the potential contradiction in democratic theory—government by majority rule can threaten the life, liberty, and property of minorities and individuals.

Yet even if it were desirable, mass government is not really feasible in a large society. Lincoln's rhetorical flourish—"a government of the people, by the people, for the people"—has no real-world meaning. What would "the people look like if all 250 million Americans were brought together in one place?

Standing shoulder to shoulder in military formation, they would occupy an area of about sixty-six square miles.

The logistical problem of bringing 250 million bodies together is trivial, however, compared with the task of bringing about a meeting of 250 million minds. Merely to shake hands with that many people would take a century. How much discussion would it take to form a common opinion? A single round of five-minute speeches would require five thousand years. If only one percent of those present spoke, the assembly would be forced to listen to over two million speeches. People could be born, grow old and die while they waited for the assembly to make one decision.

In other words, an all-American town meeting would be the largest, longest, and most boring and frustrating meeting imaginable. What could such a meeting produce? Total paralysis. What could it do? Nothing.[12]

The democratic solution to the practical problem of popular government is the development of institutions of representation—elections, parties, organized interest groups—as bridges between individuals and their government. But this solution leads inevitably to elitism, not democracy.

Individuals in all societies, including democracies, confront the iron law of oligarchy. As organizations and institutions develop in society, power is concentrated in the hands of the leadership. Society becomes "a minority of directors and a majority of directed." Individuals are no match for the power of large institutions.

Power is the ability to influence people and events by granting or withholding valuable resources. To exercise power, one must control valuable resources. Resources are defined broadly to include not only wealth, but also position, status, celebrity, comfort, safety, and power itself. Most of the nation's resources are concentrated in large organizations and institutions—in corporations, banks, and financial institutions; in television networks, newspapers, and publishing empires; in organized interest groups, lobbies, and law firms; in foundations and think tanks; in civic and cultural organizations; and, most important, in government. The government is the most powerful of all these organizations, not only because it has accumulated great economic resources, but because it has a monopoly on physical coercion. Only government can legitimately undertake to imprison and execute people.

Thus, power in a democratic society is concentrated in the hands of the relatively few people who control its largest organizations and institutions. These are the people who direct, manage, and guide the programs, policies, and activities of the major institutions of society. Collectively, these people constitute the nation's elite.

In a democratic society, unlike a totalitarian one, multiple elites exist. A defining characteristic of Western democratic nations is the *relative autonomy* of various elites—governmental, economic, media, civic, cultural, and so on. In contrast, a defining characteristic of totalitarian societies is the forced imposition of unity on elites. Fascism asserted the unity of the state in Hitler's words: "Ifinen Volk, Ifinen Reich, Ifinen Fuhrer" (one people, one state, one leader). Socialism asserts the government's control of economic as well as political resources, and communism extols "the dictatorship of the proletariat" and assigns the Communist party the exclusive right to speak for the proletariat.

Reprinted with special permission of North America Syndicate.

But in Western democracies, elites have *multiple institutional bases* of power. Not all power is lodged in government, nor is all power derived from wealth. Democracies legitimize the existence of opposition parties as well as of organized interest groups. The power and independence of a media elite is a distinctive feature of U.S. democracy. Even within U.S. government, relatively autonomous multiple elites have emerged—in the Congress; in the judiciary; in the executive; and even within the executive, in a variety of bureaucratic domains. But it is really the power and autonomy of nongovernmental elites, and their recognized legitimacy, that distinguishes the elite structures of democratic nations from those of totalitarian states.

THE MEANING OF PLURALISM

No scholar or commentator, however optimistic about life in the United States, would assert that the U.S. political system has fully realized all the goals of democracy. No one contends that citizens participate in all decisions shaping their lives or that majority preferences always prevail. Nor does anyone argue that the system always protects the rights of minorities, always preserves the values of life, liberty, and property, or provides every American with an equal opportunity to influence public policy.

However, pluralism seeks to affirm that American society is nevertheless democratic by asserting that:

1. Although citizens do not directly participate in decision making, their many leaders make decisions through a process of bargaining, accommodation, and compromise.

2. Competition among leadership groups helps protect individuals' interests. Countervailing centers of power—for example, competition among business leaders, labor leaders, and government leaders—can check one another and keep each interest from abusing its power and oppressing the individual.

3. Individuals can influence public policy by choosing among competing elites in elections. Elections and parties allow individuals to hold leaders accountable for their actions.

4. Although individuals do not participate directly in decision making, they can exert influence through participating in organized groups.

5. Leadership groups are open; new groups can form and gain access to the political system.

6. Although political influence in society is unequally distributed, power is widely dispersed. Access to decision making is often determined by how much interest people have in a particular decision. Because leadership is fluid and mobile, power depends on one's interest in public af-

fairs, skills in leadership, information about issues, knowledge of democratic processes, and skill in organization and public relations.

7. Multiple leadership groups operate within society. Those who exercise power in one kind of decision do not necessarily exercise power in others. No single elite dominates decision making in all issues.

8. Public policy does not necessarily reflect majority preference but is an equilibrium of interest interaction—that is, competing interest-group influences are more or less balanced, and the resulting policy is therefore a reasonable approximation of society's preferences.

Pluralism, then, is the belief that democratic values can be preserved in a system where multiple, competing elites determine public policy through bargaining and compromise, voters exercise meaningful choices in elections, and new elites can gain access to power.

───── ELITISM VERSUS PLURALISM

Elite theory differs from the prevailing pluralist vision of democracy in several key respects. Both theories agree that societal decision making occurs through elite interaction, not mass participation; that the key political actors are the leaders of large organizations and institutions, not individual citizens; and that public policy generally reflects the interests of large organizations and institutions, not majority preferences. Indeed, because of these similarities, some critics of pluralism assert that it is really a disguised form of elitism—that is, elitism hiding in democratic rhetoric. Critics of pluralism have charged that pluralists are closer to the elitist position than to the democratic tradition they claim to be upholding. Thus, political scientist Peter Bachrach describes pluralism as "democratic elitism."[13] Yet despite these recognized parallels with pluralist theory, elite theory offers a fundamentally different view of power and society.

First of all, elite theory asserts that the most important division in society is between elites and masses, between the few who govern and the many who do not. Elites in all organizations and institutions in society share a common experience—the exercise of power. Occupying positions of power provides elites with a common motive—the preservation of their organization and their position in it. Pluralism overlooks this central division of society into elites and masses and emphasizes the fragmentation of society and competition between leadership groups. Elitism emphasizes the importance to leaders of maintaining their positions of power, while pluralism emphasizes their devotion to their group interests.

Elite theory asserts that the mass membership of organizations, parties, interest groups, and institutions in society rarely exercises any direct control over the elite leadership. Group membership does *not* ensure effective individual participation in decision making. The organizations and institutions on which pluralists rely "become oligarchic and restrictive insofar as they monopolize access to government power and limit individual participation."[14] Henry Kariel writes, "The voluntary organizations or associations, which the early theorists of pluralism relied upon to sustain the individual against a unified omnipotent government, have themselves become oligarchically governed hierarchies."[15] Individuals may provide organizations' numerical strength, but what influence does an individual member have on leadership? Rarely do corporations, unions, armies, churches, governmental bureaucracies, or professional associations have any internal democratic mechanisms. They are usually run by a small elite of officers and activists. Leaders of corporations, banks, labor unions, interest groups, television networks, churches, universities, think tanks, and civic associations remain in control year after year. Very few people attend meetings, vote in organizational elections, or make their influence felt within their organization. The pluralists offer no evidence that the giant organizations and institutions in American life really represent the views or interests of their individual members.

Elite theory suggests that accommodation and compromise among leadership groups is the prevailing style of decision making, not competition and conflict. Pluralism contends that competition among leadership groups protects the individual. But why should we assume that leadership groups compete with each other? More likely, each elite group allows other elite groups to govern in their own spheres of influence without interference. According to elite theory, accommodation rather than competition is the prevailing style of elite interaction: "You scratch my back and I'll scratch yours." Where interests occasionally overlap, elite differences are compromised in order to maintain stability. It is true that multiple, relatively autonomous elites exist in a democratic society; but this multiplicity does not guarantee competition or a balance among centers of power.

Elite theory takes account of all power holders in society, private as well as public. Pluralism focuses on governmental leaders and those who interact directly with them. Because governmental leaders are chosen in elections, pluralism asserts that leaders can be held accountable to the people. But even if governmental elites can be held accountable through elections, how can corporation executives, media elites, union leaders, and other persons in positions of private leadership be held accountable? Pluralism usually dodges this important question by focusing primary attention on *public*, government-elite decision making and largely ignoring *private*, nongovernment-elite decision making. Pluralists focus on rules and orders enforced by *governments*, but certainly citizens' lives are vitally affected by decisions made by private institutions and organizations, among them corporations, banks, universities, television networks, and newspapers. In an ideal democracy, individuals participate in all decisions that significantly affect their lives; however, pluralism largely excludes individuals from participation in many vital decisions by claiming that these decisions are "private" in nature and not subject to public accountability.

Elitism emphasizes the shared characteristics of leaders, not only their common interest in preserving the social system and their place in it, but also their many shared experiences, values, and goals. Pluralism emphasizes diversity among leaders—differences in backgrounds, ideologies, and viewpoints. Even when elitists show that a disproportionate share of America's leadership is composed of wealthy, educated, prestigiously employed, white, upper- and upper-middle-class males, pluralists respond by asserting that these background characteristics are poor predictors of the decision-making behavior of leaders. Instead, pluralists argue that leaders' decisions are a product of their role perceptions, institutional constraints, interest group pressures, public opinion, and so on. Elitism focuses on leadership consensus, asserting that elites differ more over the means than the ends of public policy. Pluralism focuses on elite conflict, asserting that elites differ on a wide variety of issues of vital importance to society.

Finally, pluralism and elitism differ over the nature and extent of mass influences over societal decision making. Elitism asserts that elites influence masses more than masses influence elites. Communication flows primarily downward from elites to masses. An enlightened elite may choose to consider the well-being of the masses in decision making, either out of ethical principles or a desire to avoid instability and revolution. But even when elites presume to act in the interests of the masses, the elites act on their *own* view of what is good for the masses, not what the masses decide for themselves. In contrast, pluralists, while acknowledging that elites rather than the masses make society's decisions, nonetheless assert that the masses influence policy through both their membership in organized interest groups and their participation in elections. Interest groups, parties, and elections, according to the pluralists, provide the means by which the masses can hold elites accountable for their decisions. But elite theory contends that the principal function of elections is not to provide policy mandates to elites, but rather to legitimize elite rule by providing symbolic reassurance that democratic elites govern on behalf of the masses.

In short, while elitism and pluralism share some common views on the preeminent role of elites in a democratic society, elitism differs from pluralism in several key respects. In contrast to pluralism, *elitism* asserts:

1. The importance of the common elite experience—the exercise of power—in providing a compelling motive for the preservation of the

system and the elites' place in it, over and above whatever other interests that elites are supposed to represent.

2. The oligarchic and undemocratic nature of societal organizations and institutions, which renders individual participation in group decision making impossible and makes accurate representation of members' views by group leaders highly problematic.

3. The prevailing style of elite interaction as accommodationist rather than competitive, with no assurance that multiple groups in society will provide balance to public policy.

4. The exercise of power by private as well as public institutions, and the realization that even if the policies of government elites could be held accountable through elections, those of corporations, banks, television networks, and other private organizations are beyond the direct control of the electorate.

5. The commonality of elite experiences, values, and goals, and the assertion that elites differ more over the means than the ends of public policy.

6. The failure of parties and elections to provide effective means by which the masses can hold elites accountable for their policy decisions.

CASE STUDY

 ### Mass Confidence in America's Elite

How much confidence do the masses have in America's leadership? Is a "crisis of authority" confronting America's elite?

Elites have always been concerned about the possibility of mass disaffection and the opportunities that such disaffection might present for demagogues and revolutionaries. The Constitutional Convention of 1787 was inspired in part by Shays' Rebellion and the concern that the Revolutionary War had unleashed mass hostility toward established authority. John Adams worried about a general crisis in authority following the revolt against the British Crown:

> We have been told that our struggle has loosened the bonds of government everywhere, that children and apprentices were disobedient, that schools and college were grown turbulent, that Indians slighted their guardians, and negroes grew insolent to their masters. . . . [Now we have the] intimation that another

tribe [women], more numerous and powerful than all the rest, were grown discontent.*

A major concern of the nation's elite prior to 1980 was the decline of mass confidence in national leadership and distrust of its motives. Throughout the 1960s and 1970s public opinion polls showed dramatic erosion of mass support for the national government. Fewer people were willing to "trust the government in Washington to do what is right," (see Figure 1-1) and more people said "the government is pretty much run by a few big interests looking out for themselves."

The partial restoration of mass confidence in the nation and its leadership was one of the more significant achievements of the Reagan administration.

*Charles Francis Adams, ed., *Letters of John Adams,* vol. 1 (Boston: Charles C. L. Little and James Brown, 1841), pp. 96–97; cited in Seymour Martin Lipset and William Schneider, *The Confidence Gap* (New York: Free Press, 1988).

FIGURE 1-1   Mass support for American government

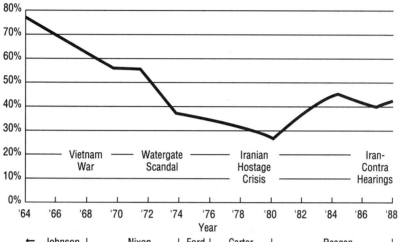

Can You Trust Government to Do What Is Right?

"How much of the time do you think you can trust the government in Washington to do what is right? Always? Most of the time? Some of the time? None of the time? " Percentage of respondents saying government can be trusted "always" or "most of the time."

SOURCE: National Election Studies Center, University of Michigan, as reported in the *New York Times*, November 19, 1984, January 21, 1987, and October 27, 1987.

The public "malaise" about which President Jimmy Carter complained was gradually lifted. Tracing the decline and restoration of public confidence over the years is easier than determining what causes these shifts in mass opinion. But it seems clear that mass confidence responds to a combination of real events, media coverage of these events, and the character of the nation's leadership.

Defeat and humiliation in war always and everywhere undermines mass support for a nation's leadership. Perhaps the most important negative influence on mass confidence in America's elite was the experience of the Vietnam War. This tragic war was followed immediately by the Watergate scandal and the first forced resignation of a president. President Carter did little to reverse the decline in mass confidence; America's humiliation by Iranian revolutionaries who took U.S. embassy personnel as hostages produced the nadir of confidence in 1979.

The long-term effect of negative media reporting—of world events and of political, military, and business leadership—is to increase social distrust and political cynicism (see Chapter Six). Television in particular has lowered general levels of trust and confidence. Because the strongest bias in network news reporting is toward conflict and controversy, scandal and corruption—bad news drives out the good news—it is unlikely in the media age that mass confidence in American institutions and leadership can ever be restored to previous high levels.

Yet clearly mass confidence can be increased. No doubt the relative peace and prosperity of the 1980s made improvement possible. But the personality of Ronald Reagan and his calculated efforts to restore optimism, pride, and patriotism had a profound effect on Americans. It is somewhat ironic that Ronald Reagan, a conser-

(continued)

CASE STUDY *(continued)*

vative critic of big government, helped to restore public confidence in "the government in Washington."

But the spurt proved to be transient. Although the Gulf War of 1991–1992 produced the usual "rally 'round the flag" effect, the exuberance evaporated quickly and, by the summer of 1992, the masses were so angry that the candidacy of Texas billionaire Ross Perot, which would have been ignored in "normal" times, created a sensation.

Mass confidence in the leadership of specific institutional sectors of society tends to follow generalized measures of confidence. Thus, for example, confidence in the leadership of business corporations, government, and the military declined during the 1970s and then rebounded in the 1980s (see Figure 1-2). However, note that mass confidence in the leadership of the media and organized labor appears to be on a continuing downward course.

FIGURE 1-2   Percentage with a great deal/quite a lot of confidence in . . .

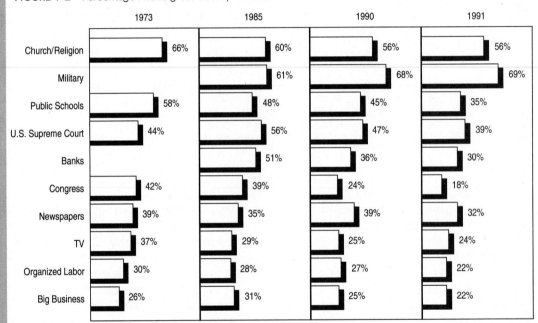

SOURCE: Gallup, *Annual Surveys.*

ELITE AND MASS THREATS TO DEMOCRACY

It is the irony of democracy that the survival of democratic values—individual dignity, limited government, equality of opportunity, private property, freedom of speech and press, religious tolerance, and due process of law—depends on enlightened elites. The masses respond to the ideas and actions of elites. When elites abandon democratic principles or the masses lose confidence in elites, democracy is in peril.

Elite Distemper

Yet democratic elites do not always live up to their responsibilities to preserve the system and its values. Elite behavior is not always enlightened and farsighted, but instead frequently shortsighted and narrowly self-serving. The relative autonomy of separate elites in a democracy—governmental, corporate, financial, media, legal, civic and cultural—often encourages narrow visions of the common good and a willingness to sacrifice societal values for relative advantage.

Examples of narrowly self-serving elite behavior abound. Politicians resort to divisive, racial appeals or to class antagonisms—setting black against white or poor against rich—to win elections, knowing that these tactics undermine mass confidence in national leadership. Corporate officials sacrifice long-term economic growth for short-term, windfall, paper profits, knowing that the nation's competitive position in the world is undermined by shortsighted "bottom-line" policies. Banking and savings and loan executives finance risky ventures in search of quick profits, knowing that their failures will be paid for by depositors and taxpayers. Members of Congress in pursuit of personal pay and perks as well as lifetime tenure cater to the political activists in their home districts, with little regard for national concerns. Bureaucrats, seeking to expand their powers and budgets, create a regulatory quagmire and huge government deficits, disadvantaging the the nation in global competition and burdening future generations with enormous debts. Interest group leaders, particularly the zealous champions of single issues, pursue their quest for special privileges, treatments, and exemptions from law, at the expense of common principles. Network television executives "hype" both news and entertainment shows with violence, scandal, sex, corruption, and scares of various sorts, knowing that these stories undermine mass confidence in the nation's institutions. Lawyers and judges pervert the judicial process for personal advantage, drowning the nation in a sea of litigation, clogging the courts and delaying justice, reinterpreting laws and the Constitution to suit their purposes, and undermining mass respect for the law.

In short, elites do not always act with unity and purpose. They all too frequently put narrow interests ahead of broader, shared values. These behaviors grow out of the relative autonomy of various elites in a democracy. They are encouraged by the absence of any external checks on the power of elites in their various domains. The only effective check on irresponsible elite behavior is their own realization that the system itself will become endangered if such behavior continues unrestrained. So periodically elites undertake reforms, mutually agreeing to curb the most flagrant abuses of the system. The stimulus to reform is the restoration of mass confidence in elite government, and ultimately the preservation of the elite system itself. But reforms often succeed only in creating new opportunities for abuse, changing the rules but failing to restrain self-interested elites.

Mass Unrest

But mass politics can also threaten democratic values. Despite a super-ficial commitment to the symbols of democracy, the masses have surpris-ingly weak commitments to the principles of individual liberty, toleration of diversity, and freedom of expression when required to apply these prin-ciples to despised or obnoxious groups or individuals. In contrast, elites, and the better-educated groups from which they are recruited, are gen-erally more willing than the masses to apply democratic values to specific situations and to protect the freedoms of unpopular groups.

Masses are dangerously vulnerable to demagogic appeals to intoler-ance, racial hatred, anti-intellectualism, class antagonisms, anti-Semi-tism, and violence. Counterelites, or demagogues, are mass-oriented leaders who express hostility toward the established order and appeal to the mass sentiments. These counterelites, whether they are on the left or right, are extremist and intolerant, impatient with due process, con-temptuous of individual rights, anxious to impose their views by sweep-ing measures, and often willing to use violence and intimidation to do so.[16] Right-wing counterelites talk of "the will of the people," while left-wing radicals cry, "All power to the people." Both appeal to mass extrem-ism: the notion that compromise and coalition-building, and working within the democratic system for change, is pointless or even immoral. Democratic politics is viewed with cynicism.[17] Counterelites frequently resort to conspiracy theories to incite the masses. The left charges that the capitalist conspiracy exploits and oppresses the people for its own profit and amusement; the right charges that the nation is falling prey to a communist conspiracy whose goal is to deprive the people of their liberty and property. Political historian Richard Hofstadter refers to this popu-larity of conspiracy theories as "the paranoid style of politics."[18] A related weapon in the arsenal of demagogues is scapegoating—the designation of particular minority groups in society as responsible for the evils suffered by the people. U.S. history has seen a variety of scapegoats, among them Catholics, immigrants, Jews, blacks, intellectuals, Communists, Wall Street bankers, and the "military-industrial complex." These tactics ap-peal to mass desire for simplistic solutions to societal problems. Simplis-tic explanations relieve the masses of the drudgery of difficult thinking and allow complex problems to be expressed in simple, emotion-laden terms. Anti-intellectualism and antirationalism are important parts of mass politics.

It is the irony of democracy that democratic values can survive only in the absence of mass political activism. Democratic values thrive best when the masses are absorbed in the problems of everyday life and involved in groups and activities that distract their attention from mass political movements. Political stability depends on mass involvement in work, family, neighborhood, trade union, hobby, church, group recreation, and other activities. When the masses become alienated from home, work, and community—when their ties to social organizations and institutions weaken—they become vulnerable to the appeals of demagogues, and democratic values are endangered.

Mass activism inspires elite repression. Mass political movements, when they gain momentum and give rise to hatred, generate fear and insecurity among elites. They respond by limiting freedom and strengthen security, banning demonstrations, investigating and harassing opposition, arresting activists, and curtailing speech, writing, and broadcasting—usually under the guise of preserving law and order. Ironically, elites resort to these repressive actions out of a genuine belief that they are necessary to preserve democratic values.

Elite theory, then, recognizes multiple threats to democracy: *elite misdeeds*—shortsighted and self-interested behavior that undermines popular support for the political system; *mass activism*—extremist and intolerant political movements, led by counterelites appealing to racial hatred, class antagonism, and personal fears; and *elite repression*—forced indoctrination in "political correctness"; limitations on dissent, speech, and assembly in the name of law and order; and the subversion of democratic values in a paradoxical effort to preserve the system.

AN ELITIST THEORY OF DEMOCRACY

All societies are governed by elites, even democratic societies. The elitist theory of democracy is not an attack upon democracy, but rather an aid in understanding the realities of democratic politics.

Elite theory is not an apology for elite rule; it is not defense of official misdeeds or repression. Rather, it is a realistic explanation of how democracy works, how democratic values are both preserved and threatened, how elites and masses interact, how public policy is actually determined, and whose interests generally prevail.

Critics of this elitist theory of democracy claim that it is "conservative," that it legitimizes elite rule, that it obstructs social progress of the masses. But elite theory neither endorses nor condemns elite governance, but rather seeks to expose and analyze the way in which elites function in a democracy. It is true that elite theory denies the possibility of ever abolishing elite rule; it denies the now discredited Marxist vision of a classless, socialist society. But, by providing a better understanding of how elites in a democratic society go about gaining, exercising, and maintaining power, elite theory identifies both the obstacles and opportunities for social progress. Rather than an idealized vision of social changes through mass citizen participation, elite theory provides a realistic assessment of how and when democratic elites are moved to initiate change. It warns the naive that leaders of "citizens' movements" are themselves elites with their own self-interests.

Elite theory poses the central question of American politics: Who governs the nation? How do people acquire power? How are economic and political power related? What interests shaped the U.S. Constitution? How have American elites changed over two centuries? How have victory and defeat in war strengthened and weakened elite governance? How widely is power shared in the United States today? Are leaders in government, business, banking, the media, law, foundations, interest groups, and cultural affairs separate, distinct, and competitive—or are they concentrated, interlocked, and consensual? Do elites or masses give greater support to democratic values? Are masses generally informed, sensible, and considerate—or are they largely ill informed, apathetic, and intolerant? Does public opinion shape elite behavior—or do elites shape public opinion through the mass media? How successful are media elites in molding mass opinion and influencing public debate? Are American political parties "responsible" instruments of popular control of government—or are they weakened oligarchies, dominated by ideologically motivated activists? Do elections serve as policy mandates from the people—or are they primarily an exercise in citizenship, choosing personnel, not policy? Are political campaigns designed to inform voters and assess their policy preferences—or are they expensive, commercial adventures in image-making? How politically active, informed, knowledgeable, and consistent in their views are the American people? Do organized interest groups fairly represent the views of their members—or do they reflect the views and interests of leaders who are largely out of touch with the members? Does competition among interest groups create a reasonable balance in public policy—or do the special interests dominate policy making at the expense of the mass public? How much influence do masses have over the actions of presidents, Congress, and courts? What role does the president play in America's elite system? Why are presidents more influential in shaping foreign policy than domestic policy? Is power shifting from elected officials to "faceless bureaucrats"? What are the sources of bureaucratic power, and can bureaucracy be restrained? Who do members of Congress really represent? Are members of Congress held accountable for their policy decisions by the voters back home—or are they free to pursue their personal interests in Washington, knowing that their constituents are generally unaware of their policy positions? Why are the nation's most important domestic policy questions usually decided by the most elitist branch of the government, the unelected, lifetime-tenured justices of the Supreme Court? Can political decentralization—decision making by sub-elites in states and communities—increase mass involvement in government? How do elites respond to mass protest movements? Do protest movements themselves become oligarchic over time and increasingly divorced from the views of the masses?

This text will address questions such as these from the perspective of *elite* theory. But it will also compare and evaluate the answers suggested by *pluralist* theory and *democratic* theory. The goal is a better understanding not only of U.S. politics but also of elitism, pluralism, and democracy.

——— NOTES

1. Robert A. Dahl, "Power, Pluralism, and Democracy: A Modest Proposal," paper delivered at American Political Science Association annual meeting, 1964, p. 3. See also Peter Bachrach, *The Theory of Democratic Elitism: A Critique* (Boston: Little, Brown, 1967).
2. Harold Lasswell and Abraham Kaplan, *Power and Society* (New Haven, Conn.: Yale University Press, 1950), p. 219.
3. Gaetano Mosca, *The Ruling Class* (New York: McGraw-Hill, 1939), p. 50.
4. Roberto Michels, *Political Parties: A Sociological Study of the Oligarchical Tendencies of Modern Democracies* (1915; reprint, New York: Free Press, 1962), p. 70.
5. Harold Lasswell and Daniel Lerner, *The Comparative Study of Elites* (Stanford, Calif.: Stanford University Press, 1952), p. 7.
6. David Truman, "The American System in Crisis," *Political Science Quarterly* 74 (December 1959): 489.
7. Richard Hofstadter, *The American Political Tradition* (New York: Knopf, 1948), p. viii.
8. John Stuart Mill, *Representative Government* (New York: Dutton, Everyman's Library, 1962), p. 203.
9. For a discussion of John Locke and the political philosophy underlying democracy, see George Sabine, *A History of Political Theory* (New York: Holt, Rinehart & Winston, 1950), pp. 517–541.
10. Roland Pennock, "Democracy and Leadership" in *Democracy Today,* eds. William Chambers and Robert Salisbury (New York: Dodd, Mead, 1962), pp. 126–127.
11. James Madison, *The Federalist* Number 10 (New York: Modern Library, 1937).
12. E. E. Schattschneider, *Two Hundred Americans in Search of a Government* (New York: Holt, Rinehart & Winston, 1969), p. 63.
13. Peter Bachrach, *The Theory of Democratic Elitism: A Critique* (Boston: Little, Brown, 1967), p. xi.

14. Robert Presthus, *Men at the Top* (New York: Oxford University Press, 1964), p. 20.

15. Henry Kariel, *The Decline of American Pluralism* (Stanford, Calif.: Stanford University Press, 1961), p. 74.

16. See Seymour Martin Lipset and Earl Raab, *The Politics of Unreason* (New York: Harper & Row, 1970).

17. See John H. Bunzel, *Anti-Politics in America* (New York: Knopf, 1967).

18. Richard Hofstadter, *The Paranoid Style of American Politics* (New York: Knopf, 1965).

SELECTED READINGS

Bachrach, Peter. *The Theory of Democratic Elitism: A Critique.* Boston: Little, Brown, 1967. In addition to giving a good review of classic elitist literature, Bachrach discusses the distinctions among democracy, pluralism, and elitism. He observes that whereas pluralists claim that their model is the practical adaptation of democratic theory to the modern technological state, pluralism in fact makes so many alterations in democratic theory as to render it unrecognizable. Bachrach coins a new term for the model produced by the combination of democratic theory with group theory; he calls it "democratic elitism." We call it "pluralism."

Bachrach, Peter, and Baratz, Morton. "Two Faces of Power." *American Political Science Review* 56 (1962): 947–952. The authors argue that power is tied to decision making but that power also comes from preventing a decision (called a "nondecision"). Thus power has two faces.

Dahl, Robert A. "A Critique of the Ruling Elite Model." *American Political Science Review* 52 (1958): 369–463. This essay is a classic critique of elitism from a pluralist point of view.

Dahl, Robert A. *Pluralist Democracy in the United States: Conflict and Consensus.* Chicago: Rand McNally, 1967. Most of Dahl's important theoretical work was at the community level. This book extended pluralism to the national level.

Domhoff, G. William, and Dye, Thomas R., eds. *Power Elites and Organizations.* Newbury Park, Calif.: Sage, 1987. This volume combines original research reports on elites in corporations, think tanks, foundations, communities, and states with theoretical essays on elitism in modern organizations.

Michels, Roberto. *Political Parties: A Sociological Study of the Oligarchical Tendencies of Modern Democracies.* New York: Free Press, 1962. This book first appeared in 1911 in German. Michels was a disciple of Mosca. Like Mosca, he sees elitism as an outcome of social organization. Michels argues that the very fact of organization in society leads inevitably to an elite. His often-quoted thesis is, "Who says organization, says oligarchy." Political scientists have called this "the iron law of oligarchy."

Mosca, Gaetano. *The Ruling Class.* Edited by A. Livingston. New York: McGraw-Hill, 1939. This book was first published in 1896 in Italy. Mosca added to it later in a 1923 edition that reflects the impact of World War I on his ideas. Along with the work of Vilfredo Pareto, Mosca's *Ruling Class* forms the basis of "classical elitism."

Pareto, Vilfredo. *The Mind and Society: Treatise of General Sociology.* New York: Harcourt, Brace & World, 1935 (originally published in 1915–1916 in four volumes). Pareto begins with a very broad definition of elite. He suggests that in any human activity, those who are the top practitioners are the elite in that activity. Thus he groups elites into two classes—the governing elite and the nongoverning elite—depending on whether the activity of which they are a top practitioner is important to government. Pareto also introduces psychological notions into his work. He speaks of "residues," which are human instincts, sentiments, or states of mind that remain constant over time and from state to state.

Parry, Geraint. *Political Elites.* New York: Praeger, 1969. This book is an excellent discussion of classical elitism. It includes extensive treatment of Mosca, Pareto, Michels, Max Weber, James Burnham, C. Wright Mills, and other elitist writers.

2

The Founding Fathers:
The Nation's First Elite

★ *All communities divide themselves into the few and the many. The first are the rich and well-born, the other the masses of people.*

Alexander Hamilton, Records of the Federal Convention of 1787

The Founding Fathers—those fifty-five men who wrote the Constitution of the United States and founded a new nation—were a truly exceptional elite, not only "rich and well-born" but also educated, talented, and resourceful. When Thomas Jefferson, then the nation's minister in Paris, first saw the list of delegates to the Constitutional Convention of 1787, he wrote to John Adams, the minister to London, "It is really an assembly of demigods."[1] The men at the Convention belonged to the nation's intellectual and economic elites; they were owners of landed estates, important merchants and importers, bankers and financiers, real estate and land speculators, and government bond owners. Jefferson and Adams were among the nation's very few notables who were not at the Constitutional Convention.

The Founding Fathers were not typical of the four million Americans in the new nation, most of whom were small farmers, tradespeople, frontier dwellers, servants, or slaves. However, to say that these men were not a representative sample of the American people, or that the Constitution was not a very democratic document, does not discredit the Founding Fathers or the Constitution. To the aristocratic society of eighteenth-century Europe, the Founding Fathers were dangerous revolutionaries who were establishing a government in which men with the talent of acquiring property could rise to political power even though not born into the nobility. And the Constitution has survived the test of time, providing the basic framework for an ever-changing society.

ELITES AND MASSES IN THE NEW NATION

Many visitors from the aristocratic countries of Europe noted the absence of an American nobility and commented on the spirit of equality that prevailed. Yet class lines existed in America. At the top of the social structure, a tiny elite dominated the social, cultural, economic, and political life of the new nation. The French chargé d'affaires reported in 1787 that America had "no nobles" but that certain "gentlemen" enjoyed "preeminence" because of "their wealth, their talents, their education, their families, or the offices they hold."[2] Some of these prominent gentlemen were Tories who fled America after the Revolution, but Charleston still had its Pinckneys and Rutledges; Boston its Adamses, Lowells, and Gerrys; New York its Schuylers, Clintons, and Jays; Philadelphia its Morrises, Mifflins, and Ingersolls; Maryland its Jenifers and Carrolls; and Virginia its Blairs and Randolphs.

Below this thin layer of educated and talented merchants, planters, lawyers, and bankers was a substantial body of successful farmers, shopkeepers, and independent artisans—of the "middling" sort, as they were known in revolutionary America. This early middle class was by no means a majority in the new nation; it stood considerably above the masses of debt-ridden farmers and frontier dwellers who made up most of the population. This small middle class had some political power, even at the time of the Constitutional Convention; it was entitled to vote, and its views were represented in governing circles, even if these views did not prevail at the Convention. The middle class was especially well represented in state legislatures and was championed by several men of prominence in the revolutionary period—Patrick Henry, Luther Martin, and Thomas Jefferson.

The great mass of white Americans in the revolutionary period were "freeholders," small farmers who worked their own land, scratching out a bare existence for themselves and their families. They had little interest in, or knowledge of, public affairs. Usually the small farmers who were not barred from voting by property-owning or tax-paying qualifications were too preoccupied with debt and subsistence, or too isolated in the wilderness, to vote anyway. Nearly eight out of ten Americans made a marginal living in the dirt; one in ten worked in fishing or lumbering; and one in ten worked in commerce in some way, whether as a dockhand, sailor, lawyer, or merchant.

At the bottom of the white social structure in the new republic were indentured servants and tenant farmers; this class, which was perhaps 20 percent of the population, apparently exercised little, if any, political power. Finally, still further below, were the black slaves. Although they made up almost another 20 percent of the population and were an important component of the American economy, they were considered property, even in a country that proclaimed the natural rights and equality of "all men."

ELITE DISSATISFACTION WITH THE CONFEDERATION

In July 1775, Benjamin Franklin proposed to the Continental Congress a plan for a "perpetual union"; following the Declaration of Independence in 1776, the Congress appointed a committee to consider the Franklin proposal. The committee, headed by John Dickinson, made its report in the form of the Articles of Confederation, which the Congress debated for more than a year before finally adopting them on November 15, 1777. The Articles of Confederation were not to go into effect until every state approved; Delaware withheld its consent until 1779, Maryland until 1781.

The Articles of Confederation, effective from 1781 to 1789, established a "firm league of friendship" among the states "for their common defense, the security of their liberties, and their mutual and general welfare." The document reassured each state of "its sovereignty, freedom, and independence, and every power, jurisdiction, and right, which is not by this confederation expressly delegated to the United States, in Congress assembled." The Confederation's delegated powers included power to declare war, to send and receive ambassadors, to make treaties, to fix standards of weights and measures, to regulate the value of coins, to manage Indian affairs, to establish post offices, to borrow money, to build and equip an army and navy, and to make requisitions (requests) to the several states for money and people. Certain powers remained with the states, including two of the most important ones of government: to regulate commerce and to levy taxes. Moreover, Congress had no authority to compel the states to honor its requisitions for revenues. Since Congress could not regulate commerce, the states were free to protect local trade and commerce even at the expense of the emerging national economy.

The Founding Fathers were very critical of the first government of the United States under the Articles of Confederation, but the government was not a failure. Between 1774 and 1789, the American Confederation declared its independence from the world's most powerful colonial nation, fought a successful war, established a viable peace, won powerful allies in the international community, created a successful army and navy, established a postal system, created a national bureaucracy, and laid the foundations for national unity.

But despite the successes of the Confederation in war and diplomatic relations, the American elites found the political arrangements under the Articles unsatisfactory, even threatening. Generally the Founding Fathers most lamented the "weaknesses" of the Articles that allowed political arrangements threatening the interests of merchants, investors, planters, real estate developers, and owners of public bonds and securities.

The inability of Congress to levy taxes under the Articles of Confederation was a serious threat to those patriots who had given financial backing to the new nation during the Revolutionary War. The Continental Congress and the states had financed the war with money borrowed through the issuance of government bonds. Congress was unable to tax the people to pay off those debts, and the states became less and less inclined, as time passed, to meet their obligations to the central government. The states paid only one-tenth the sums requisitioned by the Congress under the Articles. During the last years of the Articles, the national government was unable even to pay interest on its debt. As a result, the bonds and notes of the national government lost most of their value, sometimes selling on the open market for only one-tenth their original value. Investors who had backed the American war effort were left with nearly worthless bonds.

Without the power to tax, and with the credit of the Confederation ruined, the prospects of the central government for future financial support—and survival—looked dim. Naturally the rich planters, merchants, and investors who owned government bonds had a direct financial interest in helping the national government acquire the power to tax and to pay off its debts.

The inability of Congress under the Articles to regulate commerce, among the states and with foreign nations, and the states' practice of laying tariffs on the goods of other states as well as on those of foreign nations created havoc among commercial and shipping interests. "In every point of view," Madison wrote in 1785, "the trade of this country is in a deplorable condition."[3] The American Revolution had been fought, in part, to defend American commercial and business interests from oppressive regulation by the British government. Now the states themselves were interfering with the development of a national economy. Merchants and shippers with a view toward a national market and a high level of commerce were vitally concerned that the national government acquire the power to regulate interstate commerce and to prevent the states from imposing crippling tariffs and restrictions on interstate trade.

State governments under the Articles posed a serious threat to investors and creditors through issuing cheap paper money and passing laws impairing contractual obligations. Paper money issued by the states permitted debtors to pay off their creditors with money worth less than the money originally loaned. Even the most successful farmers were usually heavily in debt, and many of them were gaining strength in state legislatures. They threatened to pass laws delaying the collection of debts and even abolishing the prevailing practice of imprisonment for unpaid debts. Obviously creditors had a direct financial interest in establishing a strong central government that could prevent the states from issuing public paper or otherwise interfering with debt collection.

A strong central government would help protect creditors against social upheavals by the large debtor class in America. In several states, debtors had already engaged in open rebellion against tax collectors and sheriffs attempting to repossess farms on behalf of creditors. The most serious rebellion broke out in the summer of 1786 in Massachusetts, when bands of insurgents—composed of farmers, artisans, and laborers—captured the courthouses in several western districts and briefly held the city of Springfield. Led by Daniel Shays, a veteran of Bunker Hill, the insurgent army posed a direct military threat to the governing elite of Massachusetts. Shays' Rebellion was put down by a smaller mercenary army, paid for by well-to-do citizens who feared a wholesale attack on property rights.

The states' growing radicalism intimidated the propertied classes, who began to advocate a strong central government to "insure domestic tranquility," guarantee "a republican form of government," and protect property "against domestic violence." The American Revolution had disturbed the masses' tradition of deferring to those in authority. Extremists like Thomas Paine, who reasoned that it was right and proper to revolt against England because of political tyranny, might also call for revolt against creditors because of economic tyranny. If debts owed to British merchants could be legislated out of existence, why not also the debts owed to American merchants? Acts of violence, boycotts, tea parties, and attacks on tax collectors frightened all propertied people in America.

A strong central government with enough military power to oust the British from the Northwest and to protect western settlers against Indian attacks could open the way for the development of the American West. In addition, the protection and settlement of western land would cause land values to skyrocket and make land speculators rich.

Men of property in early America very actively speculated in western land. George Washington, Benjamin Franklin, Robert Morris, and even the popular hero Patrick Henry were involved in land speculation. During the Revolutionary War, the Congress had often paid the Continental soldiers with land certificates. After the war, most of the ex-soldiers sold the certificates to land speculators at very low prices. The Confederation's military weakness along its frontiers had kept the value of western lands low, for ravaging Indians discouraged immigration to the lands west of the Alleghenies, and the British threatened to cut off westward expansion by continuing to occupy (in defiance of the peace treaty) seven important fur-trading forts in the Northwest. The British forts were also becoming centers of anti-American influence among the Indians.

The development of a strong national navy was also important to American commercial interests, for the states seemed ineffective in preventing smuggling, and piracy was a very real danger and a vital concern of American shippers.

Manufacturing was still in its newborn stages during the revolutionary era in America, but farsighted investors were anxious to protect infant American industries against the import of British goods. Although all thirteen states erected tariff barriers against foreign goods, state tariffs could not provide the same protection for industry as a strong central government with a uniform tariff policy, because the state tariff system allowed low-tariff states to bring in foreign goods and circulate them throughout the country.

Finally, a strong sense of nationalism appeared to motivate America's elites. While the masses focused on local affairs, the educated and cosmopolitan leaders in America were concerned about the weakness of America in the international community. Thirteen separate states failed to manifest a sense of national purpose and identity. The Confederation was held in contempt not only by Britain, as evidenced by the violations of the Treaty of Paris, but even by the lowly Barbary states. Hamilton expressed the indignation of America's leadership over its inability to swing weight in the world community:

> There is something . . . diminutive and contemptible in the prospect of a number of petty states, with the appearance only of union, jarring, jealous, and perverse, without any determined direction, fluctuating and unhappy at home, weak and insignificant by their dissentions in the eyes of other nations.[4]

In short, America's elite wanted to assume a respectable role in the international community and exercise power in world affairs.

FORMATION OF A NATIONAL ELITE

In the spring of 1785, delegates from Virginia and Maryland met at Alexandria, Virginia, to resolve certain difficulties that had arisen between the two states over the regulation of commerce and navigation on the Potomac River and Chesapeake Bay. It was fortunate for the new nation that the most prominent man in America, George Washington, took a personal interest in this meeting. As a rich planter and land speculator who owned more than 30,000 acres of western lands upstream on the Potomac, Washington was keenly aware of commercial problems under the Articles. He lent great prestige to the Alexandria meeting by inviting participants to his home at Mount Vernon. Out of this conference came the idea for a general economic conference for all the states. The Virginia legislature issued a call for such a convention to meet at Annapolis in September 1785.

Judged by its publicly announced purpose—securing interstate agreement on matters of commerce and navigation—the Annapolis Convention was a failure; only twelve delegates appeared, representing five commercial states: New York, New Jersey, Pennsylvania, Delaware, and Virginia. But these twelve men saw the opportunity to use the Annapolis meeting to achieve greater political successes. Alexander Hamilton, with masterful political foresight, persuaded the others in attendance to strike out for a full constitutional solution to America's ills. The Annapolis Convention adopted a report, written by Hamilton, that outlined the defects in the Articles of Confederation and called upon the states to send delegates to a new convention to suggest remedies for these defects. The new convention was to meet in May 1787 in Philadelphia. Rumors at the time suggested that Hamilton, with the behind-the-scenes support of James Madison in the Virginia legislature, had intended all along that the Annapolis Convention fail in its stated purposes and that it provide a stepping-stone to larger political objectives.

Shays' Rebellion was very timely for men like Hamilton and Madison, who sought to galvanize America's elite into action. Commencing in the fall of 1786, after the Annapolis call for a new convention, the rebellion convinced men of property in Congress and state legislatures that there was cause for alarm.

On February 21, 1787, Congress confirmed the call for a convention to meet in Philadelphia

> for the sole and express purpose of revising the Articles of Confederation and reporting to Congress and the several legislatures such alterations and provisions therein as shall, when agreed to in Congress and confirmed by the states, render the federal Constitution adequate to the exigencies of government and the preservation of the union.

Delegates to the Convention were appointed by the legislatures of every state except Rhode Island, the only state in which the debtor classes had wrested political control from the legislature.

The fifty-five men who met in the summer of 1787 to establish a new national government quickly chose George Washington, their most prestigious member—indeed the most prestigious man on the continent—to preside over the assembly. Just as quickly, the Convention decided to hold its sessions behind closed doors and to keep all proceedings a carefully guarded secret. Delegates adhered closely to this decision and informed neither close friends nor relatives of the nature of the discussions. Apparently the Founding Fathers were aware that elites are most effective in negotiation, compromise, and decision making when operating in secrecy.

The Convention was quick to discard its congressional mandate to "revise the Articles of Confederation"; without much hesitation, it proceeded to write an entirely new constitution. Only men confident of their powers and abilities, men of principle and property, could proceed in this bold fashion. Let us examine the characteristics of the nation's first elite more closely.

One cannot overestimate the prestige of George Washington at this time in his life. As the commander-in-chief of the successful revolutionary army and founder of the new nation, he had overwhelming charismatic appeal among both elites and masses. Preeminent not only as a soldier, statesman, and founder of the nation, he was also one of the richest men in America. Through all the years that he had spent in the revolutionary cause, he had refused any payment for his services. He often paid his soldiers from his own fortune. In addition to his large estate on the Potomac, he possessed many thousands of acres of undeveloped land in western Virginia, Maryland, Pennsylvania, Kentucky, and the Northwest Territory. He owned major shares in the Potomac Company, the James River Company, the Bank of Columbia, and the Bank of Alexandria. And he held large amounts in U.S. bonds and securities. Washington stood at the apex of America's elite structure.

The Founding Fathers had extensive experience in governing. These same men had made all the key decisions in American history from the Stamp Act Congress to the Declaration of Independence to the Articles of Confederation. They controlled the Congress of the United States and had conducted the Revolutionary War. Eight delegates had signed the Declaration of Independence. Eleven delegates had served as officers in Washington's army. Forty-two of the fifty-five Founding Fathers had already served in the U.S. Congress. Even at the moment of the Convention, more than forty delegates held high offices in state governments; Franklin, Livingston, and Randolph were governors. The Founding Fathers were unsurpassed in political skill and experience.

In an age when no more than a handful of men on the North American continent had gone to college, the Founding Fathers were conspicuous for their educational attainment. More than half the delegates had been educated at Harvard (founded in 1636), William and Mary (1693), Yale (1701), University of Pennsylvania (1740), Columbia College (1754), Princeton (1756), or in England. The tradition of legal training for political decision makers, which has continued in the United States to the present, was already evident. About a dozen delegates were still active lawyers in 1787, and about three dozen had had legal training.

The fifty-five men at Philadelphia formed a major part of the nation's economic elite as well. The personal wealth represented at the meeting was enormous. It is difficult to determine accurately who were the richest men in America at that time because the finances of the period were chaotic and because wealth assumed a variety of forms—land, ships, credit, slaves, business inventories, bonds, and paper money of uncertain worth (even George Washington had difficulty at times converting his land wealth into cash). But at least forty of the fifty-five delegates were known to be holders of government bonds; fourteen were land speculators; twenty-four were money-lenders and investors; eleven were engaged in commerce or manufacturing; and fifteen owned large plantations.[5] (See Table 2-1.)

Robert Morris was perhaps the foremost business and financial leader in the nation in 1787. This Philadelphia merchant owned scores of ships that traded throughout the world; he engaged in iron manufacturing, speculated in land in all parts of the country, and controlled the Bank of North America in Philadelphia, probably the nation's largest financial institution at the time. He earned his title "the patriot financier" by underwriting a large share of the debts of the United States during and after the Revolutionary War. Later in his life, his financial empire collapsed, probably because of overspeculation, and he died in debt. But at the time of the Convention, he stood at the center of America's financial structure.

Perhaps what most distinguished the men at Philadelphia from the masses was their cosmopolitanism. They approached political, economic, and military issues from a "continental" point of view. Unlike the masses, members of the elite extended their loyalties beyond their states; they experienced the sentiment of nationalism half a century before it would begin to seep down to the masses.[6]

ELITE CONSENSUS IN 1787

By focusing on the debates within the Convention, many historical scholars have overemphasized the differences of opinion among the Founding Fathers. True, the Convention was the site of many conflicting views and innumerable compromises; yet the more striking fact is that the delegates were in almost complete accord on essential political questions.

TABLE 2-1 Founding Fathers' known membership in elite groups

Holders of public security interests		Real estate and land speculators	Lenders and investors	Merchants, manufacturers, and shippers	Planters and slaveholders
Major	Minor				
Baldwin	Bassett	Blount	Bassett	Broom	Butler
Blair	Blount	Dayton	Broom	Clymer	Davie
Clymer	Brearly	Few	Butler	Ellsworth	Jenifer
Dayton	Broom	Fitzsimons	Carroll	Fitzsimons	A. Martin
Ellsworth	Butler	Franklin	Clymer	Gerry	L. Martin
Fitzsimons	Carroll	Gerry	Davie	King	Mason
Gerry	Few	Gilman	Dickinson	Langdon	Mercer
Gilman	Hamilton	Gorham	Ellsworth	McHenry	C. C. Pinckney
Gorham	L. Martin	Hamilton	Few	Mifflin	C. Pinckney
Jenifer	Mason	Mason	Fitzsimons	G. Morris	Randolph
Johnson	Mercer	R. Morris	Franklin	R. Morris	Read
King	Mifflin	Washington	Gilman		Rutledge
Langdon	Read	Williamson	Ingersoll		Spaight
Lansing	Spaight	Wilson	Johnson		Washington
Livingston	Wilson		King		Wythe
McClurg	Wythe		Langdon		
R. Morris			Mason		
C. C. Pinckney			McHenry		
C. Pinckney			C. C. Pinckney		
Randolph			C. Pinckney		
Sherman			Randolph		
Strong			Read		
Washington			Washington		
Williamson			Williamson		

Protecting Liberty and Property

They agreed that the fundamental end of government is the protection of liberty and property. They accepted without debate many of the precedents set by the English constitution and by the constitutions of the new states. Reflecting the advanced ideas of their times, the Founding Fathers were much less religious than most Americans today. Yet they believed in a law of nature with rules of abstract justice to which human laws should conform. They believed that this law of nature endowed each person with certain inalienable rights essential to a meaningful existence—the rights to life, liberty, and property—and that these rights should be recognized and protected by law. They believed that all people were equally entitled to respect of their natural rights regardless of their station in life.

Most of the Founding Fathers were even aware that this belief ran contrary to the practice of slavery and were embarrassed by this inconsistency in American life.

But "equality" did *not* mean to the Founding Fathers that people were equal in wealth, intelligence, talent, or virtue. They accepted inequalities in wealth and property as a natural product of human diversity. They did not believe that government had a responsibility to reduce these inequalities; in fact, they saw "dangerous leveling" as a serious violation of the right to property and the right to use and dispose of the fruits of one's own industry.

Government as Contract

The Founding Fathers agreed that the origin of government is an implied contract among people. They believed that people pledge allegiance and obedience to government in return for protection of their persons and property. They felt that the ultimate legitimacy of government—sovereignty—rests with the people themselves and not with gods or kings and that the basis of government is the consent of the governed.

Republicanism

The Founding Fathers believed in republican government. They opposed hereditary monarchies, the prevailing form of government in the world at the time. Although they believed that people of principle and property should govern, they were opposed to an aristocracy or a governing nobility. To them, a "republican government" was a representative, responsible, and nonhereditary government. But they certainly did *not* mean mass democracy, with direct participation by the people in decision making. They expected the masses to consent to government by men of principle and property, out of recognition of their abilities, talents, education, and stake in the preservation of liberty and order. The Founding Fathers believed that the masses should have only a limited role in selecting government leaders. They bickered over how much direct participation is appropriate in selecting decision makers and they bickered over the qualifications necessary for public office, but they generally agreed that the masses should have only a limited, indirect role in selecting decision makers and that decision makers themselves should be men of wealth, education, and proven leadership ability.

Limited Government

The Founding Fathers believed in limited government that could not threaten liberty or property. Since the Founding Fathers believed that power is a corrupting influence and that the concentration of power is dangerous, they believed in dividing government power into separate bodies capable of checking, or thwarting, one another should any one branch pose a threat to liberty or property. Differences of opinion among honest people, particularly differences among elites in separate states, could best be resolved by balancing representation of these several elites in the national government and by creating a decentralized system that permits local elites to govern their states as they see fit, with limited interference from the national government.

Nationalism

Finally, and perhaps most important, the Founding Fathers believed that only a strong national government, with power to exercise its will directly on the people, could "establish justice, insure domestic tranquility, provide for the common defense, promote the general welfare, and secure the blessings of liberty."

This consensus on fundamentals dwarfed the differences requiring compromise in the Convention. It was the existence of a national elite and its agreement on the fundamentals of politics that made possible the formation of the U.S. government. If the elites had faced substantial divisiveness in 1787, any substantial competition or conflict, or any divergent centers of influence, a new government would never have emerged from the Philadelphia Convention. Elite consensus in 1787 was profoundly conservative; the elites wished to preserve the status quo in the distribution of power and property in the United States. Yet at the same time, this elite consensus was radical compared with the beliefs of their elite contemporaries elsewhere in the world. Nearly every other government adhered to the principles of hereditary monarchy and privileged nobility, whereas American elites were committed to republicanism. Other elites asserted the divine rights of kings, but American elites talked about government by the consent of the governed. While the elites in Europe rationalized and defended a rigid class system, American elites believed in equality and inalienable human rights.

——— AN ELITE IN OPERATION: CONCILIATION AND COMPROMISE

On May 25, 1787, sessions of the Constitutional Convention opened in Independence Hall, Philadelphia. After the delegates had selected Washington as president of the Convention and decided to keep the proceedings of the Convention secret, Governor Edmund Randolph, speaking for the Virginia delegation, presented a draft of a new constitution.*

*James Madison kept secret notes on the Convention, which he published many years later. Most of our knowledge about the Convention comes from Madison's notes. See Max Ferrand, ed., *The Records of the Federal Convention of 1787* (New Haven, Conn.: Yale University Press, 1911).

Representation Compromise

The Virginia plan gave little recognition to the states in its proposed composition of the national government. The plan suggested a two-house legislature, the lower house to be chosen by the people of the states, with representation according to the population. The upper house was to be chosen by the first house. This Congress would have power to "legislate in all cases in which the separate states are incompetent, or in which the harmony of the United States may be interrupted by the exercise of individual legislation." Moreover, Congress would have the authority to nullify state laws that it felt violated the Constitution, thus ensuring national supremacy. The Virginia plan also proposed a parliamentary form of government, with Congress choosing members of the executive and judiciary branches.

The most important line of cleavage at the Convention was between elites of large states and elites of small states over the representation scheme in the Virginia plan. This question was not one of economic interest or ideology, since delegates from large and small states did not divide along economic or ideological lines. After several weeks of debate over the Virginia plan, delegates from the small states presented a counterproposal in a report by William Paterson of New Jersey. The New Jersey plan may have been merely a tactic by the small-state elites to force the Convention to compromise on representation, for the plan was set aside after only a week of debate with little negative reaction. The New Jersey plan proposed to retain the representation scheme outlined in the Articles of Confederation, which granted each state a single vote. But the plan went further, proposing separate executive and judiciary branches and expansion of the powers of Congress to include the right to levy taxes and regulate commerce.

The New Jersey plan was not an attempt to retain the Confederation. Indeed, the plan included words that later appeared in the Constitution as the famous national supremacy clause that provides that the U.S. Constitution and federal laws supersede each state's constitution and laws. Thus even the small states did not envision a confederation. Both the Virginia and New Jersey plans were designed to strengthen the national government; they differed only on how much to strengthen it and on its system of representation.

On June 29, William Samuel Johnson of Connecticut proposed the obvious compromise: that representation in the lower house of Congress be based upon population, whereas representation in the upper house would be equal—two senators from each state. The Connecticut compromise also provided that equal representation of states in the Senate could not be abridged, even by constitutional amendment.

Slavery Compromises

The next question requiring compromise was that of slavery and the role of slaves in the system of representation, an issue closely related to economic differences among America's elite. It was essentially the same question that seventy-four years later divided that elite and provoked the nation's bloodiest war. Planters and slaveholders generally believed that wealth, particularly wealth in slaves, should count in apportioning representation. Nonslaveholders felt that "the people" should include only free inhabitants. The decision to apportion direct taxes among the states in proportion to population opened the way to compromise, since the attitudes of slaveholders and nonslaveholders reversed when counting people in order to apportion taxes. The result was the famous three-fifths compromise: three-fifths of the slaves of each state would be counted for the purpose of both representation and apportioning direct taxes.

A compromise was also necessary on the question of trading in slaves. On this issue, the men of Maryland and Virginia, states already well supplied with slaves, were able to indulge in the luxury of conscience and support proposals for banning the further import of slaves. But the less-developed southern states, particularly South Carolina and Georgia, could not afford this posture since they still wanted additional slave labor. Inasmuch as the southern planters were themselves divided, the ultimate compromise permitted Congress to prohibit slave trade—but not before the year 1808. The twenty-year delay would allow the undeveloped southern states to acquire all the slaves they needed before the slave trade ended.

Export Tax Compromise

Agreement between southern planters and northern merchants was still relatively easy to achieve at this early date in American history. But latent conflict was evident on issues other than slavery. Although all elite groups agreed that the national government should regulate interstate and foreign commerce, southern planters feared that the unrestricted power of Congress over commerce might lead to the imposition of export taxes. Export taxes would bear most heavily on the southern states, which depended on foreign markets in order to sell the indigo, rice, tobacco, and cotton the southern states produced. However, planters and merchants were able to compromise again in resolving this issue: articles exported from any state should bear no tax or duty. Only imports could be taxed by the national government.

Voter Qualification Compromise

Another important compromise, one that occupied much of the Convention's time (though it has received little recognition from later writers), concerned qualifications for voting and holding office in the new government. Although no property qualifications for voters or officeholders appear in the text of the Constitution, the debates revealed that members of the Convention generally favored property qualifications for officeholding. The delegates showed little enthusiasm for mass participation in democracy. Elbridge Gerry of Massachusetts declared that "the evils we experience flow from the excess of democracy." Roger Sherman protested that "the people immediately should have as little to do as may be about the government." Edmund Randolph continually deplored the turbulence and follies of democracy, and George Clymer's notion of republican government was that "a representative of the people is appointed to think for and not with his constituents." John Dickinson considered property qualifications a "necessary defense against the dangerous influence of those multitudes without property and without principle, with which our country like all others, will in time abound." Charles Pinckney later wrote to Madison, "Are you not . . . abundantly depressed at the theoretical nonsense of an election of Congress by the people; in the first instance, it's clearly and practically wrong, and it will in the end be the means of bringing our councils into contempt." Many more such elitist statements appear in the records of the Convention.[7]

Given these views, how do we explain the absence of property qualifications in the Constitution? Actually a motion was carried in the Convention instructing a committee to fix property qualifications for officeholding, but the committee could not agree upon the qualifications to be imposed. Various propositions to establish property qualifications met defeat on the floor, not because delegates believed they were inherently wrong but, interestingly enough, because the elites at the Convention represented different kinds of property holdings. Madison pointed out that fact in the July debate, noting that a land ownership requirement would exclude from Congress the mercantile and manufacturing classes, who would hardly be willing to turn their money into landed property just to become eligible for a seat in Congress. Madison rightly observed that "landed possessions were no certain evidence of real wealth. Many enjoyed them to a great extent who were more in debt than they were worth." The objections by merchants and investors defeated the "landed" qualifications for congressional representatives.

Thus the Convention approved the Constitution without property qualifications on voters, except those that the states themselves might see fit to impose. Failing to come to a decision on this issue of suffrage, the delegates merely returned the question to state legislatures by providing that "the electors in each state should have the qualifications requisite for electors of the most numerous branch of the state legislatures." At the time, this expedient course of action did not seem likely to produce mass democracy. Only one branch of the new government, the House of Representatives, was to be elected by popular vote. The other three controlling bodies—the president, the Senate, and the Supreme Court—were removed from direct voter participation. The delegates were reassured that nearly all the state constitutions then in force included property qualifications for voters.

Finally, the Constitution did not recognize women as legitimate participants in government. For nearly one hundred years, no state accorded women the right to vote. (The newly formed Wyoming Territory first gave women the right to vote and hold public office in 1869.) Not until 1920 was the U.S. Constitution amended to guarantee women the right to vote.

THE CONSTITUTION AS AN ELITIST DOCUMENT

The text of the Constitution, together with interpretive materials in *The Federalist* papers written by Hamilton, Madison, and Jay, provides ample evidence that elites in America benefited both politically and economically from the adoption of the Constitution. Although both elites and nonelites—indeed all Americans—may have benefited from the Constitution, elites benefited more directly and immediately than did nonelites. And we can infer that the elites would not have developed and supported the Constitution if they had not stood to gain substantially from it.

Elite Philosophy

We can discover the elitist consensus by examining the underlying philosophy of government contained in the Constitution. According to Madison in *The Federalist,* "the principal task of modern legislation" was to control factions.[8] A faction is a number of citizens united by a common interest adverse to the interest of other citizens or of the community as a whole. The causes of factions lie in human diversity:

> A zeal for different opinions concerning religion, concerning government, and many other points, as well of speculation as of practice; an attachment to different leaders ambitiously contending for preeminence and power; or to persons of other descriptions whose fortunes have been interesting to human passions.

Factions arise primarily because of inequality in the control of economic resources:

> But the most common and durable source of factions has been the various and unequal distribution of property. Those who hold and those who are without property have ever formed distinct interests in society. Those who are creditors and those who are debtors fall under like discrimination. A landed interest, a manufacturing interest, a mercantile interest, a monied interest, with many lesser interests, grow up of necessity in civilized nations, and divide them into different classes, actuated by different sentiments and views [*The Federalist* Number 10].

In Madison's view, a national government is the most important protection against mass movements that might threaten property. By creating such a government, encompassing a large number of citizens and a great expanse of territory, you take in a greater variety of parties and interests; you make it less probable that a majority of the whole will have a common motive to invade the rights of other citizens; or if such a common motive exists it will be more difficult for all who feel it to discover their own strength, and to act in unison with each other.

The structure of the new national government should ensure suppression of "factious" issues (those that would generate factions). And Madison did not hedge in naming these factious issues: "A rage for paper money, for an abolition of debts, for an equal division of property, or any other improper or wicked project." Note that Madison's factious issues are all challenges to the dominant economic elites. His defense of the new Constitution was that its republican and federal features would help keep certain threats to property from ever becoming public issues. In short, the Founding Fathers deliberately designed the new U.S. government to make it difficult for any mass political movement to challenge property rights.

Impact of the Constitution on Elites

Now let us examine the text of the Constitution itself and its impact on American elites. Article I, Section 8, grants seventeen types of power to Congress, followed by a general grant of power to make "all laws which shall be necessary and proper for carrying into execution the foregoing powers."

Levying taxes.   The first and perhaps most important power is the "power to lay and collect taxes, duties, imposts, and exercises." The taxing power is the basis of all other powers, and it enabled the national government to end its dependence upon states. This power was essential to the holders of public securities, particularly when combined with the provision in Article VI that "All debts contracted and engagements entered into, before the adoption of this Constitution, shall be as valid against the United States under this Constitution, as under the Confederation." Thus the national government was committed to paying off all those investors who held bonds of the United States, and the taxing power guaranteed that commitment would be fulfilled.

The text of the Constitution suggests that the Founding Fathers intended Congress to place most of the tax burden on consumers in the form of custom duties and excise taxes rather than direct taxes on individual income or property. Article I, Section 2, states that government can levy direct taxes only on the basis of population; it follows that it could not levy such taxes in proportion to wealth. This provision prevented the national government from levying progressive income taxes; not until the Sixteenth Amendment in 1913 did this protection for wealth disappear from the Constitution.

Southern planters, whose livelihoods depended on the export of indigo, rice, tobacco, and cotton, strenuously opposed giving the national government the power to tax exports. Article I, Section 9, offered protection for their interests: "No tax or duty shall be laid on articles exported from any State." However, Congress was given the power to tax imports so that northern manufacturers could erect a tariff wall to protect American industries against foreign goods.

Regulating commerce.   Congress also had the power to "regulate commerce with foreign nations, and among the several States." The interstate commerce clause, together with the provision in Article I, Section 9, prohibiting the states from taxing either imports or exports, created a free trade area over the thirteen states. This arrangement was very beneficial for American merchants.

Protecting money and property.   Following the Article I, Section 8, powers to tax and spend, to borrow money, and to regulate commerce is a series of specific powers designed to enable Congress to protect money and property. Congress is given the power to make bankruptcy laws, to coin money and regulate its value, to fix standards of weights and measures, to punish counterfeiting, to establish post offices and post roads, to pass copyright and patent laws to protect authors and inventors, and to punish piracies and felonies committed on the high seas. Each of these powers is a specific asset to bankers, investors, and shippers, respectively. Obviously the Founding Fathers felt that giving Congress control over currency and credit in the United States would result in better protection for financial interests than would leaving the essential responsibility to the states. Similarly, they believed that control over communication and transportation (by establishing post offices and post roads) was too essential to trade and commerce to be left to the states.

Creating the military.   The remaining powers in Article I, Section 8, deal with military affairs: raising and supporting armies; organizing, training, and calling up the state militia; declaring war; suppressing insurrections; and repelling invasions. These powers—together with the provisions in Article II making the president the commander-in-chief of the army and navy and of the state militia when called into the federal service, and giving the president power to make treaties with the advice and consent of the Senate, and to send and receive ambassadors—centralized diplomatic and military affairs at the national level. Article I, Section 10, confirms this centralization of diplomatic and military powers by prohibiting the states from entering into treaties with foreign nations, maintaining ships of war, or engaging in war unless actually invaded.

Clearly the Founding Fathers had little confidence in the state militias, particularly when they were under state control; General Washington's painful experiences with state militias during the Revolutionary War were still fresh in his memory. The militias had proved adequate when defending their own states against invasion, but when employed outside their own states, the militias were often a disaster. Moreover, if western settlers were to be protected from the Indians and if the British were to be persuaded to give up their forts in Ohio and open the way to westward expansion, the national government could not rely upon state militias but must have an army of its own. Similarly, a strong navy was essential to the protection of U.S. commerce on the seas (the first significant naval action under the new government was against the piracy of the Barbary states). Thus a national army and navy were not so much protection against invasion (for many years the national government continued to rely primarily upon state militias for this purpose) as they were protection and promotion of the government's commercial and territorial ambitions.

Protecting against revolution.   A national army and navy, as well as an organized and trained militia that could be called into national service, also provided protection against class wars and debtor rebellions. In an obvious reference to Shays' Rebellion, Hamilton warned in *The Federalist* Number 21:

> The tempestuous situation from which Massachusetts has scarcely emerged evinces that dangers of this kind are not merely speculative. Who could determine what might have been the issue of her late convulsions if the malcontents had been headed by a Caesar or a Cromwell? A strong military force in the hands of the national government is a protection against revolutionary action.

Further evidence of the Founding Fathers' intention to protect the governing classes from revolution is found in Article IV, Section 4, where the national government guarantees to every state "a republican form of government" as well as protection against "domestic violence." Thus in addition to protecting western land and commerce on the seas, a strong army and navy would enable the national government to back up its pledge to protect governing elites in the states from violence and revolution.

Protection against domestic insurrection also appealed to the southern slaveholders' deep-seated fear of a slave revolt. Madison drove this point home in *The Federalist* Number 23:

> I take no little notice of an unhappy species of population abounding in some of the states who, during the calm of regular government were sunk below the level of men; but who, in the tempestuous seeds of civil violence, may emerge into human character and give a superiority of strength to any party with which they may associate themselves.

Protecting slavery.   As we have noted, the Constitution permitted Congress to outlaw the import of slaves after 1808. But most southern planters were more interested in protecting their existing property and slaves than they were in extending the slave trade, and the Constitution provided an explicit advantage to slaveholders in Article IV, Section 2:

> No person held to service or labor in one State, under the laws thereof, escaping into another, shall in consequence of any law or regulation therein, be discharged from such service or labor, but shall be delivered up on claim of the party to whom such service or labor may be due.

This provision was an extremely valuable protection for one of the most important forms of property in the United States at the time. Although the U.S. slave trade lapsed after twenty years, slavery itself, as a domestic institution, was better safeguarded under the new Constitution than under the Articles.

Limiting states in monetary affairs.   The restrictions placed upon state legislatures by the Constitution also provided protection to economic elites in the new nation. States could not coin money, issue paper money, or pass legal-tender laws that would make any money other than gold or silver coin tender in the payment of debts. This restriction would prevent the states from issuing cheap paper money, which debtors could use to pay off creditors with less valuable currency. Moreover, the states were prohibited from passing legal-tender laws obliging creditors to accept paper money in payment of debts.

Limiting states in business affairs.   The Constitution also prevents states from passing any law "impairing the obligation of contracts." The structure of business relations in a free-enterprise economy depends on governmental enforcement of private contracts, and economic elites seek to prevent government from relieving people of their contractual obligations. If state legislatures could relieve debtors of their contractual obligations, relieve indentured servants of their obligations to their masters, prevent creditors from foreclosing on mortgages, declare moratoriums on debt, or otherwise interfere with business obligations, then the interests of investors, merchants, and creditors would be seriously damaged.

Elitism and the Structure of the National Government

National supremacy.   The heart of the Constitution is the supremacy clause of Article VI:

> This Constitution, and the laws of the United States which shall be made in pursuance thereof; and all treaties made, or which shall be made, under the authority of the United States, shall be the supreme law of the land; and the

judges in every State shall be bound thereby, any thing in the Constitution or laws of any State to the contrary notwithstanding.

This sentence made it abundantly clear that laws of Congress would supersede laws of the states, and it made certain that Congress would control interstate commerce, bankruptcy, monetary affairs, weights and measures, currency and credit, communication, transportation, and foreign and military affairs. Thus the supremacy clause ensures that the decisions of the national elite will prevail over those of the local elites in all vital areas allocated to the national government.

Republicanism.   The structure of the national government—its republicanism and its system of separated powers and checks and balances—was also designed to protect liberty and property. To the Founding Fathers, a republican government meant the delegation of powers by the people to a small number of citizens "whose wisdom may best discern the true interest of their country, and whose patriotism and love of justice will be least likely to sacrifice it to temporary or partial consideration."[9] Madison explained, in classic elite fashion, "that the public voice, pronounced by representatives of the people, will be more consonant to the public good than if pronounced by the people themselves." The Founding Fathers clearly believed that representatives of the people were more likely to be enlightened persons of principle and property than the voters who chose them and would thus be more trustworthy and dependable.

Voters also had a very limited voice in the selection of decision makers. Of the four major decision-making entities established in the Constitution—the House of Representatives, the Senate, the presidency, and the Supreme Court—the people were to elect only one. The others were to be at least twice removed from popular control. In the constitution of 1787, the people elected only House members, and for short terms of only two years. In contrast, state legislatures were to elect U.S. senators for six-year terms. Electors, selected as state legislatures saw fit, selected the president. The states could hold elections for presidential electors, or the state legislatures could appoint them. The Founding Fathers hoped that presidential electors would be prominent men of wealth and reputation in their respective states. Finally, federal judges were to be appointed by the president for life, thus removing those decision makers as far as possible from popular control.

Separation of powers and checks and balances.   The Founding Fathers also intended the system of separated powers in the national government—separate legislative, executive, and judicial branches—as a bulwark against majoritarianism (government by popular majorities) and an additional safeguard for elite liberty and property. The doctrine derives from the French writer Montesquieu, whose *Spirit of Laws* was a political textbook for these eighteenth-century statesmen. *The Federalist* Number 51 expressed the logic of the system of checks and balances:

Ambition must be made to counteract ambition. . . . It may be a reflection on human nature, that such devices should be necessary to control the abuses of government. But what is government itself, but the greatest of all reflections on human nature? If men were angels, no government would be necessary. If angels were to govern men, neither external or internal controls on government would be necessary. In framing a government which is to be administered by men over men, the greatest difficulty lies in this: you must first enable the government to control the governed; and in the next place oblige it to control itself.

The Constitution states the separation-of-powers concept in the opening sentences of the first three articles:

[Article I:] All legislative powers herein granted shall be vested in a Congress of the United States. . . . [Article II:] The executive power shall be vested in a President of the United States. . . . [Article III:] The judicial power of the United States shall be vested in one Supreme Court, and in such inferior courts as the Congress may from time to time ordain and establish.

Insofar as this system divides responsibility and makes it difficult for the masses to hold government accountable for public policy, it achieves one of the purposes intended by the Founding Fathers. Each of the four major decision-making bodies of the national government is chosen by different constituencies. Because the terms of these decision-making bodies are of varying length, a complete renewal of government at one stroke is impossible. Thus the people cannot wreak havoc quickly through direct elections. To make their will felt in all the decision-making bodies of the national government, they must wait years.

Moreover, each of these decision-making bodies has an important check on the decisions of the others. No bill can become law without the approval of both the House and the Senate. The president shares in the legislative power through the veto and the responsibility to "give to the Congress information of the state of the Union, and recommend to their consideration such measures as he shall judge necessary and expedient. . . ." The president can also convene sessions of Congress. But the appointing power of the president is shared by the Senate; so is the power to make treaties. Also Congress can override executive vetoes. The president must execute the laws but cannot do so without relying on executive departments, which Congress must create. The executive branch can spend only money appropriated by Congress. Indeed, "separation of powers" is a misnomer, for we are really talking about sharing, not separating, power; each branch participates in the activities of every other branch.

Even the Supreme Court, which was created by the Constitution, must be appointed by the president with the consent of the Senate, and Congress may prescribe the number of justices. More important, Congress must create lower and intermediate courts, establish the number of judges, fix the jurisdiction of lower federal courts, and make "exceptions" to the Supreme Court's jurisdiction over appeals.

Those who criticize the U.S. government for its slow, unwieldy processes should realize that the government's founders deliberately built in this characteristic. These cumbersome arrangements—the checks and balances and the fragmentation of authority that make it difficult for government to realize its potential power over private interests—aim to protect private interests from governmental interference and to shield the government from an unjust and self-seeking majority. If the system handcuffs government and makes it easy for established groups to oppose change, then the system is working as intended.

This system of intermingled powers and conflicting loyalties is still alive today. Of course, some aspects have changed; for example, voters now elect senators directly, and the president is more directly responsible to the voters than was originally envisioned. But the basic arrangement of checks and balances endures. Presidents, senators, representatives, and judges are chosen by different constituencies; their terms of office vary, and their responsibilities and loyalties differ. This system makes majority rule virtually impossible.

Judicial review.   Perhaps the keystone of the system of checks and balances is the idea of judicial review, an original contribution by the Founding Fathers to the science of government. In *Marbury* v. *Madison* in 1803, Chief Justice John Marshall argued convincingly that the Founding Fathers intended the Supreme Court to have the power to invalidate not only state laws and constitutions but also any laws of Congress that came into conflict with the Constitution. The text of the Constitution nowhere specifically authorizes federal judges to invalidate acts of Congress; at most, the Constitution implies this power. (But Hamilton apparently thought that the Constitution contained this power, since he was careful to explain it in *The Federalist* Number 78 before the ratification of the Constitution.) Thus, the Supreme Court stands as the final defender of the fundamental principles agreed upon by the Founding Fathers against the encroachments of popularly elected legislatures.

RATIFICATION: AN EXERCISE IN ELITE POLITICAL SKILLS

When its work ended on September 17, 1787, the Constitutional Convention sent the Constitution to New York City, where Congress was then in session. The Convention suggested that the Constitution "should afterwards be submitted to a convention of delegates chosen in each state by the people thereof, under the recommendation of its legislature for their assent and ratification." Convention delegates further proposed that ratification by nine states be sufficient to put the new constitution into effect. On September 28, Congress sent the Constitution to the states without further recommendations.

The ratification procedure suggested by the Founding Fathers was a skillful political maneuver. Since Convention proceedings had been secret, few people knew that the delegates had gone beyond their instructions to amend the Articles of Confederation and had created a whole new scheme of government. Their ratification procedure was a complete departure from what was then the law of the land, the Articles of Confederation. The Articles provided that Congress make amendments only with the approval of *all* states. But since Rhode Island was firmly in the hands of small farmers, the unanimity required by the Articles was obviously out of the question. The Founding Fathers felt obligated to act outside the existing law.

The Founding Fathers also called for special ratifying conventions in the states rather than risk submitting the Constitution to the state legislatures. This extraordinary procedure gave clear advantage to supporters of the Constitution, since submitting the plan to the state legislatures would weaken its chances for success. Thus the struggle for ratification began under ground rules designed by the national elite to give them the advantage over any potential opponents.

In the most important and controversial study of the Constitution to date, Charles A. Beard compiled a great deal of evidence supporting the hypothesis "that substantially all of the merchants, moneylenders, security holders, manufacturers, shippers, capitalists and financiers, and their professional associates are to be found on one side in support of the Constitution, and that substantially all of the major portion of the opposition came from the non-slaveholding farmers and debtors."[10] While historians disagree over the solidarity of class divisions in the struggle for ratification, most concede that only about 160,000 people voted in elections for delegates to state ratifying conventions and that not more than 100,000 of these voters favored the adoption of the Constitution. This figure represents about one in six of the adult males in the country, and no more than 5 percent of the general population. Thus, whether or not Beard is correct about class divisions in the struggle for ratification, it is clear that the number of people who participated in any fashion in ratifying the Constitution was an extremely small minority in the population.*

---

*Beard's economic interpretation differs from an elitist interpretation in that Beard believes that the economic elites supported the Constitution and the masses opposed it. Our elitist interpretation asserts only that the masses did not participate in writing or adopting the Constitution and that elites benefited directly from its provisions. Our interpretation does not depend upon showing that the masses opposed the Constitution but merely that they did not participate in its establishment. Attacks on Beard appear in Forrest McDonald, *We the People: The Economic Origins of the Constitution* (Chicago: University of Chicago Press, 1958) and Robert E. Brown, *Charles Beard and the Constitution* (Princeton, N.J.: Princeton University Press, 1956). Lee Benson provides a balanced view in *Turner and Beard: American Historical Writing Reconsidered* (New York: Free Press, 1960).

Some men of property and education did oppose the new Constitution. These were men who had greater confidence in their ability to control state governments than to control the new federal government. They called themselves "Anti-Federalists," and they vigorously attacked the Constitution as a counterrevolutionary document that could undo much of the progress made since 1776 toward freedom, liberty, and equality. According to the opponents of the Constitution, the new government would be "aristocratic," all powerful, and a threat to the "spirit of republicanism" and the "genius of democracy." They charged that the new Constitution created an aristocratic upper house and an almost monarchical presidency. The powers of the national government could trample the states and deny the people of the states the opportunity to handle their own political and economic affairs. The Anti-Federalists repeatedly asserted that the Constitution removed powers from the people and concentrated them in the hands of a few national officials who were largely immune to popular control; moreover, they attacked the undemocratic features of the Constitution and argued that state governments were much more representative of the people. Also under attack were the secrecy of the Constitutional Convention and the actions of the Founding Fathers, both contrary to the law and the spirit of the Articles of Confederation.

While the Anti-Federalists deplored the undemocratic features of the new Constitution, their most effective criticism centered on the absence of any bill of rights. The omission of a bill of rights was particularly glaring since the idea was very popular at the time, and most new state constitutions contained one. It is an interesting comment on the psychology of the Founding Fathers that the idea of a bill of rights did not come up in the Convention until the final week of deliberations; even then it received little consideration. The Founding Fathers certainly believed in limited government, and they did write a few liberties into the body of the Constitution, such as protection against bills of attainder and *ex post facto* laws, a guarantee of the writ of *habeas corpus,* a limited definition of treason, and a guarantee of jury trial. However, they did not create a bill of rights labeled as such.

When criticism about the absence of a bill of rights began to mount, supporters of the Constitution presented an interesting argument to explain the deficiency: (1) the national government was one of enumerated powers and could not exercise any powers not expressly delegated to it in the Constitution; (2) the power to interfere with free speech or press or otherwise to restrain liberty was not among the enumerated powers in the Constitution; (3) it was therefore unnecessary to deny the new government that power specifically. But this logic was unconvincing; the absence of a bill of rights seemed to confirm the suspicion that the Founding Fathers were more concerned with protecting property than with protecting the personal liberties of the people. Many members of the elite and nonelite alike were uncomfortable with the thought that personal liberty depended on a thin thread of inference from enumerated powers. Supporters of the Constitution thus had to retreat from their demand for unconditional ratification; the New York, Massachusetts, and Virginia conventions agreed to the new Constitution only after receiving the Federalists' solemn promise to add a bill of rights as amendments. Thus the fundamental guarantees of liberty in the Bill of Rights were political concessions by the nation's elite. Whereas the Founding Fathers deserved great credit for the document that they produced at Philadelphia, the first Congress to meet under that Constitution was nonetheless obliged to submit twelve amendments to the states, ten of which were ratified by 1791.

——— SUMMARY

Elite theory provides us with an interpretation of the U.S. Constitution and the basic structure of U.S. government. Our analysis of constitutional policies centers on the following propositions:

1. The Constitution of the United States was not "ordained and established" by "the people." Instead it was written by a small, educated, talented, wealthy elite in America, representative of powerful economic interests: bondholders, investors, merchants, real estate owners, and planters.

2. The Constitution and the national government that it established had its origins in elite dissatisfaction with the inability of the central government to pay off its bondholders, the interference of state governments with the development of a national economy, the threat to investors and creditors posed by state issuance of cheap paper money and laws relieving debtors of contractual obligations, the threat to propertied classes arising from post–Revolutionary War radicalism, the inability of the central government to provide an army capable of protecting western development or a navy capable of protecting American commercial interests on the high seas, and the inability of America's elite to exercise power in world affairs.

3. The elite achieved ratification of the Constitution through its astute political skills. The masses of people in the United States did not participate in the writing of the Constitution or in its adoption by the states, and they probably would have opposed the Constitution had they had the information and resources to do so.

4. The Founding Fathers shared a consensus that the fundamental role of government is the protection of liberty and property. They believed in a republican form of government by men of principle and property. They opposed an aristocracy or a governing nobility, but they also opposed mass democracy with direct participation by the people in decision making. They feared mass movements seeking to reduce inequalities of wealth, intelligence, talent, or virtue. "Dangerous leveling" was a serious violation of men's rights to property.

5. The structure of American government was designed to suppress "factious" issues—threats to dominant economic elites. Republicanism, the division of power between state and national governments, and the complex system of checks and balances and divided power were all designed as protections against mass movements that might threaten liberty and property.

6. The text of the Constitution contains many direct and immediate benefits to America's governing elite. Although all Americans, both elite and mass, may have benefited by the adoption of the Constitution, the advantages and benefits for U.S. elites were their compelling motives for supporting the new Constitution.

NOTES

1. Lester Cappon, ed., *The Adams-Jefferson Letters* (Chapel Hill: University of North Carolina Press, 1959), vol. I, p. 106.
2. Max Farrand, ed., *The Records of the Federal Convention of 1787* (New Haven, Conn.: Yale University Press, 1937), vol. III, p. 15.
3. Ibid., p. 32.
4. See Clinton Rossiter, *1787, The Grand Convention* (New York: Macmillan, 1966), p. 45.
5. Charles A. Beard, *An Economic Interpretation of the Constitution of the United States* (New York: Macmillan, 1913), pp. 73–151.
6. John P. Roche, "The Founding Fathers: A Reform Caucus in Action," *American Political Science Review* 55 (December 1961): 799.
7. See especially Beard, *Economic Interpretation.*
8. James Madison, Alexander Hamilton, and John Jay, *The Federalist* (New York: Modern Library, 1937).
9. Ibid.
10. Beard, *Economic Interpretation,* pp. 16–17.

SELECTED READINGS

Beard, Charles A. *An Economic Interpretation of the Constitution of the United States.* New York: Macmillan, 1913. The Free Press issued a paperback edition in 1965. Much of this chapter reflects data presented by Beard in this classic work. Beard traces the events leading up to the writing of the Constitution and the events surrounding ratification from an economic point of view. He discovers that economic considerations played a major, if not central, role in the shaping of the Constitution.

For several critiques of Beard, see:
1. Beale, Howard K., ed. *Charles A. Beard: An Appraisal.* Lexington: University of Kentucky Press, 1954.

2. Benson, Lee. *Turner and Beard: American Historical Writing Reconsidered.* New York: Free Press, 1960.

3. McDonald, Forrest. *We the People: The Economic Origins of the Constitution.* Chicago: University of Chicago Press, 1958.

Corwin, Edward S., and Peltason, J. W. *Understanding the Constitution,* 6th ed. New York: Holt, Rinehart & Winston, 1973. Of the many books that explain parts of the Constitution, this paperback is one of the best. It contains explanations of the Declaration of Independence, the Articles of Confederation, and the Constitution. The book is written clearly and is well suited for undergraduate as well as graduate and faculty use.

Lipset, Seymour Martin. *The First New Nation.* Garden City, N.Y.: Doubleday, Anchor Books, 1963. This book offers a comparative treatment of the factors necessary for the development of a new nation. Lipset argues that any new nation must develop legitimacy of government, national identity, national unity, opposition rights, and citizen payoffs. The book is important because it examines the United States as the first "new nation" in light of these five factors and then compares it to other developing nations.

Madison, James, Hamilton, Alexander, and Jay, John. *The Federalist.* New York: Modern Library, 1937. This collection of the articles published in support of the Constitution offers perhaps the most important contemporary comments available on the Constitution.

Rossiter, Clinton L. *1787, The Grand Convention.* New York: Macmillan, 1966. This readable and entertaining account of the men and events of 1787 contains many insights into the difficulties the Founding Fathers had writing the Constitution.

Wills, Gary. *Explaining America.* New York: Penguin Books, 1982. This book is a rigorous examination of *The Federalist* and the intellectual influences on its authors.

3

The Evolution of American Elites

★ *The fierceness of political struggles has often been misleading; for the range of vision embodied by the primary contestants in the major parties has always been bounded by the horizons of property and enterprise.*

Richard Hofstadter, The American Political Tradition, *1948*

A stable elite system depends on the movement of talented and ambitious individuals from the lower strata into the elite. An open elite system providing for "a slow and continuous modification of the ruling classes" is essential for continuing the system and avoiding revolution. Popular elections, party competition, and other democratic institutions in the United States have not enabled the masses to govern, but these institutions have helped keep the elite system an open one. They have assisted in the circulation of elites, even if they have never been a means of challenging the dominant elite consensus.

In this chapter, a historical analysis of the evolution of American elites, we show that American elite membership has evolved slowly, without any serious break in the ideas or values underlying the U.S. political and economic system. The United States has never experienced a true revolution that forcibly replaced governing elites with nonelites. Instead American elite membership has been open to those who acquire wealth and property and who accept the national consensus about private enterprise, limited government, and individualism. Industrialization, technological change, and new sources of wealth in the expanding economy have produced new elite members, and the U.S. elite system has permitted the absorption of the new elites without upsetting the system itself.

Policy changes and innovations in the structure of American government over the decades have been *incremental* (step-by-step) rather than revolutionary. Elites have modified public policies but seldom replaced them. They have made structural adaptations in the constitutional system designed by the Founding Fathers but have kept intact the original framework of U.S. constitutionalism.

Policy changes in the United States have not come about through demands by the people. Instead changes and innovations in public policy have occurred when elites have perceived threats to the system and have instituted reforms to preserve the system and their place in it. Reforms have been designed to strengthen the existing social and economic fabric of society with a minimum of dislocation for governing elites.

Political conflict in the United States has centered on a very narrow range of issues. Only once, in the Civil War, have elites been deeply divided over the nature of American society. The Civil War reflected a deep cleavage between southern elites—dependent upon a plantation economy, slave labor, and free trade—and northern industrial and commercial elites, who prospered under free labor and protective tariffs.

——— HAMILTON AND THE NATION'S FIRST PUBLIC POLICIES

The most influential figure in George Washington's administration was Alexander Hamilton, secretary of the treasury. More than anyone else, Hamilton was aware that the new nation had to win the lasting confidence of business and financial elites in order to survive and prosper. Only if the United States were established on a sound financial basis could it attract investors at home and abroad and expand its industry and commerce. Great Britain remained the largest source of investment capital for the new nation, and Hamilton was decidedly pro-British. He also favored a strong central government as a means of protecting property and stimulating the growth of commerce and industry.

Paying the National Debt

Hamilton's first move was to refund the national debt at face value. Most of the original bonds were no longer in the hands of the original owners but had fallen to speculators who had purchased them for only a fraction of their face value. Since these securities were worth only about twenty-five cents on the dollar, the Hamilton refund program meant a 300 percent profit for the speculators. Hamilton's program went beyond refunding the debts owed by the United States; he also undertook to pay the debts incurred by the states themselves during the Revolutionary War. His object was to place the creditor class under a deep obligation to the central government.

Establishing a National Bank

Hamilton also acted to establish a Bank of the United States, which would receive government funds, issue a national currency, facilitate the sale of national bonds, and tie the national government even more closely to the banking community. The Constitution did not specifically grant Congress the power to create a national bank, but Hamilton was willing to interpret the "necessary and proper" clause broadly enough to include the creation of a bank to help carry out the taxing, borrowing, and currency powers enumerated in the Constitution. Hamilton's broad construction of the "necessary and proper" clause looked in the direction of a powerful central government that would exercise powers not specifically enumerated in the Constitution. Thomas Jefferson, who was secretary of state in the same cabinet with Hamilton, expressed growing concern over Hamilton's tendency toward national centralization. Jefferson argued that Congress could not establish the bank because the bank was not strictly "necessary" to carry out delegated functions. But Hamilton won out, with the support of President Washington; in 1791 Congress voted to charter the Bank of the United States. For twenty years the bank was very successful, especially in stabilizing the currency of the new nation.

Expanding the "Necessary and Proper" Clause

Not until 1819 did the Supreme Court decide the constitutionality of the Bank of the United States. In the famous case of *McCulloch* v. *Maryland,* the Supreme Court upheld the broad definition of national power suggested by Hamilton under the "necessary and proper" clause. At the same time, the Court established the principle that a state law that interferes with a national activity is unconstitutional.[1] "Let the end be legitimate," Chief Justice John Marshall wrote, "let it be within the scope of the Constitution, and all means which are appropriate, which are plainly adopted to that end, which are not prohibited, but consistent with the letter and spirit of the Constitution, are constitutional." The *McCulloch* case firmly established the principle that Congress has the right to choose any appropriate means for carrying out the delegated powers of the national government. The "necessary and proper" clause is now sometimes called the "implied powers" clause or the "elastic" clause because it gives to Congress many powers that the Constitution does not explicitly grant. Congress still traces all its activities to some formal grant of power, but this task is usually not difficult.

RISE OF THE JEFFERSONIANS

The centralizing effect to Hamilton's programs and their favoring of merchants, manufacturers, and shipbuilders aroused some opposition in elite circles. Southern planters and large landowners benefited very little from Hamilton's policies, and they were joined in their opposition by local and state elites who feared that a strong central government threatened their own powers. These agrarian groups were first called "Anti-Federalists," and later "Republicans" and "Democratic Republicans" when those terms became popular after the French Revolution. When Thomas Jefferson resigned from Washington's cabinet in protest of Hamilton's program, Anti-Federalists began to gather around Jefferson.

Jefferson as a Wealthy Plantation Owner

Historians portray Jefferson as a great democrat and champion of the "common man." And in writing the Declaration of Independence, the Virginia Statute for Religious Freedom, and the famous *Notes on Virginia*, Jefferson indeed expressed concern for the rights of all "the people" and a willingness to trust in their wisdom. But when Jefferson spoke warmly of the merits of "the people," he meant those who owned and managed their own farms and estates. He firmly believed that only those who owned their own land could make good citizens. Jefferson disliked aristocracy, but he also held the urban masses in contempt. He wanted to see the United States become a nation of free, educated, landowning farmers. Democracy, he believed, could be founded only on a propertied class in a propertied nation. His belief that land ownership is essential to virtuous government explains in part his Louisiana Purchase, which he hoped would provide the American people with land "to the hundredth and thousandth generation."[2]

The dispute between Federalists and Anti-Federalists in the early United States was not between elites and masses. It was a dispute within elite circles between two propertied classes: merchants and bankers on one side, and plantation owners and slaveholders on the other.[3]

Rise of Political Parties

The Anti-Federalists, or "Republicans," did not elect their first president, Thomas Jefferson, until 1800. John Adams, a Federalist, succeeded Washington in the election of 1796. Yet the election of 1796 was an important milestone in the development of the American political system. For the first time, two candidates, Adams and Jefferson, campaigned not as individuals but as members of political parties. For the first time, the candidates for the electoral college announced themselves before the election as either "Adams's men" or "Jefferson's men." Most important, for the first time, American political leaders realized the importance of molding mass opinion and organizing the masses for political action. The Republican party first saw the importance of working among the masses to rally popular support. The Federalist leaders made the mistake of assuming that they could maintain the unquestioning support of the less educated and less wealthy without bothering to mold their opinions.

Early Attempts at Elite Repression

Rather than trying, as the Republicans did, to manipulate public opinion, the Federalists tried to outlaw public criticism of the government by means of the Alien and Sedition Acts of 1798. Among other things, these acts made it a crime to publish any false or malicious writing directed against the president or Congress, or to "stir up hatred" against them. The acts directly challenged the newly adopted First Amendment guarantee of freedom of speech and press.

In response to the Alien and Sedition Acts, Jefferson and Madison put forward their famous Kentucky and Virginia resolutions. These measures proposed that the states assume the right to decide whether Congress has acted unconstitutionally and, furthermore, that the states properly "interpose" their authority against "palpable and alarming infractions of the Constitution." The Virginia and Kentucky legislatures passed these resolutions and declared the Alien and Sedition Acts "void and of no force" in these states.

REPUBLICANS IN POWER: THE STABILITY OF PUBLIC POLICY

In the election of 1800, the Federalists went down to defeat; Thomas Jefferson and Aaron Burr were elected over John Adams and C. C. Pinckney.

Only the New England states, New Jersey, and Delaware, where commercial and manufacturing interests were strongest, voted Federalist. Because the vast majority of American people won their living from the soil, the landed elites were able to mobilize those masses behind their bid for control of the government. The Federalists failed to recognize the importance of agrarianism in the nation's economic and political life. Another half-century would pass and America's industrial revolution would be in full swing before manufacturing and commercial elites would reestablish their dominance.

But the real importance of the election of 1800 is *not* that landed interests gained power in relation to commercial and industrial interests. The importance of 1800 is that for the first time in U.S. history, control of the government passed peacefully from one faction to an opposing faction. Even today few nations in the world see government office change hands in an orderly or peaceful fashion. The fact that an "out" party peacefully replaced an "in" party is further testimony to the strength of the consensus among the new nation's elite.*

The "Virginia dynasty"—Thomas Jefferson, James Madison, and finally James Monroe—governed the country for six presidential terms, nearly a quarter of a century. Interestingly, once in office, the Republicans made few changes in Federalist and Hamiltonian policy. (The only major pieces of legislation repealed by the Republicans were the Alien and Sedition Acts. And it seems clear that in passing these acts the Federalists had violated elite consensus.) The Republicans did not attack commercial or industrial enterprise; in fact commerce and industry prospered under Republican rule as never before. They did not attempt to recover money paid out by Hamilton in refunding national or state debts. They allowed public land speculation to continue. Instead of crushing the banks, Republicans soon supported the financial interests they had sworn to oppose.

Jefferson was an ardent expansionist; to add to America's wealth in land, he purchased the vast Louisiana Territory. Later a stronger army

*The original text of the Constitution did not envision an opposing faction. Presidential electors could cast two votes for president, with the understanding that the candidate with the second highest vote total would be vice-president. Seventy-three Republican electors pledged to Jefferson and sixty-five Federalists pledged to Adams went to the electoral college. Somewhat thoughtlessly, all the Republicans cast one vote for Jefferson and one vote for Aaron Burr, his running mate, with the result that each man received the same number of votes for the presidency. Because of the tie vote, the decision went to the Federalist-controlled House of Representatives, where a movement was begun to elect Burr, rather than Jefferson, in order to embarrass the Republicans. But Alexander Hamilton used his influence in Congress to swing the election to his old political foe Jefferson, suggesting again that their differences were not so deep that either would deliberately undermine the presidency to strike at the other. Once in power, the Republicans passed the Twelfth Amendment to the Constitution, providing that each presidential elector should thereafter vote separately for president and vice-president. Both Federalists and Republicans in the states promptly agreed with this reform and ratification was completed by the election of 1804.

and a system of internal roads were necessary to help develop western land. Jefferson's successor, James Madison, built a strong navy and engaged in another war with England, the War of 1812, to protect U.S. commerce on the high seas. The Napoleonic wars and the War of 1812 stimulated American manufacturing by depressing trade with Britain. In 1816 Republicans passed a high tariff in order to protect domestic industry and manufacturing from foreign goods. As for Republican tax policies, Jefferson wrote in 1816:

> To take from one, because it is thought his own industry and that of his fathers has acquired too much, in order to spare to others, who, or whose fathers, have not exercised equal industry and skill, is to violate arbitrarily the first principle of association, "the guarantee to everyone the free exercise of his industry and the fruits acquired by it."[4]

In short, the Republicans had no intention of redistributing wealth in the United States. Indeed, before the end of Madison's second term in 1817, the Republicans had taken over the whole complex of Hamiltonian policies: a national bank, high tariffs, protection for manufacturers, internal improvements, western land development, a strong army and navy, and a broad interpretation of national power. So complete was the elite consensus that by 1820 the Republicans had completely driven the Federalist party out of existence, largely by taking over its programs.

RISE OF WESTERN ELITES

According to Frederick Jackson Turner, "The rise of the New West was the most significant fact in American history."[5] Certainly the American West had a profound impact on the political system of the new nation. People went west because of the vast wealth of fertile lands that awaited them there; nowhere else in the world could one acquire wealth so quickly as in the new American West. Because aristocratic families of the eastern seaboard seldom had reason to migrate westward, the western settlers were mainly middle- and lower-class immigrants. With hard work and good fortune, penniless migrants could become wealthy plantation owners or cattle ranchers in a single generation. Thus the West offered rapid upward social mobility.

New elites arose in the West and had to be assimilated onto America's governing circles. No one exemplifies the new entrants into the U.S. elite better than Andrew Jackson. Jackson's victory in the presidential election of 1828 was not a victory of the common people against the propertied classes but rather one of the new western elites against established Republican leadership in the East. Jackson's victory forced established U.S. elites to recognize the growing importance of the West and to open their ranks to the new rich west of the Alleghenies.

The "Natural Aristocracy"

Since Jackson was a favorite of the people, it was easy for him to believe in the wisdom of the common people. But Jacksonian democracy was by no means a philosophy of leveling egalitarianism. The ideal of the frontier society was the self-made man, and people admired wealth and power won by competitive skill. Wealth and power obtained only through special privilege offended the frontiersmen, however. They believed in a *natural aristocracy* rather than an aristocracy by birth, education, or special privilege. Jacksonians demanded not absolute equality but a more open elite system—a greater opportunity for the rising middle class to acquire wealth and influence through competition.

Expansion of the Electorate

In their struggle to open America's elite system, the Jacksonians appealed to mass sentiment. Jackson's humble beginnings, his image as a self-made man, his military adventures, his frontier experience, and his rough, brawling style endeared him to the masses. As beneficiaries of popular support, the new elites of the West developed a strong faith in the wisdom and justice of popular decisions. The new western states that entered the Union granted universal white male suffrage, and gradually the older states fell into step. Rising elites, themselves often less than a generation away from the masses, saw in a widened electorate a chance for personal advancement that they could never have achieved under the old regime. Therefore, the Jacksonians became noisy and effective advocates of the principle that all men should have the right to vote and to hold public office. They also successfully attacked the congressional caucus system of nominating presidential candidates. After his defeat in Congress in 1824, Jackson wished to sever Congress from the nominating process. In 1832, when the Democrats held their first national convention, they renominated Andrew Jackson by acclamation.

Character of the Elite

Nonetheless, the changes in the character of elites from the administrations of John Adams through Thomas Jefferson to Andrew Jackson were very minor. Sociologist Sidney H. Aronson's historical research reveals that, contrary to the general assumption, Jackson's administration was clearly upper-class, college educated, prestigiously employed, professionally trained, and probably wealthy. (See Table 3-1.) In fact, the class character of Jackson's administration was not much different from that of the Federalist John Adams. More than half of Jackson's top appointees were born into distinguished upper-class families, and three-quarters enjoyed

TABLE 3-1   Social class characteristics of three presidents' appointments

Characteristics	Adams (N = 96)	Jefferson (N = 100)	Jackson (N = 127)
Father political officeholder	52%	43%	44%
Father college educated	17	13	12
Class I family social position[a]	62	58	51
High-ranking occupation	92	93	90
Political officeholder before appointment	91	83	88
Class I social position[a]	86	74	74
Family in America in seventeenth century	55	48	48
College educated	63	52	52
Professionally trained	69	74	81
Relative an appointive elite	40	34	34

[a]"Class I" is the highest of the following four classes:
Class I: "national and international aristocracy";
Class II: "prosperous and respectable";
Class III: "respectable";
Class IV: "subsistence or impoverished."
Breakdowns by each class are as follows:
Adams: I: 62%; II: 19%; III: 5%; IV: 1%; unknown: 13%.
Jefferson: I: 58%; II: 15%; III: 6%; IV: 1%; unknown: 20%.
Jackson: I: 51%; II: 25%; III: 11%; IV: 2%; unknown: 11%.
SOURCE: Sidney H. Aronson, *Status and Kinship in the Higher Civil Service* (Cambridge, Mass.: Harvard University Press, 1964), p. 195. Reprinted by permission.

high class standing before their appointment, through either birth or achievement.

ELITE CLEAVAGE: THE CIVIL WAR

During the nation's first sixty years, American elites substantially agreed about the character and direction of the new nation. Conflicts over the national bank, the tariff, internal improvement (such as roads and harbors), and even the controversial war with Mexico in 1846 did not threaten the basic underlying consensus. In the 1850s, however, the status of blacks in American society—the most divisive issue in the history of American politics—drove a wedge into the elites and ultimately led to the nation's bloodiest war. The national political system was unequal to the task of negotiating a peaceful settlement to the slavery problem because America's elites divided deeply over the question.

Southern Elites

In 1787 the southern elites—cotton planters, landowners, exporters, and slave traders—foresaw an end to slavery, but after 1820 the demand for cotton became insatiable, and southern planters could not profitably produce cotton without slave labor. Cotton accounted for more than half the value of all U.S. goods shipped abroad before the Civil War. Although Virginia did not depend on cotton, it sold great numbers of slaves to the cotton states, and "slave raising" itself became immensely profitable.

It was the white *elites* and not the white *masses* of the South who had an interest in the slave and cotton culture. On the eve of the Civil War, probably no more than 400,000 southern families—approximately one in four—held slaves, and many of those families held only one or two slaves each. The number of great planters—men who owned fifty or more slaves and large holdings of land—was probably not more than 7,000, yet their views dominated southern politics.

Northern Elites

The northern elites were merchants and manufacturers who depended on free labor, yet they had no direct interest in abolishing slavery in the South. But both northern and southern elites realized that control of the West was the key to future dominance of the nation. Northern elites wanted a West composed of small farmers who produced food and raw materials for the industrial and commercial East and provided a market for eastern goods. Southern planters feared the voting power of a West composed of small farmers and wanted western lands for expansion of the cotton and slave culture. Cotton ate up the land and, because it required continuous cultivation and monotonous rounds of simple tasks, was suited to slave labor. Thus to protect the cotton economy, it was essential to protect slavery in western lands. This conflict over western land eventually precipitated the Civil War.

Attempts at Compromise

Despite these differences, the underlying consensus of American elites was so great that they devised compromise after compromise to maintain unity. The Missouri Compromise of 1820 divided the land in the Louisiana Purchase exclusive of Missouri between free territory and slave territory at 36°30' and admitted Maine and Missouri as free and slave states, respectively. After the war with Mexico, the elaborate Compromise of 1850 caused one of the greatest debates in American legislative history, with Senators Henry Clay, Daniel Webster, John C. Calhoun, Salmon P. Chase, Stephen A. Douglas, Jefferson Davis, Alexander H. Stevens, Robert Tombs, William H. Seward, and Thaddeus Stevens all participating. Elite divisiveness was apparent, but it was not yet so destructive as to split the nation. Congress achieved a compromise admitting California as a free state; creating two new territories, New Mexico and Utah, out of the Mexican cession; enacting a drastic fugitive slave law to satisfy southern planters; and prohibiting slave trade in the District of Columbia. Even the Kansas-Nebraska Act of 1854 was to be a compromise; each new territory would decide for itself whether to be slave or free, with the expectation that Nebraska would vote free and Kansas slave. But gradually the spirit of compromise gave way to cleavage and conflict.

Elite Cleavage

Beginning in 1856, proslavery and antislavery forces fought it out in "bleeding Kansas." Intemperate language in the Senate became commonplace, with frequent threats of secession, violence, and civil war.

In 1857 the Supreme Court decided, in *Dred Scott* v. *Sandford*, that the Missouri Compromise was unconstitutional because Congress had no authority to forbid slavery in any territory.[6] The Constitution protected slave property, said Chief Justice Roger B. Taney, as much as any other kind of property.

In 1859 John Brown and his followers raided the U.S. arsenal at Harpers Ferry as a first step to freeing the slaves of Virginia by force. Brown was captured by Virginia militia under the command of Colonel Robert E. Lee, tried for treason, found guilty, and executed. Southerners believed that northerners had tried to incite the horror of a slave insurrection, while northerners believed that Brown had died a martyr.

The conflict between North and South led to the complete collapse of the Whig party and the emergence of a new Republican party composed exclusively of northerners and westerners. For the first time in the history of American parties, one of the two major parties did not spread across both sides of the Mason-Dixon line; 1860 was the only year in American history that four major parties sought the presidency. The nation was so divided that no party came close to winning the majority of popular votes. Lincoln, the Republican candidate, and Douglas, the Democratic candidate, won most of their votes from the North and West, while John C. Breckinridge (Kentucky), the Southern Democratic candidate, and John Bell (Tennessee), the Constitutional Union candidate, received most of their votes from the South.

More important, the cleavage had become so deep that many prominent southern leaders announced that they would not accept the outcome of the presidential election if Lincoln won. Threats of secession were not new, but this time it was no bluff. For the first and only time in American history, prominent elite members were willing to destroy the American political system rather than compromise their interests and principles. Shortly after the election, on December 20, 1860, the state of South Carolina seceded from the Union. Within six months, ten other southern states followed.

Lincoln and Slavery

Abraham Lincoln never attacked slavery in the South; his exclusive concern was to halt the spread of slavery in the western territories. He wrote in 1845, "I hold it a paramount duty of us in the free states, due to the union of the states, and perhaps to liberty itself (paradox though it may seem), to let the slavery of the other states alone."[7] Throughout his political career, he consistently held this position. On the other hand, with regard to the western territories he said, "The whole nation is interested that the best use shall be made of these territories. We want them for homes and free white people. This they cannot be, to any considerable extent, if slavery shall be planted within them."[8] In short, Lincoln wanted to tie the western territories economically and culturally to the northern system. As for Lincoln's racial views, as late as 1858 he said:

> I will say, then, that I am not, nor ever have been, in favor of bringing about in any way the social and political equality of the white and black races; that I am not, nor ever have been, in favor of making voters or jurors of Negroes, nor qualifying them to hold office, nor to intermarry with white people . . . and in as much as they cannot so live while they do remain together, there must be a position of superior and inferior; and I as much as any other man am in favor of having the superior position assigned to the white race.[9]

Lincoln's political posture was essentially conservative. He wished to preserve the long-established order and consensus that had protected American principles and property rights so successfully in the past. He was not an abolitionist, and he did not want to destroy the southern elites or to alter the southern social fabric. His goal was to bring the South back into the Union, to restore orderly government, and to establish the principle that the states cannot resist national authority with force.

Emancipation as Political Opportunism

As the war continued and casualties mounted, northern opinion toward southern slaveowners became increasingly bitter. Many Republicans joined the abolitionists in calling for emancipation of the slaves simply to punish the "rebels." They knew that the South's power depended on slave labor. Lincoln also knew that if he proclaimed that the war was being fought to free the slaves, foreign intervention was less likely. Yet even in late summer of 1862, Lincoln wrote:

> My paramount object in this struggle is to save the Union. If I could save the Union without freeing any slaves, I would do it; if I could save it by freeing some and leaving others alone, I would also do that. I shall do less whenever I shall believe what I am doing hurts the cause, and I shall do more whenever I believe doing more will help the cause. I shall adopt new views as fast as they shall appear to be true views.[10]

Finally, on September 22, 1862, Lincoln issued his preliminary Emancipation Proclamation. Claiming his right as commander-in-chief of the army and navy, he promised that "on the first day of January 1863, all persons held as slaves within any state or designated part of a state, the people whereof shall then be in rebellion against the United States shall be then, thence forward, and forever free." Thus one of the great steps forward in human freedom in this nation, the Emancipation Proclamation, did not come about as a result of demands by the people, and certainly not as a result of demands by the slaves themselves. It was a political and military action by the president for the sake of helping to preserve the Union. It was not a revolutionary action but a conservative one.

RISE OF THE NEW INDUSTRIAL ELITE

The Civil War's importance to U.S. elite structure lies in the commanding position that the new industrial capitalists won in the course of struggle. Even before 1860, northern industry had been altering the course of American life; the economic transformation of the United States from an agricultural to an industrial nation reached the crescendo of a revolution in the second half of the nineteenth century. Canals and steam railroads had been opening new markets for the growing industrial cities of the East. The rise of corporations and of stock markets for the accumulation of capital upset old-fashioned ideas of property, The introduction of machinery in factories revolutionized the conditions of American labor and made the masses dependent on industrial capitalists for their livelihood. Civil War profits compounded the capital of the industrialists and placed them in a position to dominate the economic life of the nation. Moreover, when the southern planters were removed from the national scene, the government in Washington became the exclusive domain of the new industrial leaders.

Political Plunder

The protective tariff, long opposed by the southern planters, became the cornerstone of the new business structure of the United States. The industrial capitalists realized that the Northwest Territory was the natural market for their manufactured goods, and the protective tariff restricted the vast and growing American market to American industry alone. The passage of the Homestead Act in 1862 threw the national domain wide open to settlers, and the Transcontinental Railroad Act of 1862 gave the railroads plentiful incentives to link expanding western markets to eastern industry. The northeastern United States was rich in the natural resources of coal, iron, and water power; and the large immigrant population streaming in from Europe furnished a dependable source of cheap labor. The Northeast also had superior means of transportation—both water and rail—to facilitate the assembling of raw materials and the marketing of finished products. With the rise of the new industrial capitalism, power in the United States flowed from the South and West to the Northeast, and Jefferson's dream of a nation of small free farmers faded.

Social Darwinism

The new industrial elite found a new philosophy to justify its political and economic dominance. Drawing an analogy from the New Darwinian biology, Herbert Spencer undertook to demonstrate that just as an elite was selected in nature through evolution, so also society would near perfection as it allowed natural social elites to be selected by free competition. In defense of the new capitalists, Herbert Spencer argued: "There cannot be more good done than that of letting social progress go on unhindered; an immensity of mischief may be done in . . . the artificial preservation of those least able to care for themselves."[11] Spencer hailed the accumulation of new industrial wealth as a sign of "the survival of the fittest." The "social Darwinists" found in the law of survival of the fittest an admirable defense for the emergence of a ruthless ruling elite, an elite which defined its own self-interest more narrowly, perhaps, than any other in American history.

Industrial Capitalism

As business became increasingly national in scope, only the strongest or most unscrupulous of the competitors survived. Great producers tended to become the cheapest ones, and little companies tended to disappear. Industrial production rose rapidly, while the number of industrial concerns steadily diminished. Total capital investment and total output of industry vastly increased, while ownership became concentrated. One result was the emergence of monopolies and near monopolies in the major industries of the United States. Another result was the accumulation of great family fortunes.[12] (See Table 3-2, compiled from 1924 tax returns.

TABLE 3-2   The great industrial fortunes, 1924

Ranking by 1924 income tax	Family	Primary source of wealth
1	Rockefeller	Standard Oil Co.
2	Morgan Inner Group (including Morgan partners and families and eight leading Morgan corporation executives)	J. P. Morgan & Co., Inc.
3	Ford	Ford Motor Co.
4	Harkness	Standard Oil Co.
5	Mellon	Aluminum Company
6	Vanderbilt	New York Central Railroad
7	Whitney	Standard Oil Co.
8	Standard Oil Group (including Archbold, Bedford, Cutler, Flagler, Pratt, Rogers, and Benjamin, but excepting others)	Standard Oil Co.

(continued)

TABLE 3-2 The great industrial fortunes, 1924 *(continued)*

Ranking by 1924 income tax	Family	Primary source of wealth
9	duPont	E. I. duPont de Nemours
10	McCormick	International Harvester Co. and Chicago Tribune, Inc.
11	Baker	First National Bank
12	Fisher	General Motors
13	Guggenheim	American Smelting and Refrigerating Co.
14	Field	Marshall Field & Co.
15	Curtis-Bok	The Curtis Publishing Company
16	Duke	American Tobacco Co.
17	Berwind	Berwind-White Coal Co.
18	Lehman	Lehman Brothers
19	Widener	American Tobacco and Public Utilities
20	Reynolds	R. J. Reynolds Tobacco Company
21	Astor	Real estate
22	Winthrop	Miscellaneous
23	Stillman	National City Bank
24	Timken	Timken Roller Bearing Company
25	Pitcairn	Pittsburgh Plate Glass Company
26	Warburg	Kuhn, Loeb & Company
27	Metcalf	Rhode Island textile mills
28	Clark	Singer Sewing Machine Company
29	Phipps	Carnegie Steel Company
30	Kuhn	Kuhn, Loeb & Company
31	Green	Stocks and real estate
32	Patterson	Chicago Tribune, Inc.
33	Taft	Real estate
34	Deering	International Harvester Co.
35	De Forest	Corporate law practice
36	Gould	Railroads
37	Hill	Railroads
38	Drexel	J. P. Morgan & Company
39	Thomas Fortune Ryan	Stock market
40	H. Foster (Cleveland)	Auto parts
41	Eldridge Johnson	Victor Phonograph
42	Arthur Curtiss James	Copper and railroads
43	C. W. Nash	Automobiles
44	Mortimer Schiff	Kuhn, Loeb & Company
45	James A. Patten	Wheat market
46	Charles Hayden	Stock market
47	Orlando F. Weber	Allied Chemical & Dye Corp.
48	George Blumenthal	Lazard Freres & Co.
49	Ogden L. Mills	Mining
50	Michael Friedsam	Merchandising
51	Edward B. McLean	Mining
52	Eugene Higgins	New York real estate
53	Alexander S. Cochran	Textiles
54	Mrs. L. N. Kirkwood	
55	Helen Tyson	
56	Archer D. Huntington	Railroads
57	James J. Storrow	Lee Higgins & Co.
58	Julius Rosenwald	Sears, Roebuck and Co.
59	Bernard M. Baruch	Stock market
60	S. S. Kresge	Merchandising

SOURCE: Ferdinand Lundberg, *America's Sixty Families* (Secaucus, N.J.: Citadel Press, 1937). Reprinted by permission.

Admittedly it fails to record other great personal fortunes, such as Armour and Swift in meat packing, Candler in Coca-Cola, Cannon in textiles, Fleischmann in yeast, Pulitzer in publishing, Golet in real estate, Harriman in railroads, Heinz in foods, Manville in asbestos, Cudahy in food processing, Dorrance in Campbell's Soup, Hartford in A&P, Eastman in film, Firestone in rubber, Sinclair in oil, Chrysler in automobiles, Pabst in beer, and others.)

The Rockefeller Fortune

Typical of the great entrepreneurs of industrial capitalism was John D. Rockefeller. By the end of the Civil War, Rockefeller had accumulated a modest fortune in wholesale grain and meat. In 1865, with extraordinarily good judgment, he invested his money in the wholly new petroleum business. He backed one of the first oil refineries in the nation and continually reinvested his profits in his business. In 1867, backed by two new partners—H. M. Flagler and F. W. Harkness—Rockefeller founded the Standard Oil Company of Ohio, which in that year refined 4 percent of the nation's output. By 1872, with monopoly as his goal, he had acquired twenty of the twenty-five refineries in Cleveland and was laying plans to bring him control of more than 90 percent of the country's oil refineries within a decade. Rockefeller bought pipelines, warehouses, and factories and was able to force railroads to grant him rebates. In 1882 he formed a giant trust, the Standard Oil Company, with a multitude of affiliates. Thereafter the Standard Oil Company became a prototype of American monopolies. As Rockefeller himself put it, "The day of combination is here to stay. Individualism has gone, never to return." A series of antitrust cases inspired by President Theodore Roosevelt culminated in the Supreme Court decision *U.S.* v. *Standard Oil Co.* (1911), which forced the Rockefellers to divide the company into several separate corporations: Exxon Corporation, Standard Oil Co. of California, Standard Oil Co. (Indiana), Standard Oil Co. (Ohio), Atlantic Richfield Company, Mobil Corporation, and Marathon Oil Company. The Rockefellers continue to hold large blocks of stock in these companies.

Elite Political Dominance

The only serious challenge to the political dominance of eastern capital came over the issue of "free silver." Leadership of the "free silver" movement came from mine owners in the silver states of the Far West. Their campaigns convinced thousands of western farmers that the unrestricted coinage of silver was the answer to their economic distress. The western mine owners did not care about the welfare of small farmers, but the prospect of inflation, debt relief, and expansion of the supply of money and purchasing power won increasing support among the masses in the West and South.

When William Jennings Bryan delivered his famous Cross of Gold speech at the Democratic convention in 1896, he undid the Cleveland "Gold Democrat" control of the Democratic party. Bryan was a westerner, a talented orator, an anti-intellectual, and a deeply religious man; he was antagonistic to the eastern industrial interests and totally committed to the cause of free silver. Bryan tried to rally the nation's have-nots to his banner; he tried to convince them that Wall Street was exploiting them. Yet he did not severely criticize the capitalist system, nor did he call for increased federal regulatory powers. In his acceptance speech he declared, "Our campaign has not for its object the reconstruction of society. . . . Property is and will remain the stimulus to endeavor and the compensation for toil."[13]

The Republican campaign, directed by Marcus Alonzo Hanna of Standard Oil, aimed to persuade the voters that what was good for business was good for the country. Hanna raised an unprecedented $16 million campaign fund from his wealthy fellow industrialists (an amount unmatched in presidential campaigns until the 1960s) and advertised his candidate, William McKinley, as the man who would bring a "full dinner pail" to all.

Bryan's attempt to rally the masses was a dismal failure; McKinley won by a landslide. Bryan ran twice again under the Democratic banner, in 1900 and 1908, but he lost by even greater margins. Although Bryan carried the South and some western states, he failed to rally the masses of the populous eastern states or of the growing cities. Republicans carried working-class, middle-class, and upper-class neighborhoods in the urban industrial states.

LIBERAL ESTABLISHMENT: REFORM AS ELITE SELF-INTEREST

In 1882 William H. Vanderbilt of the New York Central Railroad expressed the ethos of the industrial elite: "The public be damned." This first generation of great American capitalists had little sense of public responsibility. They had built their empires in the competitive pursuit of profit. They believed that their success arose from the immutable laws of natural selection, the survival of the fittest; they believed that society was best served by allowing those laws to operate freely.

Wilson's Early Warning

In 1912 Woodrow Wilson, forerunner of a new elite ethos, criticized America's elite for its lack of public responsibility. Wilson urged America's elite to value the welfare of the masses as an aspect of its own long-run welfare. Wilson did not wish to upset the established order; he merely wished to develop a sense of public responsibility within the establishment. He believed that the national government should see that industrial elites operate in the public interest, and his New Freedom program reflected his high-minded aspirations. The Federal Reserve Act (1914) placed the nation's banking and credit system under public control. The Clayton Antitrust Act (1914) attempted to define specific business abuses, such as charging different prices to different buyers, granting rebates, and making false statements about competitors. Wilson's administration also established the Federal Trade Commission (1914) and authorized it to function in the "public interest" to prevent "unfair methods of competition and unfair and deceptive acts in commerce." Congress established an eight-hour day for railroad workers in interstate commerce (1914) and passed the Child Labor Act (1914) in an attempt to eliminate the worst abuses of children in industry (the Supreme Court, much less "public-regarding," declared this act unconstitutional). Wilson's program aimed to preserve competition, individualism, enterprise, opportunity—all considered vital in the American heritage. But he also believed fervently that elites must function in the public interest and that some government regulation might be required to see that they do so.

The Great Depression

Herbert Hoover was the last great advocate of the rugged individualism of the old order. The economic collapse of the Great Depression undermined the faith of both elites and nonelites in the ideals of the old order. Following the stock market crash of October 1929, and despite elite assurances that prosperity lay "just around the corner," the American economy virtually stopped. Prices dropped sharply, factories closed, real estate values declined, new construction practically ceased, banks went under, wages dropped drastically, and unemployment figures mounted. By 1932 one out of every four persons in the United States was unemployed, and one out of every five persons was on welfare.

Elite Reform

The election of Franklin Delano Roosevelt to the presidency in 1932 ushered in a new era in American elite philosophy. The Great Depression did not bring about a revolution or the emergence of new elites, but it did have an important impact on the thinking of America's governing elites. The victories of fascism in Germany and communism in the Soviet Union and the growing restlessness of the masses in America combined to convince America's elite that reform and regard for the public welfare were essential to the continued maintenance of the American political system and their dominant place in it.

Roosevelt sought a New Deal philosophy that would permit government to devote much more attention to the public welfare than did the philosophy of Hoover's somewhat discredited "rugged individualism." The New Deal was not new or revolutionary but rather a necessary reform

From *Feiffer: Jules Feiffer's America from Eisenhower to Reagan*, Edited by Steven Heller. Copyright © 1982 by Jules Feiffer. Reprinted by permission of Alfred A. Knopf, Inc.

of the existing capitalist system. It had no consistent unifying plan; it was a series of improvisations, many of them adopted very suddenly and some of them even contradictory. Roosevelt believed that government needed to undertake more careful economic planning to adapt "existing economic organizations to the service of the people." And he believed that the government must act humanely and compassionately toward those who were suffering hardship. Relief, recovery, and reform—not revolution—were the objectives of the New Deal.

CASE STUDY

Elites in American History

What has been the relationship between economic elites and governmental leadership in American history? Political scientist Phillip H. Burch has explored this central question in a three-volume study evaluating the social and economic backgrounds of top cabinet-level and diplomatic appointments from the administration of President George Washington to that of President Jimmy Carter.* Burch defines one of the "economic elite"

*Phillip H. Burch, Jr., *Elites in American History,* 3 vols. (New York: Holmes and Meier, 1980).

as a person who has held an important post (executive or director) in a major business enterprise or corporate law firm and/or whose family owned great wealth or occupied an important corporate position. Collectively, the economic elite never constituted more than 1 percent of the U.S. population. Yet, according to Burch, over the years since 1789 they constituted 78.7 percent of top governmental leaders.

According to Burch, the accompanying table shows that "the United States has certainly not been a land of equality of political opportunity. Rather, it has been an elitist-dominated nation." Nonetheless, economic elites occupied fewer top governmental posts in some periods than in others. During the New Deal years and World War II, President Roosevelt brought many noneconomic elites into top government posts, although Roosevelt himself possessed the very highest elite credentials. In earlier periods of American political history, government was almost exclusively directed by economic elites (95.8 percent elite-dominated in the pre-Civil War period, compared with 74.4 percent in more recent years).

Overall, nearly 80 percent of the nation's top appointed leaders have been elite figures, a considerably higher percentage than the proportion of presidents with elite backgrounds (only 58 percent by Burch's estimate). Burch concludes: "Regardless of its changing form, America has almost always been dominated by some form of wealth."**

**Ibid., vol. III, p. 388.

Elites in government, 1789–1980

	Elite cabinet and diplomatic appointees
Federalist period (1789–1801)	100.0%
Jeffersonian Republican years (1801–1829)	95.7
Jackson era (1829–1841)	93.8
Pre-Civil War decades (1841–1861)	95.2
Pre-Civil War period (1789–1861)	**95.8**
Civil War and Reconstruction (1861–1877)	81.1
Late nineteenth-century period (1877–1897)	86.8
McKinley-Taft years (1897–1913)	91.7
Wilson regime (1913–1921)	57.1
Harding-Hoover years (1921–1933)	80.9
Post-Civil War to New Deal period (1861–1933)	**83.5**
New Deal years (1933–1940)	47.4
World War II years (1940–1945)	57.9
Truman years (1945–1953)	55.6
Eisenhower years (1953–1961)	81.1
Kennedy-Johnson years (1961–1969)	62.7
Nixon-Ford years (1969–1977)	68.6
Carter years (1977–1980)	65.4
New Deal to Carter period (1933–1980)	**64.4**
Overall (1789–1980)	**78.7**

NOTE: An elite appointee is a person who has held a prior important position (executive or director) in a major business enterprise or corporate law firm and/or whose family has considerable wealth or an important corporate link.
SOURCE: Phillip H. Burch, Jr., *Elites in American History*, vol. III (New York: Holmes and Meier, 1980), p. 383. Reprinted by permission.

Noblesse Oblige

For anyone of Roosevelt's background, it would have been surprising indeed to try to do anything other than preserve the existing social and economic order. Roosevelt was a descendant of two of America's oldest elite families, the Roosevelts and the Delanos, patrician families whose wealth predated the Civil War and the industrial revolution. The

Roosevelts were not schooled in the scrambling competition of the new industrialists. From the beginning Roosevelt expressed a more public-regarding philosophy. Soon his personal philosophy of noblesse oblige—elite responsibility for the welfare of the masses—became the prevailing ethos of the new liberal establishment.

Emergence of the Liberal Establishment

The success of Roosevelt's liberal philosophy was in part a product of the economic disaster of the Great Depression and in part a tribute to the effectiveness of Roosevelt himself as a mobilizer of opinion among both elites and masses. But the acceptance of liberal establishment ideas may also be attributed in part to the changes taking place in the economic system.

One such change was a declining rate of new elite formation. Most of America's great entrepreneurial families had built their empires before World War I. The first-generation industrialists and entrepreneurs were unfriendly toward philosophies of public responsibility and appeals to the public interest. But among the children and grandchildren of the great empire builders, these ideas won increasing acceptance. Those who are born to wealth seem to accept the idea of noblesse oblige more readily than do those who must acquire wealth for themselves, and available evidence indicates that more self-made men were around in 1900 than in 1950. Figure 3-1 shows that only 39 percent of America's richest men in 1900 came from the upper classes, whereas 68 percent of the nation's richest men in 1950 were born to wealth. Moreover, 39 percent of the

FIGURE 3-1   Social origins of America's richest men, 1900–1950

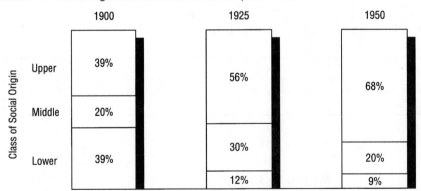

NOTE: The percentages are derived from biographies of the 275 people who were and are known to historians, biographers, and journalists as the richest people living in the United States—the ninety richest of 1900, the ninety-five of 1925, and the ninety of 1950. At the top of the 1900 group is John D. Rockefeller; at the top in 1925 is Henry Ford I; at the top in 1950 is H. L. Hunt.
SOURCE: Data based on C. Wright Mills, *The Power Elite* (New York: Oxford University Press, 1956), pp. 104–105.

richest men in 1900 had struggled up from the bottom, whereas only 9 percent of the richest men of 1950 had done so. These data suggest that the American elite in the mid-twentieth century was more receptive to the idea of responsibility for the common good and concern for the welfare of the masses. Wilson's appeals for elite responsibility fell on the deaf ears of John D. Rockefeller in 1910, but a sense of public responsibility motivated the careers of his grandsons: Nelson Rockefeller, former governor of New York and vice-president of the United States; Winthrop Rockefeller, former governor of Arkansas; David Rockefeller, former chairman of the board of the Chase Manhattan Bank of New York; and John D. Rockefeller III, former chairman of the board of the Lincoln Center for Performing Arts in New York City.

VIETNAM: ELITE FAILURE TO LEAD

America's failure in Vietnam—the nation's longest war and only decisive loss—was not the result of military defeat. Rather, it resulted from the failure of the nation's political leadership to set forth clear objectives in Vietnam, to develop a strategy to achieve those objectives, and to rally mass support behind the effort.

A national elite that seeks to lead a society into war must clearly set forth the objectives of the war and convince itself and the mass of citizens that the objectives are worth the costs. But the objectives of the United States in Vietnam were vague and continually shifting. U.S. involvement was initiated by an intelligent and well-meaning liberal elite convinced of its wisdom and idealism and confident that government power, including military force, could be used to do good in the world.

Incremental Involvement

Initially the United States sought to resist communist aggression from North Vietnam and ensure a strong and independent democratic South Vietnamese government. President John F. Kennedy sent a force of more than 12,000 advisors and counterinsurgency forces to assist in every aspect of training and support for the Army of the Republic of Vietnam (ARVN). President Kennedy personally inspired the development and deployment of U.S. counterinsurgency Special Forces ("Green Berets") to deal directly with a guerrilla enemy and help "win the hearts and minds" of the Vietnamese people. Kennedy personally approved a military coup that ended in the assassination of the unpopular Catholic President Ngo Dinh Diem in the largely Buddhist nation. But one military coup followed another, and the South Vietnamese government never achieved stability or won popularity in the countryside.

Indeed, it is not clear how U.S. military assistance can contribute to the long-term stability or popularity of any government. That is a political and not a military objective. Nonetheless, President Kennedy's actions were consistent with long-standing U.S. policy of containing the spread of communism and assisting free people in resisting internal subversion and external aggression. The "best and the brightest" of the nation's liberal leadership in the early 1960s were convinced of the wisdom of using American power in Southeast Asia; these key decision makers included Secretary of State and former Rockefeller Foundation president Dean Rusk, Secretary of Defense and former Ford Motor Company President Robert McNamara, and National Security Advisor and former Harvard University dean McGeorge Bundy.[14]

By 1964 units of the North Vietnamese Army (NVA) had begun to supplement the communist guerrilla forces (Vietcong) in the south. President Lyndon B. Johnson, informed that the South Vietnamese government was on the "verge of collapse," authorized major increases in U.S. supporting forces and began planning for a U.S. combat role. Yet in the presidential election of that year, Johnson assumed the pose of a dove and portrayed his Republican opponent Barry Goldwater as a hawk.

In August 1964, unconfirmed reports of an attack on U.S. Navy vessels by North Vietnamese torpedo boats led to the "Gulf of Tonkin" resolution by the Congress, authorizing the president to take "all necessary measures" to "repel any armed attack" against any U.S. forces in Southeast Asia. The Tonkin Gulf Resolution would be cited throughout the war by Presidents Johnson and Nixon as congressional authorization for direct U.S. military intervention.

In February 1965 President Lyndon B. Johnson ordered U.S. combat troops into South Vietnam and authorized a gradual increase in air strikes against North Vietnam. Marines landing on the beaches near Da Nang on March 8 in full battle gear were greeted by young girls selling flowers, souvenirs, and themselves; the heavy fighting would come later.

Political Limits

The fateful decision to commit U.S. ground combat forces to Vietnam was made without any significant effort to mobilize American public opinion, the government, or the economy for war. On the contrary, the president minimized the U.S. military effort, placed numerical limits on U.S. troop strength in Vietnam, limited bombing targets, and underestimated North Vietnam's military capabilities as well as expected U.S. casualties. No U.S. ground troops were permitted to cross into North Vietnam, and only once (in Cambodia in 1970) were they permitted to attack NVA forces elsewhere in Indochina. President Johnson's gradualist approach (operation "Rolling Thunder" called for U.S. air strikes to move northward from the South Vietnamese border toward Hanoi at a slow and steady pace) gave the enemy precious time to construct a heavy air defense system, organize civilian repair brigades, disperse its military depots, and develop alternative transportation routes to the south. But more important, the U.S. leadership provided no clear-cut military objectives:

> The President and his advisors did not seek the defeat of North Vietnam. They did not speak of conquest on the battlefield . . . as men from time immemorial had talked of victory! Their objective rather was to inflict sufficient pains on the North Vietnamese and Vietcong to force them to negotiate on terms acceptable to the United States.[15]

The president sought to apply "some, but not too much" military force. To avoid "undue excitement" the president failed to inform the public of the significance of the military actions undertaken. He wished to keep America on a peacetime footing, to continue his "Great Society" domestic programs, to provide both "guns *and* butter." "Quietly and without fanfare, he launched what would become America's longest, most frustrating, and most divisive war, with only a dim perception of what lay ahead and with no firm mandate from the nation."[16]

Search and Destroy Tactics

U.S. ground combat troops were initially placed in the northern-most Quang Tri province of South Vietnam in order to block the march of North Vietnamese troops directly into the south. The United States built a large military port at Da Nang to supply its forces. In the important battle of Khe Sanh in January 1968, U.S. soldiers and Marines defeated NVA efforts to dislodge those blocking forces. But the NVA had already established its Ho Chi Minh Trail, which swung around the U.S. blocking position, through "neutral" Laos and Cambodia and into the central highlands and eventually into the Mekong Delta near the South Vietnamese capital of Saigon. The U.S. commander, General William C. Westmoreland, dispersed his troops throughout South Vietnam in widespread "search and destroy" missions against infiltrating NVA forces. By late 1967 more than 500,000 U.S. troops were committed to Vietnam.

These military forces were committed to a war of attrition, a war in which U.S. firepower was expected to inflict sufficient casualties on the enemy to force them to negotiate a settlement. U.S. casualties were supposed to be minimal. With attrition defined as the military objective, the enemy "body count" became notoriously unreliable. "Americanization" of the war had a debilitating effect on the South Vietnamese army, and a genuinely popular South Vietnamese government never emerged. The air war became a farce, with the president personally selecting targets and occasionally ordering "bombing halts" in the hopes of luring the enemy to the bargaining table. North Vietnamese population centers were carefully avoided; the principal targets were roads and bridges and troop concentrations. Yet NVA troops and supplies continued to move south in increasing amounts throughout the war. The United States never struck decisively at Hanoi until the famous "Christmas bombing" in 1973. Modern, sophisticated Soviet surface-to-air missiles exacted a heavy toll of U. S. aircraft. Perhaps more important, downed U.S. airmen became tortured hostages whose fate would weigh heavily on U.S. negotiators later in the war.

Military Victory, Political Defeat

The failure of the nation's leadership to set forth a clear military objective in Vietnam made "victory" impossible. *The Pentagon Papers,*[17] composed of official memos and documents of the war, reveal increasing disenchantment with military results throughout 1967 by Secretary of Defense Robert McNamara and others who had originally initiated U.S. military actions. But President Johnson sought to rally support for the war by claiming that the United States was "winning." General Westmoreland was brought home to tell Congress that there was a light at the end of the tunnel. "We have reached an important point where the end begins to come into view."[18] But these pronouncements only helped set the stage for the enemy's great political victory—the Tet offensive.

On January 30, 1968, Vietcong forces blasted their way into the U.S. embassy compound in Saigon and held the courtyard for six hours. The attack was part of a massive, coordinated Tet offensive against all major cities of South Vietnam. The offensive caught the United States and ARVN forces off guard. The ancient city of Hue was captured and held by Vietcong for nearly three weeks. But U.S. forces responded and inflicted very heavy casualties on the Vietcong. The Vietcong failed to hold any of the positions they captured; the people did not rise up to welcome them as "liberators," and their losses were high. Indeed, after Tet the Vietcong were no longer an effective fighting force; almost all fighting would be conducted thereafter by regular NVA troops. (Hanoi may have planned the elimination of Vietcong forces this way in order to ensure its eventual domination of the South.) By any *military* measure, the Tet offensive was a "defeat" for the enemy and a "victory" for U.S. forces.

Yet the Tet offensive was Hanoi's greatest political victory. "What the hell is going on?" asked a shocked television anchorman, Walter Cronkite. "I thought we were winning the war."[19] Television pictures of bloody fighting in Saigon and Hue seemed to mock the administration's reports of an early end to the war. The media, believing they had been duped by Johnson and Westmoreland, launched a long and bitter campaign against the war effort. Elite support for the war plummeted.

Elite Opinion Shifts

Elite opinion in the United States shaped the course of the Vietnam War, not mass opinion. Evidence for this thesis is provided by John F. Mueller, who traced support for the war over time among various segments of the nation's population.[20] In the early stages of the war, there was great public support for the fighting, especially among college-educated groups (see Figure 3-2), from which elites are drawn. The masses supported the war at the outset, but not as strongly as did the better-informed and better-educated groups. But after the Tet offensive in 1968, support of the Vietnam War by college-educated Americans declined. When elites supported the war in its early stages, the United States escalated its participation, despite less-than-enthusiastic support by less-educated groups. The United States withdrew from the war and sought a negotiated settlement after elites, not masses, made a dramatic shift in opinion. Elites agreed on escalation in the early phases of the Vietnam War, and they agreed on withdrawal in its later phases. Their only disagreements among themselves occurred over the speed of withdrawal.

The antiwar protesters had no significant effect on the course of the war. Indeed, if anything, the protesters strengthened the war effort. After a careful analysis of change in elite and mass opinion of the war, Mueller concludes, "The protest against the war in Vietnam may have been counterproductive in its impact on public opinion: that is, the war might have been somewhat more unpopular if protest had not existed."[21] Most Americans disapproved of Jane Fonda's broadcasting enemy propaganda from Hanoi while U.S. prisoners were being tortured in prisons a few blocks away.

Deserted by the very elites who had initiated American involvement in the war, hounded by hostile media, and confronting a bitter and divisive presidential election, Lyndon Johnson made a dramatic announcement on national television on March 31, 1968: he halted the bombing of North

FIGURE 3-2 Trends in support of the Vietnam War, by education

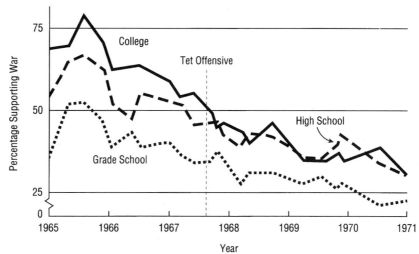

SOURCE: From John F. Mueller, *War, Presidents, and Public Opinion* (1973), p. 125. Used with permission of John Wiley & Sons, Inc.

Vietnam and asked Hanoi for peace talks, and concluded: "I shall not seek, and I will not accept, the nomination of my party for another term as your president." He also declined Westmoreland's request for more troops and for permission to attack North Vietnamese territory. U.S. ground operations were scaled down to reduce casualties. Formal peace talks opened in Paris on May 13.

Shifting Political Objectives

U.S. objectives in Vietnam shifted again with the arrival in Washington of the new president, Richard M. Nixon, and his national security advisor, Henry A. Kissinger. In the presidential election campaign of 1968, both candidates—Democratic Vice-President Hubert H. Humphrey and Republican Richard Nixon—presented nearly identical positions supporting U.S. military efforts and endorsing a negotiated peace. But when the Nixon administration took office, it immediately began a gradual withdrawal of U.S. forces from Vietnam.

Nixon and Kissinger knew the war must be ended. But they sought to end it "honorably." The South Vietnamese could not be abruptly abandoned without threatening the credibility of U.S. commitments everywhere in the world. They sought a peace settlement that would give South Vietnam a reasonable chance to survive. They hoped that "detente" with the Soviet Union, and a new relationship with the People's Republic of China, might help to bring about "peace with honor" in Vietnam. But even in the absence of a settlement, they began the withdrawal of U.S. troops under the guise of "Vietnamization" of the war effort. ARVN forces were required to take up the burden of fighting as U.S. forces withdrew.

Unable to persuade Hanoi to make even the slightest concession at Paris, President Nixon sought to demonstrate American strength and resolve. He wished to make clear to Hanoi that he would not necessarily be bound by his predecessors' restraints. In the spring of 1970 Nixon authorized an attack on an NVA sanctuary inside the territory of Cambodia—an area known as the Parrot's Beak—not far from Saigon. The Cambodian operation was brief and probably achieved very little militarily. (However, Henry Kissinger argued, "The attack on the sanctuaries made our withdrawal from Vietnam easier; it saved lives."[22]) But it mobilized the antiwar movement in the United States. Demonstrations centered on American campuses, and six students were killed in an angry confrontation with the National Guard at Kent State University. Congress broke with the president, and for the first time it gave serious consideration to proposals requiring the immediate withdrawal of U.S. troops from Vietnam.

North Vietnam launched a new massive conventional invasion of the south in March 1972. Only 6,000 American combat troops remained, and Hanoi believed that the antiwar movement in the United States would prevent Nixon from reinforcing the ARVN. Spearheaded by Soviet tanks and artillery, NVA forces struck directly across the 17th parallel and its "DMZ," or demilitarized zone. At that time Nixon was just concluding the SALT I Agreement with the Soviets, and a Moscow summit was planned. Dismissing advice that a strong U.S. response to the new NVA invasion might disrupt talks with the Soviets, Nixon authorized the heaviest bombing campaign of the war, as well as a naval blockade of North Vietnam and the mining of its Haiphong Harbor. The ARVN fought better than either Hanoi or Washington had expected. The Soviets publicly denounced the renewed U.S. bombing, but they did not disrupt the SALT talks or Nixon's summit visit to Moscow.[23] The NVA suffered heavy casualties, and the attack was thrown back.

The End Game

Meanwhile, National Security Advisor Henry Kissinger and Hanoi's Le Duc Tho had begun meeting secretly in Paris, away from the formal negotiations, to work out "the shape of a deal." U.S. prisoners of war were a major bargaining chip for Hanoi. After the heavy fighting of 1972 and the success of the ARVN and U.S. airpower, Kissinger and Le Duc Tho began inching toward an agreement. In the presidential election of 1972, the war became a partisan issue. Democratic candidate George McGovern had earlier stated that he would "crawl on his hands and knees to Hanoi" for peace, while Nixon continued his "peace with honor" theme. Nixon's landslide reelection strengthened his position in negotiations. In October Kissinger believed he had worked out a peace agreement, and he announced prematurely that "peace is at hand." But the agreement collapsed, in part because of the reluctance of the South Vietnamese to go along with the provisions worked out between Hanoi and Washington and in part because of last-minute new demands by Hanoi.[24]

The United States unleashed a devastating air attack directly on Hanoi for the first time in December 1972. U.S. B-52s from Guam joined with bombers based in Thailand to destroy factories, power plants, and transportation facilities in Hanoi itself. Critics at home labeled Nixon's action "the Christmas bombing," and congressional doves again planned to force an end to the war by law. But when negotiations resumed in Paris in January, the North Vietnamese quickly agreed to peace on the terms that Kissinger and Le Duc Tho had worked out earlier. Both Nixon and Kissinger contend that the Christmas bombing secured the final peace.[25]

The Paris Peace Agreement of 1973 called for a cease-fire in place, with NVA troops remaining in its areas of control in the south. The South Vietnamese government and the ARVN also remained in place. All U.S. forces were withdrawn from South Vietnam and U.S. prisoners returned. But the major question of the war—the political status of South Vietnam—was unresolved. The United States promised "full economic and military aid" to the South Vietnamese government and promised to "respond with full force" should North Vietnam violate the cease-fire. The

U.S. also agreed to provide Hanoi with billions of dollars in aid for reconstruction.

Abandoning Commitments

The South Vietnamese government lasted two years after the Paris Peace Agreement. The U.S. fulfilled none of its pledges, either to South or North Vietnam. Congress refused to provide significant military aid to the South Vietnamese. Congress passed the War Powers Act in 1973 over Nixon's veto, obligating the president to withdraw U.S. troops from combat within sixty days in the absence of an explicit congressional endorsement. The Watergate affair forced Nixon's resignation in August 1974. In early 1975 Hanoi decided that the United States would not "jump back in," and therefore "the opportune moment" was at hand. The NVA attacked first in the central highlands, and President Thieu unwisely ordered a withdrawal to the coast. The retreat quickly became a rout. When NVA forces attacked Hue and Da Nang, the ARVN and thousands of civilians fled southward toward Saigon.

President Gerald Ford never gave serious consideration to the use of U.S. military forces to repel the new invasion, and his requests to Congress for emergency military aid to the South Vietnamese fell on deaf ears. U.S. Ambassador Graham Martin, embarrassed by his government's abandonment of Vietnam, delayed implementation of escape plans until the last moment. The United States abandoned hundreds of thousands of loyal Vietnamese who had fought alongside the Americans for years.[26] The spectacle of U.S. Marines using rifle butts to keep desperate Vietnamese from boarding helicopters on the roof of the U.S. embassy "provided a tragic epitaph for twenty-five years of American involvement in Vietnam."[27]

The Costs of Defeat

The United States' humiliation in Vietnam had lasting national and international consequences. The United States suffered 47,318 battle deaths and missing-in-action among the 2.8 million who fought in Vietnam. This is more than the 33,629 U.S. battle deaths in Korea (1950–1953), but far fewer than the 292,131 U.S. battle deaths in the Second World War (1941–1945). Perhaps one million Vietnamese, military and civilian, in both North and South Vietnam, were killed during the war years. But the "peace" was more bloody than the war. In Cambodia more than two million people were murdered by victorious communist forces in genocidal "killing fields." More than 1.5 million South Vietnamese were forcibly relocated to harsh rural areas and "reeducation camps." Nearly one-half million "boat people" tried to flee their country; eventually the United States took in nearly 250,000 Vietnamese refugees. Unlike past wars, there were no victory parades, and no one could answer the question of the mother whose son was killed in Vietnam: "What did he die for?"

Trust and confidence in America's leadership declined to historic lows in the aftermath of the Vietnam War and Watergate. National surveys conducted over the years show the 1970s to be a period of national self-doubt. Not until the 1980s did measures of national pride and trust in government begin to turn upward again. In the immediate aftermath of the war, many Americans preferred to forget the Vietnam experience. The memories were too painful. Liberals and conservatives, Democrats and Republicans, were all equally implicated in the defeat. No one debated "who lost the war." More than a decade would pass before memorials were built to those who died in Vietnam and serious discussions of the war were undertaken.

THE GULF WAR: ELITE LEADERSHIP RESTORED

America's leadership performed markedly better in the Gulf War. Clear strategic objectives were established by President George Bush: to force the immediate and unconditional withdrawal of Iraqi troops from Kuwait; to destroy Saddam Hussein's nuclear, chemical, and biological weapons facilities; and to ensure that Iraqi military forces would no longer be capable of posing a threat to the region. The president relied upon his military commanders to devise a plan to achieve these objectives, to assemble the necessary forces to carry out the plan without artificial ceilings or limitations, and to execute the plan effectively and with minimum casualties. The president relied on a single direct chain of military command, from Secretary of Defense Richard Cheney, to the Chairman of the Joint Chiefs of Staff, General Colin Powell, to a single battlefield commander, General Norman Schwarzkopf, who controlled all Army, Navy, Air Force, and Marine units in the operation, as well as all allied forces.

The U.S. military leadership had learned its lessons from Vietnam: define clear military objectives, use overwhelming and decisive military force, move swiftly and avoid protracted stalemate, minimize casualties, and be sensitive to the image of the war projected back home. The president concentrated his attention on winning political support for the war in world capitals, at the United Nations, and, most important, at home.

Saddam Hussein's miscalculations contributed heavily to the U.S. political and military victory. His invasion of Kuwait on August 2, 1990, was apparently designed to restore his military prestige following eight years of indecisive war against Iran, to secure additional oil revenues to finance the continued buildup of Iraqi military power, and to intimidate and perhaps to invade Saudi Arabia and the Gulf states and thereby secure control over a major share of the world's oil reserves. The Iraqi invasion met with surprisingly swift response from the United Nations in Security

Council Resolution 660, condemning the invasion and demanding an immediate withdrawal, and Resolution 661, imposing a trade embargo and economic sanctions. A summit meeting of Arab states reinforced the condemnation and sanctions, with only Libya, Yemen, and the Palestine Liberation Organization (PLO) supporting Iraq. And President Bush immediately sent Secretary of Defense Cheney to Saudi Arabia to arrange for U.S. deployment of force to resist an Iraqi attack. The Saudi king was initially skeptical of U.S. resolve; the United States had deserted its friends too often in the past when the fighting got tough and public opinion shifted. But on August 7, the first U.S. forces were sent to Saudi Arabia in Operation Desert Shield to assist in the defense of the kingdom.

President Bush immediately set to work to stitch together a coalition military force that would eventually include thirty nations. While the military contributions made by many coalition nations was very modest (for example, Poland sent a hospital ship), the political symbolism was important: it was not Saddam Hussein against the United States, but Saddam Hussein against the world. Bush extracted pledges of financial support from Japan, Germany, and other nations that did not send military forces. And he maintained close contact and the political support of the Soviet Union and China whose votes in the UN Security Council were essential.

On paper, Iraq possessed the fourth largest military force in the world, with one million troops battle-hardened from eight years of war with Iran. Iraqi weapons included more than 5,000 tanks, 10,000 other armored vehicles, 4,000 artillery pieces, 700 combat aircraft, and a heavy surface-to-air missile air defense system. Iraq also possessed more than 1,000 Soviet-made Scud surface-to-surface missiles, and it had used deadly chemical weapons against Iran and its own Kurdish population.

U.S. forces faced the greatest danger in the early days of Operation Desert Shield. The first ground forces to arrive—the 82nd Airborne Division and 101st Air Assault Division—could deploy rapidly by air to trouble spots anywhere in the world, but they had no heavy tanks or artillery. Even with the support of Air Force and Navy fighters and ground-attack aircraft, these "light" forces would be vulnerable to attack by "heavy" Iraqi tank and artillery columns. But Saddam ordered his forces in Kuwait to dig into defensive positions, believing that a long standoff would eventually weaken the political coalition aligned against him and allow him to keep his stolen prize.

Early on, the president described the U.S. military deployment as "defensive," but he soon became convinced that neither diplomacy nor an economic blockade would dislodge Saddam from Kuwait. Saddam moved forty-two divisions, nearly one-half million troops, into Kuwait and southern Iraq, including his elite Republican Guard. He dug ditches and planted mine fields, erected earth berms to stop tanks, set up antiaircraft defenses, and rigged Kuwait's oil wells with explosives. He took hundreds of foreign hostages as "insurance" against attack, but this brutality only hardened Western opinion. The president ordered the military to prepare an "offensive" option.

The top U.S. military commanders, including Generals Powell and Schwarzkopf, had been field officers in Vietnam, and they were resolved not to repeat the mistakes of that war. They were reluctant to go into battle without the full support of the American people. If ordered to fight, they wanted to employ overwhelming and decisive military force; they wanted to avoid gradual escalation, protracted conflict, target limitations, and political interference in the conduct of the war. They presented the president with an "offensive" plan that called for a very large military buildup: elements of six Army divisions and two Marine divisions, with 1,900 tanks, 930 artillery pieces, and 500 attack helicopters; more than a thousand combat aircraft from B-52 "Big Uglies" to F15 and F16 fighter bombers, A-10 tank killers, and "stealthy" F117As, plus hundreds of tanker and transport aircraft; and six Navy carrier battle groups with nearly 500 combat aircraft, plus Marine amphibious forces afloat. Coalition forces included British and French heavy armored units and Egyptian, Syrian, Saudi, and other Arab units.

The president announced this massive buildup of forces on November 8, but immediately faced a barrage of criticism at home for abandoning his earlier defensive posture. U.S. Senator Sam Nunn, respected chairman of the Senate Armed Forces committee, opened hearings that urged the president to continue economic sanctions and avoid the heavy casualties that a land war was expected to produce. But the president was convinced that sanctions would not work, that Saddam would hold out for years, that eventually the political coalition backing the embargo would break up, and that Saddam would become increasingly powerful on the world stage. He argued that Saddam would soon acquire nuclear weapons, that if unchecked he would soon dominate the Arab world and Mideast oil reserves, and that aggression must not be allowed to succeed. Secretary of State James Baker convinced the UN Security Council members, including the Soviet Union (with China abstaining), to support Resolution 678 authorizing states to "use all necessary means" against Iraq unless it withdrew from Kuwait by January 15. Bush had won the support of the world body for offensive action, but the Democratic-controlled Congress balked. The president believed he had constitutional authority as commander-in-chief to attack Baghdad, whether or not Congress approved. The Democratic leadership thought otherwise, but after long debate in the Senate, enough Democrats deserted their party to give the president a close 52–47 vote in favor of the use of force. To reassure the American people and world opinion that he had exhausted all diplomatic means to free Kuwait, the president sent Secretary Baker to Geneva with a letter for Saddam. The Iraqi foreign minister refused to accept the letter and the insult reinforced support for the president's decision to use force.

From Baghdad, CNN reporters Bernard Shaw and Peter Arnett were startled the night of January 16 when Operation Desert Storm began with an air attack on key installations in the city. Iraqi forces were also surprised, despite the prompt timing of the attack; Saddam had assured them that the United States lacked the resolve to fight, and that even if war broke out, U.S. public opinion would force a settlement as casualties rose. The air war had three objectives: first, to win air supremacy by destroying radar installations, air defense control centers, SAM launchers and airfields, and any Iraqi fighters that managed to get into the air; second, to destroy strategic targets, including nuclear facilities, chemical warfare plants, command centers, and military communications; third, to degrade Iraqi military forces by cutting off supplies, destroying tanks and artillery, and demoralizing troops with round-the-clock bombardment. More than 110,000 combat missions were flown with only 39 aircraft losses, none in air combat. Smart weapons performed superbly, and U.S. television audiences were treated to videotapes of laser-guided smart bombs entering the doors and air shafts of enemy bunkers. Collateral civilian damage was lower than in any previous air war. After five weeks of air war, intelligence estimated that nearly half the Iraqi tanks and artillery in the field had been destroyed, demoralized troops were hiding in deep shelters, and the battlefield had been isolated and "prepared" for ground operations.

General Schwarzkopf's plan for the ground war emphasized deception and maneuver. He wanted to make the Iraqis believe that the main attack would come directly against Kuwait's southern border and be supported by a Marine landing on the coast. While Iraqi forces prepared for attacks from the south and the east coast, Schwarzkopf sent heavy armed columns in a "Hail Mary" play—a wide sweep to the west, outflanking and cutting off Iraqi forces in the battle area. The Iraqi forces, blinded by air attacks and obliged to stay in their bunkers, would not be able to know about or respond to the flanking attack. On the night of February 24, the ground attack began with Marines easily breaching berms, ditches, and mine fields and racing directly to the Kuwait city airport; helicopter air assaults lunged deep into Iraq; armored columns raced northward across the desert to outflank Iraqi forces and then attack them from the west; and a surge in air attacks kept Iraqi forces holed up in their bunkers. Iraqi troops surrendered in droves; highways from Kuwait city were turned into massive junkyards of Iraqi vehicles; Iraqi forces that tried to fight were quickly destroyed. After 100 hours of ground fighting, President George Bush declared a cease-fire.

The United States had achieved a decisive military victory, quickly and with precious few casualties. The president resisted calls to expand the original objectives of war—that is, to capture Baghdad, to destroy Iraq's economy, to encourage its disintegration as a nation, or to kill or capture Saddam, although it was expected that his defeat would lead to his ouster. While the war left many political issues unresolved, it was the most decisive outcome the United States had achieved since the end of World War II.

In retrospect, the president's decision to end the war after only 100 hours of ground operations appears to have been premature. Not all of the president's original objectives had been fully accomplished. Units of Saddam's elite Republican Guard, which would have been surrounded and destroyed with another's day's fighting, escaped back to Baghdad. With these surviving forces, Saddam maintained his cruel grip on the country and proceeded to attack his regime's opponents brutally, especially the Kurdish minority in northern Iraq. Later investigations revealed that his nuclear weapons facilities had not been completely destroyed. And finally, Saddam's continuation in power appeared to mock the sacrifices in lives exacted by the war.

Nonetheless, America's elite learned important political lessons from the Gulf War:

- Decisive military victory inspires confidence in a nation's elite. It inspires patriotism, national unity, and support for the nation's values and institutions. George Bush achieved an all-time high in presidential approval ratings in the polls immediately following the Gulf War victory. The military rose to the top of the list of "trusted" institutions in American society.
- A rapid conclusion of hostilities ensures that public support will not erode over time and that protracted combat and a steady stream of casualties will not fuel anitwar sentiments.
- The rapid employment of overwhelming forces is both politically and militarily superior to gradual escalation and the employment of minimum force. The use of overwhelming force reduces total casualties and achieves an earlier and more decisive victory. Such force reduces the opportunity for diplomatic interventions that may produce compromised, indecisive resolutions.
- The nation's political leadership is vastly more effective when it concentrates on developing and maintaining foreign and domestic political support for the war, while leaving the planning and execution of military operations to the military leadership.

SUMMARY

According to elite theory, the movement of nonelites into elite positions must be slow and continuous in order to maintain stability and avoid revolution. Furthermore, potential elite members must demonstrate their commitment to the basic elite consensus before being admitted to elite positions. Elite theory recognizes competition among elites but contends that elites share a broad consensus about preserving the system essentially as it is. It views public-policy changes as a response to elites' redefinition of their own self-interest rather than as a product of direct mass influence. Finally, elite theory views changes in public policy as incremental rather than revolutionary. American political history supports these propositions:

1. America's elite membership evolved slowly, with no serious break in the ideas or values of the American political and economic system. When the leadership of Hamilton and Adams—Federalists—shifted to that of Jefferson, Monroe, and Madison—Republicans—government policies changed very little because of the fundamental consensus among elite members.

2. As new sources of wealth opened in an expanding economy, America's elite membership opened to new groups and individuals who had acquired wealth and property and who accepted the national consensus about private enterprise, limited government, and individualism. The West produced new elites, who were assimilated into the governing circle. Public policies changed but were not replaced. The Jacksonians wanted a more open elite system in which the newly wealthy could acquire influence, but they were no more in favor of "dangerous leveling" than were the Founding Fathers.

3. The Civil War reduced southern planters' influence in America's elite structure and paved the way for the rise of the new industrial capitalists. The industrial revolution produced a narrowly self-interested elite of industrial capitalists. Mass movements resulted—chiefly one for free silver—but they met with failure.

4. America's elites have divided deeply on the nature of American society only once. This division produced the Civil War, the nation's bloodiest conflict. The Civil War was a conflict between southern elites, dependent on a plantation economy, slave labor, and free trade, and northern industrial commercial elites, who prospered under free labor and protective tariffs. But before, during, and after the Civil War, northern and southern elites continued to strive for compromise in recognition of shared consensus on behalf of liberty and property.

5. The new liberal establishment sought to preserve the existing social and economic order, not to overthrow it. The Great Depression, the victories of fascism in Germany and communism in the Soviet Union, and growing restlessness of the American masses combined to convince America's elites that a more public-regarding philosophy was essential to preserving the American political system and their prominent place in it. Eventually Franklin D. Roosevelt's philosophy of noblesse oblige—elite responsibility for the welfare of the masses— won widespread acceptance among established American leadership.

6. Political conflict in the United States has centered on a narrow range of issues. Consensus rather than conflict has characterized American elite history. Political rhetoric and campaign slogans should not obscure the fundamental consensus of America's elites. Whatever the popular political label has been—"Federalist," "Democratic," "Whig,"

"Republican," "Progressive," "Conservative," or "Liberal"—American leadership has been essentially conservative.

7. Policy changes have been incremental. Policy changes, including those launched by the New Deal, occurred when events threatened the system; governing elites—acting on the basis of enlightened self-interest—instituted reforms to preserve the system. Even the reforms and welfare policies of the New Deal were designed to strengthen the existing social and economic fabric of society while minimally dislocating elites.

8. America's defeat and humiliation in Vietnam was a result of the failure of the nation's elite to set forth clear policy objectives, develop a strategy to achieve those objectives, and rally mass support behind the war. Elites, not masses, initially favored the war; and the United States began its withdrawal when elite, not mass, opinion shifted against the war.

9. The Gulf War restored mass confidence in presidential leadership. The decisive use of overwhelming military force to achieve quick victory with minimum U.S. casualties propelled President Bush to all-time highs in approval ratings and established the military as the most trusted institution in American society.

———— NOTES

1. *McCulloch* v. *Maryland,* 4 Wheaton 316 (1819).
2. See Richard Hofstadter, *The American Political Tradition* (New York: Knopf, 1948), pp. 18–44.
3. Ibid., pp. 32–33.
4. Ibid., p. 38.
5. Frederick Jackson Turner, "The West and American Ideals," in *The Frontier in American History* (New York: Holt, Rinehart & Winston, 1921).
6. *Dred Scott* v. *Sandford,* 19 Howard 393 (1857).
7. Hofstadter, op. cit., p. 109.
8. Ibid., p. 113.
9. Ibid., p. 116.
10. Ibid., p. 119.
11. Herbert Spencer, *Social Statistics* (1851).
12. See Gustavus Myers, *A History of the Great American Fortunes,* 3 vols. (Chicago: Kerr, 1910).
13. V. O. Key, Jr., *Politics, Parties, and Pressure Groups* (New York: T. Y. Crowell, 1942), pp. 189–191.
14. See David Halberstam, *The Best and the Brightest* (New York: Random House, 1973).

15. George C. Herring, *America's Longest War* (New York: Random House, 1979), p. 143.
16. Ibid., p. 144.
17. New York Times, *The Pentagon Papers* (New York: Bantam Books, 1971).
18. Herring, op. cit., p. 182.
19. Ibid., p. 188.
20. John F. Mueller, *War, Presidents, and Public Opinion* (New York: Wiley, 1973).
21. Ibid., p. 164.
22. Henry Kissinger, *The White House Years* (Boston: Little, Brown, 1979), p. 507.
23. Nixon correctly judged that the Soviets would not jeopardize the SALT I Agreement for North Vietnam. See *RN: The Memoirs of Richard Nixon*, vol. 2 (New York: Warner Books, 1978), pp. 59–87.
24. See Kissinger, op. cit., pp. 1301–1446.
25. Ibid., p. 1461; Nixon, op. cit., p. 251.
26. See Frank Snepp, *Decent Interval* (New York: Random House, 1977).
27. Herring, op. cit., p. 262.

—— SELECTED READINGS

Beard, Charles A. *The Economic Basis of Politics.* New York: Knopf, 1947. Beard provides a brief reinterpretation of American political history from the perspective of economic determinism. America's foremost historian and political scientist first published this essay in 1916.

Burch, Phillip H., Jr. *Elites in American History.* Vol. I: *The Federalist Years to the Civil War.* Vol. II: *The Civil War to the New Deal.* Vol. III: *The New Deal to the Carter Administration.* New York: Holmes and Meier, 1980. The most thorough study available of the class backgrounds of American leaders throughout history. Burch describes the socioeconomic status and financial interests of top government officials from the Washington to the Carter administrations. He links the elite status of these decision makers to their public actions and policy positions.

Hartz, Louis. *The Liberal Tradition in America.* New York: Harcourt, Brace, & World, 1955. The absence of a feudal aristocracy in the United States obstructed the development of social class consciousness, which in turn prevented the emergence of socialism in this country. The United States as a nation was "born free," and most Americans consider themselves middle class.

Hofstadter, Richard. *The American Political Tradition.* New York: Knopf, Vintage Books, 1948. This book is an important political history from an elite perspective. Hofstadter traces the development of American political elites and their philosophies from Jefferson and the Founding

Fathers through Jackson, Bryan, Wilson, and Franklin Roosevelt. He emphasizes that at every stage of U.S. history, elites have been in considerable agreement over major issues (with the possible exception of the Civil War). Finally Hofstadter discusses the elite practice of incrementalism: that elite leaders have always moved to preserve the established order with as little change in the system as possible.

Lundberg, Ferdinand. *America's Sixty Families*. Secaucus, N.J.: Citadel Press, 1937. This book is a classic work on elites that systematically traces the development of the entrepreneurial elite of the late nineteenth and early twentieth centuries.

4

Positions of
Power in America

★ *The leading men in each of the three domains of power—the warlords, the corporation chieftains, the political directorate—tend to come together to form the power elite of America.*

C. Wright Mills, The Power Elite, 1956

Power in the United States is organized into large institutions. Positions at the top of the major institutions in American society are sources of great power. Sociologist C. Wright Mills described the relationship between institutional authority and power in this way:

> If we took the one hundred most powerful men in America, the one hundred wealthiest, and the one hundred most celebrated away from the institutional positions they now occupy, away from their resources of men and women and money, away from the media of mass communication that are now focused upon them—then they would be powerless and poor and uncelebrated. For power is not of a man. Wealth does not center in the person of the wealthy. Celebrity is not inherent in any personality. To be celebrated, to be wealthy, to have power, requires access to major institutions, for the institutional positions men occupy determine in large part their chances to have and to hold these valued experiences.[1]

In this chapter we describe the people who occupy high positions in the major private and governmental institutions of American society. We include the major *private* institutions—in industry, finance, law, and other "nongovernmental institutions"—because we believe that they allocate values for our society and shape the lives of all Americans. Remember, we defined an elite member as anyone who participates in decisions that allocate values for society, not just those who participate in decision making as part of the government. The decisions of automobile companies to raise prices, of banks to raise or lower interest rates, of electrical companies to market new products, of the mass media to determine what is "news," and of schools and colleges to decide what shall be taught—all affect the lives of Americans as much as do government decisions. Moreover, these private institutions have the power and resources to enforce their decisions.

NONDECISIONS

Nondecisions occur when individuals or institutions limit the scope of decision making to exclude issues that disturb established elites. Keeping issues *out* of politics is an important aspect of power, one that is just as important as deciding the issues that *are* presented to public officials—perhaps more important. So power really has two manifestations: decisions and nondecisions. Power is not only deciding the issues but also deciding what the issues will be.

Nondecisions can occur (1) when influential elites act directly to exclude an issue from the political arena; (2) when subordinates anticipate the negative reaction of elites and ignore proposals or suggestions that would "cause trouble"; or (3) when the underlying values of society and its institutional structure prevent serious consideration of alternative programs and policies.

In nondecision making, those at the top of institutional structures need not exercise their power overtly; the subordinates who carry on the day-to-day business of industry, finance, government, and so on know the values of the top elite and understand the great potential for power that the top elite possesses. These subordinates obtained their jobs in part because they exhibited dominant values in their thinking and actions. Whether consciously or unconsciously, their decisions reflect the values of those at the top.

The institutional structure of society also exercises power when it limits the scope of public decision making to issues that are relatively harmless to the elite. Institutions support the achievement of some values while obstructing the achievement of others. For example, we already know that the Founding Fathers deliberately constructed the American government system to suppress certain values and issues. James Madison, in *The Federalist* Number 10, defended the structure of the new American government, particularly its republican and federal features, on the grounds that it would suppress "factious issues." And Madison named outright the factious issues that must be avoided: "a rage for paper money, for an abolition of debts, for an equal division of property, or any other improper or wicked project."[2] Note that all the issues Madison wished to avoid involved challenges to the dominant economic interests. As a nongovernment example, consider the following: by placing owners of large blocks of company stock on governing boards of directors and by increasingly allocating large blocks of stock to top management personnel, American corporations tend to encourage the values of profit and investment security in corporate decision making. The structure of the American corporation deters it from pursuing a policy of public welfare at the expense of profit.

The fact that institutional structures maximize certain values (private enterprise, limited government, the profit system) while obstructing other values (absolute equality or "leveling," government ownership of industry) is an important aspect of politics in the United States. It is another reason for examining the major institutions of society and those who occupy high positions in them.

GOVERNING ELITES

Politicians specialize in office seeking. They know how to run for office, but they may not know how to run the government. After victory at the polls, wise politicians turn to experienced executive elites to run the government. Both Democratic and Republican presidents select essentially the same type of executive elite to staff the key positions in their administrations. Frequently, these top government executives—cabinet members, presidential advisers, special ambassadors—have occupied key posts in private industry, finance, or law or influential positions in education, the arts and sciences, or social, civic, and charitable associations. The executive elites move easily in and out of government posts from their positions in the corporate, financial, legal, and educational world. They often assume government jobs at a financial sacrifice, and many do so out of a sense of public service.

The elitist model of power envisions a single group of people exercising power in many different sectors of American life. Elitists do not necessarily expect to see individuals simultaneously occupying high positions in both business and government, but they do expect to see a "revolving door" by which elites move from power positions in banking, industry, the media, law, the foundations, and education to power positions in government, then frequently returning to prestigious private posts after a term of "public service." This revolving door pattern contrasts with the pluralist model of power (described in Chapter 1), which suggests very little overlapping among centers of power. Pluralists envision *different* groups of people exercising power in the various sectors of American life.

Let us briefly examine the career backgrounds of occupants of the three key cabinet posts of U.S. government—secretaries of state, defense, and treasury—over the past thirty-five years. We believe these biographies clearly illustrate the elitist notion of a "revolving door" of power. It is true that less important cabinet and executive staff positions are sometimes filled with career government bureaucrats or people with few elite credentials. But presidents almost always turn to the "heavyweights" to staff the key posts in the federal government.

Secretaries of State

John Foster Dulles: 1953–1960; partner of Sullivan and Cromwell (one of the twenty largest law firms on Wall Street); member of the board of directors of the Bank of New York, the Fifth Avenue Bank, the American Bank Note Company, the International Nickel Company of Canada, Babcock and Wilson Corporation, Gold Dust Corporation, the Overseas Security Corporation, Shenandoah Corporation, United Cigar Stores, American Cotton Oil Company, United Railroad of St. Louis, and European Textile Corporation; a trustee of the New York Public Library, the Union Theological Seminary, the Rockefeller Foundation, and the Carnegie Endowment for International Peace; a delegate to the World Council of Churches.

Dean Rusk: 1961–1968; former president of the Rockefeller Foundation.

William P. Rogers: 1969–1973; U.S. attorney general during Eisenhower administration; senior partner in Royall, Koegal, Rogers, and Wells (one of the twenty largest Wall Street law firms).

Henry Kissinger: 1973–1977; former special assistant to the president for national security affairs; former Harvard professor of international affairs and project director for Rockefeller Brothers Fund and for the Council on Foreign Relations.

Cyrus Vance: 1977–1980; senior partner in New York law firm of Simpson, Thatcher, and Bartlett; a director of IBM and Pan American World Airways; a trustee of Yale University, chairman of the board of trustees of the Rockefeller Foundation, and member of the Council on Foreign Relations; former secretary of the army and undersecretary of defense; U.S. negotiator in the Paris Peace Conference on Vietnam.

Edmund S. Muskie: 1980–1981; the only "political" figure to serve in this office in recent times; U.S. senator (D-Maine), 1959–1980, and chairman of the Senate Budget Committee; former governor of Maine, 1955–1959; member of Maine House of Representatives, 1946–1951; small-town attorney.

Alexander M. Haig, Jr.: 1981–1982; president of United Technologies and former four-star general, U.S. Army; former supreme allied commander, NATO; former White House chief of staff under President Richard Nixon; former deputy assistant for national security affairs under Henry Kissinger.

George P. Shultz: 1982–1988; president of Bechtel Corporation, the world's largest construction company; former secretary of the treasury and secretary of labor; former dean of the Graduate School of Business of the University of Chicago; a director of J. P. Morgan & Company, Morgan Guaranty Trust Co., Sears, Roebuck and Co., and the Alfred P. Sloan Foundation.

James A. Baker III: 1989–; former secretary of the treasury; former White House chief of staff; Bush campaign manager; wealthy Houston attorney and oilman.

Secretaries of Defense

Charles E. Wilson: 1953–1957; president and member of the board of directors of General Motors Corporation.

Neil H. McElroy: 1957–1959; former president and member of the board of directors of Procter & Gamble Co.; member of the board of directors of General Electric Co., Chrysler Corporation, and Equitable Life Insurance Company; member of the board of trustees of Harvard University, the National Safety Council, and the National Industrial Conference.

Thomas S. Gates: 1959–1960; secretary of the navy, 1957–1959; chairman of the board and chief executive officer, Morgan Guaranty Trust Co. (J. P. Morgan, New York); member of the board of directors of General Electric Co., Bethlehem Steel Corp., Scott Paper Co., Campbell Soup Co., Insurance Co. of North America, Cities Service Co., Smith, Kline and French (pharmaceuticals), and the University of Pennsylvania.

Robert S. McNamara: 1961–1967; president and member of the board of directors of the Ford Motor Co.; member of the board of directors of Scott Paper Co.; president of the World Bank, 1967–1982.

Clark Clifford: 1967–1969; senior partner of Clifford and Miller (Washington law firm); member of the board of directors of the National Bank of Washington and the Sheraton Hotel Corporation; special counsel to the president, 1949–1950; member of the board of trustees of Washington University in St. Louis.

Melvin Laird: 1969–1973; former Republican congressman from Wisconsin.

James R. Schlesinger: 1973–1977; former director, Central Intelligence Agency; former chairman, Atomic Energy Commission; former economics professor and research associate, Rand Corporation.

Harold Brown: 1977–1981; former president, California Institute of Technology; member of the board of directors of IBM and the Times-Mirror Corporation; former secretary of the air force under President Lyndon Johnson; U.S. representative to the Strategic Arms Limitation Treaty talks under President Richard Nixon.

Caspar W. Weinberger: 1981–1988; former vice-president of Bechtel Corporation; former secretary of health, education, and welfare; former director of Office of Management and Budget; former chairman of Federal Trade Commission; a director of PepsiCo and Quaker Oats Co.; former San Francisco attorney and California state legislator.

Richard B. Cheney: 1989–; former Wyoming congressman and Republican whip in the House of Representatives; former assistant to the president under Gerald Ford; White House chief of staff under Richard Nixon; former Washington attorney and congressional staffer.

Secretaries of the Treasury

George M. Humphrey: 1953–1957; former chairman of the board of directors of the M. A. Hanna Company; member of the board of directors of National Steel Corp., Consolidated Coal Company, Canada and Dominion Sugar Company; a trustee of the Massachusetts Institute of Technology.

Robert B. Anderson: 1957–1961; secretary of the navy, 1953–1954; deputy secretary of defense, 1954–1955; member of the board of directors of the Goodyear Tire & Rubber Company; member of the executive board of the Boy Scouts of America.

C. Douglas Dillon: 1961–1965; chairman of the board of Dillon, Reed, and Company (Wall Street investment firm); member of the New York Stock Exchange; director of U.S. and Foreign Securities Corporation and of U.S. International Securities Corporation; member of the board of governors of the New York Hospital and of the Metropolitan Museum.

Henry H. Fowler: 1965–1969; senior partner, Washington law firm of Fowler, Leva, Hawes, and Symington; former undersecretary of the treasury, 1961–1964; member of the Council on Foreign Relations.

David Kennedy: 1969–1971; president and chairman of the board of Continental Illinois Bank and Trust Company; a director of International Harvester Company, Commonwealth Edison, Pullman Company, Abbot Laboratories, Swift and Company, U.S. Gypsum, and Communications Satellite Corporation; trustee of the University of Chicago, the Brookings Institution, the Committee for Economic Development, and George Washington University.

John B. Connally: 1971–1972; former secretary of the navy, governor of Texas, administrative assistant to Lyndon B. Johnson; attorney for Murcheson Brothers Investment (Dallas); former director of New York Central Railroad.

George P. Shultz: 1972–1974; former secretary of labor and director of the Office of Management and Budget; former dean of the University of Chicago Graduate School of Business; former senior partner of Salomon Brothers (one of Wall Street's largest investment firms) and Stein, Roe and Farnham (investments).

William E. Simon: 1974–1977; former director, Federal Energy Office, and former deputy secretary of the treasury; former senior partner of Salomon Brothers.

Werner Michael Blumenthal: 1977–1979; former president of the Bendix Corporation; a trustee of Princeton University and member of the Council on Foreign Relations.

G. William Miller: 1979–1981; chairman and chief executive officer of the Textron Corporation; formerly a partner in the prestigious New York law firm of Cravath, Swaine, and Moore; a director of Allied Chemical and Federated Department Stores; former chairman of the Council of Economic Advisors.

Donald T. Regan: 1981–1985; former chairman of Merrill Lynch & Co., the nation's largest investment firm; former vice-chairman of the New York Stock Exchange; a trustee of the University of Pennsylvania, Committee for Economic Development, and the Business Roundtable.

James A. Baker III: 1985–1988; wealthy Houston attorney and White House chief of staff in Reagan's first term.

Nicholas Brady: 1988–; former chairman of the Wall Street firm of Dillon, Read & Co.; a director of Purolator, Bessermer Securities, Doubleday & Co., George International, ASA Ltd., Media General Inc., and NCR Corp.

These brief biographies generally confirm the revolving-door pattern of recruitment suggested by elite theory. It is true that some top officials rose to their positions through service to government (for example, Alexander Haig, Melvin Laird, Richard Cheney) and some others through universities and foundations (for example, Dean Rusk, James Schlesinger, Henry Kissinger). But most occupants of these top posts were recruited from the ranks of directors of large corporations and partners of prestigious law firms.

——— THE CONCENTRATION OF CORPORATE POWER

Economic power in the United States is concentrated in a small number of large corporations and banks. Traditionally, pluralism portrays business as just another interest group, competing with all other interest groups to influence public policy. Corporate power, according to the pluralists, depends on the political skills and resources of particular individuals, groups, and industries within the corporate world, on the performance of the economy, on the climate of public opinion, and on the relative strength of competing groups. In contrast, elitism views economic elites as distinctly powerful, not only in shaping government policy but, more important, in making decisions that directly influence all our lives.

Economic Elites

Economic elites decide what will be produced, how it will be produced, how much it will cost, how many people will be employed, who will be employed, and what their wages will be. They decide how goods and services will be distributed, how much money will be available for loans, what interest rates will be charged, and what new technologies will be developed. Of course, these decisions are influenced by governmental regulations, consumer demand, international competition, federal fiscal and monetary policy, and other public and private market forces. But in a free market economy, business elites, not government officials, make most of the key economic decisions.

Even the leading pluralist scholars have revised their views about corporate power in the United States. For many years pluralist political scientists, notably Yale University's Robert A. Dahl and Charles E. Lindblom, argued that no single interest group, including "business," dominated American politics. But Lindblom later recanted in an important book *Politics and Markets,* acknowledging "the privileged position of business." Dahl and Lindblom publicly confessed their "error":

> In our discussion of pluralism we made another error—and it is a continuing error in social science—in regarding business and business groups as playing the same interest-group role as the other groups in polyarchal systems, though more powerful. Businessmen play a distinctive role in polyarchal politics that is qualitatively different from that of any interest group. It is also much more powerful than an interest group role.[3]

Today these scholars lament that the private corporation is "hierarchical" and not governed democratically by its employees. This is true, of course, but what the pluralists still do not understand is that *all organizations are hierarchical.* Corporate governance is not unique. "Virtually all nongovernment institutions can be described in similar terms.

Universities, foundations, labor unions, many professional and trade associations, religious institutions and organizations, charitable organizations, and even public-interest groups—all exercise political power, and yet none is governed according to democratic principles or precepts. In its internal system of authority, the corporation is actually quite typical of the social structures that characterize democratic societies."[4]

Formal control of the nation's economic life rests in the hands of a relatively small number of senior officers and directors of the nation's largest corporate institutions. This concentration has occurred chiefly because economic enterprise has increasingly consolidated into a small number of giant corporations. The following statistics only suggest the scale and concentration of modern U.S. corporate enterprise.

There are 200,000 industrial corporations in the United States, but the 100 corporations listed in Table 4-1 control about 60 percent of all industrial assets in the nation. The 5 largest industrial corporations (General Motors, Exxon, Ford Motor Co., IBM, and General Electric) control 15 percent of the nation's industrial assets. Concentration in utilities, transportation, and communications is even greater.

TABLE 4-1   The 100 largest industrial corporations

Rank	Company	Sales (millions of dollars)
1.	General Motors	184,325.5
2.	Exxon	87,560.0
3.	Ford Motor	174,429.4
4.	Intl. Business Machines	92,473.0
5.	General Electric	168,259.0
6.	Mobil	42,187.0
7.	Philip Morris	47,384.0
8.	E. I. du Pont de Nemours	36,117.0
9.	Texaco	26,182.0
10.	Chevron	34,636.0
11.	Chrysler	43,076.0
12.	Boeing	15,784.0
13.	Procter & Gamble	20,468.0
14.	Amoco	30,510.0
15.	Shell Oil	27,998.0
16.	United Technologies	15,985.0
17.	Pepsico	18,775.1
18.	Eastman Kodak	24,170.0
19.	Conagra	9,420.3
20.	Dow Chemical	24,727.0
21.	McDonnell Douglas	14,841.0
22.	Xerox	31,658.0
23.	Atlantic Richfield	24,492.0
24.	USX	17,039.0
25.	RJR Nabisco Holdings	32,131.0
26.	Hewlett-Packard	11,973.0
27.	Tenneco	18,696.0
28.	Digital Equipment	11,874.7
29.	Minnesota Mining & Mfg.	11,083.0
30.	Westinghouse Electric	20,159.0

(continued)

TABLE 4-1   The 100 largest industrial corporations *(continued)*

Rank	Company	Sales (millions of dollars)
31.	International Paper	14,941.0
32.	Phillips Petroleum	11,473.0
33.	Sara Lee	8,122.0
34.	Johnson & Johnson	10,513.0
35.	Rockwell International	9,478.9
36.	Allied-Signal	10,382.0
37.	Coca-Cola	10,222.4
38.	Georgia-Pacific	10,622.0
39.	Motorola	9,375.0
40.	Bristol-Myers Squibb	9,416.0
41.	Goodyear Tire & Rubber	8,510.5
42.	Anheuser-Busch	9,986.5
43.	Occidental Petroleum	16,114.6
44.	Sun	7,143.0
45.	Caterpillar	12,042.0
46.	Aluminum Co. of America	11,178.4
47.	Lockheed	6,617.0
48.	Unocal	9,836.0
49.	Coastal	9,487.3
50.	General Dynamics	6,207.0
51.	Raytheon	6,087.1
52.	Ashland Oil	5,449.1
53.	Monsanto	9,227.0
54.	Citgo Petroleum	3,261.7
55.	Baxter International	9,340.0
56.	Unilever U.S.	N.A.
57.	Weyerhaeuser	16,927.5
58.	Unisys	8,432.0
59.	Merck	9,498.5
60.	Archer-Daniels-Midland	6,260.6
61.	American Brands	15,115.5
62.	TRW	5,635.0
63.	Textron	15,737.3
64.	Emerson Electric	6,364.4
65.	Ralston Purina	4,632.1
66.	Union Carbide	6,826.0
67.	Borden	5,481.3
68.	General Mills	3,901.8
69.	Pfizer	9,634.6
70.	Hanson Industries NA	13,222.5
71.	American Home Products	5,938.8
72.	Deere	11,649.4
73.	W. R. Grace	6,007.1
74.	Abbott Laboratories	6,255.3
75.	Hoechst Celanese	6,630.0
76.	Kimberly-Clark	5,650.4
77.	Texas Instruments	5,009.0
78.	Whirlpool	6,445.0
79.	H. J. Heinz	4,935.4
80.	Amerada Hess	8,841.4
81.	Apple Computer	3,493.6
82.	Campbell Soup	4,149.0
83.	Honeywell	4,806.7
84.	CPC International	4,510.0
85.	Miles	5,110.5

(continued)

TABLE 4-1   The 100 largest industrial corporations *(continued)*

Rank	Company	Sales (millions of dollars)
86.	Cooper Industries	7,148.6
87.	LTV	6,685.2
88.	Martin Marietta	3,896.9
89.	Quaker Oats	3,016.1
90.	Colgate-Palmolive	4,510.7
91.	North American Philips	3,043.7
92.	Kellogg	3,925.8
93.	Reynolds Metals	6,685.3
94.	Lyondell Petrochemical	1,479.0
95.	Eli Lilly	8,298.6
96.	PPG Industries	6,056.2
97.	Northrop	3,127.8
98.	Stone Container	6,902.9
99.	Litton Industries	4,998.1
100.	Warner-Lambert	3,602.0

SOURCE: *Fortune,* April 20, 1992, pp. 220–221.

Banks

The financial world is equally concentrated. Of 1,400 banks serving the nation, the 50 largest control 66 percent of all banking assets; three banks (Citicorp, BankAmerica, and Chase Manhattan) control 15 percent of all banking assets (see Table 4-2).

TABLE 4-2   The 50 largest commercial banking companies

Rank	Company	Assets (millions of dollars)	Cumulative percentage*
1.	Citicorp	216,986.0	6.9
2.	BankAmerica Corp.	110,728.0	10.4
3.	Chase Manhattan Corp.	98,064.0	13.5
4.	J. P. Morgan & Co.	93,103.0	16.5
5.	Security Pacific Corp.	84,731.0	19.2
6.	Chemical Banking Corp.	73,019.0	21.5
7.	NCNB Corp.	65,284.5	23.6
8.	Bankers Trust New York Corp.	63,596.0	25.6
9.	Manufacturers Hanover Corp.	61,530.0	27.6
10.	Wells Fargo & Co.	56,198.5	29.4
11.	First Interstate Bancorp.	51,356.5	31.0
12.	C&S/Sovran Corp.	51,237.5	32.6
13.	First Chicago Corp.	50,779.0	34.2
14.	PNC Financial Corp.	45,533.5	35.6
15.	Bank of New York Co.	45,389.9	37.0
16.	First Union Corp.	40,780.7	38.3
17.	Suntrust Banks	33,411.1	39.4
18.	Bank of Boston Corp.	32,529.1	40.4
19.	Fleet/Norstar Financial Group	32,507.0	41.4
20.	Barnett Banks	32,213.9	42.4
21.	Norwest Corp.	30,625.9	43.4
22.	Banc One Corp.	30,336.0	44.4

(continued)

TABLE 4-2   The 50 largest commercial banking companies *(continued)*

Rank	Company	Assets (millions of dollars)	Cumulative percentage*
23.	Republic New York Corp.	29,597.0	45.3
24.	First Fidelity Bancorporation	29,110.3	46.2
25.	Mellon Bank Corp.	28,762.0	47.1
26.	Continental Bank Corp.	27,143.0	48.0
27.	NBD Bancorp	26,746.6	48.8
28.	MNC Financial	26,375.8	49.6
29.	First Wachovia Corp.	26,270.8	50.4
30.	National City Corp.	23,742.6	51.2
31.	Shawmut National Corp.	23,703.3	52.0
32.	Midlantic Corp.	23,586.2	52.8
33.	Corestates Financial Corp.	23,520.3	53.6
34.	National Westminster Bancorp.	23,322.8	54.3
35.	Bank of New England Corp.	23,049.0	55.0
36.	Marine Midland Banks	20,106.9	55.6
37.	Keycorp	19,265.7	56.2
38.	First Bank System	19,001.0	56.8
39.	U.S. Bancorp	17,613.1	57.4
40.	Boatmen's Bancshares	17,468.5	58.0
41.	Union Bank	16,313.0	58.5
42.	Society Corp.	15,110.2	59.0
43.	First of America Bank Corp.	14,038.6	59.4
44.	Southeast Banking Corp.	13,390.4	59.8
45.	First City Bancorp. of Texas	13,343.5	60.2
46.	Comerica	13,300.4	60.6
47.	UJB Financial	12,817.9	61.0
48.	Harris Bankcorp	12,481.2	61.4
49.	Manufacturers National Corp.	12,078.3	61.8
50.	Crestar Financial Corp.	11,881.1	62.2

Total commercial banking assets: $3,131 billion
Total number of commercial banks: 13,139

*Cumulative percentage is the amount of the nation's total commercial banking assets encompassed at a specific ranking.
SOURCES: *Fortune,* June 6, 1988, p. D13, for individual banks; *Statistical Abstract of the United States,* 1988, p. 472, for total bank assets.

Directors

Control of these corporate resources is officially entrusted to the presidents and directors of these corporations. Approximately 3,600 people are listed as presidents or directors of these top corporations. Collectively these people control half the nation's industrial assets and nearly half of all banking assets.

A. A. Berle, Jr., a corporation lawyer and corporation director who has written extensively on the modern corporation, explains that corporate power rests with these corporations' directors and with the holders of *control blocks* of corporate stock:

> The control system in today's corporations, when it does not lie solely in the directors as in the American Telephone & Telegraph Company, lies in a com-

bination of the directors of a so-called control block (of stock) plus the directors themselves. For practical purposes, therefore, the control or power element in most large corporations rests in its group of directors, and it is autonomous—or autonomous if taken together with a control block. . . . This is self-perpetuating oligarchy.[5]

Corporate power thus does not rest in the hands of the masses of corporate employees or even in the hands of the millions of middle- and upper-class Americans who own corporate stock.

Corporate power is further concentrated by a system of interlocking directorates and by a corporate ownership system in which control blocks of stock are owned by financial institutions rather than by private individuals. Interlocking directorates, in which a director of one corporation also sits on the boards of other corporations, enable key corporate elites to wield influence over a large number of corporations. It is not uncommon for top members of the corporate elite to hold four, five, or six directorships.

MANAGERIAL ELITES

Corporate power is wielded by the managers of the nation's large industrial corporations and financial institutions. Theoretically, stockholders have ultimate power over management, but in fact individual stockholders seldom have any control over the activities of the corporations they own.

The millions of middle-class Americans who own corporate stock have virtually no influence over the decisions of directors. When confronted with mismanagement, these stockholders simply sell their stock, rather than try to challenge the powers of the directors. Indeed, most stockholders sign over "proxies" to top management so that top management may cast these proxy votes at the annual meetings of stockholders. Management itself usually selects its own slate for the board of directors and easily elects them with the help of proxies.

Large control blocks of stock in corporations are usually held by banks and financial institutions or pension trusts or mutual funds. Occasionally, the managers of these institutions will demand the replacement of corporate managers who have performed poorly. But more often than not, banks and trust funds will sell their stock in corporations whose management they distrust rather than use the voting power of their stock to replace management. Generally banks and trust funds vote their stock for the management slate. This inaction by institutional investors allows the directors and management of corporations essentially to appoint themselves and to become increasingly unchallengeable; this policy freezes absolute power in the corporate management.

Corporations, banks, insurance companies, mutual funds, investment companies, and pension trusts own most of the capital in the United States, not individual investors. Of course, the profit motive is still important to corporate managers, since profits are the basis of capital formation within the corporation. The more capital corporate managers have at their disposal, the more power they have; losses decrease the capital available to the managers and decrease their power (perhaps spelling eventual extinction of the organization).

Adolf A. Berle, Jr., summarizes the dominance of managers in corporate America:

> Management control is a phrase meaning merely that no large concentrated stockholding exists which maintains a close working relationship with the management or is capable of challenging it, so that the board of directors may regularly expect a majority, composed of small scattered holdings, to follow their lead. Thus they need not consult with anyone when making up their slate of directors, and may simply request their stockholders to sign and send in a ceremonial proxy. They select their own successors. . . . Nominal power still resides in the stockholders; actual power in the board of directors.[6]

I CLEANED SOME OF YOUR WINDOW, BUT DON'T WORRY... ...NATURE WILL DO THE REST....

MIKE PETERS reprinted by permission of UFS, Inc.

GREED IN THE BOARDROOM

Increasing evidence shows that the corporate managers put *personal motives*—especially their own pay, benefits, and perquisites—above the interests of the corporation and its stockholders. The pay of chief executive officers (CEOs) of the largest U.S. corporations has mushroomed in recent years, as has the pay of corporate directors. A $5 million annual salary is no longer uncommon, even in corporations that are losing money! The average CEO in the 365 largest corporations in 1990 took home nearly $2 million in pay and benefits.[7] During the 1980s, average CEO compensation jumped by 212 percent, while the average factory worker gained only 53 percent. According to business professor Edward E. Lawler, "It just seems to get more absurd each year. What is outrageous one year becomes a standard for the next. And no one is in a position to say no."[8] The average CEO of a major U.S. corporation makes 85 times the pay of the average factory worker. (In Japan, by contrast, the average CEO receives only 17 times the pay of an ordinary worker.) Boards of directors are supposed to oversee top executive pay and protect stockholders. But CEOs generally win approval for their own salaries from compliant directors.

It is true that "corporate raiders" have emerged in recent years to challenge the cozy life of the corporate managers.[9] Indeed, Carl Icahn, perhaps the nation's most successful corporate raider, generates more fear in corporate boardrooms than any communist revolutionary ever did. Icahn *claims* to be defending stockholders from greedy self-serving managers:

> They're out on their jet planes with their wives going on safari and the company is going to the dogs, and then they'll give parties for themselves to celebrate how great they are.[10]

So Icahn defends the role of the corporate raider as forcing U.S. management to be more accountable, more aggressive, and more competitive in the world marketplace. But the corporate takeover movement has probably had the opposite effect—adding to the burden of U.S. corporate debt, focusing management attention on short-term profit rather than long-term growth, and further eroding the competitive position of the United States in the world economy.

A hostile takeover begins with a corporate raider buying the stock of a corporation on the open market, usually with money borrowed for this purpose. The raider may wish to keep early purchases secret for a while to avoid rapid rises in the price of the stock; but federal Security and Exchange Commission rules require disclosure when a person acquires 5 percent of a corporation's stock. The raider may then offer a takeover bid to existing management. Management may reject the bid outright or try to buy back the stock purchased by the raider at a higher price—that is, to offer the raider "greenmail." If the raider and management cannot reach agreement, the hostile takeover proceeds. The raider arranges to borrow additional money—perhaps several billion dollars—to make a purchase offer to the target corporation's stockholders, usually at a price higher than the current stock exchange price. Management may search for a "white knight"—someone willing to offer even more money to purchase the corporation from its stockholders but who promises to keep the existing management. If the raider wins control of the corporation, the raider replaces management.

Following a successful takeover, the corporation is heavily laden with new debt. The raider may have borrowed billions to buy out shareholders. The investment firms that provided the loans to finance the corporation's purchase then issue "junk bonds" with high interest rates to attract investors to these risky ventures. The corporation must pay off these bonds with its own revenues. Additionally, there may be many millions of dollars in bond-sale commissions and attorneys' fees to pay out. The raider may be forced to sell off parts of the corporation or some of its valuable assets in order to help pay off part of the debt. Thus, the target corporation itself must eventually bear the burden of the takeover battle.

"Greed is good," at least for the players in the takeover game. The banks and the Wall Street investment firms that finance hostile takeovers charge high fees and commissions on the transactions, and they levy excessive interest rates on the junk bonds. The mergers and acquisitions (M & A) divisions of these firms are where the action is for ambitious young men and women.

But greed weakens the American economy over the long term. The fear of the raider forces management to focus on near-term profits at the expense of long-range research and development. Management must keep the current price of its stock high in order to deter a takeover attempt. Even worse, management often resorts to "poison pills" to deliberately weaken its own corporation to make it unattractive to raiders; it may increase its debt, buy other poorly performing corporations, devalue stockholders' voting powers, and provide itself with "golden parachutes" (rich severance benefits) in the event of ouster. Corporate raiders may enrich shareholders and speculators, but the industry itself pays the price.

The debt incurred in corporate takeovers is a concern to employees, consumers, and taxpayers. While the raider pays original stockholders handsomely, the corporation must labor intensively to pay off the debt incurred. The corporation may be broken apart and its separate pieces sold, which may disrupt and demoralize employees. Consumers may be forced to pay higher prices. If the corporation cannot meet the high interest payments, bankruptcy looms. The corporation's heavy interest payments are tax-deductible, thus depriving the U.S. Treasury of corporate tax revenues. And the diversion of American capital from productive investments to takeovers threatens to weaken future national productivity.

ELITE RECRUITMENT: GETTING TO THE TOP

How do people at the top get there? Certainly we cannot provide a complete picture of the recruitment process in all sectors of society, but we can learn whether the top leadership in government comes from the corporate world or whether these two worlds depend on separate and distinct channels of recruitment.

Biographical information on individuals in positions of authority in top institutions in each sector of society reveals separate paths to authority. Figure 4-1 shows the principal lifetime occupational activity of individuals at the top of each sector of society. (This categorization de-

FIGURE 4-1   Recruitment to top institutional positions

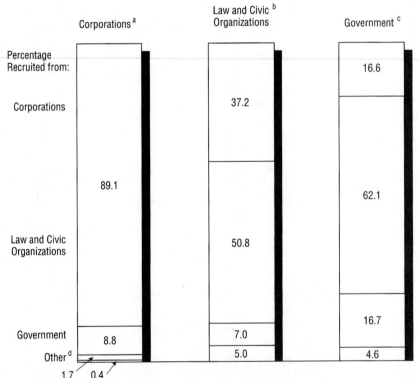

[a]Presidents and directors of the largest corporations in industry, communication, transportation, utilities, banking, and insurance. (See listings in previous tables.) $N = 3,572$.
[b]Trustees of prestigious private colleges and universities; directors of the twelve largest private foundations; senior partners of top law firms; directors or trustees of twelve prestigious civic and cultural organizations. $N = 1,345$.
[c]President and vice-president; secretaries, undersecretaries, and assistant secretaries of all executive departments; White House presidential advisors; congressional leaders, committee chairpersons, and ranking minority-party members; Supreme Court justices; Federal Reserve Board; Council of Economic Advisors; all four-star generals and admirals. $N = 286$.
[d]Labor, press, religion, and so forth.
SOURCE: Thomas R. Dye, *Who's Running America? The Conservative Years* (Englewood Cliffs, N.J.: Prentice-Hall, 1986).

pends largely on the way they identified their principal occupation in *Who's Who.*)

It turns out that the corporate sector supplies a majority of the occupants of top positions only in the corporate sector (89.1 percent). The corporate sector supplies just 37.2 percent of the top elites in law and civic organizations and only 16.6 percent of government elites. Top leaders in government are recruited primarily from the legal profession (62.1 percent); some have based their careers in government itself (16.6 percent). This finding is important. Government and law apparently provide independent channels of recruitment for high public office. High position in the corporate world is *not* a prerequisite to high public office.

What do we know about those who occupy authoritative positions in American society? A number of excellent social-background studies of political decision makers,[11] federal government executives,[12] military officers,[13] and corporate executives[14] consistently show that top business executives and political decision makers are *atypical* of the American public. They are recruited from the well-educated, prestigiously employed, older, affluent, urban, white, Anglo-Saxon, upper- and upper-middle-class male population (see Table 4-3).

Age

The average age of the corporate leaders (directors and chief executive officers) identified in one study was sixty-one.[15] Leaders in foundations,

TABLE 4-3   Social characteristics of corporate, public interest, and government elites

	Corporate	Law and civic organizations	Government
Average age	61 years	64 years	58 years
Female	0.3%	7.2%	1.4%
Schools			
Public	81.8	73.2	90.9
Private	7.0	8.8	3.0
Prestigious[a]	11.2	18.0	6.1
Colleges			
Public	31.8	12.8	43.9
Private	13.3	8.4	12.1
Prestigious[b]	55.0	78.8	43.9
Education			
College educated	90.1	95.7	100.0
Advanced degree	49.2	75.7	77.4
Urban	89.0	84.9	69.7

[a]Andover, Buckley, Cate, Catlin, Choate, Cranbrook, Country Day, Deerfield, Exeter, Episcopal, Gilman, Groton, Hill, Hotchkiss, Kingswood, Kent, Lakeside, Lawrenceville, Lincoln, Loomis, Middlesex, Milton, St. Andrew's, St. Christopher's, St. George's, St. Mark's, St. Paul's, Shatluck, Taft, Thatcher, Webb, Westminister, Woodbary Forest.

[b]Harvard, Yale, Chicago, Stanford, Columbia, MIT, Cornell, Northwestern, Princeton, Johns Hopkins, University of Pennsylvania, and Dartmouth.

SOURCE: Thomas R. Dye, *Who's Running America: The Conservative Years* (Englewood Cliffs, N.J.: Prentice-Hall, 1986).

law, education, and civic and cultural organizations were slightly older; there the average age was sixty-four. Top positions in government are filled by slightly younger people.

Sex

The female segment of the population is seriously underrepresented at the top of the nation's institutional structure.[16] Male dominance in top positions is nearly complete in the corporate world. A very few women have entered corporate boardrooms in recent years; fewer than 2 percent of the directors of large corporations are women.

Race

Of 7,000 positions of authority surveyed in top-ranked institutions in the 1980s, blacks occupied only twenty.[17] Only one black, Patricia Roberts Harris, served in the cabinet under President Jimmy Carter, and Andrew Young, former congressman from Atlanta, an early associate of Martin Luther King, Jr., and former mayor of Atlanta, served as U.S. ambassador to the United Nations. President Reagan's cabinet included one black, Samuel R. Pierce, secretary of Housing and Urban Development, and President Bush named Louis W. Sullivan, medical dean at Morehouse College, to serve as secretary of Health and Human Services. President Bush nominated Clarence Thomas to the U.S. Supreme Court seat vacated by Thurgood Marshall, the first black ever to serve on the high Court.

Education

Nearly all top U.S. leaders are college educated, and more than half hold advanced degrees. About 25.8 percent hold law degrees, and 31.1 percent hold advanced academic or professional degrees (earned degrees only, not honorary degrees). Government leaders are somewhat more likely than corporate leaders to hold advanced degrees.

A glance at the precollegiate education of our top elites reveals that many are "preppies": 11 percent of corporate leaders and 6 percent of government leaders attended one of the thirty prestigious preparatory schools in America—Groton, Hotchkiss, Exeter, Loomis, Choate, and so on.[18] Needless to say, only a infinitesimal proportion of the population receives an education at a prestigious preparatory school. Even more impressive, 55 percent of corporate leaders and 44 percent of government leaders are alumni of twelve prestigious, heavily endowed private universities: Harvard, Yale, Chicago, Stanford, Columbia, MIT, Cornell, Northwestern, Princeton, Johns Hopkins, University of Pennsylvania, and Dartmouth. Elites in America are notably "Ivy League," as Table 4-3 shows.

INEQUALITY IN AMERICA

Income inequality is and has always been a significant component of the American social structure.[19] The top fifth (20 percent) of income recipients in the United States receives more than 40 percent of all income in the nation, while the bottom fifth receives less than 5 percent (see Table 4-4). The income share of the top fifth has declined since the pre-World War II years. And the income share of the top 5 percent of families has declined dramatically from 30.0 to 16.9 percent. But the bottom fifth of the population still receives a very small share of the national income. In 1987 the bottom fifth was composed of families receiving less than $14,450 per year; the top 5 percent were those families receiving more than $86,800.

Income inequality increased in the United States during the 1980s. While the increase was slight by historical standards, and the United States remains one of the most equalitarian nations in the world, nonetheless this increase reverses the historical tendencies toward greater equality. Various theories have been put forward to explain this reversal: the decline of the manufacturing sector of the economy with its relatively high-paying blue-collar jobs; a rise in the number of two-wage families, making single-wage households relatively less affluent; and demographic trends, which include larger proportions of aged as well as larger proportions of female heads of households. The popular notion that miserly government welfare and social insurance payments caused the increase in inequality is untrue; aggregate government transfer payments did not decline in the 1980s (in any event these payments have little to do with overall income distribution). Nor is there any evidence that income taxation has any significant effect on the distribution of income. Before-tax and after-tax income distributions are nearly identical.

TABLE 4-4   Distribution of family income in the United States

Quintiles*	Percentage of total income received							1987	
	1929	1936	1950	1962	1972	1980	1983	%	$ limits
Lowest	3.5	4.1	4.8	4.6	5.5	5.2	4.7	4.6	0–14,450
Second	9.0	9.2	10.9	10.9	12.0	11.6	11.1	10.8	14,450–25,100
Third	13.8	14.1	16.1	16.3	17.4	17.5	17.1	16.9	25,100–36,600
Fourth	19.3	20.9	22.1	22.7	23.5	24.2	24.4	24.1	36,600–52,900
Highest	54.4	51.7	46.1	45.5	41.6	41.5	42.7	43.7	over 52,900
Total	100.0	100.0	100.0	100.0	100.0	100.0	100.0	100.0	
Top 5 percent	30.0	24.0	21.4	19.6	14.4	15.7	15.8	16.9	over 86,800

*Each quintile is 20 percent of the population.
SOURCES: U.S. Bureau of the Census, *Current Population Reports;* data for early years from Edward C. Budd, *Inequality and Poverty* (New York: Norton, 1967).

Wealth is even more unequally distributed than income. Millionaires in America are no longer considered rich. More than two million people have a net worth exceeding $1 million. To be truly rich today, one must be worth more than $200 million. In 1988, *Forbes* magazine identified "The *Forbes* Four Hundred"—400 Americans with an individual net worth of at least $200 million.[20] Most of the nation's wealthy are reluctant to reveal their net worth; thus any listing is only an estimate. There may be 200 individuals and families in the world worth more than $1 *billion*. *Forbes* magazine claims to have identified 192 individuals or families worth this much; only 68 of them are American. *Fortune* identifies 129, of whom 49 are Americans.[21] The richest person in the world is the Sultan of Brunei, who is worth around $25 billion, despite lower oil prices. *Fortune* lists Forrest Mars and his children, makers of Milky Way and other candies, as the richest American family; *Forbes* lists Sam Walton, the late owner of Wal-Mart Stores.

Surprisingly, most billionaires in the United States made their own fortunes. It is not necessary to inherit great wealth to be rich. The era of the self-made tycoon is far from over. It is true that the fortunes listed by *Forbes* and *Fortune* include many familiar names: Annenberg, Bechtel, Cabot, Chandler, Cox, Dorrance, du Pont, Duke, Ford, Haas, Heinz, Hearst, Hunt, Houghton, Kennedy, Kleberg, Kroc, Lykes, McCormick, Mellon, Pew, Phipps, Pitcairn, Pulitzer, Rockefeller, Uihlein, Upjohn, Weyerhaeuser. But there is an even larger number of self-made fortunes, from New York real estate mogul Donald Trump to the youthful computer wizard and Harvard dropout William Gates III, co-founder of Microsoft. The prevalence of self-made tycoons among the world's wealthiest people is testimony to the great social mobility in the United States and other free-market societies.

However, *personal wealth is insignificant next to institutional wealth.* Individuals may control millions, but institutions control billions. A president of a major corporation may receive an annual salary of $500,000 to $1 million and possess a net worth of $5 million, but these amounts are insignificant when compared to the monies that the same president may control—perhaps annual revenues of $5 billion and assets worth $10 billion or $20 billion. The contrast between individual wealth and institutional wealth is even greater when we consider that a bureaucrat in the federal government may make only $80,000 but control an agency budget of $50 *billion* annually.

Thus by far the greatest inequalities are between institutional wealth and personal wealth. Even if the government confiscated the entire personal wealth of every centimillionaire, the resulting revenue (about $80 billion) would be less than 10 percent of the federal budget for a single year. The greatest disparities in the United States are not between the rich and poor but between individuals and institutions. Wealth and power are concentrated in large corporate and government institutions. The people who control power and wealth in this nation do so by virtue of their high positions in these institutions, not because of their personal wealth or income.

THE LIBERAL ESTABLISHMENT

Elites in the United States share a consensus about the fundamental values of private property, limited government, individual liberty, and due process of law. Moreover, since the Roosevelt era, American elites have generally supported liberal, public-regarding social-welfare programs, including social security, fair labor standards, unemployment compensation, a graduated income tax, a federally aided welfare system, governmental regulation of public utilities, and countercyclical fiscal and monetary policies. Today elite consensus also includes a commitment to equality of opportunity for black Americans and desire to remove direct discrimination from the law.

The prevailing philosophy of the American elite is liberal and public-regarding, with a willingness to take the welfare of others into account as part of one's own well-being and a willingness to use governmental power to correct perceived wrongs done to others. It is a philosophy of noblesse oblige—elite responsibility for the welfare of the poor and downtrodden, particularly blacks. Traditionally the liberal elite has believed that it could change people's lives—end discrimination, abolish poverty, eliminate slums, ensure employment, uplift the poor, eliminate sickness, educate the masses, and instill dominant cultural values in everyone. America's masses do not widely share this philosophy.

Leadership for liberal reform has always come from the upper social classes—usually from established old family segments of the elite, rather than the newly rich, self-made segments. Before the Civil War, abolitionist leaders were "descended from old and socially dominant Northeastern families" and were clearly distinguished from the new industrial leaders of that era.[22] Later, when the children and grandchildren of the rugged individualists of the industrial revolution inherited positions of power, they turned away from the social-Darwinist philosophy of their parents and moved toward the more public-regarding ideas of the New Deal. Liberalism was championed not by the working class but by men like Franklin D. Roosevelt (Groton and Harvard), Adlai Stevenson (Choate School and Princeton), Averell Harriman (Groton and Yale), and John F. Kennedy (Choate School and Harvard).

The liberal, public-regarding character of the U.S. elite defies simplistic Marxian interpretations of American politics; wealth, education, sophistication, and upper-class cultural values foster attitudes of public service and do-goodism. Liberal elites are frequently paternalistic toward segments of the masses they define as "underprivileged," "culturally deprived," and "disadvantaged," but they are seldom hostile toward them. Indeed, hostility toward blacks is more characteristic of white masses than of white elites.

The liberal philosophy of noblesse oblige leads inevitably to a sense of national responsibility for the welfare of the world, which in turn involves the United States in war. The missionary spirit of liberalism strives to bring freedom—self-determination, civil liberty, limited government, and private enterprise—to all the peoples of the world. America's major wars of the twentieth century occurred during the administrations of liberal Democratic presidents: Wilson (World War I), Roosevelt (World War II), Truman (Korea), and Johnson (Vietnam). The United States fought both world wars to "make the world safe for democracy." Following World War II, the nation embarked upon a policy of worldwide involvement in the internal and external affairs of nations in an effort to halt the expansion of communism. The "good" that liberal U.S. leadership seeks to do throughout the world is neither appreciated nor understood by the elites and masses of many nations. The result has been a great deal of bloodshed and violence committed by well-meaning liberal administrations for the finest of motives. An American field commander in Vietnam summed up the liberal dilemma: "It was necessary to destroy the village in order to save it."[23]

THE CONSERVATIVE MOOD

A mood of disillusionment penetrated elite circles in the 1980s and dampened enthusiasm for government intervention in society. The war in Vietnam, President Lyndon Johnson's Great Society, urban rioting, campus unrest, Watergate, and inflation all had raised doubts about the size and scope of government power. Elite interest in liberal reforms was tempered by the failures and costs of well-meaning yet ineffective (and sometimes harmful) public programs. Elites learned that government cannot solve society's problems simply by passing a law, creating a new bureaucracy, and spending a few billion dollars. War, poverty, ill health, discrimination, joblessness, inflation, crime, ignorance, pollution, and unhappiness have afflicted society for a long time. Elites no longer assume that these problems can be erased from society by finding and implementing the "right" public policies.

The "neoconservatives" among America's elite continue to be liberal, reformist, and public-regarding, but they oppose the paternalistic state. They are not as confident or ambitious (bordering on arrogant) as the liberals of the 1960s were. The neoconservatives have more faith in the free market system and less confidence that governmental regulations will be effective. They have more respect for the traditional values and institutions, including religion, family, and the community. They believe in equal opportunity for everyone, but they do not believe in absolute equality, whereby the government ensures that everyone gets equal shares of everything. Neoconservatives, like all other liberals, disapprove of unequal treatment of racial minorities, but they generally oppose affirmative action that involves racial quotas. Finally, neoconservatives believe that the United States must maintain a strong national defense and that American democracy cannot survive for long in a world that is overwhelmingly hostile to American values.[24]

The conservative mood does not alter the underlying commitment to liberal, reformist values. But it represents a more realistic view of what government can achieve and a more traditional view of the importance of personal initiative, enterprise, work, and family. This view did not reside solely in the Reagan and Bush administrations; it enjoys wide acceptance among the nation's top leaders in every sector of society.

CASE STUDY

 ## Where to Find the Establishment

The American establishment—with its old school ties, inherited wealth, upper-class lifestyle, position, and privilege—flourishes even in a democratic society. Not only is the establishment found in the higher echelons of business and government but, more important, it is said to "inhabit" the nation's most influential universities, foundations, and think tanks. Its unifying mission is to advance a public ethos—a civic morality emphasizing tolerance, individual liberty, reform, and do-goodism. Members of the establishment are generally from the upper social class in origin and have benefited from educations at prestigious private preparatory schools and Ivy League universities.

The establishment is not an institution itself but rather a "collective entity" or "third force" (the other two being business and government) that links all the institutions of American society together to pursue liberal values and goals. The establishment seeks to protect the United States from vulgar mass impulses—religious fundamentalism, racism, narrow patriotism, and selfish, short-sighted competition. *New York Times* columnist Leonard Silk and his son Harvard historian Mike Silk write:

Although the origins of the Establishment are ecclesiastical and aristocratic, in America it is firmly joined to both democratic and capitalist institutions. But its ambitions go beyond: it seeks to protect and advance social, moral, and aesthetic values that transcend the interest of any single person, economic group, or political organization; it affects to be a harmonizer, an arbiter, a wise instructor of the nation—and particularly of its political and business leaders.*

The "familiar Establishment type" is "one of those Ivy League lawyer-doers able to move lightly among the worlds of business, government, and good works." The politics of the establishment run from "the reasonable right to the responsible left." The establishment is influential whether a Republican or Democratic administration is in Washington. "A change in the guard in Washington pulls to the new President those prominent establishmentarians most friendly to his aims, while pushing their counterparts from the previous administration back to the staffs and boards of the Establishment's private institutions."

The institutions that the establishment "inhabits" are said to be Harvard University, the *New York Times*, the Ford Foundation, the Brookings Institution, the Council on Foreign Relations, and the Committee for Economic Development. Not every person associated with these institutions is a

*Leonard Silk and Mark Silk, *The American Establishment* (New York: Basic Books, 1980), p. 325.

(continued)

member of the establishment. And there are other institutions that also possess establishment connections: Yale University, Princeton University, Columbia University, the University of Chicago, Stanford University, the Carnegie Endowment, the RAND Corporation, Twentieth Century, the Russell Sage Foundation, the Century Club, the Metropolitan Museum of Art, the Museum of Modern Art, and the Metropolitan Opera. But the establishment is not defined by these instruments. Instead the establishment is defined as "a national force, outside of government, dedicated to truth, liberty, and, however defined, the broad public interest."**

**Ibid., p. 20.

SUMMARY

Elite theory does not limit its definition of elites to those who participate in *government* decision making. Anyone who participates in decisions that allocate values for society is an elite. Power in the United States is organized into large institutions, private as well as public: corporations, banks and financial institutions, universities, law firms, churches, professional associations, and military and government bureaucracies. This chapter develops several propositions in analyzing power and the institutional structure of the United States:

1. The giant institutions and bureaucracies of American society carry great potential for power.

2. The institutional structure of American society concentrates great authority in a relatively small number of positions. About 3,500 presidents and directors of the nation's largest corporations have formal authority over half the nation's industrial assets; half its assets in communications, transportation, and utilities; nearly half of all banking assets; and two-thirds of all insurance assets.

3. Wealth in America is unequally distributed. The top fifth of income recipients receive more than 40 percent of all income in the nation, while the bottom fifth receives less than 5 percent. Inequality is lessening only very slowly over time.

4. Managerial elites are replacing owners and stockholders as the dominant influence in American corporations. Most capital investment comes from the retained earnings of corporations and bank loans rather than from individual investors.

5. Despite concentration of institutional power, different elite segments tend to exercise their power in separate sectors of society. Fewer than 20 percent of top government officeholders come from the corporate world. Most come from the legal profession; some have based their careers in government itself and in education. Thus separate channels of recruitment lead to top elite positions.

6. American elites disproportionately represent the well-educated, prestigiously employed, older, affluent, urban, white, Anglo-Saxon, upper- and upper-middle-class male population.

7. Elites in the United States share a consensus about the fundamental values of private enterprise, due process of law, liberal and public-regarding social-welfare programs, equality of opportunity, and opposition to the spread of communism. The prevailing impulse of the "liberal establishment" is to do good, to perform public services, and to use governmental power to change lives. In world affairs, this missionary spirit has involved the United States in a great deal of bloodshed and violence, presumably in pursuit of high motives: the self-determination of free peoples resisting aggression and suppression.

8. In recent years American elites have reflected a more conservative mood, derived from their disappointments with government—Vietnam, Watergate, and the failures of many Great Society programs. This "neoconservatism" is skeptical of large-scale governmental interventions to achieve social good and more respectful of free markets, traditional values, and private institutions.

9. The term *establishment* has been employed to describe an upper-class, educated "third force" in American society, separate from business and government yet frequently moving between those sectors of society. The establishment is concerned primarily with advancing a broad civic ethos—good government, tolerance, reformism, and internationalism. The establishment is said to "inhabit" the nation's most prestigious private universities, foundations, and think tanks.

NOTES

1. C. Wright Mills, *The Power Elite* (New York: Oxford University Press, 1956), pp. 10–11.
2. James Madison, Alexander Hamilton, and John Jay, *The Federalist* Number 20 (New York: Modern Library, 1937).
3. Robert A. Dahl and Charles E. Lindblom, *Politics and Economic Welfare,* 2nd ed. (University of Chicago Press, 1976). See preface.
4. David Vogel, "The New Political Science of Corporate Power," *The Public Interest* 87 (Spring 1987): 63–79.
5. A. A. Berle, Jr., *Economic Power and the Free Society* (New York: Fund for the Republic, 1958), p. 10.
6. Adolf A. Berle, Jr., *Power Without Property* (New York: Harcourt Brace Jovanovich, 1959).
7. *Business Week* (May 8, 1991): 90–112.
8. Ibid., p. 90.
9. See Thomas R. Dye, *Who's Running America? The Conservative Years* (Englewood Cliffs, N.J.: Prentice-Hall, 1986), pp. 39–41.
10. *Newsweek* (October 20, 1986): 51.

11. Donald R. Matthews, *The Social Background of Political Decision-Makers* (New York: Doubleday, 1954).

12. David T. Stanley, Dean E. Mann, and Jameson W. Doig, *Men Who Govern* (Washington, D.C.: Brookings, 1967)

13. Morris Janowitz, *The Professional Soldier: A Social and Political Portrait* (New York: Free Press, 1960).

14. Lloyd Warner and James C. Abegglen, *Big Business Leaders in America* (New York: Harper & Brothers, 1955).

15. Dye, op. cit.

16. See Thomas R. Dye and Julie Strickland, "Women at the Top," *Social Science Quarterly* 63 (March 1982).

17. See Dye, op. cit.

18. See Lisa Birnback, ed., *The Official Preppy Handbook* (New York: Workman, 1980).

19. Gabriel Kolko, *Wealth and Power in America* (New York: Praeger, 1962). See also Clair Wilcox, *Toward Social Welfare* (Homewood, Ill.: Irwin, 1969), pp. 7–24.

20. *Forbes* (July 25, 1988): 89–91.

21. *Fortune* (September 12, 1988): 46–105.

22. David Donald, *Lincoln Reconsidered* (New York: Knopf, 1956), p. 33.

23. See David Halberstam, *The Best and the Brightest* (New York: Random House, 1973), for a full account of how U.S. involvement in Vietnam grew out of the "good" motives of "good" men.

24. Irving Kristol, "What Is a Neoconservative?" *Newsweek* (January 19, 1976), p. 87.

—— SELECTED READINGS

Baltzell, E. Digby. *Philadelphia Gentlemen: The Making of a National Upper Class.* Glencoe, Ill.: Free Press, 1958. *The Protestant Establishment: Aristocracy and Caste in America.* New York: Random House, Vintage Books, 1964. The first of these books details how a national and associational upper class replaced the local and communal gentry in the United States between the close of the Civil War and 1940. The second book considers another question: will the Anglo-Saxon-Protestant caste that evolved into a national upper class remain intact, or will the descendants of new immigrants gain access to upper-class status? Baltzell concludes that this caste is still powerful but has lost its position as an authoritative aristocracy, leaving it in an uneasy state with an uncertain future.

Berle, Adolf A., Jr. *Power Without Property.* New York: Harcourt, Brace & World, Harvest Book, 1959. This work by a corporate lawyer and upper-class "insider" presents some interesting views of the American corporate economy. Berle argues that control of the corporate economy has passed from the hands of owners into the hands of managers. The effect of this change will be a return of the corporation to public accountability. This view has been widely debated. See, for example, the Kolko book cited below.

Domhoff, G. William. *Who Rules America?* Englewood Cliffs, N.J.: Prentice-Hall, Spectrum Books, 1967. *The Higher Circles.* New York: Random House, Vintage Books edition, 1970. *Who Rules America Now?* Englewood Cliffs, N.J.: Prentice-Hall, 1983. In these books, Domhoff argues that there is a governing class in the United States. By the term *governing class,* he means the part of the national upper class that holds positions of power in the federal government and industry and their upper-middle-class hired executives. He spends a great deal of time in these books developing the notion of class indicators. In *Who Rules America?* he examines elite control of the federal government; in *The Higher Circles* he develops in detail the role of private planning organizations in the formation of foreign and domestic policy; and in *Who Rules America Now?* he revises and updates his theory of upper-class dominance of American life.

Dye, Thomas R. *Who's Running America? Institutional Leadership in the United States.* Englewood Cliffs, N.J.: Prentice-Hall, 1976. This book studies 5,000 top institutional leaders in industry, banking, utilities, government, the media, foundations, universities, and civic and cultural organizations. The book names names, studies concentration of power and interlocking at the top, examines recruitment and social backgrounds, discusses elite values, examines cohesion and competition among leaders, and outlines the policy-making process. *Who's Running America? The Bush Era* (1990) updates this original work.

Galbraith, John Kenneth. *The New Industrial State.* Boston: Houghton Mifflin, Sentry Books, 1969. Galbraith presents the notion of an intimate partnership between government officials and corporate specialists, which produces general national goals (which, Galbraith observes, are "trite"). The atmosphere of interrelationship between government and business is the context for many decisions. Needs and interests of the industrial system are "made to seem coordinate with the purposes of society" (p. 379).

Halberstam, David. *The Best and the Brightest.* New York: Random House, 1973. This book assesses the men who advised presidents Kennedy and Johnson on conduct of the war in Vietnam. Based on interviews conducted by the author, a former *New York Times* Vietnam correspondent, the book reveals an excellent view of the men and processes responsible for decision making at the highest levels of the federal executive branch.

Kolko, Gabriel. *Wealth and Power in America.* New York: Praeger, 1962. Kolko discusses the distribution of wealth and income in the United States, the inequality of taxation, and the concentration of corporate power. He considers these questions: Does a small group of very wealthy people have the power to guide industry, and thereby much of the total economy, toward ends compatible with their own interests? And do they own and control the major corporations? He answers yes to both questions and then relates these facts to the problem of poverty in the United States.

Lundberg, Ferdinand. *The Rich and the Super Rich.* New York: Lyle Stuart, 1968. This book is an extensive, well-documented, popularly written but unsystematic discussion of both the corporate-governmental power partnership and elite lifestyles. Lundberg is the author of the more systematically written but dated book *America's Sixty Families* (1937).

Mills, C. Wright. *The Power Elite.* New York: Oxford University Press, 1956. This book is a classic of elite literature. Mills takes an institutional approach to roles within an "institutional landscape." Three institutions—the big corporations, the political executive, and the military—are of great importance. The individuals who fill the positions within these institutions form a power elite. These higher circles share social attributes (such as similar lifestyles, preparatory schools, and clubs) as well as positions of power. Thus Mills' power elite is relatively unified. It is also practically free from mass accountability, which leads Mills to complain of the "higher immorality" of the power elite.

Silk, Leonard, and Silk, Mark. *The American Establishment.* New York: Basic Books, 1980. A lively description of the establishment and the institutions it "inhabits," including Harvard University, the *New York Times,* the Ford Foundation, the Brookings Institution, the Council on Foreign Relations, and the Committee for Economic Development. The Silks portray the establishment as a largely upper-class "third force" linking the leadership of the corporate and government sectors of American society.

5

Elites and Masses: The Shaky Foundations of Democracy

★ *Let us transport ourselves into a hypothetical country that, in a democratic way, practices the persecution of Christians, the burning of witches, and the slaughtering of Jews. We should certainly not approve of these practices on the ground that they have been decided on according to the rules of democratic procedure.*

Joseph Schumpeter, Capitalism, Socialism, and Democracy, *1942*

Many people believe that the survival of democracy depends on widespread agreement among the American people on the principles of democratic government. However, only a small portion of the people is committed to those principles of freedom of speech and press, tolerance of diversity, due process of law, and guarantees of individual liberty and dignity. Although most people voice superficial agreement with abstract statements of democratic values, most people do not translate these principles into actual patterns of behavior. The real question is how democracy and individual freedom can survive in a country where most people do not support these principles in practice.

ANTIDEMOCRATIC ATTITUDES AMONG THE MASSES

The public gives only superficial support to fundamental democratic values—freedom of speech and press and due process of law. People say they believe in those values when they are expressed as abstract principles; for example, they answer yes to the question "Do you believe in freedom of speech for everyone?" However, the public is unable or unwilling to apply the principles to specific situations, especially situations involving

Reprinted by permission: Tribune Media Services.

despised or obnoxious groups or individuals. In contrast, elites and the well-educated groups from which they are recruited are much more willing than the masses to apply democratic values in specific situations and to protect the freedoms of unpopular groups.

After years of studying the differences between elites and masses in their attitudes toward freedom, political scientists Herbert McClosky and Alida Brill reached the following conclusions regarding the masses in the United States:

> If one judges by the responses of the mass public to survey questions, one has little reason to expect that the population as a whole will display a sensitive understanding of the constitutional norms that govern the free exercise of speech and publication. Only a minority of the mass public fully appreciate why freedom of speech and press should be granted to dissenters and to others who challenge conventional opinion.[1]

In contrast, these scholars are much more optimistic regarding freedom and tolerance among elites:

> Insofar as these matters are better understood and more firmly believed by those who, in one role or another, help to govern the society, one is tempted to conclude that, owing to the vagaries of the social process, the protection of First Amendment rights rests principally upon the very groups the Amendment was mainly designed to control—the courts, the legislature, political leaders, and the opinion elites of the society.[2]

Differences between elites and masses in support of democratic values are illustrated in Table 5-1. These questions were asked of a national sample of community leaders (the press, clergy, teachers, men and women in business, lawyers and judges, union officials, and leaders of voluntary organizations), as well as a national sample of the public.

TABLE 5-1   Comparative support of democratic values

	Percentage of mass public	Percentage of community leaders
ACADEMIC FREEDOM		
When inviting guest speakers to a college campus:		
___students should be free to invite the ones they want to hear.	41	60
___speakers should be screened beforehand to be sure they don't advocate dangerous or extreme ideas.	45	26
___neither/undecided	14	14
On issues of religion, morals, and politics, high school teachers have a right to express their opinions in class:		
___even if they go against the community standards.	28	46
___only if those opinions are acceptable to the community.	32	12
___neither/undecided	40	42

(continued)

TABLE 5-1   Comparative support of democratic values *(continued)*

	Percentage of mass public	Percentage of community leaders
FREEDOM OF SPEECH		
Should foreigners who dislike our government or criticize it be allowed to visit or stay here?		
___yes	41	69
___no	47	24
___neither/undecided	12	7
If a group asks to use a public building to hold a meeting denouncing the government, their request should be:		
___granted	23	51
___denied	57	26
___neither/undecided	20	23
If the majority votes in a referendum to ban the public expression of certain opinions, should the majority opinion be followed?		
___No, because free speech is a more fundamental right than majority rule.	49	69
___Yes, because no group has a greater right than the majority to decide which opinions can or cannot be expressed.	23	15
___neither/undecided	28	17
"Crackpot" ideas:		
___have as much right to be heard as sensible ideas.	50	81
___sometimes have to be censored for the public good.	32	10
___neither/undecided	18	9
RELIGIOUS FREEDOM		
The freedom of atheists to make fun of God and religion:		
___should be legally protected no matter who might be offended.	26	53
___should not be allowed in a public place when religious groups gather.	53	30
___neither/undecided	21	17
DUE PROCESS OF LAW		
In dealing with crime, the most important consideration is to:		
___protect the rights of the accused.	40	46
___stop crime, even if we have to violate the rights of the accused.	23	9
___neither/undecided	37	45
A person suspected of serious crimes:		
___should have the right to be let out on bail.	16	31
___should be kept safely in prison until the trial.	68	36
___neither/undecided	16	33
HOMOSEXUALITY		
Should a community allow its auditorium to be used by gay liberation movements to organize for homosexual rights?		
___yes	26	46
___no	58	40
___It depends/undecided	16	15
Complete equality for homosexuals in teaching and other public service jobs:		
___should be protected by law.	29	49
___may sound fair but is not really a good idea.	51	33
___neither/undecided	21	19

SOURCE: Herbert McClosky and Alida Brill, *Dimensions of Tolerance: What Americans Believe About Civil Liberties.* Copyright © 1983 by Sage Publications, Inc. Reprinted by permission.

Social Class and Democratic Attitudes

Clearly the masses do not fully understand or support the ideas and principles on which the U.S. political system rests. We are left asking how the system survives.

The distribution of antidemocratic attitudes among various social classes may provide part of an answer. Upper social classes (from which members of elites are largely recruited) give greater, more consistent support to democratic values than do lower social classes. Political sociologist Seymour Martin Lipset has observed that "extremist and intolerant movements in modern society are more likely to be based on the lower classes than on the middle and upper classes."[3] Analyzing the ideologies of the lower class, Lipset notes:

> The poorer strata everywhere are more liberal or leftist on economic issues; they favor more welfare state measures, higher wages, graduated income taxes, support of trade unions, and so forth. But when liberalism is defined in noneconomic terms—as support of civil liberties, internationalism, and so forth—the correlation is reversed. The more well-to-do are more liberal; the poorer are more intolerant.[4]

Lipset formulated the concept of *working-class authoritarianism.* (Authoritarianism is belief in the need for a strong central authority that compels submission.) He argued that several aspects of lower-class life contribute to an authoritarian or antidemocratic personality, among them low levels of education, low participation in political organizations, little reading, economic insecurity, and rigid family patterns.

Various theories have been offered to explain why lower-class life fosters authoritarian attitudes. One theory focuses on the work life of the lower classes. Unskilled workers are far less satisfied with their jobs than are skilled workers and, as a partial result, have a more fatalistic attitude toward life. Workers who feel little control over their lives tend to view the social and political worlds as unchangeable. Unskilled workers are also more likely to view both big business and big government as cynically manipulative. Mental health scores consistently show that people working in unskilled jobs have greater anxiety, hostility, negative self-feelings, and social alienation than do people in skilled occupations.[5]

Another theory argues that authoritarianism is a rational and necessary response to *scarcity.*

> Where food is scarce, where people rub elbows all the time, where someone must have the last word over who gets to use the TV or record-player—in other words, even in families a good deal above destitution—permissiveness simply is not possible; domestic routines and strict discipline are imperative. Because of that, sanctions must quickly be invoked when orders are breached.[6]

It is difficult for children raised in such an environment to cultivate the patience for different opinions and the attendant compromise that characterize the American democratic process. Reflecting their child-hood, 74 percent of the mass public, compared with 54 percent of political leaders, believe that "we need a strong central government to handle modern economic problems efficiently."[7]

Education and Democratic Attitudes

Education is a very important factor in developing tolerance and respect for civil liberty. Clearly, Americans' level of education is related to their degree of tolerance, as is illustrated by Figure 5-1. Each increment of education adds to the respondents' willingness to allow racists, Communists, or homosexuals to teach. In two of three examples, only those groups educated above the high school level contain tolerant majorities.

Indeed, a lack of education may be more important than any other characteristic of lower-class life in shaping authoritarian attitudes. By examining the responses of people of various educational and occupational strata, Lipset found that within each occupational level, higher educational status makes for greater tolerance. He also found that increases in tolerance associated with educational level are greater than those related to occupation. No matter what the occupation, tolerance and education were strongly related. Social psychologist William Kornhauser found that within a given occupation (auto workers), the better the education, the less authoritarian the person.[8] When education is constant, very few other relationships between class and authoritarianism remain strong. Thus the greater authoritarianism of the working classes is largely a product of their low levels of education.[9]

Education also affects tolerance by influencing an individual's ability to apply an abstract principle to a concrete situation. It is one thing to agree that peaceful demonstrations are legitimate; it is quite another to allow an *unpopular* demonstration. For example, even when less-

FIGURE 5-1   Educational levels and tolerance

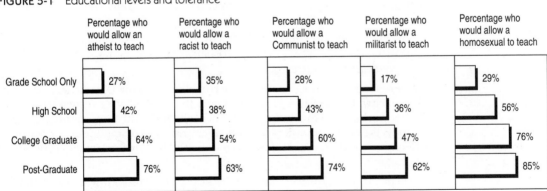

SOURCE: General Social Survey, 1989.

educated people disagree with the general statement "People should be allowed to hold a protest demonstration to ask the government to act on some issue," only about one-third of them would allow a demonstration in favor of legalizing marijuana. But well-educated people are able to apply their abstract principles to specific situations: among the well-educated who agree with this general statement, more than 80 percent would allow a pro-marijuana demonstration.

> Consistency in applying a general norm does increase with education. . . . College educated respondents rarely abandon their tolerant general norm. . . . Among the less educated, however, inconsistency is far more common. . . . The less educated are . . . considerably more likely than others to abandon a tolerant general norm.[10]

One key, then, to variations in tolerance is education.

Elite Experience and Democratic Attitudes

Leadership experience itself also contributes to tolerance. Elites are more tolerant than masses even at the same level of education. While education is the most influential factor in promoting tolerance, leadership and activity in public affairs also develops tolerance. Political scientists Herbert McClosky and Alida Brill compared mass attitudes with those of community leaders—local government officials, judges and lawyers, journalists, clergy, school administrators, and leaders of unions and civic organizations. McClosky and Brill asked a variety of questions designed to ascertain support for civil liberty. For example, they asked, "Should demonstrators be allowed to hold a mass protest march for some unpopular cause?" with possible answers being "Yes, even if most people in the community do not want it" and "No, not if the majority is against it." (Among community leaders, 71 percent said yes, but among the mass public only 41 percent would allow a mass demonstration protest for an unpopular cause.) Using questions such as these, they constructed a civil liberties scale and averaged mass and elite scores. The results in Table 5-2 show that *at each level of education*, elites are more tolerant than masses.

Perhaps leadership activity socializes people to democratic norms; they may become more familiar with democratic values because they are active in the democratic process. Or perhaps their public activity exposes them to a wider variety of attitudes, opinions, and lifestyles, broadens their perspective, and generates empathy for people different from themselves.

—— ARE THE MASSES BECOMING MORE TOLERANT?

If education reduces intolerance, the United States should be experiencing an increase in tolerance. Each year the proportion of high school grad-

TABLE 5-2   Elite support for democratic norms at different educational levels

	Mass	Community elites
Percentage of college graduates		
High	56	67
Middle	26	21
Low	18	11
Percentage with some college		
High	45	50
Middle	32	27
Low	23	23
Percentage of high school graduates		
High	22	29
Middle	37	46
Low	41	26

SOURCE: Adapted from Herbert McClosky and Alida Brill, *Dimensions of Tolerance* (New York: Russell Sage Foundation, 1983), p. 249.

uates entering college increases, pushing the median education of the population upward. Additionally, when elites send clear signals that an "out-group" is no longer a legitimate target of hostility, masses gradually pick up the signals. The status of blacks is a good example. Not only has federal legislation moved consistently toward equality, but also political candidates—Democrats and Republicans, liberals and conservatives—universally accept the premise that blacks deserve equal treatment.

For example, white Americans are generally more sympathetic toward blacks' rights today than they were in years past. From 1942 to 1982, a national sample of white Americans was asked the question "Do you think white and black students should go to the same schools or separate schools?" In 1942, not one white American in three approved of integrated schools (see Table 5-3). In 1956, two years after the historic *Brown* v. *Topeka* court decision, white attitudes had shifted markedly. Nationwide support for integration characterized about half of the white population. By 1963, two out of every three whites supported integrated schools. In recent years, there has been a continuation of the upward trend in the proportion of white Americans who favor school integration. (Note, however, that despite increasing tolerance of integration in principle, white parents do not want their children to become a minority in their schools.) Additional survey information suggests that whites are becoming increasingly accommodating toward equal rights for blacks over time in other areas as well. But it should be noted that white opinion generally *follows* public policy, rather than leading it.

There is a wide gap between the attitudes of masses and elites on the subject of black rights. The most hostile attitudes toward blacks are found among the less privileged, less educated whites. Whites of lower socioeconomic status are much less willing to have contact with blacks than are whites of higher socioeconomic status, whether it is a matter of

TABLE 5-3   White attitudes toward school integration

Question: Do you think white students and Negro students should go to the same school or to separate schools?

			Percentage answering "same schools"				
	1942	1956	1963	1966	1973	1980	1982
Total whites	30%	49%	62%	67%	82%	88%	91%

Question: Would you send your child to a school where more than half the children are black?

			Percentage answering yes				
	1942	1956	1963	1966	1973	1980	1982
Total whites	a	a	25%	33%	45%	36%	46%

SOURCES: Paul B. Sheatsley, "White Attitudes Toward the Negro," *Daedalus* 95, no. 1 (Winter 1966). Reprinted by permission of Daedalus, Journal of American Academy of Arts and Sciences, Boston, Mass., Winter 1966, *The Negro American-2.* Updating from *Gallup Opinion Index* (October 1973) and *Public Opinion* (April/May 1981 and October/November 1982). Prior to 1973 the term *Negro* was used in the question instead of *black.*
ªQuestion not asked in these years.

using the same public restrooms, going to a movie or restaurant, or living next door. It is the affluent, well-educated white who is most concerned with discrimination and who is most willing to have contact with blacks.

The political implication of this finding is obvious: opposition to civil rights legislation and to black advancement in education, jobs, income, housing, and so on, is likely to be strongest among less educated and less affluent whites. Within the white community, support for civil rights will continue to come from the educated and affluent.

The extent to which prejudice lingers is well illustrated by the relationship between education and willingness to vote for an "out-group" member (see Table 5-4). Whereas acceptance of integration is virtually universal, poorly educated populations retain their suspicions. Hence, of people with only a grade school education, substantially fewer would vote for a black president than would college-educated people.

It appears, then, that increasing levels of education and the elimination of prejudice against selected out-groups in the mass media have increased the masses' tolerance. However, the relation between education and tolerance still exists. Whereas the undereducated are more tolerant than they were a generation ago, they are substantially less tolerant than more educated citizens are.

TABLE 5-4   Percentage of voters willing to vote for a minority candidate, by educational level

Educational level of voter	Candidate					
	Catholic	Jew	Woman	Atheist	Homosexual	Black
College	96	95	87	54	42	85
High school	93	89	80	43	27	78
Grade school	81	71	69	16	12	59

SOURCE: *Gallup Political Index* (September 1983): 10–14.

CHANGING TARGETS OF INTOLERANCE

The targets of intolerance change over time, and attacks on freedom come from both liberals and conservatives. Radical right groups strive to control instruction and reading material in public schools by removing literature that they consider offensive. For decades, such groups have sought to eliminate science books with an evolutionary bias, sex education materials judged to be threatening to the institution of marriage, political literature judged to be anti-American, and economic material assessed as hostile to capitalism. Now, however, liberal groups are becoming equally vocal on behalf of censorship. These groups seek to remove literature they consider sexist and racist from schools and libraries, to ban pornography, and to reduce the display of violence on television. Television networks and public schools both report increased activity by liberal groups seeking to impose their values.

In short, the targets of legitimate discrimination are changeable; they vary with the times. In the 1950s when U.S. foreign policy was vigorously anticommunist and the Cold War was at its zenith, the masses' fear of communist activity led them to reject the legitimacy of Communists' speaking, writing, or seeking public office. But by the 1960s many people saw internal social protest as the greatest threat. The percentage of people who believed that members of the Communist party were harmful to the "American way of life" decreased, while the percentage believing student demonstrators were harmful increased. Later, increased fear of crime led to growing mass willingness to curtail the rights of accused criminals.

Public opinion is reactive: "Fear is transferred to new objects" as the political climate and issues change.[11] To discover the true nature of intolerance, one needs to know the real targets of fear and hatred. One study allowed respondents to identify the group they most strongly opposed and then asked them whether a member of this group, whatever its cause, should be allowed to seek political office, teach, make a speech, hold public rallies, and the like.

Hatred tends to vary with individual ideology. As we can see in Table 5-5, self-identified liberals hate the radical right, and self-identified conservatives hate Communists and Socialists. Overall, as shown in Table

TABLE 5-5   Personal ideology and least liked group

	Percentage of liberals	Percentage of moderates	Percentage of conservatives
Communists/Socialists	21	32	44
New Left	7	15	21
Radical Right	59	34	17
Others	8	11	7
N	293	512	372

SOURCE: John L. Sullivan, James Pierson, and George E. Marcus, *Political Tolerance and American Democracy* (Chicago: University of Chicago Press, 1982), p. 276.

TABLE 5-6   Tolerance toward least liked group

Member of least liked group . . .	Percentage answering "yes"
Should be allowed to become president	28
Should be allowed to teach	26
Should not be outlawed	33
Should be allowed to make a speech in this city	70
Should be allowed to hold public meetings	57

SOURCE: John L. Sullivan, James Pierson, and George E. Marcus, *Political Tolerance and American Democracy* (Chicago: University of Chicago Press, 1982), p. 65.

5-6, two-thirds of the sample wanted to outlaw the group named as least liked! The conclusion was that "over half of the . . . respondents . . . believe that their least liked group should be outlawed, hardly consistent with the recent conclusion that the mass public is increasingly tolerant."[12]

Thus tolerance may not have declined but simply found new targets. The public is more tolerant of groups such as Communists and atheists that have faded from attention as threats, but other targets of intolerance have emerged to take their place. This changeableness of mass attitudes suggests that, given the right circumstances, effective counterelites could mobilize people against a particular scapegoat, as has occurred in the past.

IGNORANCE AND APATHY

Ignorance and apathy also characterize mass politics. Nearly half of eligible voters in the United States stay away from the polls, even in presidential elections. Voter turnout is even lower in off-year congressional elections, when it falls to 35 percent of the voting-age population. City or county elections, when they are held separately from state or national elections, usually produce turnouts of 20 to 35 percent of eligible voters.

Political information is very scarce among the masses. Ignorance extends not only to political issues but to the basic structures and processes of government. Only about half the public knows the elementary fact that each state has two U.S. senators; fewer still know the terms of members of Congress or the number of Supreme Court justices.[13] While most Americans can name the president, only a little more than one-third can name their congressional representative. About half can come up with the name of one of their U.S. senators, but fewer than one-third can name both of them. Knowledge of state and local officeholders is even worse (see Table 5-7).

Apathy and ignorance are, of course, closely related to education, although age also plays a role. Older, better-educated Americans (the groups most elites belong to) are better informed than younger, less-educated Americans.

Ignorance breeds intolerance. Among the masses, information about the various feared and hated groups is not readily available. Threats are

TABLE 5-7   Ignorance and apathy

Percentage of adult Americans			
Political participation	Percentage of adults	Political awareness	Percentage of adults
Vote in presidential elections	53	Know name of congressional representative	36
Vote in congressional elections	35–40	Know names of both U.S. senators	29
Vote in local elections	20–30	Know name of state senator	13
Belong to interest groups	30–35	Know name of state representative	12
Ever write or call public officials	15–20		
Make campaign contributions	5–10		
Ever active in political campaign	3–5		

SOURCE: Selected polls. University of Michigan Interuniversity Consortium for Political Research (Ann Arbor: University of Michigan Survey Research Center, 1987–1988).

more symbolic than actual, and many conclude, inaccurately, that their least liked group is dangerous. Not having any clear appraisal of the probability that the feared and hated group will actually achieve its detested goals, the masses assume the worst. Among elites, however, with greater information the true nature of the danger is more apparent, and fewer groups are feared. This point becomes important when we learn that when elites do feel threatened, they too become intolerant.[14] When threatened, virtually everyone—elites and masses—is likely to become intolerant. Active, informed people are more realistic and therefore less afraid.

HOW DOES DEMOCRACY SURVIVE?

It is the irony of democracy that democratic ideals survive because the masses are generally apathetic and inactive. Thus the capacity of the American lower classes for intolerance, authoritarianism, scapegoating, racism, and violence seldom translates into organized, sustained political movements.

The survival of democracy does *not* depend on mass support for democratic ideals. It is apparently not necessary that most people commit themselves to a democracy; all that is necessary is that they fail to commit themselves actively to an antidemocratic system. Though this fact suggests that American democracy is on shaky foundations, the masses' tendency to avoid political activity makes their antidemocratic attitudes less destructive. Those with the attitudes most dangerous for democracy are the least involved in politics.[15]

Occasionally, however, mass apathy gives way to mass activism. Reflecting the masses' antidemocratic, extremist, hateful, and violence-prone sentiments, this activism seriously threatens democratic values.

Mass activism tends to occur in crises—defeat or humiliation in war, economic depression and unemployment, or threats to public safety. William Kornhauser correctly observes:

There appears to be a close relation between the severity of crises and the extent of mass movements in Western societies. The more severe the depression in industrial societies, the greater the social atomization, and the more widespread are mass movements (for example, there is a high [inverse] association between level of employment and increase in the extremist electorate). The stronger a country's sense of national humiliation and defeat in war, the greater the social atomization, and the greater the mass action (for example, there is a close association between military defeat and the rise of strong mass movements).[16]

Defeat in war, or even failure to achieve any notable victories in a protracted military effort, reduces mass confidence in established leadership and makes the masses vulnerable to the appeals of counterelites. Both fascism in Germany and communism in Russia followed on the heels of national humiliation and defeat in war. The antiestablishment culture of the late 1960s and early 1970s owed a great deal to the mistakes and failures of the nation's leadership in Vietnam.

Mass anxiety and vulnerability to counterelites also increase in periods of economic dislocation—depression, unemployment, or technological change—that threatens financial security. Poverty alone causes less anxiety than does change or the threat of change in people's level of affluence. Another source of anxiety among the masses is their perceived level of personal safety. Crime, street violence, and terrorism can produce disproportionately strong anxieties about personal safety. Historically, masses that believe their personal safety is threatened have turned to vigilantes, the Ku Klux Klan, and "law and order" movements.

The masses are most vulnerable to extremism when they are alienated from group and community life and when they feel their own lives are without direction or purpose.[17] Mass participation in the established organizations of the community—church groups, PTAs, Little League, fraternal orders—provides a sense of participation, involvement, and self-esteem. Involvement shields the masses from the despairing appeals of demagogues who play on latent mass fears and hatreds. People who are socially isolated are most likely to become mobilized by totalitarian movements. Thus a thriving group and community life very much serves the interest of elites; it helps protect them from the threat of demagogues who wish to challenge the established system of values.

COUNTERELITES: THE DEMAGOGUE AS VOICE OF THE PEOPLE

Threats to established elite values occur periodically, from both left and right. The counterelite pattern is similar regardless of the ideology behind it. Both left and right counterelite movements appeal to the desire of the "powerless" to overthrow the established elites.

Although left counterelites in the United States are just as antidemocratic, extremist, and intolerant as are right counterelites, their appeal is not as broadly based as is the appeal to the right. Left counter-elites have no mass following among workers, farmers, or middle-class Americans. In contrast, right counterelites in the United States histori-cally have been more successful in appealing to broad mass followings. Many changes in American society have contributed to the popular appeal of right counterelites: shifts in power and prestige from the farms to the cities, from agriculture to industry, from the North to the West; shifts away from individual enterprise toward collective action; shifts away from racial segregation toward special emphasis on opportunities for blacks; shifts from old values to new, from religion to secularism, from work to leisure; shifts in scale from small to large, from personal to im-personal, from individual to bureaucratic; increases in crime, racial dis-order, and threats to personal safety. Any genuine "people's" revolution in the United States would undoubtedly take the form of a right-wing, na-tionalist, patriotic, religious-fundamentalist, racist, anti-intellectual, antistudent "law and order" movement.[18]

Right-wing extremism is nothing new in American history: it in-cludes the "Know Nothings" of the nineteenth century (who opposed im-migration and Catholicism); the turn-of-the-century populists led by William Jennings Bryan (who opposed all forms of social liberalism, es-pecially the teaching of evolution); George Wallace and the early American Independent party; the "taxpayers' revolt" of the late 1970s; and the cru-sading of television evangelists in the 1980s.

The early career of George C. Wallace was typical of many counter-elites in its populism, extremism, antielitism, and egalitarianism. But Wallace was atypical in the breadth of his mass base: in the 1968 presi-dential election, 14 percent of the American electorate completely aban-doned the two-party system to support Wallace's independent candidacy. Given the historic, institutional role of the two-party system in the United States and the strength of traditional party loyalties, family ties, and socialization patterns, the fact that so many people would abandon both parties for an independent candidate testifies to the strength of Wallace's mass appeal.

In both North and South, Wallace appealed to *racial sentiments*— a mass characteristic of whites that he successfully exploited.* But it is a mistake to dismiss Wallace as merely a racist. He appealed to "little

---

*Whether Wallace was personally a racist is open to question. In his first run for gov-ernor of Alabama in 1958, Wallace shunned KKK support and ran as a "moderate" against strong-segregationist John Patterson. Wallace was badly beaten and was widely quoted as saying, "They out-niggered me that time, but they'll never do it again." One Wallace observer says, "I would term the Governor a pseudo-demagogue, because he doesn't really believe what he says about the race question. He uses it only as a technique to get the vote of the unsophisticated white man." But another observer adds, "He used to be anything but a racist, but with all his chattering he managed to talk himself into it." See Robert Sherrill, *Gothic Politics in the Deep South* (New York: Grossman, 1968), p. 283.

people" throughout the nation by expressing a wide variety of mass sentiments.

Wallace was *egalitarian* on everything but race. He attacked the "Eastern money interests" and the "over-educated ivory tower folks with pointed heads looking down their nose at us." He identified communism with wealth: "I don't believe in all this talk about poor folks turning Communist! It's the damn rich who turn Communist. You ever seen a poor Communist?" Republicans were attacked as "bankers and big money people" who exploit "us ordinary folks." Wallace's welfare and public-works programs, when he was governor of Alabama, were the most liberal in the state's history, and he was regarded as a threat to conservative business interests in that state.

Mass *fears about personal safety* were just as influential as racial prejudice in stimulating Wallace support. Wallace frequently referred to demonstrators as "the scum of the earth"; he pledged that if a demonstrator ever tried to lie down in front of a Wallace motorcade "it would be the last car he ever lies down in front of." Wallace's simplistic solution to rioting was "to let the police run this country for a year or two and there wouldn't be any riots." Wallace correctly judged that this mass audience would welcome a police state in order to ensure their personal safety. Opinion surveys in the 1960s consistently reported that "crime and violence," "riots," and "law and order" were rated as the most important issues by Wallace's mass following.

Religious fundamentalism, when it turns to political activity, frequently assumes counterelitist, demagogic rhetoric. For example, television evangelists have often been successful in mobilizing mass opinion, raising money, and achieving celebrity status. When they turn to political activity, their agenda generally reflects mass concerns about threats to traditional moral values; media approval of sexual deviance; the prevalence of abortion, pornography, and crime in society; the absence of religion in schools and public life; and communist influence at home and abroad. But established media elites (see Chapter 6) have been largely successful in discrediting these independent television preachers and in frustrating their political ambitions. The Reverend Jerry Falwell was modestly successful in shaping Republican party platforms in the Reagan era. But once in office, the Reagan administration quietly placed fundamentalist goals very low on the policy agenda. The Reverend Pat Robertson tried to mobilize fundamentalists in his bid for the Republican presidential nomination in 1988 but met with little success.

One of the important functions of the major parties is to absorb and de-radicalize mass political movements. In the 1976 Democratic presidential primaries, Jimmy Carter won over most of Wallace's followers with antiestablishment posturing. His southern background and his pretended remoteness from the circles of power in Washington appealed to many who had cast third-party votes in the previous election. (Wallace himself, crippled in a 1972 assassination attempt, did not campaign with his earlier vigor and volatility.) In subsequent elections the Republican party absorbed most of the politically active religious fundamentalists, with the Reverend Pat Robertson endorsing the Bush candidacy in 1988.

ELITE REPRESSION IN RESPONSE TO MASS ACTIVISM

Elites are more committed to democratic values than the masses, but they frequently abandon those values in periods of crisis and become repressive. Antidemocratic mass activism has its counterpart in elite repression. Both endanger democratic values.

Mass activism and elite repression frequently interact to create twin threats to democracy. Mass activism—riots, demonstrations, extremism, violence—generates fear and insecurity among elites, who respond by curtailing freedom and strengthening security. Convincing themselves that they are preserving liberal democratic values, elites may cease tolerating dissent, curtail free speech, jail potential counterelites, and strengthen police and security forces in the name of "national security" or "law and order." Ironically, these steps make society less democratic rather than more so.

Repressive behavior is typical of elites who feel threatened in crises, as some notable events in American history show. The Alien and Sedition Acts (1798), passed in the administration of John Adams, closed down Jeffersonian newspapers and jailed their editors. Abraham Lincoln suspended due process rights and imposed military law in many areas, both North and South, where citizens opposed his efforts to preserve the Union. The "Red Scare" of 1919–1920 resulted in the roundup of suspected Bolsheviks in the administration of Woodrow Wilson, even after the end of World War I. During World War II the Roosevelt administration imprisoned thousands of Japanese-American families in West Coast detention camps. And during the Truman and Eisenhower administrations, suspected Communists and "fellow travelers" were persecuted by dismissal from their jobs, blacklisting, and, occasionally, imprisonment. During the Cold War federal security agencies used such means as wiretapping, monitoring mail, paid informants, surveillance, infiltration, and "surreptitious entry" (burglary). These practices began with the Roosevelt administration and continued through the Truman, Eisenhower, Kennedy, Johnson, and Nixon years. The Watergate affair (the break-in at Democratic party headquarters in the Watergate apartments, Washington, D.C., in June 1972, and subsequent White House attempts at a coverup of those involved) grew out of a more general atmosphere of fear and repression that surrounded the White House in the early 1970s. No evidence suggests that the major figures participated in Watergate for personal financial gain. Rather, they appeared genuinely to believe that the political system was in jeopardy and that only extraordinary measures could preserve it (see Chapter 10).

Elite repression is a continuing threat to democratic values. And this threat to democratic values will always be greatest in periods of mass unrest, when elites believe that their repressive acts are necessary to preserve the political system.

——— SUMMARY

Elite theory suggests that attitudes and values, as well as socioeconomic background, distinguish elites from masses. Elites give greater support to the principles and beliefs underlying the political system. Our analysis of elite and mass attitudes suggests the following propositions:

1. Elites give greater support to democratic values than do masses. Elites are also more consistent than masses in applying general principles of democracy to specific individuals, groups, and events.

2. Extremist and intolerant movements in modern society are more likely to arise from the lower classes than from the middle and upper classes. The poor may be more liberal on economic issues, but on non-economic issues—support for civil liberties, for example—the upper classes are more liberal and the lower classes more conservative. Masses demonstrate antidemocratic attitudes more often than elites do. The masses are less committed to democratic rules of the game than elites are and are more likely to go outside those rules and engage in violence. Mass movements exploit the alienation and hostility of lower classes by concentrating on scapegoats.

3. The survival of democracy depends on elite rather than mass commitment to democratic ideals.

4. Political apathy and nonparticipation among the masses contribute to the survival of democracy. Fortunately for democracy, the antidemocratic masses are generally more apathetic than elites are. Only an unusual demagogue or counterelite can arouse the masses from their apathy and create a threat to the elite consensus.

5. Occasionally mass apathy turns into mass activism, which is generally extremist, intolerant, antidemocratic, and violence-prone. Conditions that encourage mass activism include defeat or humiliation in war, economic dislocation, and perceived threats to personal safety.

6. Counterelites appeal to mass sentiments and express hostility toward the established order and its values. Both left and right counterelites are antidemocratic, extremist, impatient with due process, contemptuous of law and authority, and violence-prone. Counterelites express racial prejudice, populism, egalitarianism, anti-intellectualism, and simplistic solutions to social problems.

7. Although left counterelites are as antidemocratic as right counterelites, their appeal is not as broadly based as the appeal of the right. Right counterelites have mobilized mass support among large numbers of farmers, workers, and middle-class Americans.

8. Although more committed to democratic values than the masses are, elites may abandon these values in crises. When war or revolution threatens the existing order, elites may deviate from democratic values to maintain the system. They may then cease tolerating the dissent, censor mass media, curtail free speech, jail counterelites, and strengthen police and security forces.

──── NOTES

1. Herbert McClosky and Alida Brill, *Dimensions of Tolerance* (New York: Russell Sage Foundation, 1983), p. 92.
2. Ibid.
3. Seymour Martin Lipset, *Political Man* (Garden City, N.Y.: Doubleday, 1963), p. 87.
4. Ibid., p. 92.
5. Lewis Lipsitz, "Work Life and Political Attitudes: A Study of Manual Workers," *American Political Science Review* 58 (December 1964): 959.
6. Harry Eckstein, "Civic Inclusion and Its Discontents," *Daedalus* 113 (Fall 1984): 130.
7. Herbert McClosky and John Zaller, *The American Ethos* (Cambridge: Harvard University Press, 1984), p. 147.
8. William Kornhauser, *The Politics of Mass Society* (Glencoe, Ill.: Free Press, 1959), p. 174.
9. Lewis Lipsitz, "Working-Class Authoritarianism: A Reevaluation," *American Sociological Review* 30 (1965): 108–109.
10. David G. Lawrence, "Procedural Norms and Tolerance: A Measurement," *American Political Science Review* 70 (March 1976): 89.
11. Hazel Erskine and Richard L. Siegel, "Civil Liberties and the Public," *Journal of Social Issues* 31 (1975): 22.
12. John Sullivan, James Pierson, and Gregory Marcus, "An Alternative Conceptualization of Political Tolerance," *American Political Science Review* 73 (September 1979): 788.
13. The actual figures vary from year to year, survey to survey, and ax (as in "ax to grind") to ax. About two-thirds can recognize *either* the name or the party. Thomas Mann and Raymond Wolfinger, "Candidates and Parties in Congressional Elections," *American Political Science Review,* 74 (1981): 595–607, bump up the numbers by allowing people to earn credit for correct identification if they are willing to rate the incumbent on a feeling thermometer (thus substantially inflating the proportion who can "recognize" an incumbent).

14. James L. Gibson, "Political Intolerance and Political Depression During the McCarthy Red Scare," *American Political Science Review*, 82, no. 11 (June 1988): 529.

15. Herbert H. Hyman, "England and America: Climates of Tolerance and Intolerance, 1962," in Daniel Bell, ed., *The Radical Right* (Garden City, N.Y.: Doubleday, 1963), p. 229.

16. Kornhauser, op. cit., p. 174.

17. Ibid., p. 33.

18. Seymour Martin Lipset and Earl Raab, *The Politics of Unreason* (New York: Harper & Row, 1970), p. 348.

——— SELECTED READINGS

Davis, James A. "Communism, Conformity, Cohorts, and Categories: American Tolerance in 1954 and in 1972–1973." *American Journal of Sociology* 81 (1975): 491–513. This replication of the original Stouffer study argues that tolerance is increasing.

Edelman, Murray. *The Symbolic Uses of Politics.* Chicago: University of Illinois Press, Illini Books, 1967. Edelman discusses the general uses of symbols in society and then specifically the uses of political phenomena as symbols. He points out that myth and symbolic reassurances have become key elements in the governmental process and argues that the masses are generally uninterested in and inattentive to political phenomena as symbols. Only when the masses perceive symbolic or real threats or reassurances do they notice things political. Masses react to stimuli. Therefore, it is political actions that "shape men's political wants and 'knowledge,' not the other way around" (p. 172). Edelman also argues that mass demands, when they are articulated, are most often met with "symbolic" rather than "tangible" rewards.

Fromm, Eric. *Escape from Freedom.* New York: Avon Books, 1941. Fromm examines the notion of authoritarianism as an escape from the isolation produced by a large society. Written primarily from a popular psychoanalytic point of view, the book offers interesting comparative reading with the political science and sociological works on authoritarianism.

Grabb, Edward G. "Working Class Authoritarianism and Tolerance of Outgroups: A Reassessment." *Public Opinion Quarterly* 3 (Spring 1979): 36–47. The relation between education and tolerance among the masses remains as strong as ever.

Huntington, Samuel P. *American Politics: The Promise of Disharmony.* Cambridge, Mass.: Harvard University Press. Huntington compares the individualistic American culture with European cultures and explains our "credal passion."

Lawrence, David G. "Procedural Norms and Tolerance: A Reassessment." *American Political Science Review* 70 (1975): 80–108. Lawrence finds more tolerance for "democratic" norms than was true in the 1950s.

Lipset, Seymour Martin, and Raab, Earl. *The Politics of Unreason*. New York: Harper & Row, 1970. This book is a historical study of right-wing extremism from colonial times to 1970.

McClosky, Herbert, and Brill, Alida. *Dimensions of Tolerance*. New York: Russell Sage Foundation, 1983. The most pessimistic of recent studies, this book offers little evidence that elite–mass differences in tolerance are narrowing.

Schattschneider, E. E. *The Semisovereign People: A Realistic View of the Democracy in America*. New York: Holt, Rinehart & Winston, 1960. This book discusses the nature of conflict and change in the United States. Schattschneider argues against the pluralist-group theory bias, which he perceives as the common view of the political system today. He also recognizes the elite–masses dichotomy that exists in the U.S. social and political system. For example, he develops the notion that elites, by virtue of their organizational strengths, can manage conflict within the political system. They can alter it, exploit it, and/or suppress it.

Stouffer, Samuel A. *Communism, Conformity, and Civil Liberties*. New York: Wiley, 1966. This book, originally published in 1955, reports the results of a national survey of 6,000 people to "examine in some depth the reactions of Americans to two dangers. One, from the communist conspiracy outside and inside the country. Two, from those who in thwarting the conspiracy would sacrifice some of the very liberties which the enemy would destroy." The study was one of the first systematic attempts to examine the intolerant frame of mind and indicates that a large portion of the masses in the United States would be willing to restrict severely even legitimate activities of unpopular minorities.

Sullivan, John L., Pierson, James, and Marcus, Gregory. "An Alternative Conceptualization of Political Tolerance." *American Political Science Review* 73 (1979): 781–794. Sullivan concludes that tolerance has not increased but that new targets of hostility have been found. See also, by the same authors, *Political Tolerance and American Democracy* (Chicago: University of Chicago Press, 1982).

Zaller, John. *The American Ethos*. Cambridge, Mass.: Harvard University Press, 1984. Zaller analyzes and explains popular ideologies.

6

Elite–Mass Communication: Television, the Press, and the Pollsters

★ *For most people most of the time politics is a series of pictures in the mind, placed there by television news, newspapers, magazines, and discussions. . . . Politics for most of us is a passing parade of symbols.*

Murray Edelman, The Symbolic Uses of Politics, *1967*

Communication in the American political system flows downward from elites to masses. Television and the press are the means by which elites communicate to the masses not only information but also values, attitudes, and emotions. Professional pollsters in turn try to measure mass response to these elite communications. But elite–mass communication often fails. Masses frequently misinterpret elite messages to them, and elites cannot always shape mass opinion as they intend.

THE NEWSMAKERS

Elites instruct masses about politics and social values chiefly through television, the major source of information for the vast majority of Americans. Those who control this flow of information are among the most powerful people in the nation.

Television is the first true *mass* communication form. Nearly everyone, including children, watches the evening news. Nearly two-thirds of the public testifies that television provides "most of my views about what is going on in the world." And most Americans say that television is their "most believable" news source.[1] (See Figure 6-1.)

Television has great impact because it is visual: it can convey emotions as well as information. Police dogs attacking blacks, people loading sacks of dead American soldiers onto helicopters, angry crowds burning and looting in cities—all convey emotions as well as information.

The power to determine what most Americans will see and hear about the world rests largely with three private corporations: Capital Cities–ABC Inc. (ABC); CBS Inc. (CBS); and the National Broadcasting Corporation (NBC), a division of General Electric Corporation. Local television stations are privately owned and licensed to use broadcast channels by a government regulatory agency, the Federal Communications Commission (FCC). But because of the high cost of producing news and entertainment at the station level, virtually all stations must use news and programming from the three networks.

Recently cable and satellite technology have eroded the traditional dominance of the three television networks. Today more than half of all television homes in the United States are cable subscribers, and that number is steadily increasing. Atlanta-based Cable News Network (CNN) now provides alternative (and politically less biased) news broadcasting, and pay channels such as HBO and specialized channels for sports (ESPN) and music (MTV) provide entertainment alternatives. ABC, NBC, and CBS still draw about 60 percent of total TV viewers, although that figure is down from 95 percent only a decade ago.

The top network executives—presidents, vice-presidents, and producers—determine the news and entertainment Americans see. These

FIGURE 6-1   Where the masses get their news and which source they believe

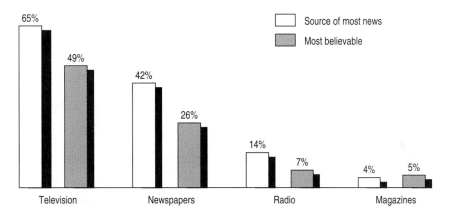

Questions: First, I'd like to ask you where you usually get most of your news about what's going on in the world today—from the newspapers or radio or television or magazines or talking to people or where?

If you got conflicting or different reports of the same news story from radio, television, the magazines, and the newspapers, which of the four versions would you be most inclined to believe—the one on radio or television or magazines or newspapers?

☐ Source of most news

▨ Most believable

65% 49% 42% 26% 14% 7% 4% 5%

Television   Newspapers   Radio   Magazines

Note: Percentages (for sources of news) add up to 125 percent due to multiple responses. For trend line on these questions, see Harold W. Stanley and Richard G. Niemi, *Vital Statistics on American Politics* (Washington: Congressional Quarterly Press, 1988. Between 1962 and 1964, television passed newspapers as a source of most news. Between 1958 and 1960, television passed newspapers as the most believable medium.

SOURCE: Television Information Office, "America's Watching: Public Attitudes Toward Television" (New York: Television Information Office, 1989).

executives are indeed "a tiny, enclosed fraternity of privileged men."* Top news anchors like Dan Rather, Peter Jennings, and Tom Brokaw assist in putting together the evening news show, but decisions about stories are made by the producers under supervision of the network executives. The leading television reporters—Ted Koppel, Ed Bradley, Mike Wallace, Barbara Walters, and others—occasionally pursue their own story ideas, but the decision to put their stories on the air rests with the news executives. Moreover, network executives exchange views with the editors of the *New York Times*, the *Washington Post, Newsweek, Time,* and a few of the largest newspaper chains. The television executives and producers and print editors and publishers collectively are the "newsmakers."

The newsmakers frequently make contradictory remarks about their own power. They sometimes claim that they do no more than "mirror" reality. The "mirror" myth is nonsense. A mirror makes no choices about

*So called by former Vice President Spiro T. Agnew, who also described them more colorfully as "super-sensitive, self-anointed, supercilious electronic barons of opinion." (See *Newsweek*, November 9, 1970, p. 22.)

what images it reflects, but television executives have the power to create some national issues and ignore others; to elevate obscure people to national prominence; to reward politicians they favor and punish those they disfavor. Indeed, at times the newsmakers proudly credit themselves with the success of the civil rights movement, ending the Vietnam War, and forcing two presidents—Johnson and Nixon—out of office. These claims contradict the mirror image theory, but they more accurately reflect the power of the mass media.

THE POLITICAL FUNCTIONS OF THE MASS MEDIA

The political power of the mass media arises from several of its vital functions: newsmaking, interpretation, socialization, persuasion, and agenda setting.[2]

Newsmaking

Newsmaking is deciding what and who are "newsworthy" and allocating precious television time and newspaper space accordingly. Television producers and newspaper and magazine editors focus attention on certain people, issues, and events, and that attention in turn generates public concern and political action. Without media coverage, the mass public would not know about these personalities, issues, or events. And without public interest, government officials would not consider the topics important.

The media must select from a tremendous oversupply of information and decide what is "news," and the selection process is the root of their power. Television cannot be "a picture of the world" (as some television executives pretend) because the whole world cannot squeeze into the picture (or into the twenty-four noncommercial minutes of the network evening news). Media attention creates events, issues, and personalities; media inattention means obscurity, even nonexistence. Of course, politicians, public relations people, interest-group leaders, and aspiring "celebrities" know that the decision of news executives are vital to their success and even to their existence. So they try, sometimes desperately, to attract the media's attention—to get just thirty seconds on the network news. The result is the "media event"—an activity arranged primarily to stimulate media coverage and attract public attention to an issue or personality. The more bizarre, dramatic, and sensational the event, the more likely it is to attract media attention. It may be a march or demonstration, a dramatic confrontation, an illustration of injustice, a press conference, a visit to a home for the elderly, or a walk down a ghetto street. A media event for television must provide opportunities for interesting or dramatic pictures; television networks are likely to ignore topics or issues without such "good visuals."

Interpretation

Interpretation of events, issues, and personalities begins when news-makers search for an "angle" on the story—a way to put it into context and speculate about its meaning and consequences. Through interpretation, newsmakers provide the masses with explanations and meanings for events and personalities.

Most network news broadcasts now include a "special segment" or "news special"—two or three minutes of "in-depth" coverage of a particular topic, such as gun control, nuclear plant safety, or international terrorism. News staffs prepare the specials well in advance of their showing and use film or videotape and a script with a "lead-in," "voice-over," and "recapitulation." The interpretive function is clearest in these stories, but interpretation takes place in every news story.

Socialization

The media's socialization function is to teach mass audiences the elite's preferred political norms and values. Both news and entertainment programming contribute to socialization. Election night coverage shows "how democracy works" and reinforces the values of political participation. Advertising shows Americans how they should live—it illustrates desirable lifestyles and encourages viewers to buy such products as automobiles, beer, soap, and perfume.

Entertainment programs also socialize the mass public by introducing social themes and ways of life—for example, racial tolerance (racially mixed neighborhoods as settings, situation comedies with cute black children), new sexual mores (sex outside marriage, unmarried couples living together), divorce and feminism (divorced mothers raising children and living happily outside marriage; successful, happy, and single professional women), and even homosexuality (well-adjusted, likable, sensitive, humorous homosexuals). Television executives and producers frequently congratulate themselves on such socially progressive themes.

Persuasion

Persuasion occurs when governments, corporations, unions, political parties, and candidates make deliberate attempts, usually but not always through paid advertising, to affect people's beliefs, attitudes, or behavior. The Department of Defense has become a major advertiser in its efforts to recruit for all-volunteer forces—"Be all that you can be!" Corporate advertisers ask Americans not only to buy products but also to believe that the corporations are concerned with the environment or with health or with the economic welfare of the nation. Unions ask television viewers to "Look for the union label."

The most obvious efforts at political persuasion take place during political campaigns. Candidates no longer rely on Democratic and

Republican party organizations to run their campaigns but instead seek out advertising and public relations specialists to direct sophisticated media campaigns. Candidates can use television to bypass party organizations and go directly to the people. As the image makers have taken over political campaigns, the importance of political parties has declined. When voters can see and hear candidates in their own living rooms, they need not rely so heavily on party leaders to provide them with information and advice. Thus candidate image has become a major factor in voters' choices (see the Case Study: Setting the Presidential Campaign Agenda).

Agenda Setting

The real power of the mass media lies in deciding what will be decided. Defining the issues, identifying alternative policies, focusing on political, economic, or social "crises"—these are critical aspects of national policy

CASE STUDY

 ### Setting the Presidential Campaign Agenda

What are people thinking about when they cast their votes in a presidential election? Setting the agenda for a presidential election is the key to victory. Bill Clinton and his campaign team understood that their success depended on making the election a referendum on the *economy.* George Bush and his advisors sought to make the election a referendum on *personal character.* But it was the news media that played the leading role in shaping the election agenda.

The media's reporting of bad economic news was unremitting from early 1991, when the nation did in fact stumble into recession, through to election day in November 1992, more than a year after the economic recovery had begun. The 1991 recession had not been as deep as the 1982 recession early in Reagan's term. (The unemployment rate reached a high of 9.6% in 1982 versus a high of 7.9% in 1991–1992.) It is true that recovery in 1992 was sluggish; but the media portrayed the economy as hopelessly mired in deficits and joblessness and under assault from global competitors. Bush's claim that the economy was "not all that bad" was technically correct, but it was treated by

the media as evidence that the president was "out of touch" with the suffering of the people. Early favorable media coverage of Ross Perot, and his message that government deficits were sapping the nation's economic strength, detached many middle-class voters from Bush. Early in the campaign, the Bush camp tried to make family values the leading issues, with only limited success. Later in the campaign, Bush focused on "taxes and trust": "Slick Willie" was a taxer and spender, as well as a draft-dodger and anti-war demonstrator. But despite doubts the voters may have had about Clinton's character, they were more concerned about the economy than anything else.

What was on the voter's mind on election day? The economy and jobs were twice as important as the next highest issue, the deficit, and almost three times as important as Bush's issues—family values, taxes, and foreign policy. The economic issue, together with health care, favored Clinton. The deficit issue favored Perot. Bush won heavy majorities of people concerned with family values, taxes, and foreign policy, but there were fewer people concerned with these issues.

making. We can refer to these activities as *agenda setting.* Conditions in society that are *not* defined as "crises," or even as "problems," by the mass media never become policy issues. Such conditions do not get on political leaders' agendas. Political leaders, anxious to get coverage on the evening news programs, speak out on the issues the mass media have defined as important. These issues are placed on the agenda of decision makers. Governments must then decide what to do about them.

Clearly, then, the power to decide what will be a "crisis" or "problem" or "issue" is critical to the policy-making process.[3] Deciding what the problems are is even more important than deciding what the solutions will be.

Pluralist textbooks imply that issues or problems or crises just happen. Pluralists argue that in a free, competitive society such as ours, channels of access and communication to government are open to everyone, so any problem can be discussed and placed on the agenda of decision makers.

But in reality, policy issues do not just happen. Creating an issue, dramatizing it, calling attention to it, turning it into a "crisis," and pressuring government to do something about it are important political tactics. Influential individuals, organized interest groups, political candidates and officeholders, and, perhaps most important, the mass media all employ these tactics.

The power of television is not in persuading viewers to take one side of an issue or another or to vote for one candidate or another. Instead the power of television is in setting the agenda for decision making: deciding which issues and candidates will be given attention and which will be ignored. Systematic research has shown that issues that receive the greatest attention in the mass media are most likely to be viewed by voters as "important."[4] (In Chapter 8, we describe the role of the mass media in defining the "serious" presidential candidates.)

LIBERAL BIAS IN TELEVISION NEWS

Network television—through entertainment, newscasts, and news specials—communicates established liberal elite values to the masses. These are the values of the media elite: liberal reform and social welfare, a concern for the problems of minorities and the poor, skepticism toward organized religion and the "traditional" family, suspicion of business, hostility toward the military, and an urge to use government power to "do good."[5] (See the case study "Media Elites Confront the Social Issues.")

There is far less diversity of views on television than in the press. Individual newspapers and magazines present conventionally "liberal" or "conservative" views—for example, the *New York Times* versus the

Wall Street Journal, Newsweek versus *U.S. News and World Report,* or *Harper's* versus the *National Review*—and thus balance one another to some degree. But all three major television networks present a conventional liberal point of view. (William F. Buckley's *Firing Line,* representing a "conservative" viewpoint, is carried only by public television stations; CNN's program *Crossfire* presents a liberal and a conservative commentator together.)

The liberal bias of the news originates in the values of the newsmakers. The owners (stockholders) of the major corporations that own the television networks, magazines, and newspaper chains usually share the moderate conservatism and Republicanism of the business community, but the producers, directors, and reporters are clearly left-leaning and Democratic in their political views. One study of news executives reported that 63 percent described themselves as "left-leaning," only 27 percent as "middle-of-the-road," and 10 percent as "right-leaning."[6] Newsmakers describe themselves as either "independent" (45 percent) or Democratic (44 percent); very few (9 percent) admit to being Republican. And most are male and upper middle class in origin. Another study asked members of the Washington press corps to describe their own politics: 42 percent of the press corps called themselves "liberal," 39 percent "middle-of-the-road," and 19 percent "conservative."[7]

CASE STUDY

 ### Media Elites Confront the Social Issues

In summarizing the social and political bias of the mass media in America, political scientist Doris A. Graber wrote, "Economic and social liberalism prevails, as does a preference for an internationalist foreign policy, caution about military intervention, and some suspicion about the ethics of established large institutions, particularly government."*

To test for these biases in television, sociologists Robert Lichter and Stanley Rothman interviewed three groups: (1) a sample of 240 news executives, editors, and reporters from ABC, CBS, NBC television, the *New York Times,* the *Washington Post,* the *Wall Street Journal, Time,* and *Newsweek;* (2) a sample of 104 producers, writers, and television network executives responsible for prime-time entertainment shows; and (3) for purposes of comparison, a sample of 218 top business exec-

utives from the leading *Fortune* industrial firms, banks, and utilities.

News and entertainment elites are decidedly more liberal and reformist in their social and political views than are other elites. Most media elites believe that government should redistribute income from the rich to the poor and that government should guarantee everyone a job. These views are not shared by business elites. Media elites are also more likely than business elites to believe that American institutions are in need of reform. However, few media elites are socialists: they reject the idea that government should take over ownership of big corporations, and they generally support private enterprise. Moreover, they reject egalitarianism and support the notion that people with more ability (presumably including themselves) should be paid more than others with less ability.

Mass Media and American Politics (Washington, D.C.: Congressional Quarterly, 1980), p. 49.

(continued)

CASE STUDY *(continued)*

Media elites are also liberals on social and cultural issues. They support affirmative action for blacks and women's rights more strongly than do business elites. The media elites give less support to traditional moral values than other elites. Few believe that homosexuality is wrong and fewer still would place any restrictions on homosexuals.

SOURCE: Thomas R. Dye and Harmon Zeigler, *American Politics in the Media Age,* 3rd ed. (Pacific Grove, Calif.: Brooks/Cole, 1989), p. 107.

	Percentage agreeing with viewpoint		
Social issue and viewpoint	Business leaders	Newsmakers	Entertainment producers
ECONOMIC LIBERALISM			
Government should redistribute income.	23	68	69
Government should guarantee jobs.	29	48	45
Big corporations should be publicly owned.	6	13	19
Private enterprise is fair.	89	70	69
People with more ability should earn more.	90	86	94
REFORMISM			
Structure of society causes alienation.	30	49	62
Institutions need overhaul.	28	32	48
SOCIAL LIBERALISM			
Strong affirmative action for blacks.	71	80	83
Women have the right to abortions.	80	90	97
Homosexuals should not teach in schools.	51	15	15
Homosexuality is wrong.	60	25	20
Adultery is wrong.	76	47	49

SOURCES: Lichter and Rothman, "Media and Business Elites," *Public Opinion* (October/November 1981): 42–46; Richter, Lichter, and Rothman, "Hollywood and America: The Odd Couple," *Public Opinion* (December/January 1983): 54–58.

BASHING AMERICA FOR FUN AND PROFIT

American television and the news media in general have a bad-news bias. They cover bad news very well. They do not cover good news very well or very often. Bad news is big news: it is dramatic and sensational. Scandal, rip-offs, violent crime, threatening budget cuts, sexual deviance, environmental scares, and similar fascinations all capture audience attention. But the good news—improved health statistics, longer life spans, better safety records, higher educational levels, and so on—does not stir audience interest so easily. The result is an overwhelming bias toward negative news stories in the media, especially on television. Bad news stories outnumber good news stories ten to one.[8]

The networks select news for its emotional impact. Stories that inspire mass fears (the crack cocaine epidemic, nuclear power plant accidents, toxic shock syndrome, AIDS, and so on) are especially favored. Violence, sex, and government corruption are favorite topics because they attract popular interest. When faced with more complex problems—inflation, government deficits, foreign policy—the newsmakers feel they must simplify, dramatize, or else altogether ignore them.

Entertainment programs reinforce the negative picture of American life. Consider the popularity of crime programs. In the real world, about three out of a hundred Americans will be victims of a crime *in a year*. In prime-time television entertainment, approximately ten crimes are committed *each night*.[9] Murder is the least common crime in the real world, but it is by far the most common crime on television, which averages one killing every two and a half programs! It is little wonder that Americans who watch a great deal of television tend to overestimate the real amount of crime in society greatly.

Why are the media so negative? One explanation is the commercial value of exciting and sensational news. It attracts viewers and increases television ratings. Higher ratings mean more advertisers and more profit for the networks. Another contributing explanation is the liberal ideology of the newsgathering establishments. The most influential journalists at the television networks and influential newspapers are political liberals. They believe that spotlighting negative aspects of American life will lead to social reforms. Their focus on the problems of American society leaves little time or space for good news. Still another explanation derives from the professional norms of journalism today. Many journalists believe that the media should be adversarial—that is, the media should act as critics of society. Investigative journalism is popular among young journalists; they believe that a vigilant, investigative press must aggressively seek to expose corruption and scandal in high places.

But fun and profit for the media come with high costs for American society. People heavily exposed to political scandal and corruption by the media lose trust and confidence in government and its institutions. Increased mass cynicism and declining voter participation can be attributed to "television malaise"—feelings of distrust, powerlessness, and disaffection from government stemming from television's emphasis on the negative in politics.[10] Taxpayers who believe that—despite billions of dollars of government spending—poverty is always getting worse, education and housing are declining, crime is worsening, and the environment is deteriorating, are likely to revolt. Why would anyone want to pay taxes if the prevailing image of government is one of scandals, waste, and rip-offs?

———— BIAS AND SLANDER: FREEDOMS OF THE PRESS

Media elites claim that the First Amendment's guarantee of freedom of the press gives them a constitutional right to be biased. Certainly the drafters of the Bill of Rights agreed with Thomas Jefferson that a free and critical press was essential to the proper functioning of democracy.

The media argue that they must be free to say and print whatever they wish, whether or not it is biased, unfair, negative, sensational, unfounded, dangerous, or offensive. Generally, the U.S. Supreme Court has agreed.

No Prior Restraint

The Court has interpreted freedom of the press to mean that government may place "no prior restraint" on speech or publication (that is, *before* it is said or published). Originally this doctrine was designed to prevent the government from closing down or seizing newspapers. Today the doctrine prevents the government from censoring any news items. For example, the Supreme Court ruled against the federal government and in favor of the *New York Times* in the famous case of the Pentagon Papers. The *New York Times* and the *Washington Post* undertook to publish secret information stolen from the files of the State Department and Defense Department regarding U.S. policy in Vietnam while the war was still in progress. No one disputed the fact that stealing the secret material was illegal. What was at issue was the ability of the government to prevent publication of the stolen materials in order to protect national security. But the Supreme Court rejected the national security argument and reaffirmed that the government may place no prior restraint on publication. If the government wishes to keep military secrets, it must not let them fall into the hands of the U.S. press.

No More "Fairness"

In the early days of radio, broadcast channels were limited and anyone with a radio could broadcast on any frequency. Interference was a common frustration of early broadcasters. The industry petitioned the federal government to regulate and license the assignment and use of broadcast frequencies.[11]

The Federal Communications Commission (FCC) was established in 1934 to allocate broadcast frequencies and license stations for the "public interest, convenience, and necessity." The enabling act clearly instructed the FCC: "Nothing in this Act shall be understood or construed to give the Commission the power of censorship. . . . " For many years a "fairness doctrine" required radio and television stations that provided air time to a political candidate to offer competing candidates the same amount of air time at the same price. In addition, stations that broadcast editorials had to provide an opportunity for responsible individuals to present conflicting views. But there was always a huge hole in the fairness doctrine: news programs were exempt. Newscasts, news specials, even long documentaries were all exempt from the fairness doctrine. A biased news presentation did *not* require the network or station to grant equal time to opponents of its views. Moreover, the FCC did little to enforce the fairness doctrine. No station ever lost its license because of the doctrine.

But this modest check on media bias was eliminated by the FCC itself in 1987. As part of an effort to deregulate the broadcasting industry, the FCC scrapped the fairness doctrine despite strong opposition from Congress and watchdog groups. (The decision did not affect the equal-time provision for political candidates.) The FCC defended its decision by arguing that (1) the doctrine chilled debate by leading broadcasters to avoid controversy, and (2) the rapid rise in the number of broadcast outlets (for example, through cable television) showed that market competition rather than government regulation best served the public interest in receiving a variety of perspectives on public affairs. Congress tried to overrule the FCC by passing legislation designed to make the fairness doctrine legally binding, but President Reagan successfully vetoed it. Thus, for the first time since television became a mass medium, broadcasters have no legal obligation to be "fair" in their presentation of public issues.

Libel and Slander

Communications that wrongly damage an individual are known in law as libel (written) and slander (spoken). The injured party must prove in court that the communication caused actual damage and that it was either false or defamatory. A damaging falsehood, or words or phrases that are inherently defamatory ("Joe Jones is a rotten son of a bitch"), are libelous and not protected by the First Amendment from lawsuits seeking compensation.

Media elites have sought over the years to narrow the individual's protection against libel and slander. They were successful in *New York Times* v. *Sullivan* (1964) in depriving *public officials* of the right to recover damages for false statements unless they are made with "malicious intent." The "Sullivan rule" requires public officials not only to show that the media published or broadcast false and damaging statements but also to prove that they did so *knowing at the time* that their statements were false and damaging, or that they did so with "reckless disregard" for the truth or falsehood of their statements. The effect of the Sullivan rule is to free the media to say virtually anything about public officials. Indeed, the media have even sought to expand the definition of "public officials" to "public figures"—that is, virtually anyone the media choose as the subject of a story.

Do the Media Ever Lie?

Bob Woodward is a managing editor for the *Washington Post* and perhaps the most famous of all "investigative reporters." His book *All the President's Men* celebrated his role in exposing government deceit in the Watergate scandal; Robert Redford gave an heroic portrayal of him in the movie version. A later book, *The Brethren*, claimed to expose the private deliberations of the U.S. Supreme Court. Woodward was the most feared and respected newsman in Washington.

Thus Woodward's astonishing report that CIA director William J. Casey admitted having approved the secret diversion of funds to the Nicaraguan Contras made big news on television, in the press, and in the news magazines. Woodward released this news in his book *The Veil*, which he moved to the top of the best-seller lists with personal appearances on "60 Minutes," Ted Koppel's "Nightline," and even "Donahue."

The "news" that the CIA director was behind the Iran-Contra affair was based on a claim by Woodward that he had interviewed Casey as he lay dying after brain surgery in Georgetown University Hospital. *Newsweek* (owned by the *Washington Post*) even supplied an artist's drawing of the deathbed scene.

The only problem was that the interview was a complete fabrication. Woodward never interviewed Casey, and Casey never admitted CIA involvement in the Iran-Contra scandal. Casey was guarded twenty-four hours a day in the hospital by CIA guards, and Casey's wife and daughter stayed in the room throughout his ordeal. Casey was paralyzed from the

CASE STUDY

 ## The New Talk-Show Politics

Political campaigning via talk shows is understandably popular with candidates. They can reach millions of voters directly without the "filters" of anchors, news reporters, and commentators with their interpretations, criticisms, and perhaps distortions of the candidates' messages. Studio and audience call-in questions are usually "soft balls." Few citizens have the information necessary to point out contradictions or inconsistencies in a candidate's statements, nor do they usually get the opportunity to ask follow-up questions and press for specific answers. So appearing on Larry King, or Oprah Winfrey, or Merv Griffin is much preferred to appearing on established news shows such as *Meet the Press, Face the Nation,* or *Sixty Minutes.* Talk-show hosts generally let guests tell their own stories. They are less adversarial than reporters.

Bill Clinton and Ross Perot mastered the new talk-show politics early in the 1992 campaign. Perot, with his Texas twang, blunt talk, and folksy style, was a favorite talk-show guest even before he announced his candidacy on *Larry King Live.* Bill Clinton adopted a "town meeting" format for his campaign appearances early in the primaries. Like Oprah and Merv, he would wander through the audience with microphone in hand, take questions, empathize with people, and tell them how he would solve their problems. But George Bush never really warmed to the talk-show format; he viewed it as undignified and "unpresidential." When the Bush and Clinton campaign teams came together to decide on a format for the presidential debates, Bush's people wanted to continue the "joint press conference" style of previous debates, while the Clinton team pressed for an open "town meeting" with a moderator and questions from the audience. The compromise was a first debate in the traditional format, the second as town meeting, and the third a combination of both.

Talk-show experience paid off for Clinton in the second debate. The studio audience and millions of viewers saw Clinton triumph. Bush would do better in later appearances, but never fully recover. After the election, a confident President Clinton pledged to continue talk-show appearances.

brain surgery and could not communicate. Mrs. Casey, her daughter, and the doctors testified that Woodward had invented his story. But so great was Woodward's prestige and influence that it is still widely circulated and believed.

Media Power

In summary, no effective governmental checks on media power really exist. The constitutional guarantee of freedom of the press is more broadly interpreted in the United States than in any other democracy. The First Amendment guarantees a powerful, independent, and critical media elite.

ASSESSING MEDIA IMPACT

What impact do media elites have on mass opinion and behavior? For many years political scientists advanced the curious notion that the mass media had only "minimal effects" on political behavior. Of course, wiser business elites never believed the minimal-effects theory, as the growth of the multibillion-dollar advertising industry attests. Nor did the politicians believe it, as they turned increasingly to expensive television advertising. Presumably political scientists were basing their theory on the fact that newspaper editorial endorsements seldom changed people's votes. Systematic research on the political effects of the mass media, particularly television, is fairly recent. This research tells a far different story.

It is not easy to sort out the effects of media communications from the effects of many other social, cultural, political, economic, and psychological influences on mass attitudes and behavior. Even when we find strong correlations between the opinions expressed in the mass media and the opinions expressed by the general public, it is difficult to determine systematically whether the media shaped public opinion, public opinion shaped media broadcasts, or both were shaped simultaneously by political events. In other words, it is difficult to prove that the media *causes* changes in opinions or behavior. Nonetheless, systematic research on media effects has progressed to the point where some generalizations are possible.

Media effects can be categorized as influencing (1) cognition and comprehension, (2) attitudes and values, and (3) behavior. These categories of effects are ranked by the degree of influence the media are likely to have over us. That is to say, the strongest effects of the media are in cognition and comprehension—in generating awareness and increasing information levels. The media also influence attitudes and values, but the strength of media effects is diluted by many other sources of attitudes and values. Finally, it is most difficult to establish the independent effect of the media on behavior.

Cognition and Comprehension

Media elites strongly influence what we know about our world and how we think and talk about it. Years ago foreign policy expert Bernard Cohen, in the first book to assess the effects of media on foreign policy, put it this way: "The mass media may not be successful in telling people what to think, but the media are stunningly successful in telling their audience what to think about."[12]

However, the masses generally suffer from *information overload;* so many communications are directed at them that they cannot possibly process them all in their minds. A person's ability to recall a media report is dependent upon repeated exposure to it and reinforcement through personal experience. For example, an individual who has a brother in a trouble spot in the Middle East is more likely to be aware of reports from that area of the world. But most viewers become narcotized by information overload; too many voices with too many messages cause them to block out nearly all information. Information overload may be especially heavy in political news. Television tells most viewers more about politics than they really want to know. Political scientist Austin Ranney writes: "The

Harley L. Schwadron

"YOUR OPINION IS POLITICALLY INCORRECT."

fact is that for most Americans politics is still far from being the most interesting and important thing in life. To them, politics is usually confusing, boring, repetitive, and above all irrelevant to the things that really matter in their lives."[13]

Attitudes and Values

Media elites can create new opinions more easily than they can change existing ones. The media often tell the masses how they should feel about news events or issues—those about which the masses have no prior feelings or experiences. And the media can reinforce values and attitudes that the masses already hold. But there is very little evidence that the media can change existing mass values.

The masses defend against bias in news and entertainment programming by *selective perception*—mentally screening out information or images with which one disagrees. Selective perception causes people to tend to see and hear only what they want to see and hear. Selective perception reduces the impact of media elites on mass attitudes and behavior.

The networks' concentration on scandal, abuse, and corruption in government, for example, has not always produced the desired liberal, reformist notions in the minds of the masses of viewers. Contrary to the expectations of network executives, their focus on governmental scandals—Watergate, illicit activities by the Central Intelligence Agency, abuses by the Federal Bureau of Investigation, congressional sex scandals, and power struggles between Congress and the executive branch—has produced feelings of general political distrust and cynicism toward government and the political system.

The Talk Show Culture

Ross Perot, a truly "electronic" candidate, announced his candidacy on *Larry King Live*, a cable talk show. The choice of venue was delicious. The original TV journalists, Walter Cronkite, David Brinkley, and the like, were relatively serious students of politics. They were followed by a cohort of attractive entertainers with little interest in much beyond personalities. Next came the prime-time "trash-news" shows and, in hot pursuit, were the network daytime talk shows—Donahue and Oprah, for example—with stronger emphasis on the bizarre.

Sleaze and conspiracy, two popular themes in talk shows, fit in well with Perot's predilections. Talk-show hosts and callers inhabit a world of appalling conspiracies, a world in which the outlandish becomes commonplace. Simple solutions, ignored by conspirators, await those bold enough to seize the day. Perot is "the apotheosis of this talk show culture . . . a candidate created and sustained by television, launched on 'Larry King Live,' . . . a candidate whose only substantive proposal is to replace representative democracy with a live TV talk show for the entire nation."[14]

Perot's candidacy was entirely media-generated. He entered no primary elections, preferring instead to use the talk shows, and to use satellite TV to address disparate audiences. His announced intention to use an "electronic town hall" (rather than Congress) as a governing body illustrates the depth of his commitment to the media as a tool for governing as well as campaigning. He is an eccentric. He funds implausible schemes (to rescue MIAs, for example), hangs out with conspiracy aficionados, and believes—no matter what the problem—that "It's just that simple." He asserts, for example, that a government attempt to cover up the existence of MIAs in Vietnam and Laos was actuated by "government officials in the drug trade who can't break the habit." This allegation is in the best talk show tradition.

Perot's disdain for both traditional politics and the established media led him to create a new electronic campaign style. He sought to avoid the traveling campaign shows. Instead, he addressed the American voter through television.

Perot was a master at the talk-show game. He even spoke seriously of running the government by "electronic town meeting." Citizens' questions, unlike those of reporters, were usually friendly and no one demanded specificity in his policy positions. The talk-show format fit Perot's style because he had no real political philosophy, no studied policy positions. He was at his best describing in blunt terms what was wrong with the system and promising to "get under the hood, and fix things." At first the established news media gave very favorable coverage to the plain-speaking billionaire; he was a welcome relief from "politics as usual." But after Perot became the leader in the polls, the media took an adversarial stance, reporting on Perot's sharp business dealings and Rambo-like involvements in covert affairs. Perot became enraged at the media and quit the race on July 16, saying "I don't have to prove anything to you people!"

Upon reentering the presidential race, Perot launched his electronic campaign. He spent more on direct media advertising than Bush and Clinton combined. His spot ads were slick commercials by an experienced Dallas advertising agency. But his most effective format was the "infomercial"—a series of broadcasts starring Perot himself with pointer in hand, ripping through graphs and charts that showed how bad the economy was. To the astonishment of pundits and political scientists, these shows were a success, with Neilsen ratings that challenged prime-time sit-coms.

TABLE 6-1 Media treatment of candidates, May 1992

	Favorable evaluations	Favorable prospects
Perot	74%	82%
Clinton	58	72
Bush	19	57

SOURCE: Robert Lichter, "Election '92: The Perot Factor," *Media Monitor*, 6 (May, 1992), p. 6.

Perot's vote totals on election night also surprised the professionals. Historically, independent candidates have lost the vote of people who expressed a preference for them in the polls but who, in the voting booth, decide not to "waste" their votes on a long shot. But Perot's well-financed media campaign effectively countered the "wasted vote" trend. Moreover, the Perot campaign played a major part in increasing voter turnout for the first time in more than thirty years.

Public Opinion

Can media elites change public opinion? This question was directly confronted by political scientists Benjamin I. Page, Robert Y. Shapiro, and Glenn R. Dempsey in an extensive study of eighty policy issues over fifteen years. They examined public opinion polls on various policy issues at a first point in time, then media content over a following interval of time, and finally public opinion on these same issues at the end of the interval. The purpose was to learn whether media content—messages scored by their relevance to the issue, their salience in the broadcast, their pro or con direction, the credibility of the news source, and quality of the reporting—changed public opinion. Although most people's opinions remained constant over time (opinion at the first time period is the best predictor of opinion at the second time period), opinion changes were heavily influenced by media messages. Page, Shapiro, and Dempsey concluded that "news variables alone account for nearly half the variance in opinion change."

They also learned that:

- *Anchors, reporters, and commentators* had the greatest impact on opinion change. Television newscasters have high credibility and trust with the general public. Their opinions are crucial in shaping mass opinion.
- *Independent experts* interviewed by the media have a substantial impact on opinion but not as great as newscasters themselves.
- A *popular president* can also shift public opinion somewhat. On the other hand, unpopular presidents do not have much success as opinion movers.
- *Interest groups* on the whole have a slightly negative effect on public opinion. "In many instances they seem to actually have antagonized the public and created a genuine adverse effect"; such cases include Vietnam War protesters, nuclear freeze advocates, and other demonstrators and protesters, even peaceful ones.[15]

Behavior

Media elites have a difficult task in *changing* behavior. But television can motivate people who are already predisposed to act in a certain way.

Many studies have been conducted concerning the effect of the media on behavior—the effect of TV violence, the effect of television on children,

"BUSH'S POLLS ARE DOWN! QUICK, HEAD FOR THE BUNKERS!!"

Reprinted with special permission of King Features Syndicate.

and the effects of obscenity and pornography. It is difficult to generalize from these studies. However, it appears that television is more likely to reinforce behavioral tendencies than to change them. For example, televised violence may trigger violent behavior in children who are already predisposed to such behavior, but televised violence has little behavioral effect on the average child. Likewise, there is little evidence that pornography itself causes rape or other deviant sexual behavior among viewers.

Nonetheless, we know that television advertising sells products. And we know that political candidates spend millions to persuade audiences to go out and vote for them on election day. Both manufacturers and politicians create name recognition, employ product differentiation, try to associate with audiences, and use repetition to communicate their messages. These tactics are designed to affect our behavior both in the marketplace and in the election booth.

Political ads are more successful in motivating a candidate's supporters to go to the polls than they are in changing opponents into supporters. It is unlikely that a voter who dislikes a candidate or is committed to a candidate, and who has a lot of information about both candidates, will be persuaded by political advertising to change his or her vote. But many potential voters are undecided, and the support of many others is "soft."

Going to the polls on election day requires effort—people have errands to do, it may be raining, they may be tired. Television advertising is more effective with the marginal voters.

ELITES AND PUBLIC OPINION

Opinions flow downward from elites to masses. Public opinion rarely affects elite behavior, but elite behavior shapes public opinion. Elites are relatively unconstrained by public opinion for several reasons. First, few people among the masses have opinions on most policy questions confronting the nation's decision makers. Second, public opinion is very unstable; it can change in a matter of weeks in response to "news" events precipitated by elites. Third, elites do not have a clear perception of mass opinion. Most communications decision makers receive are from other elites—newsmakers, interest-group leaders, influential community leaders—not from ordinary citizens.

Absence of Public Opinion

Masses do not have opinions on most policy issues. Public opinion polls frequently create opinions by asking questions that respondents never thought about until they were asked.[16] Few respondents are willing to say they have no opinion; they believe they should provide some sort of answer, even if their opinion is weakly held or was nonexistent before the question was asked. Thus they produce "doorstep" opinions (see Chapter 8).

Instability of Public Opinion

Public opinion is very unstable: asked the same question at a later date, many respondents forget their earlier answers and give the pollster the opposite reply. One study estimates that less than 20 percent of the public holds meaningful, consistent opinions on key issues, even though two-thirds or more will respond to questions asked in a survey.[17]

Opinions also vary according to the wording of questions. One can word almost any public policy question to elicit mass approval or disapproval. Thus differently worded questions on the same issue can produce contradictory results.[18] Opinion polls that ask the same question at different times are more reliable indicators of public opinion than are one-time polls, in which respondents may be responding to the wording of the question. If pollsters use the same wording over time, they can more accurately observe changes in opinion.

Bias in Communication

Elites can easily misinterpret public opinion because most of the communications they receive have an upper-class bias. Members of the masses seldom call or write their senators or representatives, much less converse with them at dinners, cocktail parties, or other social occasions. Most of the communications that decision makers receive are *intra-elite* communications—communications from newspeople, organized group leaders, influential constituents, wealthy political contributors, and personal friends—people who for the most part share the same views. Not surprisingly, therefore, legislators say that most of their mail agrees with their position; their world of public opinion is self-reinforcing. Moreover, people who initiate communication with decision makers, by writing or calling or visiting their representatives, are decidedly more educated and affluent than the average citizen.

Elite Response to Mass Opinion

Do elites respond to public opinion, or do they shape public opinion to conform to their own attitudes? When government policy and public opinion are in agreement, is it because elites adapted policy to prevailing opinion or because elites molded opinion to conform to predetermined policy? These questions are difficult to answer. Yet policies are so often enacted in the face of widespread public opposition, which eventually melts away into acquiescence, that public opinion seems to follow elite decisions rather than the other way around.

Consider national policy on civil rights, one of the few areas in which Americans demonstrably have opinions. Here the decisions of courts, Congress, and executive bureaucracies have consistently run contrary to public opinion.

When the Supreme Court decided in *Brown* v. *Board of Education of Topeka* (1954) that segregation of the races in public schools violated the equal protection clause of the Fourteenth Amendment of the Constitution, a majority of Americans opposed sending their children to integrated schools. Not until several years after that historic decision did a majority of Americans come to favor school integration. In 1967 a public referendum in California resulted in an overwhelming defeat of a "fair housing" proposal, which would have forbidden discrimination in the sale or rental of housing. One year later, Congress passed the Civil Rights Act of 1968, which, among several things, outlawed discrimination in the sale or rental of housing. Several states have held referenda on busing—the assignment and transportation of children to public schools to achieve racial balance in the classroom. Voters have rejected busing in every such referendum, sometimes by margins of 75 to 80 percent; yet the Supreme Court has held that busing may be necessary in schools with a history of racial segregation. The Court's policy answers to the requirements of the Constitution, not to public opinion. In short, elite support for civil rights at the national level is not a response to mass opinion.

When political scientist V. O. Key, Jr., wrestled with the same problem—what impact, if any, does mass opinion have on public policy?—he concluded that the "missing piece of the puzzle" was "that thin stratum of persons referred to variously as the political elite, the political activists, the leadership echelons, or the influentials."[19] In other words, elite opinion, not mass opinion, shapes public policy. Elite preferences are more likely to agree with public policy than are mass preferences. Of course, this fact does not prove that elite preferences determine policies. Policy makers may be acting rationally in response to events and conditions, and well-educated, informed elites understand and approve of government actions more than masses do.

—— SUMMARY

Communications in the American political system flow downward from elites to masses. Elites are generally isolated from public opinion—not only because the masses do not have opinions on most issues but also because of the many barriers to accurate assessment of public opinion. Our analysis fits the elitist notion that elites are subject to relatively little direct influence from masses. Elites influence mass opinion more than masses influence elite opinion.

1. Television is the principal means by which elites communicate to masses. Control of the flow of information to the masses is highly concentrated. Three television networks and a handful of prestigious news organizations decide what will be the "news."

2. The political functions of the mass media include newsmaking (deciding what to report), interpretation (providing the masses with explanations of events), socialization (teaching about preferred norms, values, and lifestyles), persuasion (making direct efforts to affect behavior), and agenda setting.

3. The most important power of the mass media is agenda setting—deciding what will be decided. The media decide what conditions in society to label "crises" or "problems" or "issues" and thereby place these topics on the agenda of national decision makers.

4. Bias in the news arises from the newsmakers' own liberal-establishment views, plus the need to dramatize and sensationalize the news. However, the newsmakers' concentration on scandal and corruption in government often produces "television malaise"—social distrust, political cynicism, and feelings of powerlessness—instead of reform.

5. "Selective perception" among the masses—the tendency to screen out information with which one disagrees—frequently causes them to resist elite indoctrination through the mass media. In such situations, the masses see violence, disorder, or war on television but ignore the elite messages attached to what they see.

6. Television has brought about major changes in politics. It has contributed to the decline of political parties; it has replaced parties as kingmakers; it has encouraged image voting; it has fostered the use of

professional advertising techniques for media campaigns; and it has added to the cost of running for public office.

7. Masses seldom have opinions on specific issues. Pollsters may create "doorstep" opinions by asking questions that respondents had not thought of before the survey. Moreover, public opinion is unstable; it changes over time and may respond to the wording of the question. Elites receive most communications from other elites. This intra-elite communication usually reinforces elite views.

8. No evidence suggests that public policy reflects mass opinion. Civil rights laws, for example, came about despite majority opposition. Public policy changes with shifts in elite, not mass, opinion.

——— NOTES

1. *Public Opinion,* August/September 1979.
2. For a comprehensive examination of the power of the mass media in American politics, see Thomas R. Dye and Harmon Zeigler, *American Politics in the Media Age,* 3rd ed. (Pacific Grove, Calif.: Brooks/Cole, 1989).
3. E. E. Schattschneider, *The Semisovereign People* (New York: Holt, Rinehart & Winston, 1961), p. 61.
4. J. M. McCleod, L. B. Becker, and J. F. Byrne, "Another Look at the Agenda-Setting Function of the Press," *Communications Research* 1 (April 1974): 131–166; see also "The Political Consequences of Agenda-Setting," *Mass Communications Review* (Spring 1976): 8–15; and D. L. Shaw and M. E. McCombs, eds., *The Emergence of American Political Issues* (New York: West, 1977).
5. Doris A. Braber, *Mass Media and American Politics* (Washington, D.C.: Congressional Quarterly, 1980), p. 41.
6. John Johnstone, Edward Slawski, and William Bowman, *The Newspeople* (Urbana: University of Illinois Press, 1976), pp. 225–226.
7. Stephen Hess, *The Washington Reporters* (Washington, D.C.: Brookings Institution, 1981).
8. Ben J. Wattenberg, *The Good News Is the Bad News Is Wrong* (New York: Simon and Schuster, 1984).
9. Linda S. Lichter and S. Robert Lichter, *Prime Time Crime* (Washington, D.C.: The Media Institute, 1986).
10. See Michael J. Robinson, "Public Affairs Television and the Growth of Political Malaise," *American Political Science Review* 70 (June 1976): 409–432.
11. See Erwin G. Krasnow, Lawrence D. Longley, and Herbert A. Terry, *The Politics of Broadcast Regulation,* 3rd ed. (New York: St. Martin's, 1982), Chap. 1.
12. Bernard Cohen, *The Press and Foreign Policy* (Princeton: Princeton University Press, 1963), p. 10.

13. Austin Ranney, *Channels of Power* (New York: Basic Books, 1983), p. 11.
14. Carl Bernstein, "The Idiot Culture," *The New Republic,* June 8, 1992, p. 24.
15. Benjamin I. Page, Robert Y. Shapiro, and Glenn R. Dempsey, "What Moves Public Opinion," *American Political Science Review* 81 (March 1987): 23–24, 37.
16. Robert S. Erikson and Norman R. Luttbeg, *American Public Opinion: Its Origins, Content, and Import* (New York: Wiley, 1973).
17. Philip Converse, "Attitudes and Non-Attitudes," in Edward R. Tufte, ed., *Quantitative Analysis of Social Problems* (Reading, Mass.: Addison-Wesley, 1970), pp. 168–189.
18. Erikson and Luttbeg, op. cit., p. 38.
19. V. O. Key, Jr., *Public Opinion and American Democracy* (New York: Knopf, 1967), p. 537.

SELECTED READINGS

Dye, Thomas R., Zeigler, Harmon, and Lichter, S. Robert. *American Politics in the Media Age,* 4th ed. Pacific Grove, Calif.: Brooks/Cole, 1992. A comprehensive examination of the influence of the mass media in all aspects of American politics.

Epstein, Edward J. *News from Nowhere.* New York: Random House, 1973. Epstein discusses the mirror myth of television and discloses in detail how network television executives create news.

Graber, Doris A. *Mass Media and American Politics,* 3rd ed. Washington, D. C.: Congressional Quarterly Press, 1989. A wide-ranging description of media effects on campaigns and elections, as well as on social values and public policy.

Halberstam, David. *The Powers That Be.* New York: Knopf, 1979. This history of the growth of power of the mass media focuses on CBS, the *New York Times, Time* magazine, and the *Washington Post.*

Lichter, S. Robert, Rothman, Stanley, and Lichter, Linda S. *The Media Elite.* Bethesda, Md.: Adler & Adler, 1986. A comprehensive study of the social, psychological, and political orientations of the leadership of the mass media, based on extensive interviews in the most influential media outlets.

Page, Benjamin I., Shapiro, Robert, and Dempsey, Glenn R. "What Moves Public Opinion." *American Political Science Review* 81 (March 1987): 23–43. Results of an experimental study, over fifteen years, of the effects of network television news on viewer policy preferences, which show that the opinions of news commentators have a strong impact on viewers.

Ranney, Austin. *Channels of Power.* New York: Basic Books, 1983. A general assessment of how television has changed American politics, especially how television has weakened political parties, undermined the credibility of political leaders, and reduced the time available to elected officials to put their programs into effect.

Robinson, Michael J. "Public Affairs Television and the Growth of Political Malaise." *American Political Science Review* 70 (1976): 409–432. Robinson examines the impact of negative television journalism on mass attitudes, including increases in feelings of distrust, cynicism, and powerlessness.

Robinson, Michael J. "Television and American Politics: 1956–1976." *Public Interest* 52 (Summer 1978): 3–29. This thoughtful essay about videopolitics explores the impact of both news and entertainment programming on mass attitudes.

7

American Political Parties: A System in Decay

★ *Organization implies the tendency to oligarchy. Every party . . . becomes divided into a minority of directors and a majority of directed.*

Roberto Michels, Political Parties, *1915*

Traditional political science asserted that parties were indispensable to democracy: "Political parties created modern democracy and modern democracy is unthinkable save in terms of parties."[1]

Parties were once viewed as necessary instruments of popular control of government. But we will show, in this chapter, that the two major political parties in the United States have little incentive to offer clear policy alternatives; that Democratic and Republican voters do not divide clearly along liberal and conservative lines; that most voters describe themselves as moderate to conservative, but they do not always hold policy views consistent with their self-descriptions; that party organizations are oligarchic and dominated by activists who are largely out of touch with the voters; that candidates are selected in primary elections in which personal organization and financial assets, not party organizational support, are crucial to victory; that party voting in general elections is declining over time; and that television has replaced party organizations as a means of linking candidates to voters. In short, the American party system fails to provide the masses with an effective means to direct public policy.

PARTIES: PLURALIST THEORY IN DISARRAY

Pluralist political theory developed a "responsible party" model of the American system that viewed the parties as principal instruments of popular control of government. "Responsible parties" were supposed to:

1. develop and clarify alternative policy positions for the voters;
2. educate the people about the issues and simplify choices for them;
3. recruit candidates for public office who agreed with party policy positions;
4. organize and direct their candidates' campaigns to win office;
5. hold their elected officials responsible for enacting party policy positions after they were elected; and
6. organize legislatures to ensure party control of policy making.

In carrying out these functions, responsible parties were supposed to modify the demands of special interests, build a consensus that could win majority support, and provide simple and identifiable, yet meaningful, choices for the voters on election day. In this way, disciplined, issue-oriented, competitive parties would be the principal means by which the people would direct public policy.

But this responsible party model fell into disarray over the years, if indeed it ever accurately described the American political system. There are some very fundamental problems with this pluralist model of the parties:

1. *The parties do not offer the voters clear policy alternatives.* Instead, each tries to capture the broad center of most policy dimensions, where it believes most Americans can be found. There is no incentive for parties to stand on the far right or far left when most Americans are found in the center. So the parties echo each other, and critics refer to them as "Tweedledee and Tweedledum." Indeed, *voter decisions are seldom based on the policy stands of candidates or parties.* As we shall see in Chapter 8, most voters cast their votes on the basis of candidate "image," the "goodness" or "badness" of the times, and traditional voting habits. As a result, the parties and candidates have little incentive to concentrate on issues. Party platforms are seldom read by anyone. Modern campaign techniques focus on the image of the candidate—compassion, warmth, good humor, experience, physical appearance, ease in front of a camera, and so forth—rather than positions on the issues.

2. *The parties themselves are oligarchies, dominated by active, ideologically motivated elites.* The active party elites, for example, delegates to the national conventions, hold policy views that do not reflect the opinions of the rank and file. Democratic party activists are far more liberal than Democratic voters, and Republican party activists are more conservative than Republican voters.

3. *Primary elections determine nominees, not party organizations.* The progressive reformers who introduced primary elections at the beginning of the twentieth century wanted to undercut the power of party machines in determining who runs for office, and the reformers succeeded in doing so. Nominees now establish personal organizations in primary elections; they do not have to negotiate with party leaders.

4. *Party loyalties have been declining over the years.* Most people remain registered as Democrats or Republicans in order to vote in party primary elections, but increasing numbers of people identify themselves as "independent" and cast their vote in general elections without reference to party. Split-ticket voting (where a single voter casts his or her vote for a Democrat in one race and a Republican in another) is also increasing.

5. *The mass media, particularly television, have replaced the party as a means of political communication.* Candidates can come directly into the voter's living room via television. Campaigning is now largely a media activity. Candidates no longer need party workers to carry their message from block to block.

Despite these problems, the American political parties survive. They are important in the selection of *personnel* for public office, if not for the selection of public policy. Very few Independents are ever elected to high political office. Serious candidates for the presidency, the U.S. Senate, the House of Representatives, state governorships, and state legislatures (in every state except nonpartisan Nebraska) must first win Democratic or Republican party nomination.

DEMOCRATIC AND REPUBLICAN PARTIES: CONSENSUS OR COMPETITION?

The " Tweedledum and Tweedledee" image of American political parties contains a great deal of truth; the Democratic and the Republican parties do in fact share the same fundamental political ideology.* Both parties reflect prevailing elite consensus on basic democratic values: the sanctity of private property, a free-enterprise economy, individual liberty, limited government, majority rule, and due process of law. Moreover, since the 1930s both parties have supported the public-oriented, mass-welfare domestic programs of the "liberal establishment": social security, fair labor standards, unemployment compensation, a graduated income tax, a national highway program, a federally aided welfare system, countercyclical fiscal and monetary policies, and government regulation of banking, transportation, food and drugs, labor relations, and the environment. Finally, both parties have supported the basic outlines of U.S. foreign and military policy since World War II: international involvement, containing Soviet expansion, European recovery, the North Atlantic Treaty Organization, military preparedness, and even the Korean and Vietnam wars. Rather than promoting competition over national goals and programs, the parties reinforce social consensus and limit the area of legitimate political conflict.[2]

The major parties are not, of course, identical. The social bases of the parties are slightly different. Both parties draw their support from all social groups in the United States, but the Democrats draw disproportionately from labor, urban workers, Jews, Catholics, and blacks, and the Republicans draw disproportionately from rural, small-town, and suburban Protestants; business interests; and professionals. To the extent that the aspirations of these two broad groups differ, the thrust of party ideology also differs. The difference, however, is not very great. Democratic identifiers—those who identify themselves as Democrats—are only slightly more to the left than Republicans are. The more active partisans, however, are more ideologically distinct. Republican and Democratic activists are more conservative and more liberal, respectively, than less active supporters of the parties are (see Figure 7-1).

However, both parties' nominees, if they are to succeed, must appeal to the center. With only two parties and an overwhelmingly nonideological electorate, "consumer demand" requires that party ideologies be ambiguous and moderate. Therefore we cannot expect the parties, which seek

*Marxists traditionally attacked the American two-party system on the grounds that both parties supported capitalism. At one time the Communist party of the USSR justified its own one-party monopoly by comparing it to the American party system: "In the USSR we have one party with one name; in the USA you have one party with two names."

FIGURE 7-1   Comparison of party officials to public in political ideology (self-described)

"How would you describe your views on most political matters?
Generally, do you think of yourself as liberal, moderate, or conservative?"

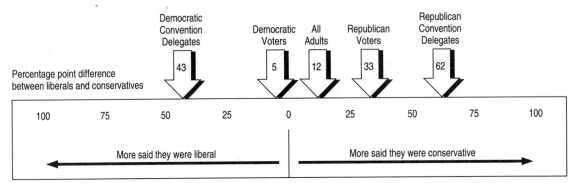

SOURCE: *New York Times*, August 21, 1992, p. A-12. Copyright © 1992 by The New York Times Company. Reprinted by permission.

to attract the maximum number of voters, to take up liberal and conservative positions supported by only minorities in the population.

Republican conservative Barry Goldwater in 1964 and Democratic liberal George McGovern in 1972 demonstrated that strong ideological stances will *not* win presidential elections in the United States. In 1964 the Republicans offered a clear ideological alternative to the majority party that is notable in recent American political history. Goldwater, the Republican presidential candidate challenging Democrat Lyndon Johnson, specifically rejected moderation ("Moderation in defense of liberty is no virtue") and defended extremism ("Extremism in defense of liberty is no vice.") His overwhelming defeat counters the argument that the masses want a party that offers a clear ideological choice. A party with a pure liberal position will suffer disastrous defeat as well. In 1972 Democrat McGovern seriously overestimated the liberalism of the electorate in his race against Republican Richard Nixon. Like Goldwater, McGovern lost in a landslide. It is true that Ronald Reagan won two presidential elections with conservative rhetoric. But Reagan's conservatism was closer to mainstream opinion than Goldwater's. More important, Reagan's personal charm, relaxed manner, and reassuring words convinced voters that he was no extremist. Indeed his most effective appeals were non-ideological; for example, when running against President Jimmy Carter in 1980, he asked voters, "Are you better off than you were four years ago?" In the 1988 presidential election, George Bush sought to avoid a conservative label, calling for a "kinder, gentler America" and successfully labeling his opponent Michael Dukakis as someone "out there, out of the mainstream."

In short, since the first goal of a party is to win elections, strong ideology and policy innovation are counterproductive. Firmer, more precise statements of ideology by the political parties would probably create new

TABLE 7-1   Vote in presidential elections, 1968–1992, by demographic factors

Demographic factors	1972 McGovern	1972 Nixon	1976 Carter	1976 Ford	1980 Carter	1980 Reagan	1980 Anderson	1984 Mondale	1984 Reagan	1988 Dukakis	1988 Bush	1992 Bush	1992 Clinton	1992 Perot
National	**38%**	**62%**	**50%**	**48%**	**41%**	**51%**	**7%**	**41%**	**59%**	**46%**	**54%**	**38%**	**43%**	**19%**
SEX														
Male	37	63	53	45	38	53	7	37	61	41	57	38	41	21
Female	38	62	48	51	44	49	6	42	57	49	51	37	46	17
RACE														
Whites	32	68	46	52	36	56	7	34	66	40	59	41	39	20
Blacks	87	13	85	15	86	10	2	90	9	86	12	11	82	7
EDUCATION														
College	37	63	42	55	35	53	10	40	59	31	62	41	40	19
High school	34	66	54	46	43	51	5	39	60	49	50	36	43	20
Grade school	49	51	58	41	54	42	3	49	50	56	43	28	56	17
OCCUPATION														
Prof. & business	31	69	42	56	33	55	10	37	62	40	59	48	36	16
White-collar	36	64	50	48	40	51	9	40	59	42	57	38	42	20
Manual	43	57	58	41	48	46	5	46	53	50	49	23	59	18
AGE														
Under 30 years	48	52	53	45	47	41	11	41	58	47	52	34	44	22
30–49 years	33	67	48	49	38	52	8	40	59	45	54	38	42	20
50 years & older	36	64	52	48	41	54	4	37	62	46	54	40	45	15
RELIGION														
Protestant	30	70	46	53	39	54	6	26	73	33	66	46	33	12
Catholic	48	52	57	42	46	47	6	44	55	47	52	36	44	20
REGION														
East	42	58	51	47	43	47	9	47	52	49	50	35	47	18
Midwest	40	60	48	50	41	51	7	38	61	47	52	37	42	21
South	29	71	54	45	44	52	3	36	63	41	58	43	42	16
West	41	59	46	51	35	54	9	40	49	46	52	34	44	22
Members of labor union families	46	54	63	36	50	43	5	53	45	57	42	24	55	21

Note: 1976 and 1980 results do not include vote for minor-party candidates.
SOURCES: *Gallup Political Indexes*, 1968–1989; *New York Times*, November 5, 1992.

lines of cleavage and eventually fragment the parties. The development of a clear liberal or conservative ideology by either party would only cost it votes.

DECLINING MASS ATTACHMENTS TO PARTIES

For many years party identification among voters remained remarkably stable. (Party identification is determined by survey responses to the

TABLE 7-2 Partisan identification, national election studies, 1952–1990 (percent)

	1952	1954	1956	1958	1960	1962	1964	1966	1968	1970	1972	1974	1976	1978	1980	1982	1984	1986	1988	1990
Strong Democrat	22	22	21	27	20	23	27	18	20	20	15	17	15	15	18	20	17	18	17	20
Weak Democrat	25	25	23	22	25	23	25	28	25	24	26	21	25	24	23	24	20	22	18	19
Independent Democrat	10	9	6	7	6	7	9	9	10	10	11	13	12	14	11	11	11	10	12	12
Independent	6	7	9	7	10	8	8	12	11	13	13	15	15	14	13	11	11	12	11	11
Independent Republican	7	6	8	5	7	6	6	7	9	8	10	9	10	10	10	8	12	11	13	12
Weak Republican	14	14	14	17	14	16	14	15	15	15	13	14	14	13	14	14	15	15	14	15
Strong Republican	14	13	15	11	16	12	11	10	10	9	10	8	9	8	9	10	12	10	14	10
Apolitical	3	4	4	4	2	4	1	1	1	1	1	3	1	3	2	2	2	2	2	2
Total	101	100	100	100	100	99	101	100	101	100	99	100	101	101	100	100	100	100	101	101
Number of interviews	1,784	1,130	1,757	1,808	1,911	1,287	1,550	1,278	1,553	1,501	2,694	2,505	2,850	2,283	1,613	1,418	2,236	2,166	2,032	1,991

Note: Question: "Generally speaking, do you consider yourself a Republican, a Democrat, an Independent, or what?" If Republican or Democrat: "Would you call yourself a strong (R/D) or a not very strong (R/D)?" If Independent or other: "Do you think of yourself as closer to the Republican or Democratic party?"
SOURCE: Calculated by the editors from National Election Studies data (Ann Arbor, Mich.: Center for Political Studies, University of Michigan).

question, "Generally speaking, do you usually think of yourself as a Republican, a Democrat, an Independent, or what?") However, indications of a weakening of the American party system are found in the steady rise of self-described "Independents" and "weak" Democrats and Republicans. Today fewer than 30 percent of voters are strong party identifiers (see Table 7-2).

This decline in party identification among voters is possibly the most "dramatic change in the American public over the past two decades." For political party organizations, the need to attract independent voters makes candidates with strong partisan images unattractive.

The Democratic party has long held a decided edge among American voters in both registration and self-identification. Nationwide Democratic registration exceeds Republican registration by almost two to one. But this Democratic party loyalty has been gradually eroded by popular Republican presidents.

Party identification is very closely associated with voter choice at the polls. Most voters cast their ballots for the candidates of their party. This is true in presidential elections (see Table 7-3) and even more true in congressional and state elections. Democratic party identifiers are somewhat more likely to vote for a Republican presidential candidate than Republican party identifiers are likely to vote for a Democrat. And Independents have tended to vote Republican in presidential elections. Indeed, the key to the success of Republican presidential candidates over the years has been their ability to win the votes of Independents and Democrats.

TABLE 7-3 Party and voter choice in presidential elections

	Percentage of Republicans	Percentage of Democrats	Percentage of Independents
1992			
Republican: Bush	73	10	32
Democrat: Clinton	10	77	38
Perot	17	13	30
1988			
Republican: Bush	92	17	55
Democrat: Dukakis	8	82	43
1984			
Republican: Reagan	92	26	63
Democrat: Mondale	7	73	35
1980			
Republican: Reagan	86	26	55
Democrat: Carter	8	69	29
Independent: Anderson	5	4	14
1976			
Republican: Ford	91	18	57
Democrat: Carter	9	82	38
1972			
Republican: Nixon	95	33	69
Democrat: McGovern	5	67	31

Voters in general are losing their party allegiances, even though partisan affiliation remains the best explanation of individual voting choice in presidential elections. But the drift has been more damaging to the Democratic party. The percentage of the population identifying with the Republican party is increasing, while the percentage identifying with the Democratic party is declining. Figure 7-2 shows that these changes appear to be long-term, rather than dependent upon the attraction of a particular candidate. Among all voters, the Democratic advantage has shrunk to three points (34 percent of voters are Democrats, and 31 percent are Republicans). Among whites, the Republicans have enjoyed a slight advantage since 1985. Significantly, the largest part of the population (unreported in the figure) is without party identification (35 percent). Moreover, the Republican gains go against the general trend of decline in party loyalty.

FIGURE 7-2   Changes in party allegiance

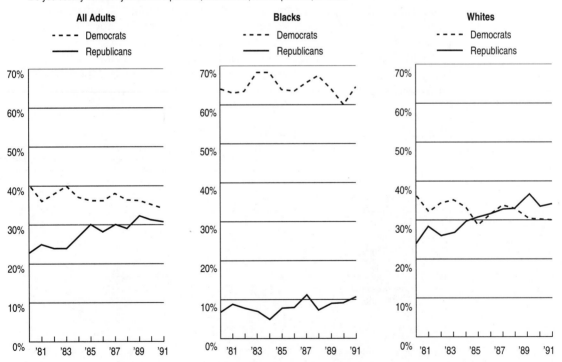

Do you usually consider yourself a Republican, a Democrat, an independent, or what?

Based on 120 polls by the *New York Times* and CBS News that have been pooled for each year. A total of 162,589 adults were interviewed by telephone nationwide from January 1980 through June 1991. Independents and those with no response are not shown.

SOURCE: *New York Times,* July 14, 1992, p. 1. Copyright © 1992 by The New York Times Company. Reprinted by permission.

ARE DEMOCRATS LIBERAL AND REPUBLICANS CONSERVATIVE?

Democratic and Republican voters cannot be clearly differentiated along liberal and conservative lines. If they could be—if the Republican party attracted most conservatives and the Democratic party most liberals—the Democratic party would no longer be the majority party, because more voters describe themselves as conservative than liberal.

The terms *liberal* and *conservative* have been used with different meanings over the years, so it is difficult to know whether Americans are really liberal or conservative. We can ask them questions like "How would you describe your own political philosophy—conservative, moderate, or liberal?" The results of surveys over recent years are shown in Figure 7-3. Self-described conservatives outnumber liberals by a large margin.

What do Americans mean when they label themselves as liberal, moderate, or conservative? This question has no clear answer. People who label themselves conservative do not consistently oppose social welfare programs or government regulation of the economy. People who label themselves liberals do not consistently support social welfare programs or government regulation of the economy. Nonetheless, more people prefer to label themselves conservative than liberal.

FIGURE 7-3   Ideology among all American adults

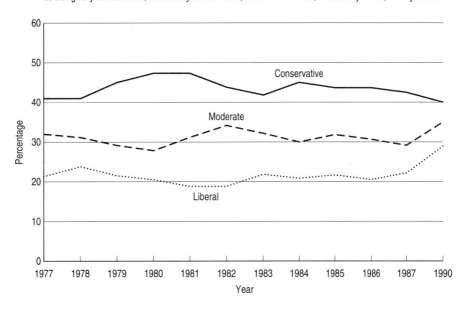

Question: Now, thinking politically and socially, how would you describe your general outlook—as being very conservative, moderately conservative, middle-of-the-road, moderately liberal, or very liberal?

SOURCE: *Public Opinion* (November/December 1987): 23. Reprinted with the permission of the American Enterprise Institute for Public Policy.

Democratic elites are far more liberal than the general electorate or even Democratic voters. Table 7-4 reveals that in 1988 conservatives in the electorate outnumbered liberals by about 30 to 20 percent. Democratic voters were fairly evenly split between liberals and conservatives. But among Democratic elites, self-identified liberals overwhelmed conservatives 39 percent to 5 percent. The liberal predisposition of Democratic leaders was even more obvious on the issues. While 33 percent of Democratic voters and 43 percent of the total electorate would prefer to reduce the size of the federal government, only 16 percent of Democratic leaders agree. In domestic policy only 43 percent of Democratic voters support current abortion laws, compared to 72 percent of Democratic leaders; only 45 percent of Democratic voters believe government does too

TABLE 7-4 Party and ideology

	Percentage of all adults	Percentage of Democratic voters	Percentage of Republican voters	Percentage of Democratic leaders*	Percentage of Republican leaders*
POLITICAL PHILOSOPHY					
Conservative	30	22	43	5	60
Liberal	20	25	12	39	1
GOVERNMENT ROLE					
Prefer smaller government, fewer services	43	33	59	16	87
Prefer larger government, more services	44	56	30	58	3
DOMESTIC POLICY					
Favor increased federal spending for day care	52	56	44	87	36
Abortion should remain legal	40	43	39	72	29
Government pays too little attention to blacks	34	45	19	68	14
FOREIGN POLICY					
Keep defense spending at least at current levels	66	61	73	32	84
Worry about Communist takeover of Central America	37	25	55	12	80

*Delegates to 1988 presidential nominating conventions
SOURCE: *New York Times*, August 14, 1988. Copyright © 1988 by The New York Times Company. Reprinted by permission.

little for blacks, compared to 68 percent of Democratic leaders. A large majority of Democratic voters want to keep defense spending at least at current levels, compared to only 32 percent of Democratic leaders.

While exact percentages and specific questions vary from one election to the next, the general pattern is clear: Democratic party activists are far more liberal than Democratic party voters or the general electorate. These party activists play the major role in the selection of the Democratic candidate. As a result, Democratic presidential candidates have been selected from the liberal wing of their party. The selection of liberal candidates provides an opportunity for the Republicans to win over Democratic party identifiers, particularly those who are conservative.

Thus, party elites in both parties are ideologically separated from their voters. Republican leaders are more conservative than either Republican voters or the general electorate. But because conservative positions are generally more popular than liberal positions among the electorate, the conservatism of Republican elites has not hurt their party in presidential elections as much as the liberalism of Democratic elites has hurt their presidential candidates.

POLITICAL PARTIES AS PAPER OLIGARCHIES

It is something of an irony that the parties, as the agents of democratic decision making, are not themselves democratic in their structures. One of the most sweeping indictments of political parties on this count comes from the political philosopher Roberto Michels, whose "iron law of oligarchy" leads him to conclude that "every party . . . becomes divided into a minority of directors and a majority of directed."[3]

American political parties are skeletal organizations, "manned generally by small numbers of activists and involving the great masses of their supporters scarcely at all."[4] In essence, power in the parties rests in the hands of those who have the time and the money to make it a full-time, or nearly full-time, occupation. Party activists—no more than 3 or 4 percent of the adult population—can decide what product is to be offered to political consumers (the party in the electorate). Beyond this link, the party activists and electorate have little interaction.

Who are the party activists? We know, from research cited in other chapters, that the activists are strongly ideological and committed to the norms of the democratic decision-making process. Since these characteristics describe the upper socioeconomic groups, it is not surprising that party activists are of relatively high socioeconomic status and come from families with a history of party activity. The highest socioeconomic levels are found in the highest echelons of the party organization. More than 70 percent of delegates to the Democratic and Republican national conventions are college graduates and almost half have graduate degrees. All but a handful are professionals or managers, and most enjoy incomes well above that of the average American (see Table 7-5). As political scientist Frank Sorauf notes, "The parties . . . attract men and women with the time and financial resources to be able to afford politics, with the information and knowledge to understand it, and with the skills to be useful in it."[5]

Political Parties: The End of Organization

Political parties are said to be agents of democratic decision making. Traditionally, political parties have been oligarchies; the infamous "smoke-

TABLE 7-5   Party delegates, 1988 presidential nominating conventions

	Democrats	Republicans
AGE		
18–29	4%	4%
30–39	22	13
40–49	33	28
50–59	25	30
60 +	16	25
DELEGATE TO LAST CONVENTION		
Yes	38%	41%
No	62	59
RELIGION		
Protestant	51%	70%
Catholic	30	24
Jewish	6	2
RACE		
Black	21%	3%
White	70	96
EDUCATION		
High school	9%	10%
Some college	18	21
College graduate	21	26
Post graduate	52	42
SEX		
Male	48%	63%
Female	52	37
POLITICAL PHILOSOPHY		
Very liberal	15%	*
Somewhat liberal	24	1%
Moderate	50	36
Somewhat conservative	3	41
Very conservative	8	19

*Less than half of 1 percent.
SOURCE: *New York Times,* August 14, 1988. Copyright © 1988 by The New York Times Company. Reprinted by permission.

filled room" phrase was coined to inculpate the party bosses who, as late as 1968, picked presidential candidates without having to heed public opinion. One of the most sweeping indictments of political parties comes from the political philosopher Roberto Michels, whose "iron law of oligarchy" leads him to conclude that "every party . . . becomes divided into a minority of directors and a majority of directed."[6] Michels assumed a party organization with genuine power to select candidates, a condition that no longer exists in the United States. There are indeed party activists, state and national committees that meet and compete for the allocation of intraparty spoils. Both the Democratic and Republican parties have national committees with full-time staffs, and both parties have various policy commissions and caucuses that attract the attention of the energetic few. 1992 Democratic party nominee Bill Clinton was an active member of the Democratic Leadership Council, a group of moderate party activists seeking to avert another in a string of defeats. The participants in the various party organizations and the delegates to the national conventions are hardly typical of the ordinary voters (see Table 7-5). But, as Herrnson explains, "Most candidates for elective office in the United States are self-recruited and conduct their own nominating campaigns."[7] Members of Congress are individual entrepreneurs who raise their own money to direct their own campaigns. Nor do party organizations select nominees for the presidency. Equally important, the party organizations cannot keep a candidate out of the race. Pat Buchanan, running against the incumbent Republican George Bush in the primary elections of 1992, embarrassed the president with higher than expected support among voters. In the Democratic primaries, former California Governor Jerry Brown, without a chance of success, harassed Bill Clinton and temporarily reduced the probability of Clinton's eventual success. No party organization could influence the behavior of either Buchanan or Brown.[8]

PRESIDENTIAL PRIMARIES AND THE DETERIORATION OF PARTIES

The growth of presidential primaries is an institutional change as important as the decline in party identification among the masses. In their efforts to make the party organization more "responsive," Democratic reformers developed a set of rules for state nominating caucuses and conventions that were so complex that many states chose the primary election for selecting delegates to their national nominating conventions.

Consequently presidential primaries have increased beyond the reformers' original expectations. In 1968 the parties held 34 presidential primaries. In 1972, the year of the reforms, they held 45. Given the thrashing the Democrats received in 1972, one might have expected the party regulars to try to reverse the reforms. However, the presidential primary was too popular to banish. By 1976, 30 states held presidential primaries, and in 1980 the number had grown to 36. By 1980 three-fourths of all delegates were chosen by primaries (see Table 7-6). Though the Democrats have led the push toward democratization, the Republicans have moved in the same direction. The increased use of primaries has been written into state law and now generally applies to both parties.

Given the expanded role of primaries, do "the voters" now select the presidential nominees? Actual participation in presidential primaries is far less than in general elections. Whereas voting in general elections hovers around 50 percent, participation in presidential primaries does not exceed 30 percent of eligible voters. Clearly, with an average turnout of this size, primaries do not even in sheer numerical terms represent the voice of "the people."

In low-turnout elections, the higher social classes are the principal participants. Such is the case in primary elections. Participants come disproportionately from the college-educated, professionally employed, upper-middle classes. Conspicuously underrepresented in the primary electorate are working-class voters and ethnic minorities. The primary electorate is "the New Class—the young, college educated, professional, and managerial groups."[9]

Primary elections strengthen the influence of the ideological activists in each party. Liberals are overrepresented among Democratic primary voters and conservatives are overrepresented among Republican primary voters (see Table 7-6). But as the national electorate has been somewhat more conservative in its self-identification over the last decade, the Republican party has not suffered as much from the primary system as the Democratic party.

In the past, the primary system produced Democratic presidential nominees who were far more liberal in their views than rank-and-file Democrats in the electorate. Only Jimmy Carter's victory on the heels of Watergate in 1976 interrupted a string of Democratic presidential defeats that began in 1968, and it is important to note that Carter was the most conservative of the Democratic nominees—Humphrey, McGovern, Mondale, and Dukakis. Clinton succeeded as a moderate "new" Democrat.

TABLE 7-6 Influence of presidential primaries in convention votes, 1968–1992

	Democrats			Republicans		
Year	No. of primaries	No. of delegate votes	Percentage of all votes	No. of primaries	No. of delegate votes	Percentage of all votes
1968	17	983	37.5	16	458	34.3
1972	23	1,862	60.5	22	710	52.7
1976	30	2,183	72.6	29	1,533	67.9
1980	35	2,378	71.8	36	1,516	76.0
1984	25	2,431	62.1	30	1,551	71.0
1988	35	2,842	68.0	36	1,771	78.0
1992	37	3,261	76.0	38	1,840	84.0

The nomination process begins with the Iowa caucuses in February, followed by the first primary election: New Hampshire, a tiny state that has jealously guarded its position as the first state to hold a primary in a presidential year. The tradition certainly has nothing to do with the strategic importance of New Hampshire in terms of delegate strength. New Hampshire's voters account for less than 1 percent of all votes cast in Democratic primaries, and they choose less than 1 percent of the delegates to the Democratic convention. Were it not for the fact that New Hampshire kicks off the season, it would be ignored. However, the extensive media coverage in the state might lead one to conclude that New Hampshire is a crucial state in the general election. Thus New Hampshire *is* crucial—as a media event.

Primaries provide an ideal opportunity for the media to separate the serious candidates from the aspirants (see Chapter 6). Although the primary electorate is more ideological than the electorate in general elections, the candidates rarely develop the issues well. Not only are early primaries frequently crowded with candidates, but the fact that the candidates are from the same party reduces the opportunity for exploring issues.

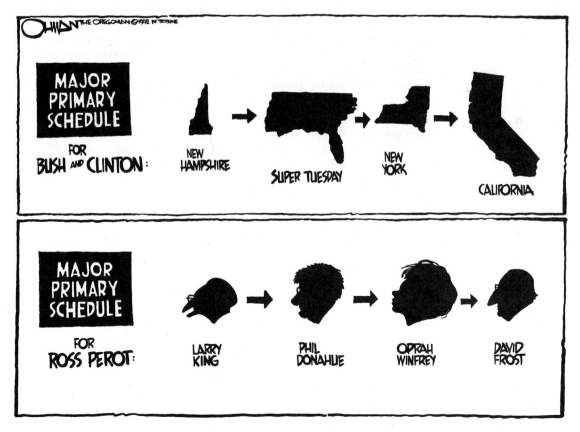

Reprinted by permission: Tribune Media Services.

TABLE 7-7   Primary and general election voters' ideology

	Florida	Illinois	Tennessee	Texas
Percentage of Democratic primary voters who call themselves liberals	30	38	30	34
Percentage of general election voters who call themselves liberals	21	25	18	21
Percentage of Republican primary voters who call themselves conservatives	60	55	59	65
Percentage of general election voters who call themselves conservatives	49	42	46	49

SOURCE: Derived from Elaine Ciyulla Kamark, "Structure as Strategy: Presidential Nominating Politics in the Post-Reform Era," in L. Sandy Maisel, ed., *The Parties Respond* (Boulder: Westview Press, 1990), p. 174.

Thus, a candidate's media image becomes crucial. Before the primary season, candidates seek to establish credibility as serious contenders of presidential caliber. They attempt to generate name familiarity (as revealed in public opinion surveys) and thus recognition first as serious candidates, not necessarily as front-runners. The proliferation of primaries and attendant media attention makes it possible for a candidate to become well known quickly. A reputation can be created by "a strong organization, plenty of funds, shrewd advisors, an appealing campaign style, and a good image on television, even if his position on issues is not well known and is likely to antagonize many voters once they have become familiar with it."[10]

The consequence of the primary system is that political party leaders—governors, senators, representatives, mayors, the heads of state party organizations, and the like—cannot control the selection of presidential candidates. Without the anchor of party identification, public opinion becomes more volatile, more susceptible to media manipulation. Politics without parties becomes even more issueless than it was in the past. The primary system has been a major factor in the demise of parties and the creation of the new media elite: "Because the competing candidates often share most ideological orientations, personal attributes such as appearance, style, and wit attain new importance (presidents today must be fit and not fat, amusing not dull, with cool not hot personalities)."[11]

Turnout in the Democratic primaries is quite low, averaging at most 20 percent of the eligible electorate. Although intended to make the nomination process more representative, the Democratic primaries attract only a small stratum of voters who are much more liberal than Democratic rank-and-file voters. (In 1992 about 19 percent of the general public claimed to be liberal, compared to 51 percent of the voters in Democratic primaries.) Thus, Democratic presidential hopefuls must project a *liberal* image to win primary elections and earn enough delegates for the nomination. Yet this liberal image has proved fatal in general elections with their moderate to conservative voters.

REALIGNMENT OR DEALIGNMENT?

In recent decades two clear trends have appeared in party identification among the public. First, the percentage of voters preferring *neither* party has increased substantially, and, second, the Democratic party has lost adherents. The rise of Independents and the decline of Democratic partisans are two major developments that tend to complement one another.

Dealignment refers to the decline in the attractiveness of either party. Dealignment is suggested by the growing number of people who have negative or neutral images of the parties and the growth in the belief that neither party can provide solutions for important problems.

Realignment is a more long-term change. Scholars are not in agreement as to whether a single election can be said to realign party identi-

CASE STUDY

 ### The Real Parties

In recent years, survey researchers have begun to suspect that the old liberal–conservative party dichotomy was of limited value. To better understand voting groups in the electorate, survey responses were factor-analyzed to discover eleven "real parties." Where do you fit?

	Percentage of electorate	Percentage of Bush voters
REPUBLICANS (30 PERCENT OF THE LIKELY ELECTORATE)		
Enterprisers: Affluent, educated, probusiness, antigovernment, worry about the deficit.	16	98
Moralists: Middle-aged, middle-income, antiabortion, pro-school prayer and promilitary.	14	96
INDEPENDENTS (24 PERCENT OF THE LIKELY ELECTORATE)		
Upbeats: Young, optimistic, strongly patriotic, progovernment, worry about the deficit.	9	83
Disaffected: Middle-aged, alienated, pessimistic, antigovernment and antibusiness, promilitary.	7	68
Followers: Young, little faith in America or interest in politics, worry about unemployment.	4	40
Seculars: Middle-aged, educated, nonreligious, pro-personal freedoms.	4	24
DEMOCRATS (41 PERCENT OF THE LIKELY ELECTORATE)		
'60s Democrats: Upper middle-class, identify with '60s peace, civil rights, and environmental movements.	11	12
New Dealers: Older, middle-income, religious, protectionist, pro-unions and progovernment.	15	27
Partisan poor: Militantly Democratic, pro-social spending, anti-tax hikes.	9	19
God and Country Democrats: Older, strong faith in America's institutions, pro-social spending and pro-tax hikes.	6	38

SOURCE: "The People, The Press, and Politics: Post-Election Typology Survey," November 1988, p. 22. Times-Mirror. Reprinted with permission.

fication, or whether it takes several elections. But scholars do share a basic understanding of what realignment looks like; it occurs when

> social groups change their party alignment; the party system realigns when the partisan bias of groups changes in ways that alter the social group profile of the parties. The changes may result from a previously Democratic group becoming Republican, [they] may reflect the development of a partisan cleavage among a group of voters who had not displayed any distinctive partisan bias, [and they] might also come about as a highly aligned group begins to lose its partisan distinctiveness.[12]

The major party realignment in recent decades has been the erosion of the Democratic party loyalty of white southern voters. White southerners, conservatives in disposition, have been drifting away from their traditional Democratic ties. Republican candidates swept the southern states in four presidential elections (Nixon in 1972, Reagan in 1980 and 1984, and Bush in 1988). Only in 1976 did Georgian Jimmy Carter and in 1992 Arkansan Bill Clinton move the southern states back into the Democratic column.

Yet many of the characteristics of great historical party realignments (such as the creation of the New Deal coalition that elected Franklin Roosevelt in the 1930s) are absent. Realignments in the past resulted in increased turnout, because massive shifts in preference generally were accompanied by increased interest in politics. But this effect did not occur in the Reagan victories. Traditionally, realignment also has changed the fortunes of the parties at the congressional and state levels. But Republican presidential victories in the South have *not* been accompanied by many victories at the state or local levels.

At the same time, short-term changes have been observed among other groups. Men, union members, and Catholics are more Republican now than they were in 1952, and so are younger voters. But these changes do not necessarily suggest that the Republican party will become a majority party. They do suggest that the Democratic advantage will not be as large as it once was.

Thus, there is a little bit of both realignment and dealignment going on. The rise of independents is strongly associated with the entry into the electorate of younger voters (see Figure 7-4). In the 1984 election, 61 percent of first-time voters chose Reagan, although their choice is less stable than the long-term change in the votes of white Southerners. In 1988, Bush drew 51 percent of first-time voters. As younger voters resist partisan identification throughout their lives, it is likely that the electorate will continue its independent course. This trend suggests dealignment. The independents, the young voters, are not establishing party ties as they grow older. The growth in the number of independents is not a result of the rejection of former loyalties by partisans; rather, it is a reflection of a changing electorate. Those who became eligible to vote after 1964 are less partisan than their predecessors. As time passes, the pre-

FIGURE 7-4   Age composition of Independent voters

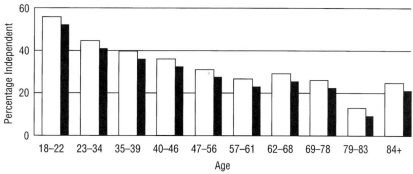

SOURCE: Survey Research Center, University of Michigan; data for 1984.

1964 generation of voters will be replaced by younger ones, with a continuing decline of partisan loyalties. Dealignment makes the future of either party more dependent upon a "star."

PARTY CAMPAIGN STRATEGIES

In general, political campaigns are designed to accomplish two important objectives: first, to win over the undecided or weak partisans among the voters; second, to motivate one's own supporters to turn out on election day. For Democratic candidates, the campaign strategy is simply to guarantee that Democratic identifiers vote for the Democratic candidate. Since more voters are Democratic identifiers than Republican identifiers, the Democrats should win, barring short-term forces. For example, if Democratic and Republican candidates had no image impact, if the issues were of no relevance, and if the turnout for each party matched predictions, the "normal vote" for the Democrats would be 54 percent. The normal vote is a model, not an actual occurrence, but like any other model it helps in understanding reality. For Republican candidates, the strategy is to attract independents and weak Democrats from their partisan affiliation, persuading them to vote more on issues or on the personalities or images of the candidates.

Strong partisan attitudes are generally stable; individual voters rarely change their party affiliation, Although the percentage of Independents is increasing and that of party identifiers decreasing, it is not because voters are converting from one party to another; rather it is because the new, younger voters lack strongly developed party affiliations.

The increased number of Independent voters adds an element of volatility in presidential elections. During these election campaigns, Independents, who are not tied to parties and who respond primarily to short-term forces such as candidate image, contribute to surges and declines in the polls.

Finally, although an individual's party identification may remain stable, individual Democratic identifiers increasingly have voted for the opposition party's candidate. Consequently, since 1960 the correlation between party identification and party voting has gradually weakened.

Strategic considerations must take into account another complicating factor of partisan identification: turnout. Despite the preponderance of Democratic identifiers, variations in turnout can favor Republican candidates. Since Republican voters typically are of higher socioeconomic status than are Democratic voters, their turnout rates are substantially higher. Hence, "getting out the vote" is a Democratic strategy, while stimulating short-term defection from party affiliation is a Republican strategy.

──── MEDIA CAMPAIGNS

Mass media campaigns, directed by professional public relations and advertising specialists, have replaced party organizations in political campaigns. Television has contributed to the decline of political parties; it has replaced party leaders as "kingmakers"; it has encouraged voting on the basis of candidate image; it has fostered the development of media campaigns with professional advertising techniques; and it has significantly increased the costs of running for public office. All these changes reduce the influence of masses in politics and contribute to the power of elites.

The Decline of Parties

The media have replaced the party organization as the principal link between the candidates and the voters. Candidates can take their campaigns directly to the voters. They can capture party nominations in primary elections dominated by television advertising. Party organizations have little to say about who wins the party's nomination and next to nothing to say about who wins in the general election. Aspiring candidates no longer begin their quest for public office by calling on party leaders but start instead by hiring professional media advertising firms. Both primary and general elections are now fought largely in the media.

Media as Kingmakers

Heavy media coverage creates candidates. The media provide name recognition, the first requirement for a successful candidate. Indeed, heavy media attention can transform previously unknown figures into instant candidates; candidates no longer need to spend long years in political apprenticeship in minor offices to run for Congress or a governorship. The media can also condemn an aspiring candidate to obscurity and defeat simply by failing to report his or her activities. Newsmakers select the "serious" candidates for coverage at the beginning of a race. In primary elections, the media even select "the real winner": if the favorite does not win by as large a margin as the media predicted, the media may declare the runner-up "the real winner" even when his or her vote total is less than that of the favorite. People who cannot perform well in front of a camera are no longer feasible candidates for major public office.

Image Elections

In covering elections, television largely ignores policy questions and focuses on candidate image—the personal traits of the candidates. Candidates are presented on television not in terms of their voting records or policy positions but instead on their ability to project a personal image of charm, warmth, "compassion," youth and vigor, honesty and integrity, and so forth. Elections are presented on television as struggles between competing personalities.

The media cover elections as a political game, made up of speeches, rallies, press conferences, travels, and perhaps debates. The media report on who is winning or losing, what their strategies are, how much money they are spending, how they look in their public appearances, the response of their audiences, and so on. It is not surprising that policy issues do not play a very large role in voters' decisions, because the media do not pay much attention to policy issues.

The Media Campaign

Professional media campaigns, usually directed by commercial advertising firms, have replaced traditional party-organized or amateur grass-roots campaigns. Today, professional media people may plan an entire campaign; develop computerized mailing lists for fund-raising; select a (simple) campaign theme and desirable candidate image; monitor the progress of the campaign with continuous voter polls; produce television tapes for commercials, as well as signs, bumper stickers, and radio spots; select the candidate's clothing and hairstyle; write speeches, schedule appearances that will attract new coverage; and even plan the victory party.

Professional campaign management begins with assessing the candidate's public strengths and weaknesses, evaluating those of the opponent, and determining the concerns uppermost in voters' minds. Early polls can test for name recognition, favorable or unfavorable images, and voter concerns; these polls then feed into the campaign strategy—helping to select a theme, choose an image for the candidate, and identify the opponent's weaknesses. Polls during the campaign chart the candidate's progress, assess the theme's effectiveness, and even identify undecided groups as targets for last-minute campaign efforts. "Negative" campaigns can stress the opponent's weaknesses. Most professional campaigning takes the form of paid television commercials, produced by experienced advertising agencies and shown in specific voter "markets." But a good media campaign manager also knows how to get the candidate "free" time on the evening news. Candidates must attract the media and convey a favorable image: they may visit an old people's home, a coal mine, a ghetto, or a pig farm to appeal to specific groups of voters. A candidate may work a day digging ditches (particularly if perceived as a playboy millionaire), or walk from city to city (particularly if the opponent flies in a chartered airplane), or participate in a hog-calling contest (particularly if viewed as too intellectual). Such activities are more likely to win a spot on the evening news than is a thoughtful speech on nuclear disarmament.

Elitist Effects of the Media

All these media effects on elections contribute to the relative power of elites. Local party organizations have been replaced by national media campaigns. Policy questions are largely ignored in elections, in favor of easily manipulated candidate images. (More about campaigning and voter choice appears in Chapter 8.) Grass-roots campaigning has been displaced by expensive, professional media campaigns, usually directed by commercial advertising agencies. The costs of campaigning have risen dramatically because of the high cost of television advertising. The first question any aspiring candidate faces today—from city hall to county courthouse to state capital to Washington—is how much money can be raised for the campaign. The high costs of a media campaign require that (1) the candidate be personally wealthy or have wealthy friends or (2) the candidate receive financial support from organized interests, usually the political action committees (or PACs) established by corporations, banks, professional associations, industry groups, unions, and other special interests. (The power of interest groups is discussed in Chapter 9.)

MONEY AND POLITICS

Political campaigns are becoming very costly. The costs of running for public office are being driven up primarily by the increased use of the mass media.

The "Bad Old Days"

Prior to the introduction of public financing for presidential elections, Republicans generally outspent Democrats. In the days before reform, serious candidates for national office needed to attract the support of wealthy "angels." Farsighted angels would select a politician early in his career and continue support for many years. Richard Nixon had his W. Clement Stone, a Chicago insurance tycoon; George McGovern had Steward Mott, heir to the General Motors fortune; Jimmy Carter had Paul Austin, chairman of the board of Coca-Cola; and Ronald Reagan had the "Ronald Reagan Trust Fund," overseen by William French Smith (later attorney general in the Reagan administration, and for years associated with Crocker National Bank) and Justin Dart, whose holding company controls Rexall Drugs. After public financing was introduced, individual contributions became less important than contributions of groups.

Democrats usually received less money than Republicans from the corporate world, although about half of Democratic funds came from corporations. Traditionally Democrats turned to big labor for support, notably to the AFL-CIO and the larger international unions like the United Auto Workers and United Steel Workers. Liberal Democrats also received support from upper-class liberal philanthropists.

"Reform" in Presidential Elections

Chronic Democratic campaign deficits were a stimulus to campaign "reform," especially when Democrats controlled both houses of Congress with a close presidential election approaching in 1976. In 1974, Congress passed a comprehensive campaign spending law, which created a Presidential Election Campaign Fund from voluntary checkoffs from individual income taxes of $1 per person, and established the Federal Election Commission (two members selected by the House, two by the Senate, and two by the president) to oversee federal election spending. The election commission distributes campaign monies from the fund to (1) candidates in the primaries (who could raise $5,000 in each of twenty states), (2) the Democratic and Republican parties for their national conventions, and (3) the Republican and Democratic candidates in the general election. The law also limits individual contributions in any election to $1,000 and organizational contributions to $5,000. Candidates must report all contributions to the Federal Election Commission.

The Supreme Court modified these provisions by declaring that, as an exercise of First Amendment rights, an individual can spend unlimited personal wealth on his or her own election campaign.[13] Moreover, also as an exercise of First Amendment rights, a person may spend any amount of personal wealth to advertise his or her own political views. As long as these independent expenditures are not tied directly to a political campaign, no legal limits apply. Although the campaign spending law, as modified by the Supreme Court, reduces the role of the financial angels, it permits wealthy people to spend large amounts on their own campaigns, thus keeping direct exercise of political power in the hands of the affluent (see Figure 7-5 and Table 7-8).

FIGURE 7-5 Average amount spent by the winners of congressional races each year, in millions of dollars

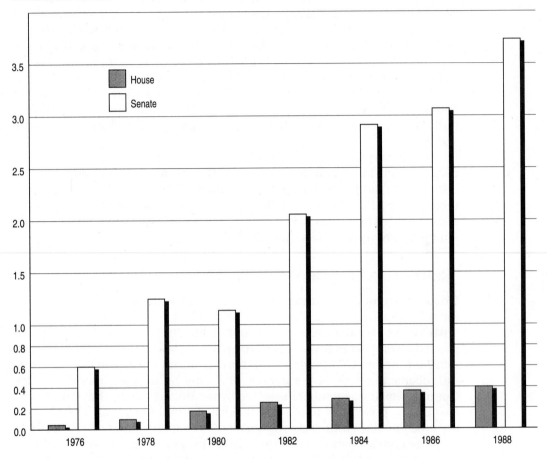

TABLE 7-8   Congressional campaign costs: 1972–1990 (millions of dollars)

	1972	1974	1976	1978	1980	1982	1984	1986	1988	1990
Senate	26	29	46	87	103	128	150	183	201	180
House	40	45	79	111	136	172	176	211	256	265
Total	66	74	125	198	239	300	326	394	457	445

SOURCE: Federal Election Commission

   PACs give most of their money to incumbents. (For more on PAC contributions, see Chapter 9.) The propensity of PACs for supporting incumbents gives incumbents of either party an advantage. The advantage has lain with the Democrats, since Democrats outnumber Republicans in Congress.

What Does the Money Buy?

Money does not guarantee victory, but it does guarantee the *opportunity* for victory. Without good financing, potential candidates do not become candidates. With good financing, potential candidates can hire consultants—media experts, pollsters, direct mailing specialists, voice coaches, statisticians, speech writers, and makeup artists—to give their campaigns appeal. Not only do the consultants charge a lot (perhaps $250 per hour) but the technology they employ—computers, interviews, and television—is costly. Some candidates have paid for daily surveys, seeking to monitor every nuance of voter reaction. Because consultants need success in order to build their reputations, they too shun underfunded candidates. One student of consulting concludes that "you need $150,000 just to get in the door to see a consultant."[14]

Indeed, consultants, fueled by PACs, are far more important to candidates than political parties are. Not only have they usurped the role of parties in the campaign (volunteer doorbell-ringers are fast becoming a relic of the past), but they also encourage candidates to deemphasize issues and concentrate on image. The "three Ps"—polling, packaging, and promotion—are more important than parties, grass-roots support, and the development of strong positions on the issues.

The Return of the "Fat Cats"

Although the political action committees foot a good part of the bill, wealthy individual candidates, unrestrained by campaign contribution limitations, are still in a strong position after the "reforms." Those who have the money to get into a consultant's office can be off and running early in a campaign. Wealthy candidates, armed with their consultants, can meet start-up costs promptly and attract the attention of the political action committees, building upon their initial advantage. Candidates who are personally wealthy are given a substantial head start.

Whatever the reformers' goals, their work has made the electoral process even more the property of wealthy candidates, consultants, and political action committees. Party "bosses" are gone, but these new elites have replaced them.

——— SUMMARY

Elitism asserts that elites share a consensus about the fundamental values of the political system. The elite consensus does not mean that elite members never disagree or never compete with one another for preeminence. But elitism implies that competition centers on a narrow range of issues and that elites agree on more matters than they disagree on. The single elite model suggests that parties agree about the direction of public policy and disagree only on minor details. Our analysis of the party system in the United States suggests the following propositions:

1. The parties share a consensus both on basic democratic values and on major directions of U.S. policy. They believe in the sanctity of private property, the free enterprise economy, individual liberty, and limited government. Moreover, both parties have supported the same general domestic and foreign policies—including social security, a graduated income tax, countercyclical fiscal and monetary policies, anticommunism, the Cold War, and the Korean and Vietnam wars.

2. The parties do not present clear ideological alternatives to the American voter. Both major parties are overwhelmingly middle class in organization, values, and goals. Deviation from the shared consensus by either party is more likely to lose than attract voters.

3. Both parties draw support from all social groups in the United States, but the Democrats draw disproportionately from labor, workers, Jews, Catholics, and blacks, and the Republicans draw disproportionate support from rural, small-town, and suburban Protestants, business interests, and professionals.

4. Democratic and Republican party leaders differ over public policy more than Democratic and Republican mass followers do. The consensus about welfare economics extends to Democratic leaders, Democratic followers, and Republican followers; only the Republican leadership is outside this consensus, with a more laissez-faire position. However, all observed party differences fall well within the range of elite consensus on the values of individualism, capitalism, and limited government.

5. The parties are dominated by small groups of activists who formulate party objectives and select candidates for public office. The masses play a passive role in party affairs. They are not really members of the party; they are more like consumers.

6. Party activists differ from the masses because they have the time and financial resources to be able to "afford" politics, the information and knowledge to understand it, and the organization and public relations skills to be successful in it.

7. The choice of party nominees is a choice of party activists, not a choice of the masses of party members.

8. Individual political party identification is reasonably stable. However, recent years have seen a rapid growth of Independent voters, particularly among younger people.

9. Political campaigns are designed to focus on images of candidates, not issues. They are also designed to increase the turnout of a candidate's supporters.

10. The "normal vote" in the United States today yields approximate equality for both parties.

NOTES

1. E. E. Schattschneider, *Party Government* (New York: Rinehart, 1942), p. 1.
2. See Walter Dean Burnham, "The Changing Shape of the American Political Universe," *American Political Science Review* 59 (March 1965): 28, and "Party Systems and the Political Process," in William Nisbet Chambers and Walter Dean Burnham, eds., *The American Party Systems: Stages of Political Development* (New York: Oxford University Press, 1967), pp. 305–307.
3. Roberto Michels, *Political Parties: A Sociological Study of the Oligarchical Tendencies of Modern Democracy* (1915; reprint, New York: Dover, 1959), p. 32.
4. Frank J. Sorauf, *Party Politics in America* (Boston: Little, Brown, 1968), pp. 79–80.
5. Ibid., p. 94.
6. Roberto Michels, op. cit., p. 32.
7. Paul S. Herrnson, "Reemergent National Party Organizations," in L. Sandy Maisel, ed., *The Parties Respond: Changes in the American Party System* (Boulder: Westview Press, 1990), p. 54.
8. However, former President Nixon, for whom Buchanan had once worked, did persuade him to reduce the intensity of his attacks.
9. Everett C. Ladd, *Where Have All the Voters Gone?* (New York: Norton, 1978), p. 63.
10. Malcom E. Jewell, "A Caveat on the Expanding Use of Presidential Primaries," *Policy Studies Journal* (Summer 1974): 282.
11. Jeane Kirkpatrick, *Dismantling the Parties* (Washington, D.C.: American Enterprise Institute, 1978), p. 7.
12. John Petrocik, "The Post New Deal Party Coalitions and the Election of 1984," paper presented at the meeting of the American Political Science Association, New Orleans, 1985, p. 7.
13. *Buckley* v. *Valeo*, 424 U.S. 1 (1976).
14. Norman Ornstein, quoted in *Newsweek* (November 8, 1982): 31.

SELECTED READINGS

Alexander, Herbert. *Financing Politics.* Washington, D.C.: Congressional Quarterly Press, 1992. This book clearly explains the intricacies of the campaign finance reform legislation.

Crotty, William T. *Political Reform and the American Experiment.* New York: T. Y. Crowell, 1977. This book is a provocative analysis of reform, including reform in political parties, as cyclical, frequently resulting in unanticipated consequences.

Downs, Anthony. *An Economic Theory of Democracy.* New York: Harper & Row, 1959. Downs develops an abstract model of party politics based on traditional democratic political theory. He discusses the relationships among voters, parties, and governmental policy according to the democratic model and deduces empirical propositions.

Eldersveld, Samuel. *Political Parties in American Society.* New York: Basic Books, 1982. Eldersveld discusses parties as organizations, as policy makers, and as competitors for votes, emphasizing changes in their impact on government and elections.

Iyengar, Shanto, and Kinder, Donald R. *News That Matters.* (Chicago: University of Chicago Press, 1987. Television news *does* influence attitudes; this book explains how.

Kamark, Elaine C. "Structure as Strategy: Presidential Nominating Politics in the Post-Reform Era," in L. Sandy Maisel, ed., *The Parties Respond* (Boulder: Westview Press, 1990). This collection of essays argues that, rather than declining in influence, American political parties are changing their structure to adapt to a newer, more fluid environment. Resoundingly upbeat, the book is a useful counterbalance to skeptics, such as the authors of this text.

Ladd, Everett C., Jr. *Where Have All the Voters Gone?* 2nd ed. New York: Norton, 1982. This brief, very readable book highlights recent changes in parties and elections.

Lipset, Seymour Martin, ed. *Party Coalitions in the 1980s.* San Francisco: Institute for Contemporary Studies, 1981. This book contains, along with other valuable essays, thoughtful remarks by Reagan's and Carter's principal consultants.

Miller, Warren E. *Without Consent.* Lexington: University of Kentucky Press, 1988. Miller provides an analysis of the attitudes of delegates to the national conventions.

Polsby, Nelson W., and Wildavsky, Aaron. *Presidential Elections,* 7th ed. New York: Scribner's, 1988. This book is the established leader in the field, with clear writing and minimal use of jargon.

Ranney, Austin. *Curing the Mischiefs of Faction.* Berkeley: University of California Press, 1975. This book of essays focuses on the role of political parties in maintaining political stability.

Shafer, Byron E. *Bifurcated Politics.* Cambridge, Mass.: Harvard University Press, 1988. Shafer examines how the primary system has reduced accountability.

Sorauf, Frank J., and Beck, Paul A. *Party Politics in America,* 6th ed. Glenview, Ill.: Scott, Foresman & Co., 1988. Sorauf employs the organizing concept of the political system in this theoretical work. He focuses on the parties within the American political system—their structure and the functions they perform.

8

Elections: Imperfect Instruments of Accountability

★ *As long as people are people, democracy, in the full sense of the word, will always be no more than an ideal. One may approach it as one would the horizon in ways that may be better or worse, but it can never be fully attained. In this sense, you, too, are merely approaching democracy.*

Vaclav Havel, to the United States Congress, 1992

——ELECTIONS: THE MYTH OF THE POLICY MANDATE

Traditional "pluralist" textbooks in American government tell us that elections are a means by which masses can hold elites responsible for their policy decisions. The traditional argument is that elections enable masses to direct future public policy by voting for one candidate or another on election day.

We argue that elections do not serve as policy mandates; instead they function as symbolic reassurance to the masses. By allowing the masses to participate in a political activity, elections contribute to the legitimacy of government. But elections only allow the masses to help choose *personnel* for public office; elections do not allow the masses to choose the direction of public *policy*.

For elections to serve as policy mandates—that is, for voters to exercise influence over public policy through elections—four conditions would be necessary: (1) competing candidates would offer clear policy alternatives, (2) voters would be concerned with policy questions, (3) election

results would clarify majority preferences on these questions, and (4) elected officials would be bound by their campaign positions.

In this chapter we contend that politics in the United States fulfills none of these conditions. Voters consequently cannot directly control public policy, for several reasons:

1. The parties do not offer clear policy alternatives. Because both parties agree on the major direction of public policy (see Chapter 7), the voters cannot influence it by choosing between the parties.

2. Policy considerations are not the primary motivators of voter decisions. For a mandate to be valid, the electorate must make informed, policy-oriented choices. But most voters are poorly informed on policy questions and have no strong, consistent policy positions. Traditional party ties and candidate personalities influence voters more than policy questions do. These factors dilute the voters' influence over policy.

3. Majority preferences on policy questions cannot be determined from election results. Victory for a candidate's party need not mean that the voters support all of its programs. Among the voters for a candidate are opponents as well as advocates of the candidate's position on a given issue. A popular majority may be composed of many policy minorities. How is a candidate to know which (if any) of his or her policy positions brought electoral victory?

4. Finally, for voters to exercise control over public officials, elected officials would have to be bound by their campaign pledges. However, elected officials frequently ignore their campaign pledges.

IGNORANCE, CONTRADICTIONS, AND INCONSISTENCIES IN VOTER OPINION

If elections are to be a means of popular control over public policy, voters must be reasonably well informed about policy issues and must hold opinions about them. Yet large numbers of the electorate are politically uninformed, have no real opinions on policy issues, and therefore respond inconsistently to policy questions.

Ignorance

Public opinion surveys regularly report what is now the typical finding of a low level of political information among adult Americans (see Chapter 5 and Table 8-1). Elites view such political ignorance as irrational. For active and influential elites, the stakes of competition in politics are high, and the cost of information is cheap; their careers, self-esteem, and prestige are directly and often daily affected by political decisions. For such elites, ignorance would be irrational.

TABLE 8-1 Ignorance of the electorate

Percentage of electorate that . . .		Year	Source
94	Know the capital city of United States	1945	[AIPO]
94	Know the president's term is 4 years	1951	[AIPO]
93	Recognize photograph of the current president	1948	[AIPO]
89	Can name governor of their home state	1973	[Harris]
83	Aware of right to jury trial	1987	[Hearst]
80	Know meaning of term "veto"	1947	[AIPO]
79	Can name the current vice president	1978	[NORC]
78	Know what initials FBI stand for	1949	[AIPO]
74	Know meaning of the term "wiretapping"	1969	[AIPO]
70	Can name their mayor	1967	[AIPO]
69	Know which party has most members in U.S. House of Representatives	1978	[NORC]
68	Know president limited to two terms	1970	[CPS]
63	Know China to be communist	1972	[CPS]
63	Have some understanding of term "conservative"	1960	[SRC]
58	Know meaning of term "open housing"	1967	[AIPO]
52	Know that there are two U.S. senators from their state	1978	[NORC]
46	Can name their congressman	1973	[Harris]
41	Aware Bill of Rights is the first 10 amendments to U.S. Constitution	1987	[Hearst]
39	Can name both U.S. senators from their state	1973	[Harris]
38	Know Russia is not a NATO member	1964	[AIPO]
34	Can name the current U.S. secretary of state	1978	[NORC]
31	Know meaning of "no-fault" insurance	1977	[AIPO]
30	Know term of U.S. House member is 2 years	1978	[NORC]
28	Can name their state senator	1967	[AIPO]
23	Know which two nations involved in SALT	1979	[CBS/NYT]

SOURCES: American Institute of Public Opinion (Gallup); Center for Political Studies; Lou Harris and Associates; National Opinion Research Center; CBS/NYT; Hearst Corporation. See Robert S. Erikson, Norman R. Luttbeg, and Kent L. Tedin, *American Public Opinion*, 3rd ed. (New York: Macmillan, 1988), p. 42.

Among the masses, however, political ignorance may be a rational stance—that is, the cost of informing oneself about politics may outweigh the benefits. Most people do not have friends in public office and do not benefit directly from the victory of one candidate or another. Moreover, because one vote among millions is only infinitesimally influential, to most people it must seem quite reasonable to remain ignorant about politics. Thus the average voter systematically tunes out political information. As political scientist Philip Converse puts it, "For many people, politics does not compete in interest with sports, local gossip, and television dramas."

Phantom Opinion

Inconsistencies in mass opinion are frequently revealed in public opinion polls. Because opinion polls ask questions that are meaningless to many people, the answers are often meaningless as well. Many people have never thought about the question before it is asked and will never think about it again. Their spontaneous responses do not reflect preexisting

FIGURE 8-1   American voters' level of information

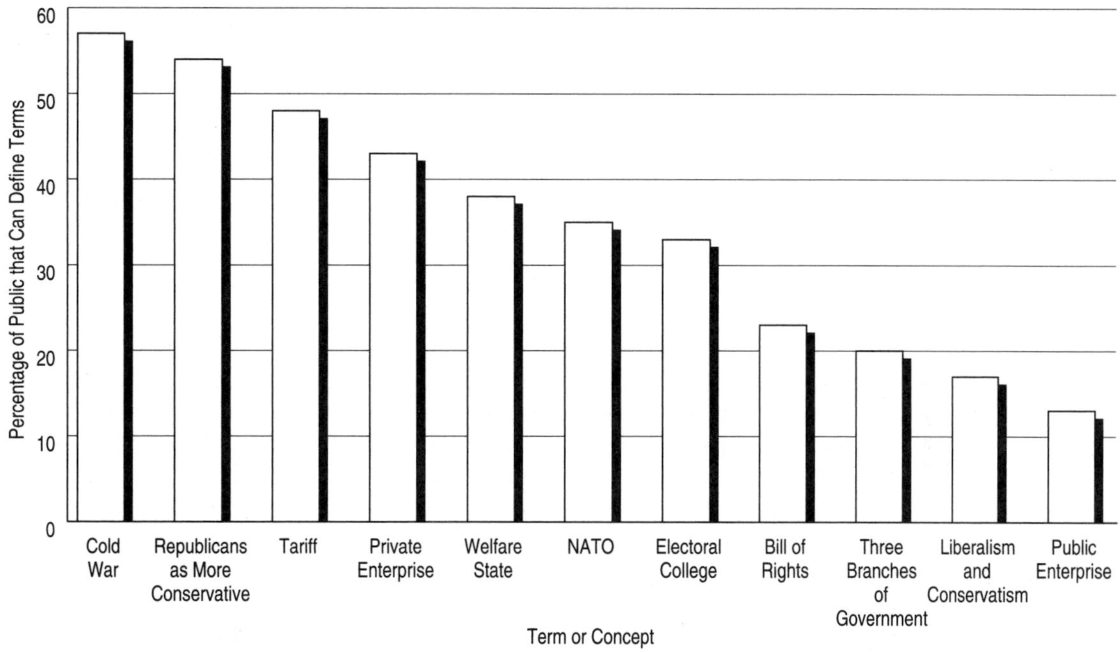

SOURCE: Adapted from W. Russell Neuman, *The Paradox of Mass Politics* (Cambridge, Mass.: Harvard University Press, 1986), p. 17.

opinion. Many respondents do not wish to appear uninformed, and therefore they offer an "opinion" even though they had never thought about the issue prior to the interview. Few people acknowledge they have no opinion, even when that option is provided on a survey question. Many respondents simply react to question wording, responding positively to positive phrases ("helping poor people," "improving education," "cleaning up the environment," and the like) and negatively to negative phrases (such as "raising taxes," "expanding governmental power," "restricting choice"). Many respondents succumb to a "halo effect"—giving socially approved responses to questions, regardless of their true feelings.

Inconsistent Opinion

Since so many people hold no real opinion on political issues, question wording frequently produces inconsistent responses. For example, when asked whether they agreed or disagreed with the statement "Professors in state-supported institutions should have freedom to speak and teach the truth as they see it," Californians appeared to support academic freedom by a ratio of 52 to 39. But when opinions were sought on the statement "Professors who advocate controversial ideas or speak out against official policy have no place in a state-supported college or university," the same ratio of 52 to 39 was found, but this time the majority was on the side favoring restrictions on academic freedom.[1] A study of attitudes toward pornography provides an even clearer example of inconsistent response. When respondents were asked whether they agreed that "people should have the right to purchase a sexually explicit book, magazine, or movie, if that's what they want to do," an overwhelming 80 percent endorsed the statement. However, when the same respondents were also asked whether they agreed with the opposite statement that "community authorities should be able to prohibit the selling of magazines or movies they consider to be pornographic," 65 percent approved of this opposite view as well.[2]

Unstable Opinion

Weakly held opinions not only result in inconsistent responses, they can also produce directly contradictory responses to the same question when asked at different times. Many people who offer opinions in successive interviews change their position from one side to the other. For example, the same respondents were interviewed shortly before and shortly after the 1984 presidential election. In each of the two surveys, the respondents were asked their views on whether the federal government should guarantee everyone "a good job and a good standard of living" or whether the "government should let each person get ahead on his own." Overall opinion shifted on the issue—37 percent of respondents on the preelection survey answered that the government should let people get ahead on their own, whereas 44 percent agreed with that statement in the postelection survey. More important, more than half of the respondents *shifted opinion,* giving a response different from the response they gave in the first interview only a few weeks earlier.[3]

IN SEARCH OF ISSUE-ORIENTED VOTERS

The ideal "responsible party" model requires not only that the parties offer clear and divergent policy alternatives to the voters, but that the voters make their electoral choices on the basis of their policy preferences. As we have already noted, most voters have no information or opinion about many specific policy issues and therefore cannot be expected to base their electoral choices on these issues. However, it is sometimes argued that, in lieu of specific policy stances, voters have broad liberal or conservative policy dispositions they use as a basis for voting. The "responsible party" model would be strengthened if it could be shown that voters think of themselves ideologically as liberals or conservatives and select candidates to match their own ideological position. In contrast, if voters largely overlook ideology, as well as specific policy positions, in their electoral decisions, then the argument of elite theory that elections fail to give the masses control over policy is strengthened.

To assess the electorate's ability to conceptualize (to think abstractly), the University of Michigan Survey Research Center (SRC) examined the responses of a sample to questions about the good and bad points of the two major parties. Researchers derived the following categories as a result. *Ideologues* are respondents who are either "liberal" or "conservative" and are likely to rely on abstract principles in evaluating candidates and issues. *Near ideologues* are those who mentioned an abstract principle, but did not rely on it as much as the ideologues did and may not have clearly understood the meaning of abstract political terms. At the next level, the *group benefits* class contained those who did not exhibit any overriding ideology in their thinking but were able to evaluate parties and candidates by expected favorable or unfavorable treatment for social groups. Subjects favored candidates they considered sympathetic to a group with which they identified. A fourth group is respondents who base their judgment on their perception of the "goodness" or "badness" of the times. They blame or praise parties and candidates because of their association with conditions of war or peace, prosperity or depression. The last level includes respondents whose evaluations of the political scene hold *no relationship whatever to policy,* even in the broadest and most symbolic sense. Some of these profess loyalty to one of the two parties but have no understanding of the party's positions.

When social scientists first examined the entire electorate, they found that ideological commitments were significant in the political decisions of only a tiny fraction of people (see Figures 8-2 and 8-3). Of the total electorate, 3 percent were ideologues, 10 percent were near ideologues, and the remainder displayed no ideological content in their evaluations. Since these initial investigations, the proportion of the electorate that casts a vote based on ideology has stabilized at about 20 percent. There is no evidence that ideological voting is increasing.

FIGURE 8-2   Voters classified as ideologues and near ideologues

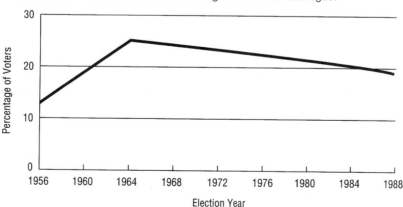

SOURCE: Paul R. Hagner and John C. Pierce, *Conceptualization and Consistency in Political Beliefs.* Paper presented at the annual meeting of the Midwest Political Science Association, Cincinnati, 1981.

FIGURE 8-3   Percentages of ideologues at three educational levels

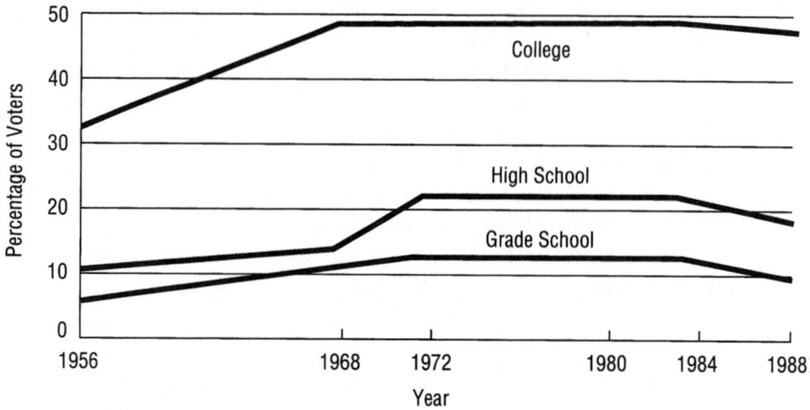

Note: Combines ideologues and near ideologues.
SOURCE: Data provided through the courtesy of Arthur Miller, University of Michigan, Survey Research Center.

Clearly, then, the majority of the public does not conceptualize politics in the same way as the minority of ideologically oriented voters. The ideological debate between liberals and conservatives has very little meaning for most Americans.

Do liberal voters regard themselves as Democrats and conservatives as Republicans, as the popular images of the major parties suggest? In general, yes. Those who identify themselves as Republicans are more conservative than those who regard themselves as Democrats. Furthermore, liberals tend to vote for Democratic presidential candidates, and conservatives tend to vote for Republicans. These patterns persist even when the candidates and issues change from one election to another.

However, voters who label themselves "liberal" do not necessarily agree with one another on the issues, and the same is true of "conservatives." *Elites* link attitudes toward various policies with an overreaching liberal or conservative ideology. For elites, ideology is a summary of various specific policy attitudes. But *masses* do not link their policy positions with their "liberalism" or "conservatism."

For example, the proper role of the federal government in guaranteeing jobs and a good standard of living has been the source of enduring partisan debate between liberal and conservative party activists and officeholders. Liberal elites, especially liberal Democratic elites, believe that the federal government should take an active role in the economy. Thus a self-described "liberal" *should* know that a liberal position on this issue is to favor governmental guarantees, and a conservative position is to favor individual self-reliance. But the masses do not approach the issue in this way (see Table 8-2). Only among the college educated and among strong conservatives do more than half of respondents know that a liberal policy is one of federal intervention. The masses of non-college-educated

"Should anyone inquire, Harrington, our portions are generous, not liberal."

voters have very little knowledge of the policy implications of the " liberal" and "conservative" labels.

In summary, ideology does not mean very much. Describing oneself as liberal or conservative does not mean that one advocates or even recognizes policies consistent with one's professed ideology.[4]

Elites themselves frequently make the mistake of confusing the educated minority with the mass of uninformed voters. As Warren Miller concludes, "Levels of conceptualization have not altered much in recent years, but it remains difficult to convey to politically interested and active

TABLE 8-2   "Liberals" and "conservatives" correctly associating liberalism with an active role for federal government in the economy

Political stance of respondent	College (%)	High school (%)	Grade school (%)
Strong liberal	78	22	0
Liberal	50	35	30
Weak liberal	51	47	0
Centrist	30	28	26
Weak conservative	50	30	0
Conservative	56	42	23
Strong conservative	81	67	54

Note: Percentages reflect the proportion of respondents who associate liberalism with an active role for government and conservatism with individual self-help.
SOURCE: Survey Resource Center, University of Michigan, 1980.

citizens the lack of complexity or sophistication in the ways most Americans talk and apparently think about politics."[5]

THE GROUP BASIS OF VOTING

The social group basis of voting is easily observed in presidential elections. Different social groups give disproportionate support to Republican and Democratic candidates. No group is *wholly* within one party or the other; and group differences are modest, with the exception of the strong Democratic loyalty shown by black voters over the years. If *no* group influences were involved in voter choices, we would expect that the percentage of each group's vote for Democratic and Republican candidates would be the same as the national percentages. But it is clear that Democratic presidential candidates have drawn disproportionate support from blacks, union members, less-educated manual workers, Catholics, and Jews; Republican presidential candidates, meanwhile, have drawn disproportionate support from whites, the college educated, professional and business people, and Protestants. A small but significant "gender gap" also exists, with recent Republican candidates doing better among men than women, even though both gave majority support to Reagan in 1984 and Bush in 1988.

Pluralists argue that these social group differences in voting are evidence of a "responsible" electorate. Pluralists may acknowledge that most voters have no knowledge of specific policy issues, and some pluralists will even acknowledge that most voters do not consistently or accurately apply liberal or conservative policy dimensions to their electoral choice. However, pluralists argue that many voters use a *group benefits* standard in making their electoral choice. For example, many black voters may not follow specific arguments on civil rights legislation or study the candidates' records on the issue. But they have a general idea that the Democratic party, beginning with President Franklin D. Roosevelt and continuing through the administration of President Lyndon Johnson, took the lead in supporting the interests of black Americans. Thus, it is not irrational for black voters to give disproportionate support to Democratic candidates, even when particular Republican and Democratic candidates have similar records in support of civil rights. Likewise, voters in other social groups may employ a group benefits standard in evaluating parties and candidates. In short, group identification becomes the essential mediating device between the individual voter and electoral choice.

For many years the group basis of voter choice directed political campaign strategy. Candidates conscientiously solicited the support of identifiable social groups—union members, teachers, farmers, small business owners, Jews, the aged, ethnic groups, and so on—by appearing at rallies, securing the endorsement of group leaders, pledging to look after a group's interests, or citing their personal (sometimes manufactured) identification with the group they were addressing. And indeed, all candidates continue to be sensitive to group identifications among voters.

Group identifications in the electorate constitute the strongest arguments in support of pluralist political theory (see Chapter 1). However, there is evidence that these group identifications may be declining in importance in electoral politics.

Over time, the social class basis of voter choice appears to be diminishing. During the Great Depression of the 1930s, economic issues dominated American politics to the exclusion of almost all other issues. President Franklin D. Roosevelt's efforts to restore prosperity, ameliorate suffering, and provide for economic security created a strong partisan alignment, with low-income, manual workers voting Democratic and high-income professional and business people voting Republican. This link between class and party is visible today, although it is gradually weakening. Many pundits and commentators erroneously claimed that during the 1980s Ronald Reagan was splitting America along class and income lines, but just the opposite was in fact true. Consider, for example, the evidence presented in Figure 8-4. In general, the partisan difference in presidential elections between manual workers on the one hand, and professional, managerial, and sales workers on the other, has been diminishing over time.

Today's media-oriented campaigning, emphasizing direct television communication with individual voters, reduces the mediating function of groups. Media campaigning emphasizes candidate image—personal qualities such as leadership, compassion, character, humor, and charm—rather than group identification. Since a television ad reaches a very broad audience, unlike a candidate's appearance at a group meeting, these ads usually address themes *all* viewers can relate to—creating jobs, cleaning up the environment, winning wars, and so on—rather than specific group interests.

Thus, over time it is likely that group differences in voting will become only moderate. Indeed, even today both Democratic and Republican

FIGURE 8-4   Party differences between manual and nonmanual workers

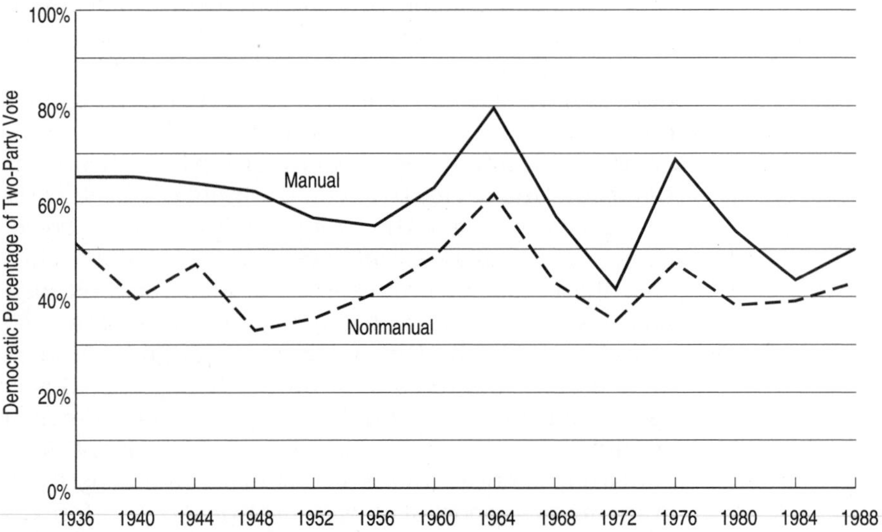

SOURCES: Data for 1936–1960 from Robert A. Alford, *Party and Society* (Chicago: Rand McNally, 1963). Data for 1964–1988 from National Election Studies, University of Michigan. See also Robert S. Erikson, Norman R. Luttbeg, and Kent L. Tedin, *American Public Opinion*, 3rd ed. (New York: Macmillan, 1988), p. 177.

parties draw support from all social groups. Consequently both parties find it difficult to formulate overt group or class appeals. Social group differences between the parties are likely to remain indistinct and overlapping.

Table 8-3 shows the decay of political parties as "glue" for voters, holding them together across categories of candidates and making diverse pieces of political information into a fathomable whole. High correlations (those approaching 1.0) mean that a vote in congressional elections is tautly joined to a vote in presidential elections; in other words, a Democrat votes the Democratic ticket, and a Republican votes Republican. An immense deterioration in this correlation occurred in the 1960s, and it has

TABLE 8-3   Decline of the relationship between presidential and congressional votes in electoral combinations

Decade	President–House	President–Senate
1900s	.85	
1910s	.54	.84
1920s	.40	.55
1930s	.44	.65
1940s	.65	.82
1950s	.63	.67
1960s	.26	.26
1970s	.16	.04
1980s	.14	.13

SOURCE: Martin Wattenberg, *The Rise of Candidate Centered Politics* (Cambridge: Harvard University Press, 1991), p. 37.

continued unabated. Candidates do not emphasize their party affiliation—in fact they seldom allude to it—and voters are no longer led by partisan passions.

THE FLOATING VOTERS

"Floating voters" are those not closely tied by party or group affiliations, who switch their support from one party to the other in different elections and change their voting decision in response to campaign-generated forces or last-minute developments. These floating voters may only constitute 15 to 20 percent of the electorate; more than 80 percent of voters have fairly stable party and group affiliations to guide their choice. Yet these floating voters generally determine the outcome of elections.

If these floating voters were well-informed about policy issues and attentive to candidates' policy statements, then we might conclude that election outcomes were policy-driven, even though the overwhelming majority of voters were not policy-oriented. But the reverse is true: the crucial floating voters are even *more* ignorant of policy issues and *less* attentive to politics than the average voter is. Political scientist Philip Converse comments on the floating voters:

> Not only is the electorate as a whole quite uninformed, but it is the least informed members of the electorate who seem to hold the critical "balance of power" in the sense that alternatives in the governing party depend disproportionately on shifts in their sentiments.[6]

Since the floating voters are most likely to change their decisions during a presidential campaign, the candidates' campaign strategies are aimed directly at these most ignorant and least policy-oriented voters.

CASE STUDY

 ### "Change"—Clinton's Winning Strategy

Clinton's campaign strategy was to hammer home a single theme: the economy is in bad shape and the nation demands change. In the Democratic primaries, Clinton was able to best lesser-known candidates but the White House seemed an impossible dream. He was running **third** in the polls, trailing both President Bush and the new wild card in the deck, independent billionaire Ross Perot.

Clinton had spent a political lifetime managing his career. So when strategists suggested that he jettison his moderate image in favor of cultivating the core liberal constituency of the Democratic Party in order to eke out a victory in an expected three-man race, he rejected the idea. He insisted on sticking with the original game plan—moderation and change. When Perot unexpectedly pulled out of the race on the eve of the Democratic convention, Clinton's strategy was amply rewarded. Perot had detached many moderate white voters from Bush; when he dropped out of the race, his supporters flocked to Clinton's banner. By the end of the Democratic convention, Clinton had a twenty-point lead in the race.

Clinton's single-minded focus on the economy and the need for change contrasted with the clumsy, unfocused Bush campaign. The Bush team first tried to claim the popular "change" theme for themselves, only to hear voters ask why the presi-

(continued)

CASE STUDY *(continued)*

dent hadn't sought change in the previous four years. Then they turned to "family values" with only limited success. Bush's efforts to remind voters of America's victories in the Cold War and the Gulf War seemed to backfire: they only proved that the president had focused his energies on foreign affairs rather than on problems at home. Bush's claims that the economy was not all that bad only seemed to show that he was "out of touch" with the people. Bush was frustrated by the media's continued portrayal of the economy as sick and faltering, despite growth in output and declining unemployment. The Republican convention appeared to be dominated by social conservatives who gave the campaign an intolerant, mean-spirited, image.

Clinton went into the debates with two simple goals—to keep the focus of the campaign on the economy and the need for change, and to avoid making mistakes that would threaten his lead in the polls. Bush had a much more challenging task—to refocus the campaign on Clinton's character and somehow overcome his huge lead in the polls. But in the first debate Clinton nimbly deflected Bush's attack on his organizing of anti-war demonstra-

tions. Bush was awkward and uncomfortable in the attack mode; Clinton was boyish and knowledgeable. Ross Perot clearly "won" the battle of sound bites in the debates. But what mattered most was that Clinton had achieved his goals, while Bush had failed to hit the home run that he so badly needed.

In the final days of the campaign, Bush finally hit his stride with a fierce attack on Clinton's character. While Bush's theme was negative and failed to give voters a reason to vote *for* the president, it began to erode Clinton's support. But just as Bush appeared to be narrowing the gap, the media undercut him by rehashing old news about his role in the Iran-Contra affair. The Clinton team wanted the election to be a referndum on the economy. In the end, that is what they got.

The voter's anxieties about the economy determined the election outcome. While Clinton emerged only five percentage points ahead of Bush in the popular vote, the nation's desire for change was clear. He prevailed in one of the toughest political campaigns in American history because he skillfully presented himself to the voters as an agent of change.

ELECTIONS AS SYMBOLIC REASSURANCE

If elections do not enable voters to control public policy directly, what are their purposes? Elections are a symbolic exercise to help tie the masses to the established order. Political scientist Murray Edelman agrees that voters have little effect on public policy and contends that elections are primarily "symbolic reassurance." According to Edelman, elections serve to "quiet resentments and doubts about particular political acts, reaffirm belief in the fundamental rationality and democratic character of the system, and thus fix conforming habits of future behavior."[7]

Elections Give Legitimacy to Government

Virtually all modern political systems—authoritarian and democratic, capitalist and communist—hold elections. Indeed, communist dictatorships took elections very seriously and strove to achieve 90 to 100 percent voter turnout rates, despite the fact that the Communist party offered only one candidate for each office. Why did these nations bother to hold elections when the outcome had already been determined? All political regimes seek to tie the masses to the system by holding symbolic exercises in political participation to give the ruling regime an aura of legitimacy. Of course, democratic governments gain even greater legitimacy from elections; democratically elected officeholders can claim that the voters' participation legitimizes their activities and their laws.

Elections Choose Personnel, Not Policy

In democratic nations, elections serve a second function: choosing personnel to hold public office. In 1992 the American voters decided that Bill Clinton and not George Bush would occupy "the nation's highest office" for the next four years. (The vast majority of people in the world today have never had the opportunity to participate in such a choice.) However, this choice is one of personnel, not policy. Parties do not offer clear policy alternatives in election campaigns; voters do not choose the candidates' policy positions; and candidates are not bound by their campaign pledges anyway. Political scientist Gerald M. Pomper explains:

> To choose a government is not to choose governmental policies. Whereas the voters largely do determine the players in the game of American politics, they have far less control over the signals the players will call, the strategies they will employ, or the final score. The popular will, as represented by a majority of voters, does not determine public policy.[8]

Elections Allow for Retrospective Judgments

The third function of elections is to give the masses an opportunity to express themselves about the conduct of the public officials who have been in power. Elections do not permit the masses to direct *future* events, but they do permit the masses to render retrospective judgment about *past* political conduct.

Elections give voters the opportunity to express their displeasure by ousting incumbents from office. But it is not always easy to decipher what the incumbents did wrong that aroused the voters' displeasure. Consider, for example, the crucial 1968 presidential election at the height of the Vietnam War. Democrat Lyndon Johnson, who had first committed U.S. ground combat troops to battle in 1965, announced that he would not be a candidate for reelection, and he halted bombing raids and opened peace talks with the North Vietnamese. In the general election that year, voters could choose between Republican Richard Nixon, Democrat Hubert Humphrey, and Independent George Wallace. All three promised to "end" the war, but none provided a specific program for doing so—whether surrender, all-out bombing, or anything in between. But the voters were able to express their discontent with Johnson's handling of the war by voting against a continuation of the Democratic administration.

The voters were able to express their distaste for the Watergate scandal (see Chapter 10) by ousting the Republican administration of Gerald Ford in 1976 and turning the White House over to Democrat Jimmy

Carter, who piously promised "a government as good as its people." But aside from expressing a preference for honesty in government, it is not clear what other policy directions the voters were giving in that election. President Nixon ended the Vietnam War, opened relations with the People's Republic of China, and negotiated the first strategic arms limitation agreement with the Soviet Union. It is not likely that the voters were expressing their opposition to these policies by ousting the Republicans.

What policy lessons can political elites learn from President Carter's defeat in 1980? Perhaps the only clear retrospective judgment rendered by the American people in that election is that an American president should never appear weak and helpless in the face of international terrorism. Carter's inability to handle the Iranian embassy hostage-taking effectively probably sealed his fate; if the military rescue mission had been successful, Ronald Reagan may never have won the presidency.

Was Ronald Reagan's landslide reelection victory in 1984 over Democrat Walter Mondale a policy mandate for cutting taxes, reducing domestic spending, and a military buildup—the key policy directions in Reagan's first term? Or was it simply an expression of approval of Reagan's presidential style—his warmth, patriotism, good humor, and optimism about America? Throughout the eight years of Reagan's presidency, liberal academics and journalists argued strongly that Reagan's victories reflected his personal popularity, not support for his conservative message. In contrast, conservative commentators urged Reagan to use his voter "mandate" to advance a conservative policy agenda.

Perhaps the strongest support for the retrospective voting argument is found in the relationship between economic downturns and the vote for the incumbent party. In presidential elections, the candidate of the incumbent party (whether a president seeking reelection or the president's party nominee) tends to lose votes if the economy is experiencing a downturn during the election year. Incumbent Republican President Herbert Hoover lost in a landslide in the Great Depression in 1932. However, this message from the voters—keep the U.S. economy strong and growing—is hardly a policy directive.

Retrospective voting clearly dominated the voters' decisions in 1992. The voters opted for **change**! Fully 62 percent of the voters cast their votes against President Bush—43 percent for Clinton and 19 percent for Perot. Voters cited the economy as the primary issue on their minds in polls taken as they exited the voting booth. But few voters knew what plans Clinton and Perot had offered to remedy the nation's economic ills. Clinton's stump speech offered everything to everybody: "We can be pro-growth and pro-environment, we can be pro-business and pro-labor, we can make government work again by making it more aggressive and leaner and more effective at the same time, and we can be pro-family and pro-choice." What kind of policy mandate can Clinton claim from such promises? What kind of policy mandate can be claimed by a president who won only 43 percent of the vote?

Elections are notoriously poor instruments for determining the policy preferences of the electorate. Even a staunch defender of the pluralist interpretation of American politics, political scientist Gerald Pomper, concedes that

> Policy choices in elections are difficult to accomplish. They require, at least, that candidates take definable positions, that the voters correctly perceive these positions, and that the voters then cast their ballots on the basis of these positions. Even when all of these conditions are met, an election may still not be clearly the result of issue voting.[9]

Although none of these conditions exists, and elections in the United States seldom serve as policy mandates, elites nevertheless *believe* that they can be held to account for their actions, and so they are more responsive than they otherwise would be. Elections, even if they are simple retrospective judgments on style, can still make elites more constrained in their behavior. Even if the electorate cannot issue policy mandates, voters can "throw the rascals out" and bring in new ones.

Elections Provide Protection Against Official Abuse

Elections can also protect individuals and groups from official abuse. John Stuart Mill wrote, "Men, as well as women, do not need political rights in order that they might govern, but in order that they not be misgoverned."[10] He went on:

> Rulers in ruling classes are under a necessity of considering the interests of those who have the suffrage; but of those who are excluded, it is in their option whether they will do so or not, and however honestly disposed, they are in general too fully occupied with things they must attend to, to have much room in their thoughts for anything which they can with impunity disregard.[11]

Certainly the long history of efforts to ensure black voting rights in the South suggests that many concerned Americans believed that if blacks could secure access to the polls, they could better protect themselves from discrimination. Some major steps in the struggle for voting rights were the abolition in 1944 of the "white primary" (blacks had not been allowed to participate); the Civil Rights Acts of 1957, 1960, 1964, and 1965, all of which contained provisions guaranteeing free access to the polls; and the Twenty-Fourth Amendment to the Constitution, which eliminated poll taxes (see Chapter 15). In signing the Voting Rights Act of 1965, President Johnson said:

> The right to vote is the most basic right, without which all others are meaningless. It gives people—people as individuals—control over their own destinies. . . . The vote is the most powerful instrument ever devised by man for breaking down injustice and destroying the terrible walls which imprison men because they are different from other men.

But the high hopes stirred by the development of voting laws often deteriorated into frustration and disillusionment when blacks realized that the electoral process alone could not solve their problems. The vote is a symbol of full citizenship and equal rights that can contribute to black self-respect,[12] but questions remain about how much blacks can gain through the exercise of their vote.

It has proven much more difficult to resolve social and economic inequities through the electoral process than to eliminate directly discriminating laws and regulations.

ELECTORAL PARTICIPATION AND NONPARTICIPATION

Another problem with the pluralist theory of popular control over public policy through elections is the fact that *half the adult population fails to vote,* even in presidential elections. Since the 1960 Kennedy-Nixon race, voter turnout has steadily slipped from 64 percent of the eligible voters to 63 percent in the 1964 Johnson-Goldwater race, 60 percent in the 1968 Nixon-Humphrey-Wallace race, 56 percent in the 1972 Nixon-McGovern race, 53 percent in the 1976 Carter-Ford race, and about 52 percent in both the 1980 Reagan-Carter race and the 1984 Reagan-Mondale race. Turnout for the 1988 Bush-Dukakis election hit a new low of 50 percent of eligible voters. Off-year (nonpresidential) elections bring out fewer than half the eligible voters. In 1990, only 32 percent of eligible voters came to the polls. Yet in these off-year contests the nation chooses all its U.S. representatives, one-third of its senators, and about half of its governors (see Figure 8-5).

FIGURE 8-5 Participation in presidential and congressional elections, 1960–1988

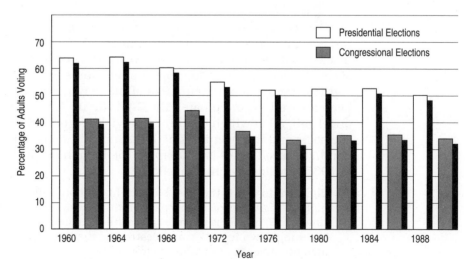

Lester Milbrath listed six forms of "legitimate" political participation.[13] Individuals may run for public office, become active in party and campaign work, make financial contributions to political candidates or causes, belong to organizations that support or oppose candidates, attempt to influence friends while discussing candidates or issues, and vote in elections. Activities at the top of this list require greater expenditure of time, money, and energy than those at the bottom, and they involve only a tiny minority of the population. Less than 1 percent of adults in the United States ever run for public office. Only about 5 percent are ever active in parties and campaigns, and only about 10 percent make financial contributions. About one-third of the population belongs to organizations that could be classified as political interest groups, and only a few more people ever try to persuade their friends to vote a certain way. And finally, only about 50 to 55 percent of the U.S. electorate will vote in a hard-fought presidential campaign.

Participation is not uniform throughout all segments of the population (see Table 8-4). High voter turnout relates to such factors as college education, white-collar occupation, and high income. Although these figures pertain only to voting, other forms of participation follow substantially the same pattern. White, middle-class, college-educated, white-collar Americans participate more in all forms of political activity than do nonwhite, lower-class, grade-school-educated Americans.

Election turnout figures in the United States are lower than those of several other democracies. The turnout in recent elections has been 74 percent in Japan, 77 percent in Great Britain, 83 percent in Israel,

TABLE 8-4 Percent turnout in presidential elections by selected groups, 1988

AGE		RACE	
18–25	36	Whites, non-Hispanic	58
26–40	57	Blacks	45
41–54	68	Hispanics	38
55 +	64		
EDUCATION		OCCUPATION	
Eighth grade or less	44	Unskilled	49
Some high school	45	Skilled	53
High school graduate	57	Clerical	60
Some college	59	Self-employed	68
College graduate	76	Professional	69
INCOME (FAMILY)		PARTY IDENTIFICATION	
Less than $5,000	39	Strong Democrats	64
$5,000 to $9,999	44	Weak Democrats	49
$10,000 to $14,999	57	Independent Democrats	56
$15,000 to $19,999	56	Independents	43
$20,000 to $24,999	64	Independent Republicans	62
$25,000 to $29,999	71	Weak Republicans	65
$30,000 to $34,999	65	Strong Republicans	70
$35,000 to $49,999	70		
$50,000 and more	68		

SOURCE: *New York Times*, November 10, 1988, p. 18.

88 percent in West Germany, and 93 percent in Italy. The lower U.S. turn-outs may reflect stricter residence and registration requirements and greater frequency of elections. But Americans may also be less "political" than citizens of other democracies, less likely to care about the outcome of elections, and less likely to feel that government has much effect on their lives. Interest in politics may be lacking because differences are less significant between opposing parties and candidates, so that the elector-ate has less invested in which party or candidate wins.[14] In 1988, the non-southern percentage of turnout was the lowest since the election of Andrew Jackson in 1824.

SUMMARY

Elite theory contends that the masses do not participate in policy making and that the elites who do are subject to little direct influence from apa-thetic masses. But many scholars who acknowledge that even democratic societies are governed by elites seek to reaffirm democratic values by contending that voters can influence elite behavior in elections. In other words, modern pluralists sometimes challenge elitism on the ground that elections give the masses a voice in policy making by holding governing elites accountable to the people.

Our analysis suggests that elections are imperfect instruments of accountability. Even if the people can hold *government* elites accountable through elections, how can they hold accountable corporate elites, finan-cial elites, union leaders, and other private leadership? The accountabil-ity argument usually ignores the realm of *private* decision making, to focus exclusively on public decision making by elected elites. But cer-tainly our lives are vitally affected by the decisions of private institutions and organizations. So the first problem with the accountability thesis is that, at best, it applies only to elected government elites. However, our analysis of elections also suggests that it is difficult for the voters to hold even government elites accountable.

1. Competing candidates in elections do not usually offer clear policy alternatives; hence voters seldom can affect policy by selecting a particular candidate for public office.

2. Voters are not well informed about the policy stands of candi-dates, and relatively few voters are concerned with policy questions. The masses cast their votes in elections based on traditional party ties, can-didates' personalities, group affiliations, and a host of other factors with little relation to public policy.

3. Mass opinion on public policy is inconsistent and unstable. Rel-atively few voters (generally well-educated, upper-class voters from whom elites are drawn) hold reasonably consistent political ideologies. Mass opinion is unguided by principle, is unstable, and is subject to change.

4. Available evidence suggests that elites influence the opinion of masses more than masses influence the opinion of elites. The masses respond to political symbols manipulated by elites, not to facts or political principles.

5. The only reasonably stable aspect of mass politics is party identification. But party identification in the mass electorate does not allow for any significant policy choices, since Democrats and Republicans hold fairly similar opinions on most issues.

6. Election results do not necessarily reflect majority preferences on policy questions for a number of reasons. Campaigns generally stress the presentation of political ideologies rather than the content of the ideologies. Victory for a party or a candidate may not indicate support for a specific policy position. Voters frequently misinterpret candidates' policy preferences. Often a candidate's voters include not only advocates of the stated position but some who oppose it and some who vote for the candidate for other reasons. A candidate may take positions on many different issues, so observers cannot know which policy positions resulted in election. Finally, for voters to influence policy through elections, winning candidates would have to be bound to follow their campaign pledges.

7. Elections are primarily a symbolic exercise that helps tie the masses to the established order. Elections offer the masses an opportunity to participate in the political system, but electoral participation does not enable them to determine public policy.

8. Elections are means of selecting personnel, not policy. Voters choose on the basis of a candidate's personal style, filtered through partisan commitment. A candidate's election does not imply a policy choice by the electorate.

9. At best, elections provide the masses with an opportunity to express themselves about the conduct of past administrations, but they do not help them direct the course of future events. Again, a vote against the party or candidate in power does not identify the policy being censured. Moreover, voters have no guarantee that a newly elected official will pursue any specific policy alternatives.

10. Few individuals participate in any political activity other than voting. Nearly half the adult population fails to vote even in presidential elections.

——— NOTES

1. *Gallup Opinion Index,* March 1968, p. 11; cited in Robert S. Erikson, Norman R. Luttbeg, and Kent L. Tedin, *American Public Opinion,* 3rd ed. (New York: Macmillan, 1988), p. 55.
2. *Public Opinion* (September/October 1986): 32; also cited by Erikson et al., *op. cit.,* p. 55.
3. Ibid., p. 45.

4. Teresa Levitin and Warren E. Miller, "Ideological Interpretations of Presidential Elections," *American Political Science Review* 73 (September 1979): 769.

5. Warren E. Miller and Teresa E. Levitin, *Leadership and Change: The New Politics and the American Electorate* (Cambridge, Mass.: Winthrop Publishers, 1976), p. 15.

6. Philip Converse, "Information Flow and the Stability of Partisan Attitude," *Public Opinion* 26 (Winter 1962): 588; cited in Erikson et al, *op. cit.,* p. 251.

7. Murray Edelman, *The Symbolic Uses of Power* (Urbana: University of Illinois Press, 1964), p. 17.

8. Gerald M. Pomper, *Elections in America: Control and Influence in Democratic Politics* (New York: Dodd, Mead, 1980), p. 51.

9. Gerald M. Pomper, "The Presidential Election," in Gerald M. Pomper et al., *The Election of 1984* (Chatham, N.J.: Chatham House, 1985), p. 81.

10. John Stuart Mill, *Considerations on Representative Government* (Chicago: Henry Regnery, Gateway, 1962), p. 144.

11. Ibid., pp. 130–131.

12. William R. Keech, *The Impact of Negro Voting: The Role of the Vote in the Quest for Equality* (Chicago: Rand McNally, 1968), p. 3.

13. Lester Milbrath, *Political Participation* (Chicago: Rand McNally, 1965), pp. 23–29.

14. Robert E. Lane, "The Politics of Consensus in an Age of Affluence," *American Political Science Review* 61 (December 1965): 880.

SELECTED READINGS

Campbell, Angus, Converse, P., Miller, W., and Stokes, D. *The American Voter: An Abridgement.* New York: Wiley, 1964. An abridged version of the classic study of voting behavior in the United States conducted by the Survey Research Center at the University of Michigan.

Chubb, John E., and Peterson, Paul, eds. The *New Direction in American Politics.* Washington, D.C.: The Brookings Institution, 1985. These authors argue that Reagan was a "phenomenon," the instrument of potentially major changes in politics.

Epstein, Leon. *Political Parties in the American Mold.* Madison: University of Wisconsin Press, 1986. Epstein provides a jargon-free, balanced, historical and theoretical view of parties in the United States.

Owen, Gary R. and Polsby, Nelson, eds. *Media and Momentum.* Chatham, N.J.: Chatham House, 1987. This book examines the primaries, especially New Hampshire as a curious, aberrant development.

Sorauf, Frank J. *Money in Elections.* Glenview, Ill.: Scott, Foresman, 1988. This is the essential guide to the labyrinths of campaign finance, its laws, their violation, and the impact of money on the political process.

CHAPTER

9

Organized Interests: Defenders of the Status Quo

★ *There is overwhelming evidence that participation in voluntary organizations is related to upper social and economic status. . . . The flaw in the pluralist heaven is that the heavenly chorus sings with a strong upper class accent.*

E. E. Schattschneider, The Semisovereign People, *1960*

Organized interest groups, not the "the people," have the most direct day-to-day influence over government. The public interest is a fiction, but the organized interests are potent political realities, in Washington, state capitals, and city halls. Interest-group activity, including lobbying, is generally protected by the First Amendment to the U.S. Constitution—"the right of the people peaceably to assemble and to petition the government for redress of grievances." But how democratic is the interest-group system? Do interest groups represent "the people" fairly? Or is the interest-group system a means of elite control over government?

INTEREST GROUPS: DEMOCRATIC OR ELITIST?

Pluralists contend that interest groups perform several important functions for their members and for a democratic society. First, the organized group links the individual and the government. Political scientists Gabriel Almond and Sidney Verba state:

> Voluntary associations are the prime means by which the function of mediating between the individual and the state is performed. Through them the individual is able to relate himself effectively and meaningfully to the political system.[1]

But is mediation by an organized group any more efficient than direct citizen-government interaction? Why do we need a middleman?

Pluralists also argue that interest groups enhance individual well-being. In a complex society, with primary associations (small groups, such as the family) diminishing in importance, secondary associations (less intimate but more goal-oriented) may help people overcome the sense of powerlessness characteristic of mass societies. Groups help integrate the individual with society.

Finally, the pluralists feel that interest groups help reduce potentially divisive conflicts. According to the theory of overlapping group memberships, all citizens are members of groups (some organized, some not).[2] Each person is a product of group affiliations. A person may be, for example, a lawyer, a southerner, a military veteran, and a Protestant, with each affiliation imposing its own values. No single group affiliation could claim the individual's total, undivided loyalty. Hence multiple group affiliations help modify the demands of any one group and reduce societal conflict.

Thus the supposition that interest groups are "bad" because they oppose the "public interest" is no longer in favor. Pluralists now consider groups "good" because (1) they provide a more effective voice for citizens who are competing for resources, (2) they reduce the anxiety produced by feelings of powerlessness, and (3) they provide an element of stability.

However, the pluralist interest-group theory rests on several assumptions that may or may not be correct:

1. Membership in organizations is widespread and thus broadly represents all individual interests.
2. Organized groups efficiently translate members' expectations into political demands; nothing is lost in the translation, and members gain a great deal by presenting demands through a representative association.
3. Although interest groups are not always and uniformly successful (some win and some lose), each group, whatever its demands, has equal access to the political resources necessary for success.
4. Organizations help make individuals politically effective; thus they strengthen the social fabric.

We shall refute the first three of these assumptions; and, although the fourth assumption is true, we will argue that *because* groups strengthen the social fabric, they guide their members toward accepting the status quo. We suggest that interest groups, rather than articulating the demands of masses, protect the values of established elites.

THE CLASS BIAS OF INTEREST-GROUP AFFILIATION

It is widely believed that Americans are joiners, and a majority of the population does in fact belong to at least one formal organization. Yet membership in organized interest groups is clearly linked to socioeconomic status. Membership is greatest among the professional and managerial classes, college-educated and high-income people. The upper-middle and upper classes are the primary joiners of organized groups.[3]

The class bias of organized groups varies according to the organization. Unions (which frequently are not voluntary) and the Ku Klux Klan recruit from the lower strata. Upper-middle-class blacks lead civil rights organizations. Liberal causes, such as the women's movement and Common Cause, draw disproportionately from the university-educated and academically connected liberal establishment and rarely appeal to the lower classes. The social bias in association membership, whether or not the association is political, is complemented by the high social origins of lobbyists and the predominance of business organizations in *effective* lobbying.

One sure guide to the class bias of an organization is the extent to which it evokes the image of the "average American." Common Cause, the "people's lobby," stands out as an especially egregious case. Its literature invariably invokes the symbols of the common people. Powerless in the face of the "interest groups," the average American should join Common Cause. However, the average member of Common Cause has a family income twice the national average; 43 percent have completed graduate school or a professional school.[4] Studies of comparable groups document the upper-class bias of liberal, reformist groups, as do studies of environmental groups (see Table 9-1). Because such groups are the intellectual and organizational heirs of the nineteenth-century reform movement, a movement that combated urban political machines in the name of good government, it is hardly surprising that blue-collar workers, the heart of the old urban machines, are conspicuous by their absence. Common Cause is one of numerous "people's lobbies" with goals unrelated to mass aspirations.

TABLE 9-1   Characteristics of environmental/conservation group members

	Environmental Action (N = 705)	Environmental Defense Fund (N = 630)	National Wildlife Federation (N = 509)	Sierra Club (N = 661)	The Wilderness Society (N = 623)
EDUCATION (%)					
High school graduate or less	7	6	34	7	9
Some college	13	11	23	16	14
College graduate	80	83	43	77	77
INCOME (%)					
Under $10,000	15	7	17	9	13
$10,000–$19,999	29	24	38	31	26
$20,000–$39,999	33	38	36	41	36
$40,000 and over	23	31	9	19	25
MEDIAN AGE	39	46	51	38	47
SEX (%)					
Male	63	58	54	68	57
Female	37	42	46	32	43
PARTY IDENTIFICATION (%)					
Democrat	31	29	12	29	20
Independent	65	62	60	59	64
Republican	4	9	28	12	16
POLITICAL IDEOLOGY (%)					
Conservative	9	13	46	23	29
Middle-of-the-road	9	13	31	16	18
Liberal	72	67	21	57	51
Radical	10	7	2	4	2
RELIGIOUS AFFILIATION (%)					
No organized group/none	56	47	22	54	40
Protestant	27	34	60	29	45
Catholic	6	8	16	11	10
Jewish	11	11	2	6	5
TOTAL GROUP MEMBERSHIP (1977)	**16,000**	**45,000**	**620,000**	**178,000**	**68,000**

SOURCE: Ronald G. Shaiko, "Grass Roots Lobbying: Environmentalists as Constituents," paper presented at the meeting of the American Political Science Association, New Orleans, 1985. Used with permission.

This bias has obvious implications for the functions of interest groups. Their activities mostly benefit the upper-middle and upper classes. Whether or not interest groups are an effective link between the citizen and government, many citizens do not avail themselves of this benefit. Even if the formal organization reduces anxiety or increases feelings of power, it does not serve the poor and the uneducated, whose alienation from the society is the greatest and whose need for such services is most extreme.[5]

Among members of organizations, active participation—and holding formal office—relates directly to social status. Whereas the majority of Americans are members of organizations, only a minority of members are active. Control typically rests with a small elite. The "iron law of oligarchy" states that even the most democratically inclined organizations gradually evolve into oligarchies. The oligarchs, who help shape the goals of the organizations, come disproportionately from the upper social classes.[6]

Thus our first empirical test of contemporary pluralist interest-group theory fails to corroborate one of its basic assumptions. Those who are active in interest groups constitute only a small portion of the populace, and they tend to be of higher socioeconomic status than those who are not active. In short, the elites are the most active in interest groups in the United States. And as E. E. Schattschneider concludes:

> The business or upper-class bias of the pressure system shows up every-where. . . . The data raise a serious question about the validity of the proposition that special interest groups are a universal form of political organization reflecting all interests.[7]

HOW WELL DO GROUPS TRANSMIT MEMBERS' DEMANDS?

The next test of pluralist group theory is how well interest groups translate members' demands into political action—or whether they do so at all.

The size of the group is an important variable in its leadership's political effectiveness. Since elected officials are sensitive to numbers, a large membership enhances a group's access to legislators. However, large groups find it difficult to commit themselves to an explicit position since their membership is so heterogeneous. The policy positions of mass membership organizations are often vague and broad, devoid of specific content—and thus harmless. The U.S. Chamber of Commerce, for example seeks to represent "businesspeople," without regard for the nature of the business. Since intrabusiness disputes are often as bitter as labor-management disputes, the chamber cannot take a position on many of the legislative and administrative details that affect the economic health of various segments of the business community. The American Petroleum

Institute, representing only the oil industry, is far more effective than the broad-based Chamber of Commerce.

Leaders and followers differ. *All* groups are afflicted with the curse of misrepresentation.[8] For example, civil rights organization leaders and the majority of black Americans differ in their views of affirmative action. By surveying the leaders of civil rights groups and asking identical questions of random samples of blacks, Linda Lichter discovered that black leaders do not necessarily represent the views of black masses (see Table 9-2). Black leaders think black people are going backward, whereas followers think they are making progress. Leaders have experienced discrimination, whereas followers perceive they have not. Leaders support affirmative action and followers do not. Leaders think they have been abandoned by the Democrats but followers do not.

Black followers are *social* conservatives, but for leaders the opposite is true. Given this evidence, Lichter concludes:

> Only about half of all blacks said that the leaders they see on television and read about in the newspapers represent a majority of black people. This split may be related to the small proportion of blacks, 14 percent, who said they belonged to any civil rights organization. Many blacks, therefore, may not be in close touch with the policies of some black leaders and civil rights groups.[9]

TABLE 9-2   Black leaders and followers: Do they agree?

	Black leaders (%)	All blacks (%)
Most blacks today making progress or going backward?		
Making progress	39	66
Going backward	61	34
Have you, personally, ever experienced racial discrimination against blacks in terms of applying for a job, or not?		
Have experienced racial discrimination	74	40
Have not	26	60
Some people say that to make up for past discrimination, members of minority groups should be given preferential treatment in getting jobs and places in college. Others say that ability, as determined by test scores, should be the main consideration. Which point of view comes closer to how you feel on this matter?		
Minorities should be given preference	77	23
Ability should be the main consideration	23	77
Would you say the Democratic party is now more interested, as interested, or less interested in helping solve the problems of black Americans as compared with four years ago?		
More interested	10	46
As interested	31	26
Less interested	59	28
Prayer in the public schools (percentage in favor)	40	83
The death penalty for murder (percentage in favor)	33	55
Allowing homosexuals to teach in the public schools (percentage in favor)	59	40

SOURCE: Excerpted from *Public Opinion*, August/September 1985, pp. 42–43.

In contrast to large groups, small and highly organized groups have attained very tangible benefits. Small groups with narrow interests can achieve cohesion more readily and can concentrate their resources on a limited, tangible objective.[10] They can act decisively and persistently based on precise information. Such organizations are most frequently business, professional, or industrial; they are the major employers of lobbyists at the state and national level. Many businesspeople organize into trade associations representing many industrial and commercial activities. Because their membership represents a specific form of business activity—for example, insurance—many trade associations are quite small, some with as few as twenty-five members. Their power to advocate specific values is disproportionate, while the business community as a whole fights symbolic battles.

SINGLE-INTEREST-GROUP POLITICS

"Representative government . . . is in the worst shape I have seen it in my sixteen years in the Senate. The heart of the problem is that the Senate and the House are awash in a sea of special-interest campaign contributions and special-interest lobbying."[11] This complaint by Senator Edward Kennedy reflects his belief that "new" groups, unfamiliar with the processes of bargaining, negotiation, and compromise, are competing with "old" groups that are well established, well connected, and sophisticated about the need for compromise.

Single-issue or single-interest groups are the powers that gave rise to Senator Kennedy's complaint. Such groups are indeed more prevalent, or at least more visible, than they were in the past. Older, established groups have a variety of interests that concern their staffs and active members. Single-interest groups live, as their name implies, for the defeat or passage of one law, one cause.

Because single-issue groups focus on one narrow concern (abortion or gun control, for example), they do not have much flexibility for bargaining or compromise. Their strength is almost solely the intensity of their beliefs. They offer no benefits to members other than political commitment that ranges from "merely strong" to "fanatical." Although not writing explicitly about single-issue groups, Jeffrey Berry described well their characteristics: "For the most part, these people are zealots, and they derive a great deal of satisfaction from their jobs. In contrast to the more mildly committed private interest lobbyists, the public interest activists are more likely to seek out the work they are doing, rather than merely 'drift' into it."[12]

This intense commitment has at least two important consequences. First, leaders have far less freedom of action than they would have with a membership recruited for nonpolitical reasons. The second consequence is that the clearer link between leaders and followers and the dedication of both to the cause hampers leaders from fully using the traditional processes of political compromise. Clearly, a person who sees abortion as a form of murder cannot compromise by saying, "I would agree to thirty thousand federally funded abortions and no more."

Why have single-issue groups proliferated in the past decade? Much of the explanation lies in the reforms of political parties and Congress (see Chapter 7). As political parties reformed to increase their responsiveness, the strength of party organization declined. More and more states hold open primaries. Candidates rely more on personal organization and media exposure than on party organization support (see Chapter 8). As parties weaken, popular attachment to the parties deteriorates so that neither party attracts the loyalty of a majority of voters. In Congress, party influence has diminished, with reforms creating a larger role for subcommittees and reducing the importance of seniority (see Chapter 12). Candidates turn to single-interest organizations, whose elective influence appears significant in contrast to the decline of parties and the continuing decline of mass participation in elections. Such groups, of course, represent minorities, but so do all other interest groups. The essential difference is that they are *more* representative of the views of their members—because they cannot compromise—than are the established groups. They are not the functional equivalent of political parties, for their causes are limited. They are, however, more responsive to issues than parties and traditional interest groups are.

LOBBYING: HOW ORGANIZED INTERESTS INFLUENCE GOVERNMENT

Lobbying is any communication directed at a government decision maker with the hope of influencing decisions. For organized interests, lobbying is a continuous activity—in congressional committees, in congressional staff offices, at the White House, at executive agencies, at Washington cocktail parties. If a group loses a round in Congress, it continues the fight in the agency in charge of executing the policy, or it challenges the policy in the courts. The following year it resumes the struggle in Congress: it fights for repeal of the offending legislation, for weakening amendments, or for budget reductions that would cripple enforcement efforts. The process can continue indefinitely.

We can classify lobbying techniques in four categories: (1) access, (2) information, (3) grass-roots mobilization, and (4) campaign support. In the real world of Washington power struggles, all these techniques may be applied simultaneously, or innovative techniques may be discovered and applied at any time.

One technique that most experienced lobbyists shun is the *threat*. Amateur lobbyists may threaten legislators by vowing to defeat them at the next election, a tactic guaranteed to produce a defensive reaction among members of Congress. Out of self-respect, legislators are likely to respond to crude pressures by demonstrating their independence and voting against the threatening lobbyist. Moreover, experienced members of Congress know that such threats are empty; lobbyists can seldom deliver enough votes to influence the outcome of an election.

Access

To communicate with decision makers, an organized interest first needs access to them. As a prominent Washington lobbyist explained: "Number 1 is the access—to get them in the door and get a hearing for your case . . . knowing the individuals personally, knowing their staffs and how they operate and the kind of information they want . . . that kind of personal knowledge can help you maximize the client's hearing."[13]

"Opening doors" is a major business in Washington. Individuals who have personal contacts with decision makers (or who say they do) sell their services at high prices. Washington law firms, public relations agencies, and consultants all offer their insider connection and their advice to potential clients. Many professional lobbyists are former members of Congress, former White House aides, or former congressional staff personnel who "know their way around." The personal prestige of the lobbyist, together with the group's perceived political influence, helps open doors in Washington.

Access is also the object of socializing. This too is becoming institutionalized. There are, of course, the usual dinners with lobbyists, but more often lobbyists are showing up at various fund-raising affairs. Lobbyists pay thousands of dollars a plate at the president's dinner, the Democratic Congressional Dinner, and fund-raisers for individual members of Congress. Few legislators can be bought for the price of an individual dinner, but how about a sixty-thousand-dollar dinner (the take in the average fund-raiser)?

Another form of contribution is the honorarium. Organizations pay two thousand dollars per speech, plus expenses, and twenty-two thousand dollars a year is the limit on legislators. Each year, fifty or so legislators meet or exceed this limit.

Then there are the really big boondoggles. For example, in 1985 Congress members and their spouses flew at government expense to the Paris air show, where the aerospace industry entertained.

Information

Once lobbyists gain access, their knowledge and information become their most valuable resources. A lobbyist may contribute such information as (1) knowledge of the legislative process, (2) expertise on the issue under debate, and (3) information about the group's position on the issue.

Because legislators and their aides value all three types of knowledge, lobbyists can often trade their knowledge for congressional support.

Lobbyists must spend considerable time and effort keeping information about bills affecting their interests. They must be thoroughly familiar with the ins and outs of the legislative process—the relevant committees and subcommittees, their schedules of meetings and hearings, their key staff members, the best moments to act, the precise language for proposed bills and amendments, the witnesses for hearings, and the political strengths and weaknesses of the legislators themselves.

The lobbyist's policy information must be accurate as well as timely. A successful lobbyist never supplies faulty or inaccurate information; his or her success depends on maintaining the trust and confidence of the decision makers. A reputation for honesty is as important as a reputation for influence. Lobbyists provide the information and argumentation that members of Congress use in legislative debate and in speeches back home. In this role, the lobbyist complements the functions of congressional staff. Testimony at legislative hearings is a common form of information exchange between lobbyists and legislators. Lobbyists also provide the technical reports and analyses used by congressional staffs in their legislative research.

Grass-Roots Mobilization

Many organized interests also lobby Congress by mobilizing constituents to apply pressure on their behalf. Many lobbyists believe that legislators, especially insecure ones, pay close attention to letters, telegrams, and calls from "folks back home." The larger organized interests often have local chapters throughout the nation and can mobilize these local affiliates to apply pressure when necessary. Lobbyists encourage influential local elites to visit a Congress member's office personally or to make a personal phone call on behalf of the group's positions.

Of course, experienced lawmakers recognize attempts by lobby groups to orchestrate "spontaneous" grass-roots outpourings of cards and letters. Pressure mail is often identical in wording and content. Nevertheless, members of Congress dare not ignore a flood of letters and telegrams from home, for the mail shows that constituents are aware of the issue and care enough to sign their names. Sophisticated lobbyists, such as Richard A. Viguerie, a widely recognized conservative and expert on mass mailings, have refined modern computerized mail techniques.

Another grass-roots tactic is to mobilize the press in a Congress member's home district. Lobbyists may provide news, analyses, and editorials to local newspapers and then clip favorable articles to send to lawmakers. Lobby groups may also buy advertisements in hometown newspapers. And nearly every *Washington Post* carries full- or half-page ads placed by lobby groups.

Campaign Support

Increasingly, the key to success in lobbying is the campaign contribution. Interest-group contributions not only help lobbyists gain access and a favorable hearing but also help elect people friendly to the group's goals. As the costs of campaigning increase, legislators must depend more heavily on the contributions of organized interests.

It is politically stupid for a lobbyist to extract a specific vote pledge from a legislator in exchange for a campaign contribution. Crude "vote buying" is usually (not always, though) avoided. Instead, organized interests contribute to the campaign fund of an incumbent number of Congress over a long period of time and leave it to the lawmaker to figure out how to retain their support. When a legislator consistently votes against an organized interest, that interest may then contribute to the opposition candidate in the next election.

Regulation of Lobbies

Although the First Amendment protects lobbying, government can regulate lobbying activities. The principal method is disclosure: the law requires lobbyists to register as lobbyists and to report how much they spend. But definitions of lobbying are unclear and enforcement is weak. Many of the larger lobby groups—for example, the National Association of Manufacturers, the National Bankers Association, and Americans for Constitutional Action—have never registered as lobbyists. These organizations claim that because lobbying is not their "principal" activity, they need not register under the law. Financial reports of lobbyists grossly underestimate the extent of lobbying in Congress because the law requires reports only on money spent on direct lobbying before Congress, not on money spent for public relations or for campaign contributions. Another weakness in the law is that it applies only to attempts to influence Congress and does not regulate lobbying activities in administrative agencies or the executive branch. However, restrictive legislation might violate the First Amendment freedom to "petition the government for a redress of grievances."

PACs: THE NEW POLITICAL PARTIES

Political parties are large, disorganized, and largely devoid of ideology. A contributor wishing to support a specific political cause gets more for his or her money by contributing to a PAC. A PAC, or political action committee, is a nonparty organization that solicits voluntary contributions to disburse to political candidates. PACs have been organized by labor unions, trade associations, and liberal and conservative groups: environmental groups, for example, all have organized PACs. However, the largest number of PACs is in the corporate sector. Contributions to PACs must be voluntary; corporations and labor unions cannot legally use corporate or union treasuries for political campaigns.

The PACs have become a major force in Washington politics in recent years. An estimated one-third of all campaign contributions now originates with them. The increasing cost of television campaigning makes many legislators dependent on PAC contributions to run their campaigns.

The PACs give most of their money to *incumbent* members of Congress (see Table 9-3). Not only does this practice strengthen incumbents against their opponents, but it also makes incumbents less likely to change the law governing PAC contributions. The object is *access*. Rarely will money be contributed in an explicit contract for a vote. Whereas some PACs are largely concerned with one set of policies, others are more interested in a long-term, institutionally structured relationship with the legislature. Thus the preference for incumbents is reasonable. In 1990, political action committees spent $159 million on elections to the Senate and House. In the House, most of the money went to Democratic incumbents; in the Senate, Republicans fared better, but incumbents—irrespective of party—continued to dominate. Political action committees have therefore contributed to the creation of two congressional parties, not Democrats and Republicans, but incumbents and challengers.

Copyright, 1989, *Boston Globe*. Distributed by Los Angeles Times Syndicate. Reprinted by permission.

TABLE 9-3   Distribution of PAC contributions to congressional elections, 1990

	Total (millions)	Democrats	Republicans	Incumbents	Challengers	Open seats
House	110.4	73.4 (67%)	36.9 (33%)	80.3 (73%)	7.7 (7%)	13.6 (9%)
Senate	48.8	24.9 (51%)	23.9 (49%)	36.9 (76%)	8.4 (17%)	3.4 (7%)

It is a mistake to view PACs as interested solely in the immediate election of incumbents. PACs also give money to officeholders not up for election in a particular year, in order to help them retire debts or prepare for a future election. Additionally, PACs spend money in "indirect" expenditures. Indirect expenditures include ads and endorsements that are not paid for directly by the candidates' campaign organizations.

In an account of all PAC spending, indirect expenditures are said to be more than direct expenditures. The top fifteen PACs in direct campaign expenditures are listed in Table 9-4.

TABLE 9-4   The top money raisers

	Millions of dollars
CORPORATE PACs	
American Telephone and Telegraph Company Inc. PAC (AT&T PAC)	2.83
United Parcel Service (UPS PAC)	1.86
Federal Express Corporation Political Action Committee (FEPAC)	1.56
Philip Morris Political Action Committee (PHIL-PAC)	.937
Waste Management Inc. Employees' Better Government Fund (WMI PAC)	.893
LABOR PACs	
Democratic/Republican/Independent Voter Education Committee	10.51
National Education Association Political Action Committee	4.50
UAW V CAP (UAW Voluntary Community Action Program)	4.04
American Federation of State, County and Municipal Employees	3.89
Machinists Nonpartisan Political League	3.12
IDEOLOGICAL (NON-CONNECTED) PACs	
Voter Guide	5.08
National Congressional Club (Sen. Jesse Helms)	3.54
Auto Dealers and Drivers for Free Trade PAC	3.08
American Citizens for Political Action	2.77
Campaign America	2.43
TRADE ASSOCIATIONS	
American Medical Association Political Action Committee	5.69
Realtors' Political Action Committee	5.30
Association of Trial Lawyers of America Political Action Committee	3.86
NRA Political Victory Fund	3.69
Dealers Election Action Committee of the National Automobile Dealers Association (NADA)	2.76

SOURCE: Federal Election Commission Report, March 31, 1991.

LABOR AND THE DEMOCRATS

The PACs have a strong preference for incumbents. Since more Democratic than Republican incumbents are in Congress, Democrats usually receive more PAC money than Republicans do. Moreover, Democrats benefit from organized labor's unwillingness to court Republicans. The Democrats have a solid base in labor and expand to corporations.

If Democrats were dependent upon organized labor and Republicans upon corporations, the Democrats would be at a major disadvantage. The corporate PACs are the growth sector (see Figure 9-1). Labor is suffering from a decline in union membership, as the economy shifts from an industrial to a service base. Once 30 percent of the work force, unionized labor is now only 18 percent and dropping. Young, educated, and female workers have traditionally been less likely to join unions, and they are now the most rapidly growing segments of the work force. In 1960, one-third of the work force was female; now one-half is female. In 1960, one in ten workers was a college graduate, but now one in four is.[14] Surveys consistently show that organized labor ranks dead last among public and

FIGURE 9-1   Growth of PACs

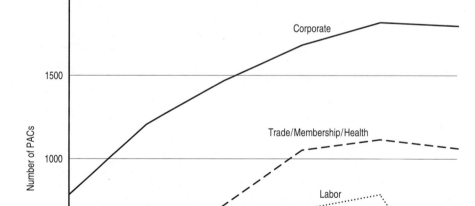

SOURCE: Federal Election Commission

private institutions on the question of confidence.[15] Labor's decline and the rise of corporate PACs suggest a further decrease in the diversity of the interest-group system.

FOLLOW THE MONEY: INTEREST GROUPS AND THE BUDGET

Interest groups naturally flock to those committees and institutions that spend or collect money. Myriad organizations play a role in the annual budget process.

Consider, for example, the budget "summit agreement" in 1990, in which President Bush abandoned his "no new taxes" pledge, and Congress raised income and gasoline taxes and imposed a "luxury tax." While media attention was focused upon the income tax increase, many backroom deals were struck. Narrowly targeted tax breaks—"rifle shots"—are part of the culture of Congress. The rebellion against leadership was generated partly because the rifle shots were available only to the leadership, not the rank and file. For example, a proposed 10 percent luxury tax was to be applied to all private airplanes that cost more than $100,000, to all boats that cost more than $30,000, and to all jewelry and furs priced over $500. In the Senate, the counterproposal raised the cost to $250,000 and exempted planes that were used 80 percent of the time for business. Why the change? Senate Minority Leader Robert Dole is from Kansas, where Cessna Aircraft Company and Beechcraft Aircraft Corporation are located. The summit budget plan had set the cost floor for boats at $30,000. However, Senate Majority Leader George Mitchell is from Maine, where the boat-building industry would be damaged by that provision. Therefore, the floor was raised to $100,000. Simultaneously, Mitchell secured a break for UNUM, the Life Insurance Company of Portland, the largest private employer in Maine's largest city. The Fur Information Council of America lobbied for a higher "luxury" threshold for fur coats; the threshold was raised to $10,000. The threshold price for "luxury" cars was set at $30,000. The vast majority of such cars are made by European and Japanese manufacturers. No lobbyists were around to plead their case, and the American automakers had no strong objection to the threshold.

In early conversations about "sin taxes" on tobacco and alcohol, talk of a cigarette tax of sixteen cents a pack was common; the tax eventually enacted was half that amount, as a result of intense tobacco industry lobbying and the savvy of Senator Wendell Ford of Kentucky. He importuned House Ways and Means Committee Chairman Daniel Rostenkowski to accept a deal: if Rostenkowski would buy the tobacco tax reduction, Ford would support legislation permitting airport passenger fees for airport construction. Rostenkowski is from Chicago, where O'Hare Airport is in serious need of funds, and he eagerly traded tobacco taxes for passenger fees. When this bargain was struck, the cigar manufacturers of southern Florida were exempted. The tax on cigarettes, but not cigars, was increased.

Meanwhile, the liquor and wine industry, aided by House Majority Leader Richard Gephardt of Missouri, held down the increase in excise taxes on wine and beer (Anheuser-Busch is in St. Louis). Senate budget bargainers were said to be more worried about protecting California's Pete Wilson in a tough reelection campaign. Since California is the nation's leading wine producer, Wilson was given "something to take credit for." Oregon's Bob Packwood could "take credit" for another wrinkle. Wineries producing less than two hundred thousand gallons a year were exempt from the tax—a criterion satisfied by every vineyard in Oregon.

CONSERVATIVE INFLUENCE OF ORGANIZATIONS

Organizations perform a conservative, stabilizing function for society. Formal organizations seldom cause social change. Of course, the goals of associations vary, some being more radical than others. But in general, organizations gradually become more moderate as the goal of perpetuating themselves takes priority over their original goals:

> The day-to-day behavior of the permanent staff and active participants (a minority of the membership) becomes centered around proximate goals of primary internal importance, modifying or "displacing" the stated goals of the organization.[16]

In other words, as organizations grow older, they shift from trying to implement their original values to maintaining their structure, even if they thereby sacrifice the organization's central mission.[17] The people who have the greatest stake in the existing social system thus come to dominate the organization. Of course, organizations do not stop seeking change, but the extent of change they seek is minimal. Once they achieve even a few of their goals, they then have a stake in the ongoing system and a rational basis for moderate politics. Social stability is apparently a product of this organizational system—not simply because people have overlapping affiliations but because of the intrinsic nature of organizations.

Since groups serve society by cementing their members to the established social system, those who seek to alter this system find organizations an unsatisfactory mechanism. True, some groups develop with radical change in mind, but the process of bureaucratization leadership from "have-nots" to "haves" gradually reduces any organization's commitment to substantial change. Impoverished people and blacks have gained little from groups because the group structure is dominated by people with a favored position in society. For segments of society effectively barred from other forms of participation, violent protest may be the only method of entry into the political process. Ironically, if deprived peoples succeed in organizing themselves, violence will probably decline, to be replaced by organizational activity. But in time, the new organizations will develop their own commitment to the status quo, thus again leaving the truly deprived with little to show for their sacrifices.

THE CASE AGAINST INTEREST GROUPS

Pluralist theory rejects the notion of a "public interest." Regarding such an idea as naive, pluralist writers prefer to regard the public interest as the sum of the competing demands; a Darwinian notion that the strongest coalition will—and should—win.

But in the absence of a recognized public interest, governments become so ensnared in interest group squabbles that they cannot address broader, more distant goals. The example most often given is the American budget deficit, which in spite of innumerable warnings continues to spiral out of control (see Chapter 11). Thomas Mann, a serious and reflective student of American government, in a masterly bit of understatement, grieves that "when effective action on the country's most pressing problems requires the imposition of losses on organized interests, with benefits to all on the distant horizon, the odds of success in the U.S. political system are not very high."[18] Only a government strong enough to impose costs on interest groups could resolve the budget crisis and serve the public interest. But the United States does not have that government. Mann therefore settles on a realistic if bleak prediction about the future of American politics: "a continuation of the escapism and deadlock of recent years. . . ."[19] In a similar vein, political scientist Terry Moe predicts that the "current administrative tangle may actually get worse over time." Moe thinks so for the same reasons as does Mann: the proliferation of interest groups and the attendant "structural disarray."[20]

The same interest-group deadlock that destroys fiscal responsibility in Washington also destroys effective energy conservation and environmental protection. For example, the United States does not lack an energy policy because Reagan and Bush were indisposed toward government intervention. It lacks such a policy because interest-group bargaining provides no incentives for conservative or thinking beyond today.

> The pluralism form of interest intermediation produces dissensus and instability. Pluralism encourages interest groups to pursue their own particular interests in coalitions with other groups that are pursuing their particular interest. Such coalitions generally adopt policies that are concerned more with existing distributional inequities than with long-term collective gain.[21]

Since gasoline in the United States is far less expensive than in other industrial democracies, so the argument runs, only a steep tax will slow our guzzling habits. But a phalanx of interest groups is opposed to increases in gasoline taxes. This tax increase not only would raise revenue;

it also would have at least a marginal impact on Americans' eagerness to consume energy at rates far greater than those of the other industrial democracies. (U.S. gasoline taxes in 1990 were about $0.25 per gallon; they were $3.80 in Italy, $3.10 in France, $2.10 in Britain, $2.05 in West Germany, $1.80 in Japan, and $0.90 in Canada.) However, few, if any, organized interests have an incentive to lobby for a gasoline tax, whereas many have incentives to assail it. A gasoline tax lacks allies among energy producers of any kind; a decline in the use of gasoline does not lead to an increase in the demand for other fuels. Therefore, notably, the tax offers coal and natural gas companies no clear opportunities to improve their market share. Meanwhile, as far as the petroleum industry is concerned, reduced demand for its principal product is bad news. Others think so too. Alongside the gasoline sellers will stand road contractors, engineers, truckers, taxicab companies, the nation's biggest automakers, and the United Auto Workers, as well as service industries such as motels, fast-food chains, shopping malls, and countless other roadside businesses for whom patronage by motorists (and therefore inexpensive gasoline) is lifeblood. Elected officials in other industrialized democracies some-times confront similar pressure groups, but never on the same scale.[22]

Pluralism (open and unconstrained group access to the institutions where decisions are made) relies on market incentives to provoke competing group pressures. But interest groups do not meet the traditional pluralist claims made for them. They do not represent masses of people any more efficiently than political parties do. Interest groups do, however, create pressures to pursue the shortsighted domestic policies that are driving the United States to economic decline. Thus, although theorists of pluralism continue to sing the praises of interest groups because of their presumed representative capacity, fewer and fewer voices are joining in the chorus today.

SUMMARY

Pluralism asserts that organized interest groups provide the individual with an effective way to participate in the political system. It contends that individuals can make their voices heard through membership in the organized groups that reflect their views on public affairs. Pluralists further believe that competition among organized interests provides a balance of power that protects the individual's interests. Interest groups divide power among themselves and hence protect the individual from rule by a single oppressive elite.

Earlier we pointed out that pluralism diverges from classical democratic theory. Even if the plural elite model accurately portrays the reality of American politics, it does not guarantee the implementation of democratic values. Our analysis of interest groups produced the following propositions:

1. Interest groups draw disproportionately from middle- and upper-class segments of the population. The pressure-group system is not representative of the entire community.

2. Leadership of interest groups is recruited from the middle- and upper-class population.

3. Business and professional organizations predominate among organized interest groups.

4. Generally mass membership groups achieve only symbolic success, and smaller, more cohesive groups are able to achieve more tangible results.

5. Considerable inequality exists among organized interest groups. Business and producer groups with narrow membership but cohesive organization achieve their tangible goals at the expense of broad, unorganized groups seeking less tangible goals.

6. Organized interest groups are governed by small elites whose values do not necessarily reflect the values of most members.

7. Business groups and associations are the most highly organized and active lobbyists in Washington and in the state capitals. Their influence is especially evident in the growth of political action committees.

8. Organizations tend to become conservative as they acquire a stake in the existing social order. Therefore, pressures for substantial social change must generally come from forces outside the structure of organized interest groups.

———NOTES

1. Gabriel A. Almond and Sidney Verba, *The Civic Culture: Political Attitudes and Democracy in Five Nations* (Boston: Little, Brown, 1965), p. 245.
2. David B. Truman, *The Governmental Process* (New York: Knopf, 1951).
3. Almond and Verba, op. cit., p. 249.
4. Andrew S. McFarland, *Common Cause* (Chatham, N.J.: Chatham House, 1984), pp. 48–49.
5. Sidney Verba and Norman H. Nie, *Participation in America* (New York: Harper & Row, 1972), p. 208.
6. Roberto Michels, *Political Parties: A Sociological Study of the Oligarchical Tendencies of Modern Democracy* (1915; reprint, New York: Dover, 1959), esp. p. 248.
7. E. E. Schattschneider, *The Semisovereign People: A Realist's View of Democracy in America* (New York: Holt, Rinehart & Winston, 1960), pp. 31–34.
8. Norman R. Luttbeg and Harmon Zeigler, "Attitude Consensus and Conflict in an Interest Group: An Assessment of Cohesion," *American Political Science Review* 60 (September 1966): 658.

9. Linda S. Lichter, "Who Speaks for Black America?" *Public Opinion* (August/September 1985): 44.
10. Murray Edelman, *The Symbolic Uses of Politics* (Urbana: University of Illinois Press, 1964), pp. 24–26.
11. *Newsweek* (November 6, 1979): 50.
12. Jeffrey M. Berry, *Lobbying for the People* (Princeton, N.J.: Princeton University Press, 1977), pp. 100, 109.
13. Congressional Quarterly, *The Washington Lobby*, 4th ed. (Washington, D.C.: Congressional Quarterly Press, 1982), p. 5.
14. Steven M. Bloom, "American Labor at the Crossroads," *American Demographics*, September 1985, p. 31.
15. See, for example, *Gallup Political Index*, July 1985, p. 3.
16. Harmon Zeigler and Wayne Peak, *Interest Groups in American Society*, 2nd ed. (Englewood Cliffs, N.J.: Prentice-Hall, 1972), p. 81.
17. Sheldon L. Messinger, "Organizational Transformation: A Case Study of a Declining Social Movement," *American Sociological Review* 20 (February 1955): 10.
18. Thomas E. Mann, "Breaking the Political Impasse," in Henry J. Aaron, ed., *Setting National Priorities: Policy for the Nineties* (Washington, D.C.: The Brookings Institution, 1990), p. 303.
19. Ibid., p. 313.
20. Terry Moe, "The Politics of Bureaucratic Structure," in John E. Chubb and Paul E. Peterson, eds., *Can the Government Govern?* (Washington, D.C.: The Brookings Institution, 1989), pp. 327–328.
21. Freeman, op cit., p. 91.
22. Pietro S. Nivola, "Déjà Vu All Over Again: Revisiting the Politics of Gasoline Taxation," *The Brookings Review* 9 (1990/1991): 33.

SELECTED READINGS

Bayes, Jane H. *Ideologies and Interest Group Politics.* Novato, Calif.: Chandler and Sharp Publisher, 1982. Bayes argues that the United States is a special-interest group in the world economy.

Berry, Jeffrey M. *Lobbying for the People.* Princeton, N.J.: Princeton University Press, 1977. Berry describes the activities of organizations whose efforts do not provide a selective advantage to their members (such as environmental groups and Common Cause).

Boles, Janet K. *The Politics of the Equal Rights Amendment.* New York: Longman, 1979. This case study describes the campaigns for and against the equal rights amendment in various states.

Dye, Thomas R. *Who's Running America?* 3rd ed. Englewood Cliffs, N.J.: Prentice-Hall, 1982. In a detailed examination, by name, position, and so on, Dye does not dismiss the possibility that there *is* a "they."

Edelman, Murray. *The Symbolic Uses of Politics.* Urbana: University of Illinois Press, 1964. Edelman discusses the general uses of symbols in society and then the specific uses of political phenomena as symbols. He points out that myth and symbolic reassurance have become key elements in the governmental process. Edelman argues that the masses are generally uninterested in and inattentive to political phenomena as symbols. Only when the masses perceive symbolic or real threats or reassurances do they notice things political. Masses react to stimuli. Therefore, political actions "shape men's political wants and 'knowledge,' not the other way around" (p. 172). Edelman also argues that mass demands, when they are articulated, are most often met with "symbolic" rather than "tangible" rewards.

Malbin, Michael J. "Campaign Finance Reform and the 'Special Interests.' " *Public Interest* 56 (Summer 1979): 21–42. This article is a history and analysis of the growth of political action committees.

McFarland, Andrew S. *Common Cause.* Chatham, N.J.: Chatham House, 1984. The backgrounds of members, relationships between leaders and followers, and processes of intra-organizational decision making are covered in a brief, valuable book.

Moe, Terry M. *The Organization of Interests.* Chicago: University of Chicago Press, 1980. Moe concentrates solely on interest groups as organizations, with special attention to group formation, membership maintenance, and the development of political goals.

Olson, Mancur, Jr. *The Logic of Collective Action: Public Goods and the Theory of Groups.* New York: Schocken Books, 1968. This well-written work outlines the rational basis for interest-group activity. Individuals are the units of analysis, and Olson constructs a model of individual motivation for collective behavior given an assumption of rationality.

Schattschneider, E. E. *The Semisovereign People: A Realist's View of Democracy in America.* New York: Holt, Rinehart & Winston, 1960. This book analyzes the nature of conflict and change in the United States. Schattschneider argues against the pluralist bias on interest groups, which he perceives as the common view of the political system today. He also recognizes the elite–masses dichotomy that exists in the American social and political system. For example, he develops the notion that elites, by virtue of their organizational strengths, can manage conflict within the political system. They can alter it, exploit it, and/or suppress it.

Schlozman, Kay Lehman, and Tierney, John T. *Organized Interests and American Democracy.* New York: Harper & Row, 1986. This is the best text in a segmented market.

Verba, Sidney, and Nie, Norman H. *Participation in America.* New York: Harper & Row, 1972. The authors examine the causes and effects of political participation, including participation in organizations.

Wright, John. "PACs, Contributions, and Roll Calls: An Organizational Perspective." *American Political Science Review* 79 (June 1985): 400–414. The author finds no appreciable relationship between PAC contributions and roll call votes.

10 The Presidency

★ *The Presidency is the focus for the most intense and persistent emotions. . . . The President is . . . the one figure who draws together the people's hopes and fears for the political future.*

James David Barber, The Presidential Character, *1985*

Governmental elites in the United States do not command; they seek consensus with other elites. Decision making by governmental elites is a process of bargaining, accommodation, and compromise among the dominant interests in American society. Governmental elites act essentially as go-betweens and mediators, seeking policies that are mutually beneficial to the major interests—industrial, financial, labor, farm, military, bureaucratic, and so on.

The presidency stands at the center of elite interaction in the American political system. For the *elite*, the president proposes policy initiatives, mobilizes influence within the political system, and supervises the management of government and the economy. For the *masses*, the president is a symbol of national unity, an outlet to express their emotions toward government, and a vicarious means of taking political action. For *both* elites and masses, the presidency provides a means of handling national crises—taking whatever actions are necessary in an emergency to stabilize the nation, protect its security, and calm its citizens.

THE PRESIDENT AS SYMBOLIC LEADER

More than any other political figure, the president attracts the attention and emotion of the American masses. The people look to the presidency for leadership and reassurance. They want a president who will personalize government, simplify political issues, and symbolize the "compassionate" and protective role of the state. They want someone who seems concerned with them.

The people also look for toughness, competence, and decisiveness in the presidency. They are prepared to support a president who is willing to *do something*, whether "something" is a good idea or not. National surveys regularly gauge presidential popularity by asking, "Do you approve or disapprove of the way (Bush or Reagan or Carter, etc.) is handling his job as president?" (see Figure 10-1). Presidential popularity goes up when the president takes dramatic action or when the nation faces an external crisis or threat.

The people *want* to support the president. All presidents begin their terms with broad public support. Over time, however, support wanes as troubles pile up and the president is unable to cope with them. Indeed, the popular expectations of a president far exceed the president's powers to meet them. The result is an inevitable decline in public support until a new crisis occurs or dramatic action is necessary.

A brief overview of presidential popularity ratings over time confirms these notions: that a president takes office with broad public support, that support tends to decline over time, and that renewal of support can occur with dramatic action or crisis. Figure 10-1 compares approval ratings of five presidents. Each took office, whether through election or assassination or resignation, with broad popular support. Over time this support

FIGURE 10-1   Presidential approval ratings, 1981–1992

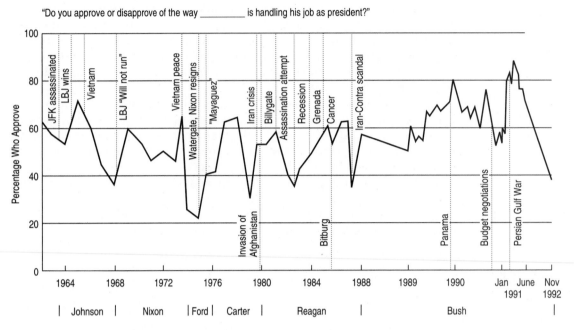

"Do you approve or disapprove of the way _____ is handling his job as president?"

SOURCE: Data based on *Gallup Opinion Index*, 1981–1992.

declined. But dramatic action—peace in Vietnam for Nixon, the *Maya-guez* affair for Ford, the Iranian crisis for Carter, the assassination attempt on Reagan—produced dramatic increases in presidential support. International humiliations or scandals erode presidential popularity.

Nothing inspires elite support among the masses more than decisive military victory. President George Bush achieved the highest public approval ratings in history following victory in the Persian Gulf War. This unprecedented peak occurred only months after the low approval ratings he earned following the abandonment of his "no new taxes" pledge. As the nation turned to domestic concerns following the Gulf War, Bush's approval ratings slipped.

THE PRESIDENT'S FORMAL POWERS

The president has many sources of formal power as chief administrator, chief legislator, party leader, chief diplomat, commander in chief, and chief of state and crisis manager (see Table 10-1). But despite the great powers of the office, no president can monopolize policy making. The president functions within an established elite system and can exercise power only within the framework of that system. The choices available to the president are only those alternatives for which elite support can be mo-

TABLE 10-1   Formal presidential powers

CHIEF ADMINISTRATOR

Implement policy—"Take care that laws be faithfully executed" (Art. II, Sec. 3).

Supervise executive branch of government.

Appoint and remove policy officials.

Prepare executive budget.

CHIEF LEGISLATOR

Initiate policy—"give to the Congress information of the State of the Union and recommend to their consideration such measures as he shall judge necessary and expedient" (Art. II, Sec. 3).

Veto legislation passed by Congress.

Convene special session of Congress "on extraordinary occasions" (Art. II, Sec. 3).

PARTY LEADER

Control national party organization.

Control federal patronage.

Influence (not control) state and local parties through prestige.

CHIEF DIPLOMAT

Make treaties ("with the advice and consent of the Senate") (Art. II, Sec. 2).

Make executive agreements.

Exercise power of diplomatic recognition—" receive ambassadors and other public ministers" (Art. II, Sec. 3).

COMMANDER IN CHIEF

Command U.S. armed forces—"The President shall be Commander-in-Chief of the army and navy" (Art. II, Sec. 2).

Appoint military officials.

Initiate war.

Exercise broad war powers.

CRISIS MANAGER AND CHIEF OF STATE

Oversee formal national action—"The executive Power shall be vested in a President" (Art. II, Sec. 1).

Represent the nation as chief of state.

bilized. The president cannot act outside existing elite consensus—outside the "rules of the game"—and must be sensitive to the interests of major elites—business, agriculture, military, education, bureaucracy, and so on.

PRESIDENTIAL POWERS OF PERSUASION

The presidency's real power depends not on formal authority but on the president's abilities at persuasion. The president does not command American elites but stands in a central position in the elite structure. Responsibility for initiating public policy falls principally on the president and the presidential staff and executive departments. The president has a strong incentive to fulfill this responsibility, since a large segment of the American public holds the president responsible for everything that happens in the nation during that term of office, whether or not the president has the authority or capacity to do anything about it.

Through the power to initiate policy alone, the president's impact on the nation is considerable. The president sets the agenda for public decision making. The president presents programs to Congress in various presidential messages and in the budget and thereby largely determines the business of Congress in any session. Few major undertakings ever get off the ground without presidential initiation; the president frames the issues, determines their context, and decides their timing.

Presidents: Weak and Strong

The powers of the presidency and the importance of this office in the American political system vary with political circumstances and with the personalities of those who occupy the office. The contrasting views of presidents William Howard Taft and Theodore Roosevelt often come up in debates about the true nature of executive power. Taft said:

> The true view of the executive function is, as I conceive it, that the president can exercise no power which cannot be fairly and reasonably traced to some specific grant of power or justly implied and included within such express grant as proper and necessary to its exercise. Such specific grants must be either in the federal constitution or in the pursuance thereof. There is no undefined residuum of power which can be exercised which seems to him to be in the public interest.[1]

Theodore Roosevelt offered an alternative view:

> I decline to adopt the view that what was imperatively necessary for the nation could not be done by the president unless he could find some specific authorization to do it. My belief was that it was not only his right but his duty to do anything that the needs of the nation demanded, unless such action was forbidden by the Constitution or by the laws.[2]

Most evaluations of presidential performance favor the more activist approach to the office. Political analysts usually downgrade Taft, Herbert Hoover, and Dwight Eisenhower, who took more restricted views of the presidency, in comparison with Woodrow Wilson, Theodore and Franklin Roosevelt, and Harry Truman, who were much more active presidents (see Table 10-2).

Growth of Presidential Power

On the whole, presidents of the twentieth century have exercised greater power and initiative than those of the nineteenth century. First, the United States has assumed greater involvement in world affairs, with a resulting increase in the importance of military and foreign policy. In foreign and military affairs, the Constitution gives the president unmis-

TABLE 10-2   Rating the presidents

THE "GREAT" PRESIDENTS	THE "AVERAGE" PRESIDENTS
Lincoln	McKinley
F. Roosevelt	Taft
Washington	Van Buren
Jefferson	Hoover
THE "NEAR GREAT" PRESIDENTS	Hayes
	Arthur
T. Roosevelt	Ford
Wilson	Carter
Jackson	B. Harrison
Truman	THE "BELOW AVERAGE" PRESIDENTS
THE "ABOVE AVERAGE" PRESIDENTS	Taylor
J. Adams	Tyler
L. Johnson	Fillmore
Eisenhower	Coolidge
Polk	Pierce
Kennedy	THE "FAILURES"
Monroe	
J. Q. Adams	A. Johnson
Cleveland	Buchanan
	Nixon
	Grant
	Harding

SOURCE: Robert K. Murray and Tim H. Blessing, *Greatness in the White House*, University Park: Pennsylvania State University Press, 1988, p. 16. Copyright 1988 by The Pennsylvania State University. Reproduced by permission of The Pennsylvania State University Press.

takable and far-reaching powers: to send and receive ambassadors, to make treaties (with the advice and consent of the Senate), and to direct the armed forces as commander in chief. In effect, these powers give the president almost exclusive authority over the nation's foreign and military policy.

A second contributor has been the growth of the executive branch. The federal bureaucracy has grown into a giant elite structure, and the Constitution places the chief executive at the top of the structure. The Constitution gives the president broad, albeit vague, powers to "take care that the laws be faithfully executed" and to "require the opinion in writing of the principal officer in each of the executive departments upon any subject relating to the duties of their respective offices." This clause gives the president general executive authority over the three million civilian employees of the federal bureaucracy. Moreover, the president has the right to appoint (and the right to remove) the principal officers of the executive branch. The Senate must consent to appointments but not to removals. Budgetary control is a major presidential weapon. Although Congress still must appropriate all monies spent by executive departments, the president nonetheless has responsibility for formulating the budget. Congress may cut a presidential budget request and even appropriate more than the president asks for a particular agency or program, but in practice Congress tends to accept the bulk of the president's budget.

The third reason for the importance of the presidency in the twentieth century is technological improvements in the mass media, which have strengthened the role of the president as symbolic leader and molder of mass opinion. Television brings the president directly into contact with the masses, and the masses' attachment to the president is unlike their attachment to any other public official or symbol of government. Fred I. Greenstein has classified the "psychological functions of the presidency." The president

1. "Simplifies perception of government and politics" by serving as "the main cognitive 'handle' for providing busy citizens with some sense of what their government is doing."
2. Provides "an outlet for emotional expression" through public interest in his and his family's private and public life.
3. Is a "symbol of unity" and of nationhood (as the national shock and grief over the death of a president clearly reveal).
4. Provides the masses with a "vicarious means of taking political action" in that the president can act decisively and effectively while they cannot do so.
5. Is a "symbol of social stability" in providing the masses with a feeling of security and guidance. Thus, for the masses, the president is the most visible elite member.[3]

THE PERSONAL PRESIDENCY

The president is the nation's leading celebrity. When the president chooses to address the entire nation, the television networks cancel their regular programming and provide free television time.

The presidency possesses enormous symbolic significance. The president affects popular images of authority, legitimacy, and confidence in the American political system. The president can arouse feelings of patriotism or cynicism, hope or despair, honor or dishonor. Political scientist James David Barber writes:

> The Presidency is the focus for the most intense and persistent emotions. . . . The President is . . . the one figure who draws together the people's hopes and fears for the political future. On top of all of his routine duties, he has to carry that off—or fail.[4]

Effects of Popularity

Presidents are aware of their power as symbolic leader. Abraham Lincoln once declared, "Public sentiment is everything. With public sentiment nothing can fail, without it nothing can succeed."

A president's public popularity in part determines presidential power in interactions with other elites. A president with high ratings in the polls for any reason can get better cooperation from other elites than when low in the polls. For example, Congress is more likely to support legislation by the president when the president's popularity is high. Political scientist George C. Edwards reports that the overall correlation between presidential popularity and support in Congress is .50 for the House and .40 for the Senate. These correlations are not perfect (1.00), which suggests that Congress frequently ignores the president's popularity. But popularity with the masses is certainly one basic component of presidential power.

Popularity has little to do with a president's position on the issues. In recent years, both Republican and Democratic and both liberal and conservative presidents have all at one time or other enjoyed high ratings and suffered low ratings in the polls. As Richard Neustadt has written, "Presidential standing outside of Washington is actually a jumble of imprecise impressions held by relatively inattentive men."[5]

The American president receives more veneration, even though possessing less power, than European heads of state: "He is the nation's spokesman, the personification of the nation—the closest thing Americans have to a royal sovereign. Upon his election he and his family dominate the news in America."[6]

Presidential Lifestyle

Americans also expect their presidents to be exemplary in their personal lives, setting an example, like royalty. Presidents must provide not only political salvation, but moral cleansing as well: "The President is expected to personify our bitterness in an inspiring way, to express in what he does and is (not just what he says) a moral idealism which, in the public mind, is the very opposite of politics."[7] When a president does not, as is often the case, the shock is profound: Nixon's profanity and vulgarity, as revealed by the Watergate tapes, generated outrage. Even scholars are appalled at John Kennedy's astonishing sexual promiscuity. Reeves writes of John Kennedy that:

> Kennedy abused his high position for personal gratification. His reckless liaisons with women and mobsters were irresponsible, dangerous and demeaning to the office. . . . Had Kennedy lived to see a second term, the realities of his lechery and his dealings with [mobsters] might have leaked out while he was still in office, gravely damaging the presidency, debilitating his administration and severely disillusioning a populace which, no matter how jaded it seemed, looks to a president with hope for reassurance and leadership.[8]

Between one-fourth and one-third of Americans object to presidents' not belonging to a church, using tranquilizers, using profanity, having seen a psychiatrist, or wearing jeans in the oval office.[9]

——— THE PRESIDENCY IN ECLIPSE?

Presidential power to govern the nation is weakened by divided party control of government. One of the most striking manifestations of the decline of political parties (see Chapter 7) is the emergence of divided government, with the president from one party and a majority of one or both houses of Congress composed of the opposition. The "normal" divided government is one with a Republican president and a Democratic legislative majority. The Republicans have won seven of eleven presidential elections since 1952, while the Democrats have dominated the legislature, especially the House of Representatives. There the Republicans have not won a majority since 1952. Divided government was once rare: only once (1888) in twenty-five presidential elections between 1856 and 1952 did the party winning the presidency not also win a majority in the House of Representatives. But given the durability of the Democratic majority in the House, and the success of Republicans in presidential elections ensured "gridlock" government. Indeed, Clinton's victory was inspired, in part, by the demand to break the gridlock.

Voters are increasingly willing to divide their party loyalties. In 1988, 81 percent of the voters in the presidential election were party-liners (that is, they voted for the candidate who matched their party identification), up from 67 percent in 1972. However, the proportion of party-liners among voters in elections for seats in the House of Representatives is much lower, causing political scientist Morris Fiorina to conclude that

> party identification in the population was a stronger correlate of voting in the 1930s and 1940s than it is today. Although the increased independence of the electorate has clearly been exaggerated . . . there has been a general weakening in the strength of partisanship. In addition there has been a decline in the capacity of partisanship to "structure" the vote . . . even those who report that they are strong partisans are less likely to support their party's candidate *across the board* than they were a generation ago.[10]

About one-fourth of the electorate votes for the presidential candidate of one party and the congressional candidate of the other.[11]

The United States holds many more elections than other industrial democracies and thus provides more opportunities for voters to divide their party loyalty from one election to another. The total percentage of those who voted for Democrats for some offices and Republicans for others is much higher than the proportion who split their votes in national elections. In 1960, about one-third of voters divided their allegiance; in 1988, two-thirds did.[12] Political parties are weaker than they once were. A longer view reveals how much has changed about the American voter. In the 1900s, one could predict 85 percent of the variance of state votes for candidates for the House of Representatives by knowing the state's vote for the candidates for president; in other words, a reliable prediction of a state's vote for its congressional delegation could be made simply by knowing its vote for president. In the 1980s, this information would be of no predictive help at all; the two sets of votes had become virtually completely independent.

But divided government is only part of the story. Power in Congress has continued to become decentralized (see Chapter 12), and independent centers of power have grown in influence, in a process of "fragmentation" that nobody—not even the president—can control. Political scientist Richard Rose, viewing the United States in comparison with Europe, seeks a government institutionally capable of managing:

> In seeking to exercise influence on subgovernments [that is, combinations of interest groups, bureaucracies, and legislative committees], the basic problem of the President is simple: there is no government there. The President does not have in his own hands the authority to override the preferences of subgovernments in the name of broader national interests. . . . Parliamentary systems have subgovernments too . . . but in a parliamentary system there is government as well as subgovernments.[13]

The presidency today is show without substance: "The more a president holds to the initiative and keeps it personal, the more he reinforces the mythology that there actually exists in the White House a capacity to govern."[14] But presidents are, at best, opportunists and facilitators rather than policy leaders. Good facilitators (Roosevelt, Reagan) exercise leadership "at the margins."[15]

It is true that the president is relatively free of ensnaring and entangling group alliances. Presidents and their staffs are less accessible to interest groups; with partial public financing, their campaigns are less dependent upon interest groups for money. Interest groups operate best in the deep confines of Congress. But presidents cannot make full use of their relative independence from interest groups, because presidents' power, in comparison to that of Congress, is in decline. Seligman and Covington explain the "presidential paradox":

> Developments in the presidential election system [primaries] and in the general governing context [increased fragmentation] have made the process of translating electoral support into a governing coalition more difficult. The striking consequence of these developments is that at a time when the scope of the president's responsibilities has expanded, the bases of his political support have become less reliable.[16]

Presidents "struggle to get control of the government," but "few of them succeed."[17] Three recent American presidents illustrate the scope and limitations of the job. They are Richard Nixon, Ronald Reagan, and George Bush.

WATERGATE AND THE RESIGNATION OF A PRESIDENT

The president must govern the nation within the boundaries of elite consensus. Mass opinion can be manipulated, but elite opinion is a powerful restraint on executive action. Voters may elect the president, but elites determine what is done in office.

The forced resignation of President Nixon is one of the most dramatic illustrations in American history of the president's dependence on elite support. A president reelected by an overwhelming majority had to resign his office less than two years after his landslide victory. We contend that Nixon's threatened impeachment and subsequent resignation were not a result of specific misdeeds or improprieties in office. Instead Nixon's demise was a result of (1) his general isolation from established elites, (2) his failure to adopt an accommodating style of politics, and (3) his frequent disregard of traditional "rules of the game."

The Constitution defines an impeachable offense as "treason, bribery, or other high crimes and misdemeanors." But impeachment is not really a legal process; it is a political process, and Nixon's offenses were more political than criminal.*

Isolation from Established Elites

Nixon's ouster was chiefly a result of his isolation from established elites and the suspicion, distrust, and hostility generated by his isolation. Established Eastern elites never fully accepted him. Despite his apprenticeship in a top Wall Street law firm, he was always regarded as opportunistic, uncultured, and middle class by the Eastern corporate and financial leaders he served, by influential segments of news media, and by intellectuals in prestigious universities and foundations. Nixon was upwardly mobile, competitive, self-conscious, boorish; he stood in marked contrast to the wealthy, cool, self-assured, aristocratic John F.

---

*The only precedent for a presidential impeachment—the impeachment and trial of Andrew Johnson in 1868—was also political. No evidence proved President Johnson's personal involvement in a crime for which he could be indicted and found guilty in a court of law. Johnson was a southern Democrat, a U.S. Senator from a seceding state (Tennessee) who had remained loyal to the Union. Lincoln chose him as vice-president in 1864 as a gesture of national unity. When Johnson acceded to the presidency after Lincoln's assassination, he resisted attempts by "radical" Republicans in Congress to restructure southern society by force. When Johnson dismissed some federal officials who opposed his conciliatory policies, Congress passed the Tenure of Office Act over Johnson's veto, forbidding executive removals without Senate consent. Johnson contended that the act was an unconstitutional infringement of his powers as chief executive. (Years later the Supreme Court agreed, holding that the power of removal is an executive power and specifically declaring that the Tenure of Office Act had been unconstitutional.) When Johnson dismissed his "radical" Republican secretary of war, Edwin M. Stanton, Congress was enraged. The House impeached Johnson on a party-line vote, charging that Johnson had violated the Tenure of Office Act. The Civil War had left a legacy of bitterness against Johnson as a southerner and a Democrat. But following a month-long trial in the Senate, the result was thirty-five "guilty" votes and nineteen "not guilty" votes—one vote short of the necessary two-thirds vote for removal. Seven Republicans joined the twelve Democrats in supporting the president. John F. Kennedy, in his book *Profiles in Courage,* praised the strength and courage of those senators who resisted popular emotions and prevented the president's removal. See Michael Les Benedict, *The Impeachment and Trial of Andrew Johnson* (New York: Norton, 1973).

Kennedy. Nixon fought his way up—from rooms over his father's grocery store, through the local, unprestigious Whittier College (California), to Duke Law School (North Carolina)—by self-sacrifice and hard work, long hours of studying, and postponement of pleasures and luxuries.

When Nixon came to the presidency, he found a giant Washington bureaucracy, overwhelmingly liberal in its politics and more responsive to the news media, influential interest groups, and key senators and House members than to the chief executive. This is how it has always been in Washington. But Nixon sought to exert power over the bureaucracy by adding to the size and powers of his own White House staff and centralizing decision making. His national security adviser, Henry Kissinger, became more powerful than the secretary of state (which he later became) or the secretary of defense; his domestic affairs adviser, John Ehrlichman, became more powerful than the secretaries who headed the domestic departments; and his chief of staff, H. R. Haldeman, became more powerful than anyone else, determining what information the president received and carrying out presidential orders. This style of administration won the president the lasting enmity of the Washington bureaucracy, and it also contributed to his isolation from other elites.

Nixon's long-standing hostility toward the press, a hostility that was more than reciprocated, contributed immeasurably to his isolation. But it was Nixon himself who, in reaction to a hostile press, cut himself off from the dialogue with influential publics. James David Barber writes, "As Watergate deepened, this famous loner of a president got loner and loner. His contacts with the press, which already had been in steep decline, became even rarer. Not only did his cabinet members have trouble seeing him; even his own lawyers were sometimes cut out."[18]

Failure at Accommodation

Nixon's personality made it difficult for him to engage in the friendly, handshaking, backslapping politics that his predecessor Lyndon Johnson had developed into a fine art. As a consequence Nixon never fit comfortably into the accommodationist style of elite interaction. Nixon did not enjoy politics; he was by nature a loner. He made his major decisions alone in the presidential retreat at Camp David or at his San Clemente or Key Biscayne homes far from the hubbub of Washington.

Nixon also cut himself off from other elites. House members and senators could not reach him; aides handled his telephone calls; and he seldom, if ever, consulted key influential persons outside the government. Only the "Germans" at the White House—Haldeman, Ehrlichman, Ziegler (the press secretary) and Kissinger—had direct access to him. They stood as a "Berlin Wall," isolating the president from other elites because the president wanted it that way. Those who directed the influential news media (such as CBS News, the *Washington Post*, and the *New York Times*), whom Nixon (correctly) perceived as his enemies, were aggressively shut out; Nixon held fewer press conferences than any other president since Herbert Hoover.

Nixon's style was to confront crisis directly, to avoid surrender, to test his own strength of character against adversity. His instinct in a crisis was to "fight like hell" rather than to bargain, accommodate, and compromise. Nixon viewed politics as a burden to be borne rather than an art to enjoy. James David Barber believes that such political figures eventually become rigid.[19]

As the Watergate affair broadened and intensified, Nixon increasingly viewed it as a test of his strength and character. He perceived a conspiracy of liberal opponents in Congress and the news media to reverse the 1972 election outcome. He became unyielding in his stance on executive privilege, withholding tapes and documents. He came to believe that he was defending the presidency itself.

Violating Rules of the Game

The Watergate bugging and burglary of Democratic national headquarters violated established "rules of the game." Elites and masses in the United States have generally condoned repressive acts against communists, subversives, and "radicals." But turning these tactics against established political opposition—Democrats, liberals, and assorted presidential critics—clearly violates elite consensus.

Yet despite all the media's revelations, Nixon would *not* have had to resign if he had publicly repented and cooperated with Congress, the news media, and representatives of the Eastern establishment in cleansing his administration.

Nixon's final line of defense was legal and technical: a feeble plea to abide by the constitutional definition of impeachment, "high crimes and misdemeanors." But the president was really forced to resign because of political acts: his isolation from establishment elites, his failures in accommodationist politics, and his misunderstanding of the rules of elite interaction.

The Irony of Richard Nixon

It is ironic that Richard Nixon saw himself as a tribune of the people— "the great silent majority," as he identified them—pitting himself against a liberal establishment that was not properly elected and did not reflect grass-roots sentiments. Nixon believed he understood "middle America," and he probably did, since he was middle American himself. But in the end, established elites turned middle America against him. Public opinion is unstable, changeable, and susceptible to manipulation by the mass media. In six months in 1973, Nixon suffered the steepest plunge in public opinion approval ratings ever recorded.

Richard Nixon failed to understand that without elite support, even landslide victories at the polls are meaningless. Popular majorities elect a president, but a president can govern only with the support of the nation's elite. Nixon learned this costly lesson in his "final crisis."[20]

RONALD REAGAN: THE "GREAT COMMUNICATOR" AS PRESIDENT

Ronald Reagan has never been the right-wing extremist portrayed by his political opponents. His ties to the nation's corporate and financial establishment are long-standing. When his Hollywood acting career nose-dived in the 1950s, Ralph J. Cordiner, chairman of the board of General Electric, selected Reagan not only to host the *G.E. Theater* on television but also to give lectures throughout the country on the merits of the free enterprise system. When Reagan lost viewer ratings to one of his own favorite programs, *Bonanza,* he turned more and more to the business-lecture circuit as a source of income. Reagan had always been a Democrat and a six-time elected president of his union, the Screen Actors Guild. But in 1964 he delivered an impressive television appeal for Republican presidential candidate Barry Goldwater. A group of prominent business-men decided that Reagan had political potential; they agreed to establish a "Ronald Reagan trust fund" to help guide his financial and political future. Two years later, in 1966, Reagan defeated Edmund G. "Pat" Brown (Jerry Brown's father) to become governor of California.

Reagan served two terms as governor of the nation's largest state, waiting impatiently for the opening that would lead him to the Oval Office. As governor, Reagan was closer to the center of the political spectrum, and more willing to bargain and compromise with a Democratic legislature, than his earlier conservative speech making suggested. In 1976 Reagan almost succeeded in taking the Republican presidential nomination away from Gerald Ford. Reagan posed as the conservative and Ford as the moderate within the Republican party. But in 1980, when it was clear that Reagan was the front-runner for the GOP nomination, he began to portray himself as a moderate. His "aw, shucks," mannerisms and "nice guy" image sheltered him from accusations that he was a fanatic of the radical right.

Reagan's cabinet appointments reaffirmed the establishment character of his administration: Alexander M. Haig, his first secretary of state (former NATO commander, president of United Technologies Corp.); George Shultz, secretary of state (president of the Bechtel Corporation and former secretary of the treasury); Caspar Weinberger, secretary of defense (vice-president of the Bechtel Corporation and former secretary of health, education and welfare); and Donald T. Regan, secretary of the treasury and later White House chief of staff (chairman of the Wall Street investment firm of Merrill Lynch & Co.). The name and party of the president may change, but governing elites are drawn from the same pool of established leaders.

The President as TV Host

Other presidents appreciated the role of the media, but none had the ability to use it as purposively as Reagan. His presidency was organized around television. The "awesome" burden was not a problem for a media president. Reagan's job was always the *public presentation* of his presidency, not the management of its policy implementation.

Reagan as president was analogous to Reagan as host of the popular television show *G.E. Theater.* He was not part of that show but was rather a mediator who introduced the drama to the viewers. His role in his administration was similar. He was the genial host who explained to the viewers what was happening in some otherwise confusing place called "the government." Reagan, while part of the government, just as he was part of *G.E. Theater,* was somehow distanced from it.

Yet Reagan clearly had a vision of his presidency. His mission, as he viewed it, was to reduce the role of government in Americans' everyday affairs, to establish and maintain a strong military force, and to lighten the tax burden. Like Franklin Roosevelt, to whom he liked to be compared, Reagan entered the White House committed to reversing an es-

BORGMAN FOR THE CINCINNATI ENQUIRER

Reprinted with special permission of King Features Syndicate.

tablished pattern of policy. Roosevelt intended to reduce the commitment to laissez-faire economics and increase the role of the government in the economic life of the country. Reagan was committed to a reduction of the role of government in economic life. Both proposed seemingly radical changes (although they were far less radical than the media claimed). However, unlike Roosevelt, who had no clearly thought-out ideology, Reagan had, if not a blueprint, at least a strong personal commitment to individualism.

GEORGE BUSH: SQUANDERING PRESIDENTIAL POPULARITY

If George Bush had any serious ambitions about public policy, he would be frustrated—but since he has no program, that has not been a problem. The *Economist* characterized the president this way: "In a sense the man and the hour have met. America is equipped with a president without a vision at a time when visions are out of fashion."[21] The conservative British journal is not alone in its assessment. Representative John LaFalce (D.–N.Y.), invited to the White House for the "full treatment" with the president, provided a revealing portrait of the "Great Administrator." He emerged from the White House saying that "nobody knows what this president is serious about."[22] Bush's "pragmatism," to use the term he prefers, was highlighted by the 1990 budget fiasco. As one disappointed Republican consultant explained: "The White House has just been floating, without any strong ties to causes or issues or philosophy. George Bush doesn't understand people who are really committed and who don't want to compromise on principles in the budget process, because he is the ultimate pragmatist who just wants to make government work."[23]

Nothing—of any major import—that Bush sought from Congress was granted. But Bush, even when he tried, just did not have a domestic program. George Bush served. He was a public man. He ran for office. His most compelling cause, indeed his only consistent one, was to be president. Therefore, while he appeared to be losing when his various initiatives—rare though they were—were routinely tossed aside by Congress, he was not really losing at all. As his mentor, Secretary of State James Baker, pointed out when asked if Bush was—as he appeared—largely bereft of ideas: "He's rocketing along at a 70 percent approval rating." Bush's approval rating was his sole criterion of success. It is not just that Bush was vacuous: his "no-policy" probably improves his approval rating. The do-nothing strategy was effective as long as there was nothing that— from the point of view of the masses—needed to be done. Immense deficits and the slide of the American standard of living are not deleterious issues. But, after the apparent success of the Gulf War, the economy sputtered along, then drifted into recession. As the economy weakened, Bush's popularity went into a precipitous decline. The failure of the economy was more in image than in reality, a problem not helped by the

President's description of it as "in free fall." However, the response from Bush's "image makers" virtually guaranteed a continued plunge. He participated in a pitiful trip to Japan, where he vomited on the Japanese Prime Minister and was described by the Japanese press as an "American auto-parts salesman." Then, early in the primary season, he resurrected the image of Bush-the-country-music-enthusiast and "good ole boy." He spoke of "bidness," said he was so full he was "about to bust my britches," quoted lyrics from a song by the Nitty Gritty Dirt Band (whom he called the "Nitty Ditty Nitty Gritty Great Bird"), and proudly admitted "When I need a little free advice about Saddam Hussein, I turn to country music." Liberal commentator Tom Wicker got it right when he noted that "the more a president does or even tries to do in difficult domestic affairs, the more likely he is to outrage one or more powerful interests or constituencies; but the less he attempts, the less he risks rocking the boat or pulling down the approval rating."[24]

Traditionally it has been thought that presidential popularity had a purpose—that is, to achieve policy goals. The president uses popularity to persuade Congress to do what the president wants. Presidents are thought to exchange some of their popularity in order to gain passage of a desired proposal. Since Bush did not want anything much except to maintain his popularity, when he did take a position, he had the lowest "batting average" with Congress among first-year presidents since World War II. He was unwilling to give up some of his popularity in order to prod Congress into action.

Bush's distaste for domestic policy contrasted markedly with his performance in his preferred domain, foreign policy. Whereas Reagan regularly lobbied Congress and even went over the head of Congress to lobby the American people directly via television, Bush preferred the "old-boy network." Bush was not comfortable with bargaining, and he did not really care about domestic policy. Thus, at the same time as he was earning the just plaudits of the world for his coordination of an international response to the Iraqi invasion of Kuwait in August 1990, he was regarded, equally justly, as weak and rudderless on the subject of the federal budget. Unfortunately for the president, no one had invaded Congress. Bush had more success forging an agreement among Gorbachev and the European democracies than in striking a deal with the leaders of his own political party. He could handle Gorbachev and Thatcher, but not House Minority Whip Newt Gingrich, who led the Republican revolt against the president's budget agreement.

Bush's most severe domestic defeat, his 1990 defeat on the budget and his acceptance of tax increases, came about for three reasons. First, unlike Reagan, Bush lacked a guiding public philosophy and a vision of what he wanted to achieve. Second, also unlike Reagan, Bush's distaste for lobbying led him to leave the arm-twisting to his principal negotiators, Chief of Staff John Sununu and Budget Director Richard Darman, both of whom were unpopular in Congress. Third, Bush's personal style was not that of the media-savvy Reagan, and Bush's television appeal for pub-

Give the gift that Keeps on giving...

Deficits are forever.

By permission of Doug Marlette and Creators Syndicate.

lic support on the budget backfired. Thus Bush accepted new taxes in spite of his emphatic campaign pledge, "Read my lips. No new taxes." Bush's popularity plunged (see Figure 10-1); it was restored only by the Gulf War.

In 1990 *Time* magazine named George Bush its "*men* of the year," a sobriquet meaning that Bush was two presidents. The domestic president was the Bush who suffered humiliating defeats at the hands of an independent Congress. As the foreign-policy president, however, Bush responded forcefully to the Iraqi invasion of Kuwait, constructing and holding together a diverse coalition of nations and armies to inflict a demeaning rout upon Saddam Hussein's armies. The stark differences in the two presidents is a consequence not only of Bush's frankly conceded lack of interest in domestic politics, but also of the institutional constraints imposed by "American exceptionalism." As the *only* industrial democracy with both separation of powers and federalism, the United States invites presidential retreat into foreign and defense affairs, where cooperation with diverse allies is more easily obtained than cooperation from a hostile and decentralized Congress. Add to these constitutional inhibitions the demise of strong party loyalty among members of the

Senate and the House and the growing independence of "iron triangles" and subcommittees, and George Bush's difficulties became clear. As Richard Rose explained, "The basic problem of the President is simple: There is no government there."[25]

ISSUES IN PRESIDENTIAL POWER: THE WAR-MAKING CONTROVERSY

For decades, the liberal intellectuals in the United States praised the presidency and scorned Congress. Textbooks taught students that the hope of the nation rested with a powerful president. They presented Congress as unprogressive, dilatory, even reactionary. Strong presidents—Lincoln, Roosevelt, Truman—were eulogized; weak presidents—Coolidge, Hoover, Eisenhower—were ridiculed. Leading establishment scholars—for example, Harvard political scientist Richard Neustadt—taught that presidents should conduct themselves so as to maximize their power.[26] These political analysts led Americans to believe that because the president is the only official elected by *all* the people, the presidential powers would be used to "do good."

But then came several presidents—Johnson, Nixon, and Reagan—whom the nation's liberal intellectuals distrusted. As a result, establishment views of the presidency did an about-face. The Vietnam War and Watergate convinced liberal intellectuals that the presidency was too powerful and that Congress must more actively check the actions of unruly presidents. Many commentators, journalists, intellectuals, and, of course, senators and House members argued the importance of curtailing the president's war-making powers, overseeing White House activities, and protecting the nation from the abuses of presidential power.

War and the Constitution

The American colonists who declared their independence from Britain in 1776 were deeply suspicious of standing armies and of a king who would send British troops to the colonies. Their distrust carried over after independence, causing the Founding Fathers to make military affairs subject to civilian control. The Second Continental Congress had overseen the conduct of the military during the Revolutionary War. It commissioned George Washington to be commander in chief but instructed him "punctually to observe and follow such orders and directions . . . from this or a future Congress." Washington chaired the Constitutional Convention of 1787, and he recognized the need for a strong chief executive who could respond quickly to threats to the nation. Moreover, he was aware of the weaknesses of civilian militia and favored a national army and navy.

The Constitutional Convention of 1787 divided the war power between Congress and the president. Article I, Section 8, states, "The Congress shall have the power to . . . provide for the common defense . . . to declare war . . . to raise and support armies . . . to provide and maintain a navy . . . to make rules for the government and regulation of the land and naval forces." Article II, Section 2, states, "The President shall be Commander in Chief of the army and navy of the United States." In defending the newly written Constitution, the *Federalist* papers construed the president's war powers narrowly, implying that the war-making power of the president was little more than the power to defend against imminent invasion when Congress was not in session.

Historically the president has exercised the nation's war-making powers. Since 1789 U.S. forces have participated in military actions overseas on more than 150 occasions, but Congress has declared war only five times: the War of 1812, the Mexican War, the Spanish-American War, World War I, and World War II. Supreme Court Justice William H. Rehnquist wrote before he was elevated to the Court:

> It has been recognized from the earliest days of the Republic, by the President, by Congress and by the Supreme Court, that the United States may lawfully engage in armed hostilities with a foreign power without Congressional declaration of war. Our history is replete with instances of "undeclared wars" from the war with France in 1789–1800 to the Vietnamese War.[27]

The Supreme Court has generally refused to take jurisdiction in cases involving the war powers of the president and Congress.

Thus, whereas Congress retains the formal power to "declare war," in modern times wars are seldom "declared." Instead they begin with direct military actions, and the president, as commander in chief of the armed forces, determines what those actions will be. Over the years Congress generally recognized the supremacy of the president in military affairs. Not until the Vietnam War was there serious congressional debate over who has or should have the power to commit the nation to war. In the past, Congress tended to accept the fact that under modern conditions of war only the president has the information-gathering facilities and the ability to act with the speed and secrecy required for military decisions during periods of crisis.

The War in Vietnam

The war in Vietnam was not an unprecedented use of the president's war-making powers. John Adams fought a war against the French without a congressional declaration; Thomas Jefferson fought the Barbary pirates; every president in the nineteenth century fought the Indians; Abraham Lincoln carried presidential war-making powers further than any president before or since; Woodrow Wilson sent troops to Mexico and a dozen Latin American nations; Franklin D. Roosevelt sent U.S. destroyers to protect British convoys in the north Atlantic before Pearl Harbor; and

Harry Truman committed American forces to a major war in Korea. So when President Johnson ordered bombing attacks on North Vietnam in 1965, and eventually committed more than half a million men to the battle, he was not really assuming any greater powers than those assumed by presidents before him. Perhaps his greatest mistake was his failure to achieve either a military or diplomatic solution to the war.

In the early days of the Vietnam War, the liberal leadership of the nation strongly supported the effort, and no one questioned the president's power to commit the nation to war. However, by 1969 most liberal congressional leaders who had supported the war in its early stages had rushed to become doves. Indeed, senators argued over who had been the first to change his mind about the war. Moreover, with a new, Republican president and a Democratic Congress, congressional attacks on presidential policy became much more partisan. As public opposition to the Vietnam War grew, and with the presidency and Congress now controlled by different parties, Congress sought to reassert its role in war-making decisions.

Congress made several attempts to curtail the president's war-making powers by cutting off money for U.S. military activity in Southeast Asia. Most people recognized that Congress did not have the authority to end the Vietnam War by congressional declaration, but Congress could set a cutoff date for spending government funds in support of U.S. troops in Southeast Asia. Nonetheless, antiwar legislators could not get their colleagues to cut off funds for the war until *after* President Nixon announced a peace agreement in 1973. Congress then cut off funds for Vietnam (an action that former Secretary of State Henry Kissinger says led to the collapse of South Vietnam). Significantly, Congress has never voted to cut off funds to support American armies in the field.

The War Powers Act

In 1973 the Congress passed the War Powers Act, designed to restrict presidential war-making powers. President Nixon vetoed the bill, but the Watergate affair appeared to undermine his support in this struggle with Congress, and Congress overrode his veto. The act is an interesting example of the continuing struggle over checks and balances in the U.S. government. The act has these provisions:

1. In the absence of a congressional declaration of war, the president can commit armed forces to hostilities or to "situations where imminent involvement in hostilities is clearly indicated by the circumstances" only:
   a. To repel an armed attack on the United States or to forestall the "direct and imminent threat of such an attack."
   b. To repel an armed attack against U.S. armed forces outside the United States or to forestall the threat of such attack.

    c. To protect and evacuate U.S. citizens and nationals in another country if their lives are threatened.

    d. With specific statutory authorization by Congress, not to be inferred from any existing or future law or treaty unless Congress so specifies.

2. The president must report promptly to Congress the commitment of forces for such purposes.

3. Involvement of U.S. forces must be no longer than sixty days unless Congress authorizes their continued use by specific legislation.

4. Congress can end a presidential commitment by a concurrent resolution, an action that does not require the president's signature.

The War Powers Act raises constitutional questions. Clearly a commander in chief can order forces to go anywhere. Presumably, Congress cannot constitutionally command troops, yet that is what the act attempts to authorize by specifying that troops must come home if Congress orders them to do so or if Congress simply fails to endorse the president's decision to commit them. No president—Democrat or Republican—can allow Congress to usurp this presidential authority.

After President Reagan had committed troops to Lebanon in 1983, Congress tried to invoke the War Powers Act by authorizing an eighteen-month stay for U.S. marines. The president proclaimed the act unconstitutional and Secretary of State George Shultz made it clear that the administration would keep the troops there as long as it desired. Only the death of more than two hundred marines in a suicide pact by an Islamic faction persuaded Reagan to withdraw U.S. troops from Lebanon. Immediately thereafter, U.S. troops invaded the tiny Caribbean island of Grenada. Informing Congress *after* the fact, Reagan made no mention of the sixty-day limitation imposed by the War Powers Act. As the success of the invasion became apparent, Congress avoided any discussion of the act.

President Ford ignored the act in sending U.S. forces to rescue the U.S. ship *Mayaguez* from the Cambodians in 1976. When President Reagan launched two air strikes against Libya in 1986 in reprisal for terrorist activities, he did not consult congressional leaders prior to his decision and gave them, at best, perfunctory notification. Still, he was given strong congressional endorsement for his actions. Swift and decisive victories are still the best presidential defense against the War Powers Act.

The Iraqi invasion of Kuwait threw a new light on the debate. Congress initially wanted to be involved in the framing of the U.S. response; Bush ignored Congress's pleas and went about his own agenda. Miffed by the slight, Congress attempted to formulate a policy the weekend before the United Nations' deadline for Iraqi withdrawal. In the end, despite cries that Bush's action had brought the U.S. to the edge of a constitutional crisis, Congress capitulated, passed a "practical" declaration of war, and allowed Bush to do whatever he pleased.[28]

—— OTHER EXECUTIVE ELITES

The presidency is not one person but more than five thousand permanent employees in the executive office of the president, which includes the White House Office, the Office of Management and Budget, the Council of Economic Advisers, the National Security Council, the National Aeronautics and Space Council, the Office of Emergency Planning, and the Office of Science and Technology. In addition there is the presidential cabinet, consisting of heads of thirteen major executive departments. Finally, more than forty independent agencies function outside the regular departmental organization of the executive branch, including the Interstate Commerce Commission, the Federal Reserve Board, the Federal Trade Commission, the Federal Power Commission, the Federal Communications Commission, the Securities and Exchange Commission, the National Labor Relations Board, the Civil Aeronautics Board, and the Atomic Energy Commission (see Chapter 11).

Closest to the president is a group of aides and assistants who work with the chief executive in the White House Office, which the president can organize as he sees fit. These aides and assistants perform whatever duties the president assigns them. They usually include a chief of staff, a press secretary, an appointment secretary, and one or more special assistants for liaison with Congress. Some of the president's assistants have ad hoc assignments, while others have a specialty.

Staff Power

Increasingly White House staff members have come to exercise great power in the name of the president. They frequently direct affairs in the name of the president ("The president has asked me to tell you . . ."), but the president may have little direct oversight of their activities. Even more serious is the fact that staff members may come into power with little preparation or experience for elite membership. Often their training consists of nothing more than serving as "advance guard" in presidential election campaigns: scheduling presidential appearances, handling campaign advertising, and fetching coffee and doughnuts. These staff are valued not for their independent contributions to policy but rather for their personal loyalty to the president.

Frequently in recent presidential administrations, staff members have embarrassed the president. Truman's personal secretary went to jail for fixing a tax case. Eisenhower's assistant to the president, Sherman Adams, retired in disgrace for accepting expensive gifts. Johnson's White House adviser, Walter Jenkins, was convicted of a homosexual assault. Almost all of Nixon's original White House staff were indicted in the Watergate scandal. Carter's director of the Office of Management and Budget, Bert Lance, was forced to resign after disclosures of irregularities in his banking business.

Perhaps it was inevitable that the Reagan administration would fall prey to a major scandal. Reagan delegated more authority to the various executive staffs than any of his predecessors. The rise of such powerful staffers as Donald Regan, Robert McFarlane, John Poindexter, and Edwin Meese greatly increased the likelihood of presidential embarrassment.

The Iran-Contra Scandal

The Iran-Contra scandal grew out of President Reagan's strong personal commitment to secure the release of hostages held by Iranian-backed terrorists in Lebanon, together with "a management style that put the principal responsibility for policy review and implementation on the shoulders of his advisors."[29] When Secretary of State George Shultz and Secretary of Defense Caspar Weinberger strongly recommended that the president *not* undertake to trade arms for hostages, the president turned to his National Security Council staff to carry out the assignment. National Security Adviser John McFarlane and his staff assistant Marine Lieutenant Colonel Oliver North traveled secretly to Iran to negotiate the exchange. Although President Reagan denies that a deal trading arms for hostages deal was what he intended, investigators concluded that "whatever the intent, almost from the beginning the initiative became in fact a series of arms for hostages deals."[30] To further complicate matters, Lieutenant Colonel North, with the knowledge and approval of National Security Advisor John Poindexter (who had replaced McFarlane), diverted money from the arms sales to support the Contra forces in Nicaragua in their fight against the communist Sandinista government. President Reagan claims to have had no knowledge of this use of the funds, and no evidence emerged in the many investigations of the matter to contradict his claim. But the president generally backed the Contras at a time when Congress by law had directed that no U.S. funds be spent for their military support. At the very least, President Reagan was guilty of loose supervision of his White House staff. The Iran-Contra scandal seriously tarnished the Reagan presidency.

Bush's Old-Boy Network

George Bush depended upon friends to staff his office and relied heavily on his cabinet friends—substantially more than Reagan did. Bush did not manage a "cabinet government," since many cabinet members are of little import. However, some cabinet members—who were also his friends—became powerful. Secretary of State James Baker, fellow Houston oilman and long-time Bush tennis partner, did not face any formidable challenge to his influence. Baker was powerful, not because of his position as secretary of state, but because of his friendship with the president. Bush was also very close to Secretary of Commerce Robert A. Mosbacher, another Texas oilman, and Treasury Secretary Nicholas Brady, who attended Yale with Bush's brother and became the president's friend when they served as directors of Purolator Courier Corporation, a company partially owned by Brady's family.

Bush's reliance on friends also meant that his friends were friends with one another and that, as upper-class values require, they avoided impolite remarks. The secretaries of defense and state and the Director of the National Security Council, Brent Scowcroft, got along famously, in spite of an institutional history of discord between these agencies. Those who were not within this circle of close friends, Budget Director Richard Darman for instance, may have suffered ebbs and flows of fortunes and power, but the old-boy network survived the occasional mistake intact.

Personal Power Is Fleeting

Power in the White House staff is personal, temporary, and fleeting; it is not institutionally based. Some chiefs of staff have been quite powerful, whereas others have not. The key to finding out who is "in" or "out" at the White House is to locate the people the president trusts, irrespective of their formal position. Since power is more personal than institutional, today's power brokers are tomorrow's has-beens. One can play endless rounds of "whatever happened to . . . ?" Try Jody Powell (Carter's chief of staff), John Ehrlichman (Nixon's chief of staff), Donald Regan (Reagan's chief of staff), or David Stockman (Reagan's first budget director), all at one time said to be at the heart of the American political power structure. This predicament is a consequence of the blitz on Washington that ensues when a new president is sworn in: many campaign lackeys are paid off with jobs. Using the campaign organization as the primary source for recruitment leads to predictable excess. "The natural choice of campaign aides . . . may lead to problems because the nature of governing is different in important ways from the nature of political campaigns."[31] The president's reliance on amateurs leads, almost inevitably, to serious gaffes, since the president's men are political operatives. Watergate, Iran-Contra, and John Sununu's abuse of travel are only the most well-known examples of such gaffes.

—— SUMMARY

The president is the popular symbol of governmental authority. However, presidents are substantially less able to control decisions than they would like to be.

1. Governmental elites in the United States do not command; they seek consensus. Governmental decision making involves bargaining, accommodation, and compromise among government and nongovernment elites. Our examination of the presidency provides clear evidence of the consensual nature of elite interaction and the heavy price a president must pay for failure to pursue accommodationist policies.

2. Of elites in the United States, the president is the first among equals. Presidential power depends not on formal authority but on personal abilities of persuasion. Moreover, the president must still function within the established elite system. The choices available to presidents are limited to alternatives for which elite support can be mobilized. Despite access to mass opinion, the president can be effectively checked by other public and private elites.

3. In the twentieth century, presidential power has increased as a result of the growing importance in national life of military and foreign policy, areas in which the president has the greatest constitutional powers. The growth of the executive branch of government and the increased visibility of the president in the mass media also contribute to the growth of presidential power.

4. Controversies over presidential power are always linked to their political context. While liberal writers generally praise strong presidents in history, they turned against the presidency under Johnson and Nixon. Congress passed the War Powers Act to try to restore control over armed interventions such as Vietnam.

5. The forced resignation of President Nixon was a dramatic illustration of the president's dependence on elite support. A president must govern within the boundaries of elite consensus or face removal from office. The president can be removed not only for "high crimes and misdemeanors" but also for *political* offenses—violating elite consensus.

6. Nixon's resignation was a product not only of specific improprieties in office but also of his isolation from established elites, his failure to adopt an accommodationist style of politics, and his disregard of traditional rules of the game.

7. Established elites who are concerned with declining public trust and confidence frequently turn to "new faces" to provide the appearance of change. But the change is cosmetic only and does not include fundamental change in programs, policies, or values. Jimmy Carter's rapid rise to the presidency probably resulted from this need to find a "new face" to reassure the masses.

8. Reagan's presidency allows a second look at media presidents. As the first president in the decade to last, and to maintain strong public approval through a second term, he brings the media presidency to full fruition.

9. Bush, not Reagan's equal in charisma or mass appeal, was not comfortable with the media style mandated by the Reagan presidency and followed slavishly by his advisors. He was presented in a variety of guises, none of which bore any resemblance to his true personality, and he suffered appalling losses in popular esteem for these mistakes.

NOTES

1. William Howard Taft, *Our Chief Magistrate and His Powers* (New York: Columbia University Press, 1938), p. 138. Reprinted in John P.

Roche and L. W. Levy, eds., *The Presidency* (New York: Harcourt Brace Jovanovich, 1964), p. 23.

2. From Arthur B. Tourtellot, *President on the Presidency* (Garden City, N.Y.: Doubleday, 1964), pp. 55–56.

3. Fred I. Greenstein, "The Psychological Functions of the Presidency for Citizens," in Elmer E. Cornwell, ed., *The American Presidency: Vital Center* (Chicago: Scott, Foresman, 1966), pp. 30–36.

4. James David Barber, *The Presidential Character,* 3rd ed. (Englewood Cliffs, N.J.: Prentice-Hall, 1977), p. 2.

5. Richard Neustadt, *Presidential Power* (New York: New American Library, 1960), pp. 88–89.

6. George C. Edwards III and Stephen J. Wayne, *Presidential Leadership,* 2nd ed. (New York: St. Martin's, 1990), p. 99.

7. Barber, op. cit., p. 4.

8. Thomas Reeves, *John F. Kennedy* (New York: Kreiger, 1990), p. 190.

9. Robert E. Denton, Jr., *The Symbolic Dimensions of the American Presidency* (Prospect Heights, Ill.: Waverly Press, 1982), p. 52.

10. Morris P. Fiorina, "The Electorate in the Voting Booth," in L. Sandy Masiel, ed., *The Parties Respond* (Boulder: Westview Press, 1990), p. 120.

11. Fiorina, op. cit., p. 122.

12. Austin Ranney, "Broadcasting, Narrowcasting, and Politics," in Anthony King, ed., *The New American Political System* (Washington: AEI Press, 1991), p. 188.

13. Richard Rose, *The Postmodern President* (Chatham, N.J.: Chatham House, 1989), p. 71.

14. Theodore J. Lowi, *The Personal President* (Ithaca: Cornell University Press, 1985), p. 154.

15. George C. Edwards III, *At the Margins* (New Haven: Yale University Press, 1989).

16. Lester G. Seligman and Cary R. Covington, *The Coalitional Presidency* (Chicago: Dorsey Press, 1989), p. 30.

17. C. Calvin MacKenzie, "Partisan Presidential Leadership: The President's Appointees," in Maisel, op. cit., p. 288.

18. Barber, op. cit., p. 382.

19. James David Barber, "Tone-Deaf in the Oval Office," *Saturday Review* (January 12, 1974): 14.

20. For further information on Richard M. Nixon's career, see his political autobiography, *Six Crises* (Garden City, N.Y.: Doubleday, 1962).

21. *The Economist* (December 9, 1989), p. 21.

22. Quoted in *Congressional Quarterly* (November 4, 1989): 2921.

23. Ibid.

24. Tom Wicker, "Bush Hits the Political Jackpot," *New York Times,* January 23, 1990.

25. Rose, op. cit., p. 71.

26. Neustadt, op. cit.

27. Congressional Quarterly, *The Power of the Pentagon* (Washington, D.C.: Congressional Quarterly Press, 1972), p. 42.
28. Jack Germond and Jules Witcover, "This One's Not Like 1917 and 1941," *National Journal* (January 19, 1991): 178.
29. *The Tower Commission Report* (New York: Times Books, 1987), p. 80.
30. Ibid., p. 80.
31. James P. Pfiffner, *The Strategic Presidency: Hitting the Ground Running* (Pacific Grove, CA: Brooks/Cole, 1988), p. 21.

SELECTED READINGS

Barber, James David. *The Presidential Character: Predicting Performance in the White House,* 3rd ed. Englewood Cliffs, N.J.: Prentice-Hall, 1985. This extremely readable book seeks to classify presidents along two continua: an "active–passive" baseline, according to the amount of energy and enthusiasm displayed in the exercise of presidential duties, and a "positive–negative" baseline, dealing with the degree of happiness or "fun" each president displays in manipulating presidential power. Using these two baselines, Barber classifies the modern presidents into four types: active-positive (FDR, Truman, Kennedy), active-negative (Wilson, Hoover, Johnson), passive-positive (Taft, Harding), and passive-negative (Coolidge, Eisenhower). President Nixon was analyzed while in office to demonstrate the predictive capacity of these concepts.

Buchanan, Bruce. *The Citizen's Presidency.* Washington, D.C.: Congressional Quarterly Press, 1987. Buchanan examines how the president has become a symbol as much as—if not more than—a center of power.

Edwards, George C., III. *The Public Presidency.* New York: St. Martin's Press, 1983. A deliberation on the relationship between presidential success and public opinion.

Edwards, George C., III, and Wayne, Steven J. *Presidential Leadership.* New York: St. Martin's Press, 1985. This book explores the premise that success and failure are linked less to personality than to politics.

Halberstam, David. *The Best and the Brightest.* New York: Random House, 1972. This book deals with the men who advised presidents Kennedy and Johnson with regard to the conduct of the war in Vietnam. Based on interviews by former *New York Times* Vietnam correspondent David Halberstam, this book reveals an excellent view of the men and processes responsible for decision making at the highest levels of the federal executive.

Lowi, Theodore. *The Personal President.* Ithaca, N.Y.: Cornell University Press, 1985. Lowi traces the process by which "the president" and "the government" become synonymous terms.

11

The Bureaucratic Elite and Public Policy

★ *The problem is not conspiracy or corruption, but unchecked rule. And being unchecked, the rule reflects not the national need but the bureaucratic need.*

John K. Galbraith, The New Industrial State, 1967

Power in the United States is gradually shifting from those who control economic and political resources to those who control technology and organized expertise. Indeed, Washington bureaucracy has become a major base of power in American society—independent of Congress, the president, the courts, and the people. Government bureaucracies invade every aspect of modern life: the home, communications, transportation, the environment, the work place, schools, the streets.

In theory, a *bureaucracy* is a form of social organization that the German sociologist Max Weber described as having (1) a chain of command (hierarchy); (2) a division of labor among subunits (specialization); (3) specification of authority for positions and units by rules and regulation (span of control); (4) impersonality in executing tasks (neutrality); (5) adaptation of structure, authority, and rules to the organization's goals (goal orientation); and (6) predictability of behavior based on maintenance of records and assurance of rules (standardization).[1] If we use Weber's definition, then both corporations and governments, and many other organizations in society, are bureaucracies. Indeed, not only the U.S. Department of Health and Human Services but also General Motors, IBM, the Catholic Archdiocese of Boston, and the American Red Cross are bureaucracies. In theory, bureaucracies are organized to achieve specified goals through hierarchy, specialization, control, neutrality, and standardization.

In practice, *bureaucracy* has become a negative term. People have come to view bureaucracy as bringing with it red tape, paper shuffling, duplication of effort, waste and inefficiency, impersonality, insensitivity, and overregulation. More important, people have come to view governmental bureaucracy as unresponsive to the needs of the nation or the people.

The "faceless bureaucrats" in Washington are not really accountable to anyone. The president, Congress, and courts can place only the broadest restrictions on bureaucratic power. And certainly "the people" have no direct means of altering bureaucratic decisions. Even the president, the White House staff, and cabinet officials have great difficulty establishing control over the bureaucracy. The bureaucrats control information and technology, and they almost invariably outlast their political superiors in office. Very often, in fact, the bureaucrats feel a certain contempt for their superiors because political leaders do not share the information, technical expertise, and experience of the bureaucrats.

SOURCES OF BUREAUCRATIC POWER

Public policy is whatever governments choose to do or not to do. Public policies are the activities of governmental agencies and bureaucrats, acting within their official capacities. By far the overwhelming majority of these activities are initiated by bureaucrats themselves, not by any elected officials and certainly not by the American people.

The power of bureaucracies grows with advances in technology and increases in the size and complexity of society. Large, complex, technological societies cannot be governed by a single president and 535 members of Congress who lack the expertise, time, and energy to look after the myriad details involved in nuclear power or environmental protection or occupational safety or communications or aviation or trucking or fair employment or hundreds of other aspects of American life. So the president and Congress create bureaucracies, appropriate money for them, and authorize them to draw up detailed rules, regulations, and "guidelines" to govern us. The bureaucracies receive only vague and general directions from the president and Congress. Actual governance is in the hands of the Nuclear Regulatory Commission, the Environmental Protection Agency, the Occupational Safety and Health Administration, the Federal Communications Commission, the Federal Aviation Administration, the Interstate Commerce Commission, the Equal Employment Opportunity Commission, and hundreds of similar bureaucratic agencies. (There are approximately two thousand federal government agencies with rule-making powers.) One estimate suggests that the bureaucracies announce *twenty* rules or regulations for every *one* law of Congress. In this way, the power to make policy has passed from the president and Congress to the bureaucratic elite.

Why is policy making shifted to the bureaucracy? The standard explanation is that Congress and the president do not have the time, energy, or expertise to handle the details of policy making. A related explanation is that the increasing complexity and sophistication of technology require technical experts ("technocrats") to actually carry out the intent of Congress and the president. No single bureaucrat can master the complex activities of even a single large governmental agency—from budgeting, purchasing, personnel, accounting, planning, communication, and organization to the complexities of nuclear plants, energy transmission, the internal revenue (tax) code, or the computerized social security files. Each bureaucrat has relatively little knowledge of overall policy. But that person's narrow expertise, when combined with the narrow expertise of thousands of other bureaucrats, creates an organized base of power that political leaders find difficult to control.

A second reason policy making is shifted to the bureaucracy is that Congress and the president deliberately pass vague and ambiguous laws, largely for symbolic reasons—to ensure nuclear safety, protect the environment, ensure occupational safety, allocate broadcasting channels, guarantee flight safety, prevent unfair interstate charges, guarantee "equal employment opportunity," and so on. The bureaucrats' role is to use the "authority" of these symbolic laws to decide what actually will be done. Thus bureaucrats must give meaning to symbolic measures. Frequently Congress and the president do not want to take public responsibility for unpopular policies. They find it easier to blame the bureaucrats and pretend that unpopular policies are a product of an ungovernable Washington bureaucracy. This explanation allows an elected president and an elected Congress to impose regulations without accepting responsibility for them.

Finally, the bureaucracy itself is now sufficiently powerful to have its own laws passed—laws that allow agencies to expand in size, acquire more authority, and obtain more money. Bureaucracy has become its own cause. Political scientist James Q. Wilson comments on "the great, almost overpowering, importance of the existing government and professional groups in shaping policy":

> I am impressed by the extent to which policy making is dominated by the representatives of those bureaucracies and professions having a material stake in the management and funding of the intended policy and by those political staffs who see in a new program a chance for publicity, advancement, and a good reputation for their superiors.[2]

ORGANIZATION OF THE WASHINGTON BUREAUCRACY

How big is big government? The United States now has more than eighty thousand separate governments, including federal, state, and local governments, as well as public school districts. These governments collectively spend about 35 percent of the gross national product (GNP), the sum of all goods and services produced in the nation. The federal government alone accounts for 23 percent of the GNP, and other governments account for 12 percent. The "private sector" accounts for the remaining 65 percent of the GNP; however, most, if not all, of the private sector comes under governmental regulation.

The executive branch of the U.S. government includes fourteen departments, forty independent executive agencies operating outside of these departments, and the large Executive Office of the President (see Figure 11-1).

Cabinet.   The cabinet rarely functions as a group. It consists of the secretaries of the fourteen executive departments, the vice president, the UN ambassador, the CIA director, and the special trade representative, with the president as its head. Cabinet officers in the United States are powerful because they head giant administrative organizations. The secretary of state, the secretary of defense, the secretary of the treasury, the attorney general, and to a lesser extent the other departmental secretaries are all people of power and prestige in America. But the cabinet, as a council, rarely makes policy.[3] Seldom does a strong president hold a cabinet meeting to decide important policy questions. More frequently, the president knows what he wants and holds cabinet meetings only to help him sell his views.

FIGURE 11-1 The organization of the U.S. government

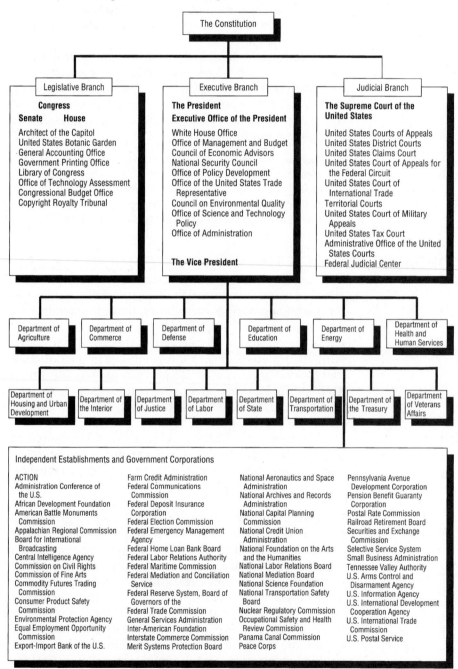

SOURCE: Census, Statistical Abstract of the United States 1988, p. 288.

NSC.   The National Security Council (NSC) resembles a cabinet; the president is chairman and the vice president, secretary of state, secretary of defense, and director of the Office of Emergency Planning (a minor unit in the executive office) are participating members. The chairman of the Joint Chiefs of Staff and the director of the Central Intelligence Agency are advisers to the NSC. A special assistant to the president for national security affairs heads the NSC staff. The purposes of the council are to advise the president on security policy and to coordinate foreign, military, and domestic policies. However, in the Iran-Contra scandal a staff member of the NSC, Lieutenant Colonel Oliver North, undertook an operational role in security policy. As a result, various investigative committees strongly recommended that the NSC staff confine itself to an advisory role.

OMB.   The Office of Management and Budget (OMB) is the largest agency in the Executive Office of the President. Its function is to prepare the budget of the United States for the president to submit to Congress. The federal government cannot spend money without appropriations by Congress, and all requests for congressional appropriations must clear OMB first, a requirement that gives OMB great power over the executive branch. Since all agencies request more money than they can receive, OMB has primary responsibility for reviewing, reducing, and approving estimates submitted by departments and agencies (subject, of course, to appeal to the president); it also continuously scrutinizes the organization and operations of executive agencies in order to recommend changes promoting efficiency and economy. Like members of the White House staff, the top officials of OMB are responsible solely to the president; thus they must reflect the president's goals and priorities in their decision making.

CEA.   The president, with Senate consent, appoints three professional economists of high standing to the Council of Economic Advisers. Created by the Employment Act of 1946, the CEA analyzes trends in the economy and recommends to the president the fiscal and monetary policies necessary to avoid depression and inflation. In addition, the CEA prepares the economic report that the act requires the president to submit to Congress each year. The economic report, together with the annual budget message to Congress, gives the president the opportunity to outline the administration's major policies.

PRESIDENTIAL CONTROL OF THE BUREAUCRACY

Constitutionally the president has authority over the federal bureaucracy. The president has the formal power to appoint all secretaries, undersecretaries, and deputy secretaries and most bureau chiefs in the federal government. The president also has the power to reorganize the federal bureaucracy, subject to congressional veto. And, of course, the president exercises formal control over the budget. OMB works directly under presidential supervision.

The president's formal powers over the bureaucracy center on appointments, reorganization, and the budget. We should, however, consider the *real* limitations on these three powers.

Appointments

Although the federal bureaucracy consists of three million employees, the president actually appoints only about twenty-five hundred people. Approximately six hundred of those appointments are policy-making positions; the rest are subordinate positions often used for patronage. Many patronage positions go to professional bureaucrats by default because a president cannot find qualified political appointees. Many political appointees are baffled by the career bureaucrats in the agencies. The bureaucrats have the knowledge, skills, and experience to continue existing programs with little or no supervision from their nominal political chiefs. Many political heads "go native"; they yield to the pressures of the career bureaucrats. The president's appointee whose charter is to control a bureau ends up the bureau's captive instead.

Since a majority of career bureaucrats are Democrats, exercising policy control over the bureaucracy is particularly difficult for a Republican president. Richard Nixon attempted to deal with this problem by increasing the power of his immediate White House staff; he placed control of major programs in the White House staff at the expense of the cabinet departments. The unhappy result was that the White House staff itself became a powerful bureaucracy, frequently locked in conflict with executive departments and duplicating much of the departments' research and policy-planning activities. More serious for Nixon and the country, members of the White House staff, speaking "in the name of the president," developed power bases independent of the president.

Ronald Reagan's approach was to appoint conservatives and Republicans to head many key agencies. But the bureaucracy fought back by isolating and undermining Reagan's appointees within the agencies. Lower-level bureaucrats often supplied damaging information to the press and to Congress, claiming that Reagan appointees did not enforce the laws properly. Then they sought to protect their jobs with special legislation preventing the president from firing "whistle blowers."

George Bush experienced less conflict with the bureaucracy because he did not pursue any clear domestic policy goals. Unlike his predecessor Ronald Reagan, Bush did not seek to slow the growth of government, to deregulate the economy, or to reduce taxing and spending—all policies that are strongly opposed by government bureaucrats. Bush himself held a variety of bureaucratic posts during his career—UN ambassador, CIA director, ambassador to the People's Republic of China. Because Bush did not seek to change bureaucratic ways in Washington, he did not encounter the vocal opposition of the bureaucracy.

Reorganization

The president can choose to reorganize the bureaucracy to reflect his priorities. However, most presidents limit this practice to one or two key presidential programs (presidential reorganizations are subject to legislative veto). For example, to emphasize his commitment to cancer research, President Nixon created the National Cancer Institute and gave it substantial independence from its parent organization, the U.S. Public Health Service. In the 1960s President Kennedy created the National Aeronautics and Space Administration as an independent agency to carry out his commitment to a national space program. President Carter created the new Department of Education to fulfill his campaign pledge to emphasize educational matters, even though the new department's parent organization, the Department of Health, Education, and Welfare, bitterly opposed it. President Reagan promised in his 1980 campaign to eliminate the Department of Education as well as the Department of Energy. But reorganization is a difficult task. Nothing arouses the fighting instincts of bureaucrats as much as the rumor of reorganization. President Reagan was eventually forced to drop his plans to eliminate these two departments. Instead, Reagan ended his administration by creating a new cabinet-level department—the Department of Veterans' Affairs—in response to demands for greater status and prestige by veterans' interests.

The Budget

The president exercises budgetary power over the bureaucracy through OMB. Thus the OMB director must be a trusted ally of the president, and OMB must support the president's programs and priorities if presidential control over the bureaucracy is to be effective. But even OMB must accept the budgetary base of each department (the previous year's budget, adjusted for inflation) and engage in "incremental" budgeting. Despite its own expertise, OMB rarely challenges the budgetary base of agencies but instead concentrates its attention on requested increases.

Any agency that feels shortchanged in the president's budget can leak the fact to its supporting interest groups and congressional subcommittee. Any resulting "public outcry" may force the president to restore the agency's funds. Or Congress can appropriate money not requested by the president. The president may go along with the increased expenditures simply to avoid another confrontation with Congress.

CASE STUDY

 ### Bureaucratic Maneuvers

How can bureaucrats outmaneuver the president? One illustration of bureaucratic leeway and discretion in implementing presidential decisions has been widely quoted:

> Half of a President's suggestions, which theoretically carry the weight of orders, can be safely forgotten by a cabinet member. And if the President asks about a suggestion the second time, he can be told that it is being investigated. If he asks a third time, the wise cabinet officer will give him at least part of what he suggests. But only occasionally do Presidents ever get around to asking three times.*

Bureaucratic maneuvers can become even more complex. Morton Halperin, former staff member of the National Security Council under Henry Kissinger (Halperin later charged Kissinger and others with bugging his telephone), describes "ten commandments" of bureaucratic infighting.** These suggest the power of the bureaucracy and the frequently bitter nature of bureaucratic warfare:

1. Never play "politics" with security. But use your own notions of politics to screen out information from the president that conflicts with your own objectives.

2. Tell the president only what is necessary to persuade him of the correctness of your own position. Avoid giving him "confusing" information. Isolate the opposition by excluding them from deliberations.

3. Present your own policy option in the middle of two other obviously unworkable alternatives to give the president the illusion of choice.

4. If the president selects the "wrong" policy anyhow, demand "full authority" to deal with the undesirable consequences, which you say are sure to arise.

5. Always predict the consequences of not adopting your policy in terms of worst cases, making predictions of dire consequences that will follow.

6. If the president chooses your own policy, urge immediate action; if he selects another policy, you may agree in principle but argue that "now is not the time."

7. If the opposition view looks very strong, "leak" damaging information to your supporters in the press or Congress and count on "public opposition" to build.

8. Fully implement orders that result from the selection of your own policy recommendation; circumvent or delay those that do not.

9. Limit the issues that go to the president. Bring up only those favorable to your position or that he is likely to favor.

10. Never oppose the president's policy in such extreme terms that you lose his trust. Temper your disagreements so that you can live to argue another day.

Bureaucrats do not really consider these "commandments" cynical. Indeed they may not realize when they are following them. They often sincerely believe that their own policies and projects are in the nation's best interest.

*Graham T. Allison, *Essence of Decision* (Boston: Little, Brown, 1971), p. 172.
**Leslie H. Gelb and Morton H. Halperin, "The Ten Commandments of the Foreign Policy Bureaucracy," *Harper's* (June 1972): 28–36.

THE BUDGET MAZE

The budget is the single most important policy statement of any government. The expenditure side of the budget shows "who gets what" from government, and the revenue side shows "who pays the costs." The budget lies at the heart of the policy-making process.

Deciding about taxing and spending each year is a long and difficult process. Former budget director David Stockman, who both critics and admirers concede knew more about the federal budget than anyone else in Washington, was quoted: "I just wish that there were more hours in the day or that we didn't have to do this so fast. . . . None of us really understands what's going on with these numbers."

The president is responsible for submitting the annual federal budget, with estimates of revenue and recommendations for expenditures, to the Congress. The Congress controls the purse strings; no federal monies may be spent without congressional appropriation. The president relies on the Office of Management and Budget to prepare a budget for the Congress. The president's budget is usually submitted in January of each year. The federal fiscal year (FY) begins October 1; this gives Congress nearly nine months to consider the president's budget and pass the appropriations act for the coming fiscal year.

Preparation of the budget by OMB starts more than a year before the beginning of the fiscal year for which it is intended. (Fiscal years are named for the year in which they *end*, so, for example, OMB prepares FY 91 in 1989 for presentation to Congress in January 1990 and passage before October 1, 1990; FY 91 ends September 30, 1991.) OMB considers budget requests by all executive departments and agencies, adjusting them to fit the president's overall policy goals. It prepares the *Budget of the United States Government* for the president to submit to Congress. Table 11-1 summarizes the steps in the overall schedule for budgetary preparation.

The Constitution gives Congress the authority to decide how the government should spend its money: "No money shall be drawn from the Treasury but in consequence of appropriations made by law" (Article I, Section 9). The president's budget is sent initially to the House and Senate budget committees, whose job it is to draft a budget resolution for the Congress, setting future target goals for appropriations in various areas. The House and Senate budget committees rely on their own bureaucracy, the Congressional Budget Office (CBO), to review the recommendations made by the president and OMB. Congress is supposed to pass a budget resolution by late spring. The resolution should guide the House and Senate appropriations committees and their subcommittees in writing the appropriations acts. There are usually thirteen separate appropriations acts each year. Each one covers a broad area of government; for example, defense, labor, human services and education, commerce, justice, state, and judiciary. These appropriations bills must pass both House and Senate in identical form, just as any other legislation must. All the acts are supposed to be passed before the start of the fiscal year, October 1. These procedures were mandated in the Congressional Budget and Impoundment Control Act of 1974. However, Congress rarely follows its own timetable or procedures.

The common goal of the congressional budget procedures, the House and Senate budget committees, and the Congressional Budget Office is

TABLE 11-1   The budget process

Approximate schedule	Actors	Tasks
PRESIDENTIAL BUDGET MAKING		
January–March	President and OMB	OMB presents long-range forecasts for revenues and expenditures to the president. The president and OMB develop general guidelines for all federal agencies. Agencies are sent guidelines and forms for their budget requests.
April–July	Executive agencies	Agencies prepare and submit budget requests to OMB.
August–October	OMB and agencies	OMB reviews agency requests and holds hearings with agency officials. OMB usually tries to reduce agency requests.
November–December	OMB and president	OMB presents revised budget to president. Occasionally agencies may appeal OMB decisions directly to the president. President and OMB write budget messages for Congress.
January	President	President presents budget for the next fiscal year to Congress.
CONGRESSIONAL BUDGET PROCESS		
February–May	CBO and congressional committees	Standing committees review taxing and spending proposals for reports to House and Senate budget committees. Congressional Budget Office (CBO) also reviews entire presidential budget and reports to budget committees.
May–June	Congress; House and Senate budget committees	House and Senate budget committees present first concurrent resolution, which sets overall total for budget outlays in major categories. Full House and Senate vote on resolution. Committees are instructed to stay within budget committee's resolution.
July–September	Congress; House and Senate appropriations committees and budget committees	House and Senate appropriations committees and subcommittees draw up detailed appropriations bills. Bills are submitted to House and Senate budget committees for second concurrent resolution. Budget committees may force reductions through "reconciliation" provisions to limit spending. The full House and Senate vote on "reconciliations" and second (firm) concurrent resolution.
September–October	Congress and president	House and Senate pass various appropriations bills (nine to sixteen bills, by major functional category, such as "defense"). Each is sent to president for signature. (If vetoed by president, the appropriations bills go back to House and Senate, which must override veto with two-thirds vote in each body or revise bills to gain president's approval.)

(continued)

TABLE 11-1   The budget process   *(continued)*

Approximate schedule	Actors	Tasks
EXECUTIVE BUDGET IMPLEMENTATION		
After October 1	Congress and president	Fiscal year for all federal agencies begins October 1. If no appropriations bill has been passed by Congress and signed by president for an agency, Congress must pass and the president sign a continuing resolution to allow the agency to spend at last year's level until a new appropriations act is passed. If no continuing resolution is passed, the agency must officially cease spending government funds and must officially shut down.

to allow Congress to consider the budget in its entirety rather than in separate segments. But after the budget resolution is passed, the thirteen separate appropriations bills begin their long and tortuous journeys through specialized appropriations subcommittees. Agency and department leaders from the administration are frequently called to testify before these subcommittees to defend the president's request. Lobbying activity is very heavy in these subcommittees. If the appropriations committees report bills that exceed the ceilings established by the budget resolution, Congress must prepare a *reconciliation bill* to reconcile the amounts set by the budget resolution and the amounts set by the appropriations committees. This procedure tends to match the power of the House and Senate budget committees against the House and Senate appropriations committees. When passed, the reconciliation bill binds the appropriations committees and the Congress to ceilings in each area. However, all this congressional infighting generally runs beyond the October 1 deadline for the start of the fiscal year. Congress is usually forced to pass a *continuing resolution,* which allows executive agencies to continue to spend money, generally at last year's level, until the appropriations act passes. If no appropriations act or continuing resolution is passed, theoretically a government agency would have to shut down completely.

Despite highly publicized wrangling between the president and Congress over the budget each year, final congressional appropriations rarely deviate by more than 2 or 3 percent from the original presidential budget.[4] This means that the president and the Office of Management and Budget have real budgetary power over executive departments, with Congress only rarely setting aside presidential budgetary recommendations.

Congressional appropriations acts cover broad areas of government. Once the appropriations act passes Congress—for example, the huge labor, human resources, and education appropriations act—the president is forced either to sign or to veto the entire act. The president does *not* have the power of line-item veto, which would allow him to veto individual expenditures within a broad appropriations act. This limitation permits Congress to force unwanted spending items on the president by including those items in a broad bill that the president needs to have passed so that the government can keep functioning.

THE PRIORITIES OF AMERICAN GOVERNMENT

Over the years, total federal spending has grown not only in real dollars but also as a percentage of the gross national product (see Figure 11-2). This means that the government in Washington is taking a larger share of the nation's resources. Defense spending is not what is driving the growth of the federal government. Defense spending *declined* after the Vietnam War from 10 percent of the GNP to less than 5 percent; it recovered briefly to about 6 percent under President Reagan and has now

FIGURE 11-2   Federal spending as a percentage of gross national product

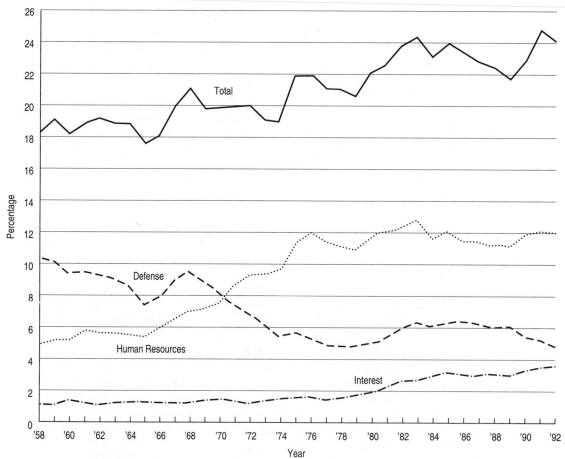

SOURCE: Fiscal 1992 Budget.

declined to about 4 percent. Governmental growth has been driven primarily by social security, health, and welfare spending.

In the decade of the 1970s, the United States changed its "national priorities," and for the first time in history social welfare spending took precedence over national defense. Indeed, as Figure 11-2 shows, it was during the administration of Richard Nixon that social welfare spending began to outrun defense spending in the federal budget. Note that the general direction of trend lines changed in the Reagan administration. Welfare spending no longer grew as a percentage of the GNP, although social security payments continued their upward direction. Defense spending rose temporarily in the early 1980s and then began to decline again.

The federal government relies primarily on the individual income tax (37 percent) and the social security payroll tax (30 percent) for its revenue, as Figure 11-3 shows. Corporate taxes have declined over the years to only 7 percent of federal revenues, while government borrowing has expanded to 19 percent.

MORTGAGING THE FUTURE: ELITE FISCAL IRRESPONSIBILITY

Every year the U.S. government goes deeper into debt. It is now about four *trillion* dollars in debt, a figure equal to sixteen thousand dollars for every man, woman, and child in the nation. The debt is more than half the size of the gross national product. The debt is owed to banks, insurance companies, investment firms, and anyone else who buys U.S. government

FIGURE 11-3   The federal government dollar

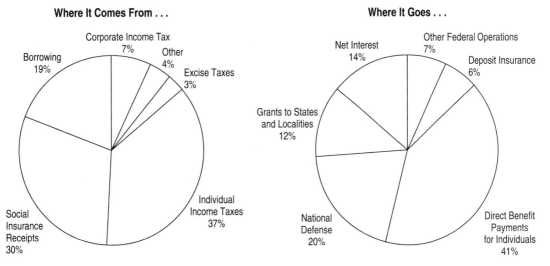

Where It Comes From . . .

Corporate Income Tax 7%
Other 4%
Excise Taxes 3%
Borrowing 19%
Individual Income Taxes 37%
Social Insurance Receipts 30%

Where It Goes . . .

Net Interest 14%
Other Federal Operations 7%
Deposit Insurance 6%
Grants to States and Localities 12%
National Defense 20%
Direct Benefit Payments for Individuals 41%

SOURCE: Fiscal 1992 Budget.

bonds. International investors own about 20 percent of the national debt. Government interest payments to holders of the debt now amount to about 14 percent of governmental expenditures. The debt need not ever be paid off, but future generations of American taxpayers must continue to pay the annual interest on it as long as it is not.

Governmental expenditures have exceeded revenues for every one of the last thirty years. Democrats and Republicans, liberals and conservatives, have all contributed to government deficits; they differ only in placing blame. Conservatives blame runaway government entitlement programs with built-in inflation protections, such as in Social Security and Medicare, as well as large-scale spending programs in welfare, education, job training, and agriculture. Liberals blame defense spending and Reagan's tax cuts. The Economic Recovery Tax Cut Act in 1981 reduced individual income taxes by 25 percent and lowered the top rate from 70 to 50 percent. The Tax Reform Act of 1986 was revenue-neutral; it lowered the top rate to 28 percent but closed many loopholes to make up for lost revenue. Democrats claim that the nation's high deficits result largely from these tax cuts. Republicans argue that Democrats in the Congress are responsible for the deficit because they failed to cut domestic spending as the president wished.

Copyright 1991 by HERBLOCK in the Washington Post.

FIGURE 11-4   Interest on the debt: A growing bite of the budget dollar

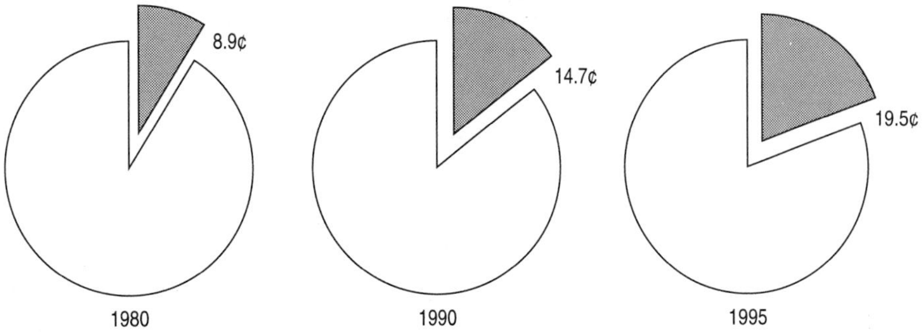

| 1980 | 1990 | 1995 |

8.9¢   14.7¢   19.5¢

If the trend set in 1980–1990 continues, net interest in 1995 will consume approximately 19.5 percent of the budget.

Mortgaging the Future

Young Americans today are being burdened by irresponsible deficit spending by the government. The painful legacy of these annual deficits will linger for generations. Very soon interest payments on the debt will consume about one out of every five dollars of federal expenditures (see Figure 11-4). This means that future taxpayers can receive at most only four dollars of public goods and services for every five dollars paid to the federal government. Today we spend more on interest payments than on welfare benefits, Medicare, health, transportation, or education; and soon interest payments will exceed defense spending.

Avoiding Responsibility

The simple and responsible solution to the federal deficit is to have the president and Congress prepare and pass only balanced budgets. But that solution has eluded policy makers for more than thirty years. No president or Congress, Democrat or Republican, has been willing to reduce expenditures or raise taxes in order to produce a balanced budget. American politics has reached a level of irresponsibility at which calls for a balanced budget are considered "naive" and "unrealistic." So Washington searches for politically "painless" remedies.

The Balanced Budget Constitutional Amendment

Constitutions govern government. Presumably, if the American people wish to discipline their government they can do so by amending the Constitution to restrict the actions of officials; indeed, according to the National Taxpayers Union, some thirty-one states have petitioned Congress to call a constitutional convention to balance the budget. Yet during the very same years that President Ronald Reagan proposed a balanced budget amendment to the U.S. Constitution, he also submitted budgets with the largest peacetime deficits in history.

Gramm-Rudman-Hollings

Congress devised its own deficit reduction plan in 1985 calling for "mandatory" reductions in annual federal deficits each year until a balanced budget is reached. The plan was originally proposed by Senators Phil Gramm (R.–Tex.), Warren B. Rudman (R.–N.H.), and Ernest F. Hollings (D.–N.C.). Of course, no Congress can really mandate that future Congresses do anything they do not wish to do; but Gramm-Rudman established automatic budget cuts that would take effect if Congress and the president could not agree on deficit reductions. However, the plan failed to bring about a balanced budget. Congress frequently resorted to "smoke and mirrors" to obscure the real size of the deficit and to claim that Gramm-Rudman ceilings were being met. Some deficit spending, including the massive bailout of the savings and loan industry, was placed "off-budget." Revenue estimates were inflated, thus obscuring deficits until after the fiscal year was over and the ceilings bypassed; and Congress itself set back the deficit reduction schedule year after year.

Budget Summits

While the reluctance of politicians to raise taxes or cut spending to balance budgets is the principal cause of the nation's continuing deficit woes, partisan conflict between Republican presidents and Democrat-controlled Congresses prevents the adoption of meaningful remedies. Even when political and economic pressures build to reduce the size of these deficits, Republican presidents and Democratic Congresses offer opposing budget solutions. Republican presidents Ronald Reagan and George Bush generally sought to reduce deficits through cuts in domestic spending, not tax increases. Democratic Congresses generally sought to reduce deficits through reductions in defense spending as well as tax increases. Inasmuch as the U.S. constitutional system gives both the president and Congress a check on the actions of the other, some agreement is necessary to achieve reductions. Hence the frequent call for a "budget summit" between leaders of Congress and the president, the director of the Office of Management and Budget, and key presidential advisers.

Yet budget summits have failed to achieve significant reductions in annual federal deficits. In 1990, President George Bush was forced to retract his campaign pledge—"Read my lips. No new taxes!"—and agree to an increase in the top marginal income tax rate from 28 to 31 percent. Military spending was cut dramatically, and token reductions were made in domestic programs. But these modest efforts were washed away in a sea of red ink. Slowing economic growth, with lower projected government revenues and higher interest rates promised the nation continuing deficits in excess of two to three hundred billion dollars a year.

INCREMENTALISM AND PUBLIC POLICY

Ideally, governments should decide policy questions by identifying society's goals, examining all possible policies to achieve the goals, researching the benefits and costs of each policy alternative, calculating the benefits and costs of each policy alternative, and then selecting the policy that maximizes benefits and minimizes costs. In other words, policy making should be *rational*. In fact it is not. Instead, policy makers, in both Congress and the White House, tend to continue existing governmental programs, policies, and expenditure levels with only incremental changes each year. This practice is called *incrementalism*.

Why is decision making incremental rather than rational? Why do presidents, members of Congress, and especially bureaucrats generally agree to continue the policies of the past, accept existing budget levels, and avoid annual reexamination of all previous decisions?

First, policy makers do not have the time, intelligence, or money to investigate all possible alternatives to existing policy. The cost of collecting the necessary information is too great. And policy makers do not have the predictive capabilities, even in an age of computers, to forecast accurately the consequences of each policy alternative; nor can they accurately calculate all benefits and costs when many diverse and noncomparable political, social, economic, and cultural values are at stake.

Second, policy makers accept previous policies and decisions because of the inherent uncertainty of a completely new or different approach. They find it safer to stick with known programs.

Third, heavy investment in existing programs ("sunk costs") may preclude really fundamental changes. Investments may be in money, buildings, or other hard items, or they may be in popular expectations, perceived entitlements, administrative practices, or organizational structures. Accepted wisdom holds, for example, that bureaucracies tend to persist long after their usefulness is over. People develop routines that are difficult to unlearn, and groups acquire a stake in organizations and practices. Change is very difficult.

Fourth, incrementalism is politically expedient. Agreement is easier when disputed items are only increases, decreases, or modifications in existing programs. Political conflict lessens with continuity of policies. It would "overload the system" with political tension to reconsider every policy or decision every year. Incrementalism reduces conflict, maintains stability, and helps preserve the political system.

Fifth, policy makers cannot always agree about society's goals and values, or about what constitute benefits and costs. One group's benefits may be another group's costs, and vice versa. Since no rational, comprehensive understanding of goals or values is possible, each administration finds it easier to continue existing policies into the future.

Finally, policy makers, like most of us, do not always act to maximize all desirable values. Instead, they try to satisfy particular demands. Rather than search for one best way, they end their search when they find a way that works. This search usually begins with the familiar—that is, policy alternatives close to current policies. Only if minor modifications appear unsatisfactory will policy makers venture out toward more radical policy innovations.

Incrementalism is particularly apparent in governmental spending. Today more than three-quarters of the federal budget is "uncontrollable"—that is, determined by previous congressional decisions and not easily changed in the annual budget-making process.

One source of uncontrollable spending is interest on the federal debt. Interest payments have grown rapidly as a percentage of all federal spending. The federal government must make these payments to maintain its credit and the nation's banking system. The interest payments are a product of a long history of federal deficits. As the deficit increases each year, interest payments go up.

Entitlement programs are the largest source of uncontrollable spending. These programs provide classes of people with a legally enforceable right to benefits. Entitlement programs account for *two-thirds* of all federal spending and include Social Security, welfare payments, Medicaid, and Medicare. Although these entitlements are benefits that past Congresses have pledged the federal government to pay, they are not really uncontrollable: Congress could amend or repeal the laws that established them. But such actions are difficult politically. Legislators would be vulnerable to charges of breach of faith or failure of trust by those who have come to depend on the benefits.

INSIDE WASHINGTON: THE IRON TRIANGLES

Traditionally it was assumed that when Congress passed a law and then created a bureaucracy and appropriated money to carry out the intent of the law, that was the end of the political process. It was assumed that the intent of Congress would be carried out—the political battle having been resolved—and government would get on with the job of "administering" the law.

It turns out, however, that political battles do not end with victory or defeat in Congress. Organized interests do not abandon the fight and return home simply because the site of the battle shifts from the political arena to an administrative one. We tend to think that "political" questions are the province of the president and Congress, and "administrative" questions the province of the bureaucracy. Actually "political" and "administrative" questions do not differ in content; they differ only in who decides them.

Once the bureaucracy takes over an issue, three major power bases—the "iron triangles"—come together to decide its outcome: the executive agency administering the program; the congressional subcommittee charged with its oversight; and the most interested groups, generally those directly affected by the agency.[5] The interest groups develop close relationships with the bureaucratic policy makers. And both the interest groups and the bureaucrats develop close relationships with the congressional subcommittees that oversee their activities. Agency–subcommittee–interest group relationships become established; even the individuals involved remain the same over fairly long periods of time, as senior members of Congress retain their subcommittee memberships.

Note that the parts of this triumvirate do *not* compete (as pluralist ideology suggests). Instead bureaucratic agency, congressional subcommittee, and organized interest come together and cooperate in bureaucratic policy making.

CONTROLLING THE BUREAUCRACY: CONGRESS AND COURTS

Congress or the courts can overturn the decisions of bureaucracies if sufficient opposition develops to bureaucratic policies. But such opposition is unlikely if bureaucracies work closely with their congressional subcommittees and their interested groups.

Congressional Constraints

Congress can restrain the bureaucracy by

1. Passing direct legislation changing rules or regulations or limiting bureaucratic activity.
2. Altering or threatening to alter the bureau's budget.
3. Retaining specific veto powers over certain bureaucratic actions (agencies must submit some proposed rules to Congress; if Congress does not act within a specified time, the rules take effect).
4. Conducting investigations, usually during legislative or appropriations hearings, that publicize unpopular decisions, rules, or expenditures by bureaus.
5. Making direct complaints to the bureaucracy through formal contacts.

Yet it is difficult for Congress to use these powers as a truly effective check on the bureaucracy.

Judicial Constraints

The federal courts exercise more direct control over the bureaucracy than Congress does. Decisions by executive agencies usually can be appealed to federal courts. Moreover, federal courts can issue injunctions (orders) to executive agencies before they institute their rules, regulations, projects, or programs.

Judicial control of the bureaucracy has its limitations, however:

1. Judicial oversight usually emphasizes *procedural* fairness rather than policy content.
2. Bureaucracies have set up elaborate administrative processes to protect their decisions from challenge on procedural grounds.
3. Lawsuits against bureaucracies are very expensive; the bureaucracies have armies of attorneys paid for out of tax monies to oppose anyone who attempts to challenge them in court.
4. Excessive delays in federal courts add to the time and expense of challenging bureaucratic decisions.

In fact, citizens have not had much success in court cases against bureaucracies. Political scientists Bradley Cannon and Michael Giles report that the courts rarely reverse the decisions of federal regulatory commissions. For example, the Federal Power Commission and the Federal Trade Commission win 91 percent of the cases they argue before the Supreme Court; the National Labor Relations Board wins 75 percent; and the Internal Revenue Service wins 73 percent. Only the Immigration and Naturalization Service has a mediocre record of 56 percent.[6]

THE BUREAUCRATIC ELITE

What kind of person inhabits the Washington bureaucracy? In a study of more than a thousand people who occupied top federal positions during five presidential administrations, the prestigious Brookings Institution reported that 36 percent rose through the ranks of government, 26 percent came from law firms, 24 percent from business, and 7 percent from a variety of other fields.[7] A plurality of top federal executives are career bureaucrats. Most top federal executives (63 percent) were federal bureaucrats at the time of their appointment to a top post; only 37 percent had no prior experience as federal bureaucrats. Thus the federal bureaucracy is producing its own leadership, with some limited recruitment from business and law.

Like other sectors of the elite, the bureaucracy recruits its top federal executives primarily from the middle- and upper-middle-class segments of the population. More than 99 percent of top federal executives are college educated, and 68 percent have advanced degrees (44 percent in law, 17 percent with earned master's degrees, and 11 percent with earned

CASE STUDY

 ### The President's Cabinet: Only the Faces Change

Each new presidential administration promises dramatic change in government—change in personnel as well as policy. Indeed, "pluralists" often portray the American political system as a struggle between broad coalitions of groups, represented by the Republican and Democratic parties, to capture control of the government and to determine personnel and policy. According to this interpretation, a change in the party in power should bring significant change in interest-group representation as well as in programs and policies.

Critics of this pluralist view contend that changes in administration do not bring different kinds of people to Washington and in fact bring only incremental changes in policy. According to this "elitist" interpretation, a change in the party in power may bring new faces into high office, but new personnel will rarely differ from past administrations in their social backgrounds, corporate ties, educational credentials, Ivy League connections, and government experience.

Consider the evidence on cabinet-level officials in the nine presidential administrations since World War II (those of Truman, Eisenhower, Kennedy, Johnson, Nixon, Ford, Carter, Reagan, and Bush):

- 47.8 percent had Ivy League educations.
- 69.4 percent had advanced degrees (18.6 percent had Ph.D.s and 39.5 percent had law degrees).
- 60.4 percent had served as officers or directors of corporations, banks, or investment firms before their appointment; their average age upon taking office was fifty-two.
- Only 3.7 percent of cabinet-level appointees were black, and only 3.7 percent were women.

The political significance of these observations can be debated. One might argue, for example, that social background, educational experience, and corporate ties are poor predictors of decision-making behavior. Even if top administrative officials have homogeneous backgrounds, they often view

policy questions very differently. The link between social backgrounds and decision-making behavior is very weak.

Nonetheless, it is an interesting comment on the recruitment process that characteristics of top cabinet officials do not change very much from one administration to the next. Names and faces change but characteristics of top leaders remain the same.

Given the different social bases of the Democratic and Republican parties, we might expect modest differences in the composition of Democratic and Republican cabinets. But in fact few significant differences exist between members of the four Democratic administrations (Truman, Kennedy, Johnson, Carter) and the five Republican administrations (Eisenhower, Nixon, Ford, Reagan, Bush) since World War II. The Republicans are only slightly more "Ivy League" than the Democrats (55.1 percent versus 40.0 percent), and the Democrats tend to recruit more lawyers than the Republicans (44.6 percent versus 34.8 percent). The greatest party difference is the Republicans' tendency to call upon corporate directors (71 percent of cabinet-level appointees). Although Democratic presidents also call upon corporate directors (49.2 percent of cabinet-level appointees), the difference is statistically significant.

The occupational backgrounds of cabinet-level appointees confirm the homogeneity of Democratic and Republican administrations. About one-quarter of the top posts generally go to lawyers. Almost one-quarter go to corporate executives, with Republican appointees more likely to be corporate executives (30.4 percent) than Democratic appointees (15.4 percent). About 15 percent of all appointees have based their careers on public office; Democratic appointees are more likely to have centered their careers in government (20.0 percent) than are Republican appointees (11.6 percent).

(continued)

CASE STUDY *(continued)*

Academe has contributed about 18 percent of cabinet-level appointees since World War II, nearly all of whom had earned a Ph.D. Economics is the leading field of study among academics in cabinet-level positions. The Carter administration had more Ph.D.s (seven) than any other; the Truman administration had none.

Cabinet-level recruitment in the Bush administration clearly fit the pattern of other administrations. We may lament the absence of pluralism in the social character of the nation's elites, but Bush's top leaders were no different from previous administrators in their corporate ties, government experience, Ivy League connections, and educational credentials (see table).

Who's running the government in Washington? Backgrounds of cabinet-level appointees in presidential administrations from Truman through Bush

	Truman through Carter			Reagan (1st term)	Reagan (2nd term)	Bush
	Total	Democratic	Republican			
Previous government posts (%)	79.1	81.5	76.8	68.4	95.0	90.0
Previous corporate posts (%)	60.4	49.2	71.0	73.7	65.0	35.0
Education (%)						
Advanced degree	69.4	76.9	65.2	68.4	60.0	80.0
Law degree	39.5	44.6	34.8	26.3	50.0	40.0
Ivy League	47.8	40.0	55.1	57.9	60.0	50.0
Harvard	23.9	23.1	24.6	26.3	30.0	20.0
Ph.D.s	18.6	20.0	18.2	15.8	10.0	25.0
No degree	0	0	0	0	5.0	0
Average age	52.5	50.4	54.5	55.1	56.1	56.0
Women (%)	3.7	3.1	4.4	5.3	10.0	10.0
Blacks (%)	3.7	4.6	3.0	5.3	5.0	5.0
Career Occupation (%)						
Law	28.3	32.3	24.6	11.1	30.0	40.0
Big business	23.1	15.4	30.4	26.3	40.0	40.0
Small business	5.2	1.5	9.1	5.3	5.0	15.0
Government/public office	15.7	20.0	11.6	15.8	10.0	5.0
Academia	18.6	21.5	15.9	15.8	10.0	25.0
Agriculture	2.2	1.5	3.0	5.3	5.0	5.0
Military	3.0	3.1	3.0	5.3	10.0	10.0
Other	3.7	4.6	3.0	5.3	5.0	5.0

SOURCES: For Reagan and Bush administrations, see Thomas R. Dye, *Who's Running America?*, 5th ed. (Englewood Cliffs, N.J.: Prentice-Hall, 1990); for totals from Truman through Carter, see Philip H. Burch, Jr., *Elites in American History*, vol. III (New York: Holmes and Meier, 1980).

doctorates). The Brookings Institution reports that the Ivy League schools plus Stanford, Chicago, Michigan, and Berkeley educated more than 40 percent of the top federal executives, with Yale, Harvard, and Princeton leading the list.[8]

Little difference exists between Republican and Democratic administrators. Of course, Democratic presidents tend to appoint Democrats to top posts and Republican presidents tend to appoint Republicans. However, few discernible differences are evident in the class backgrounds, educational levels, occupational experiences, or previous public service of Democratic and Republican appointees.

One troublesome problem at the top of the federal bureaucracy is federal executives' short tenures. The median tenure in office of top federal executives is only two years. Only the regulatory commissions have significantly longer tenure. Such a short tenure at the top has obvious disadvantages. The head of a large department or agency needs a year or more to become fully productive by learning the issues, programs, procedures, technical problems, and personalities involved in the work. If such a person resigns after two years, the federal bureaucracy is not getting continuous, knowledgeable direction from its top officials.

THE REGULATORY QUAGMIRE

The Washington bureaucracy has become the regulator of the national economy, the protector of business against its rivals, and the guardian of the American people against everything from tainted foods to rickety stepladders. Federal regulatory bureaucracies began in 1887 with the creation of the Interstate Commerce Commission to regulate railroad rates. Since then thousands of laws, amendments, court rulings, and executive orders have expanded the powers of the regulatory commissions over every aspect of our lives (see Figure 11-1 for a list of independent commissions and agencies).

Federal regulatory bureaucracies are legislatures, investigators, prosecutors, judges, and juries—all wrapped into one. They issue thousands of pages of rules and regulations each year; they investigate thousands of complaints and conduct thousands of inspections; they require businesses to submit hundreds of thousands of forms each year; they hold hearings, determine "compliance" and "noncompliance," issue corrective orders, and levy fines and penalties. Most economists agree that overregulation adds greatly to the cost of living (perhaps one to two hundred billion dollars a year), that it is an obstacle to innovation and productivity, and that it hinders economic competition. Most regulatory commissions are *independent;* they are not under an executive department, and their members are appointed for long terms by a president who has little control over their activities.

The Captured Regulators

Over the years, the reform movements that led to the establishment of the older regulatory agencies have diminished in influence. Many regulatory agencies have become closely identified with regulated industry. The capture theory of regulation describes how regulated industries come to benefit from government regulation and how regulatory commissions come to represent the industries they are supposed to regulate rather than "the people." From time to time, various regulatory commissions have behaved as if "captured" by their industry. These have included the Interstate Commerce Commission (ICC) with railroads and trucking, the Federal Reserve Board (FRB) with banking, the Food and Drug Administration (FDA) with the drug industry, the Federal Communications Commission (FCC) with television and radio, the Securities and Exchange Commission (SEC) with the stock market, the Federal Power Commission (FPC) with the natural gas industry, and the National Highway Traffic and Safety Administration (NHTSA) with the auto industry.

Historically, regulatory commissions have acted only against the most wayward members of an industry. By attacking the businesses giving the industry bad publicity, the commissions actually helped improve the public's opinion of the industry as a whole. Regulatory commissions provided symbolic reassurance to the public that the behavior of the industry was proper.

By limiting entry into an industry by smaller firms (either directly, by denying them routes or broadcast channels, for example; or indirectly, by making the requirements for entry very costly), the regulatory commissions reduce competition. This function is an important asset to larger established businesses; they no longer fear new, cut-rate competitors.

The close relationships between the regulatory bureaucracies and their client industries stem from a common resource: expertise. Not only do the regulatory commissions frequently turn to the regulated industries for information but they also recruit bureaucrats from industry leaders. Commission members usually come from the industry they are supposed to regulate.[9] And after a few years in government, the "regulators" return to high-paying jobs in the industry. This practice is known as the "revolving door" problem.

Many federal regulatory commissions attract young attorneys, fresh from law school, to their staffs. When the attorneys are successful, they frequently are offered much higher-paying jobs in the industries they are regulating. So industry siphons off "the best and the brightest" to become defenders against government regulation. And of course these people have already learned the intricacies of government regulation, with taxpayers paying for their training. People see jobs in federal regulatory agencies as stepping-stones to lucrative careers in private (regulated) industry.

Over the years, then, industry came to *support* the regulatory bureaucracies. Industry often strongly opposes proposals to reduce government control—deregulation. Proposals to deregulate railroads, interstate trucking, and airlines have met with substantial opposition from both the regulating bureaucracies and the regulated industries, working together. Thus industry views most regulation favorably.

The New Bureaucracies

Recently Congress has created or expanded several bureaucracies to cover areas in which they have little or no expertise. To make matters worse, their jurisdiction extends to all industries rather than specific ones. Prime examples are the Equal Employment Opportunity Commission (EEOC), the Occupational Safety and Health Administration (OSHA), and the Environmental Protection Agency (EPA). The business community widely resents regulations by these agencies. Rules developed by EEOC to prevent discrimination in employment and promotion (affirmative action guidelines) have been awkward, and the EEOC enforcement of these rules has been nearly chaotic. Many businesses do not believe that EEOC has the expertise to understand their industry or their labor market. The same is true of the much-despised OSHA, which has issued thousands of safety regulations that appear costly and ridiculous to those in the industry. The complaint about EPA is that it seldom considers the *costs* of its rulings to business or the consumer. Industry representatives contend that EPA should weigh the costs of the regulations against the benefits to the environment.

Note that the EEOC, OSHA, and EPA have general responsibilities across all business and industry. Thus these agencies are unlikely to develop expertise in the fashion of the FCC, ICC, or other single-industry regulators. On the other hand, after a few years of interaction between business and these new regulators, conflict may diminish and cooperation may become the prevailing style of interaction.

Deregulation

The demand for deregulation has echoed in Washington for many years. Complaints about excessive regulation include the following:

1. The increased costs to businesses and consumers of complying with many separate regulations, issued by separate regulatory agencies, are excessive. Environmental regulation alone may be costing Americans one to two hundred billion dollars a year, but the costs never appear in a federal budget because businesses and consumers absorb them.

2. Overregulation hampers innovation and productivity. New drug research has decreased more than 75 percent in the past decade because of lengthy testing by the Food and Drug Administration (FDA). Most observers feel that FDA would not approve aspirin if it were proposed for marketing today. The costs and delays in winning permission for a new product tend to discourage invention.

3. Regulatory bureaucracies' involvement in licensing and business start-up reduces competition. The red tape involved—the cost of complying with federal reporting requirements—is in itself an obstacle to small businesses.

4. Regulatory agencies do not weigh the costs of complying with their regulations against the benefits to society. Regulators generally introduce controls with little regard for the cost-benefit trade-offs.

Not until 1978 did Congress act for the first time to significantly reduce the burden of regulation. Acting against the objections of the airline industry, which wanted continued regulation, Congress stripped the CAB of its power to allocate airline routes to various companies and to set rates. The CAB went out of existence in 1985. The airlines were "set free" (against their will) to choose where to fly and what to charge and to compete openly with one another.

Airline deregulation brought about a huge increase in airline travel, from roughly fifteen million passengers in 1980 to forty million in 1990. The airlines doubled their seating capacity and made more efficient use of their aircraft through the development of hub-and-spoke networks. Air safety continued to improve. Fatalities per millions of miles flown declined, and, because travelers were diverted from far more dangerous highway travel, overall transportation safety was improved. But these favorable outcomes were overshadowed by complaints about congestion at major airports and increased flight delays, especially at peak hours. The major airports are publicly owned, and governments have been very slow in responding to increased air traffic. Congestion and delays are widely publicized. Politicians respond to complaints by calling for regulation of airline travel.

Reregulation   Deregulation threatens to diminish politicians' power and eliminate bureaucrats' jobs. It forces industries to become competitive and diminishes the role of interest-group lobbyists. So in the absence of strong popular support for continued deregulation, pressures for *reregulation* will be strong in Washington.

The Savings and Loan Fiasco

Reregulation also gained impetus from the financial disaster in the savings and loan industry. During the 1970s, deregulation of the financial industry allowed savings and loans to expand well beyond their traditional function of providing home mortgage loans and encouraged them to make riskier loans for commercial development. Removal of limits on interest rates savings and loans could pay on deposits forced them to compete for depositors, which encouraged them to make riskier loans to recover their higher costs. But because the federal government guaranteed deposits (up to one hundred thousand dollars) through the Federal Deposit Insurance Corporation (FDIC), the savings and loans were really risking money guaranteed by American taxpayers. Fraud and mismanagement played a role in the disaster, but the real problem was the moral hazard created by allowing these companies free rein with government-guaranteed funds. If the U.S. government is going to guarantee deposits, then it must regulate their use. Alternatively, if the financial industry is deregulated, then the government should stop insuring deposits. The savings and loan disaster has resulted in tightened federal regulation of banking and savings institutions.

SUMMARY

The federal bureaucracy is a major base of power in the United States, largely independent of the other branches of government and not very responsive to the American people. Governmental bureaucracies invade every aspect of modern life, and their power is growing each year. A bureaucratic elite that both formulates and implements public policy is emerging. Elitism in bureaucracy takes several forms:

1. Bureaucratic power increases with the size and technological complexity of modern society. Official lawmaking bodies—Congress and the president—set forth only general policy statements. Bureaucracies write tens of thousands of rules and regulations and actually undertake the tasks of government.

2. Bureaucratic power increases because (a) Congress and the president do not have the time or expertise to master policy details; (b) Congress and the president deliberately pass vague laws for symbolic reasons, then turn over actual governance to bureaucracies; and (c) the bureaucracy has now amassed sufficient power to influence the president and Congress.

3. The federal government alone employs three million people and spends 22 percent of the gross national product. State and local governments hire millions more and bring the total governmental portion of the GNP to approximately 35 percent.

4. Although the president is officially in charge of the executive branch of government, presidential control is limited by (a) the relatively small number of patronage positions and large numbers of professional civil service bureaucrats, (b) the difficulty of achieving meaningful reorganization, and (c) the large number of "uncontrollable" items in the budget.

5. Once a political question shifts to the bureaucracy, an "iron triangle" of power bases comes together to decide its outcome: the executive bureaucracy, the congressional subcommittee, and the organized interest groups.

6. In theory, Congress restrains the bureaucracy directly by ordering changes in rules, altering the budget, retaining veto powers over bureaucratic action, conducting investigations, and registering complaints. In practice, however, Congress rarely reverses bureaucratic decisions and seldoms tampers with "uncontrollable" budget items.

7. In theory, the courts can also restrain the bureaucracy. But rarely do they actually reverse administrative decisions.

8. The federal regulatory commissions are investigators, prosecutors, judges, and juries—all wrapped into one. Members of these commissions serve long, overlapping terms, and they do not report to executive departments. They are relatively free from mass influence.

NOTES

1. Max Weber, *The Theory of Social and Economic Organization*, A. M. Henderson and Talcott Parsons, trans. (New York: Oxford University Press, 1947). Summary by Robert C. Fried, *Performance in American Bureaucracy* (Boston: Little, Brown, 1976).
2. James Q. Wilson, "Social Science: The Public Disenchantment, A Symposium," *American Scholar* (Summer 1976): 358; also cited by Aaron Wildavsky, *Speaking Truth to Power* (Boston: Little, Brown, 1979), p. 69.
3. See Richard F. Fenno, Jr., *The President's Cabinet* (Cambridge, Mass.: Harvard University Press, 1959).
4. See Aaron Wildavsky, *The Politics of the Budgetary Process*, 4th ed. (Boston: Little, Brown, 1984); Mark W. Huddleston, "Assessing Congressional Budget Return: The Impact on Appropriations," *Policy State Journal* 9 (Autumn 1980): 81–86.
5. Kenneth J. Meier, *Politics and the Bureaucracy* (North Scituate, Mass.: Duxbury Press, 1979), p. 51.
6. Bradley Cannon and Michael Giles, "Recurring Litigants: Federal Agencies before the Supreme Court," *Western Political Quarterly* 15 (September 1972): 183–191.
7. David T. Stanley, Dean E. Mann, and Jameson W. Doig, *Men Who Govern* (Washington, D.C.: Brookings Institution, 1967).
8. Ibid., p. 21.
9. Marver H. Bernstein, *Regulating Business by Independent Commissions* (Princeton, N.J.: Princeton University Press, 1965), p. 118.

SELECTED READINGS

Cranford, John. *Budgeting for America*, 2nd ed. Washington, D.C.: Congressional Quarterly Press, 1989. Cranford presents a readable and nonpartisan introduction to the federal government's deficit problems, the budgetary maze, tax policy, and the political gridlock that has prevented effective action.

Lindbloom, Charles E. *The Intelligence of Democracy.* New York: Free Press, 1965. Lindbloom analyzes democratic decision-making processes and offers a prescription for the best way to make collective decisions. The book discusses in depth the implications of incremental decision making.

Wildavsky, Aaron. *The Politics of the Budgetary Process,* 4th ed. Boston: Little, Brown, 1984. This book is the classic introduction to budgetary decision making and the folkways of bureaucracies. Wildavsky concludes that "budgeting turns out to be an incremental process, proceeding from a historical base, guided by accepted notions of fair shares, in which decisions are fragmented, made in sequence by specialized bodies, and coordinated through multiple feedback mechanisms." The importance of this book lies in its argument against policy formation based strictly on rational considerations.

Wildavsky, Aaron. *Speaking Truth to Power: The Art and Craft of Policy Analysis.* Boston: Little, Brown, 1979. An important essay on why policies do not always work as intended, this book examines how and why bureaucracies substitute their own purposes for their original goals, how past policies create new problems, and how national planning conflicts with good politics.

12

Congress:
The Legislative Elite

★ *The heart of the trouble is that power is exercised by minority, not majority, rule.*

Joseph S. Clark, The Senate Establishment, *1963*

The Founding Fathers established Congress to represent the people in policy making. But how does Congress "represent" the people, and who are "the people"? Because of the way its members are elected, Congress tends to represent local elites in the United States and thereby injects a strong parochial influence into national decision making. Representatives are part of local elite structures; they retain their local businesses, club memberships, and political networks. They are not responsible to national political leaders but rather to leaders within their home constituencies. Thus congressional members represent many small segments of the nation rather than the nation as a whole.

SOCIAL BACKGROUNDS OF CONGRESS: THE CLASS BIAS

The "representational bias" of Congress begins with recruitment. Senators and House members are seldom recruited from the masses; they are drawn mostly from the well-educated, prestigiously employed, affluent upper and upper-middle classes.[1] Only a small minority come from families of wage earners or salaried workers.

Occupation

Professional and business occupations dominate the halls of Congress, meaning that congressional members are generally of higher social standing than their constituents. One reason is that candidates for Congress have a better chance at election if their occupations are socially "respectable" and provide opportunities for extensive public contacts. Lawyers, bankers, insurance brokers, and realtors establish in their businesses the wide circle of friends necessary for political success.

The overrepresentation of lawyers in Congress and other public offices is particularly marked (see Table 12-1), since lawyers constitute no more than two-tenths of 1 percent of the labor force.[2] Lawyers have always played a prominent role in the American political system. Twenty-five of the fifty-two signers of the Declaration of Independence and thirty-one of the fifty-five members of the Continental Congress were lawyers. The legal profession has also provided 70 percent of the presidents, vice-presidents, and cabinet officers of the United States and more than 50 percent of the U.S. senators and House members. Lawyers are in a reasonably high-prestige occupation, but so are physicians, business executives, and scientists. Why, then, do lawyers dominate Congress?

Some people argue that lawyers bring a special kind of skill to Congress. They represent clients in their work; therefore they can use the same skill to represent constituents in Congress. Also lawyers deal with public policy as it is reflected in the statute books, so they may be reasonably familiar with public policy before entering Congress. But

TABLE 12-1   Occupations of members of Congress, 1986–1990*

Occupation	House Democrat	House Republican	Senate Democrat	Senate Republican	Total
Acting/Entertainment	1	1	0	0	2
Aeronautics	0	3	1	1	5
Agriculture	8	11	1	3	23
Business/Banking	66	72	13	15	166
Clergy	2	0	0	1	3
Education	25	17	6	5	53
Engineering	2	2	0	0	4
Journalism	9	8	5	3	25
Labor Leadership	2	0	0	0	8
Law	122	62	36	27	247
Law Enforcement	6	2	0	0	8
Medicine	2	2	0	0	4
Military	0	0	0	1	1
Professional Sports	3	1	1	0	5
Public Service/Politics	58	36	14	6	114

*Because some members have more than one occupation, the total is higher than congressional

professional skills alone cannot explain the dominance of lawyers in public office. Of all the high-prestige occupations, only lawyers can really afford to neglect their careers for political activities. Physicians, corporate managers, and scientists pay a high cost if they neglect their vocations for political activity. But political activity can help boost lawyers' careers; free public advertising and contacts with potential clients are two important benefits. Moreover, lawyers have a monopoly on public offices in law enforcement and the court system, and the offices of judge or prosecuting attorney often provide lawyers with stepping-stones to higher public office, including Congress.

Thus information on the occupational background of congressional members indicates that more than high social status is necessary for election to Congress. Experience in personal relations and public contacts, easy access to politics, and a great deal of free time to devote to political activity are also helpful.[3]

Education

Congressional members are among the most highly educated occupational groups in the United States. Their educational level is considerably higher than that of the populations they represent. Their education reflects their occupational background and their middle- and upper-class origins. White Anglo-Saxon Protestants are substantially overrepresented in Congress. About two-thirds of the House and three-fourths of the senate are Protestant. The main minority groups—blacks, Catholics, Jews, and foreign born—have disproportionately fewer seats in Congress.

Religion

Religious denominations of high social status, such as Episcopalians and Presbyterians, are regularly overrepresented in Congress. About one-third of the U.S. senators and House members are affiliated with the Congregational, Presbyterian, Episcopalian, or Unitarian churches. Although the representation of Catholics and Jews has increased in recent years, evidence indicates that these minorities can win representation in Congress only in districts in which they are a majority or near majority. Nearly all Catholic and Jewish members come from northern and industrial states, notably from major cities; Mississippi, Georgia, and South Carolina send congressional delegations composed largely of Baptists and Methodists; New York City sends delegations almost solidly Catholic and Jewish. Apparently local electorates prefer their representatives to reflect the dominant religious and ethnic backgrounds in their districts.

Race and Gender

Blacks make up just over 12 percent of the nation's population. Beginning in 1993, their membership in the House of Representatives will reach 9 percent for the first time. The leap in black membership is a product of judicial interpretations of the Voting Rights Act, which requires that minorities be given maximum opportunity to elect minorities to Congress through redistricting. Hispanic membership also rose in the House (to 18 members) as a result of redistricting.

It was not until 1966 that the first black person, Republican Edward Brooke of Massachusetts, was popularly elected to the Senate; he served until 1979. Carol Moseley Braun was the first black woman to be elected to the Senate in 1992, "the year of the woman." That same year, a record 106 women won party nominations for House seats and 11 women ran for the Senate. The result was a record number of women serving in the House (47) and the Senate (6). Yet these numbers amount to only 11 percent of the House and 12 percent of the Senate.

TABLE 12-2 Demographics of Congress

	Female	Black	Average age
HOUSE MEMBERS (435)			
1985–1987	20	20	49.7
1987–1989	23	23	50.7
1989–1991	25	24	52.1
1991–1993	28	26	52.8
1993–1995	47	38	51.7
SENATORS (100)			
1985–1987	2	0	54.2
1987–1989	2	0	54.4
1989–1991	2	0	55.6
1991–1993	2	0	57.2
1993–1995	6	1	58.0

Turnover

Turnover among members of Congress is very low. In any session of Congress, only about 10 to 20 percent of the members will be new to their jobs. Most of these freshmen will be replacing retired members; rarely are incumbents defeated for reelection.

WHOM DOES CONGRESS REALLY REPRESENT?

Elites: The Relevant Constituents

The relevant political constituencies of members of Congress are the elites of their districts rather than general district populations. In reality, their constituencies are not aggregate bodies of people, but relatively small groups of political activists with the time, interest, and skill to communicate about political events.

Constituents' ignorance.　For the great mass of people, Congress is an institution with very low visibility. A study commissioned by the Senate

"NEVER MIND MY CONSTITUENTS – HAVE YOU POLLED THE NETWORKS?"

Subcommittee on Intergovernment Relations discovered some grim facts about the public's awareness of Congress. Only 59 percent of a national sample of Americans could identify one senator from their state, and barely half could name that person's party. Only 39 percent could name both senators. Members of the House of Representatives fared even worse. Only 46 percent of the general public could identify their representative, and only 41 percent could name their representative's political affiliation.[4]

Even when constituents know a congressional member's name, few know the member's specific policy positions or, for that matter, the member's overall political position. Hence, Miller and Stokes found that among those who offered a reason for candidate choice, only 7 percent indicated that their choice had any "discernible issue content." If one asks for detailed information about policy stands, only a "chemical trace" of the population qualifies as attentive.[5]

Only about 15 percent of the population has *ever* written a letter to a senator or House representative, and 3 percent of the population accounts for more than two-thirds of congressional mail. During periods of turmoil the flow of letters becomes more urgent. However, even in critical national situations, the flow of communication is unrepresentative.[6]

Political activists of the district. A legislator's relevant constituents, then, are the home district's active, interested, and resourceful elites. In an agricultural district, they are the leaders of the American Farm Bureau Federation and the major agricultural producers—cotton producers, wheat growers, and so on; in the Southwest, oil producers or ranchers; in the mountain states, the copper, lead, and silver mining interests; in upper New England, the lumber, granite, and fishing interests; in central Pennsylvania and West Virginia, the coal interests and leaders of the United Mine Workers. More heterogeneous urban constituencies may contain a variety of influential constituents—bankers and financial leaders, real estate owners and developers, owners and managers of large industrial and commercial enterprises, top labor leaders, and the owners and editors of newspapers and radio and television facilities. In certain big-city districts with strong, disciplined party organizations, the key congressional constituents may be the city's political and governmental elites—the city or county party chairpersons or the mayor. And, of course, anyone who makes major financial contributions to a congressional candidate's campaign becomes an important constituent, for such money is hard to come by.

Sending the Message to Legislators

The elite of a constituency tends to transmit messages to its representatives that are in *agreement* with the representative's known policy preferences.[7] Representatives, like most other people, tend to associate with people with whom they agree. Thus they will maintain contact with the constituency largely through existing acquaintances. Representatives gain two-thirds of their information about constituency preferences through such personal contact and another 25 percent through mail. Representatives hear what they want to hear. Their selective perception may help explain why conflicting reports of public opinion are so common.

As we have seen, legislators' communication with local *elites* is relatively intense. When elites and masses do not share the same opinion, it is not surprising that legislators' actions do not fit mass preferences. On a few particularly visible issues, those on which the masses have strong opinions, the agreement between legislative performance and constituency demand can be relatively high. On civil rights issues, for instance, the correlation between congressional voting and constituency opinion is high. On most other issues, however, the correlation is low. If the constituents knew what their representative was doing, they would not be particularly happy. Except for the few major issues—such as civil rights—the "average" constituent would say of the representative's behavior, "I don't like it; I don't dislike it; I just don't think about it very much."

Although we cannot say with assurance what the representative process *is*, we certainly know what it is *not*. It is not the representation of the will of the people. At best, representation is intraelite communication.

Reelection of Incumbents

The ultimate reprisal for congressional members who fail to keep their ears to the ground is to be sent home. Legislators, of course, subscribe to the popular theory of representative government, summarized by Charles O. Jones: "[Election time] is the period of accounting; either the representative is instructed further, or he is defeated for malrepresentation, or he is warned, or he is encouraged."[8]

In reality very little such accounting takes place; *incumbents rarely lose.* Indeed, if we accept the standard theory of election, Americans are ecstatic over the performance of Congress. More than 85 percent of the senators who seek reelection win, and a whopping 95 percent of House members who seek reelection win.

Table 12-3 looks at Congress and its constituents from another perspective. Popular support for Congress has diminished; criticism has increased. But do the voters throw the rascals out? Clearly not. Not only does the electorate routinely return incumbents to their seats, but the general postwar trend is toward even greater safety for incumbents.

Why do incumbents win? First of all, name familiarity—in the absence of any knowledge of issues—can be a powerful advantage. The average voter, even if only vaguely aware of the incumbents, is likely to recognize their names on the ballot and vote for them.

TABLE 12-3   Popular support for Congress and reelection of incumbents

Year	Percentage of public rating Congress positively	Percentage of Senate incumbents reelected	Percentage of House incumbents reelected
1966	49	96	90
1967	38	—	—
1968	46	83	96
1969	34	—	—
1970	34	88	95
1971	26	—	—
1972	24	84	93
1974	29	92	90
1976	33	61	96
1978	34	68	95
1980	18	59	92
1982	14	93	90
1984	14	90	96
1986	15	75	98
1988	16	77	98
1990	14	96	97

SOURCE: Gallup Political Index, 1970–1990.

Reprinted by permission: Tribune Media Services.

Second, incumbents are more likely to have an effective political organization and a stable network of communication with local elites. Smart incumbents can use their franking privilege for mailing newsletters, polls, and other information; they can appear at various public events, call news conferences, address organizational meetings, and, in general, make themselves as visible as possible at minimal expense.

Finally, incumbents attract heavy campaign contributions. By developing ties with local elites, and because the "smart money" backs a winner, incumbents have more to spend in their campaigns. Incumbents generally can raise twice as much money as challengers can.

Thus the cue for voters is incumbency (name familiarity) rather than issue position or even party affiliation (as the role of incumbency grows, the role of party identification weakens). Clearly, then, Congress is an institution that can generally operate free of mass reprisals: "We have neither a Democratic nor a Republican party. Rather, we have an incumbency party which operates a monopoly."[9]

CONGRESSIONAL SELF-RECRUITMENT: THE ENTREPRENEURIAL SPIRIT

Members of Congress are self-recruited. Although both parties have national committees, they do little of substance about the essential task of political parties: deciding who earns the party's nomination. "Most candidates for elective office in the United States are self-recruited and conduct their own nominating campaigns."[10] Candidate interviews show that "the decision to run for office is extremely personal."[11] The parties are not invisible, only weak. Table 12-4 shows candidates' ratings of the influence of various agencies in their recruitment. The scores can range from 1 (no influence) to 5 (great influence). The table reveals feeble parties. The candidates rank family and friends as the major influence in their recruitment, and this response usually masks their own personal initiative. Most candidates are "self-status."[12] Among the Democratic candidates, unions and interest groups are judged more influential than, and, for Senate candidates, as influential as, the Democratic National Committee. Among both sets of contestants, the *local* party was more influential than the *national* party organizations.

When it's time to raise money, from which sources do candidates believe it comes? In Table 12-4 we find some evidence for the belief that parties are gaining ground: Republicans regard their congressional or Senate campaign committee as providing the most help. Democrats, true to their image, are more beholden to interest groups. Democrats, who have held a majority in the House of Representatives since 1953, regard unions and political action committees as more helpful in raising money than political parties. Among the other aspects of the campaign—its general

TABLE 12-4   Help in getting to Washington: congressional candidates' estimates of influence in their recruitment

	Democrats		Republicans	
	House	Senate	House	Senate
Family/Friends	3.7	3.8	4.1	3.8
Local Party	2.2	1.5	2.3	1.6
State Party	1.8	2.0	1.8	2.0
National Committee	1.5	2.0	1.8	2.1
Congressional/Senate Campaign Committee	1.5	2.3	2.0	2.7
Unions	1.8	2.0	1.7	1.3
Interest Groups	1.8	2.0	1.7	1.3
PACs	1.4	1.4	1.6	1.6

CONGRESSIONAL CANDIDATES' ASSESSMENT OF HELP IN FUND-RAISING

	Democrats		Republicans	
	House	Senate	House	Senate
Local Party	1.8	1.5	1.8	1.8
State Party	1.6	2.4	2.0	2.8
National Committee	1.6	1.8	2.2	2.0
Congressional Campaign Committee	2.5	2.8	3.1	4.0
Unions	2.8	3.0	1.1	1.0
Interest Groups	2.4	2.6	1.8	1.8
PACs	2.7	2.4	2.4	2.4

SOURCE: Derived from Paul S. Herrnson, *Party Campaigning in the 1980s* (Cambridge, Mass.: Harvard University Press, 1988), pp. 8, 112.

management, polling, advertising, turning out voters, and so on—political parties play a more active role. Among Republicans, party organizations are more important than other agencies in each activity except supplying campaign workers, where the interest groups are more important. Among Democrats, the party is regarded as less significant: it is more important in overall campaign management, but less important in developing advertising, and it is no more important than interest groups in conducting surveys, conducting efforts to get out the vote, and in recruiting campaign workers.[13] In short, parties are one of a variety of agencies upon which candidates rely.

THE LUSH LIFE ON CAPITOL HILL

Congress has created an elaborate perquisite ("perk") system for itself. In 1991, the lush life on Capitol Hill came under severe attack and members of Congress faced widespread popular disapproval for their enjoyment of the perks outlined in Table 12-5. Their expense accounts can be used for travel, but members of Congress also have access to interest-group-funded travel. When House members approved a $35,000 pay raise in 1990, the trade-off was to limit honoraria (fees paid by interest groups for speeches) to $26,850 a year. However, the interest-group-funded travel

TABLE 12-5   Congressional perks

	Senate	House
Salary	$125,000	$125,000
Expense account	$611,000	$119,000
Auto tax deduction	$3,000	$3,000
Mailing	free	free
Computing	free	free
Travel	$23,900	$23,900
Use of military aircraft	free	free
Airport parking	free	free
Courier service	free	free
Banking	free	free
Postage (personal)	free	free
Printing	free	free
Picture framing	free	free
Greeting cards	free	free
Telephones		
local	free	free
long-distance	free	free
Satellite hookups	free	free
TV/radio studios	free	free
Family membership in health/ tennis/golf/ swimming clubs	free	free
Purchase of furniture, haircuts, car wash, etc.	reduced (leather chair: $4.80) subsidized	reduced (leather chair: $4.80) subsidized
Cameras, film, video equipment, stationery	free	free
Average retirement annuity	$2.5 million	$2.5 million
Civil rights laws (affirmative action, sexual harassment)	exempt	exempt
D.C. parking violations	canceled	canceled

was not touched, and the honoraria in excess of the ceiling can be donated to a designated charity, providing the member with valuable public relations. In each session of Congress, members of Congress take about 4,000 privately sponsored trips. The leading travelers in the House of Representatives are set out in Table 12-6.

Recipients of interest-group largesse defend their travel as necessary for their representative obligations, but critics wonder why January—when Washington is usually in the grip of bitter cold—is the most popular month for travel. For instance, in January 1990, twenty-five members of the House, some with families, flew to Palm Springs at the expense of the Tobacco Institute. The Tobacco Institute wanted to achieve "better communication between individuals and legislators who face a barrage of anti-tobacco proposals every session."[14] The leading sponsors of congressional trips during 1989–1990 are shown in Table 12-7.

Scholars have been slow to understand that the perks of office are a driving motivation for reelection. The congressional lifestyle is one in which money has little meaning. The generous salary is not large enough

TABLE 12-6   Trips and honoraria provided by interest groups to representatives, 1991

	Trips	Honoraria
Patricia Shroeder (D.–Colo.)	98	$231,418
William Gray (D.–Penn.)	74	$108,098
Dan Rostenkowski (D.–Ill.)	53	$216,500
Charles Stenholm (D.–Tex.)	51	$46,250
Curt Weldon (R.–Penn.)	41	$8,000
Bill Richardson (D.–Calif.)	40	$35,000
Norman Miteta (D.–Calif.)	39	$40,000
Jim Bunning (R.–Ken.)	36	$7,030
Stephen Solarz (D.–N.Y.)	33	$46,422
John Lewis (R.–Calif.)	33	$38,100

SOURCE: Michael McCauley and Andrew Cohen, *They Love to Fly and It Shows* (Washington, D.C.: Public Citizen's Congress Watch, 1991), p. 8.

TABLE 12-7   Leading sponsors of congressional trips, 1989-1990

Organization	Trips
Chicago Mercantile Exchange	118
National Cable Television Association	75
Connell Rice and Sugar	72
National Association of Broadcasters	67
Aspen Institute	62
Electronic Industries Association	55
Textron	51
American Medical Association	49
Tobacco Institute	47
US Telephone Association	43

SOURCE: Michael McCauley and Andrew Cohen, *They Love to Fly and It Shows* (Washington, D.C.: Public Citizen's Congress Watch, 1991), p. 6.

to support the lush lifestyle of Capitol Hill. For example, former Speaker of the House Tip O'Neill and members of his personal staff flew to Dublin for St. Patrick's Day and returned to Washington immediately after the parade. Few who earn $89,000 (the salary for representatives at the time of O'Neill's trip) would have spent $100,000 for a day in Dublin.

A little bribery and a little sex does not distinguish Congress from many other institutions in society. The unique feature of congressional corruption is its legality. When the 1991 scandal—bounced checks and restaurant bills—hit the media, the public reaction was harsh. Overdrawn accounts plague most of us at one time or another; but the checks members of Congress wrote when funds in their accounts were insufficient were covered by the member's personal bank. Opinion polls showed that huge majorities of the American public believed that the bad check episode revealed members of Congress to be corrupt, pampered, and arrogant; 83 percent thought legislators overdrew their accounts because they knew they could get away with it, not because of carelessness.[15]

Politicians in the United States are *self-recruited.* They organize their own fund-raising, hire their own consultants, manage their own enterprises. They are entrepreneurs whose life is the pursuit of political office.

Sooner or later, they win, and some become members of Congress. For example, Richard Gephardt, House majority leader, has been "pursuing office all his life."[16] He was student body president in college, a St. Louis alderman, and in 1976, when an incumbent retired, he was ready for his House campaign. He made a run for the Democratic presidential nomination in 1988. Gephardt did it all by himself.

Consider also Representative Scott Klugg, a Wisconsin Republican elected in 1990. A thirty-seven-year-old former television anchorman, he defeated veteran Robert Kastenmeir. His decision to run for office illustrates well the self-selection process that encourages the excesses for which Congress is condemned. As Klugg explained, "I do have a certain entrepreneurial spirit, and I wanted to be the captain of my own ship. In a lot of ways, Congress will be fun . . . ."[17] All members of Congress are captains of their own ships, and they can use that position to enrich their lives: "It beats heavy lifting," said one member in a moment of candor.[18]

However, Congress is now so widely mistrusted that the gap between their staff's worship and the solicitation of interest groups on the one hand, and public loathing on the other, is even more vexing to Congress than in the past. Mass confidence in elite institutions is in general disarray (see the Case Study "Mass Confidence in America's Elites," p. 14); but the public's loss of confidence is greatest with regard to Congress. The percentage of people expressing "a great deal" or "quite a lot" of confidence in Congress has declined from 42 percent in 1973 to 18 percent in 1991. Congress now ranks dead last among all institutions in public confidence.

The distrust of Congress on the part of citizens is less troubling than it may seem. Nobody enjoys being hated, but members of Congress have learned that, whereas people hate *Congress,* they do not hate their *own* member of Congress (see Table 12-8). The general perception is something like this: "Members of Congress are crooks, but Representative ——— is fighting for us." Incumbents rarely lose, and although term limitation referenda generally succeed, when such a referendum was written to include sitting members of Congress (in Washington State), it failed. Viewed in the abstract, the position "member of Congress" is regarded as promoting the same level of integrity as would employment as a street peddler, TV evangelist, car dealer, or prostitute.[19] Ralph Nader, not given to moderation, phrased mass perception accurately: "Members of Congress have no shame. Scandal, fraud and corruption are rampant in Congress and they gave themselves a raise."

TABLE 12-8   Public perceptions of Congress and of their own members of Congress

	Members of Congress	Your congressman
Deserve(s) reelection (%)	20	44
Rate honesty and ethics as excellent/good (%)	46	69
Are (is) financially corrupt (%)	41	15

SOURCE: *American Enterprise* (January/February, 1991): 85. Reprinted by permission.

CONGRESS AND THE PRESIDENT: AN UNSTABLE BALANCE OF POWER

The President Initiates, Congress Deliberates

How do the roles of Congress and the other governmental elites differ? Policy proposals begin outside Congress; the role of Congress is to respond to proposals from the president, bureaucratic elites, and interested nongovernmental elites. Congress does not merely ratify or rubber-stamp decisions; it plays an independent role in the policy-making process. But the role is essentially deliberative; Congress accepts, modifies, or rejects the policies initiated by others. For example, the national budget, perhaps the most important policy document, is written by executive elites and modified by the president before Congress receives it. Congress may modify it further but does not formulate the budget. Of course, Congress is a critical conduit through which appropriations and revenue measures must pass. But sophisticated lawmakers are aware that they function as arbiters rather than initiators of public policy.

The relationship between Congress and other policy-making elites is not necessarily stable. Whether Congress merely ratifies the decisions of others or asserts its voice independently depends on many factors, such as the aggressiveness and skill of the president and the strength of congressional leadership. Congress may be tenacious in *rejecting* policy, but it rarely *initiates* policy.

The Presidential Tilt

The pendulum of power swings between Congress and the executive branch, but the general trend since the administration of Franklin D. Roosevelt has been toward the president. A key event in the power struggle between Congress and the president was the depression of the 1930s. In economic crisis, Congress, with its cumbersome decision-making process, simply gave up. Roosevelt's first act was to close all banks by executive order, explaining that he intended to use executive power to wage war against depression just as he would in the event of foreign invasion. In the early days of the New Deal, senators and House members voted for bills they had never even read.

Although Congress has recovered a more active role in domestic affairs, its role in foreign affairs remains minimal. President Truman decided to commit troops to Korea with only the most cursory communication to Congress; the decision to escalate in Vietnam—the famous Tonkin Gulf Resolution of 1965—received technical approval from Congress after only two days of debate and with only two dissenting votes.

Defeat and humiliation in Vietnam led directly to the War Powers Act in 1973, by which Congress attempted to capture control over the war-making power—control that had historically rested with the president (see Chapter 10). Although the act was passed by Congress over President Nixon's veto, all subsequent presidents, Democratic and Republican, have ignored the act. Congress may rant and rave, but the president remains commander in chief of the armed forces in reality as well as in title. Only a prolonged, unsuccessful, and unpopular war could inspire renewed efforts by Congress to assert itself in national security affairs.

However, the Congress retains the ability to embarrass a presidential administration and force it to change course through congressional investigative powers. Such an investigation, with the cooperation of the television media, can compel a president to abandon an unpopular action. In the Iran-Contra hearings in 1987, Congress exposed President Reagan's arms-for-hostages dealings with Iran and forced the administration to curtail all negotiations with terrorist regimes. Moreover, despite a spirited defense by Lieutenant Colonel Oliver North of the president's aid to the Contra forces in Nicaragua, Congress succeeded in undermining popular support for Contra aid and thus forced the president to abandon the Contras. Congress can use its access to the media to influence public opinion and pressure the president.

Theoretically, Congress can control the president through its power over the budget. The Constitution (Article I, Section 9) states that "No money shall be drawn from the Treasury, but in consequence of appropriations made by law." Congress can withhold funds or place elaborate restrictions on the use of funds in order to work its will over the president. But even through the use of budgetary power, its most effective tool, Congress has not been able to dominate the presidency. More often than not, the president's budget recommendations are accepted by the Congress with only minor changes (see Chapter 11). Occasionally, Congress and the president will engage in highly publicized budgetary battles over both domestic and foreign policy issues. For example, in recent fights the Congress succeeded in reducing the number of MX missiles from 100 to 50, in limiting production of the B-2 Stealth bomber to fifteen aircraft, and in lowering defense spending 5 to 10 percent below presidential recommendations. Nonetheless, Congress appears reluctant to use its budgetary powers to directly challenge the president in foreign policy. Congress has never voted to cut off funds for U.S. forces fighting in the field.

The ultimate congressional power over the president is impeachment. Despite the Constitution's admonition that impeachment can only be voted for "Treason, Bribery, and other high Crimes and Misdemeanors" (Article II, Section 4), all impeachment movements in U.S. history have developed on political grounds (see Chapter 10). Yet the political circumstances that would force the removal or resignation of a president are extreme—indeed, Nixon's forced resignation is unique in American history.

The Loss of the President's Coattails

The power of the president in legislative affairs depends upon initiation and persuasion, not his "coattails" (the tendency of the winning presidential candidate to pull fellow party members along to victory in their own races). Only Eisenhower in 1952, Johnson in 1964, and Reagan in 1980 succeeded in pulling significant numbers of their party's congressional candidates into office with them (see Table 12-9). Other presidential campaigns had very little effect on congressional elections. With the declining importance of political parties, the correlation between presidential and congressional voting is decreasing. The common pattern is for the congressional incumbent to be returned while the district is simultaneously voting for the presidential candidate of the other party. Democrat Bill Clinton was unable to increase his party's strength in the Congress in 1992. Republicans actually gained strength in the House.

—— THE ELABORATE PROCEDURES OF LEGISLATIVE ELITES

The rules and procedures of Congress are elaborate but important to the functioning of legislative elites. Legislative procedures and rules make the legislative process fair and orderly. Without established customs, rules, and procedures, 535 men and women could not arrive at collective decisions about the thousands of items submitted to them during a congressional session. Yet the same rules also delay or obstruct proposed changes in the status quo; they strengthen Congress's conservative role in policy making. In congressional procedures, legislation faces many opportunities for defeat and many obstacles to passage.

TABLE 12-9   Presidential elections and congressional outcomes

| | | | | President's party in Congress* | | | |
| | President's popular vote margin | | | House | | Senate | |
Date	Party	President	Percent	Seats lost/gained	Control	Seats lost/gained	Control
1956	Rep.	Eisenhower	57.4	−3	Dem.	0	Dem.
1960	Dem.	Kennedy	49.7	−21	Dem.	0	Dem.
1964	Dem.	Johnson	61.1	37	Dem.	1	Dem.
1968	Rep.	Nixon	43.4	5	Dem	7	Dem.
1972	Rep.	Nixon	60.7	12	Dem.	−2	Dem.
1976	Dem.	Carter	50.1	1	Dem	1	Dem.
1980	Rep.	Reagan	50.7	35	Dem.	12	Rep.
1984	Rep.	Reagan	58.8	17	Dem.	−1	Rep.
1988	Rep.	Bush	54.0	−4	Dem.	−1	Dem.
1992	Dem.	Clinton	43.0	−9	Dem.	0	Dem.

*Data for the beginning of first session of each Congress, excluding vacancies at beginning of session.

The elaborate procedures of Congress ensure that very few of the bills introduced are ever passed. In a given Congress (Congresses are named for their two-year sessions, starting from the first Congress of 1787–1789; the 102nd Congress convened in 1992), more than 10,000 bills will be introduced, but fewer than 800 bills will be enacted. In other words, fewer than 10 percent of the measures introduced will ever find their way through the law-making process.

The Law-Making Process

Congress follows a fairly standard pattern in the formal process of making laws; Figure 12-1 describes briefly some of the most important procedural steps. Bills generally originate in the president's office, in executive departments, or in the offices of interested elites, but a member of the House or Senate must formally introduce them into Congress. Except for bills raising revenue, which must begin in the House of Representatives according to the Constitution, bills can be introduced in either house. Upon introduction, a bill moves to one of the standing committees of the House or Senate, which may (1) recommend it for adoption with only minor

1. *Introduction.* Most bills can be introduced in either house. (In this example, the bill is first introduced in the Senate.) It is given a number and referred to the proper committee.

2. *Hearings.* The committee may hold public hearings on the bill.

3. *Committee action.* The full committee meets in executive (closed) session. It may kill the bill, approve it with or without amendments, or draft a new bill.

4. *Calendar.* If the committee recommends the bill for passage, it is listed on the calendar.

5. *Debate, amendment, vote.* The bill goes to the floor for debate. Amendments may be added. The bill is voted on.

6. *Introduction to the second house.* If the bill passes, it goes to the House of Representatives, where it is referred to the proper committee.

7. *Hearings.* Hearings may be held again.

8. *Committee action.* The committee rejects the bill, prepares a new one, or accepts the bill with or without amendments.

9. *Rules Committee consideration.* If the committee recommends the bill, it is listed on the calendar and sent to the Rules Committee. The Rules Committee can block a bill or clear it for debate before the entire House.

10. *Debate, amendment, vote.* The bill goes before the entire body and is debated and voted upon.

11. *Conference, committee.* If the bill as passed by the second house contains major changes, either house may request a conference committee. The conference—five persons from each house, representing both parties—meets and tries to reconcile its differences.

12. *Vote on conference report.* When committee members reach an agreement, they report back to their respective houses. Their report is either accepted or rejected.

13. *Submission to the president.* If the report is accepted by both houses, the bill is signed by the speaker of the House and the president of the Senate and is sent to the president of the United States.

14. *Presidential action.* The president may sign or veto the bill within ten days. If the president does not sign and Congress is still in session, the bill automatically becomes law. If Congress adjourns before the ten days have elapsed, it does not become law. (This is called the "pocket veto.") If the president returns the bill with a veto message, it may still become a law if passed by a two-thirds majority in each house.

FIGURE 12-1   How a bill becomes a law

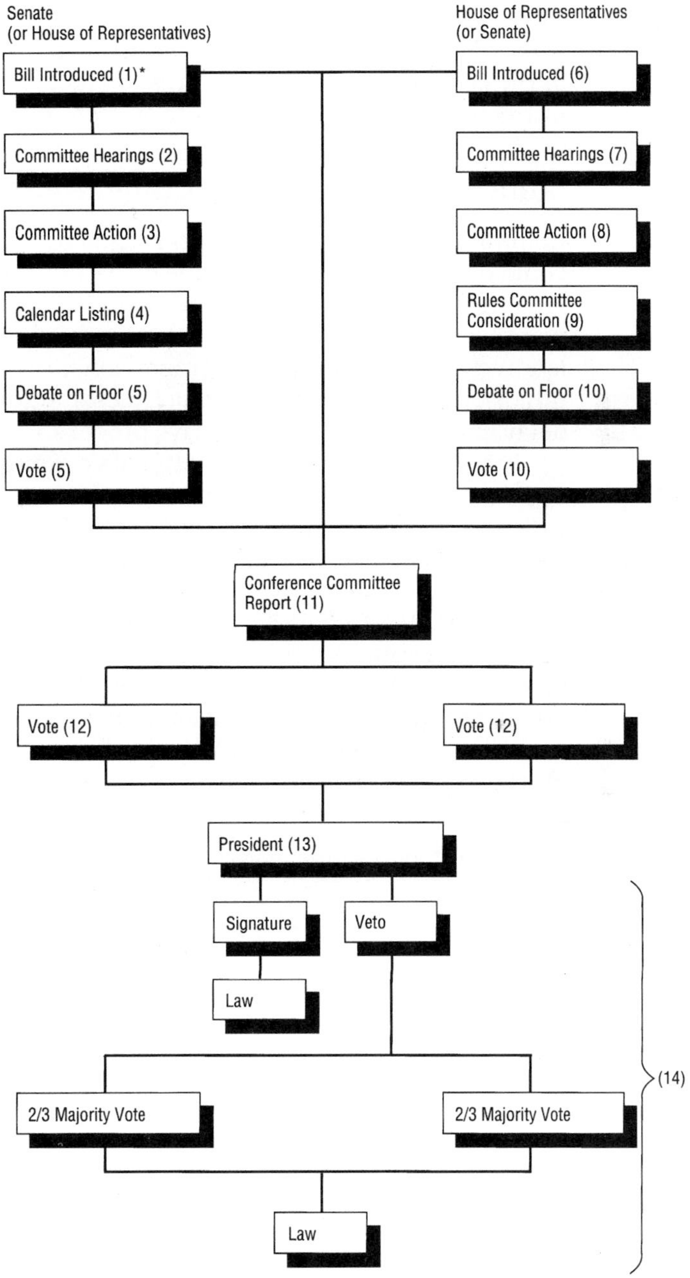

Senate
(or House of Representatives)

House of Representatives
(or Senate)

| Bill Introduced (1)* | | Bill Introduced (6) |

| Committee Hearings (2) | | Committee Hearings (7) |

| Committee Action (3) | | Committee Action (8) |

| Calendar Listing (4) | | Rules Committee Consideration (9) |

| Debate on Floor (5) | | Debate on Floor (10) |

| Vote (5) | | Vote (10) |

Conference Committee Report (11)

| Vote (12) | | Vote (12) |

President (13)

Signature   Veto

Law

| 2/3 Majority Vote | | 2/3 Majority Vote | }(14)

Law

*Numbers in parentheses are keyed to descriptions on page 310.

changes, (2) virtually rewrite it into a new policy proposal, (3) ignore it and prevent its passage through inaction, or (4) kill it by majority vote. The full House or Senate *may* overrule a committee decision but does so rarely. Most members of Congress are reluctant to upset the prerogatives of the committees and the desires of recognized leaders. Therefore committees have virtual power of life or death over every legislative measure.

Standing Congressional Committees and Subcommittees

Committee work is essential to the legislative process; Congress as a body could never hope to review all the measures put before it. As early as 1885 Woodrow Wilson described the American political process as "government by the standing committees of Congress"[20] But while reducing legislative work to manageable proportions, the committee system allows a minority of the legislators, sometimes a single committee chairman, to delay and obstruct the legislative process.

In the Senate, the most prestigious committees are Foreign Relations, Appropriations, and Finance; in the House, the most powerful are the Rules Committee, Appropriations, and Ways and Means. (Table 12-10 lists the twenty-seven standing committees of the House and the twenty of the Senate.) To expedite business, most standing committees create subcommittees to handle particular matters falling within their jurisdiction. This practice further concentrates power over particular subject matter in the hands of a very few congressional members. Considerable power lies in the hands of subcommittee members, especially the chairpersons; interested elites cultivate the favor of powerful subcommittee and committee chairpersons.

TABLE 12-10   The standing committees of Congress

Committee
SENATE
Democratic:
Policy
Steering
Republican:
Policy
Committee
Agriculture, Nutrition, and Forestry
Appropriations
Armed Services
Banking, Housing, and Urban Affairs
Budget
Commerce, Science, and Transportation
Energy and Natural Resources
Environment and Public Works
Finance

(continued)

TABLE 12-10   The standing committees of Congress   *(continued)*

Committee

Foreign Relations
Governmental Affairs
Judiciary
Labor and Human Resources
Rules and Administration
Select Ethics
Select Indian Affairs
Select Intelligence
Small Business
Special Aging
Veterans' Affairs

HOUSE OF REPRESENTATIVES

Democratic Party
Committees:
   Speaker
   Majority Leader
   Steering and Policy
   Personnel
   Congressional Campaigns

Republican Party
Committees:
   Minority Leader
   Minority Whip
   Committee on Committees
   Policy
   Research
   Congressional
Agriculture
Appropriations
Armed Services
Banking, Finance, and Urban Afairs
Budget
District of Columbia
Education and Labor
Energy and Commerce
Foreign Affairs
Government Operations
House Administration
Interior and Insular Affairs
Judiciary
Merchant Marine and Fisheries
Post Office and Civil Service
Public Works and Transportation
Rules
Science, Space, and Technology
Select Aging
Select Children, Youth, and Families
Select Hunger
Select Intelligence
Select Narcotics Abuse and Control
Small Business
Standards of Official Conduct
Veterans' Affairs
Ways and Means

Public hearings.   In examining legislation, a committee or subcommittee generally holds public hearings on bills deemed worthy by the chairperson or, in some cases, by the majority of the committee. Influenced by the legal profession, represented by a majority of legislators, the committees tend to look upon public hearings as trials in which contestants present their sides of the argument to the committee members, who act as judges. Presumably, during this trial the skillful judges will sift facts on which to base their decisions. In practice, however, committees use public hearings primarily to influence public opinion or executive action or, occasionally, to discover the position of major elite groups on the measure under consideration. Major decisions take place in secret executive session.

Committee membership.   The membership of the standing committees on agriculture, labor, interior and insular affairs, and the judiciary generally reflects the interest of particular elite groups in the nation. Legislators representing farm interests sit on the agricultural committees; representatives of land, water, and natural resource interests serve on interior and insular affairs committees; members of Congress with labor ties and urban industrial constituencies gravitate toward the labor committee; and lawyers dominate the judicial committees of both houses.

Given the power of congressional committees, the assignment of members to committees is one of the most significant activities of Congress. In the House of Representatives, the Republicans assign their members to committees through the Committee on Committees, which consists of one representative from each state that sends a Republican to Congress. Each representative votes with the strength of his or her state delegation. But the real business of this committee is conducted by a subcommittee appointed by the Republican party leader. The subcommittee fills committee vacancies with freshman members and those who request transfer from other committees. The Committee on Committees considers the career backgrounds of members, their seniority, and their reputation for soundness, which usually means support for the party leadership. Often the chairperson of a standing committee tells the Committee on Committees his or her preferences for committee members. Democrats in the House make committee assignments through the Steering and Policy Committee. This committee is composed of the party leadership; the caucus elects twelve members to represent geographic regions, and the speaker appoints the additional nine members.

In the Senate, the Committee on Committees fills Republican committee positions, and a steering committee appointed by the Democratic leader selects Democratic committee members. Usually only senators with seniority are eligible for positions on the major Senate committees, such as the foreign relations, armed services, and appropriations committees.

The power of the chair.   Committee and subcommittee chairpersons are very powerful. They usually determine the bills the committee will consider, select issues for public hearings, and establish the agenda of the committee. Governmental and nongovernmental interests officially must consult the chairperson on all questions relating to his or her committee; this procedure confers status on the chairperson with the executive branch and with interested nongovernmental elites. Only occasionally does a majority within the committee-subcommittee "baronage" overrule a chairperson's decision on a committee matter.

The Growing Power of Subcommittees

The chairperson's power has eroded somewhat, due to successful House Democratic caucus challenges of the seniority system and the growth in the power of subcommittees. Indeed, the move to strengthen the autonomy of subcommittees may be the most significant recent structural change in Congress, eclipsing the more publicized seniority issue. Many subcommittee chairpersons have overtaken full committee chairpersons in influence and autonomy. Those leading the drive to establish subcommittee autonomy were the younger Democrats, who gained more influence than they would have had without reforms. Today no House member can be chairperson of more than one subcommittee, so younger members can can gain access to these key positions. A subcommittee "bill of rights" gives the Democrats on each committee (rather than the committee chairperson) the authority to select subcommittee chairpersons, guarantees all members sufficient assignments, and provides adequate subcommittee budgets. Finally, all committees with more than twenty members must have at least four subcommittees. Thus subcommittee chairpersons assume influence almost equal to that of their committee counterparts.

The Seniority System

Guarantee of conservatism.   The practice of appointing chairpersons according to seniority guarantees conservatism in the legislative process. The member of the majority party with the longest continuous service on the committee becomes chairperson; the member of the minority party with the longest continuous service on the committee is the ranking minority member. Therefore chairpersons are not chosen by their own committees, by their own party, or by the House and Senate as a whole. They are chosen by the voters of noncompetitive congressional districts whose representatives are likely to stay in office the longest. The major decisions in Congress rest with those members from areas where party competition and voter participation are low; in the past, these areas have been southern and rural or big-city machine constituencies. In both houses, the seniority system works against the competitive urban and suburban districts. In 1971 both parties modified seniority to allow review and ratification by the party caucus. However, though the Democratic caucus will occasionally displace a committee chairperson, most senior members remain at the top of the Capitol hierarchy.

In recent years, the strengthening of the national Democratic party and the growth of the Republican party in the South have weakened southerners' overall position in Congress; once, about half the Democrats in Congress were southerners, whereas now only one-fourth are. As young southerners replace old and as Democrats from other regions build seniority, Democratic southern domination of committee chairs has diminished.

Growth of influence.   As their influence within Congress grows, high-seniority legislators tend to identify with Congress as an institution, to the detriment of possible influence of their constituencies. Two factors are at work here. Legislators get to know each other well (they see one another more regularly than they see constituents), and older legislators probably have learned from experience that a perceived unpopular vote will not bring the vigorous constituency response they once thought was inevitable. Thus the experienced legislator tends to develop a more realistic view of the electorate, expressed well in one senator's remarks: "After several terms, I don't give a damn any more. I'm pretty safe now and I don't have to worry about reaction in the district."[21] Legislators also specialize in certain kinds of legislation, thus developing expertise that draws their colleagues to them as credible sources of information. As one put it, "That's the beauty of the seniority system—there are informed, experienced people on each Committee you can consult."[22] When members of Congress need advice, they usually turn to someone of higher seniority.

Initial committee assignments do not depend strictly on seniority. But once assigned, the legislator can remain, building up seniority. First, though, each party must make its selection. Since control of Congress depends upon reelection, the party leadership tries to place party members where they can do the most good for their constituents. As we noted, this practice assures representation of the major interests in a constituency on the appropriate committee.

The seniority system has both critics and defenders. Its most active critics are (1) those with low seniority, (2) those without formal leadership positions, (3) those from urban districts, and (4) those with a more liberal voting record.[23] Supporters of seniority (with characteristics in direct contrast to those reformers listed above) talk more of the rewards of experience, the development of expertise, and the nurturing of stability in relationships. Seniority helps maintain the "subsystem": without it, the established network of relationships among interest groups, executive agencies, and committees would flounder.

Lobbyists, Committees, and Committee Reform

Lobbyists try to focus their activities as narrowly as possible, thus making possible the development of strong ties with relevant congressional committees and administrative agencies. Such a "subsystem" can develop to the benefit of all participants. Legislators benefit from campaign contributions by interest groups; lobbyists benefit from personal working relationships with committees and their staffs; administrative agencies benefit from interest groups' and congressional committees' support of their budget requests.

Decentralization: Strengthening the Iron Triangles

Each subcommittee develops its own "policy network." Policy networks are the "iron triangles" of interest groups, executive bureaucracies, and subcommittee members and staff. As they develop mutually in the acquisition of expertise, they tend to develop a common bond whose strength frequently exceeds that of loyalty to the party. There is a subcommittee chair for virtually every majority party legislator; there is also at least one subcommittee, and frequently no more than three, to attract the attention of a particular interest group. "Subgovernments" is the name given to the interaction of the participants in the various iron triangles.

Each subgovernment is theoretically answerable to the full committee and to the membership of the Senate and House. In practice, the centrifugal force tugging them away from the center is too powerful to resist. A fragmented, disjointed decision-making process is not easily controlled by party leaders and the president.[24] Such a process is easily accommodated to the needs of the political action committees, whose generosity toward members of "their" subcommittees exceeds the contribution of political parties by a ratio of 5 to 1.

Decentralization does not mean that each of the subcommittees is an independent source of policy initiation. Rather, they are instruments for the protection of the iron triangles.

Legislative Procedure

The House Rules Committee.   After a standing committee reports a bill in the House (step 8 in Figure 12-1), the Rules Committee must issue a special rule or order before the bill can go before the House membership for consideration. Consequently each bill must go through two committees. (The only exceptions are bills reported by the House Appropriations and the Ways and Means committees; the House may consider their bills at any time as privileged motions.) The Rules Committee can kill a bill by shelving it indefinitely. It can insist that the bill be amended as the price of permitting it on the floor and can even substitute a new bill for the one framed by another committee. The Rules Committee determines how much debate will be permitted on any bill and the number and kind of amendments that may be offered from the floor. The only formal limits on Rules Committee authority are the *discharge petition* (which is rarely used and hardly ever successful) and *calendar Wednesday,* a cumbersome procedure that permits standing committees to call up bills the Rules Committee has blocked. The Rules Committee, clearly the most powerful committee in Congress, is dominated by senior members elected from noncompetitive districts.

Senate filibusters.   In the Senate, control of floor debate rests with the majority leader. But the majority leader does not have the power to limit debate; a senator who has the floor may talk without limit and may choose to whom he or she yields the floor. If enough senators wish to talk a bill to death, they may do so in what is known as a filibuster. This device permits a small minority to tie up the business of the Senate and prevent it from voting on a bill. Under Rule 22 of the Senate, debate can be limited only by a process called *cloture.* Sixteen members' signatures on a petition will bring cloture to a vote; a three-fifths vote of the full Senate ends the filibuster. But cloture has been successful only six times in the history of the Senate. It has been a major weapon in civil rights legislation; the Civil Rights Act of 1964 passed the Senate through a cloture petition. But generally senators agree to protect their right of unlimited debate. Like the Rules Committee in the House, the filibuster is a means by which a small elite can defend itself against majority preferences.

The final vote.   Of the ten thousand bills introduced into Congress every year, only about a thousand, or one in ten, become law. After approval of a bill by the standing committee in the Senate or by the standing committee and the Rules Committee in the House, the bill moves to the floor for a vote. Usually the most crucial votes come on the amendments to the bill that are offered to the floor (however, the Rules Committee may prevent amendments in the House). Once the membership defeats major amendments or incorporates them into the bill, the bill usually picks up broad support, and the final vote is usually heavily in favor of it.

Conference committees.   One of the most conservative features of American government is its *bicameralism;* after following a complicated path in one house, a bill must repeat the process in the other. A bill must pass both branches of Congress in identical form before it goes to the president for signature. However, the Senate often amends a House bill, and the House usually amends Senate bills. And every time a house amends a bill, it must resubmit the bill to the originating house for concurrence with the changes. If either house declines to accept changes in the bill, an ad hoc joint committee, called a *conference committee,* must iron out specific differences. Disagreements between the houses are so frequent that from one-third to one-half of all public bills, including virtually all important ones, must go to conference committees after passage by both houses.

Conference committee members, appointed by the presiding officers of each house, usually come from the two standing committees that handled the bills in each house. Since the final bill produced by the conference committee is generally accepted by both houses, these committees have tremendous power in determining the final form of legislation. Both houses must accept or reject conference committee reports as a whole; they cannot further amend them. Most conference committee meetings are closed and unrecorded; the committees hold no hearings and listen to no outside testimony. The bill that emerges from their deliberations may not represent the view of either house and may even contain items never considered by either one. Some people have dubbed conference committees a "third house" of Congress, whose members are not elected by the people, keep no record of their work, and usually operate behind closed doors—with no debate about their products allowed.

ELITES WITHIN ELITES: THE CONGRESSIONAL ESTABLISHMENT

A power hierarchy exists among federal government elites that is supported by protocol, by the distribution of formal constitutional powers, by the powers associated with party office, by the committee and seniority systems of Congress, and by the "informal folkways" of Washington. According to the protocol of Washington society, the president holds the highest social rank, followed by former presidents and their widows, the vice-president, the speaker of the House, members of the Supreme Court, foreign ambassadors and ministers, cabinet members, U.S. senators, governors of states, former vice-presidents, and, finally, House members.

Senatorial Power

The Constitution grants greater formal powers to senators than to House members. There being only one hundred senators, individual senators are more visible than House members in the social and political life of Washington, as well as in their home states. Senators also have special authority in foreign affairs not accorded to House members, for the Senate must advise and consent by a two-thirds vote to all treaties entered into by the United States. The threat of Senate repudiation of a treaty makes it desirable for the president to solicit Senate views on foreign affairs; generally the secretary of state works closely with the Senate Foreign Relations Committee on such matters. Influential senators undertake personal missions abroad and serve on delegations to international bodies. Another constitutional power afforded senators is to advise and consent on executive appointments, including Supreme Court justices, cabinet members, federal judges, ambassadors, and other high executive officials. Although the Senate generally approves the presidential nominations, the added potential for power contributes to the difference between the influence of senators and of House members. Finally, senators serve six-year terms and represent broader and more heterogeneous constituencies. Thus they have a longer guaranteed tenure in Washington, more prestige, and greater freedom from minor shifts in opinion among nongovernmental elites in their home states.

Senators can enhance their power through their political roles; they often wield great power in state parties and can usually control federal patronage dispensed in their state. The power of the Senate to confirm nominations has given rise to the important political custom of "senatorial courtesy": senators of the same party as the president have virtual veto power over major appointments—federal judges, postmasters, customs collectors, and so on—in their states. Presidential nominations that go to the Senate are referred to the senator or senators from the state involved. If the senator declares the nominee personally obnoxious to him or her, the Senate usually respects this declaration and rejects the appointment. Thus before the president submits a nomination to the Senate, he usually makes sure that the nominee will be acceptable to his party's senator or senators from the state involved.

Party Leadership

Party leadership roles in the House and the Senate are major sources of power in Washington. (See Table 12-11 for a list of Senate and House leaders for the 102nd Congress.)

The speaker of the House.   The speaker of the House of Representatives, elected by the majority party of the House, exercises more power over public policy than any other member of either house. Before 1910 the speaker appointed all standing committees and their chairs, possessed unlimited discretion to recognize members on the floor, and served as chair of the Rules Committee. But in 1910, progressives severely

TABLE 12-11   Party leadership in the 103rd Congress

Senate	Senator	State
President Pro Tempore	Byrd	W. Virginia
Majority Leader	Mitchell	Maine
Majority Whip	Ford	Kentucky
Minority Leader	Dole	Kansas
Minority Whip	Simpson	Wyoming

House	Representative	State
Speaker	Foley	Washington
Majority Leader	Gephardt	Missouri
Majority Whip	Bonior	Michigan
Minority Leader	Michel	Illinois
Minority Whip	Gingrich	Georgia

curtailed the speaker's authority. Today the speaker shares power over committee appointments with the Committee on Committees; committee chairs are selected by seniority, not by the speaker; and the speaker no longer serves as chair of the Rules Committee. However, the speaker retains considerable authority: referring bills to committees, appointing all conference committees, ruling on all matters of House procedure, recognizing those who wish to speak, and generally directing the business of the floor. More important, the speaker is the principal figure in House policy formulation, leadership, and responsibility; although sharing these tasks with standing committee chairs, the speaker is generally "first among equals" in relation to them.

Floor leaders and whips.   Next to the speaker, the most influential party leaders in the House are the majority and minority floor leaders and the party whips. These party leaders are chosen by their respective party caucuses at the beginning of each congressional session. The party caucus, composed of all the party's members in the House, usually does little more than elect these officers; it makes no major policy decisions. The floor leaders and whips have little formal authority; their role is to influence legislation through persuasion. Party floor leaders must combine parliamentary skill with persuasion, maintain good personal relationships with party members, and cultivate close ties with the president and administration. They cannot deny party renomination to members who are disloyal to the party, but because they can control committee assignments and many small favors in Washington, they can prevent a maverick from becoming an effective legislator.

The whips, or assistant floor leaders, keep members informed about legislative business, see that members are present for important floor votes, and communicate party strategy and position on particular issues. They also serve as the eyes and ears of the leadership, counting noses before important votes. Party whips should know how many votes a particular measure has, and they should be able to get the votes to the floor when the roll is called.

The vice president.   The vice president of the United States, who serves as president of the Senate, has less control over Senate affairs than the speaker has over House affairs. The vice president votes only in case of a tie and must recognize senators in the order in which they rise. The majority party in the Senate also elects from its membership a president pro tempore, who presides in the absence of the vice president.

The majority and minority leaders.   The key power figures in the Senate are the majority and minority leaders, who are chosen by their respective parties. The majority leader usually has great personal influence within the Senate and is a power figure in national affairs. The majority leader, when of the same party as the president, is in charge of getting the president's legislative program through the Senate. Although having somewhat less formal authority than the speaker of the House, the majority leader has the right to be the first senator to be heard on the floor and, with the minority floor leader, determines the Senate's agenda. He or she can greatly influence committee assignments for party members. But on the whole, the majority leader's influence rests on powers of persuasion. Many people consider Lyndon Johnson the most persuasive, and therefore most effective, majority leader in recent times (1953–1960).

Committee chairs.   The committee system and the seniority rule also create powerful congressional figures: the chairs of the most powerful standing committees, particularly the Senate foreign relations, appropriations, and finance committees and the House rules, appropriations, and ways and means committees. The chairs of the standing committees in both houses have become powerful through members' respect for the authority of their committees. The standing committee system is self-sustaining because an attack on the authority of one committee or committee chairperson is much like a threat to all; members know that if they allow one committee or committee chairperson to be bypassed on a particular measure, they open the door to other similar infringements of power. Hence committee chairs and ranking committee members tend to stand by one another and support one another's authority over legislation assigned to their respective committees. Committee chairs and ranking committee members also earn respect because of their seniority and experience in the legislative process. They are often experts in parliamentary process as well as in the substantive area covered by their committees. Finally, and perhaps most important, committee chairs and ranking committee members acquire power through their relationships with executive and private elites who influence policy within the committee's jurisdiction.

CONFLICT AND CONSENSUS: VOTING IN CONGRESS

Party Voting

Studies of roll-call voting in Congress show that the role of party influence in legislative conflict varies according to the issue.[25]

Cohesion.   Party votes, those roll-call votes in which a majority of voting Democrats oppose a majority of voting Republicans, occur for less than half the roll-call votes in Congress. Roll-call voting follows party lines more often than it follows sectional, urban-rural, or any other divisions that have been studied. How much cohesion exists within the parties? Table 12-12 shows the number of party votes in Congress in recent years, and the average support Democratic and Republican members of Congress have given to their parties. Democrats and Republicans appear equally

TABLE 12-12   Party voting in Congress, 1971–1989

Year	Party votes as percentage of total votes	Percentage of party support: Democrats*	Percentage of party support: Republicans*
1972			
Senate	36	57	64
House	27	58	61
1973			
Senate	40	69	64
House	42	68	68
1974			
Senate	44	63	59
House	29	62	63
1975			
Senate	48	68	64
House	48	69	72
1976			
Senate	37	62	61
House	36	66	67
1977			
Senate	42	63	66
House	42	68	71
1978			
Senate	45	66	59
House	33	63	69
1979			
Senate	47	68	69
House	47	69	73
1980			
Senate	46	64	65
House	38	69	71
1981			
Senate	48	71	81
House	37	69	74
1982			
Senate	43	72	76
House	36	72	69
1983			
Senate	44	76	74
House	56	71	74
1984			
Senate	40	68	78
House	47	74	71
1985			
Senate	50	75	76
House	61	80	75
1986			
Senate	52	72	76
House	57	79	70
1987			
Senate	41	81	75
House	64	81	74
1988			
Senate	45	78	68
House	47	80	74
1989			
Senate	35	78	78
House	55	81	72
1990			
Senate	54	82	77
House	49	86	78

*Average percentage of times a member voted with majority of party of affiliation in disagreement with the other party's majority.
SOURCE: *Congressional Quarterly.*

cohesive, with members of both parties voting with their party majority more than two-thirds of the time. Party voting appears more frequent in the House than in the Senate.

Even when party-line votes do take place, they are the result more of members' personal predispositions than of explicitly formulated party policy. Political scientist Theodore Lowi makes the distinction between party "regularity," which is still strong, and party organization and discipline, of which there is none.[26]

Bipartisanship.   Bipartisan votes, those roll calls in which divisions do not fall along party lines, occur most frequently on foreign policy and defense issues. Bipartisan agreement is also likely on appropriation bills and roll calls on low-conflict issues. Recently bipartisan voting has settled issues of federal aid to education, highway beautification, water pollution, voting rights, presidential continuity, and increases in federal employees' pay and veterans' benefits.

Conflict.   Conflict between parties occurs most frequently over social welfare programs, housing and urban development, economic opportunity, medical care, antipoverty programs, health and welfare, and the regulation of business and labor. Party conflict is particularly apparent in the budget, the most important policy document in the national government. The budget is the president's product and carries the label of the president's party. On some issues, such as civil rights and appropriations, voting generally follows party lines during roll calls on preliminary motions, amendments, and the other preliminary matters but swings to a bipartisan vote on the final legislation. In such situations the parties disagree on certain aspects of the bill but compromise on its final passage.

Influence of the issue.   Many issues that cause conflict between the Democratic and Republican parties relate to the conflict between government and private initiative. In general, Democrats have favored federal subsidies for agriculture; federal action to assist labor and low-income groups through social security, relief, housing, and wage-hour regulation; and generally a larger role for the federal government in launching new projects to remedy domestic problems. Republicans, on the other hand, have favored free competition in agriculture, less governmental involvement in labor and welfare matters, and reliance on private action.

Presidential support.   The president generally receives greater support from his own party than from the opposition party in Congress. Democratic President Lyndon Johnson was the most successful president in recent history in legislative affairs (see Figure 12-2). His congressional influence declined slightly in his last year, but he regularly secured more

FIGURE 12-2   Presidential success on votes in Congress

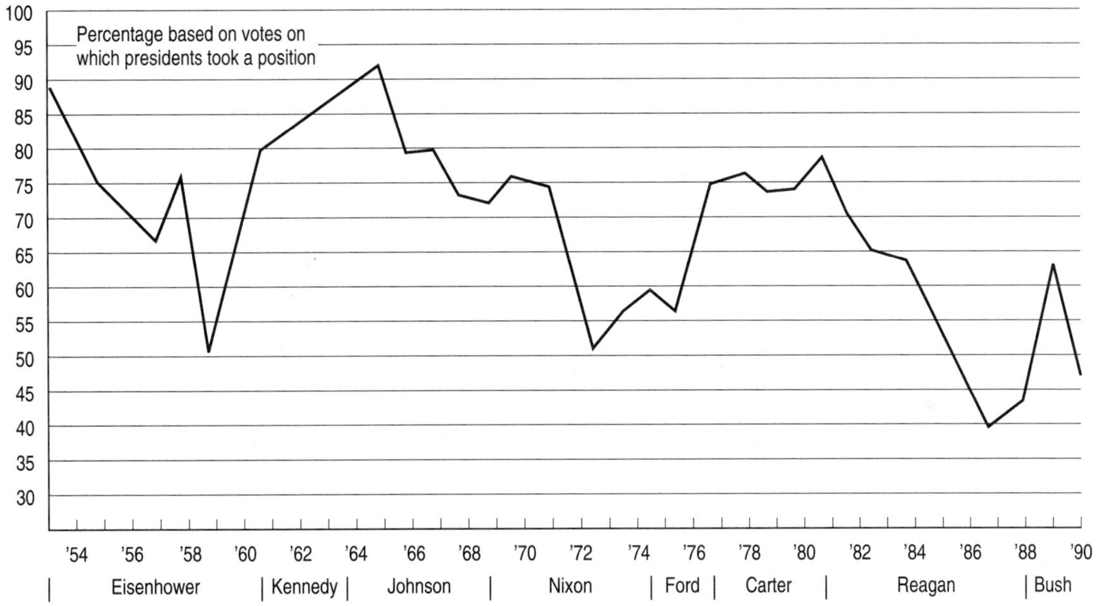

SOURCE: *Congressional Quarterly Weekly Report.*

than 80 percent of Democratic votes in the House and 70 percent of Democratic votes in the Senate. He even won a majority of Senate Republican votes (see Table 12-13). Republican President Richard Nixon won greater support from Republicans in the House and Senate than from Democrats, but he regularly won more than half of the Democrats to his side. Democrat Jimmy Carter had Democratic support in the House and Senate but much less Republican support. Republican Ronald Reagan had the most partisan pattern of congressional support and opposition: Republicans in the House and Senate gave him strong support throughout his presidency. Democrats in the House and Senate gave him more than 40 percent support in his first two years, but later their opposition increased. In his second term he faced a very hostile Democratic party in the House and only a slightly less hostile Democratic party in the Senate.

The Conservative Coalition

On a significant number of issues, a "conservative coalition" emerges. This coalition is said to appear when a majority of southern Democrats join a majority of Republicans to oppose a majority of northern Democrats. Historically this coalition has reflected conservative Republican and southern Democratic opposition to the liberal agenda and has

TABLE 12-13   Congressional voting in support of the president's position

President/Year	House (%)		Senate (%)	
	All Democrats	Republicans	All Democrats	Republicans
DEM. JOHNSON				
1964	84	42	73	52
1965	83	46	75	55
1966	81	45	71	53
1967	80	51	73	63
1968	77	59	64	57
REP. NIXON				
1969	56	65	55	74
1970	64	79	56	74
1971	53	79	48	76
1972	56	74	52	77
1973	39	67	42	70
1974	52	71	44	65
REP. FORD				
1974	48	59	45	67
1975	40	67	53	76
1976	36	70	47	73
DEM. CARTER				
1977	69	46	77	58
1978	67	40	74	47
1979	70	37	75	51
1980	71	44	71	50
REP. REAGAN				
1981	46	72	52	84
1982	43	70	46	77
1983	30	74	45	77
1984	37	64	45	81
1985	31	69	36	80
1986	26	69	39	90
1987	26	65	38	67
REP. BUSH				
1988	28	61	51	73
1989	36	69	55	82
1990	29	63	38	70

Note: Percentages are calculated as number of congressional votes supporting the president divided by the total number of votes on which the president took a position.

SOURCE: Norman Ornstein, Thomas E. Mann, and Michael J. Malbin, *Vital Statistics on Congress* (Washington, D.C.: Congressional Quarterly Press, 1990).

generally resisted new federal interventions in the economy and supported tax cuts and a strong national defense. Although the conservative coalition has appeared less frequently in recent years, it has been very successful in votes in which it did appear (see Figure 12-3). The low appearance rate and high success rate are not contradictory. Rather this pattern suggests it is difficult for southern Democratic conservatives to abandon their party; when they do, the conservative coalition prevails.

FIGURE 12-3   The conservative coalition

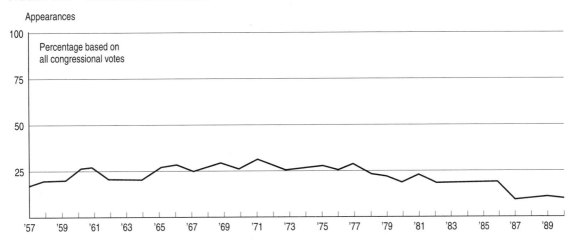

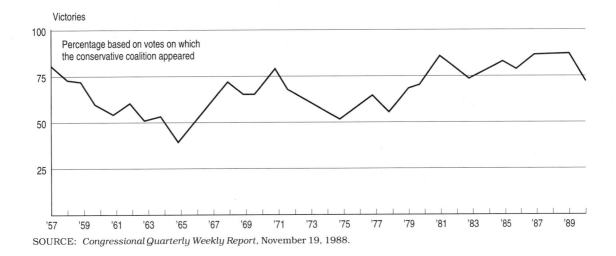

SOURCE: *Congressional Quarterly Weekly Report*, November 19, 1988.

SUMMARY

This analysis of Congress proposes several ways to refine elite theory and apply it to a specific institution.

1. Congress tends to represent locally organized elites, who inject a strong parochial influence into national decision making. Members of Congress are responsible to national interests that have a strong base of support in their home constituencies.

2. A member's relevant political constituency is not the general population of the home district but its elite. Less than half the general population of a district knows its legislator's name; fewer still have any idea

of how their representative voted on any major issue. Only a tiny fraction ever express their views to their legislators.

3. With the possible exception of civil rights questions, most members of Congress are free from the influence of popular preferences in their legislative voting. However, a member's voting record generally reflects the socioeconomic makeup of the home district. A member of Congress is the product of the social system in his or her constituency and shares its dominant goals and values.

4. Congress seldom initiates changes in public policy. Instead it responds to policy proposals initiated by the president and by executive, military, and interested nongovernmental elites. The congressional role in national decision making is usually deliberative: Congress responds to policies initiated by others.

5. Congressional committees are important to communication between governmental and nongovernmental elites. "Iron triangles" (or "policy clusters") consisting of alliances of leaders from executive agencies, congressional committees, and private business and industry tend to develop in Washington. Committee chairs are key members of the policy clusters because of their control over legislation in Congress.

6. The elaborate rules and procedures of Congress delay and obstruct proposed changes in the status quo, thus strengthening Congress's conservative role in policy making. Transforming a bill into law is a difficult process; congressional procedures offer many opportunities for defeat and many obstacles to passage.

7. An elite system within Congress places effective control over legislation in the hands of relatively few members. Most of these congressional "establishment" members are conservatives from both parties who have acquired great seniority and therefore control key committee chairs.

8. Most bills that do not die before the floor vote pass unanimously. The greatest portion of the national budget passes without debate. The conflict that exists in Congress tends to follow party lines more often than any other factional division. Conflict centers on the details of domestic and foreign policy but seldom on its major directions.

—— NOTES

1. See Donald R. Matthews, *The Social Background of Political Decision-Makers* (New York: Doubleday, 1954).
2. Heinz Eulau and John D. Sprague, *Lawyers in Politics* (Indianapolis, Ind.: Bobbs-Merrill, 1964).
3. See Joseph A. Schlesinger, *Ambition and Politics* (Chicago: Rand McNally, 1966).
4. U.S. Senate, Committee on Government Operations, Subcommittee on Intergovernmental Relations, *Confidence and Concern: Citizens*

View American Government (Washington, D.C.: U.S. Government Printing Office, 1973), pp. 72–77.

5. Warren Miller and Donald Stokes, "Constituency Influence in Congress," *American Political Science Review* 57 (March 1963).

6. Ibid., p. 55.

7. Raymond A. Bauer, Ithiel De Sola Pool, and Lewis A. Dexter, *American Business and Public Policy* (New York: Atherton Press, 1963), ch. 35.

8. Charles O. Jones, "The Role of the Campaign in Congressional Politics," in M. Kent Jennings and Harmon Zeigler, eds., *The Electoral Process* (Englewood Cliffs, N.J.: Prentice-Hall, 1966), p. 21.

9. Fred Westheimer, quoted in *Congressional Quarterly* (December 1, 1973): 3130.

10. Paul S. Herrnson, "Reemergent National Party Organizations," in L. Sandy Maisel, ed., *The Parties Respond* (Boulder: Westview Press, 1990), p. 54.

11. Paul S. Herrnson, *Party Campaigning in the 1980s* (Cambridge, Mass.: Harvard University Press, 1988), p. 86.

12. Kazee and Thornberry, in a study of thirty-six congressional candidates, found that 61 percent were self-starters. However, half of the candidates had attended party-sponsored seminars. Thus the party organization might have pricked their interest. In no case, however, did a self-starter experience organizational assessment. See Thomas A. Kazee and Mary C. Thornberry, "Where's the Party? Congressional Candidate Recruitment and American Party Organizations," *Western Political Quarterly*, 43 (1990): 48–56.

13. Herrnson, op. cit., pp. 84ff.

14. Michael McCauley and Andrew Cohen, *They Love to Fly and It Shows* (Washington, D.C.: Public Citizen's Congress Watch, 1991), p. 1.

15. *New York Times*, October 9, 1991, p. 1.

16. Alan Ehrenhalt, *The United States of Ambition* (New York: Random House, 1991), p. 253.

17. *New York Times*, January 6, 1991.

18. Quoted in Donald Lambro, *Washington: City of Scandals* (Boston: Little, Brown, 1984), p. 44.

19. James Patterson and Peter Kim, *The Day America Told the Truth* (New York: Prentice-Hall, 1991), p. 143.

20. Woodrow Wilson, *Congressional Government* (1885; reprint, New York: Meridian Books, 1956), p. 178.

21. John W. Kingdon, *Congressmen's Voting Decisions* (New York: Harper & Row, 1973), p. 62.

22. Ibid., p. 88.

23. Roger H. Davidson, David M. Kovenock, and Michael K. O'Leary, *Congress in Crisis: Politics and Congressional Reform* (Belmont, Calif.: Wadsworth, 1966), pp. 67–91.

24. Steven S. Smith, "New Patterns of Decision Making in Congress," in

John E. Chubb and Paul E. Patterson, eds., *New Directions in American Politics* (Washington, D.C.: Brookings Institution, 1985), p. 203.

25. See Malcolm E. Jewell and Samuel C. Patterson, *The Legislative Process in the United States* (New York: Random House, 1966): William J. Keefe and Morris Ogul, *The American Legislative Process* (Englewood Cliffs, N.J.: Prentice-Hall, 1964).

26. Theodore Lowi, *The Personal President* (Cornell University Press, 1985), p. 127.

SELECTED READINGS

Cain, Bruce, Ferejohn, John, and Fiorina, Morris. *The Personal Vote.* Cambridge, Mass.: Harvard University Press, 1987. The authors compare the British and U.S. systems.

Fenno, Richard. *Home-Style.* Boston: Little, Brown, 1978. This book is Fenno's impressionistic account of how members of Congress communicate with constituents.

Goldenberg, Edie N., and Traugott, Michael W. *Campaigning for Congress.* Washington, D.C.: Congressional Quarterly Press, 1984. This is a careful description, based upon a variety of sources, of what it takes to get to Capitol Hill.

Jacobson, Gary C. *The Politics of Congressional Elections.* Boston: Little, Brown, 1987. This book is more theoretical, more empirically compelling, and more difficult than the Goldenberg and Traugott book.

Mann, Thomas E., and Ornstein, Norman. *The New Congress.* Washington, D.C.: American Enterprise Institute, 1981. The authors frankly assess the myths and realities of the "reformed" Congress.

Stern, Philip M. *The Best Congress Money Can Buy.* New York: Pantheon, 1988. Stern discusses the grim truth about James Madison's hope for democracy.

13

Courts: Elites in Black Robes

★ *Scarcely any political question arises in the United States that is not resolved, sooner or later, into a judicial question.*

Alexis de Tocqueville, Democracy in America, *1835*

The Supreme Court of the United States and the federal court system comprise the most elitist institution in American government. Nine justices—none of whom is elected and all of whom serve for life—possess ultimate authority over all the other institutions of American government. These people have the power to declare void the acts of popularly elected presidents, Congresses, governors, state legislators, school boards, and city councils. No appeal is possible from their determination of the "supreme law of the land," short of undertaking the difficult task of amending the Constitution itself.

The Supreme Court, rather than the president or Congress, has made many of the nation's most important domestic policy decisions. The Supreme Court took the lead in eliminating segregation from public life, ensuring separation of church and state, defining rights of criminal defendants and the powers of law enforcement officials, ensuring voters equality in representation, defining the limits of free speech and free press, and declaring abortion a fundamental right of women. Sooner or later in American politics, most important policy questions come before these justices—who are not elected to office and cannot be removed for anything other than "treason, bribery, or high crimes and misdemeanors." As de Tocqueville observed as early as 1835, "Scarcely any political question arises in the United States that is not resolved, sooner or later, into a judicial question."[1]

JUDICIAL REVIEW AS AN ELITIST PRINCIPLE

Recognition of the undemocratic character of judicial power in the United States is not new. The Founding Fathers viewed the federal courts as the final bulwark against mass threats to principle and property:

> Limited government . . . can be preserved in practice no other way than through the medium of courts of justice, whose duty it is to declare all acts contrary to the manifest tenor of the Constitution void.[2]

In *Marbury* v. *Madison* (1803), the historic decision establishing the power of judicial review, John Marshall argued persuasively that (1) the Constitution is "the supreme law of the land" and U.S. and state laws must be congruent with it; (2) Article III of the Constitution gives to the Supreme Court the judicial power, which includes the power to interpret the meaning of laws and, in case of conflict between laws, to decide which law shall prevail; and (3) the courts are sworn to uphold the Constitution, so they must declare void a law that conflicts with the Constitution.

Since 1803 the federal courts have struck down more than one hundred laws of Congress and uncounted state laws that they believed conflicted with the Constitution. Judicial review and the power to interpret the meaning and decide the application of law are judges' major sources of power.

The Founding Fathers' decision to grant federal courts the power of judicial review over state court decisions and state laws is easy to understand. Article VI states that the Constitution and national laws and treaties are the supreme law of the land, "anything in the Constitution or laws of any state to the contrary notwithstanding." Federal court power over state decisions is probably essential in maintaining national unity, for fifty different state interpretations of the meaning of the Constitution or of the laws and treaties of Congress would create unimaginable confusion. Thus the power of federal judicial review over state constitutions, laws, and court decisions is seldom questioned.

However, at the national level, why should an appointed court's interpretation of the Constitution prevail over the views of an elected Congress and an elected president? Members of Congress and presidents swear to uphold the Constitution, and we can assume that they do not pass laws they believe to be unconstitutional. Since both houses of Congress and the president must approve laws before they become effective, why should federal courts be allowed to set aside these decisions?

The answer is that the Founding Fathers distrusted popular majorities and the elected officials subject to their influence. They believed government should be prevented from attacking principle and property, whether to do so was the will of the majority or not. So the Founding Fathers deliberately insulated the courts from popular majorities; by appointing judges for life terms, they sought to ensure their independence. The Founding Fathers originally intended that a president—who is not directly elected—would appoint judges and that a Senate—also not directly elected—would confirm the president's appointments. Only in this way, the writers of the Constitution believed, would judges be sufficiently protected from the masses to permit them to judge courageously and responsibly.

THE MAKING OF A SUPREME COURT JUSTICE

All federal judges are appointed by the president and confirmed by a majority vote of the Senate. The recruitment process is highly political. The attorney general's office assists the president in screening candidates for all federal judgeships. For positions on the Supreme Court, presidents usually nominate judges who share their political philosophy. One might assume that this practice is a democratizing influence on the Court, assuming that the people elect a president because they agree with his political philosophy. But Supreme Court justices frequently become independent once they reach the Court. Former Chief Justice Earl Warren, as Republican governor of California, had swung critical delegate votes to Eisenhower in the 1952 Republican convention. When the grateful president rewarded him with the chief justiceship, little in Warren's background suggested that he would lead the most liberal era in the

Court's history. Later Eisenhower complained that the Warren appointment was "the biggest damn mistake I ever made."[3]

Social Background

Justices' social backgrounds generally reflect close ties with the upper social strata. More than 90 percent of the Supreme Court justices have been from socially prominent, politically influential, upper-class families.[4] More than two-thirds of the justices ever serving on the Court attended Ivy League or other prestigious law schools (see Tables 13-1 and 13-2). The typical Supreme Court justice is "white, generally Protestant . . . ; fifty to fifty-five years of age at the time of his appointment; Anglo-Saxon ethnic stock . . . ; high social status; reared in an urban environment; member of a civic-minded, politically active, economically comfortable family; legal training; some type of public office; generally well educated."[5]

Of course, social background does not necessarily determine judicial philosophy. However, "if . . . the Supreme Court is the keeper of the American conscience, it is essentially the conscience of the American upper-middle class, sharpened by the imperative of individual social responsibility and political activism, and conditioned by the conservative impact of legal training and professional legal attitudes and associations."[6]

TABLE 13-1   Backgrounds of current U.S. Supreme Court justices

Justice	Year of birth	Law school	Position at time of appointment	Appointed by (year)
William H. Rehnquist	1924	Stanford	Associate Supreme Court Justice (Assistant U.S. Attorney General prior to initial Supreme Court appointment)	Chief Justice— Reagan (1986) Associate Justice—Nixon (1972)
Byron R. White	1918	Yale	U.S. Deputy Attorney General	Kennedy (1962)
Harry A. Blackmun	1908	Harvard	Judge, U.S. Court of Appeals	Nixon (1970)
John Paul Stevens	1916	Chicago	Judge, U.S. Court of Appeals	Ford (1975)
Sandra Day O'Connor	1930	Stanford	Judge, U.S. Court of Appeals	Reagan (1981)
Antonin Scalia	1936	Harvard	Judge, U.S. Court of Appeals	Reagan (1986)
Anthony M. Kennedy	1936	Harvard	Judge, New Hampshire	Bush (1990)
David Souter	1939	Harvard	Judge, New Hampshire	Bush (1990)
Clarence Thomas	1948	Yale	Judge, U.S. Court of Appeals	Bush (1991)

TABLE 13-2 Backgrounds of all U.S. Supreme Court justices

All U.S. Supreme Court justices, 1789 to present	Number of justices (105 = total)
OCCUPATIONAL POSITION BEFORE APPOINTMENT	
Private legal practice	25
State judgeship	21
Federal judgeship	24
U.S. Attorney General	7
Deputy or Assistant U.S. Attorney General	2
U.S. Solicitor General	2
U.S. Senator	6
U.S. Representative	2
State governor	3
Federal executive posts	10
Other	3
RELIGIOUS BACKGROUND	
Protestant	83
Roman Catholic	9
Jewish	5
Unitarian	7
No religious affiliation	1
AGE ON APPOINTMENT	
Under 40	4
41–50	30
51–60	56
61–70	15
POLITICAL PARTY AFFILIATION	
Federalist (to 1835)	13
Democrat-Republican (to 1828)	7
Whig (to 1861)	2
Democrat	42
Republican	41
SEX	
Male	104
Female	1
RACE	
White	103
Black	2

SOURCES: Congressional Quarterly, *Congressional Quarterly's Guide to the U.S. Supreme Court* (Washington, D.C.: Congressional Quarterly, 1979) and *Congressional Quarterly's Guide to Government, Spring 1983* (Washington, D.C., 1982). Updated.

Politicizing the Confirmation Process

Historically, the Senate Judiciary Committee, which holds hearings and recommends confirmation to the full Senate, consented to nominations by the president with a minimum of dissent; the Senate has rejected only 29 of the 132 Supreme Court nominations ever sent to it. The prevailing ethos had been that a popularly elected president deserves the opportunity to appoint judges; that the opposition party in Congress will have its own opportunity to appoint judges when it captures the presidency; and that partisan bickering over judicial appointments is undesirable. But the U.S. Senate's rejection of President Reagan's nomination of Judge Robert H. Bork in 1987 ended the traditional confirmation ethos. Securing the Senate's confirmation of a Supreme Court nominee is now a televised political campaign.

No appointee to the Supreme Court was ever more qualified in terms of scholarship, judicial experience, and knowledge of the law than Judge Bork. As a law school professor at the University of Chicago and Yale University, Bork had written many scholarly volumes and articles on constitutional law; he had served as solicitor general of the United States and as a judge of the prestigious U.S. Court of Appeals for the District of Columbia, where he had written hundreds of opinions. But Bork had a reputation for "conservative activism"—a desire to better reflect the "original intent" of the Constitution's framers by rolling back some of the Supreme Court's broad interpretations of privacy rights, free speech, and equal protection of the law. Perhaps most controversial were his views of *Roe* v. *Wade;* he had labeled the Court's striking down of state laws prohibiting abortion as a "wholly unjustifiable judicial usurpation of state legislative authority." Historically, judicial nominees were not asked to tell the Senate how they will vote on pending cases; to do so before considering evidence and hearing arguments would presumably impair the nominees' ability to render impartial judgments. But, unlike previous nominees, Bork was subjected by the Senate Judiciary Committee to extensive case-by-case questioning in nationally televised confirmation hearings. The bearded, scholarly Bork presented a poor TV image, and liberal interest groups conducted an unprecedented political campaign to derail his nomination. His public and private life was extensively investigated, and he was obliged to defend himself from a wide variety of charges. When overnight opinion polls showed the prickly professor to be losing ground, the Democratic-controlled Judiciary Committee and U.S. Senate rejected his nomination. A second unfortunate nominee, Douglas H. Ginsberg, withdrew in the face of press reports that he had smoked marijuana. Finally, when President Reagan submitted the name of a relatively unknown and ideologically bland nominee, Anthony M. Kennedy, who solemnly testified that he had "no overarching theory of [constitutional] interpretation" and "no fixed or immutable ideas," the Senate relented and confirmed the appointment. However, once on the Court, Kennedy aligned himself with the conservative bloc.

Confirmation as Sleazy Spectacle

If the Bork battle signaled the Senate's descent into bitter partisanship in the confirmation process, the battle over the nomination of Clarence Thomas to the U.S. Supreme Court marked the Senate's collapse into disgraceful spectacle. Indeed the Senate Judiciary Committee's sleazy performance in the Thomas confirmation established a new low in public ethics.

Clarence Thomas, as President Bush's nominee to replace Thurgood Marshall, the first black Supreme Court Justice, reflected the generally conservative judicial philosophy of earlier Reagan appointees. Thomas had risen from a very impoverished early childhood in rural Pinpoint, Georgia, through Catholic elementary and secondary schools, to graduate with honors from Holy Cross College and go on to Yale Law School. He began his legal career as an assistant Missouri attorney general under John C. Danforth, before Danforth became a popular Republican U.S. Senator. Thomas came to Washington with Danforth, and was appointed assistant secretary for civil rights in the U.S. Department of Education and later chairman of the U.S. Equal Employment Opportunity Commission. In the latter role, Thomas spoke out against racial quotas in favor of individual rights and against welfare programs that create permanent dependency.[7] Although Thomas had not directly spoken out on the Court's *Roe* v. *Wade* abortion decision, it was widely believed that Thomas would join the Court's abortion opponents and modify or reverse the decision. Thus, Thomas's Republicanism and conservatism challenged the

"SAME HERE—I'VE NEVER BEEN SEXUALLY HARASSED EITHER"

Copyright 1991 by HERBLOCK in the Washington Post

prevailing stereotype of black political leaders. Nonetheless, early on it was generally expected that Thomas would be confirmed; the Senate had recently confirmed his 1990 appointment to the U.S. Court of Appeals. Indeed, the prospect of his confirmation sent hordes of liberal interest-group investigators scouring the nation for dirt on the nominee.

In an early routine FBI investigation, an assistant of Thomas at both the Department of Education and later at the Equal Employment Opportunity Commission, Anita F. Hill, alleged that he had sexually harassed her. Hill had also graduated from Yale Law School; she was a professor at the University of Oklahoma Law School. Initially, the Senate Judiciary Committee, chaired by Democrat Joseph Biden, overlooked the complaint: it was more than ten years old; Hill had followed Thomas from Education to the EEOC after the alleged harassment occurred; and Hill initially refused to testify publicly. But a Senate staff member leaked the story; feminist interest groups attacked the all-male committee for ignoring the sexual harassment complaint; and a frightened committee scurried to set up televised hearings that turned into three days of sleazy public drama.

The televised hearings captured the nation's attention, touching directly on emotional issues of race and sex. Feminist groups tried to cast the issue as one of sexual harassment and male insensitivity to women's concerns. Anita Hill was an effective witness; millions of television viewers were titillated by her allegations of Thomas's pornographic talk about large breasts and penises, group sex and bestiality. But Clarence Thomas fought back hard, denying all charges and accusing the committee of conducting a "high-tech lynching." Thomas tried to cast the issue as an unscrupulous attack on an "uppity" black man who dares to have conservative opinions. Democrats found themselves in a excruciating dilemma, caught in a bitter conflict between two of their core constituencies—feminists and blacks.

The mass public may not know or care much about judicial philosophy. But race and sex elicit strong opinions. And in the end the Senate decided that the safest route was to follow the opinion polls. Clarence Thomas won the television battle: at the end of the hearings 61 percent of men and 57 percent of women supported his confirmation.[8] More important, a large majority of blacks supported Judge Thomas, despite opposition to him from black leaders. Thomas was confirmed by a Senate vote of 52 to 48, the closest such vote in more than one hundred years. But there were no real winners in the embarrassing affair, and the Senate itself and its confirmation process were the biggest losers of all.

THE SPECIAL STYLE OF JUDICIAL POLICY MAKING

An *appearance of objectivity* cloaks the power of the courts to shape American life. Because judges serve for life and are legally accountable to no one, they maintain the fiction that they are not engaged in policy making but merely "applying" the law to specific cases.[9] To admit otherwise would spotlight the conflict between judicial power and the democratic myth of policy making by elected representatives.

Many of the nation's best judicial thinkers question this mechanistic theory of judicial objectivity, however. For example, former Justice Felix Frankfurter once observed:

> The meaning of "due process" and the content of the terms like "liberty" are not revealed by the Constitution. It is the Justices who make the meaning. They read into the neutral language of the Constitution their own economic and social views. . . . Let us face the fact that five Justices of the Supreme Court are the molders of policy rather than the impersonal vehicles of revealed truth.[10]

The courts also maintain the *fiction of nonpartisanship*. Judges must not appear as if political considerations affected their decisions. Once appointed to the federal bench, they are expected to have fewer direct ties to political organizations than members of Congress do. Federal judges must not appear to base their decisions on partisan considerations or party platforms or to bargain in the fashion of legislators. Perhaps as a result of their nonpartisan appearance, courts enjoy a measure of prestige that other government institutions lack. Judicial decisions are more acceptable to the public if the public believes that the courts dispense unbiased justice.

Courts function under *special rules of access*. The Constitution gives jurisdiction to federal courts only in "cases and controversies." Courts do not issue policy pronouncements, rules, or orders on their own initiative. For example, courts do not declare a law of Congress or an action of the president unconstitutional immediately upon its passage or occurrence. Nor do the federal courts render advisory opinions prior to congressional or executive action. The courts assume a passive role and wait until a case comes before them that directly challenges a law of Congress or an action of the president.

To gain access to the federal courts, one must present a *case* in which the federal courts have *jurisdiction*. A case must involve two disputing parties, one of which must have incurred some real damages as a result of the action or inaction of the other. The federal courts will accept jurisdiction based on (1) the nature of the parties—a case in which the U.S. government is a party; or a controversy between two or more states, or between a state and a citizen of another state, or between citizens of different states; or a case involving a foreign nation or citizen; or (2) the nature of the controversy—a case that arises under the Constitution (a "constitutional question") or under the laws and treaties of the United States. Congress has further limited the jurisdiction of federal courts in cases between citizens of different states by requiring that the dispute involve more than fifty thousand dollars. State courts hear all other cases.

Judicial policy making follows a *legalistic style*. Plaintiffs and defendants present facts and arguments to the courts in formal testimony, cross-examination, legal briefs, and oral arguments, all of them highly ritualized. Legal skills are generally necessary to make presentations that meet the technical specifications of the courts. Decorum in court proceedings is highly valued because it conveys a sense of dignity; legislative or executive offices rarely function with as much decorum.

These distinctive features of judicial policy making—the appearance of objectivity, the fiction of nonpartisanship, special rules of access, limited jurisdiction, and legalistic style—all contribute to the power of the courts. They help to legitimize court decisions, to win essential support for them, and thus to contribute to the influence of judges in the political system.

THE STRUCTURE OF THE FEDERAL COURT SYSTEM

The federal court system consists of three levels of courts with general jurisdiction, together with various special courts (the Court of Claims, Customs Court, Patent Court, and Court of Military Appeals). The Constitution establishes only the Supreme Court, although Congress determines the number of Supreme Court justices—traditionally nine. Article III authorizes Congress to establish "such inferior courts" as it deems appropriate. Congress has designed a hierarchical court system consisting of nearly one hundred U.S. federal district courts and eleven U.S. circuit courts of appeals, in addition to the Supreme Court of the United States (see Figure 13-1).

Federal District Courts

Federal district courts are the trial courts of the federal system. Each state has at least one district court, and larger states have more. (New York, for example, has four.) More than five hundred judges, appointed for life by the president and confirmed by the Senate, preside over these courts. The president also appoints a U.S. marshal for each district court to carry out orders of the court and maintain order in the courtroom. Federal district courts hear criminal cases prosecuted by the U.S. Department of Justice, as well as civil cases. As trial courts, the district courts use both grand juries (juries composed to hear evidence and, if warranted, to indict a defendant by bringing formal criminal charges against that person) and petit, or regular, juries (juries that determine guilt or innocence). District courts may hear as many as three hundred thousand cases in a year.

Circuit Courts of Appeals

Circuit courts of appeals are *appellate courts*. They do not hold trials or accept new evidence but consider only the record of the trial courts and oral or written arguments (briefs) submitted by attorneys. Federal law

FIGURE 13-1   The U.S. court system

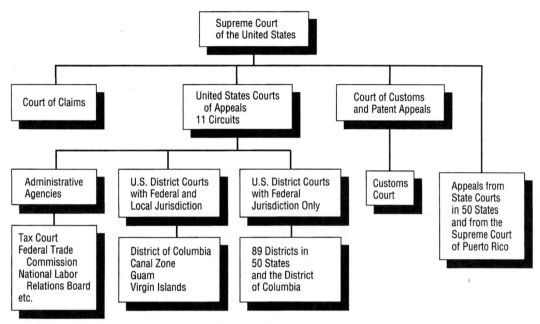

SOURCE: U.S. House of Representatives, Committee on the Judiciary, *The United States Courts: Their Jurisdiction and Work* (Washington, D.C.: U.S. Government Printing Office, 1969), p. 3.

provides that every individual has a right to appeal his or her case, so courts of appeals have little discretion in hearing appeals. Appellate judges themselves estimate that more than 80 percent of all appeals are "frivolous"—that is, they are without any real basis at all. These courts require nearly one hundred circuit court judges, appointed for life by the president and confirmed by the Senate. Normally three judges serve together on a panel to hear appeals. More than 90 percent of the cases decided by circuit courts of appeals end at this level. Further appeal to the Supreme Court is not automatic; the Supreme Court itself decides what appeals it will consider. Hence, for most cases, the decision of the circuit court of appeals is final.

U.S. Supreme Court

The Supreme Court of the United States is the final interpreter of all matters involving the U.S. Constitution and federal laws and treaties, whether the case began in a federal district court or in a state court. In some cases the Supreme Court has original jurisdiction (authority to serve as a trial court), but it seldom uses this jurisdiction. Appellate jurisdiction is the Supreme Court's major function. Appeals may come from a state court of last resort (usually a state supreme court) or from lower federal courts. The Supreme Court determines for itself whether to accept an appeal and consider a case. It may do so if a "substantial federal question" is at issue in the case, or if "special and important reasons" apply. Any four justices can grant an appeal. However, the Supreme Court denies most cases submitted to it on *writs of appeal* and *writs of certiorari;* the Court need not give any reason for denying appeal or certiorari.*

In the early days of the republic, the size of the U.S. Supreme Court fluctuated, but since 1869 its membership has remained at nine: the chief justice and eight associate justices. The Supreme Court is in session each year from October through June, hearing oral arguments, accepting written briefs, conferring, and rendering opinions.

THE JURISDICTION OF THE FEDERAL COURT SYSTEM

In the U.S. federal system, each state maintains its own court system. The federal courts are not necessarily superior to state courts; both state and federal courts operate independently. But since the U.S. Supreme Court has appellate jurisdiction over state supreme courts, as well as over lower federal courts, the Supreme Court oversees the nation's entire judicial system.

State courts have general jurisdiction in all criminal and civil cases. According to Article III of the U.S. Constitution, federal court jurisdiction extends to

1. Cases arising under the Constitution, federal laws, or treaties.
2. Cases involving ambassadors, public ministers or counsels, or maritime and admiralty laws.
3. Cases in which the U.S. government is a party.
4. Cases between two or more states.
5. Cases between a state and a citizen of another state.
6. Cases between citizens of different states.
7. Cases between a state or a citizen and a foreign government or citizen of another nation.

Obviously, it is not difficult "to make a federal case out of it," regardless of what "it" might be. The Constitution contains many vaguely worded guarantees—"due process of law," "equal protection of the laws," protection from "cruel and unusual punishment" and "unreasonable searches and seizures," and so forth—which allow nearly every party to any case to claim that a federal question is involved and that a federal court is the proper forum.

*The Court technically must hear writs of appeal, but only a few matters qualify; among them are cases involving clear constitutional issues (for example, a finding that a federal law is unconstitutional, that a state law is in conflict with federal law, or that a state law is in violation of the U.S. Constitution). Writs of certiorari are granted when four members agree that an issue involves a "substantial federal question" (as decided by the Supreme Court).

The great bulk of the national caseload begins and ends in state court systems. The federal courts do not intervene once a state court has started hearing a case, except in very rare circumstances. And Congress has stipulated that legal disputes between citizens of different states must involve fifty thousand dollars or more in order to be heard in federal court. Moreover, parties to cases in state courts must "exhaust their remedies"—that is, appeal their case all the way through the state courts—before the federal courts will hear their appeal. Appeals from state supreme courts go directly to the U.S. Supreme Court and not to federal district or circuit courts. Usually appeals from state supreme courts to the U.S. Supreme Court are made on the grounds that the case raises "a federal question"— that is, a question on the application of the U.S. Constitution or federal law. The U.S. Supreme Court reviews only a very small fraction of appeals from state court decisions.

Of the ten million civil and criminal cases begun in the nation's courts each year, only about 2 percent are in federal courts. The U.S. Supreme Court will receive about five thousand appeals each year but will hear only about two hundred of them. So state and local courts hear the great bulk of legal cases. The U.S. Constitution "reserves" general police powers to the states so that crimes and civil disputes are generally matters of state and local concern. Murder, robbery, assault, and rape are normally state offenses rather than federal crimes. Federal crimes generally center on offenses (1) against the U.S. government or its property; (2) against U.S. government officials or employees while they are on duty; (3) that involve crossing state lines (such as nationally organized crime, unlawful escape across state lines, taking kidnapping victims across state lines); (4) that interfere with interstate commerce; and (5) that occur on federal territories or on the seas.

Majority opinions of the Supreme Court are usually written by a single justice who summarizes majority sentiment. Concurring opinions are written by justices who vote with the majority but who feel that the majority opinion does not fully explain their reasons. A dissenting opinion is written by a justice who is in the minority; such opinions have no impact on the outcome of the case. Written opinions are printed, distributed to the press, and published in *U.S. Reports* and other legal reporting services.

ACTIVISM VERSUS SELF-RESTRAINT IN JUDICIAL POLICY MAKING

Great legal scholars have argued the merits of activism versus self-restraint in judicial decision making for more than a century.[11] The view for *self-restraint* argues that since justices are not popularly elected, the Supreme Court should move cautiously and avoid direct confrontation with legislative and executive authority. Justice Felix Frankfurter wrote, "The only check upon our own exercise of power is our own sense of self-restraint. For the removal of unwise laws from the statute books, appeal lies not to the courts but to the ballot and to the processes of democratic government."[12]

But Frankfurter was arguing a minority position on the Court. The dominant philosophy of the Supreme Court under Chief Justice Earl Warren (1953–1969) was one of *judicial activism*. The Warren Court believed it should shape constitutional meaning to fit its estimate of the needs of contemporary society. By viewing the Constitution as a deliberately broad and flexible document, one can avoid dozens of new constitutional amendments to accommodate a changing society. The strength of the U.S. Constitution lies in its flexibility—its relevance to contemporary society.[13]

The Supreme Court's posture of judicial activism, combined with its lifetime appointments, greatly strengthens its elitist character. If a nonelective institution such as the federal judiciary assumes a strong, activist role in national policy making, the result is an even more elitist political system. This is true whether the Supreme Court is active on behalf of liberal or conservative policies. Liberals who praise the virtues of judicial activism, who urge the Court to stand against the misguided policies of an elected president and Congress, must recognize the elitist nature of their argument.

Rules of Restraint

Even an activist Supreme Court adheres to some general rules of judicial self-restraint. These rules include the following:

1. The Court will not pass upon the constitutionality of legislation in a nonadversary proceeding but only in an actual case. Thus the Court will not advise the president or Congress on constitutional questions.

2. The Court will not anticipate a question on constitutional law; it does not decide hypothetical cases.

3. The Court will not formulate a rule of constitutional law broader than required by the precise facts to which it must be applied.

4. The Court will not pass upon a constitutional question if some other ground exists upon which it may dispose of the case.

5. The Court will not pass upon the validity of a law if the complainant fails to show that he or she has been injured by the law, or if the complainant has availed himself or herself of the benefits of the law.

6. When doubt exists about the constitutionality of a law, the Court will try to interpret the meaning of a law so as to give it a constitutional meaning and avoid the necessity of declaring it unconstitutional.

7. A complainant must have exhausted all remedies available in lower federal courts or state courts if the Supreme Court is to accept review.

8. The constitutional issue must be crucial to the case, and it must be substantial rather than trivial, before the Court will invalidate a law.

9. Occasionally the Court defers to Congress and the president and classifies an issue as a political question, and refuses to decide it. The Court has stayed out of foreign and military policy areas.

10. If the Court holds a law unconstitutional, it will confine its decision only to the particular section of the law that is unconstitutional; the rest of the statute stays intact.[14]

Stare Decisis

Courts are also limited by the principle of *stare decisis,* which means that the issue has already been decided in earlier cases. Reliance upon precedent is a fundamental notion in law. Indeed the underlying common law of England and the United States is composed simply of past decisions. Students of the law learn through the case-study method: the study of previous decisions. Reliance on precedent gives stability to the law; if every decision were new law, then no one would know what the law is from day to day. Yet the Supreme Court frequently discards precedent. Former Justice William O. Douglas, who seldom felt restrained by legal precedent, justified disregard of precedent as follows:

> The decisions of yesterday or of the last century are only the starting points. . . . A judge looking at a constitutional decision may have compulsions to revere the past history and accept what was once written. But he remembers above all else that it is the Constitution which he swore to support and defend, not the gloss which his predecessors may have put on it. So he comes to formulate his own laws, rejecting some earlier ones as false and embracing others. He cannot do otherwise unless he lets men long dead and unaware of the problems of the age in which he lives do his thinking for him.[15]

Original Intent

Should the Constitution be interpreted in terms of the intentions of the Founding Fathers or according to the morality of society today? Most jurists agree that the Constitution is a living document, that it must be interpreted by each generation in the light of current conditions, and that to do otherwise would soon render the document obsolete. But in interpreting the document, whose values should prevail—the values of the judges or the values of the Founding Fathers? The doctrine of original intent takes the values of the Founding Fathers as expressed in the text of the Constitution and applies these values to current conditions. Defenders of original intent argue that the words in the document must be given their historical meaning and that meaning must restrain courts as well as the legislative and executive branches of government. The Supreme Court should not set aside laws made by elected representatives unless they conflict with the original intent of the Founding Fathers. A Supreme Court that sets aside laws because they do not accord with today's moral standards is simply substituting its own morality for that of elected bodies. Such decisions lack democratic legitimacy, because there is no reason why judges' moral views should prevail over those of elected representatives. But this original intent doctrine has had little influence on the activist Supreme Court.

Wisdom versus Constitutionality

Distinguished jurists have long urged the Supreme Court to exercise self-restraint. A law may be unwise, unjust, unfair, or even stupid and yet still be constitutional. One cannot equate the wisdom of the law with its constitutionality, and the Court should decide only the constitutionality and not the wisdom of a law. Justice Oliver Wendell Holmes once lectured his colleague, sixty-one-year-old Justice Stone, on this point:

> Young man, about 75 years ago I learned that I was not God. And so, when the people . . . want to do something I can't find anything in the Constitution expressly forbidding them to do, I say, whether I like it or not, "Goddamn it, let 'em do it."[16]

However, the actual role of the Supreme Court in the nation's power struggles suggests that the Court indeed equates wisdom with constitutionality. People frequently cite broad phrases in the Fifth and Fourteenth Amendments establishing constitutional standards of "due process of law" and "equal protection of the laws" when attacking laws they believe are unfair or unjust. Most Americans have come to believe that laws that are simply unwise must also be unconstitutional and that the courts have become the final arbiters of fairness and justice.

THE SUPREME COURT IN ELITIST PERSPECTIVE

We can best understand the Supreme Court as an elitist institution rather than as a conservative or liberal institution in U.S. government. During the 1930s, the Supreme Court was a bastion of conservatism; it attacked the economic programs of the New Deal and clung to the earlier elite philosophy of rugged individualism. Yet many people criticized the Warren Court later as too liberal in its views of equality of the law, church-state relations, and individual rights before the law. This apparent paradox is understandable if we view the Court as an exponent of the dominant elite philosophy rather than as a constant liberal or conservative element in national politics. When the dominant elite philosophy was rugged individualism, the Court reflected this fact, just as it reflects a liberal philosophy today. Of course, owing to the insulation of the Court even from other elites, through life terms and independence from the executive and legislative branches, a *time lag* exists between changes in elite philosophy and the court decisions reflecting those changes.

The New Deal Period

The Supreme Court's greatest crisis occurred when it failed to respond swiftly to changes in elite philosophy. When Franklin D. Roosevelt became president in 1933, the Supreme Court was still committed to the philosophy of rugged individualism. In a four-year period (1933–1937), the Court made the most active use of its power of judicial review over congressional legislation in its history in a vain attempt to curtail the economic recovery programs of the New Deal. It invalidated the National Industrial Recovery Administration, nullified the Railroad Retirement Act, invalidated the National Farm Mortgage Act, and threw out the Agricultural Adjustment Act. Having denied the federal government the power to regulate manufacturing, petroleum, mining, agriculture, and labor conditions, the Court reaffirmed the notion that the states could not regulate hours and wages. By 1936 it appeared certain that the Court would declare the Social Security Act and the National Labor Relations Act unconstitutional.

The failure of the Court to adapt itself quickly to the new liberalism of the national elite led to its greatest crisis. Roosevelt proposed to "pack" the Court by expanding its size and adding new liberal members. But the nation's leadership itself was divided over such a drastic remedy; so well had the Court served the interests of the established order over its history that Congress was reluctant to accept Roosevelt's plan. Moreover, at a critical point in the debate, the Court changed its attitude, with Chief Justice Hughes and Justice Roberts making timely changes in their position. In *National Labor Relations Board* v. *Jones & Laughlin Steel Corporation*, the Court expanded the definition of interstate commerce to remove constitutional barriers to governmental regulation of the economy.[17] It also upheld the power of the federal government to establish a social security system in a series of decisions that struck down due-process objections to social and economic legislation. And it reinterpreted the contract clause to permit Congress and the states to regulate wages, hours, and work conditions.

The Warren Court

A liberal concern for the underprivileged in America characterized the Supreme Court under the leadership of Chief Justice Earl Warren. The Court firmly insisted that no person in the country should be denied equal protection of the law. It defended the right of blacks to vote, to attend integrated schools, and to receive equal justice in the courts; it upheld the power of Congress to protect blacks from discrimination in public accommodations, employment, voting, and housing. It ruled that discrimination against any group of voters by state legislatures in the apportioning of election districts was unconstitutional. It protected religious minorities (and the nonreligious) from laws establishing official prayers and religious ceremonies in public schools. The Court also protected defendants in criminal cases from self-incrimination through ignorance of their rights, confessions extracted unethically by law enforcement officials, or lack of legal counsel.

The Court, however, was noticeably less concerned with civil liberty when it involved the liberal establishment's Cold War ideology. In *Dennis v. United States* the Court permitted the prosecution of Communists for merely "advocating" the overthrow of the government, and in *Communist Party, U.S.A.* v. *Subversive Activities Control Board* it upheld the right of government to require registration of "subversive" organizations.[18] It permitted congressional committees to interrogate citizens about their political views and upheld loyalty oaths and loyalty-security programs. But by the late 1960s, after a decline of Cold War ideology among the nation's elite, the court began to protect "Communists" and "subversives" from some of the harsher provisions of federal law.

The Burger Court

Popular predictions that the Burger Court, with four Nixon appointees including Chief Justice Warren Burger, would reverse the liberal decisions of the Warren Court did not take into account the elitist character of the Court. Supreme Court efforts to end racial segregation under law, ensure equality in representation, and maintain separation of church and state are fundamental commitments of the national elite. Hence the Burger Court did not reverse any of the landmark decisions of the Warren Court in these areas. The Burger Court extended the doctrine of *Brown v. Board of Education of Topeka* to uphold court-ordered busing of children to end racial imbalance in public schools with a history of segregation under law (southern school districts).[19] However, the Court refused to extend the busing requirement to force independent suburban school districts to bus students into central cities to achieve racial balance in predominantly black city schools. Many civil rights groups hoped the Burger Court would use the Eighth Amendment prohibition against "cruel and unusual punishment" to strike down the death penalty. But the Court, while insisting on fairness and uniformity in application, upheld the death penalty itself.[20] The Court declined to substitute its own notions about "cruel and unusual punishment" for the judgment of the many state legislatures that had voted to retain the death penalty.

Liberals also hoped that the Burger Court would extend traditional concerns for minorities to uphold affirmative action programs. Affirmative action programs, which favor minorities in education and employment, were challenged on the grounds that they discriminate against nonminority individuals in violation of the federal Civil Rights Acts and the Equal Protection Clause of the Fourteenth Amendment.[21] Opponents of racial goals, ratios, and quotas argued that the Constitution and laws of the United States are "color-blind": that they protect *all* individuals against discrimination, not just minorities, and that racial classifications and differential treatments based on race or sex, even if they are designed to benefit disadvantaged groups, are illegal and unconstitutional. But the Burger Court refused to endorse a sweeping "color-blind" argument; it upheld some affirmative action programs while striking down others.[22] The Supreme Court is still struggling with the constitutionality of affirmative action; it has not rendered a sweeping decision one way or the other.

The Burger Court issued one of the most sweeping declarations of individual liberty in the Supreme Court's history: the assertion of the constitutional right of women to have abortions. In *Roe* v. *Wade* in 1973 the Supreme Court ruled that the word "person" in the Constitution did *not* include the unborn fetus.[23] Therefore the Fifth and Fourteenth Amendments' guarantee of "life, liberty, and property" did not protect the "life" of the fetus. The Court also held that the "liberty" of women included the right to decide whether or not to have an abortion.

The Rehnquist Court

Since *Roe* v. *Wade* the Supreme Court has been petitioned frequently to reverse itself, but most justices have stood by the principle that abortion is a personal liberty. The Court held that federal and state governments need not provide tax money to fund abortions; but it struck down various state attempts to limit or interfere with a woman's decision to terminate a pregnancy. However, in 1989 the Supreme Court narrowly upheld a Missouri law designed to protect unborn children by requiring physicians to test for viability after 20 weeks of pregnancy and by preventing both the abortion of a viable fetus and the use of public funds or facilities for abortions except to preserve the life and health of the mother. Justice Sandra Day O'Connor cast the swing vote in the 5-to-4 decision; her separately written opinion argued that the Missouri law did not violate a woman's constitutional right to choose abortion early in pregnancy. This decision, *Webster* v. *Reproductive Health Services,* encouraged "pro-life" groups to seek to enact laws similar to Missouri's, and inspired "pro-choice" groups to rally to oppose restrictions on abortion.

The Supreme Court may not always reflect the conservative and restrained judicial policy preferences of the Nixon, Reagan, and Bush presidencies. This is a testimony to the elitist character of the Court. Once appointed, a Supreme Court justice can become a "surprise judge," voting differently from what the appointing president would have wished or predicted.

DO THE COURTS RULE THE NATION?

George C. Wallace once put the argument bluntly: "Thugs and federal judges have just about taken charge of this country."[24] Others have also worried about the increasing role of the judiciary—the ability of courts to intrude into people's lives in ways unprecedented in history. One need not be a "conservative" in politics to be concerned about the extent to which we now rely upon a nonelected judiciary to solve our problems, rather than upon democratically elected executives and legislators.

Growing Reliance on the Courts

Harvard Law School Professor Archibald Cox, who became famous as the first Watergate prosecutor, warned that "excessive reliance upon courts instead of self-government through democratic processes, may deaden the people's sense of moral and political responsibility for their own future, especially in matters of liberty, and may stunt the growth of political capacity that results from the exercise of the ultimate powers of decision."[25] For good or for ill, Americans have come to rely on courts to solve problems once handled by legislatures, local officials, school boards, teachers, parents, or other social organizations.

Court Congestion

Each year U.S. courts try more than 10 million cases, most of them in state and local courts. Nearly 200,000 cases begin in federal courts each year. Most of these cases will be settled before trial, but about 20,000 (10 percent) go to trial. People appeal more than 20,000 cases to U.S. courts of appeal each year. And the U.S. Supreme Court receives more than 5,000 cases each year, although it can give serious attention to only about 200 of them.

About 500,000 lawyers practice in the United States. The federal government, through its Legal Services Corporation, operates its own law firm for the poor, with more than 3,500 lawyers in 300 programs throughout the country.

The growing number of legal cases not only raises questions about the increasing power of a nonelected, lifetime judicial elite, but it also overburdens the court system and creates many injustices. As more and more cases get into the judicial system, congestion and costs mount. Cases may be backed up on court dockets for years. As a result, injured parties in civil cases must suffer long delays before receiving compensation. Defendants in criminal cases who are free on bail may deliberately delay the trial, hoping that witnesses will move away or forget important details or that victims will grow frustrated and give up trying to prosecute. Most lawsuits require attorneys on both sides, and attorneys are expensive. The longer a case drags on, the more expensive it is likely to be.

Plea Bargaining

Congestion forces prosecuting attorneys in criminal cases to *plea bargain* with defendants—that is, to make special arrangements for criminal defendants to plead guilty in exchange for reduced charges. For example, a prosecutor may reduce the charge of rape to sexual assault, which usually carries a lighter penalty. The prosecutor enters into such a bargain in order to avoid the delays and costs of a trial; the defendant makes such a bargain to escape serious penalty for the crime. Estimates suggest that 90 percent of all criminal cases are now plea bargained.

Judicial Reforms

Federal courts are so well insulated from popular pressure and from congressional and presidential pressures that we will probably have to wait for them to "reform" themselves. If federal judges are slow in handling cases, if their decisions are arbitrary, if congestion and confusion reign in their courtrooms, if they bog themselves down in details of managing school districts or prisons or hospitals, if they are lazy or poorly trained in the law, if they are in poor health or senile, no one can do much about it. Only five federal court judges have *ever* been impeached and convicted by Congress. In 1989, Federal District Court Judge L. C. Hastings became the first sitting judge in more than fifty years to be impeached, tried, and found guilty by the Congress. Other judges have resigned under fire: Federal Judge Otto Kerner (former governor of Illinois) resigned his judicial post only five days before he was scheduled to enter prison for income tax evasion, perjury, bribery, and mail fraud.[26] In short, the U.S. citizenry has little control over the judiciary, despite the control it exercises over all of us.

CASE STUDY

Life or Death Decisions

It is ironic indeed that a nation that thinks of itself as a democracy must call upon a nonelective, life-time elite of nine people to decide a question as fundamental as life or death. It is even more ironic when Americans attack the Supreme Court as "conservative" because it tries to return this difficult decision to the states for other people to decide it.

Prior to 1972, thirty-five states officially sanctioned the death penalty; only fifteen states had abolished capital punishment. Federal law also retained the death penalty. However, no one had actually suffered the death penalty since 1967 because of numerous legal tangles and direct challenges to the constitutionality of capital punishment.

Several constitutional arguments are possible against the death penalty, aside from whatever moral, ethical, or religious objections one might raise. The first is that the death penalty is "cruel and unusual punishment," prohibited by the Eighth Amendment to the U.S. Constitution. The problem with this argument is that the early Jeffersonians, who wrote the amendment and the other sections of the Bill of Rights, themselves employed the death penalty. Indeed the Fifth Amendment mentions the death penalty, specifically indicating that this penalty was acceptable at the time. For nearly 200 years the general agreement was that death was not "cruel" or "unusual" unless carried out in a particularly bizarre or painful fashion. Most

(continued)

CASE STUDY *(continued)*

executions were by hanging; the electric chair was introduced in the 1920s as a "humane" alternative, and the gas chamber followed in some states. Nonetheless one can still argue that by today's standards the death penalty is "cruel and unusual," recognizing that moral standards change over time.

Another constitutional argument against the death penalty is that courts apply it in a discriminatory fashion, violating the equal protection clause of the Fourteenth Amendment. Although blacks comprise only 12 percent of the population, more than half the people executed have been black. Moreover, among both blacks and whites, the less educated and less affluent individuals tend to be the ones executed. Finally, some people argue that imposition of the death penalty is arbitrary—that no clear, consistent criteria exist for deciding who should be executed and who should be spared.

The primary advocate of abolishing the death penalty on the Supreme Court has been former Justice Thurgood Marshall, who believes that the death penalty is the ultimate form of racial discrimination. Marshall wants to see the death penalty struck down once and for all. When a series of cases, including *Furman* v. *Georgia,* came to the Court in 1972, more than 700 people throughout the nation waited under sentence of death. But Marshall was unable to convince his colleagues on the Court that the death penalty was always "cruel and unusual." Of the other liberals on the Court, only Justice William J. Brennan seemed to agree that death itself was a cruel and unusual punishment. But Justice William O. Douglas, together with Potter Stewart and Byron White, believed that application of the death penalty was arbitrary, random, unfair, and discriminatory. Some individuals, usually poor, black, and uneducated, were sentenced to die for crimes for which other individuals, usually affluent, white, and educated, were sentenced to jail. So Justice Marshall lined up five votes in 1972 to strike down the death penalty *as it was then imposed.* But Marshall was not able to

persuade a majority of the justices to abolish the death penalty altogether.

The minority view in 1972, which upheld the death penalty, was led by Chief Justice Warren Burger. Burger argued that the courts of the United States had always permitted the death penalty and had never held it to be cruel and unusual. Indeed, as an indicator of contemporary standards, Burger observed that most states and the federal government itself retained the death penalty. The federal government had recently enacted death-penalty laws for airplane hijacking when death resulted and for assassination of the president or vice president. "The word cruel," said Burger, "can mean grossly out of proportion to the severity of the crime; but certainly when the crime is murder, the death penalty is not out of proportion to the crime." Chief Justice Burger reminded the states that the majority had not abolished the death penalty itself but had merely struck down its arbitrary use. He invited the states to reconsider and rewrite their death-penalty laws. In private conversation, however, neither Burger nor Marshall believed that the states would reenact death-penalty laws. Both men believed that "there will never be another execution in this country."*

TABLE A Voting on the Supreme Court: The death penalty

Cases	Strike down death sentence	Uphold death sentence
Furman v. *Georgia* (1972)	Marshall Brennan Douglas Stewart White	Burger Rehnquist Blackmun Powell
Gregg v. *Georgia* (1976)	Marshall Brennan	Burger Rehnquist Blackmun Powell Stewart White Stevens

*Bob Woodward and Scott Armstrong, *The Brethren: Inside the Supreme Court* (New York: Simon and Schuster, 1979), p. 279.

(continued)

Thus, by a five-to-four vote, the Supreme Court struck down all capital punishment laws as they were written and administered in 1972. (See Table A.) The 700 people on death row received a permanent reprieve. But the Court was badly divided. The justices wrote nine separate opinions, totaling 50,000 words on 243 pages—the longest Supreme Court decision in history.

To the surprise of many who hoped to abolish the death penalty, the *Furman* v. *Georgia* case in 1972 stimulated thirty-five states to reenact the death penalty with specific guidelines to avoid arbitrary or discriminatory use. By 1976 another 600 people waited on death row for the Supreme Court to examine these new state laws.

The Supreme Court finally considered the new state laws in a series of death-penalty cases in 1976.** Only Marshall and Brennan believed that capital punishment always violates the "cruel and unusual" punishment clause of the Eighth Amendment. Justice John Paul Stevens had replaced the aging liberal, William O. Douglas, on the Court. Stevens, together with Burger, Blackmun, Powell, and Rehnquist, provided five votes to uphold the death penalty. And Justices White and Stewart would uphold the death penalty if it was shown not to be arbitrarily imposed or discriminatory.

Georgia, Florida, and Texas, as well as several other states, had enacted very carefully designed capital punishment laws after the 1972 *Furman* v. *Georgia* decision. The objective was to ensure fairness and uniformity of application. Most of these laws provided for two trials: one to determine guilt or innocence and another to determine whether to impose the death sentence. The second trial called for evidence of "aggravating" and "mitigating" factors; if only aggravating factors were evident, the death penalty would be mandatory.

Justices Stewart, Powell, and Stevens together wrote the majority opinion in all the death-penalty cases in 1976. They ruled on behalf of the Court

---

**Gregg* v. *Georgia*, *Profitt* v. *Florida*, *Jurek* v. *Texas*.

that "the punishment of death does *not* invariably violate the Constitution." They upheld the death penalty with the following rationale. The men who drafted the Bill of Rights, including the Eighth Amendment, accepted death as a common sanction for crime. Clearly, one must interpret the Eighth Amendment prohibition against "cruel and unusual" punishment in a dynamic fashion, reflecting changing moral values. But the decisions of more than half the nation's state legislatures to reenact the death penalty since 1972 and the decisions of juries to impose the death penalty on hundreds of people under these laws are evidence that "a large proportion of American society continues to regard it as an appropriate and necessary criminal sanction." Moreover, said the Court majority, the social purposes of retribution and deterrence justify the use of the death penalty. This ultimate sanction is "an expression of society's moral outrage at particularly offensive conduct." The Court reaffirmed that *Furman* struck down the death penalty only when inflicted in "an arbitrary and capricious manner." The Court approved the consideration of "aggravating and mitigating circumstance." The Court also approved of automatic review of all death sentences by state supreme courts to ensure that the sentence did not reveal the influence of passion or prejudice, that evidence supported aggravating circumstances, and that the sentence was proportionate to the crime. However, the Court disapproved of state laws making the death penalty mandatory in all first-degree murder cases, holding that such laws were "unduly harsh and unworkably rigid."

Marshall wrote a very emotional opinion dissenting from the majority view. And Brennan too was very upset over the changing attitude of the Court. "Justice of this kind is obviously no less shocking than the crime itself," he wrote, "and a new 'official' murder, far from offering redress for the offense committed against society, adds instead a second defilement to the first." But these dissents had no effect on the outcome of the case.

——— SUMMARY

The Supreme Court determines many of the nation's most important policies. Indeed, most political questions sooner or later end up in the courts. Any fair examination of the court system in the United States will reveal the elitist character of judicial decision making.

1. The Supreme Court is the most elitist branch of the national government. Nine justices—none of whom is elected and all of whom serve for life—can void the acts of popularly elected presidents, Congresses, governors, legislatures, school boards, and city councils.

2. The principle of judicial review of congressional acts grew out of the Founding Fathers' distrust of popularly elected officials subject to influence by popular majorities. Judicial review enables the courts to protect constitutional principles against attacks by elected bodies.

3. The social backgrounds of judges reflect close ties to upper-class segments of society. Presidents may attempt to influence court decisions through their selection of judges, but life terms make judges independent of presidential or congressional influence once they are appointed.

4. Judicial decision making takes on an appearance of objectivity, maintains the fiction of nonpartisanship, employs special rules of access, and reflects a legalistic style. These features help legitimize the decisions of people who have no electoral mandate.

5. Since justices are not popularly elected, some scholars and jurists have urged self-restraint in judicial policy making. They argue that the Supreme Court should decide only the constitutionality of a law, not its wisdom; the Court should not substitute its own judgment for the judgment of elected representatives. But over the years judicial activism has augmented the power of judges. Justices have used broad phrases in the Constitution such as "due process of law" and "equal protection of the law" to strike down laws they believe are unfair or unjust.

6. Over its history the Supreme Court has not been consistently liberal or conservative but rather has reflected dominant elite philosophy. The greatest crisis in the Court's history occurred in the 1930s when dominant elites accepted New Deal "liberalism," but the Court continued to reflect the "rugged individualism" of an earlier era. It has become almost commonplace to predict that, once a new justice is appointed, a radical swing—either to the left or to the right—will occur. Such swings are rare. The Burger Court's affirmation of the right to an abortion was *not* abrogated by the Rehnquist Court, for example. The Rehnquist Court upheld First Amendment rights against local ordinances prohibiting hateful speech and generally eschewed extremism.

NOTES

1. Alexis de Tocqueville, *Democracy in America* (New York: Mentor Books, 1956), p. 73.
2. James Madison, Alexander Hamilton, and John Jay, *The Federalist* (New York: Modern Library, 1937), p. 505.
3. Joseph W. Bishop, "The Warren Court Is Not Likely to Be Overruled," *New York Times Magazine* (September 7, 1969): 31.
4. John R. Schmidhauser, *The Supreme Court* (New York: Holt, Rinehart & Winston, 1960), p. 59.
5. Henry Abraham, *The Judicial Process* (New York: Oxford University Press, 1968), p. 58.
6. Schmidhauser, op. cit., p. 59.
7. See *Congressional Quarterly Weekly Report*, July 6, 1991, p. 1827.
8. ABC News/Washington Post poll, reported in *Congressional Quarterly Weekly Report*, October 19, 1991, p. 3028.
9. *U.S. v. Butler*, 297 U.S. 1 (1936); Carl Brent Swisher, "The Supreme Court and the Moment of Truth," *American Political Science Review* 54 (December 1960): 879.
10. Felix Frankfurter, "The Supreme Court and the Public," *Forum* 83 (June 1930): 332–334.
11. Frank Jerone, *Law and the Modern Mind* (New York: Coward-McCann, 1930); Benjamin N. Cardozo, *The Nature of the Judicial Process* (New Haven, Conn.: Yale University Press, 1921); Roscoe Pound, *Justice According to Law* (New Haven, Conn.: Yale University Press, 1951).
12. *West Virginia State Board of Education* v. *Barnette*, 319 U.S. 624 (1943).
13. Archibald Cox, *The Warren Court* (Cambridge, Mass.: Harvard University Press, 1968), p. 2.
14. See Abraham, op. cit., pp. 310–326.
15. Justice William O. Douglas, "Stare Decisis," *Record* (April 1947).
16. Quoted by Charles P. Curtis, *Lions Under the Throne* (Boston: Houghton Mifflin, 1947), p. 281.
17. *National Labor Relations Board* v. *Jones & Laughlin Steel Corporation*, 301 U.S. 1 (1937).
18. *Dennis* v. *U.S.*, 341 U.S. 494 (1951); *Communist Party, U.S.A.* v. *Subversive Activities Control Board*, 367 U.S. 1 (1961).
19. *Swann* v. *Charlotte-Mecklenburg Board of Education*, 39 L.W. 4437 (1971).
20. *Furman* v. *Georgia*, 408 U.S. 238 (1972).
21. *Gregg* v. *Georgia, Profitt* v. *Florida, Jurek* v. *Texas*, 428 U.S. 242 (1976).
22. *Regents of the University of California* v. *Bakke*, 438 U.S. 265 (1978).

23. *Roe* v. *Wade,* 410 U.S. 113 (1973); *Doe* v. *Bolton,* 410 U.S. 179 (1973).
24. *Newsweek* (January 10, 1977): 42.
25. Archibald Cox, *The Role of the Supreme Court in American Government* (New York: Oxford University Press, 1976), p. 103.
26. *Time* (August 20, 1979): 54.

SELECTED READINGS

Abraham, Henry J. *The Judicial Process.* New York: Oxford University Press, 1968. This book is one of the most comprehensive introductions to the basics of the judicial process. It provides both a sound theoretical introduction to the nature, sources, and types of law and a thorough nuts-and-bolts knowledge of the staffing, organization, and technical processes involved in the judicial process. The book provides four extensive bibliographies dealing with U.S. constitutional law, biographies and autobiographies of and by justices of the Supreme Court, a discussion of comparative constitutional law, and analysis of civil liberties.

Baum, Lawrence. *The Supreme Court,* 3rd ed. Washington, D.C.: Congressional Quarterly Press, 1989. A readable, up-to-date introduction to the Supreme Court as a political institution, the book covers the selection of justices, the nature of cases decided, the process of decision making, and the impact of the Supreme Court's decisions.

Jacob, Herbert. *Justice in America,* 2nd ed. Boston: Little, Brown, 1972. Jacob assesses how well American courts administer civil and criminal justice. He views the courts as political, policy-making institutions and examines their participants, procedures, and restraints. The book gives special attention to out-of-court settlements, plea bargaining, and political justice and injustice.

Woodward, Bob, and Armstrong, Scott. *The Brethren: Inside the Supreme Court.* New York: Simon and Schuster, 1979. This sensationalized behind-the-scenes account of decision making by the Supreme Court supposedly exposes the fact that members of the Court maneuver, argue, and compromise over major issues confronting the Court and the nation.

14

American Federalism: Elites in States and Communities

★ *The importance of denationalizing conflicts can hardly be over-estimated, particularly in a large country like the United States where there is great diversity in resources and local problems.*

Robert A. Dahl, Pluralist Democracy in the United States, *1967*

There are more than 83,000 separate governments in the United States, of which more than 60,000 have the power to levy their own taxes. These governments include 50 states; 3,042 counties; 19,205 cities; 16,691 townships; 29,487 special districts; and 14,741 school districts. The U.S. Constitution endows states with all governmental powers not vested specifically in the national government or reserved to the people. All other governmental jurisdictions are subdivisions of states. States may create, alter, or abolish these other units of government by amending state laws or constitutions.

Decentralization—decision making by sub-elites—reduces strain on the national political system and on national elites by keeping many issues out of the national arena. National conflict is reduced by allowing sub-elites to pursue their own policies within the separate states and communities; they need not battle for a single national policy to be applied uniformly throughout the land. For example, sub-elites who wish to raise taxes and spend more money for public schools can do so in their own states and communities, and those who wish to reduce taxes and eliminate what some consider to be educational "frills" can also do so within their own states and communities.

But the masses play an even smaller role in state and local politics than they do in national politics. The news media emphasize national politics rather than state or community politics. Very few citizens know who their state senator or state representative is or who their city council members or county commissioners are. We can expect 50 percent of the nation's eligible voters to cast ballots in presidential elections, but turnout in state gubernatorial elections in nonpresidential years is generally less than 50 percent. Municipal elections often attract fewer than 20 to 30 percent of the eligible voters.

Despite low rates of participation in state and local elections, most Americans believe that state and local governments are "closer to the people" and therefore "more understanding of their real needs" (see Figure 14-1). Moreover, the masses believe that state and local government is more efficient, less wasteful, and less corrupt than the government in Washington.

FEDERALISM: THE DIVISION OF POWER BETWEEN NATION AND STATES

The Constitution divides power between two separate authorities, the nation and the states, each of which can directly enforce its own laws on individuals through its own courts. American federalism differs from a "unitary" political system in that the central govenment has no legal authority to determine, alter, or abolish the power of the states. At the same time, American federalism differs from a confederation of states, in which

FIGURE 14-1   Public images of the federal system

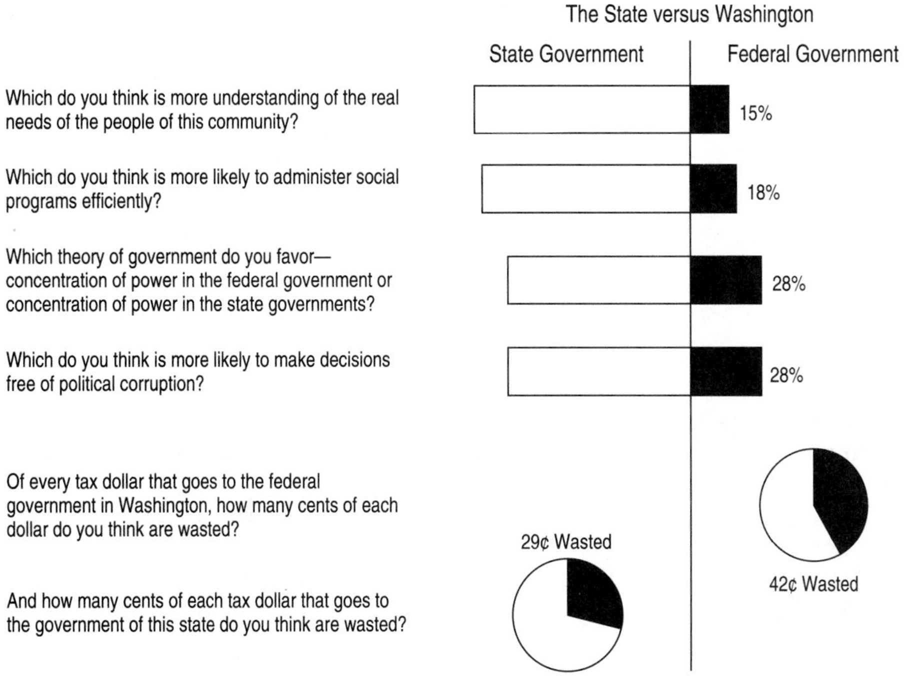

The State versus Washington

State Government | Federal Government

Which do you think is more understanding of the real needs of the people of this community?   15%

Which do you think is more likely to administer social programs efficiently?   18%

Which theory of government do you favor— concentration of power in the federal government or concentration of power in the state governments?   28%

Which do you think is more likely to make decisions free of political corruption?   28%

Of every tax dollar that goes to the federal government in Washington, how many cents of each dollar do you think are wasted?

And how many cents of each tax dollar that goes to the government of this state do you think are wasted?

29¢ Wasted

42¢ Wasted

the national government depends on its states for power. The American system shares authority and power constitutionally and practically.

The U.S. Constitution originally defined federalism in terms of (1) the powers exercised by the national government (delegated powers) and the national supremacy clause; (2) the powers reserved to the states; (3) the powers denied by the Constitution to both the national government and the states; and (4) the constitutional provisions giving the states a role in the composition of the national government.

Delegated Powers

The U.S. Constitution lists eighteen grants of power to Congress, including authority over war and foreign affairs, authority over the economy ("interstate commerce"), control over the money supply, and power to tax and spend "to pay the debts and provide for the common defense and general welfare." Finally, after seventeen specific grants of power comes the power "to make all laws which shall be necessary and proper for carrying into execution the foregoing powers and all other powers vested by this Constitution in the government of the United States or in any department or officer thereof." This statement is generally known as the "necessary and proper" clause.

These delegated powers, when coupled with the assertion of "national supremacy" in Article VI, ensure a powerful national government. The national supremacy clause is very specific in asserting the supremacy of federal laws:

> The Constitution, and the laws of the United States which shall be made in pursuance thereof; and all treaties made or which shall be made under the authority of the United States, shall be the supreme law of the land; and the judges in every state shall be bound thereby, anything in the constitution or laws of any state to the contrary notwithstanding.

Reserved Powers

Despite these broad grants of power to the national government, the states retained considerable governing power from the beginning of the republic. The Tenth Amendment reassured the states that "the powers not delegated to the United States . . . are reserved to the states respectively, or to the people." The states generally retain control over property and contract law, criminal law, marriage and divorce, the provision of education, highways, and social welfare activities. The states control the organization and powers of their own local governments. Finally, the states, like the federal government, retain the power to tax and spend for the general welfare.

Powers Denied to the States

The Constitution denies some powers to both national and state government, namely the powers to abridge individual rights. The first eight amendments to the U.S. Constitution originally applied only to the national government, but the Fourteenth Amendment, passed by Congress in 1866, provided that the states must also adhere to fundamental guarantees of individual liberty.

The Constitution denies the states some powers in order to safeguard national unity: the powers to coin money, enter into treaties with foreign nations, interfere with the "obligations of contracts," levy taxes on imports and exports, and engage in war, along with some others.

The State's Role in National Government

The states are also basic units in the organizational scheme of the national government. The House of Representatives apportions members to the states by population, and state legislatures draw up their districts. Every state has one House representative regardless of population. Each state elects two U.S. senators regardless of population. The president is chosen by the electoral votes of the states; each state has as many electoral votes as it has senators and House representatives. Finally, three-fourths of the states must ratify amendments to the U.S. Constitution.

THE GROWTH OF POWER IN WASHINGTON

Over time governmental power has centralized in Washington. While the formal constitutional arrangements of federalism remain in place, power has flowed relentlessly toward the national government since the earliest days of the nation. Perhaps the most important developments over time have been (1) the broad interpretation of the "necessary and proper" clause to obscure the notion of "delegated powers" and allow the national government to do anything not specifically prohibited by the Constitution; (2) the victory of the national government in the Civil War, demonstrating that states could not successfully resist federal power by force of arms; (3) the establishment of a national system of civil rights based upon the Fourteenth Amendment, which brought federal government into the definition and enforcement of civil rights; (4) the growth of federal power under the interstate commerce clause as a national industrial economy emerged; and (5) the growth of federal grants-in-aid to state and local governments as a major source of revenues for these governments and a major source of federal intervention into state and local affairs.

The "Necessary and Proper" Clause

Chief Justice John Marshall added immeasurably to national power in *McCullough v. Maryland* (1819) when he broadly interpreted the "necessary and proper" clause of Article I, Section 8, of the Constitution. In approving the establishment of a national bank (a power not specifically delegated to the national government in the Constitution), Marshall wrote:

> Let the end be legitimate, let it be within the scope of the Constitution, and all means which are appropriate, which are plainly adopted to that end, which are not prohibited but consistent with the letter and the spirit of the Constitution, are constitutional.

Since then, the "necessary and proper" clause has been called the "implied powers" clause or even the "elastic" clause, suggesting that the national government can do anything not specifically prohibited by the Constitution. Given this tradition, the courts are unlikely to hold an act of Congress unconstitutional solely because no formal constitutional grant of power gives Congress the power to act.

The Civil War

The Civil War was the nation's greatest crisis in federalism. Did a state have the right to oppose federal action by force of arms? The issue was decided in the nation's bloodiest war. (Combined casualties in the Civil War, military and civilian, exceeded U.S. casualties in the Second World War, even though the U.S. population in 1860 was only one-quarter of the population in 1940.) The same issue was at stake when the federal government sent troops to Little Rock, Arkansas, in 1957 and Oxford, Mississippi, in 1962 to enforce desegregation; however, in those confrontations it was clear which side held the military advantage.

Civil Rights

Over the years, the U.S. Supreme Court has built a national system of civil rights based on the Fourteenth Amendment. This amendment rose out of the Civil War: "No *state* shall . . . deprive any person of life, liberty, or property, without due process of law; nor deny to any person within its jurisdiction the equal protection of the laws." In early cases, the Supreme Court held that the general guarantee of "liberty" in the first phrase (the "due process" clause) prevents states from interfering with free speech, press, religion, and other personal liberties. Later, particularly after *Brown* v. *Board of Education of Topeka* in 1954, the Supreme Court also used the "equal protection" clause to ensure fairness and equality of opportunity throughout the nation.

The Interstate Commerce Clause

The growth of national power under the interstate commerce clause is also an important development in American federalism. The industrial revolution created a national economy governable only by a national government. Yet until the 1930s the Supreme Court placed many obstacles in the way of government regulation of the economy. Finally in *National Labor Relations Board* v. *Jones & Laughlin Steel Corporation* (1937), the Supreme Court recognized the principle that Congress could regulate production and distribution of goods and services for a national market under the interstate commerce clause. As a result, the national government gained control over wages, prices, production, marketing, labor relations, and all other important aspects of the national economy.

───── MONEY AND POWER

Money and power go together. In 1913, when the Sixteenth Amendment gave the national government the power to tax incomes, financial power shifted from the states to Washington. The income tax gave the federal government the authority to raise large sums of money, which it spent for the "general welfare," as well as for defense. Of course, federal *land* grants to the states began as far back as the famous Northwest Ordinance in 1787, when Congress gave federal land to the states to assist in building public schools. Again, by the Morrill Land Grant Act in 1862, Congress made land grants to the states to promote higher education. But the first major federal *money* grants to the states began shortly after enactment of the federal income tax. Grant programs began in agricultural extension (1914), highways (1916), vocational education (1917), and public health (1918).

Gradually the federal government expanded its power in states and communities by use of grants-in-aid. During the Great Depression of the 1930s, the national government used its taxing and spending powers in a number of areas formerly "reserved" to states and communities. Congress began grants-in-aid programs to states and communities for public assistance, unemployment compensation, employment services, child welfare, public housing, urban renewal, highway construction, and vocational education and rehabilitation. The inadequacy of state and local revenue systems contributed significantly to the increase of national power in states and communities. Federal grants-in-aid to state and local governments expanded over the years in both dollar amounts and the percentage of the total revenue of states and communities that comes from the federal government (see Table 14-1). The Reagan administration was successful in slowing the growth of federal grants and reducing state and local dependence on federal money. Nonetheless, state and local governments still rely on the federal government for about 18 percent of their total revenues.

THE EVOLUTION OF AMERICAN FEDERALISM

American federalism has undergone many changes during the more than two hundred years that it has been in existence. And it continues to change over time.

TABLE 14-1   Washington's money in state and local government finance

	Total federal grants-in-aid (millions of dollars)	Federal grants as a percentage of state and local revenue
1902	7	—
1922	118	2.1
1932	232	2.9
1938	800	7.2
1948	1,861	8.6
1950	82,858	24.4
1960	6,974	11.6
1970	25,029	14.8
1975	49,800	22.7
1980	91,500	25.8
1985	105,900	20.9
1988	116,700	18.2
1990	135,400	19.0

SOURCE: *Budget of the United States Government: 1992* (Washington, D.C.: Government Printing Office, 1991).

Dual Federalism

The pattern of federal-state relations during the nation's first hundred years has been described as *dual federalism*. The states and the nation divided most governmental functions. The national government concentrated its attention on the delegated powers—national defense, foreign affairs, tariffs, commerce across state lines, coining money, establishing standard weights and measures, maintaining a post office and building post roads, and admitting new states. State governments decided the important domestic policy issues—slavery (until the Civil War), education, welfare, health, and criminal justice. This separation of policy responsibilities was once compared to a layer cake, with local governments at the base, state governments in the middle, and the national government at the top.

Cooperative Federalism

The industrial revolution, bringing the development of a national economy; the income tax, which shifted financial resources to the national government; and the challenges of two world wars and the Great Depression all combined to end the strict distinction between national and state concerns. The new pattern of federal-state relations was labeled *cooperative federalism*. Both the nation and the states exercised responsibilities for welfare, health, highways, education, and criminal justice. This merging of policy responsibilities was compared to a marble cake. "As the colors are mixed in a marble cake, so functions are mixed in the American federal system."[1]

The Great Depression of the 1930s forced states to ask for federal financial assistance in dealing with poverty, unemployment, and old age. Governors welcomed massive federal public-works projects. In addition, the federal government intervened directly in economic affairs, labor relations, business practices, and agriculture. Through the grant-in-aid device, the national government cooperated with the states in public assistance, employment services, child welfare, public housing, urban renewal, highway building, and vocational education.

Yet even during this period when the nation and the states shared responsibility, the national government emphasized cooperation in achieving common national and state goals. Congress generally acknowledged that it had no direct constitutional authority to regulate public health, safety, or welfare. Congress relied primarily on its powers to tax and spend for the general welfare in providing financial assistance to state and local governments to achieve shared goals. Congress did not usually legislate directly on local matters.

Centralized Federalism

Over the years it became increasingly difficult to maintain the fiction that the national government was merely assisting the states in performing their domestic responsibility. By the time President Lyndon B. Johnson launched the Great Society in 1964, the federal government clearly set forth its own national goals. Virtually all problems confronting American society—from solid-waste disposal and water and air pollution to consumer safety, home insulation, noise abatement, and even metric conversion—were declared to be national problems. Congress legislated directly on any matter it chose. The Supreme Court no longer concerned itself with the reserved powers of the states; the Tenth Amendment lost most of its meaning. The pattern of national-state relations became centralized. To continue the cake analogy, the "frosting had moved to the top, something like a pineapple upside-down cake."

In 1985 the U.S. Supreme Court ended all pretense to constitutional protection of state power in its *Garcia* decision. Prior to this case it was generally believed that the states were constitutionally protected from direct congressional coercion in matters traditionally "reserved" to the states. The Congress could bribe states with grant-in-aid money to enact federal programs—or threaten them with the loss of such aid if they failed to conform to federal rules—but Congress was careful not to give direct orders to state and local government. However, in the *Garcia* case, the Supreme Court upheld a federal law requiring state and local governments to obey federal wage and hour rules. The Court dismissed the argument that the nature of American federalism and the reserved powers clause of the Tenth Amendment prevented Congress from legislating directly in state and local affairs. The Court declared that there were no constitutionally protected state powers, that the only protection given the states is their representation in the Congress and in presidential elections.

New Federalism

The term *new federalism* has been applied to proposals that would return power and responsibility to states and communities. Actually, the term was first used by President Nixon in the early 1970s to describe his general-revenue-sharing proposal: the direct allocation of federal tax revenues to state and local governments to use for general purposes with no strings attached. Later the term referred to a series of proposals by President Reagan to reduce state and local dependency on federal revenues and return powers to states and communities.

To implement the new federalism, Reagan consolidated many *categorical grants* (by which the federal government specifies individual projects or programs in cities and states) into a few large *block grant* programs (by which the federal government provides funds for use by states and cities for broad purposes, such as law enforcement and community development, with state and local officials deciding about specific projects or programs). These block grants provide greater flexibility in the use of federal funds and allow state and local officials to exercise more power over projects and programs within their jurisdictions. Reagan also ended the federal government's general-revenue-sharing program, which had funneled billions of dollars annually to states and cities.

The political response of the nation's governors and mayors to many new federalism proposals was less than enthusiastic. State and local officials generally wanted relief from federal guidelines, regulations, and conditions that came with federal grants. But they feared the financial burdens of doing without these programs. Opposition in Congress to Reagan's new federalism prevented any massive changes in federal versus state and local government responsibilities.

THE POLITICS OF FEDERALISM

In recent years political conflict over federalism—over the division of responsibilities and finances between national and state/local governments—has tended to follow traditional "liberal" and "conservative" political cleavages. Generally, liberals seek to enhance the power of the *national* government. Liberals believe that people's lives can be changed by the exercise of governmental power—to end discrimination, abolish poverty, eliminate slums, ensure employment, uplift the downtrodden, educate the masses, and cure the sick. The government in Washington has more power and resources than state and local governments, and liberals have turned to it rather than to state and local governments to cure America's ills. State and local governments are regarded as too slow, cumbersome, weak, and unresponsive. The government in Washington is seen by liberals as the principal instrument for social and economic reform. Thus, liberalism and centralization are closely related in American politics.

The liberal argument for national authority can be summarized as follows:

1. State and local governments have insufficient awareness of social problems. The federal government must take the lead in civil rights, equal employment opportunities, care for the poor and aged, the provision of adequate medical care for all Americans, and the elimination of urban poverty and blight.

2. It is difficult to achieve change when reform-minded citizens must deal with fifty state governments or eighty thousand local governments. Change is more likely to be accomplished by a strong central government.

3. State and local governments contribute to inequality in society by setting different levels of services in education, welfare, health, and other public functions. A strong national government can ensure uniformity of standards throughout the nation.

4. A strong national government can unify the nation behind principles and ideals of social justice and economic progress. Extreme decentralization can foster local or regional "special" interests at the expense of the general "public" interest.

Generally, conservatives seek to return power to *state and local* governments. Conservatives are more skeptical about the "good" that government can do. Adding to the power of the national government is not seen as an effective way of resolving society's problems. On the contrary, conservatives argue that "government is the problem, not the solution." Excessive governmental regulation, burdensome taxation, and inflationary government spending combine to restrict individual freedom, penalize work and saving, and destroy incentives for economic growth. Government should be kept small, controllable, and close to the people.

The conservative argument for state and local autonomy can be summarized as follows:

1. "Grass-roots" government promotes a sense of self-responsibility and self-reliance.

2. State and local governments can better adapt public programs to local needs and conditions.

3. State and local governments promote participation in politics and civic responsibility by allowing more people to become involved in public questions.

4. Competition between states and cities can result in improved public programs and services.

5. The existence of multiple state and local governments encourages experimentation and innovation in public policy, from which the whole nation may gain.

6. State and local governments reduce the administrative workload on the national government, as well as reducing the political turmoil that results when one single policy must govern the entire nation.

The argument over federalism will never be settled once and for all. Debates over federalism are part of the fabric of American politics.

ELITE STRUCTURES IN THE STATES

Elite structures vary among the fifty states.[2] To understand elite patterns in state politics, we can identify several categories of elite systems.

Unified Elite System

In states with nondiversified economies and weak, noncompetitive parties, a cohesive group of economic interests generally dominates state politics. For many years, Maine offered a good example of this type of elite system: "In few American states are the reins of government more openly, more completely in the hands of a few leaders of economic interest groups than in Maine."[3] Power, timber, and manufacturing interests (the "big three") formed a cohesive economic elite because of their key position in the state's economy. More than three-fourths of the state is woodland, most of it owned by a handful of timber and paper companies. The timber interests, combined with power companies and textile and shoe manufacturers, controlled Maine politics and protected their own economic well-being. Challenges to the predominance of the big three were seldom well organized or sustained.

Traditionally, the states of the Deep South displayed the cultural homogeneity and unified elites characteristic of nondiversified or agricultural economies. Occasionally "populist" candidates briefly challenged the dominance of the planting, landowning, and financial elites in southern states. But once in power, the demagogues seldom implemented populist programs; more frequently they became instruments of the established elites whom they castigated in campaign oratory.

Dominant Elites Among Lesser Elites

A second type of elite structure develops in states with a nondiversified economy, although the states may display a reasonably competitive party system, with moderate party cohesion in the legislature. This structure features a dominant elite with several lesser elites; its primary characteristic is the prevailing influence of a single industry.

Political histories abound of the power of Anaconda in Montana, Du Pont in Delaware, the oil companies in Texas and Louisiana, the coal companies in West Virginia, and so on. Doubtless their reputations for absolute control of a state far exceed their actual control over public policy. The oil industry's reputation for control of Texas politics is often exaggerated. The chairman of the Texas Democratic Executive Committee once said, "It may not be a wholesome thing to say, but the oil industry today is in complete control of state politics and state government."[4] This type of overstatement is common in political circles; in fact, many issues in state politics are of little concern to the oil interests. However, Texas politicians are unlikely to oppose the oil depletion allowance in the federal tax structure due to its direct and vital impact on the oil producers. The same is true of the dominant interests in other states: although they may not control all aspects of state politics, they control those matters that directly affect them.

Bipolar Elite Structure

A bipolar structure is most likely in an industrial, urban, competitive state with strong, cohesive political parties. Michigan is the prototype of this form. The state's economy is industrial rather than agricultural, but it is nondiversified and heavily dependent on the automotive industry, the largest single employer. But automobile manufacturers do not dominate Michigan politics because organized labor has emerged as an effective counterbalance to the manufacturers. Joseph La Palombara concludes that "no major issues of policy (taxation, social legislation, labor legislation, etc.) are likely to be decided in Michigan without the intervention, within their respective parties and before agencies of government, of automotive labor and automotive management."[5] Labor and management elites in Michigan each have "their own" political party, and polarization in the elite system accompanies strong competition between well-organized, cohesive, and disciplined Democratic (labor) and Republican (management) party organizations.

Plural Elite Structure

A state with a highly diversified economy is likely to produce a plural elite structure. California may have the most diversified economy of any state in the nation, with thriving agricultural interests, timber and mining resources, and manufacturing enterprises that run the gamut from cement to motion pictures. Railroads, brewers, racetracks, motion pictures, citrus growers, airplane manufacturers, insurance companies, utilities, defense contractors, and a host of other economic interests coexist in this state. No one economic interest or combination of interests dominates California politics. Instead a variety of elites govern within specific issue areas; each elite concentrates its attention on matters directly affecting its own economic interest. Occasionally the economic interests of elites may clash, but on the whole elites coexist rather than compete. Political parties are somewhat less cohesive and disciplined in the plural elite system. Economic elites, hesitating to identify too closely with a single party, even make financial contributions to opposing candidates to ensure protection of their interests no matter which party or candidate wins.

——— SINGLE ELITES IN AMERICAN COMMUNITIES

One of the earliest studies of community elites was the classic study of "Middletown" by Robert Lynd and Helen Lynd in the mid-1920s and again in the mid-1930s.[6] In Middletown, the Lynds found a monolithic power structure dominated by the X family, owners of the town's largest industry. ("Middletown" was actually Muncie, Indiana, and the X family was the Ball family, owners of the Ball Corporation, for whom Ball State University is named.) Community power was firmly in the hands of the business class, which controlled the economic life of the city, particularly through its ability to control the extension of credit. The city was run by a "small top group" of "wealthy local manufacturers, bankers, the local head managers of . . . national corporations with units in Middletown, and . . . one or two outstanding lawyers." Democratic procedures and governmental institutions were window dressing for business control. The Lynds described the typical city official as a "man of meager caliber" and as a "man whom the inner business control group ignores economically and socially and uses politically." Perhaps the most famous passage from the Lynds' study was a comment by a Middletown man made in 1935:

> If I'm out of work, I go to the X plant; if I need money I go to the X bank, and if they don't like me I don't get it; my children go to the X college; when I get sick I go to the X hospital; I buy a building lot or house in the X subdivision; my wife goes downtown to buy X milk; I drink X beer, vote for X political parties, and get help from X charities; my boy goes to the X YMCA and my girl to their YWCA; I listen to the word of God in a X subsidized church; if I'm a Mason, I go to the X Masonic temple; I read the news from the X morning paper; and, if I'm rich enough, I travel via the X airport.[7]

In sociologist Floyd Hunter's influential study of Atlanta, Georgia, in the 1950s, he found that community policy originated with a group composed primarily of business, financial, religious, and education leaders rather than with the people of the community.[8] According to Hunter, only those holding high positions in the business and financial community were admitted to the circle of influential persons in Atlanta. Hunter explained that the top power structure concerned itself only with major policy decisions, from which the leaders of certain substructures—economic, government, religious, educational, professional, civic, and cultural—then took their cues, communicating and implementing the policies decided at the top level.

> [The substructures] are subordinate . . . to the interests of the policy makers who operate in the economic sphere of community life in Regional City [Atlanta]. The institutions of the family, church, state, education, and the like draw sustenance from economic institutional sources and are thereby subordinate to this particular institution more than any other. . . . Within the policy-forming groups the economic interests are dominant.[9]

The top power holders seldom operated openly: "Most of the top personnel in the power group are rarely seen in the meetings attended by associational understructure personnel in Regional City."[10]

In Hunter's description of community decision making, decisions tended to flow down from top policy makers (composed primarily of business and financial leaders) to the civic, professional, and cultural association leaders, the religious and educational leaders, and the government officials who carry out the program. The masses of people had little direct or indirect participation in the process. Policy did not go *up* from associational groupings or from the people themselves.

According to Hunter, elected public officials were clearly part of the lower-level institutional substructure that executed rather than formulated policy. Finally, Hunter found that this whole power structure was held together by "common interests, mutual obligations, money, habit, delegated responsibilities, and in some cases by coercion and force."[11]

Hunter's findings in Atlanta reinforced the elite model and were a source of discomfort to those who wish to see the United States governed in a truly democratic fashion. Hunter's research challenged the notion of popular participation in decision making or grass-roots democracy; it raised doubts as to whether cherished democratic values were being realized in American community life.[12]

PLURAL ELITES IN AMERICAN COMMUNITIES

Pluralist models of community power stress the fragmentation of authority, the influence of elected public officials, the importance of organized group activity, and the roles of public opinion and elections in determining public policy. Who, then, rules in the pluralist community? "Different small groups of interested and active citizens [rule] in different issue areas with some overlap, if any, by public officials, and occasional intervention by a larger number of people at the polls."[13] Citizens' influence is felt not only through organized group activity but also through elites' anticipating their reactions and endeavoring to satisfy their demands. Leadership in community affairs is exercised not only by elected public officials but also by interested individuals and groups who confine their participation to one or two issues. The pluralist model regards interest and activity, rather than economic resources, as the key to elite membership. Competition, fluidity, access, and equality characterize community policies.

In his significant study of power in New Haven in the early 1960s, political scientist Robert A. Dahl admitted that "tiny minorities," whose social class is not representative of the community as a whole, make most community decisions.[14] However, Dahl challenged the notion that the elite system in American community life was pyramidal and cohesive and unresponsive to popular demands. Dahl studied major decisions in urban redevelopment and public education in New Haven, as well as the nominations for mayor in both political parties. In contrast to Hunter's highly monolithic and centralized power structure in Atlanta, Dahl found a polycentric and dispersed system of elites in New Haven. Many elites exercised influence from time to time, each exerting some power over some issues but not over others. One set of leaders was influential in urban renewal matters; another was powerful in public education.

Business elites, who dominated Atlanta, according to Hunter's study, were only one of the many influential elites in New Haven:

> The economic notables, far from being a ruling group, are simply one of many groups out of which individuals sporadically emerge to influence the politics and acts of city officials. Almost anything one might say about the influence of the economic notables could be said with equal justice about a half dozen other groups in the New Haven community.[15]

Yet Dahl also found that the people involved in community decisions in New Haven added up to only a tiny minority of the community. For example, Dahl wrote:

It is not too much to say that urban redevelopment has been the direct product of a small handful of leaders.[16]

The bulk of the voters had virtually no direct influence on the process of nomination.[17]

The number of citizens who participated directly in important decisions bearing on the public schools is small.[18]

Moreover, Dahl noted that people exercising leadership for each issue had higher social status than the rest of the community and that these middle- and upper-class elite members possessed more of the skills and qualities required of leaders in a democratic system.

Dahl's New Haven obviously parallels the pluralistic model. However, his New Haven clearly was not a democracy in the sense that we defined the term earlier. Not all citizens participated in the decisions that affected their lives, and not all had an equal opportunity to influence public policy.

THE OLD ECONOMIC ELITES

Most of the nation's economic resources are controlled by *national* institutions—industrial corporations, banks, utilities, insurance companies, investment firms, and the national government. Most of the forces shaping life in American communities arise outside of these communities; community leaders cannot make war or peace, or cause inflation or recession or determine interest rates or the money supply. But there is one economic resource—land—that is controlled by *community* elites. Land is a valuable resource: capital investment, labor and management, and production must be placed somewhere.

Traditionally, community power structures were composed primarily of landed interests whose goal was to intensify the use of their land and add to its value. These community elites sought to maximize land values, real estate commissions, builders' profits, rent payments, and mortgage interest and to increase revenues to commercial enterprises serving the community. Communities were traditionally dominated by mortgage lending banks, real estate developers, builders, and landowners. They were joined by owners or managers of local utilities, department stores, attorneys and title companies, and others whose wealth is affected by land use. Local bankers who financed the real estate developers and builders were often at the center of the elite structure. Unquestionably these community elites competed among themselves for wealth, profit, power, and preeminence. But they shared a consensus about intensifying the use of land.

Growth was the shared elite value. The old community elite was indeed a "growth machine."[19] The old community elite believed that capital investment in the community would raise land values, expand the labor force, generate demand for housing as well as commercial services, and enhance the local tax base. Attracting investors required the provision of good transportation facilities—highways, streets, rail access, and water and airport facilities. It required the provision of utilities—water, gas and electrical power, solid waste disposal, and sewage treatment. It required the provision of good municipal services, especially fire and police protection; the elimination of harassing business regulations and the reduction of taxes on new investments to the lowest feasible levels; the provision of a capable and cooperative labor force, educated for the needs of productive capital and motivated to work; and finally, the provision of sufficient amenities—cultural, recreational, aesthetic—to provide the corporate managers with a desirable lifestyle.

Traditional community elites strove for consensus. They believed that community economic growth—increased capital investment, more jobs, and improved business conditions—benefited the entire community. According to Paul E. Peterson, community residents share a common interest in the economic well-being of the city: "Policies and programs can be said to be in the interest of cities whenever the policies maintain or enhance the economic position, social prestige, or political power of the city as a whole."[20] Economic elites themselves would have agreed with Peterson.

Local government officials were expected to share in the elite consensus. Economic prosperity was necessary for protecting the fiscal base of local government. Growth in local budgets and public employment, as well as governmental services depends upon growth in the local economy. Governmental growth expanded the power, prestige, and status of government officials. Moreover, economic growth was usually good politics. Growth-oriented candidates for public office usually had larger campaign treasuries than antigrowth candidates. Finally, according to Peterson, most local politicians had "a sense of community responsibility." They knew that if the economy of the community declines, "local business will suffer, workers will lose employment opportunities, cultural life will decline, and city land values will fall."[21]

THE NEW POLITICAL ELITES

Today, in most American communities, the old economic elites have been replaced by new political elites. Many of the old economic elites sold their businesses to national corporations and vacated their positions of community leadership. Locally owned stores and factories became manager-directed plants and chain stores. The result was a weakening of community loyalties in the business sector. The new corporate managers could easily decide, in response to national economic conditions, to close the local plant or store with minimal concern for the impact on the community. Local banks were merged into national banking corporations and local bankers were replaced by banking executives with few community ties. City newspapers that were once independently owned by families who lived in the communities were bought up by giant newspaper and publication chains. Instead of editors and reporters who expected to live the lives of their communities, city newspapers came to be staffed with people who hope to move up in the corporate hierarchy—people who strive primarily to advance their own careers, not the interests of the local community.

The nationalization of the American economy and the resulting demise of locally owned enterprises created a vacuum of leadership in community affairs. Professional politicians moved into this vacuum in city after city, largely replacing the local bankers, real estate developers, chambers of commerce, and old-style newspaper editors who had dominated community politics for generations. The earlier economic elites were only part-time politicians who used local government to promote their economic interests. The new professional political elites work full time at local politics. They are drawn primarily by personal ambition, not so much for wealth as for the power and celebrity that accompany running for and winning public office. They are not "screened" by economic elites or political parties, but rather they nominate themselves, raise their own funds, organize their own campaigns, and create their own publicity.

The political elites are independent entrepreneurs. They win office "by selling themselves to the voters, in person, one at a time, day after day. People who do not like to do this, people who do not like to knock on strangers' doors or who find it tedious to repeat the same thirty-second personal introduction thousands of times, are at a severe disadvantage."[22] Thus, over time these full-time political elites drive out the part-time economic elites.

The new political elites seldom have a large financial stake in the community, aside from their homes. They are *not* corporate leaders, or bankers, or developers. They may be lawyers, but they are not highly successful lawyers from prestigious law firms; rather, the are "political activists with law degrees."[23] They are not strongly committed to the community's economic growth or well-being. They do not necessarily seek community consensus on behalf of prosperity.

On the contrary, it's fashionable among new political elites to complain loudly about the problems created by growth—congestion, pollution, noise, unsightly development, or the replacement of green spaces with concrete slabs. No-growth movements appeal to people who already own their houses and do not intend to sell them, people whose jobs are secure in government bureaucracies or tenured professorships, people who may be displaced from their homes and neighborhoods by new facilities, and people who see no direct benefit to themselves from growth. These no-growth movements (or, to use the current euphemism, "growth-management" movements) are *not* mass movements. They do *not* express the aspirations of workers for jobs or renters for their own homes. Instead, they reflect upper-middle-class lifestyle preferences of educated, affluent, articulate homeowners. Growth brings ugly factories, cheap commercial outlets, hamburger stands, fried chicken franchises, and "undesirable" residents. Even if new business or industry would help hold down local taxes, these affluent citizens would still oppose it, preferring to retain the appearance or lifestyle of their community.

New political elites waving the no-growth banner challenge traditional economic elites in many large and growing cities in the West and South. The no-growth leaders may themselves have been beneficiaries of community growth only five or ten years ago, but they quickly perceive their own political interest in slowing or halting additional growth.

Halting or curtailing growth serves the financial interests of homeowners, apartment owners, and owners of already-developed commercial property. Curtailing growth serves to freeze out competition from new homes, apartment complexes, and commercial centers. It allows owners of existing homes and properties to raise prices and rents to new residents. It is no surprise that "neighborhood associations" led by upper- and upper-middle-class homeowners are at the forefront of no-growth politics.

Municipal government offers the tools to challenge the old growth elites. Communities may restrict growth through zoning laws, subdivision control restrictions, utility regulations, building permits, and environmental regulations. Opposition to street widening, road building, or tree cutting can slow or halt development. Public utilities needed for development—water lines, sewage disposal facilities, fire houses, and so on—can be postponed indefinitely. High development fees, "impact fees," utility hookup charges, or building permit fees can all be used to discourage growth. Environmental laws, or even "historic preservation laws, can be employed aggressively to halt development.

———— SUMMARY

The existence of political sub-elites within the larger American political system permits some decentralization of decision making. Decentralization, or decision making by sub-elites, reduces potential strain on the consensus of national elites. Each sub-elite sets its own policies in its own state and community, without battling over a single national policy to be applied uniformly throughout the land. The following propositions summarize our consideration of American federalism and our comparative analysis of elites in states and communities.

1. American federalism divides power constitutionally between national and state governments, each of which can directly enforce its own laws on individuals through its own courts. The Constitution itself cannot be amended without the consent of the national government (two-thirds of both houses of Congress) and the states (three-fourths of the legislatures).

2. Over time, power has centralized in Washington owing to (a) a broad interpretation of the "necessary and proper" clause granting the national government the power to do anything not specifically prohibited by the Constitution, (b) the victory of the national government in the Civil War, (c) the establishment of a national system of civil rights, (d) the growth of national power under the interstate commerce clause, and (e) the growth of federal grants-in-aid to state and local governments.

3. The principal instrument of national power in states and communities is the federal "grant-in-aid." Federal grants now provide about 18 percent of all state and local government revenue. Federal rules, regulations, and guidelines accompanying the grants give the federal government great power over the activity of local governments. The "new federalism" proposed to reverse the flow of power to Washington and return responsibility to states and cities. The Reagan administration consolidated many categorical grant programs into block grants, ended general-revenue sharing, and reversed the growing dependence of state and local government on federal revenue.

4. Debate over state versus national power reflects the power of various interests at the state and national levels. Liberal elites, stronger at the national level, generally assert the supremacy of the national government. In contrast, conservative and rural interests, dominant in some states and communities but less powerful at the national level, provide the backbone of support for "states' rights."

5. States with the most unified and cohesive elite systems are likely to be one-party states, rather than competitive two-party states. Unified elite systems are more likely to be found in states whose political parties show little cohesion and states that are poor, rural, and agricultural. Wealthy, urban, industrial states have more diversified elite groups, and a single elite cannot easily dominate the political scene.

6. Scholars have described American communities in terms reflecting both single-elite and plural-elite models. Yet even the plural-elite studies conclude that "tiny minorities" make "the key political, economic, and social decisions." They also find that these "tiny minorities" come from the upper- and middle-class community.

7. Traditional community power structures concern themselves with economic growth. These community power structures are dominated by banks, real estate developers, builders, and landowners, all of whom benefit directly from increasing the value of land. These power structures mobilize mass support for local growth policies by promising more jobs.

8. New political elites have arisen in many cities to replace traditional economic elites. As the economy nationalized, locally owned businesses, banks, and newspapers were replaced by national corporations and chains, whose managers have fewer ties to community affairs. Local political elites moved into the vacuum of power. These new elites are self-nominated, full-time, professional politicians.

9. The new political elites are not necessarily committed to economic growth. They frequently endorse "growth management" proposals designed to halt or curtail growth. These new elites do *not* reflect mass interests but rather the preferences of upper-middle-class, educated, articulate homeowners for avoiding noise and pollution, ugly factories, cheap commercials, and "undesirable" residents.

NOTES

1. Morton Grodzins, *The American System* (Chicago: Rand McNally, 1966), p. 265.
2. Harmon Zeigler, "Interest Groups in the States," in Herbert Jacob and Kenneth A. Vines, eds., *Politics in American States* (Boston: Little, Brown, 1965), p. 114.
3. Duane Lockard, *New England State Politics* (Princeton, N.J.: Princeton University Press, 1959), p. 79.
4. Robert Engler, *The Politics of Oil* (New York: Macmillian, 1961), p. 354.
5. Joseph La Palombara, *Guide to Michigan Politics* (East Lansing: Michigan University, Bureau of Social and Political Research, 1960), p. 104.
6. Robert S. Lynd and Helen M. Lynd, *Middletown* (New York: Harcourt, Brace & World, 1929); and *Middletown in Transition* (New York: Harcourt, Brace & World, 1937).
7. Lynd and Lynd, *Middletown in Transition*, p. 74.
8. Floyd Hunter, *Community Power Structure* (Chapel Hill: University of North Carolina Press, 1953).
9. Ibid., p. 94.
10. Ibid., p. 90.
11. Ibid.
12. For a more pluralist view of Atlanta's power structure, see Kent Jennings, *Community Influentials* (New York: Free Press, 1964).
13. Aaron Wildavsky, *Leadership in a Small Town* (Totowa, N.J.: Bedminister Press, 1964), p. 8.
14. Robert A. Dahl, *Who Governs?* (New Haven, Conn.: Yale University Press, 1961).
15. Ibid., p. 72.
16. Ibid., p. 115.
17. Ibid., p. 106.
18. Ibid., p. 151.
19. See Harvy Molotch, "The City as Growth Machine," *American Journal of Sociology* 82 (September 1976): 309–330; and "Capital and Neighborhood in the United States," *Urban Affairs Quarterly* 14 (March 1979): 289–312.
20. Paul E. Peterson, *City Limits* (Chicago: University of Chicago Press, 1981), p. 20.

21. Ibid., p. 29.
22. Alan Ehrenhalt, *The United States of Ambition* (New York: Time Books, 1991), p. 15.
23. Ibid., p. 16.

—— SELECTED READINGS

Dahl, Robert A. *Who Governs?* New Haven, Conn.: Yale University Press, 1961. This book is perhaps the most important pluralist community power study. Using a decisional approach, Dahl finds that a number of elites make decisions in different issue areas.

Ehrenhalt, Alan. *The United States of Ambition.* New York: Time Books, 1991. A description of fundamental changes in community, state, and national politics over the last thirty years, illustrated with a series of case studies. Ehrenhalt argues that in communities across the country new professional political elites have grabbed power from the old economic elites. The new political elites nominate themselves and win elections through hard work and self-promotion. They are not committed to community prosperity so much as to their own careers.

Hunter, Floyd. *Community Power Structure.* Chapel Hill: University of North Carolina Press, 1953. Although classical elitism has its origins in European sociological theory, much of the current American controversy over elitism has resulted from community power research. This book was one of the first community power studies reporting elitist results. Hunter's use of the reputational method in this study of Atlanta set the scene for a heated debate with the pluralists.

Ricci, David M. *Community Power and Democratic Theory: The Logic of Political Analysis.* New York: Random House, 1981. This book is an excellent review of both past and current philosophical, ideological, and methodological differences between elitists and pluralists of each theory, including the contributions of Joseph Schumpeter ("process" theory of democracy), David Truman ("group" theory of democracy), Floyd Hunter ("reputational" theory of elitism), C. Wright Mills ("positional" theory of elitism), and Robert Dahl ("pluralist" theory of democracy). The text also includes an excellent discussion of "the present scholarly impasse" between advocates of each point of view, as well as an annotated bibliography of relevant literature.

15

Protest Movements: Challenge to Dominant Elites

★ *The social origins of protest leaders are rather similar to, instead of strikingly different from, the social origins of leaders of established parties with whom they clash.*

Anthony Oberschall, Social Conflict and Social Movements, *1973*

People without access to the resources of interest-group politics, and people whose values are substantially at odds with the prevailing public policy, occasionally enter mass protest movements. These protest *movements* sometimes lead to the establishment of protest *organizations* designed to "represent and shape the broadly held preferences . . . of the social movement."[1] This shaping and organizing is where protest movements and the protest organizations either succeed or fail. Generally protest movements without organizations fail because intermittent violence isolates the movement from established elites.[2] Of course, established elites do not ignore protests. Rather they may (1) make symbolic gestures to pacify the active protesters (co-opting them through programs that bring protest leaders into the "system"), (2) limit protests through repression (increased law enforcement), or (3) do both simultaneously. Often elite response is a combination of accommodation and repression, with heavier doses of accommodation handed out to movements whose goals are within the general framework of elite consensus.[3]

As organizations arise to direct the aspirations of protest movements, the advantages of accommodation increase.[4] The leaders find that by moderating their demands they can gain a portion of their original goals and also achieve for themselves and the organization a stake in the elite system. Thus protest movements that become protest organizations eventually come to share the elite consensus.

Protest movements tend to be cyclical. Many fail to achieve organizational stability and soon fade from memory. Others successfully travel the road from protest to organization to accommodation, but the price is high. Movement toward political success not only requires accommodation to the acceptable norms of established elites, it also requires organizational leadership by people with negotiating skills and willingness to sustain activity for long periods of time. Protest leaders, irrespective of the movements they represent, do *not* come from the lower strata of society.[5]

From the variety of movements that have risen and fallen during the history of the United States, the civil rights movement and the feminist movement offer interesting and contemporary examples for discussion.

THE HISTORY OF BLACK SUBJUGATION

The place of blacks in American society has been a central issue of domestic politics in the United States since the first black slaves stepped onto these shores in 1619. The American nation as a whole, with its democratic tradition, has felt strong conflicting sentiments about slavery, segregation, and discrimination. White America has harbored an ambivalence toward blacks—a recognition of the evils of inequality but a reluctance to take steps to eliminate it. This "American dilemma" reflects the larger issue of the American masses' attitudes toward democracy:

commitment to abstract ideals with substantially less commitment to their practice.[6] To a large extent, we can view blacks' struggle for full citizenship as a dialogue—sometimes violent, sometimes peaceful—between the demands of black counterelites and the response of dominant white elites.

Abolition

In 1865 the Thirteenth Amendment abolished slavery everywhere in the United States. The Fourteenth Amendment, passed in 1867 by a Republican Congress that intended to reconstruct southern society after the Civil War, made "equal protection of the laws" a command for every state to obey. The Fifteenth Amendment, passed in 1869, prohibited federal and state governments from abridging the right to vote "on account of race, color, or previous condition of servitude." In addition, Congress passed a series of civil rights statutes in the 1860s and 1870s guaranteeing the new black freedmen protection in the exercise of their constitutional rights. The Civil Rights Act of 1875 specifically outlawed segregation by privately owned businesses offering to serve the public. Between 1865 and the early 1880s the success of the civil rights movement was evident in widespread black voting throughout the South, the presence of many blacks in federal and state offices, and the almost equal treatment afforded blacks in theaters, restaurants, hotels, and public transportation.

The Rise of White Supremacy

But by 1877 support for Reconstruction policies began to crumble. In the Compromise of 1877, the national government agreed to end military occupation of the South, give up its efforts to rearrange southern society, and lend tacit approval to white supremacy in that region. In return, the southern states pledged their support to the Union, accepted national supremacy, and agreed to permit the Republican presidential candidate, Rutherford B. Hayes, to assume the presidency, although the Democratic candidate, Samuel Tilden, had received a majority of the popular vote in the disputed election of 1876. The Supreme Court adhered to the terms of this compromise. In the famous Civil Rights Cases of 1883, the Supreme Court declared unconstitutional those federal civil rights laws preventing discrimination by private individuals. By denying Congress the power to protect blacks from discrimination, the Court paved the way for the imposition of segregation as the prevailing social system of the South. In the 1880s and 1890s, white southerners imposed segregation in public accommodations, housing, education, employment, and almost every other sector of private and public life. By 1895 most southern states had passed laws *requiring* racial segregation in education and in public accommodations.

In 1896, in the famous case of *Plessy* v. *Ferguson,* the Supreme Court upheld state laws requiring segregation.[7] Although segregation laws involved state action, the Court held that segregating the races did not violate the equal protection clause of the Fourteenth Amendment so long as people in each race received equal treatment. Schools and other public facilities that were "separate but equal" won constitutional approval.

The violence that occurred during that period was almost entirely one-sided: whites attacked blacks.[8] The pattern of race relations at the turn of the century was clearly one of violent repression, exclusion of blacks from jobs and labor unions, and rigid segregation. Blacks lost most of what they had gained during Reconstruction.

TWENTIETH-CENTURY RESPONSES

The Black Response: Initial Developments

The NAACP and National Urban League.   The first black organizations emerged from the repressive pattern of the late nineteenth century; blacks formed the National Association for the Advancement of Colored People (NAACP) and the National Urban League in 1909 and 1910, respectively. Both organizations reacted against Booker T. Washington's acceptance of the inferior status of blacks, and both worked closely with white liberals. These organizations, depending as they did on the good will of whites, sought black equality through court action and other legal means. They were (and still are) dominated by middle-class blacks and upper-class whites. They accepted the premise that they could effect meaningful change within the American legal system. They were (and are) conservative in that their techniques require commitment to the institutional status quo. They disavowed attempts to change or overthrow the basic political and economic structure of the society; they simply sought to integrate blacks into the existing society. In other words, they took literally the ideology and premises of the American democratic system.

The development of counterelites.   When the concentration of blacks in northern cities increased the potential for mass action, a different pattern of violence began to emerge. First, the black community began to *express* its grievances. As grievances such as discrimination in housing and transportation built up and expression became more aggressive, a precipitating incident would occur, and blacks responded by attacking whites or their property. The northern-style riot differed substantially from southern-style violence; blacks no longer remained passive victims but became active participants. The northern-style riot made its first appearance in Springfield, Illinois, in 1908.

Perhaps the first important black counterelite was Marcus Garvey. Since the NAACP was an elitist organization in both membership and appeal, Garvey, a West Indian, organized the Universal Negro Improvement Association to articulate the latent feelings of black nationalism. Garvey's programs for a separate black nation in Africa appealed to impoverished blacks, especially as white bigotry in the form of the Ku Klux Klan spread north in the wake of black economic advance. Garvey was essentially a forerunner of the Black Muslims of the 1950s and 1960s and the more radical black nationalists of the late 1960s. Like the Muslims, Garvey urged his followers to practice personal frugality and establish a high level of morality. Like the nationalists, he sought to teach blacks that their color could be a source of pride rather than shame. At one time, Garvey had a following estimated at three million, but his movement collapsed in the mid-1920s. His appeal to the black masses, nevertheless, was very important, for Garvey asserted that blacks would never gain what the NAACP insisted that they could achieve: an equal share in the American economic system. As Myrdal observed, the Garvey movement "tells of the dissatisfaction so deep that it mounts to hopelessness of ever enjoying a full life in America."[9]

Court declaration of equality.   The period following the Korean War, marked by enormous legal and symbolic victories, was crucial in the development of the relationship between blacks and whites. The long labors of the NAACP paid off in the historic *Brown* v. *Board of Education of Topeka* decision in which the Court reversed the *Plessy* v. *Ferguson* doctrine of "separate but equal."[10] This decision symbolized the beginning of a new era of high expectations among blacks. Whereas elected elites had remained silent on civil rights and, in fact, exhibited substantial hostility, an appointed elite, the Supreme Court, declared that blacks and whites were equal in the eyes of the law.

However, *Brown* v. *Board of Education of Topeka* was only the beginning of the political battle over segregation. Segregation did not disappear simply because the Supreme Court declared it unconstitutional. Segregation was widespread and deeply ingrained. Seventeen states required segregation by law, and the U.S. Congress required segregation in Washington, D.C. Four other states (Arizona, Kansas, New Mexico, and Wyoming) authorized segregation at local option. Unless another political elite with equal resources could challenge the political power of the white majority in the South, the pattern of segregation was unlikely to change.

In not ordering immediate desegregation, the Supreme Court snatched the tangible portion of the victory away from blacks. The Court placed primary responsibility for enforcing the decision on local officials and school boards, in effect returning power to the white sub-elites in the South. As a result, during the 1950s the white South developed many schemes to resist integration. Ten years after *Brown*, only about 2 percent of the blacks in the South attended integrated schools; the other 98 percent remained in segregated schools. In short, the decision meant nothing to the overwhelming majority of blacks, whose frustrations intensified as they saw the discrepancy between the Supreme Court's intent and the behavior of local officials. Blacks had gained a legal victory, but they were impotent politically. As a result, the civil rights movement changed its focus from legal restrictions to de facto segregation and unequal socioeconomic institutions.

The politics of litigation.   Significantly, the next phase of the civil rights movement was strongly elitist. The prime players were the NAACP and the Supreme Court, both of them insulated from white and black masses. The elite orientation of the NAACP led its leaders to accept the prevailing values of white elites. It attracted the "talented tenth"—the minority of upper-class, educated blacks. It played by the "rules of the game"—litigation, not protest. White elites, especially those most removed from mass sanction, found NAACP values quite compatible with their own. The educated blacks of the NAACP sought only to remove legal barriers to equality of opportunity. Educated themselves, they regarded education as the key to success. NAACP leadership, which was economically successful on the whole, was better accepted by white elites and thus was culturally at the periphery of the black community. The NAACP's success depended largely on maintaining "good connections" with white elites, and the organizational leadership did not intend to risk its favored position by identifying with those sections of the black community unacceptable to the white elites.

Creative Disorder

The symbolic importance of the *Brown* decision is great, and despite the paucity of tangible benefits, the decision undoubtedly increased blacks' expectations and demands. Black sociologist Kenneth Clark assesses the importance of official sanction as follows:

> This [civil rights] movement would probably not have existed at all were it not for the 1954 Supreme Court school desegregation decision which provided a tremendous boost to the morale of Negroes by its clear affirmation that color is irrelevant to the rights of American citizens. Until this time the Southern Negro generally had accommodated to the separation of the black from the white society.[11]

Bus boycotts.   In 1955 a black women, Rosa Parks, refused to ride in the back of a bus in Montgomery, Alabama, lending dramatic support to Clark's hypothesis. Her act brought about the Montgomery boycott, in which blacks refused to use the public transportation system until they could sit wherever they preferred; this action was the first significant step away from the NAACP's legalism. The Montgomery bus boycott required mass-oriented leadership. Martin Luther King, Jr., who gained instant national prominence through the bus boycott, initially filled this need. His Southern Christian Leadership Conference (SCLC) emerged in 1957 as the first southern-originated civil rights group. Although substantially more militant than the older black organizations, it was nevertheless explicitly nonviolent. The purposes of mass demonstrations were to challenge the legality of both legal and de facto segregation and to prick the consciences of white elites.

Direct-action tactics.   The tactics of the SCLC were extended by the Student Nonviolent Co-ordinating Committee (SNCC), which developed in the next phase of direct action—the sit-in demonstrations and freedom rides of the 1960s. In February 1960, at Greensboro, North Carolina, students of the North Carolina Agricultural and Technical College conducted the first sit-ins. As other sit-ins followed, SNCC organized to coordinate the new student protest. SNCC, unlike the SCLC, encouraged blacks to feel proud of being black. The Congress on Racial Equality (CORE), which had begun in the 1940s, emerged from quiescence to lead the freedom rides, which challenged the Jim Crow laws of transportation facilities. Many thousands of students participated in these extremely dangerous rides, refusing to obey the segregation laws.

The vigor with which blacks pursued the freedom rides and sit-ins was a clear sign that the civil rights movement was committed to direct action. However, even this new phase of the civil rights movement was not really a mass movement; the participants were still relatively privileged in comparison with the black masses. The most frequent participants in the confrontations of the early 1960s were urban students.[12] These relatively privileged youths were disappointed in the white society's unwillingness to recognize their merits.

Birmingham demonstrations.   In 1963, in Birmingham, Alabama, blacks conducted prolonged demonstrations on the broadest front yet conceived by civil rights leaders. Blacks presented demands to end discrimination in public accommodations, employment, and housing to the white elite of Birmingham. Under the leadership of Martin Luther King, Jr., these demonstrations were committed to nonviolence. Probably because of the broad nature of the demands, the grass roots of the black community began to participate for the first time. All strata of the black community became active.

The Civil Rights Act of 1964

The Birmingham demonstrations were another landmark in the civil rights movement. Partly because of the southern elites' repressive behavior toward these peaceful demonstrations, the Kennedy administration proposed significant civil rights legislation. Thus the Birmingham demonstration of 1963 stimulated what was to become the Civil Rights

Act of 1964, Congress's first significant entry into civil rights. The act passed both houses of Congress by more than a two-thirds vote, winning the overwhelming support of both Republicans and Democrats. It ranks with the Emancipation Proclamation, the Fourteenth Amendment, and *Brown* v. *Board of Education of Topeka* as one of the most important steps toward full equality for blacks in the United States. Among its more important provisions are the following:

- It is unlawful to apply unequal standards in voter registration procedures or to deny registration for irrelevant errors or omissions on records or applications.
- It is unlawful to discriminate against or segregate people on the grounds of race, color, religion, or national origin in any place of public accommodation, including hotels, motels, restaurants, movies, theaters, sports arenas, entertainment houses, and other places that offer to serve the public. This prohibition extends to all establishments whose operations affect interstate commerce or whose discriminatory practices are supported by state action.
- Each federal department and agency must act to end discrimination in all programs or activities receiving federal financial assistance in any form. This action will include termination of financial assistance.
- It is unlawful for any employer or labor union to discriminate against any individual in any fashion in employment because of race, color, religion, sex, or national origin; an Equal Employment Opportunity Commission will enforce this provision through investigation, conference, conciliation, persuasion, and, if necessary, civil action in federal court.

Although largely symbolic, the Civil Rights Act of 1964 did bring about tangible gains for southern blacks. The withdrawal of federal grant-in-aid money as a sanction was a remarkable innovation in federal enforcement of civil rights. When the U.S. Office of Education began to apply pressure in the South, its progress was impressive compared with that of the preceding ten years.

CONTINUING INEQUALITIES BETWEEN BLACKS AND WHITES

Blacks' economic position has improved substantially in recent years, but this improvement is not bringing the black masses appreciably closer to the white standard of living (see Table 15-1). Examining the ratio of white to black income allows a comparison of the condition of blacks *relative* to that of whites. Between 1947 and 1970 the gap gradually narrowed. Whereas in 1947 the median income of black families was only 51 percent of white family income, by 1970 it had risen to 64 percent. But this narrowing of the gap between black and white family incomes did not continue in the 1970s. During the recession of 1974–1975, black family income slipped back to 58 percent of white family income. By 1982—

TABLE 15-1   Black income as ratio of white median family income

1947	.51	1974	.58
1964	.54	1975	.58
1965	.54	1976	.59
1966	.58	1977	.57
1967	.59	1978	.57
1968	.60	1980	.56
1969	.61	1982	.56
1970	.64	1984	.56
1971	.60	1986	.57
1972	.59	1988	.57
1973	.58	1990	.57

again, in the depths of a recession—black income had declined to 56 percent of white income; it is only 57 percent today.

Compared to white children, black children are:

Five times as likely to
- Be dependent on welfare
- Become pregnant as teenagers

Four times as likely to
- Live with neither parent and be supervised by a child welfare agency
- Be murdered
- Be incarcerated between 15 and 19 years of age

Three times as likely to
- Be poor
- Have their mothers die in childbirth
- Live with a parent who has separated from his or her spouse
- Live in a female-headed household
- Be placed in an educable, mentally retarded class
- Be in foster care
- Die of known child abuse
- Score below average on scholastic aptitude tests

Twice as likely to
- Die in the first year of life
- Be born prematurely
- Suffer from low birthweight
- Have a mother who received late or no prenatal care
- Be born to a teenage or single-parent family
- See a parent die
- Live in substandard housing
- Be suspended from school or suffer corporal punishment
- Live in institutions

Indeed, life in an American ghetto approximates life in a Third World country. The life expectancy of blacks is currently *falling*, a phenomenon unprecedented in industrial democracies (see Figure 15-1). (Life expectancy declined in the USSR during the 1970s and 1980s at about the same rate as did life expectancy for American blacks.)

FIGURE 15-1   Life expectancy of blacks and whites in the United States, 1972–1988.

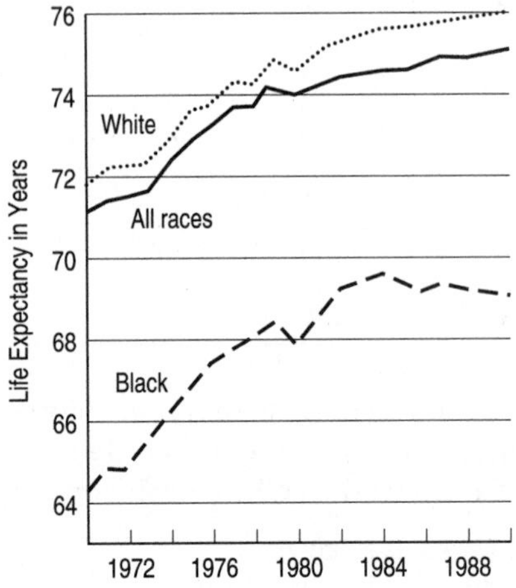

SOURCE: U.S. Bureau of the Census, 1991.

AFFIRMATIVE ACTION OR "QUOTAS"?

What public policies should be pursued to achieve equality? Is it sufficient that government eliminate discrimination, guarantee equality of opportunity to blacks and whites, and apply color-blind standards to both groups? Or should government take action to overcome the results of past unequal treatment of blacks: preferential or compensatory treatment that will favor black applicants for university admission and scholarships, job hiring and promotion, and other opportunities for advancement in life?

Increasingly, the goal of the civil rights movement has shifted from the traditional goal of equality of opportunity to one of affirmative action to establish goals and timetables to achieve equality. Although usually avoiding the term *quota*, affirmative action tests the success of equal employment opportunity by observing whether certain groups achieve admissions, jobs, and promotions in proportion to their numbers in the population, and it allows for preferential or compensatory treatment to overcome the results of past discrimination.

The constitutional question posed by affirmative-action programs is whether they discriminate against whites in violation of the equal-protection clause of the Fourteenth Amendment. Clearly, this is a question for the Supreme Court to resolve, but unfortunately the Court has failed to develop a clear-cut answer.

Higher Education

One of the most celebrated cases of reverse discrimination occurred in California. In *Regents of the University of California* v. *Bakke* (1978), the

Supreme Court struck down a special admissions program for minorities at a state medical school on the ground that it excluded a white applicant because of his race, violating his rights under the equal-protection clause.[13] Allan Bakke applied to the University of California at Davis for two consecutive years and was rejected; in both years black applicants with significantly lower grade-point averages and scores on medical aptitude tests were accepted through a special admissions program that reserved sixteen minority places in a class of one hundred.

Jobs

However, in *United Steelworkers of America* v. *Weber* (1979), the Supreme Court approved a plan developed by a private employer and a union to reserve 50 percent of higher-paying, skilled jobs for minorities.[14] Under federal government pressure, Kaiser Aluminum Corporation and the United Steelworkers union had established a program to get more blacks into skilled technical jobs. Only 2 percent of the skilled jobs in the plant where Weber, a white man, worked were held by blacks, whereas 39 percent of the local work force was black. When Weber was excluded from the training program and blacks with less seniority and fewer qualifications were accepted, he filed suit in federal court, contending that he had been discriminated against because of his race in violation of Title VII of the Civil Rights Act of 1964. (Weber could not contend that his rights under the Fourteenth Amendment's equal-protection clause had been violated, because this clause applies only to governmental discrimination.) Title VII prevents *all* discrimination in employment on the basis of race; it does not specify discrimination against blacks or other minorities.

The Supreme Court held that Title VII "left employers and unions in the private sector free to take such race-conscious steps to eliminate manifest racial imbalance in traditionally segregated job categories. We hold that Title VII does not prohibit such . . . affirmative action plans." Weber's reliance on the clear language of Title VII was held to be "misplaced." According to the Court, it would be "ironic indeed" if the Civil Rights Act were used to prohibit "all voluntary private race-conscious efforts to end traditional patterns" of discrimination.

The Civil Rights Act of 1991

In 1989 the Supreme Court, in *Wards Cove Packing Company* v. *Antonio*, denied relief to low-paid Asian-American employees of an Alaska cannery who contended that they had been the victims of racial discrimination in the workplace. The Court said that the burden of proof in such lawsuits was on the plaintiff to show actual discrimination, as opposed to showing merely that certain employment practices had a disparate impact upon racial minorities or women.

Since then, a congressional effort to overturn this and several comparable decisions has been a high priority for civil rights interest groups. In 1990, Congress passed legislation that would return the burden of proof to the employer, using the "business necessity" standard of the 1971 case *Griggs* v. *Duke Power*, in which the Court ruled that employers were required to prove that discriminatory personnel policies and practices were required by business necessity. Even though he agreed with the *Griggs* criteria, President Bush vetoed the bill, alleging it to be a "quota bill."

Bush decided that his strategy was flawed after the divisive hearings on Clarence Thomas's nomination to the Supreme Court and David Duke's success in the October 19 primary election in Louisiana. Anita Hill's sexual harassment allegations put the issue of employment discrimination at the top of the media's agenda, raising the political cost that Bush would risk if he appeared insensitive. David Duke, an ex-Klansman and candidate for governor of Louisiana, ran strongly among white voters and created the impression that opposition to affirmative action was a racist position. Bush had to distance himself from Duke. Thus, he dropped his objections to the legislation, and, in 1991, another civil rights act was on the books.

In addition to incorporating the "business necessity" language of *Griggs* (with the definition of this ambiguous phrase left to the courts), the 1991 Civil Rights Act prohibits "race norming," or adjusting test scores to boost the rankings of minorities; establishes a damages cap for intentional bias; and creates a commission to investigate the "glass ceiling" that prevents women and minorities from rising to the top positions in corporations. The upshot is, as is typically true, a mixed bag. By abolishing race norming, the legislature eliminated one of the most criticized developments in race policy. And, of course, creating a commission is a time-honored method of delay.

ELITE VERSUS MASS RESPONSE TO CIVIL RIGHTS

Progress in civil rights policy—from *Brown* v. *Board of Education of Topeka*, through the Civil Rights Act of 1964, to affirmative action programs today—has been a response of a national *elite* to conditions affecting a minority of Americans. Advances in civil rights have *not* come about because of demands by the white majority of citizens. On the contrary, the civil rights policies of the national elite have met with varying degrees of resistance from white masses in states and communities.

Mass Opinion About Discrimination

The attitudes of white masses toward blacks in the United States are ambivalent. Today most whites believe that blacks face very little discrim-

TABLE 15-2 White and black attitudes toward discrimination

	Percentage agreeing	
	Whites	Blacks
Do you feel that, compared to whites, blacks . . .		
get equal pay for equal work?	72	31
are treated equally by the justice system?	51	17
On the average blacks have worse jobs, income, and housing than white people. Do you think these differences are . . .		
because most blacks have less inborn ability to learn?	21	16
because most blacks do not have the motivation or willpower to pull themselves out of poverty?	62	36
because most blacks don't have the education that it takes to rise out of poverty?	52	68
Most people agree that on the average, blacks have worse jobs, income, and housing than whites. Do you think the differences are . . .		
mainly due to discrimination?	7	70

SOURCE: Derived from data reported in *The American Enterprise* (January/February 1990): 96–103.

ination in jobs, housing, or education and that any differences between whites and blacks in society is a result of blacks' lack of motivation (see Table 15-2). Blacks disagree. Most blacks believe that they are not treated equally in employment, housing, or education and that differences between blacks and whites in standards of living are "mainly due to discrimination." Whites constitute a large majority of the nation's population—more than 87 percent. If public policy reflected the views of this majority, there would be very little civil rights legislation.

Mass Opinion About Affirmative Action

Affirmative action is more popular among elites than masses. Overall, the American public opposes preferences in hiring and promotion, even when asked to consider "past discrimination." Opinion surveys about affirmative action are most commonly worded to ask respondents whether they agree that minorities (or women) should be accorded preferential treatment to make up for past discrimination (see Table 15-3). The results of

TABLE 15-3 Opinions about affirmative action

Question: "Some people say that because of past discrimination, blacks should be given preference in hiring and promotion. Others say that such preference in hiring and promotion is wrong because it discriminates against whites. What about your opinion—are you for or against preferential hiring and promotion of blacks?"

	Total	Whites	Blacks
For	19%	12%	51%
Against	75	79	36
Don't know/Refuse to answer	6	9	13

SOURCE: General Social Survey, 1991.

such surveys show that while whites generally oppose affirmative action, blacks are divided in their opinion. Moreover, without the "past discrimination" qualifying phrase, two-thirds of blacks and about 90 percent of whites oppose affirmative action.

According to one study:

> Americans' response to pollsters' questions leave little doubt that they believe that equality of access and opportunity rather than of condition or result should be the defining principle of our commitment to egalitarianism. . . . They disapprove of making race or ethnicity a legitimate or predominant ground for awarding jobs, social benefits, or opportunities.[15]

Affirmative action is one of the rare public policies on civil rights that a substantial minority of whites believe has personally disrupted their lives. Ten percent claim to have lost a job opportunity or educational opportunity because of reverse discrimination.[16]

JESSE JACKSON: CHANNELING PROTEST

JESSE: From charity to parity—our time has come. From aid to trade, from welfare to our share, from slaveship to championship—our time has come. From outhouse to White House—our time has come.
CHORUS: Run, Jesse, Run!

Jesse Jackson, so fluent in rhyme and alliteration, inspired millions of black voters in 1984 and 1988. Jackson was not the first black to run for president. That distinction belongs to Representative Shirley Chisholm of New York, who ran for the Democratic nomination in 1972. But Jackson demonstrated conclusively that a black man could be a serious contender for the presidency. His vision was a Rainbow Coalition of "the desperate, the damned, the disinherited, the disrespected, and the despised," but the rainbow never had many colors in it except black.

In two presidential elections Jackson captured the aspirations for power and self-determination of millions of blacks from the rural South to the northern urban ghettoes. He pushed himself into national black leadership, stepping over the more experienced black politicians—Andrew Young of Atlanta, Tom Bradley of Los Angeles, Wilson Goode of Philadelphia. But these leaders were eventually swept along by the feelings of racial pride that Jackson's campaigns unleashed.

Initially Jackson's politics were *not* the coalition politics of established black leaders. He alienated Jews and white civil libertarians with his embrace of Yasir Arafat and the Palestine Liberation Organization; his reference to Jews as "hymies" did not help him, even though he publicly apologized for the slip. The Black Muslim Louis Farrakhan and his paramilitary bodyguards provided security for Jackson throughout his

INTRODUCING THE HOT NEW RAPPER...

VICE-P

DON'T BE DISSIN' SISTER...
I WANNA BE VEEP MISTER...
GROVEL LIKE MIKE IN '88...
OR PEROT WILL BE MY RUNNING MATE...

JESSE FOR VP

THE OREGONIAN ©1992 BY TRIBUNE

Reprinted by permission: Tribune Media Services

first campaign. His proposals to dismantle the U.S. military and his visits to Fidel Castro placed him to the political left of most black leaders.

In 1984 Jackson won 18.2 percent of all the votes cast in Democratic primary elections; in 1988 he expanded his political base to 29.3 percent of all Democratic primary votes and finished second to the Democratic nominee, Michael Dukakis. Jackson's rhetoric in the primary elections was extreme, but in Democratic primaries one must be extreme.

However, in spite of his successes, Jackson's claim to leadership has not gone uncontested.

> Black leadership . . . is fractured. Those representing the Old Guard blame lingering racism and cramped economic opportunities. They see affirmative action, job training and expanded federal programs as the way out. . . . Disputing these views is a new breed of bootstrap conservatives, including some blacks, who say that race is no longer the crucial factor. . . . [Black] *Washington Post* columnist William Raspberry wrote . . . about the rise of the black middle class and warned its members that a new message was needed for

those left behind: "It would help enormously if the well-off would let the poor—especially the children—in on their vital secret: you can make it if you try."[17]

The new, more conservative black leaders think pragmatically; they move with ease among whites and do not feel hostility toward their white colleagues in the corridors of power. They are attracted to technological solutions to problems and are not repelled when the implications seem "racist." For example, they concede that black family instability must be overcome before poverty is reduced, a position that would have been unthinkable for black leaders a decade ago. Jackson too may make such points, but his rhetoric is still one of confrontation. Like many "first-generation" black leaders, Jackson's path to activism was through the church and he, like King, projects a religious fervor. But "second-generation" black leaders find the mixture of religious passion and political solutions distasteful:

> The new black officeholder's greatest problem with Jackson is one of style. Jackson continues to relish his role as a political outsider, as someone who wants to rattle the system. He speaks with passion and radiates a religious zeal. The New Breed speaks a more technocratic language and believes it is important to work within the system.[18]

THE FEMINIST MOVEMENTS

In recent years increasing numbers of women have come to view themselves as a distinct group facing economic and social discrimination similar to that suffered by blacks.

The Beginning of Modern Feminism

Early feminists sprang from the abolitionist movement; similarly, modern feminists found their voice initially through participation in the civil rights movement. As the movement reached its zenith in the late 1960s, active women had come to see the desirability of political activity and the necessity for cohesive organization. As Jo Freeman, a women's movement analyst, explains,

> The civil rights movement provided the training for many another movement's organizers, including the young women of the women's liberation movement. It would appear that the art of "constructing" a social movement requires considerable skill and experience. Even in supposedly spontaneous social movements, the professional is more valuable than the amateur.[19]

As with all other social movements, participants in the feminist movement are, as Freeman concludes, "white, middle class, and college educated."

Reprinted with special permission of King Features Syndicate

In Search of Group Identity

Are women a "group"? That is, are their attitudes, behaviors, and problems unique to them as women? Obviously, in a categoric sense, women are a group. But do they behave as an interest group?

Group self-awareness.   At the elite level, the feminist movement generally appears to make its demands as if it accurately represented the views of all women. However, since women are so diverse in background and ideology, conservative women's organizations have found it easy to challenge this claim. One valuable resource in the political process is the ability of an interest group to portray itself as representative of a broad constituency; the larger the potential clientele of the group, the more difficult this stance becomes. Just as "workers," "men," or "consumers" have few attitudes in common, few attitudes are common to all women. As a group, women do not live in ghettos as many blacks do. Women are rich, poor, black, white, Republican, Democratic, northern, southern, and so forth. Like men, they are too diverse to categorize. Thus while the feminist movement is analogous to the black movement in its style of leadership recruitment, analogies do not hold when we talk of group consciousness.

Spectrum of attitudes.   Women do not display much cohesion in their political attitudes. Majorities of both women and men oppose busing to achieve racial equality. Majorities of both women and men favor the death penalty. On the other hand, women seem to be more opposed to the use of force. Women more consistently oppose war, regardless of their attitude toward women's equality; all women are also less likely than men to regard force as a legitimate method of handling urban unrest.[20] Nevertheless, over the broad array of issues that come and go during the political lives of men and women, differences between the sexes are few.

Women and Work

Employed women and housewives* differ in their attitudes toward sexual equality. The experience of work seems to be more of a catalyst toward feminist thinking. A clear majority of working women cite economic necessity rather than intrinsic satisfaction as their reason to work.[21] However, once women enter the economic world, they find equality a more important goal than do housewives.[22]

The influence of work upon attitudes is more important for an understanding of women than for an understanding of men. Men have been assumed to derive more life satisfaction from work; women, until the new feminism, from the home. Men are said to be "married to their jobs." Since women were presumed to be more closely linked to the home, the source of their varied acceptance of feminist ideology is their experience at work or in the home: "For women, the source of false consciousness is not the economic system, but the family. The centrality of the family to the lives of both men and women lends credence to the notion that the family operates to the disadvantage of women."[23] Support for feminist ideology is *always* greater among employed women than housewives. Since 1972, between 38 and 47 percent of employed women have been strong feminists, compared with about half that many among housewives. The reluctance of housewives to accept feminism was clearly understood by Betty Friedan, who believed that "momism" (the societal acceptance of the fundamental role of women as mothers) was the enemy of feminism.[24] According to feminist author Gayle Yates, Friedan's message was that women were made into infants, "doing work that can be accomplished by an eight year old." Work should be the "central means by which women find a full new identity for themselves."[25]

If work helps to liberate women, education works doubly well. College-educated, employed women are the most committed to feminism. Two-thirds of them are strong feminists, compared with only 19 percent of less highly educated housewives. Thus the women's movement is similar to all other social movements in that its most supportive clientele is from the upper classes.

*The U.S. Census Bureau defines "working [employed] women" as women who are employed outside the home, "housewives" as women who, regardless of marital status, work solely in the home. This text uses the same convention in categorizing women.

SOCIAL CLASS AND FEMINIST IDEOLOGY

The distinguished anthropologist Margaret Mead "infuriated some feminists" when she described women's liberation as "essentially a middle class movement" spurred by "career drive." Similarly, political scientist Cynthia Epstein alleged that the National Organization for Women (NOW) suffers a "stigma" because its membership draws disproportionately from "college students or graduates, under 30, single, interested in professional careers, and to the political left."[26]

Unsympathetic masses. The inability of the women's movement to attract lower-class recruits reflects not only the lower political participation of such classes in general but also the more conservative views of the lower classes toward changing familial and social relationships. In a similar vein, the relative absence of black women from the feminist movement probably reflects their lower socioeconomic status as well as the reluctance of blacks (both female and male) to associate with a white-dominated movement for fear of being co-opted. Black women approve of feminist goals more than white working-class women do but consider racial discrimination a more serious problem.

Feminists and antifeminists. Politically active *antifeminist* groups also draw from the higher social strata. Women who actively oppose the Equal Rights Amendment largely come from the middle and upper-middle classes and from the ranks of college graduates. However, unlike feminist leaders, more than 70 percent of antifeminist nonworking leaders are housewives.[27] Thus both feminist and antifeminist movements draw disproportionately from the upper social strata; not surprisingly, political scientist Janet Boles found that activists on both sides of the ERA controversy were from the upper-middle classes.[28] As we know, the feminist movement is hardly unique in its class bias. It attracts women who are professionally oriented, highly educated, and consequently more likely to be victims of job discrimination. The antifeminist ideology appeals more to those who draw satisfaction from the traditional family.

The ideologies of the two groups of women are quite distinct. Feminists are more liberal in their social and political ideology and are more strongly Democratic in partisan affiliation. Although one cannot speak of women as a political group, one can speak of clear differences in feminists' and antifeminists' ideologies. Women are not a group, but we can identify groups of women.

Economic Status of Women

Evidence of economic discrimination against women is manifest, yet economic gains for women have been more dramatic than those enjoyed by blacks (see Table 15-4). To some extent, the continued inequality between the incomes of men and women reflects the difficulty women have in

TABLE 15-4 Median income of women as a percentage of male median income

1972	59%
1978	59%
1983	62%
1985	67%
1986	68%
1987	70%

SOURCES: U.S. Department of Labor; U.S. Department of Commerce, Bureau of the Census.

entering high-income occupations; they must settle for more drudgery and less money. Some occupations (nursing and secretarial work) are almost exclusively female; others, especially the highly paid, "hard," applied sciences (mechanical engineering) are predominately male. However, *within* occupational categories, economic discrimination is also evident. The starting salaries of women and men—assuming they are not self-employed—are virtually equal and, in some cases, show a slight bias in favor of women. The question is whether or not they can maintain parity throughout their careers, a question for which the answer is not yet available since the entry of women into male bastions is so recent. It is instructive to learn that strong majorities of working women believe they have an equal chance in earning salary increases, increased responsibility, and promotion. However, women do *not* believe they have an equal opportunity to become executives; men largely agree with this assessment.[29]

The enhanced position of women in the job market is mirrored by their entry into higher education. Since 1980, women have constituted a slight majority of the total population of entering freshmen. And educated women have made gains in male-dominated prestigious occupational fields (see Table 15-5).

The number of working women has been rising steadily since 1947 and has accelerated since 1976. Of all adult women, 57 percent are employed outside of the home, and greater increases are anticipated for younger women with high educational attainment. The percentage of employed mothers has also grown substantially. The share of all families with children in which the woman is employed is now 58 percent, and about half of the mothers of preschool children are employed outside the home.

However, women face obstacles not encountered by men. Women who work are still likely to do more housework than men (see Table 15-6). Women are still expected to follow their husbands wherever their jobs take them. Working outside the home *is* a tough decision, and some women who have made this decision later revoke it. Studying a group of women who became adults in the 1970s, sociologist Kathleen Gerson describes two types of women: domestic and nondomestic. Women who had foregone the traditional mother role typically experienced "a high degree of insta-

TABLE 15-5 Women as a percentage of all workers in selected occupations, 1975 and 1988

Occupation	Women as a percentage of total employed	
	1975	*1988*
Airplane pilot, navigator	—	3.1
Architect	4.3	14.6
Auto mechanic	0.5	0.7
Bartender	35.2	49.6
Bus driver	37.7	48.5
Cab driver, chauffeur	8.7	12.5
Carpenter	0.6	1.5
Child care worker	93.8	97.3
Computer programmer	25.6	32.2
Computer systems analyst	14.8	29.5
Data entry keyer	92.8	88.2
Data processing equipment repairer	1.8	8.8
Dental assistant	100.0	98.7
Dentist	1.8	9.3
Economist	13.1	35.3
Editor, reporter	44.6	51.1
Elementary school teacher	85.4	84.8
College/university teacher	31.1	38.5
Firefighter	—	2.1
Garage, gas station attendant	4.7	6.2
Lawyer, judge	7.1	19.5
Librarian	81.1	85.4
Mail carrier	8.7	22.0
Office machine repairer	1.7	6.4
Physician	13.0	20.0
Police officer	2.7	13.4
Registered nurse	97.0	94.6
Secretary	99.1	99.1
Social worker	60.8	66.0
Telephone installer, repairer	4.8	12.1
Telephone operator	93.3	89.8
Waiter/waitress	91.1	82.6
Welder	4.4	4.9

SOURCE: U.S. Bureau of Labor Statistics, January 1976, Table 2 and January 1989, Table 22.

bility in their relationships with men," whereas those who chose the traditional family had "established stable commitments in which male careers took precedence."[30] Other factors, such as a disappointing work experience, are more important in driving women toward domesticity than are the male-dominated institutions that figure prominently in feminist theory. Since there are abundant examples of both domestic and nondomestic women (the entry of women into the job market is slowing, and some women have left the market for the traditional "homemaker" role), Gerson's conclusions tell us much about the continued lack of cohesion among women:

> Those who developed non-domestic orientations sought to restructure the sexual division of labor at home and at work and also to redefine traditional ideologies of child rearing. They met opposition from domestically oriented

TABLE 15-6   Who's doing the housework?

Mothers are doing less housework than they once did while fathers are doing more.
(Time men and women aged 18 to 65 spent doing household tasks, by presence and age of children, in hours per week, 1965–1985)

	Men			Women			Percentage done by women*		
	1985	1975	1965	1985	1975	1965	1985	1975	1965
NO CHILDREN									
Female tasks	4.4	2.4	2.6	14.5	17.3	18.7	77	88	88
Cooking	2.3	1.5	1.4	6.4	7.4	6.4	74	83	82
Cleaning**	2.1	0.9	1.2	8.1	9.9	12.3	79	92	91
Male/shared tasks	6.0	4.7	2.1	3.4	3.0	2.6	36	39	55
Total	10.4	7.1	4.7	17.9	20.3	21.3	63	74	82
ALL CHILDREN AGED 5 AND OLDER									
Female tasks	3.9	2.2	2.0	16.6	22.0	27.0	81	91	93
Cooking	1.9	1.1	0.9	7.1	8.9	9.6	79	89	91
Cleaning**	2.0	1.1	1.1	9.5	13.1	17.4	83	92	94
Male/shared tasks	6.5	5.4	3.3	3.3	1.9	3.3	34	26	50
Total	10.4	7.6	5.3	19.9	23.9	30.3	66	76	85
CHILDREN UNDER AGE 5									
Female tasks	3.5	2.4	1.6	20.0	22.3	29.2	85	90	95
Cooking	1.4	1.2	0.8	8.4	8.9	9.9	86	88	92
Cleaning**	2.1	1.2	0.8	11.6	13.4	19.3	85	92	96
Male/shared tasks	5.5	3.5	2.3	2.5	2.8	2.8	31	44	55
Total	9.0	5.9	3.9	22.5	25.1	32.0	71	82	90

*Assuming equal numbers and backgrounds of men and women; percentages, subtotals, and totals may vary due to rounding.
**Cleaning includes meal clean-up, housecleaning, laundry, and ironing.
SOURCES: 1985: Americans' Use of Time Project, Survey Research Center, University of Maryland; 1965, 1975: Americans' Use of Time Project, Survey Research Center, University of Michigan.

women who found it in their interest to preserve traditional arrangements and beliefs. The study found emerging divisions among women that promise to add to the social turmoil generated by women's changing position.[31]

Like all other groups that strive to build consensus among disparate elements (such as consumers, businessmen, and the working class), the size of the potential clientele for women's movements, while it creates the raw material of political power, also creates the discord that diminishes political power.

One problem that groups seeking to represent women have is that women have made substantial progress. Unlike blacks, whose economic situation relative to that of whites has failed to improve, women can point to consistent progress. As a ratio of men's wages, women's wages have crept up slowly but inexorably to 70 percent in 1988, up from 60 percent in 1960.[32] This improvement reflects changes in time use: women now spend about twenty-six hours a week in economic activity, up from nineteen hours in 1965. During the same period, men's weekly hours in economic activity declined from forty-eight to forty-one. Time spent by women in child care decreased from six to two hours per week.[33] As Sylvia Nasah concludes:

> You've heard it often: The 1980's were the backlash years, when Ronald Reagan and George Bush trashed affirmative action, feminism went out of fashion and the news media convinced women that they couldn't have it all. The implication is that women's economic progress stalled.
>
> Widely accepted though it may be, that last assumption is mostly wrong. A fresh body of research—mostly by a new generation of female economists who've mined a mountain of unexplored data—shows compellingly that women were big economic winners in the 1980's expansion and that their gains are likely to keep coming in the 1990's regardless of who is in the White House.
>
> From the top of the pay scale to the bottom, from stock traders earning six-figure bonuses to $5-an-hour sales clerks, women gained on men in the 1980's. While the median annual salary for men slid 8 percent after inflation between 1979 and 1990, to $28,843 from $31,315, the comparable salary for women rose 10 percent, to $20,656 from $18,683.
>
> The most basic measure of women's status in the work force—the number of cents women earn for each dollar of men's earnings—rose to a record 72 cents in 1990. Conventional wisdom . . . has it that women made no progress in the past decade. In fact, women were stuck earning around 60 cents to the men's dollar from 1960 through 1980, but started catching up fast as the economy expanded in the 1980's.[34]*

In other words, there is no readily apparent political "enemy" to castigate. With continued progress, the feminist movement, like other social movements, is becoming part of the "establishment."

—— SEXUAL HARASSMENT

The hearings on Clarence Thomas's nomination to the Supreme Court brought unprecedented levels of media scrutiny to the issue of sexual harassment in the work place. Corporations, with considerable justification, feared that the sensational hearings, replete with graphic language, would inspire a multitude of sexual harassment lawsuits.

Sexual harassment is an emerging issue. In 1980, the Equal Employment Opportunity Commission published guidelines on two types of sexual harassment: "quid pro quo" (sex for a job, a promotion, or a salary increase) and "hostile environment." Liability for quid pro quo harassment generates little controversy, but the hostile environment criterion is more contentious. In the internal guidelines of corporations and other organizations, a "hostile environment" has been regarded as covering suggestive jokes, lustful glances, the display of provocative photographs

*Source: *New York Times,* October 18, 1992, p. B–1. Copyright © 1992 by The New York Times Company. Reprinted by permission.

of women, or any other behavior or condition that might be viewed as offensive. But how can employers know what is sexually offensive?

Courts have traditionally used a standard of reasonableness to evaluate legal liability: for example, how would a "reasonable person" react to nude photographs? However, adding to the confusion in the context of sexual harassment is the courts' interest in using the "reasonable woman" standard to assess harassment. By relying on the reasonable woman standard, courts are asserting that there are major differences in the ways men and women respond to sexual advances. Human resource professionals (consulting firms that once specialized in labor relations) are reaping a financial harvest from these confusing issues, as are lawyers.

—— SUMMARY

Elite theory helps us to understand the development of protest movements and organizations, their accommodation by governing elites, and their eventual moderation and incorporation into the elite structure. Elites modify public policy to defuse protest movements; they grant symbolic victories and elite status to protest leaders in exchange for the moderation of their demands and their support for the system. Masses frequently resist even these accommodationist policies. Progress in civil rights is an elite response to minority appeals, not to mass demands.

1. The first governmental institution to act for equality of opportunity for blacks in the twentieth century was the Supreme Court. The Court, structurally the furthest removed from the influence of white masses, was the first to apply liberal public-regarding policies to blacks. Elected elites who are more accessible to white masses were slower to act on black rights than were appointed elites.

2. Elected white elites did not respond to black requests until faced with a prolonged campaign of nonviolent civil disobedience, public demonstrations, and creative disorder and crises. Generally elites have responded by making modest changes in the system in order to maintain stability. Often these changes are only symbolic.

3. Elimination of legal discrimination and guaranteed equality of opportunity have largely resulted from the efforts of black middle-class groups who share a dominant elite consensus and who appeal to the conscience of white elites to extend that consensus to include blacks.

4. Elites have not responded to demands that go beyond accepted elite consensus; for example, demands for absolute equality that have replaced demands for equality of opportunity. New mass-oriented black counter-elites have emerged to contend with established middle-class black elites. Middle-class black elites have relatively little influence with the masses

in the ghettos. Mass counterelites have less respect for the rules of the game than do either white elites or established middle-class black leaders.

5. Protest movements have a spillover effect; they ripple from group to group. Groups only recently beginning to protest, such as women, have not developed the group consciousness of more severely repressed groups.

6. Leaders of the women's movement are professional, educated, upper-middle-class women, whose views are not universally shared by the masses of women in the United States. Yet it is difficult to mobilize masses of women on behalf of feminist goals. The economic status of women has been consistently improving while that of blacks has not.

———— NOTES

1. John D. McCarthy and Mayer N. Zald, "Resource Mobilization and Social Movements: A Partial Theory," *American Journal of Sociology* 82 (1977): 1212–1238. See also Steven E. Barkan, "Strategic, Tactical, and Organizational Dilemmas of the Protest Movement against Nuclear Power," *Social Problems* 72 (October 1979): 19–37.
2. Michael Lipsky, *Protest in City Politics* (Chicago: Rand McNally, 1970).
3. See Piven and Cloward, op. cit., on accommodation and repression.
4. Ibid., p. 5.
5. Anthony Oberschall, *Social Conflict and Social Movements* (Englewood Cliffs, N.J.: Prentice-Hall, 1973), p. 155.
6. Gunnar Myrdal, *An American Dilemma* (New York: McGraw-Hill, 1964), vol. I, p. xxi.
7. *Plessy* v. *Ferguson,* 163 U.S. 537 (1896).
8. Allen D. Grimshaw, "Lawlessness and Violence in America and Their Special Manifestations in Changing Negro-White Relationships," *Journal of Negro History* 44 (January 1959): 67.
9. Myrdal, op. cit., vol. II, p. 749.
10. *Brown* v. *Board of Education of Topeka,* 347 U.S. 483 (1954).
11. Kenneth B. Clark, "The Civil Rights Movement: Momentum and Organization," in Talcott Parsons and Kenneth B. Clark, eds., *The Negro American* (Boston: Beacon Press, 1966), p. 610.
12. Crane Brinton, *The Anatomy of Revolution* (New York: Vintage Books, 1965), pp. 100–105.
13. *Regents of the University of California* v. *Bakke,* 438 U.S. 265 (1978).
14. *United Steelworkers of America* v. *Weber,* 443 U.S. 193 (1979).
15. John H. Bunzel, "Affirmative Reactions," *Public Opinion* (February/March 1986): 49.
16. William R. Beer, "Resolute Ignorance: Social Science and Affirmative Action," *Society* (May/June 1987): 66.

17. Quoted in *U.S. News & World Report* (March 17, 1986): 18.
18. Stuart Rothenberg, "The Second Generation of Black Leaders," *Public Opinion* (July/August 1987): 43, 60.
19. Jo Freeman, *The Politics of Women's Liberation* (New York: McKay, 1975), p. 70.
20. Sidney Verba and Norman H. Nie, *Participation in America* (New York: Harper & Row, 1972); Gerald Pomper, *Voters' Choice* (New York: Harper & Row, 1975), p. 88.
21. *Public Opinion*, January/February 1979, p. 38.
22. Harmon Zeigler and Keith Poole, "Political Woman, Gender Indifference," *Public Opinion*, August/September 1985, pp. 54–55.
23. Harmon Zeigler and Keith Poole, *Women, Public Opinion, and Politics* (New York: Longman, 1985), p. 26.
24. Betty Friedan, *The Feminine Mystique* (New York: Dell, 1963).
25. Gayle Graham Yates, *What Women Want* (Cambridge, Mass.: Harvard University Press, 1975), p. 39.
26. Cynthia Epstein, *Woman's Place* (Berkeley: University of California Press, 1970), pp. 39–40.
27. David W. Brady and Kent L. Tedin, "Ladies in Pink: Religion and Political Ideology in the Anti-ERA Movement," *Social Science Quarterly* 56 (March 1976): 570.
28. Janet Boles, *The Politics of the Equal Rights Amendment* (New York: Longman, 1979), ch. 3.
29. Shirley Wilkins and Thomas A. W. Milner, "Working Women: How It's Working Out," *Public Opinion*, October/November 1985, p. 46. The authors reason that male pessimism is a consequence of men becoming more aware of the problems of employed women.
30. Kathleen Gerson, *Hard Choices* (Berkeley: University of California Press, 1985), pp. 115–116.
31. Ibid., pp. 216–217.
32. Sarah E. Rix, ed., *The American Woman*, 1990–1991 (New York: W. W. Norton, 1990), pp. 390–391.
33. *The World's Women, 1970–1990: Trends and Statistics* (New York: United Nations, 1991), p. 101.
34. Sylvia Nasah, "Women's Progress Stalled? Just Not So," *New York Times*, October 18, 1992, p. B–1.

—— SELECTED READINGS

Barkan, Steven G. "Strategic, Tactical, and Organizational Dilemmas of the Protest Movement against Nuclear Power." *Social Problems* 27 (1979): 19–37. The author discusses the single-issue focus and civil disobedience tactics of protest organizations.
Baxter, Sandra, and Lansing, Marjorie. *Women in Politics.* Ann Arbor: University of Michigan Press, 1980. This study of women's beliefs

about politics, candidates, and parties is especially helpful because of its comparative analyses.

Carden, Maren L. *The New Feminist Movement*. New York: Russell Sage, 1974. This book offers an impressionistic but informed account of the goals and membership of various kinds of women's organizations.

Clark, Kenneth B. *Dark Ghetto: Dilemmas of Social Power*. New York: Harper & Row, Harper Torchbook, 1967. Clark offers a particularly incisive analysis of the life of American blacks in urban ghetto areas and of the pathologies this life produces.

Deckard, Barbara S. *The Women's Movement*, 3rd ed. New York: Harper & Row, 1983. The authoritative study of the women's movement, its organizations, and its aims.

Gamson, William A. *The Strategy of Social Protest*. Homewood, Ill.: Dorsey Press, 1975. This is an analysis of why some protest groups lose, others become "insiders," and yet others never appear, discouraged by the incremental nature of political change.

Hewlett, Sylvia Ann. *A Lesser Life*. New York: William Morrow, 1986. Hewlett proposes that things are not getting better but worse, and she discusses what women can do about it.

Kirkpatrick, Jeane. *Political Women*. New York: Basic Books, 1978. This book explores the conditions leading to women's seeking political office.

Kirp, David L., Yudof, Mark G., and Strong Franks, Marlene. *Gender Justice*. Chicago: University of Chicago Press, 1986. Unlikely to satisfy either the left or the right, this book nevertheless proposes some *possible* solutions to the problem of inequality.

Klein, Ethel. *Gender Politics*. Cambridge: Harvard University Press, 1985. Klein believes that women are becoming more cohesive politically.

McCourt, Kathleen. *Working Class Women and Grass-Roots Politics*. Bloomington: Indiana University Press, 1977. This book describes what working-class women expect to gain from political participation.

Myrdal, Gunnar. *An American Dilemma*, 2nd ed. Vol. I: *The Negro in a White Nation*. Vol. II: *The Negro Social Structure*. New York: McGraw-Hill, 1964. Originally published in 1944, Myrdal's study is one of the most comprehensive analyses of the situation of blacks in the United States. It draws broadly from many disciplines.

Oberschall, Anthony. *Social Conflict and Social Movements*. Englewood Cliffs, N.J.: Prentice-Hall, 1973. Oberschall's book is the most authoritative and well-reasoned text on the subject. It provides an exhaustive history of significant social protest movements, including those in the United States.

Piven, Frances Fox, and Cloward, Richard A. *Poor People's Movements*. New York: Pantheon, 1977. The authors argue that such movements are ultimately co-opted and turned against the interests of the poor.

Sapiro, Virginia. *The Political Integration of Women.* Champaign, Ill.: University of Illinois Press, 1983. A well-reasoned analysis of panel data, with a focus on many of the factors discussed in this chapter.

Woodward, C. Vann. *The Strange Career of Jim Crow,* 3rd ed. New York: Oxford University Press, 1974. The apparently irrational behavior of the white South is explained.

Yates, Gayle Graham. *What Women Want.* Cambridge: Harvard University Press, 1975. Three different ideologies—feminist, liberationist, and androgynous—are described.

EPILOGUE:
Preserving Democratic Values in an Elitist System

Thomas R. Dye
Harmon Zeigler

Elitism is a necessary characteristic of all societies. The elitism we have described in American society is not a corruption of democratic ideas attributable to capitalism, war, the "military-industrial complex," the special interests, or any other events or people in this nation. There is no "solution" to elitism, any more than there is a cure for old age.

The question is not how to combat elitism, or empower the masses, or achieve revolution. Mass governance is neither feasible nor desirable. Rather, the question is how to encourage an enlightened elite to act decisively to preserve individual freedom, human dignity, and the values of life, liberty, and property.

WHY ELITE GOVERNANCE IS INEVITABLE

Many mass movements, both "left" and "right" in their political ideologies, have promised to bring power to "the people." Indeed, the phrase *the people* endures as one of the most compelling political symbols. But "the people" are not especially interested in politics, for good reason: "life is too short, work is too hard, and leisure too precious for the average citizen to spend more than a small fraction of his time gathering information about the people whose names confront him on the ballot each election year."[1] One way to explain elitism is that it reflects the natural division of labor between those who are interested in politics and those who are not. The overwhelming majority of people are unwilling to invest the time and energy to become more than marginal and transitory participants.

"The people" do not wish to govern; they wish to live peaceful, comfortable, fulfilling lives. The American people

> do not know much about politics and do not care that they do not know. In their preferences they sway with the political breezes. . . . They are easily influenced, easily disillusioned. But most important of all, they are—for all practical political purposes—functionally illiterate.[2]

As society grows larger, the individual is reduced in influence, power, and capacity to shape political decisions. About half the eligible population does not vote in presidential elections. We believe their abstention is rational. The phrase *rational ignorance* sums up the reasoning behind our point of view.

> The most endlessly discussed, and most extravagant of space in the press and of time in broadcasting, is politics; its meetings, conferences, party caucuses and personalities. The least discussed are the non-political activities that many more people enjoy far more: domestic interests, artistic pursuits, charitable works, fraternizing with friends or doing nothing at all—all ways of using leisure time that mystify the political people and mislead them into seeing non-political people as irresponsible, uncooperative or unpatriotic.[3]

Voters are not stupid; they are just more concerned with living their own lives than with politics. As Thomas Hobbes put it, "A plain husband-man is more Prudent in the Affaires of his own house, than is a Privy Counselor in the Affaires of other men."[4]

The sheer size of the nation and its government and corporate institutions is one of the great obstacles to popular democracy. In a large society, even assuming political equality, the individual's influence on societal decisions is so tiny as to render participation in mass democracy fruitless. As the society grows larger, the individual shrinks in influence, power, liberty, and the capacity to shape the decisions affecting his or her life. The chance that an individual in a society of 250 million people can affect the outcome of an election or any other collective decision is infinitesimal. An individual with less than one-two-hundred-millionth of a voice in the outcome of issues cannot be personally effective, even under conditions of perfect equality. Nearly half the eligible population does not vote in presidential elections. Many who abstain surely feel that their one vote in millions cannot affect the outcome. This assumption is *rational.* Size is one obstacle to effective individual participation in politics.

Another obstacle to effective individual participation in politics is inequality—not only in wealth but also in education, knowledge, intelligence, and leadership. Many social democrats in America and Europe complain about inequalities among individuals, especially inequalities of wealth. They propose to eliminate such inequalities by taking from the rich and giving to the poor to achieve a "leveling," which they believe is essential to democracy. But the really dangerous inequalities in society are those between institutions and individuals. If the government confiscated the wealth of every centimillionaire in the United States, the total would amount to less than half of one year's sales of General Motors or Exxon and less than 8 percent of the federal government's expenditures for a single year. Even very wealthy individuals are insignificant next to the wealth and power of the giant institutions of an advanced technological society. American democracy today faces the problem of controlling these giant institutions: corporations, banks, utilities, media networks, foundations, universities, and especially government itself.

Mature students of politics must confront the iron law of oligarchy: every political organization "becomes a minority of directors and a majority of directed."[5] As each protest movement organizes and then institutionalizes, its leadership gradually becomes a self-perpetuating oligarchy. The mass membership must delegate governing responsibilities to representatives, and by so doing it creates a governing minority distinct from the masses in behavior, role, and status. This process occurs no matter what the system of accountability; delegation of authority creates a governing elite. Organization inevitably means oligarchy.

WHY MASS GOVERNANCE IS UNDESIRABLE

Great suffering has been inflicted on humanity in the name of "the people." The world has witnessed many "successful" mass movements that have overthrown social and political systems, usually at great cost in human lives, promising to empower the masses. Hitler promised to empower *das Volk* (the people); Lenin promised a "dictatorship of the proletariat" (the workers); and Mao Tse-tung promised a "people's republic." But those movements created new elite systems that were at least as "evil" as, and certainly no more democratic than, the older systems they replaced.

> Nowhere is this penchant for creating one's own reality more apparent—and more pernicious—than in the intelligentsia's conception of "the people." Radicals insist on speaking for and acting for the "people" (sometimes described as "the popular masses") against the alleged self-seeking elite in control of the state and the nation's wealth. In their view, the establishment of a just and free society requires the destruction of the status quo. But contact with the people of flesh and blood quickly reveals that few if any of them want their familiar world to be destroyed: what they desire is satisfaction of specific grievances—that is, partial reform, with everything else remaining in place. It has been observed that spontaneous rebellions are conservative rather than revolutionary, in that those involved usually clamor for the restitution of rights of which they feel they have been unjustly deprived: they look backward. In order to promote its ideal of comprehensive change, the intelligentsia must, therefore create an abstraction called "the people" to whom it can attribute its own wishes.[6]

The aftermath of these mass movements is political and economic disaster, corruption and moral decay, and great human suffering. From the former Soviet Union to Nicaragua, we now know that corruption was not a deplorable diversion from the socialist ambition; it was the essence of state power. Economies were impoverished, environments ravished, spirits broken, not to bring power to the people but to bring power to elites.

Despite a superficial commitment to the symbols of democracy, the people are not attached to the ideals of individual liberty, toleration of diversity, freedoms of expression and dissent, and equality of opportunity. On the contrary, elites are more likely to hold these values. Masses are authoritarian, intolerant, anti-intellectual, nativistic, alienated, hateful, and violent. Mass politics is extremist, unstable, and unpredictable. The masses are not committed to democratic "rules of the game"; when they take political action, they frequently go outside the rules to engage in violence. Moreover, mass politics frequently reflects the alienation and hostility of the masses by concentrating on scapegoats— whether Jews, blacks, Catholics, immigrants, students, intellectuals, or any other minority—who are in some way different from the majority of the masses.

The masses are fatally vulnerable to tyranny. Extremist movements, reflecting authoritarianism, alienation, hostility, and prejudice, are more likely to grow from the masses than from elites. Hannah Arendt writes, "A whole literature on mass behavior and mass psychology demonstrated and popularized the wisdom, so familiar to the ancients, of the affinity between democracy and dictatorship, between mob rule and tyranny."[7] The masses, feeling in themselves the power of the majority, cannot be trusted to restrain themselves in dealing with dissenting minorities. Tolerance of diversity comes only with years of socialization. Efforts to reeducate or resocialize the masses are futile. Two hundred years ago Jefferson proposed universal free public education as a curative for mass ignorance, incompetence, and alienation. Today the masses in the United States average more than twelve years of free public education, but they appear even less capable of governing wisely and humanely than did the masses of Jefferson's time.

HOW ELITES HAVE FAILED THE NATION

Elites must govern wisely if democracy is to survive. When masses turn to the politics of rage, the disorder is serious but generally short-lived. When elites fail to govern wisely, the devastation can be more formidable and more prolonged. In this edition of *The Irony of Democracy*, we have acknowledged that the nation's elites are not governing wisely. Here is the basis for this harsh assessment:

- Federal deficit spending is out of control. The federal government's debt is now over four trillion dollars—more than sixteen thousand dollars for every man, woman, and child in the United States.
- American industry is becoming less competitive internationally.
- The country's infrastructure is deteriorating.
- America's children are poorly educated.
- The gap between the rich and poor is increasing.
- The ethics of political elites are more suspect than at any time in the past half century.

America's political class has been replaced by a new set of activists with values as dangerous to democracy as those of the masses. The new activists owe allegiance only to themselves; they made their own way to the top; their expertise is in running personal, permanent campaign organizations. Their behavior in public office is unconstrained by any larger view of the public interest. Beginning with the anti–Vietnam War and civil rights movements of the late 1960s, Americans have undertaken a sustained assault on all forms of political organization, since organization equals oligarchy. The American political culture is profoundly antiorganizational. An individualistic culture opposes the imposition of organizations between individuals and government.

Today, most politicians are self-selected, and they run for office because that is what they do: they run, and run, and run. Their expertise is not in governing, but in running for office. Lacking any connection with a political party, they raise their own money, run their own campaigns, and are, in the finest American sense of the word, individual entrepreneurs. "Who sent us the political leaders we have? There is a simple answer to that question. They sent themselves."[8] In Congress, with the decline of seniority and the expansion of the influence of subcommittees, each of these entrepreneurs can establish his or her own reelection business. The idea of "the public interest" has no meaning under these conditions.

Augmenting the individualism of the new class of politicians is the media. Concurrently with the rise of primary elections, television decision makers began their inexorable surge to the inner circles of power in the United States. Media values are sensationalist, not given to serious contemplation of major problems. The most serious domestic crisis of our time is the deficit, rarely mentioned by the media. Since politicians wish, more than anything, to remain in office, they do not say things that would come off as boring on television.

The final members of the new elite structure are the political action committees and the interest groups that support them. Interest groups are not new to American politics, but their financial power has never been so great. With huge sums for campaigns now coming from political action committees, individual political entrepreneurs would be irrational not to take their money.

Once public-regarding, elites are now less so. They are shortsighted, ignoring the broader public interest in favor of their own immediate political benefit. As a result, pressing problems facing the United States are not being addressed.

The federal debt is increasing annually and now is more than 50 percent of the gross national product.   Balanced budgets are essential to the political and economic well-being of the nation. Interest payments on the debt are now approaching 20 percent of federal spending. These payments come from current taxes, and they divert money away from all other government programs. Servicing such an enormous debt is a cruel example of income transfer: The government, of necessity, transfers our tax money to banks and other investors, many of them foreign. Deficits also transfer burdens of government from the current generation to future generations. Even if the federal government could manage to balance its current budget, debt and interest payments would remain the obligations of our children and grandchildren. There are two ways to reduce the deficit: raise taxes or cut spending. The incentives to do either, or both, do not exist: spending for entitlement programs, especially Social Security and Medicare for the aged, helps re-elect incumbents, while supporting tax hikes is considered politically fatal. Since the goal of politics is reelection, it would be irrational for the present elites to cut spending or raise taxes. The result is a budget deficit that gnaws away at the U.S. economy, eroding its international competitive capacity, and lowering the nation's standard of living.[9]

American industry is becoming less competitive internationally. A dispassionate look at U.S. industrial competitiveness is hardly reassuring. Table 1 shows how *Fortune* magazine ranks the competitiveness of U.S. industries relative to those of Japan and Europe. This is not a portrait of "the richest and most powerful nation in the world," as many political leaders—especially presidents—are prone to assert. Ten years ago, computers, telecommunications equipment, pharmaceuticals, and forest products would have earned the highest mark. Ten years from now, where

TABLE 1   The competitiveness of U.S. industries

A grade of A means an industry is in a dominant position, unlikely to erode; B suggests equity with Europe and Japan; C connotes vulnerability and likely decline; D means the industry is near death.

Pharmaceuticals	A
Forest products	A
Aerospace	B+
Chemicals	B
Food	B
Scientific and photographic equipment	B
Petroleum refining	B
Telecommunications equipment	B−
Computers	C+
Motor vehicles	C
Metals	C−
Electronics	D

SOURCE: Andrew Kupfer, "How American Industry Stacks Up," *Fortune* 125 (March 9, 1992): 30.

will U.S. industry be? We are not concerned simply out of feelings of hurt pride. The decline of our industry takes money out of our economy and reduces the standard of living of the average American. U.S. industry remains focused upon short-term profits rather than long-term research and development. Nondefense research and development in the United States is about 1.8 percent of the gross national product, whereas it is 3 percent in Japan and 2.8 percent in Germany. Presumably, then, if *Fortune* returns to the same story in a decade, our competitive position will have continued to decline. Indeed, the most reliable measure of international performance—the annual growth rate of real gross domestic product per worker—suggests that we need not wait a decade. From 1982 to 1991, the United States manifested a feeble 1.1 percent annual growth rate, compared to 3.0 in Japan, 2.1 in France, and 1.6 in Germany.

The country's infrastructure is deteriorating.   Public spending on infrastructure is down from 2.3 percent of gross domestic product twenty years ago to 1.3 percent today. A drive through any major city will show what this decrease looks like. The lack of public investment in infrastructure accounts for possibly as much as half the decline in American productivity. More than half of the federal budget is devoted to individual entitlement programs, almost 20 percent to interest payments on the debt, and less than 20 percent to national defense. This leaves less than 10 percent for *all* other spending—transportation education, community development, the environment, science, and technology.

American children are poorly educated.   American schools are among the worst in the industrialized world, if the achievement of their clients— the students—is an acceptable measure. Although the United States spends more than most countries on education, it apparently wastes most of the money. Table 2 shows how American students stack up.

Asian and European children scored higher, irrespective of the wealth of the particular country: Switzerland, France, Italy, and the other wealthy European countries have better test results than does the United

TABLE 2   American students compared to students in other countries.

	Nine-year-olds	*Thirteen-year-olds*
Math	12th among 14 countries	15th among 20 countries
Science	4th among 14 countries	14th among 19 countries
Homework	8th among 14 countries	16th among 20 countries
TV watching	1st among 14 countries	3rd among 20 countries

States but so do Ireland, Hungary, and Russia. Among myriad explanations, one of the most obvious is often overlooked: American children do not work very hard. They spend about four hours a week studying, compared to nineteen in Japan and about fourteen in Europe. Poor education hurts productivity and therefore the standard of living.

The gap between the rich and poor is increasing.   The rich are getting richer and the poor are getting poorer. This explosive issue routinely attracts simplistic explanations and demagogic cures. The facts are clear: between 1979 and 1986, the income of the wealthiest 20 percent increased by 60 percent while the income of the poorest 20 percent increased by only 30 percent. Thus, in 1979 the poorest earned one-third as much as the wealthiest group, but by 1986, the poor earned only one-fourth as much. If these trends continue, the resulting extremes of wealth and poverty may lead to increased mass dissatisfaction, increased disaffection from the elites, increased interest in the simplicity of demagogic solutions, and, ultimately, to the instability of the governing regime.

The causes of growing inequality are more complex than the evil machinations of American politicians. Inequality is also increasing in Sweden, Canada, Australia, and West Germany.[10] Among the contributing causes are (1) the growth in female-headed families, (2) the exacerbation of the income gap between older and younger men (because of the size of the baby boom cohort), and (3) the rise of more affluent two-earner families *and* less affluent no-earner families. (Two-earner families reflect the rise of women's labor force participation; in the top two quintiles, 60 percent of the families have two earners; in the bottom quintile, 44 percent of the families have *no* earners.) These causes do not respond to quick fixes, to demands that "the rich" be taxed more heavily, that the Japanese be prohibited from investment or that Japanese imports be curtailed, or that public and private institutions establish affirmative action programs. Playing self-serving games of blame and division, or expanding the welfare bureaucracy by creating yet another "war on poverty," is not a substitute for addressing the structural causes of extremes of wealth and poverty.

The ethics of political elites are more suspect than at any time in the past half century.   Corruption and politics are natural allies. Politicians have always tucked away a little bit for themselves; the United States has endured major scandals throughout its history. So what, exactly, is different now? Corruption is more ubiquitous and more publicized. Before the "reforms" of the 1960s, individual members of Congress were less interesting targets because so much influence and power lay with the leadership. The late Huey Long, the southern populist leader assassinated in 1935, coined the slogan "Every man a king." Today his dream has been realized in the House of Representatives. No longer must members wait until they have earned seniority that endows them with authority; they are influential from the moment they take the oath of office. With so many subcommittees, each lavishly funded with staff resources, almost every Representative can chair *something*. About half the Democratic membership does so, up from one-third before the "reforms." Many members of Congress have had little or no previous experience in public office. So they arrive, acquire a personal staff, a substantial travel allowance, and access to the steady flow of PAC dollars. They are not apprentices; they are—especially in the eyes of their staffs—big-time power brokers. The U.S. Congress is the most lavishly funded and powerful legislative body in the world. Who would not succumb? Take the example of Scott Klug, who was a radio announcer before his 1990 election to the House of Representatives. At a briefing for new members of Congress at Harvard's Kennedy School of Government, Representative Klug, a Republican from Madison, Wisconsin, lamented that lectures on economics were "like taking exams when you're about to get married." He expressed more interest in figuring out how to spend the $475,000 allotted to him for the eighteen full-time and four part-time aides who will help him. Representative Klug adumbrated: "I do have a certain entrepreneurial spirit, and I wanted to be the captain of my own ship. . . . In a lot of ways, Congress will be fun."

The second major difference between corruption now and in the past is the role of the media and the destruction of the barrier between public and private life. Compare President John F. Kennedy and his brother, Senator Edward "Ted" Kennedy. Reporters knew about John F. Kennedy's extramarital affairs, and back-of-the-bus jokes about his sexual prowess were common fare. But the Kennedy administration remained untouched by scandal. Ted Kennedy, on the other hand, has endured published reports of having sex on the floor of a Washington restaurant and appearing before his nephew's alleged rape victim wearing only a T-shirt; he has become a national laughingstock.

WHAT ELITES SHOULD DO

The problems outlined above are serious. To address them, elites must, first of all, *regain a sense of the public interest;* they must undertake disagreeable, essential, and politically risky policies. Admittedly, there are no incentives, as the political system is now constructed, for them to do so. Electing "good people" is futile, since the incentives even for good people are to perpetuate the policies that have contributed to the American malaise. A standard phrase to describe the elite value system in bygone years was *public-regarding.* Few would use that phrase today. Yet a public-regarding elite is precisely what is required.

Public-regarding elites would reduce federal spending and raise taxes until the deficit is under control. They would confront the education establishment with its failure and require that student performance be raised and evaluated. They would divert federal money from entitlement programs, including Social Security, to infrastructure repair and construction and nondefense research and development. They would slow the trend toward extreme inequality by understanding and addressing its causes. They would conduct their personal lives impeccably. They would eliminate useless symbolism—such as passing laws against flag-burning—from their agenda.

Political scientist Joseph Nye, Jr., wrote that the United States' decline can be arrested if we simply address "such domestic issues as the budget deficit, savings rate, educational system, and condition of our cities." He is absolutely right, of course. But how to do so when there are no incentives? Political scientist Thomas Mann, recognizing the difficulty of coming to grips with such major problems, grieves that "when effective action on the country's most pressing problems requires the imposition of losses on organized interests, with benefits to all on the distant horizon, the odds of success in the U.S. political system are not very high."[11] Only an elite courageous enough to impose costs on the public could undertake this responsibility. Regrettably, a more realistic forecast of the future of U.S. politics is "a continuation of the escapism and deadlock of recent years. . . ."[12] To rebuild order means turning back the clock, eliminating the impediments to organizational durability, and re-creating a political class—an establishment.

The United States is confronting a decline in economic productivity and a consequent decline in Americans' standard of living. High deficits, a tattered infrastructure, inferior education, a growing inequality in income distribution—all either are caused by or else cause lower productivity. High productivity yields an enhanced standard of living; low productivity means a loss in the quality of life. "Productivity isn't everything, but in the long run it is almost everything. A country's ability to improve its standard of living over time depends almost entirely on its ability to raise its output per worker."[13] U.S. productivity is declining, while that of other industrial democracies is not. In the 1980s, the United States' productivity expanded at just over 1 percent annually; Japan's grew at slightly less than 3 percent, while France and Germany enjoyed productivity betterment of about 2.5 percent. Our comparatively low status today contrasts starkly with our past stature. For the first seventy years of the twentieth century, U.S. productivity advanced at a 2.8 percent rate; since 1970, however, it has averaged only an anemic 1.2 percent. Had this decline not taken place, "our living standards would be at least 25 percent higher than they are now."[14] Yet "what is truly remarkable about our times is that the political system accepts our reduced prospects with so much equanimity."[15] Surely a responsible political elite would address—not ignore—the most momentous issue of our time. To say that "it's morning in America" is not enough.

WHAT CAN STUDENTS DO?

Regardless of what students are told by high school graduation speeches about their ability to reshape the world, elites—not students—govern the nation. It will be a long while before anyone in college today occupies a position of power allowing him or her to shape American society. In the meantime, what can students really do to help preserve democratic values?

1. *Avoid being exploited or used by demagogues of the left or right.* It is wise to lower your expectations about short-term possibilities for change. Excessive idealism, coupled with impatience to change society now, leads only to bitterness and disillusionment. In the long run, these feelings may reduce rather than increase your political effectiveness. Excessive idealism can also expose you to the demagogic appeals of those politicians who exploit others' idealism for their own advantage. Understanding your personal limits in shaping the world and resolving society's problems is important. It is time to reexamine adolescent optimism about "changing the world."

2. *Develop your powers to think critically.* You will benefit from reexamining the "truths" taught in the public schools—looking beyond the slogans of democracy (and of Marxism) to the realities of power in contemporary society. Just as this book has tried to reexamine traditional teachings about American government, concerned students should also critically reexamine the economic system, the social system, the communications system, and even the accepted "truths" of the physical and biological sciences. Developing your independent powers of social and political analysis can help you resist the flood tide of popular rhetoric, the symbolic posturing of politicians, the pseudoscience of the bureaucratic social engineers. You can learn to be wary of the politician or bureaucrat who promises to solve society's problems with a stroke of the pen: to end racism, eliminate poverty, cure the sick, prevent crime, clean the air and water, provide new energy, all without imposing any new taxes or further restricting individual freedom. You will learn that society's problems have no simple solutions.

3. *Master the technological revolution rather than letting it master you.* For example, you should endeavor to learn about one or more aspects of technology in the pursuit of your education. If computers are going to direct your life, why not learn some computer technology yourself? The same applies to social institutions. If laws regulate your life, why not master some aspects of the law yourself, even as an undergraduate? If you are going to be the object of the administrative, managerial, and budgetary practices of large bureaucracies, why not learn something about these subjects, for self-defense if nothing else? If you are not majoring in any of the physical or biological sciences, why not explore some of these courses—perhaps on a pass-fail basis if your school permits it? The more

you know about today's technology, the less impressed you will be when someone tells you that certain policies are "technological requirements."

4. *Become familiar with the meaning of individual freedom and dignity throughout the ages.* Read about and understand the human quest for freedom in many times and cultures—from St. Thomas More to Aleksandr Solzhenitsyn, from Antigone to Galileo. You should also learn to view American democracy from a world perspective, comparing the personal freedoms we enjoy with those existing in other nations. It is one thing to struggle against mindless corporate and governmental bureaucracies in this country but quite another to conclude that the United States is "not worth saving"—especially when viewing the personal liberties of Americans in the context of the personal restrictions in many other nations.

5. *Maintain a healthy distrust of government and assume responsibility for your own life.* Personal freedom is most endangered when we place too much trust in government, see great idealism in its actions, and have unquestioning faith in our public leaders. Democratic values—individual dignity, freedom of speech and press, rights of dissent, personal liberty—are safer when we are suspicious of government and its power and worry about its size and complexity. Perhaps the most important danger to a free people is that they "politicize" all the problems confronting them as individuals, they blame government and "society" for the problems that beset them, and they therefore excuse themselves from personal efforts to confront these problems. If we look to government to resolve all our problems, our social dependency will increase, and we will assume less responsibility for our lives. The traditional democratic value is to encourage individuals to shape their own destinies.

NOTES

1. Alan Ehrenhalt, *The United States of Ambition: Politicians, Power, and the Pursuit of Office* (New York: Random House, 1991), p. 10.
2. Jarol B. Manheim, *All of the People All of the Time* (Armonk, N.Y.: M. E. Sharpe, 1991), p. 239.
3. Arthur Seldon, *Capitalism* (Cambridge, Mass.: Basil Blackwell, 1990), pp. 231–232.
4. Thomas Hobbes, *Leviathan* (1651; reprint, New York: Collier Books, 1963), p. 22.
5. Roberto Michels, *Political Parties: A Sociological Study of the Oligarchical Tendencies of Modern Democracies* (1915; reprint, New York: Free Press, 1962), p. 70.
6. Richard Pipes, *The Russian Revolution* (New York: Knopf, 1990), p. 131.
7. Hannah Arendt, *The Origins of Totalitarianism* (New York: Harcourt Brace, 1951), p. 309.
8. Ehrenhalt, op. cit., pp. 18–19.

9. Michael E. Porter, *The Competitive Advantage of Nations* (New York: Free Press, 1990), p. 531; Charles L. Schultz, "The Federal Budget and the Nation's Economic Health," in Henry J. Aaron, ed., *Setting the National Priorities: Policy for the Nineties* (Washington: The Brookings Institution, 1990), pp. 19–64.

10. Gordon Green, John Coder, and Paul Ryscavage, "Comparisons of Earnings Inequality for Men in the 1980s," *The Review of Income and Wealth* 38 (March 1992), pp. 1–6.

11. Thomas E. Mann, "Breaking the Political Impasse," in Henry J. Aaron, ed., *Setting the National Priorities: Policy for the Nineties* (Washington: The Brookings Institution, 1990), p. 303.

12. Ibid., p. 313. See also Terry Moe, "The Politics of Bureaucratic Structure," in John E. Chubb and Paul E. Peterson, eds., *Can the Government Govern?* (Washington: The Brookings Institution, 1989), pp. 327–328.

13. Paul Krugman, *The Age of Diminished Expectations* (Cambridge, Mass.: MIT Press, 1992), p. 8.

14. Ibid., p. 13.

15. Ibid., p. 195.

EPILOGUE:

The Irony of Ironies

W. Lance Bennett

Elite rule may or may not be inevitable. The more important question is whether some political systems do a better job than others in holding elites accountable to the public interest. Since Professors Dye and Zeigler base much of their analysis on assumptions about human nature, they end up making breathtaking generalizations that may obscure important differences among political systems. So what if elites have ruled in Nazi Germany, the former Soviet Union, and the USA? Perhaps their main point is that no system of government, including democracy, is safe in the hands of the masses of ordinary citizens, because as the authors put it: "Masses are authoritarian, anti-intellectual, nativistic, alienated, hateful, and violent. Mass politics is extremist, unstable, and unpredictable." Hence, the irony of democracy.

The irony of this irony is that elites often behave as badly, if not worse, than these masses who are not to be entrusted with their own sovereignty. Perhaps it is even more ironic that the allegedly inattentive masses of American citizens have long been aware of the decline in public responsibility on the part of their rulers. Consider, for example, the results of polls over the last four decades. The following figures represent the percentages of the public who agree that the government is run primarily for the benefit of a few big interests:[1]

Year	Percentage
1960	25%
1970	50
1980	70
1990	77

Lance Bennett teaches political science at the University of Washington and is the author of numerous books and articles on public opinion, the news media, and political communication. His recent works include *News: The Politics of Illusion* (2nd ed., Longman, 1988) and *The Governing Crisis: Media, Money and Marketing in American Elections* (St. Martin's, 1992). As a member of the Foreign Policy Studies Committee of the Social Science Research Council, he chaired the SSRC workshop series on "The Media and Foreign Policy." His current research is concerned with the factors that regulate the "marketplace of ideas" in public policy debates, with particular emphasis on the voices and viewpoints appearing in media coverage of various domestic and foreign policy issues.

In light of these trends, it is not surprising that the vast majority of citizens these days feel that public officials don't care what they think. In short, there appear to be good reasons why people are deeply worried about the health of our society and economy.

In this edition of the book, the authors admit and, to their credit, lament that elites in the United States are behaving very badly these days. Yet their analysis offers little in the way of encouragement or concrete suggestions for improving the situation. The reason is simple: Analyses based on human nature are either optimistic or pessimistic, depending on one's view of human nature. Theirs is pessimistic. When pressed to explain why the American governing class has fallen into disgrace, the authors once again point the finger of blame at the people. With the spread of direct primary elections and other democratic reforms, the argument goes, politicians have taken to pandering to the indiscriminating masses, thereby corrupting themselves and the political process. Politicians have become political entrepreneurs bent on winning elections as individuals, not on governing wisely as a group.

While I agree completely that today's elected officials are much better at winning elections than at governing, I prefer another way of explaining this problem and thinking through the solution. Instead of a pessimistic view of human nature, I prefer a neutral one that allows people to behave well or badly, depending on the kinds of institutions and social relations they create and live with. This allows us to understand how societies differ, how political relations change, why corruption occurs, and, above all, how to fix it. Although Dye and Zeigler are right about the growing list of national problems that need attention so desperately, their call for elites to regain their sense of responsibility and govern more wisely seems to me a weak remedy. I doubt that individual leaders, no matter how well intentioned they may be, can make much of a dent in the nation's problems until the institutions of government themselves are repaired. Public officials, no matter how morally correct or politically creative, cannot accomplish much when major institutions of government, such as parties and elections, have fallen apart. Rather than blame people (and, indirectly, democracy itself) for these problems, why not abandon the question of blame altogether and think about how government works, why it breaks down, and how to reform it?

It turns out that there are other democracies in the world that have stronger parties, higher levels of citizen satisfaction, and a shorter list of big national problems than we do. Surely this is not because people in other countries, whether they be elites or masses, are inherently better human beings. If there are important differences among democracies, why not look at the designs of institutions for part of the explanation? We can learn from other models about how to create stronger party systems, more active voters, more informed citizens, and healthier economies and societies. Above all, learning from other societies and institutions enables us to stop blaming ourselves as individuals for the failings of government and to figure out how, as a group, to do something positive to change it.

—— A LESS IRONIC VIEWPOINT

Irony can be interesting. By definition, it is puzzling, fascinating, and often amusing. Unfortunately, ironic ways of thinking can also leave us pessimistic about the possibilities for change and paralyzed at the thought of taking meaningful action. Perhaps it is amusing, and a bit sad, that many more Americans recognize TV's Judge Wapner than the Chief Justice of the Supreme Court of the United States. Yet this is hardly surprising, given the deliberate reach of television and the equally deliberate efforts of the Supreme Court to stay out of the limelight, to avoid controversy and public display, and to cloak its decisions in often obscure and high-minded legal language.

If we wanted to change the way people relate to the Court, we could invent a new institutional membership of the Court to the people, such as electing Supreme Court Justices! Or, if you prefer something less drastic, how about requiring the Chief Justice to explain the Court's rulings in public, perhaps on national television? Then again, you might see some negative consequences in these reforms and decide that, for all its flaws, the present arrangement is just fine. Still, there might be some small change in the way we experience our legal institutions that would make a big difference in how we think about them. Perhaps the government could provide money to public television or even the major networks to produce prime-time programs that ask important questions about abortion or civil rights and dramatize the ways in which these issues move through the legal system. Instead of *L.A. Law* and *The People's Court*, maybe people would get hooked on the real political dramas going on in society all the time. Such programming might well increase public levels of awareness, interest in legal issues, understanding of the process, and perhaps even greater recognition of Supreme Court justices. Prime-time television in Germany, Sweden, or England, for example, is more likely to broadcast such programming and, not surprisingly, people in those nations are more knowledgeable about the issues and people involved. Looking at the other side of the coin, Americans may be ignorant of the names of their public officials but they are probably more aware of their individual legal rights and, for better or worse, exercise those rights in court more than any other people on Earth. Thus, there must be features of our social life that do promote legal awareness at some level.

When we see people as responsive to the institutions and social environments in which they live, important new questions come to mind: What kind of citizenship and political relations do we want to promote in society and how do we go about doing them? Discussions such as the one above are animated by a very different conception of human nature than the one adopted by Professors Dye and Zeigler. I find it more useful to think that people are extremely malleable and capable of responding in richly different ways to different social environments. True, there always will be a few bad actors spoiling the best of surroundings and a few saints making the best of the worst conditions but, for the most part, people learn to respond to the dominant norms, morals, and social models of the environments in which they grow up and live out their lives. Those environments consist of institutions, such as schools, churches, sports teams, families, business organizations, colleges, clubs, and, yes, political parties, courts, legislatures, and bureaucracies. When those institutions fall apart or otherwise cease to be meaningful and rewarding to people, individuals are left increasingly to their own devices and must make their own ways in life, for better or worse.

The good news in this way of thinking about society and politics is that if we can figure out what went wrong with our social or political institutions and can convince enough other people that our analysis makes sense, then we can begin to change those institutions in ways that better serve society again. In the next section I present an analysis of what has changed in American government and politics to produce the "governing crisis" with which we are currently struggling and what we can do to help resolve that crisis.[2]

FROM IRONY TO INSTITUTIONS

Many of the institutions in public life are letting the people down these days. Congress, the courts, businesses, schools, legislatures, the press, and the presidency all compete for the bottom spot in public confidence ratings. Economic and social life appear to a majority of Americans to be drifting without leadership or vision. Not surprisingly, many people point to elections, the driving engine of democratic government, when they think of the central institutional breakdown that best explains why so much of the rest of society is struggling.

Viewed from almost any angle, elections are in trouble. Parties seem unable to come up with new ideas, much less act together with the discipline required to bring them to life. Candidates seem more concerned with their personal images and pleasing their financial backers than with promoting larger social agendas. Voter participation is low, citizen mistrust of politicians is high, and many of those who continue to participate feel excluded from both major parties and declare themselves independents. Many of these political independents may feel that being neutral is better than joining a party that has run out of ideas but it must be conceded that, in politics, being neutral is of very little value when it comes to deciding what must be done with society and how to do it.

These disturbing trends in elections all have their historical roots. The Democratic party's support for civil rights legislation in the 1960s drove many conservative southern Democrats into the Republican camp in presidential voting. The Republican party's corruption scandals of the 1970s kept many voters from becoming full-fledged Republicans. The reforms of Congress and the financing of the election process during the 1970s and 1980s ended up weakening party leadership. At the same time, they opened up the parties to direct influence by interest groups who were encouraged to form political action committees (PACs) to buy legalized influence from individual candidates and parties, alike. These and other important events have created an election process that is virtually worthless for getting parties to stand behind broad programs of action, much less keeping their promises to voters once members of those parties get into office. It is hardly surprising that the rest of society is drifting without guidance when the guiding mechanism of government has gone so far off course.

In place of elections as forums in which to debate great problems, work out new ideas, and lay the foundations of understanding and political support necessary for governing, we have developed a system that minimizes problems, shrinks from ideas, and encourages candidates to do whatever it takes to scare or deceive voters into supporting them. This electoral process leaves elected officials virtually incapable of governing, even if they have a clue about what to do when they arrive in office.

What exactly has gone wrong with the election process and the institutions that link it to society and government? The historical events mentioned above have created a new electoral process that, in turn, creates a government virtually incapable of dealing with society's problems. How does this new election system work? Begin with the PAC reforms in campaign financing that created a vast but unwieldy interest group constituency for candidates and elected officials—a constituency that is bound to get more attention from government than voters can.

Instead of competing with each other for broad audience approval, today's candidates compete for the support of much more specialized and seldom recognized groups: political campaign contributors. A presidential election currently costs each candidate upward of $100 million and more than twice that if we consider the uses of party and "independent" campaign funds for support of national campaigns. Although federal funding covers the majority of a candidate's immediate costs, candidates personally must raise millions of dollars in order to win the primaries and qualify for the national largesse. Competition for these staggering sums of money is stiff and the nature of this offstage maneuvering does not reward those who expand the domain of issues and policy proposals. The problem in Congress is even more damaging. Representatives must raise money all the time in order to pay for their next elections. The thousands of promises made to often microscopic special interests leave government in a gridlock, bogged down with the problems of thousands of PACs and lobbies, without much incentive for dealing with more general social concerns.

All of this results in candidates who don't have very much to offer voters in terms of broad or credible proposals appearing every two, four, or six years. At the same time, this restricted range of political ideas makes backing candidates a safer bet for big money interests. In fact, restricting the range of ideas enables many backers to hedge their bets and support opposing candidates and parties. This is, of course, a bad thing for the health of democracy but a very good thing for those who invest their money in elections.

This brings us to the second major constraint on campaigns as places to discuss new political ideas: the wholesale use of marketing techniques to generate campaign content. Marketing experts now enter into elections in a big way. Their task is to transform a product of diminished or dubious market value (a candidate or party that has become the client of special interests) into one that wins the largest market share. The result is an emphasis on communication that short-circuits logic, reason, and linguistic richness in favor of image-making techniques. This means that candidates are not sold to a broad general public but to narrow slices or "market segments" of that public. These market segments need not understand the candidate, only vote for him or her. Thus, people are induced to vote for Candidate A over Candidate B much as soap buyers may favor Brand X over Brand Y without feeling they have established a meaningful relationship with their laundry detergent in the process. This further diminishes the importance of language, logic, and reason in the articulation of campaign issues.

Since at least 1980, the Democrats have encountered a difficult problem, one that paralyzed the early Goldwater Republicans until the party solved it with the successful marketing of the "new" Richard Nixon and the even "newer" Ronald Reagan. The problem is simple: a narrow, unpalatable issue agenda that is hard to sell to the general public. The Republican secret was to turn the liability of voter avoidance into an asset by targeting key segments of the shrinking audience that continued to vote. Since votes aren't dollars, profitability isn't an issue. Only victory counts, no matter how many voters boycott the electoral process altogether. In a classic commentary on the new political age, a Republican strategist ushered in the election of 1980 with these words: *"I don't want everyone to vote. Our leverage in the election goes up as the voting population goes down."*[3]

The preceding two constraints engage a third limiting condition operating on electoral debates and meaningful communication between leaders and citizens: the highly controlled use of the news media. The press, like the voters, generally regard issues and ideas as the most important grounds for electoral choice. Idea-less elections antagonize reporters who are searching for meaningful differences between the candidates to write home about. An aroused press can be expected to assume an adversarial role, leaping on inconsistencies, making much of candidate slips and blunders, seizing upon anything inflammatory in the absence of credible policy positions. As a result, campaigns tend to isolate their candidates from the press corps and stick to a tightly controlled and carefully scripted daily schedule. This means, in media guru Roger Ailes' words, that reporters are handed a lot of visuals and attacks, while mistakes (and ideas) are held to a minimum.

By now it is well accepted that good media strategy entails three things: keeping the candidate away from the press; feeding the press a simple, telegenic political line of the day; and making sure the daily news line echoes (magnifies may be the better word) the images from campaign ads, thus blurring the distinction between commercials and "reality."[4] Candidates and their "handlers" vary in their ability to keep the press pack at bay but, when they succeed, reporters are left with little but an impoverished set of campaign slogans to report. As ABC reporter Sam Donaldson said on an election-week news-analysis program in a tone that resembled the coroner disclosing an autopsy result: "When we cover the candidates, we cover their campaigns as they outline them."[5] And so, a willing, if unhappy, press becomes a channel for transmitting the shallow content that emerges from the interplay of advertising strategy and the concessions made to campaign contributors.

In recent years, the media have showed signs of becoming more critical of campaigns. Encouraged by a public that is angry at candidates and politicians, the news contains increased coverage of the celluloid world of marketed candidates and media manipulation. This increase in media coverage of media campaigns, however, has not brought candidates out of hiding or appreciably affected the way campaigns are run. The ironic result of media attempts to "deconstruct" candidate images and expose the techniques of news control may be to reinforce public cynicism about the whole process. Taking the public behind the political illusions has not succeeded in bringing the candidates out of hiding behind those illusions. The net result is still an election system dominated by mass marketed, Madison Avenue messages that deliver quick, emotional punches instead of lasting visions and governing ideas to voters. In other words, the way in which news organizations have exercised their critical skills may result less in changing the system than in reinforcing (albeit inadvertently) the public cynicism that helps keep it going.

Each of these related constraints on political communication imposes a substantial limit on what candidates say to voters, creating, in turn, important limits on the quality of our most important democratic experience. Taken together, these limiting conditions go a long way toward explaining the alarming absence of meaningful choices and satisfied voters in recent elections. Not surprisingly, these shallow electoral contests play best on television. In the words of a leading campaign consultant commenting on a race in California, "A political rally in California consists of three people around a television set."[6] Considering the magnitude of these forces working against the traditional forms and contents of political communication, it is not surprising that candidates say so little these days. One marvels that they are able to say anything at all.

ARE INDIVIDUAL CITIZENS TO BLAME?

Where do citizens fit into this picture? Professors Dye and Zeigler argue that reforms in elections were motivated by demands from the masses for more democracy. Yet the reforms themselves appear anything but democratic, creating a system that represents special interests far better than individual citizens. Indeed, it is understandable why so many individuals have dropped out of the political process. Yet, without some sort of effective citizen input, little is likely to change.

Even when there are signs of citizen life, it is not always clear that people are seeing the big picture. Led by Oklahoma, California, and Colorado, for example, there has been a national stirring to limit the terms of state legislators. In an action that raised constitutional questions, Colorado voters even approved limits on the length of time that their national representatives can serve. There is little doubt that elected officials at all levels hear these signals from voters. The question is whether term limits will accomplish anything beyond signaling voter displeasure to lawmakers. The larger issue here is whether most citizens understand enough about what displeases them to be able to change it effectively. The irony of the electoral breakdown that I have described briefly is that it may not be possible for people simply to vote their way out of it. And, if stronger measures are required, who will think of them? What is required is a sweeping political reform movement in the United States, aimed at restoring the democratic balance in the electoral process so that people feel represented by their government and so that government can govern once again. The analysis above contains a number of points for such a political reform program.

REFORM THE INSTITUTIONS AND THE PEOPLE WILL FOLLOW

The place to begin is with fundamental campaign finance reform. The whole system of political finance that gives rise to special interest politics and varieties of political corruption must be reformed if politicians are to develop a healthier sense of the public interest. Consider the words of Fred Wertheimer, President of Common Cause, the public interest lobby that has pushed for campaign finance reform:

> Washington has become an ethics swamp. Our nation's capital is addicted to special-interest influence money, and members of Congress are benefiting professionally and personally from these funds.
>
> In the last six years, special interests have poured more than $400 million in PAC money, $31 million in honoraria fees, and countless additional

millions in illegal soft money and other payments into our system of government. These payments represent investments in government decision making—investments which improperly and unfairly magnify the voices of special interest at the expense of representative government.

We've always experienced individual cases of corruption and impropriety in government. But today we have a system of institutionalized corruption. The rules themselves allow activities to take place legally that are improper and corrupting. . . .

Washington insiders argue that the American people don't really care about Washington's ethics mess. They're wrong. But what's happening is even more dangerous than what they perceive as indifference on the part of the American public.

The American people are moving beyond outrage to a state of deep cynicism. They are reaching a state of "no expectations" about our government leaders. And in a democracy, that's a red flag alert. There cannot be a fundamental erosion of ethical values at the seat of government without grave consequences for the nation.[7]

Reforms in campaign finance must affect all levels of politics from the president and Congress to local offices. Since we are talking about a system of influence, it will do little good to correct one part of the problem without attending to all of it. Electing a president with his or her own ideas for a change will have little consequence if Congress throws up a wall of special interest resistance to putting those ideas into action. The same applies to state and local politics.

What kind of finance reform would make a difference? *First eliminate PAC contributions to political campaigns.* (Contributions to party organizations might be permitted *but* state and national parties should be restricted severely in "soft money" spending during the several months prior to election day. Let "party-building" activities take place *between*, not during, elections.) *Next, create a system of public funding for both challengers and incumbents.* (It would be possible to adapt various European models for this.) *Finally, set spending limits on campaigns and "index" those limits according to the office and the size of the district.* (In order to observe Supreme Court rulings that political finance is a form of free speech, apply spending limits only to those who "voluntarily" accept public funding.) In conjunction with the other reforms outlined below, it is possible to imagine spending limits set at one-half or even one-third of current spending averages.

But, the critics will argue, the costs of public financing are too great. How can the government afford to back large numbers of political aspirants, many of whom stand no chance of ultimate victory? To put this in perspective, the costs of financing the entire slate of national candidates (including challengers) in a presidential-election year amounts to about 1% of the annual defense budget. Isn't the national democracy worth as much as, say, a couple of high-tech bombers or submarines every four years? Leaving aside the question of what our national tax priorities ought to be and what dollar value should be placed on reforms to save democratic institutions, there is another, more expedient answer to this criticism. The costs of campaigning could be lowered by more than half through one very simple move: Eliminate the enormously expensive practice of paid political advertising on television and radio. This could be done in ways that would end the Madison-Avenue-style candidate marketing that is so damaging to the spirit of democracy. This brings us to our next proposal.

Although it is probably unconstitutional to ban broadcast political advertising, various regulatory measures could reduce the quantity of dollars needed to mount an effective political campaign. The practice of candidate marketing sets in motion a whole antidemocratic syndrome. Rather than promoting dialogues between candidates and voters that might result in new political initiatives, political advertising of the sort that dominates American campaigns short-circuits the very chances for such communications. Skipping the stages of dialogue, reason, feedback, and debate, marketing techniques probe the subliminal minds of isolated segments of the voter market for images and themes that produce quick psychological responses. The resulting interactions between candidates and voters defy the clear understandings on which stable consensus and programs of action depend. Moreover, the practice of scientifically targeting small voter blocs and then aiming the bulk of campaign content at them violates the spirit of broad democratic involvement. Any practice that turns reduced voter participation and citizen withdrawal into a good thing rather than a cause for alarm should be outlawed as unhealthy to the principles on which the whole system rests.

The solution? Empower the Federal Communications Commission to broaden its regulation of elections within its sphere of "public service" broadcasting. *In particular, require networks to donate set amounts of "public service" air time to candidates and parties during elections, and require the time to be issued (and used by candidates) in blocks of five to fifteen minutes.* These two reforms would simultaneously cut the costs of campaigning and require candidates to actually say something in the time allocated to them. More important, these reforms would help set in motion the right kind of electoral dynamic: Free air time would cut the costs of campaigning, making strict spending limits more realistic.

There are, of course, many who will rally around the symbol of free speech on this one. We can anticipate an unholy alliance of broadcasters, who profit enormously from campaign commercial sales, and candidates who have won office through the assistance of good marketing. These forces will talk of free speech as though their lives had been dedicated to nothing but advancing that cause. However, the prohibition of political advertising on radio and TV (the media in which it is subject to greatest abuse) has at least three precedents within the liberal democratic tradition.

First, consider the fact that a number of thriving Western democracies as diverse, for example, as England, Germany, and Sweden, all regulate political advertising on the airwaves. Indeed, most other democracies regulate political advertising in ways much more drastic than called for in the present proposal. And their political processes, if not healthier than ours, are at the very least no worse for it.

Second, the United States has regulated various other forms of broadcast advertising deemed harmful to the national health: hard liquor, cigarettes, sexual services, and pornography, just to name a few. The deterioration of political life due to candidate marketing on television and radio constitutes at least as great a hazard as these already prohibited commodities.

Finally, the free speech defense crumbles even if examined in "strict constructionist" terms. Almost nobody in public life subscribes to the absolute reading of the First Amendment clause that says "Congress shall pass *no* law. . . ." Since the eminent Justice Holmes developed the "clear and present danger" doctrine in the early part of this century, most reasonable people have accepted the idea that speech may be restricted if it presents a clear and present danger to the survival of the people or their way of government. Even the Supreme Court decision in *Buckley* v. *Valeo* granted Congress some broad regulatory powers in elections. If a better case is made for the dangers of contemporary electoral speech, perhaps the Court will see fit to expand those powers in future rulings. I would suggest that the effects of candidate marketing, as they are manifest through the commercialization of elections, represent a far greater threat to the principles and practices of our democratic government than any threat that can be conjured by domestic enemies or flag burning.

The reform of candidate communication to voters would do little good if the press did not change its ways of commenting on candidates and covering their campaigns. Thus, we also must try to get the media to change their coverage patterns. For starters, it would be nice if the press did more than just grumble when political campaigns manipulate news events and restrict journalistic access to candidates. True, the media are running more stories about media manipulation, empty rhetoric, and voter dissatisfaction than ever before, but they have had little or no perceptible impact on candidate behavior.

There is, of course, nothing that reporters can do to force candidates to ride on the press plane and talk candidly about what, if anything, is on their minds. However, new ways of reporting on campaigns could exert considerable indirect pressure on candidates. For example, the *New York Times* and other leading news organizations have begun conducting "focus groups" with a broad range of citizens during recent elections, and converting their reports based on these discussions into something of a "dialogue" between candidates and voters. Building on this idea of a critical "dialogue" contained within news reports, several other innovations might be considered.

To begin with, *the leading national news organizations could stake their prestige on creating a "national agenda" reflecting a synthesis of public opinion and the views of bipartisan experts on the major concerns of the day.* This agenda could then be used as a reference for analyzing candidate responsiveness to the national interest. In other words, instead of framing the campaign story as an often baseless "horserace," journalists could compare candidates on how well they were responding to the items on the national agenda. Of course, there will always be temptations to make a "horserace" out of an election, as the metaphor has a powerful hold in the culture. (The use of this metaphor dates back at least as far as Andrew Jackson's acclaimed entry as the "Tennessee stud" in the presidential horserace of 1824.) However, there is no reason that the metaphor needs to be as empty as it has been. Making a "horserace" out of candidate responses to the national agenda would turn elections into more meaningful contests than the current weekly updates based on popularity polls. As the race progresses, news organizations could update their evaluations by asking the panels of bipartisan experts for continuing input. Opinion polls could be figured in as well but only after vague questions about "popularity" or "who would you vote for?" have been supplemented with questions about the credibility of candidate responses to the agenda items.

Creating national agendas and evaluating candidates' credibility might break down their ability to control the content of campaign news coverage and, at the same time, open up other aspects of the press-politician relationship. Who knows? Politicians might turn idle promises into more serious issues in the eyes of voters and experts alike by responding pointedly to poor showings against their competition. Moreover, if broadcast advertising were regulated, candidates might have to say something substantive just to stay even with each other in precious media exposure.

As for the objection that no two news organizations would come up with the same national agenda, so much the better. Surely there would be enough overlap to provide some continuity in the news coverage. (The tendency of the press to look over their shoulders to see what the competition is doing would ensure it.) And some level of informed disagreement about the shape of the public interest and the degree of party and candidate responsiveness would introduce a necessary critical edge into the proceedings. If many societies thrive with an avowedly partisan press, surely the American people can live with minor debates about national goals.

Finally, we need to bring citizens back into the political process. While the preceding reforms should do just that if they are successful, we also should consider removing a major barrier to voting in the United States: the difficulty and unevenness of registration procedures from one state to another. If people are registered, they tend to vote. The United States sits near the bottom of the list of world democracies in terms of the proportion of eligible citizens who are registered to vote. If registration to vote were easier and more uniform across the various states, more people would be introduced into the electoral arena, magnifying the effects of all of the reforms discussed here. Few, if any, good reasons exist for cumbersome voter registration procedures. We are beyond the age of machine politics and the corruption of voter lists that once may have justified the ordeal of seeking out a registrar and supplying proof of identity and residence. And there is no excuse for the racial discrimination that has led many states to impose one challenge after another to the registration of black voters.

The good news is that various plans have surfaced in Congress to sign up voters at government offices (post office, motor vehicle, etc.), to register by mail, and even to register on election day. The bad news is that feet are dragging on these bills. In 1990, for example, a sensible bill (The National Voter Registration Act) finally passed the House after long and difficult negotiations. However, a barrage of objections killed it in the Senate and political obstacles have been thrown in its way ever since. Some senators charged that allowing voters to register by mail would invite fraud. Others claimed that increased registration efforts would be costly without making any difference in the final outcome of elections because unregistered voters might vote the same way registered voters do. Some even argued that voting rates among registered voters are declining, thus reducing the importance of the whole issue of registration. In an era when the more who don't vote, the easier the campaign consultant's (and the candidate's) life becomes, any reluctance to simplify voter registration should be viewed skeptically.

HOPE FOR REFORMING THE SYSTEM? IN THE FINAL ANALYSIS, IT'S UP TO THE PEOPLE

Here I can cheerfully rejoin Professors Dye and Zeigler and agree that the ultimate responsibility in a democracy lies with the people. But in my view, people can overcome ignorance and apathy if they become armed with some understanding of how their governing system works and if they have some idea of what to do when it breaks down. One can only hope that Americans will convert their anger about a failing government into action. But how to get the right reforms going?

There are signs that citizen actions are stirring around the land. The important question, however, is whether those stirrings will become focused on the right problems and find the right ways to address those problems. For example, there is something of a groundswell around the country to limit terms in office. There is even a movement for a constitutional "term limit" amendment at the national level. However, before too much time and energy is consumed in this effort, it would be wise to reflect on whether this solves *any* of our problems with elections and governing. As an angry signal to politicians, term limits may be a start. But as a full-blown substitute for more basic reforms, they are way off the mark.

Similarly, it may be a mixed blessing that a number of third party initiatives are in the wind these days. There has been talk in recent years about a women's party, a labor party, a consumer party, a "green" party, and perhaps a coalition of such groups in a revitalized "Rainbow Party." In 1992, Ross Perot created hopes that his ill-fated grass-roots movement might turn into a third party. Such efforts, however, are doomed to splinter and fail unless they all recognize that their respective issues must be subordinated to the broader issue of election reform. Perhaps a Reform Party with a set of election reform proposals atop its platform would make a difference and win support among discouraged voters. If nothing else, a Reform Party would provide a focal point and, more important, an organizational base for the kind of sustained social movement that will have to emerge in the next decade if Americans are to have any hope of regaining control of their government.

The prospects for a social movement are reasonably good, particularly with a third party as its beacon. Indeed, American history can be viewed as a succession of social movements (the frontier movement, the transcendentalists, abolitionists, populists, progressives, suffragettes, prohibitionists, labor, civil rights, feminists, counter-cultures, and born-again Christians, to name a few). In this view, social movements are the noninstitutional, "hidden hand" of change in American life. The time is ripe for another one. And the stakes have never been higher. All lesser issues, interests, and groups are affected by the governing crisis. Without a grass-roots movement aimed squarely at regaining popular, idea-based control of the government, democracy may well become an electronic echo in a marketing jingle or a nostalgic image of times gone by.

— NOTES

1. The data from 1960, 1970, and 1980 are from Seymour Martin Lipset and William Schneider, *The Confidence Gap: Business, Labor, and Government in the Public Mind.* New York: Free Press, 1983. The 1990 figure is from a New York Times/CBS News Poll reported in the *International Herald Tribune,* November 5, 1990, p 1.
2. A much more detailed version of this analysis can be found in my book, *The Governing Crisis: Media, Money, and Marketing in American Elections.* New York: St. Martin's Press, 1992.
3. Paul Weyrich quoted in Thomas Ferguson and Joel Rogers, "The Reagan Victory: Corporate Coalitions in the 1980 Campaign," in Ferguson and Rogers, eds., *The Hidden Election: Politics and Economics in the 1980 Presidential Campaign,* New York: Pantheon, 1981, p. 4.
4. See, for example, Mark Hertsgaard, *On Bended Knee: The Press and the Reagan Presidency.* New York: Farrar, Strauss and Giroux, 1988.
5. "This Week with David Brinkley," *ABC,* November 6, 1988.
6. Robert Shrum, quoted in R. W. Apple, Jr., "Candidates Focus on Television Ads," *New York Times,* October 19, 1986, p. A16.
7. Fred Wertheimer, "Window of Opportunity: The Climate Is Ripe for Ethics Reforms," *Common Cause Magazine,* July/August 1989, p. 45.

The Constitution of the United States of America

We the People of the United States, in Order to form a more perfect Union, establish Justice, insure domestic Tranquility, provide for the common defense, promote the general Welfare, and secure the Blessings of Liberty to ourselves and our Posterity, do ordain and establish this Constitution for the United States of America.

—— ARTICLE I

Section 1.   All legislative Powers herein granted shall be vested in a Congress of the United States, which shall consist of a Senate and House of Representatives.

Section 2.   The House of Representatives shall be composed of Members chosen every second Year by the People of the several States, and the Electors in each State shall have the Qualifications requisite for Electors of the most numerous Branch of the State Legislature.

No Person shall be a Representative who shall not have attained to the age of twenty five Years, and been seven Years a Citizen of the United States, and who shall not, when elected, be an Inhabitant of that State in which he shall be chosen.

Representatives and direct Taxes shall be apportioned among the several States which may be included within this Union, according to their respective Numbers, *which shall be determined by adding to the whole Number of free Persons, including those bound to Service for a Term of Years, and excluding Indians not taxed, three fifths of all other persons.*[1] The actual Enumeration shall be made within three Years after the first Meeting of the Congress of the United States, and within every subsequent Term of ten Years, in such Manner as they shall by Law direct. The Number of Representatives shall not exceed one for every thirty Thousand, but each State shall have at Least one Representative, and until such enumeration shall be made, the State of New Hampshire shall be entitled to chuse three, Massachusetts eight, Rhode-Island and Providence Plantations one, Connecticut five, New York six, New Jersey four, Pennsylvania eight, Delaware one, Maryland six, Virginia ten, North Carolina five, South Carolina five, and Georgia three.

When vacancies happen in the Representation from any State, the Executive Authority thereof shall issue Writs of Election to fill such Vacancies.

The House of Representatives shall chuse their Speaker and other Officers; and shall have the sole Power of Impeachment.

Section 3.   The Senate of the United States shall be composed of two Senators from each State, *chosen by the Legislature thereof,*[2] for six Years; and each Senator shall have one Vote.

Immediately after they shall be assembled in Consequence of the first Election, they shall be divided as equally as may be into three Classes. The Seats of the Senators of the first Class shall be vacated at the Expiration of the second Year, of the second Class at the Expiration of the

[1]Superseded by the Fourteenth Amendment. Throughout, italics indicate passages altered by subsequent amendments.

[2]See Seventeenth Amendment.

fourth Year, and of the third Class at the Expiration of the sixth Year, so that one third may be chosen every second Year; *and if Vacancies happen by Resignation, or otherwise, during the Recess of the Legislature of any State, the Executive thereof may make temporary Appointments until the next Meeting of the Legislature, which shall then fill such Vacancies.*[3]

No Person shall be a Senator who shall not have attained to the Age of thirty Years, and been nine Years a Citizen of the United States, and who shall not, when elected, be an Inhabitant of the State for which he shall be chosen.

The Vice President of the United States shall be President of the Senate, but shall have no Vote, unless they be equally divided.

The Senate shall chuse their other Officers, and also a President pro tempore, in the Absence of the Vice President, or when he shall exercise the Office of President of the United States.

The Senate shall have the sole Power to try all Impeachments. When sitting for that Purpose, they shall be on Oath or Affirmation. When the President of the United States is tried, the Chief Justice shall preside: And no Person shall be convicted without the Concurrence of two thirds of the Members present.

Judgment in Cases of Impeachment shall not extend further than to removal from Office, and disqualification to hold and enjoy any Office of Honor, Trust or Profit under the United States: but the party convicted shall nevertheless be liable and subject to Indictment, Trial, Judgment and Punishment, according to Law.

Section 4.   The Times, Places and Manner of holding Elections for Senators and Representatives, shall be prescribed in each State by the Legislature thereof; but the Congress may at any time by Law make or alter such Regulations, except as to the Places of chusing Senators.

The congress shall assemble at least once in every Year, and such Meeting shall be on the first Monday in December, unless they shall by Law appoint a different Day.[4]

Section 5.   Each House shall be the Judge of the Elections, Returns and Qualifications of its own Members, and a Majority of each shall constitute a Quorum to do Business; but a smaller Number may adjourn from day to day, and may be authorized to compel the Attendance of absent Members, in such Manner, and under such Penalties as each House may provide.

Each House may determine the Rules of its Proceedings, punish its Members for disorderly Behaviour, and, with the Concurrence of two thirds, expel a Member.

Each House shall keep a Journal of its Proceedings, and from time to time publish the same, excepting such Parts as may in their Judgment

[3]See Seventeenth Amendment.
[4]See Twentieth Amendment.

require Secrecy; and the Yeas and Nays of the Members of either House on any question shall, at the Desire of one fifth of those Present, be entered on the Journal.

Neither House, during the Session of Congress, shall, without the Consent of the other, adjourn for more than three days, nor to any other Place than that in which the two Houses shall be sitting.

Section 6.   The Senators and Representatives shall receive a Compensation for their Services, to be ascertained by Law, and paid out of the Treasury of the United States. They shall in all Cases, except Treason, Felony and Breach of the Peace, be privileged from Arrest during their Attendance at the Session of their respective Houses, and in going to and returning from the same; and for any Speech or Debate in either House, they shall not be questioned in any other Place.

No Senator or Representative shall, during the Time for which he was elected, be appointed to any civil Office under the Authority of the United States, which shall have been created, or the Emoluments whereof shall have been encreased during such time; and no Person holding any Office under the United States, shall be a Member of either House during his Continuance in Office.

Section 7.   All Bills for raising Revenue shall originate in the House of Representatives; but the Senate may propose or concur with Amendments as on other Bills.

Every Bill which shall have passed the House of Representatives and the Senate, shall, before it become a Law, be presented to the President of the United States; If he approves he shall sign it, but if not he shall return it, with his Objections to that House in which it shall have originated, who shall enter the Objections at large on their Journal, and proceed to reconsider it. If after such Reconsideration two thirds of that House shall agree to pass the Bill, it shall be sent, together with the Objections, to the other House, by which it shall likewise be reconsidered, and if approved by two thirds of that House, it shall become a Law. But in all such Cases the Votes of both Houses shall be determined by Yeas and Nays, and the Names of the Persons voting for and against the Bill shall be entered on the Journal of each House respectively. If any Bill shall not be returned by the President within ten Days (Sundays excepted) after it shall have been presented to him, the Same shall be a Law, in like Manner as if he had signed it, unless the Congress by their Adjournment prevent its Return, in which Case it shall not be a Law.

Every Order, Resolution, or Vote to which the concurrence of the Senate and House of Representatives may be necessary (except on a question of Adjournment) shall be presented to the President of the United States; and before the Same shall take Effect, shall be approved by him, or being disapproved by him, shall be repassed by two thirds of the Senate and House of Representatives, according to the Rules and Limitations prescribed in the Case of a Bill.

Section 8.   The Congress shall have Power To lay and collect Taxes, Duties, Imposts and Excises, to pay the Debts and provide for the common Defense and general Welfare of the United States; but all Duties, Imposts and Excises shall be uniform throughout the United States;

To borrow Money on the credit of the United States;

To regulate Commerce with foreign Nations, and among the several States, and with the Indian Tribes;

To establish a uniform Rule of Naturalization, and uniform Laws on the subject of Bankruptcies throughout the United States;

To coin Money, regulate the Value thereof, and of foreign Coin, and fix the Standard of Weights and Measures;

To provide for the Punishment of counterfeiting the Securities and current Coin of the United States;

To establish Post Offices and post Roads;

To promote the Progress of Science and useful Arts, by securing for limited times to Authors and Inventors the exclusive Right to their respective Writings and Discoveries;

To constitute Tribunals inferior to the Supreme Court;

To define and punish Piracies and Felonies committed on the high Seas, and Offences against the Law of Nations;

To declare War, grant Letters of Marque and Reprisal, and make Rules concerning Captures on Land and Water;

To raise and support Armies, but no Appropriation of Money to that Use shall be for a longer Term than two Years;

To provide and maintain a Navy;

To make Rules for the Government and Regulation of the land and naval Forces;

To provide for calling forth the Militia to execute the Laws of the Union, suppress Insurrections and repel Invasions;

To provide for organizing, arming, and disciplining the Militia, and for governing such Part of them as may be employed in the Service of the United States, reserving to the States respectively, the Appointment of the Officers, and the Authority of training the Militia according to the discipline prescribed by Congress;

To exercise exclusive Legislation in all Cases whatsoever, over such District (not exceeding ten Miles square) as may, by Cession of particular States, and the Acceptance of Congress, become the Seat of the Government of the United States, and to exercise like Authority over all Places purchased by the Consent of the Legislature of the State in which the Same shall be, for the Erection of Forts, Magazines, Arsenals, dock-Yards, and other needful Buildings;—And

To make all Laws which shall be necessary and proper for carrying into Execution the foregoing Powers, and all other Powers vested by this Constitution in the Government of the United States, or in any Department or Officer thereof.

Section 9.   The Migration or Importation of such Persons as any of the States now existing shall think proper to admit, shall not be prohibited by the Congress prior to the Year one thousand eight hundred and eight, but a Tax or duty may be imposed on such Importation, not exceeding ten dollars for each Person.

The Privilege of the Writ of Habeas Corpus shall not be suspended, unless when in Cases of Rebellion or Invasion the public Safety may require it.

No Bill of Attainder or ex post facto Law shall be passed.

No Capitation, or other direct, Tax shall be laid, unless in Proportion to the Census or Enumeration herein before directed to be taken.

No Tax or Duty shall be laid on Articles exported from any State.

No Preference shall be given by any Regulation of Commerce or Revenue to the Ports of one State over those of another: nor shall Vessels bound to, or from, one State be obliged to enter, clear, or pay Duties in another.

No Money shall be drawn from the Treasury, but in Consequence of Appropriations made by Law; and a regular Statement and Account of the Receipts and Expenditures of all public Money shall be published from time to time.

No Title of Nobility shall be granted by the United States: And no Person holding any Office of Profit or Trust under them, shall, without the Consent of the Congress, accept of any present, Emolument, Office, or Title, of any kind whatever, from any King, Prince, or foreign State.

Section 10.   No State shall enter into any Treaty, Alliance, or Confederation; grant Letters of Marque and Reprisal; coin Money; emit Bills of Credit; make any Thing but gold and silver Coin a Tender in Payment of Debts; pass any Bill of Attainder, ex post facto Law, or Law impairing the Obligation of Contracts, or grant any Title of Nobility.

No State shall, without the Consent of the Congress, lay any Imposts or Duties on Imports or Exports, except what may be absolutely necessary for executing its inspection Laws: and the net Produce of all Duties and Imposts, laid by any State on Imports or Exports, shall be for the Use of the Treasury of the United States; and all such Laws shall be subject to the Revision and Control of the Congress.

No State shall, without the Consent of the Congress, lay any Duty of Tonnage, keep Troops, or Ships of War in time of Peace, enter into any Agreement or Compact with another State, or with a foreign Power, or engage in War, unless actually invaded, or in such imminent Danger as will not admit of delay.

——— ARTICLE II

Section 1.   The executive Power shall be vested in a President of the United States of America. He shall hold Office during the Term of four Years, and, together with the Vice President, chosen for the same Term, be elected, as follows:

Each State shall appoint, in such Manner as the Legislature thereof may direct, a Number of Electors, equal to the whole Number of Senators and Representatives to which the State may be entitled in the Congress: but no Senator or Representative, or Person holding an Office of Trust or Profit under the United States, shall be appointed an Elector.

The Electors shall meet in their respective States, and vote by Ballot for two Persons, of whom one at least shall not be an Inhabitant of the same State with themselves. And they shall make a List of all the Persons voted for, and of the Number of Votes for each; which List they shall sign and certify, and transmit sealed to the Seat of the Government of the United States, directed to the President of the Senate. The President of the Senate shall, in the Presence of the Senate and House of Representatives, open all the Certificates, and the Votes shall then be counted. The Person having the greatest Number of Votes shall be the President, if such Number be a Majority of the whole Number of Electors appointed; and if there be more than one who have such Majority, and have an equal Number of Votes, then the House of Representatives shall immediately chuse by Ballot one of them for President, and if no Person have a Majority, then from the five highest on the List the said House shall in like Manner chuse the President. But in chusing the President, the Votes shall be taken by States, the Representation from each State having one Vote: A quorum for this Purpose shall consist of a Member or Members from two thirds of the States, and a Majority of all the States shall be necessary to a Choice. In every Case, after the Choice of the President, the Person having the greatest Number of Votes of the Electors shall be the Vice President. But if there should remain two or more who have equal Votes, the Senate shall chuse from them by Ballot the Vice President.[5]

The Congress may determine the Time of chusing the Electors, and the Day on which they shall give their Votes; which Day shall be the same throughout the United States.

No Person except a natural born Citizen, or a Citizen of the United States, at the time of the Adoption of this Constitution, shall be eligible to the Office of President; neither shall any Person be eligible to that Office

---

[5]Superseded by the Twelfth Amendment.

who shall not have attained to the Age of thirty five Years, and been four-teen Years a Resident within the United States.

In Case of the Removal of the President from Office, or of his Death, Resignation, or Inability to discharge the Powers and Duties of the said Office, the Same shall devolve on the Vice President, and the Congress may by Law provide for the Case of Removal, Death, Resignation or Inability, both of the President and Vice President, declaring what Officer shall then act as President, and such Officer shall act accordingly, until the Disability be removed, or a President shall be elected.[6]

The President shall, at stated Times, receive for his Services, a Compensation which shall neither be encreased nor diminished during the Period for which he shall have been elected, and he shall not receive within the Period any other Emolument from the United States, or any of them.

Before he enter on the Execution of his Office, he shall take the following Oath or Affirmation:—"I do solemnly swear (or affirm) that I will faithfully execute the Office of President of the United States, and will to the best of my Ability, preserve, protect and defend the Constitution of the United States."

Section 2.   The President shall be Commander in Chief of the Army and Navy of the United States, and of the Militia of the several States, when called into the actual Service of the United States; he may require the Opinion, in writing, of the principal Officer in each of the executive Departments, upon any Subject relating to the Duties of their respective Offices, and he shall have Power to grant Reprieves and Pardons for Offences against the United States, except in Cases of Impeachment.

He shall have Power, by and with the Advice and Consent of the Senate, to make Treaties, provided two thirds of the Senators present concur; and he shall nominate, and by and with the Advice and consent of the Senate, shall appoint Ambassadors, other public Ministers and Consuls, Judges of the Supreme Court, and all other Officers of the United States, whose Appointments are not herein otherwise provided for, and which shall be established by Law: but the Congress may by Law vest the Appointment of such inferior officers, as they think proper, in the President alone, in the Courts of Law, or in the Heads of Departments.

The President shall have Power to fill up all Vacancies that may happen during the Recess of the Senate, by granting Commissions which shall expire at the End of their next Session.

Section 3.   He shall from time to time give to the Congress Information of the State of the Union, and recommend to their Consideration such Measures as he shall judge necessary and expedient; he may, on extraordinary Occasions, convene both Houses, or either of them, and in Case of

[6]See Twenty-Fifth Amendment.

Disagreement between them, with Respect to the Time of Adjournment, he may adjourn them to such Time as he shall think proper; he shall receive Ambassadors and other public Ministers; he shall take Care that the Laws be faithfully executed, and shall Commission all the Officers of the United States.

Section 4.   The President, Vice President, and all civil Officers of the United States, shall be removed from Office on Impeachment for, and Conviction of, Treason, Bribery, or other high Crimes and Misdemeanors.

——— ARTICLE III

Section 1.   The judicial Power of the United States, shall be vested in one supreme Court and in such inferior Courts as the Congress may from time to time ordain and establish. The Judges, both of the supreme and inferior Courts, shall hold their Offices during good Behaviour, and shall, at stated times, receive for their Services, a Compensation, which shall not be diminished during their Continuance in Office.

Section 2.   The judicial Power shall extend to all Cases, in Law and Equity, arising under this Constitution, the Laws of the United States, and Treaties made, or which shall be made, under their Authority;—to all Cases affecting Ambassadors, other public Ministers and Consuls;—to all Cases of admiralty and maritime Jurisdiction;—to Controversies to which the United States shall be a Party;—to Controversies between two or more States;—*between a State and Citizens of another State;*[7]—between Citizens of different States;—between Citizens of the same State claiming Lands under Grants of different States, and *between a State or the Citizens thereof, and foreign States, Citizens, or Subjects.*[8]

In all Cases affecting Ambassadors, other public Ministers and Consuls, and those in which a State shall be Party, the supreme Court shall have original Jurisdiction. In all the other Cases before mentioned, the supreme Court shall have appellate Jurisdiction, both as to Law and Fact, with such Exceptions, and under such Regulations as the Congress shall make.

The Trial of all Crimes, except in Cases of Impeachment, shall be by Jury; and such Trial shall be held in the State where the said Crimes shall have been committed; but when not committed within any State, the Trial shall be at such Place or Places as the Congress may by Law have directed.

Section 3.   Treason against the United States, shall consist only in levying War against them, or in adhering to their Enemies, giving them

[7]See Eleventh Amendment.
[8]See Eleventh Amendment.

Aid and Comfort. No Person shall be convicted of Treason unless on the Testimony of two Witnesses to the same overt Act, or on Confession in open Court.

The Congress shall have Power to declare the Punishment of Treason, but no Attainder of Treason shall work Corruption of Blood, or Forfeiture except during the Life of the Person attained.

──── ARTICLE IV

Section 1.   Full Faith and Credit shall be given in each State to the public Acts, Records, and judicial Proceedings of every other State. And the Congress may by general Laws prescribe the Manner in which such Acts, Records, and Proceedings shall be proved, and the Effect thereof.

Section 2.   The Citizens of each State shall be entitled to all Privileges and Immunities of Citizens in the several States.

A Person charged in any State with Treason, Felony, or other Crime, who shall flee from Justice, and be found in another State, shall on Demand of the executive Authority of the State from which he fled, be delivered up, to be removed to the State having Jurisdiction of the Crime.

No Person held to Service or Labour in one State, under the Laws thereof, escaping into another, shall, in Consequence of any Law or Regulation therein, be discharged from such Service or Labour, but shall be delivered up on Claim of the Party to whom such Service or Labour may be due.[9]

Section 3.   New States may be admitted by the Congress into this Union; but no new State shall be formed or erected within the Jurisdiction of any other State; nor any State be formed by the Junction of two or more States, or Parts of States, without the Consent of the Legislatures of the States concerned as well as of the Congress.

The Congress shall have Power to dispose of and make all needful Rules and Regulations respecting the Territory or other Property belonging to the United States; and nothing in this Constitution shall be so construed as to Prejudice any claims of the United States, or of any particular State.

Section 4.   The United States shall guarantee to every State in this Union a Republican Form of Government, and shall protect each of them against Invasion; and on Application of the legislature, or of the Executive (when the Legislature cannot be convened) against domestic Violence.

[9]See Thirteenth Amendment.

ARTICLE V

The Congress, whenever two thirds of both Houses shall deem it necessary, shall propose Amendments to this Constitution, or, on the Application of the Legislatures of two thirds of the several States, shall call a Convention for proposing Amendments, which, in either Case, shall be valid to all Intents and Purposes, as Part of this Constitution, when ratified by the Legislatures of three fourths of the several States, or by Conventions in three fourths thereof, as the one or the other Mode of Ratification may be proposed by the Congress; Provided that no Amendment which may be made prior to the Year One thousand eight hundred and eight shall in any Manner affect the first and fourth clauses in the Ninth Section of the first Article; and that no State, without its Consent, shall be deprived of its equal Suffrage in the Senate.

ARTICLE VI

All debts contracted and Engagements entered into, before the Adoption of this Constitution, shall be as valid against the United States under this Constitution, as under the Confederation.

This Constitution, and the Laws of the United States which shall be made in Pursuance thereof; and all Treaties made, or which shall be made, under the Authority of the United States, shall be the supreme Law of the Land; and the Judges in every State shall be bound thereby, any Thing in the Constitution or Laws of any State to the Contrary notwithstanding.

The Senators and Representatives before mentioned, and the Members of the several State Legislatures, and all executive and judicial Officers, both of the United States and of the several States, shall be bound by Oath or Affirmation, to support this Constitution; but no religious Test shall ever be required as a Qualification to any Office or public Trust under the United States.

ARTICLE VII

The Ratification of the Conventions of nine States, shall be sufficient for the Establishment of this Constitution between the States so ratifying the Same.

Done in Convention by the Unanimous Consent of the States present the Seventeenth Day of September in the Year of our Lord one thousand seven hundred and eighty seven and of the Independence of the United States of America the Twelfth. In witness whereof We have hereunto subscribed our Names.

Articles in Addition to, and Amendment of, the Constitution of the United States of America, Proposed by Congress, and Ratified by the Several States, Pursuant to the Fifth Article of the Original Constitution:

Amendment I

(Ratification of the first ten amendments was completed December 15, 1791.)

Congress shall make no law respecting an establishment of religion, or prohibiting the free exercise thereof; or abridging the freedom of speech, or of the press; or the right of the people peaceably to assemble, and to petition the Government for a redress of grievances.

Amendment II

A well regulated Militia, being necessary to the security of a free State, the right of the people to keep and bear Arms, shall not be infringed.

Amendment III

No Soldier shall, in time of peace be quartered in any house, without the consent of the Owner, nor in time of war, but in a manner to be prescribed by law.

Amendment IV

The right of the people to be secure in their persons, houses, papers, and effects, against unreasonable searches and seizures, shall not be violated, and no Warrants shall issue, but upon probable cause, supported by Oath or affirmation, and particularly describing the place to be searched, and the persons or things to be seized.

Amendment V

No person shall be held to answer for a capital, or otherwise infamous crime, unless on a presentment or indictment of a Grand Jury, except in cases arising in the land or naval forces, or in the Militia, when in actual service in time of War or public danger; nor shall any person be subject for the same offence to be twice put in jeopardy of life or limb; nor shall be compelled in any criminal case to be a witness against himself, nor be deprived of life, liberty, or property, without due process of law; nor shall private property be taken for public use, without just compensation.

Amendment VI

In all criminal prosecutions, the accused shall enjoy the right to a speedy and public trial, by an impartial jury of the State and district wherein the crime shall have been committed, which district shall have been previously ascertained by law, and to be informed of the nature and cause of the accusation; to be confronted with the witnesses against him; to have compulsory process for obtaining witnesses in his favor, and to have the Assistance of Counsel for his defense.

Amendment VII

In Suits at common law, where the value in controversy shall exceed twenty dollars, the right of trial by jury shall be preserved, and no fact tried by a jury, shall be otherwise reexamined in any Court of the United States, than according to the rules of the common law.

Amendment VIII

Excessive bail shall not be required, nor excessive fines imposed, nor cruel and unusual punishments inflicted.

Amendment IX

The enumeration in the Constitution, of certain rights, shall not be construed to deny or disparage others retained by the people.

Amendment X

The powers not delegated to the United States by the Constitution, nor prohibited by it to the States, are reserved to the States respectively, or to the people.

Amendment XI (1795)

The Judicial power of the United States shall not be construed to extend to any suit in law or equity, commenced or prosecuted against one of the United States by Citizens of another State, or by Citizens or Subjects of any Foreign State.

Amendment XII (1804)

The Electors shall meet in their respective states and vote by ballot for President and Vice-President, one of whom, at least, shall not be an inhabitant of the same state with themselves; they shall name in their ballots the person voted for as President, and in distinct ballots the person voted for as Vice-President, and they shall make distinct lists of all persons voted for as President, and of all persons voted for as Vice-President, and of the number of votes for each, which lists they shall sign and certify, and transmit sealed to the seat of the government of the United States, directed to the President of the Senate;—The President of the Senate shall, in the presence of the Senate and House of Representatives, open all the certificates and the votes shall then be counted;—the person having the greatest number of votes for President, shall be the President, if such number be a majority of the whole number of Electors appointed; and if no person have such majority, then from the persons having the highest numbers not exceeding three on the list of those voted for as President, the House of Representatives shall choose immediately, by ballot, the President. But in choosing the President, the votes shall be taken by states, the representation from each state having one vote; a quorum for this purpose shall consist of a member or members from two-thirds of the states, and a majority of all the states shall be necessary to a choice. And if the House of Representatives shall not choose a President whenever the right of choice shall devolve upon them, *before the fourth day of March next following,*[10] then the Vice-President shall act as President, as in the case of the death or other constitutional disability of the President.—The person having the greatest number of votes as Vice-President shall be the Vice-President, if such number be a majority of the whole number of Electors appointed, and if no person have a majority, then from the two highest numbers on the list, the Senate shall choose the Vice-President; a quorum for the purpose shall consist of two-thirds of the whole number of Senators, and a majority of the whole number shall be necessary to a choice. But no person constitutionally ineligible to the office of President shall be eligible to that of Vice-President of the United States.

Amendment XIII (1865)

Section 1.   Neither slavery nor involuntary servitude, except as a punishment for crime whereof the party shall have been duly convicted, shall exist within the United States, or any place subject to their jurisdiction.

Section 2.   Congress shall have the power to enforce this article by appropriate legislation.

Amendment XIV (1868)

Section 1.   All persons born or naturalized in the United States, and subject to the jurisdiction thereof, are citizens of the United States and the State wherein they reside. No State shall make or enforce any law which shall abridge the privileges or immunities of citizens of the United States; nor shall any State deprive any person of life, liberty, or property, without due process of law; nor deny to any person within its jurisdiction the equal protection of the laws.

[10]Altered by the Twentieth Amendment.

Section 2.   Representatives shall be apportioned among the several States according to their respective numbers, counting the whole number of persons in each State, excluding Indians not taxed. But when the right to vote at any election for the choice of electors for President and Vice President of the United States, Representatives in Congress, the Executive and Judicial officers of a State, or the members of the Legislature thereof, is denied to any of the male inhabitants of such State, being twenty-one years of age, and citizens of the United States, or in any way abridged, except for participation in rebellion, or other crime, the basis of representation therein shall be reduced in the proportion which the number of such male citizens shall bear to the whole number of male citizens twenty-one years of age in such State.

Section 3.   No person shall be a Senator or Representative in Congress, or elector of President and Vice President, or hold any office, civil or military, under the United States, or under any State, who, having previously taken an oath, as a member of Congress, or as an officer of the United States, or as a member of any State legislature, or as an executive or judicial officer of any State, to support the Constitution of the United States, shall have engaged in insurrection or rebellion against the same, or given aid or comfort to the enemies thereof. But Congress may by a vote of two-thirds of each House, remove such disability.

Section 4.   The validity of the public debt of the United States, authorized by law, including debts incurred for payment of pensions and bounties for services in suppressing insurrection or rebellion, shall not be questioned. But neither the United States nor any State shall assume or pay any debt or obligation incurred in aid of insurrection or rebellion against the United States, or any claim for the loss or emancipation of any slave; but all debts, obligations, and claims shall be held illegal and void.

Section 5.   The Congress shall have power to enforce, by appropriate legislation, the provisions of this article.

Amendment XV (1870)

Section 1.   The right of citizens of the United States to vote shall not be denied or abridged by the United States or by any State on account of race, color, or previous condition of servitude.

Section 2.   The Congress shall have power to enforce this article by appropriate legislation.

Amendment XVI (1913)

The Congress shall have power to lay and collect taxes on incomes, from whatever source derived, without apportionment among the several States, and without regard to any census or enumeration.

Amendment XVII (1913)

The Senate of the United States shall be composed of two Senators from each State, elected by the people thereof, for six years; and each Senator shall have one vote. The electors in each State shall have the qualifications requisite for electors of the most numerous branch of the State legislature.

When vacancies happen in the representation of any State in the Senate, the executive authority of such State shall issue writs of election to fill such vacancies: *Provided,* That the legislature of any State may empower the executive thereof to make temporary appointments until the people fill the vacancies by election as the legislature may direct.

This amendment shall not be so construed as to affect the election or term of any Senator chosen before it becomes valid as part of the Constitution.

Amendment XVIII (1919)

Section 1.   After one year from the ratification of this article the manufacture, sale, or transportation of intoxicating liquors within, the importation thereof into, or the exportation thereof from the United States and all territory subject to the jurisdiction thereof for beverage purposes is hereby prohibited.

Section 2.   The Congress and the several States shall have concurrent power to enforce this article by appropriate legislation.

Section 3.   This article shall be inoperative unless it shall have been ratified as an amendment to the Constitution by the legislatures of the several States, as provided in the Constitution, within seven years from the date of submission hereof to the States by the Congress.[11]

Amendment XIX (1920)

The right of citizens of the United States to vote shall not be denied or abridged by the United States or by any State on account of sex.

[11]Repealed by the Twenty-First Amendment.

Congress shall have power to enforce this article by appropriate legislation.

Amendment XX (1933)

Section 1.   The terms of the President and Vice President shall end at noon on the 20th day of January, and the terms of Senators and Representatives at noon on the 3rd day of January, of the years in which such terms would have ended if this article had not been ratified; and the terms of their successors shall then begin.

Section 2.   The Congress shall assemble at least once in every year, and such meeting shall begin at noon on the 3rd day of January, unless they shall by law appoint a different day.

Section 3.   If, at the time fixed for the beginning of the term of the President, the President elect shall have died, the Vice President elect shall become President. If a President shall not have been chosen before the time fixed for the beginning of his term, or if the President elect shall have failed to qualify, then the Vice President elect shall act as President until a President shall have qualified; and the Congress may by law provide for the case wherein neither a President elect nor a Vice President elect shall have qualified, declaring who shall then act as President, or the manner in which one who is to act shall be selected, and such person shall act accordingly until a President or Vice President shall have qualified.

Section 4.   The Congress may by law provide for the case of the death of any of the persons from whom the House of Representatives may choose a President whenever the right of choice shall have devolved upon them, and for the case of the death of any of the persons from whom the Senate may choose a Vice President whenever the right of choice shall have devolved upon them.

Section 5.   Sections 1 and 2 shall take effect on the 15th day of October following ratification of this article.

Section 6.   This article shall be inoperative unless it shall have been ratified as an amendment to the Constitution by the legislatures of three-fourths of the several States within seven years from the date of its submission.

Amendment XXI (1933)

Section 1.   The eighteenth article of amendment to the Constitution of the United States is hereby repealed.

Section 2.   The transportation or importation into any State, Territory, or possession of the United States for delivery or use therein of intoxicating liquors, in violation of the laws thereof, is hereby prohibited.

Section 3.   This article shall be inoperative unless it shall have been ratified as an amendment to the Constitution by conventions in the several States, as provided in the Constitution, within seven years from the date of submission thereof to the States by the Congress.

Amendment XXII (1951)

Section 1.   No person shall be elected to the office of the President more than twice, and no person who has held the office of President, or acted as President for more than two years of a term to which some other person was elected President shall be elected to the office of President more than once. But this Article shall not apply to any person holding the office of President when this Article was proposed by the Congress, and shall not prevent any person who may be holding the office of President, or acting as President, during the term within which this Article becomes operative from holding the office of President or acting as President during the remainder of such term.

Section 2.   This article shall be inoperative unless it shall have been ratified as an amendment to the Constitution by the legislatures of three-fourths of the several States within seven years from the date of its submission to the States by the Congress.

Amendment XXIII (1961)

Section 1.   The District constituting the seat of Government of the United States shall appoint in such manner as the Congress may direct:
A number of electors of President and Vice President equal to the whole number of Senators and Representatives in Congress to which the District would be entitled if it were a State, but in no event more than the least populous State; they shall be in addition to those appointed by the States, but they shall be considered, for the purposes of the election of President and Vice President, to be electors appointed by a State; and they shall meet in the District and perform such duties as provided by the twelfth article of amendment.

Section 2.   The Congress shall have power to enforce this article by appropriate legislation.

Amendment XXIV (1964)

Section 1.   The right of citizens of the United States to vote in any primary or other election for President or Vice President, for electors for President or Vice President, or for Senator or Representative in Congress, shall not be denied or abridged by the United States or any state by reason of failure to pay any poll tax or other tax.

Section 2.   The Congress shall have the power to enforce this article by appropriate legislation.

Amendment XXV (1967)

Section 1.   In case of the removal of the President from office or of his death or resignation, the Vice President shall become President.

Section 2.   Whenever there is a vacancy in the office of the Vice President, the President shall nominate a Vice President who shall take office upon confirmation by a majority vote of both Houses of Congress.

Section 3.   Whenever the President transmits to the President pro tempore of the Senate and the Speaker of the House of Representatives his written declaration that he is unable to discharge the powers and duties of his office, and until he transmits to them a written declaration to the contrary, such powers and duties shall be discharged by the Vice President as Acting President.

Section 4.   Whenever the Vice President and a majority of either the principal officers of the executive departments or of such other body as Congress may by law provide, transmit to the President pro tempore of the Senate and the Speaker of the House of Representatives their written declaration that the President is unable to discharge the powers and duties of his office, the Vice President shall immediately assume the powers and duties of the office as Acting President.

Thereafter, when the President transmits to the President pro tempore of the Senate and the Speaker of the House of Representatives his written declaration that no inability exists, he shall resume the powers and duties of his office unless the Vice President and a majority of either the principal officers of the executive departments or of such other body as Congress may by law provide, transmit within four days to the President pro tempore of the Senate and the Speaker of the House of Representatives their written declaration that the President is unable to discharge the powers and duties of his office. Thereupon Congress shall decide the issue, assembling within forty-eight hours for that purpose if not in session. If the Congress, within twenty-one days after the receipt of the latter written declaration, or, if Congress is not in session, within twenty-one days after Congress is required to assemble, determines by two-thirds vote of both Houses that the President is unable to discharge the powers and duties of his office, the Vice President shall continue to discharge the same as Acting President; otherwise, the President shall resume the powers and duties of his office.

Amendment XXVI (1971)

Section 1.   The right of citizens of the United States, who are 18 years of age or older, to vote shall not be denied or abridged by the United States or any state on account of age.

Section 2.   The Congress shall have the power to enforce this article by appropriate legislation.

Index

TO THE OWNER OF THIS BOOK:

We hope that you have found Dye and Zeigler's *The Irony of Democracy*, 9th Edition, useful. So that this book can be improved in a future edition, would you take the time to complete this sheet and return it? Thank you.

Instructor's name: _____

Department: _____

School and address: _____

_____

1. The name of the course in which I used this book is: _____

_____

2. My general reaction to this book is: _____

_____

_____

3. What I like most about this book is: _____

_____

_____

4. What I like least about this book is: _____

_____

_____

5. Were all of the chapters of the book assigned for you to read?   Yes   No

   If not, which ones weren't? _____

6. Do you plan to keep this book after you finish the course?   Yes   No

   Why or why not? _____

_____

7. On a separate sheet of paper, please write specific suggestions for improving this book and anything else you'd care to share about your experience in using the book.

Optional:

Your name: _____   Date: _____

May Wadsworth quote you, either in promotion for *The Irony of Democracy*, 9th Edition, or in future publishing ventures?

Yes: _____   No: _____

Sincerely,
Thomas R. Dye
Harmon Zeigler

FOLD HERE

BUSINESS REPLY MAIL
FIRST CLASS   PERMIT NO. 34   BELMONT, CA

POSTAGE WILL BE PAID BY ADDRESSEE

Thomas R. Dye/Harmon Zeigler
Wadsworth Publishing Company
10 Davis Drive
Belmont, CA 94002